INTERNATIONAL INVESTMENT LAW AND LEGAL THEORY

Expropriation is a hotly debated issue in international investment law. This is the first study to provide a detailed analysis of its norm-theoretical dimension, setting out the theoretical foundations underlying its understanding in contemporary legal scholarship and practice. Jörg Kammerhofer combines a doctrinal discussion with a theoretical analysis of the structure of the law in this area, undertaking a novel approach that critically re-evaluates existing case-law and writings. His approach critiques the arguments for a single expropriation norm based on custom, interpretation and arbitral precedents within international investment law, drawing also on generalist international legal thought, to show that both cosmopolitan and sovereigntist arguments are largely political, not legal. This innovative work will help scholars to understand the application of theory to investment law and help specialists in the field to improve their arguments.

JÖRG KAMMERHOFER is Senior Research Fellow at the University of Freiburg, Germany, and *Privatdozent* for international law and legal theory at the Vienna University of Economics and Business. His publications include *Uncertainty in International Law* (2010), and *International Legal Positivism in a Post-Modern World*, co-edited with Jean d'Aspremont (Cambridge, 2014).

CAMBRIDGE STUDIES IN INTERNATIONAL AND COMPARATIVE LAW: 158

Established in 1946, this series produces high quality, reflective and innovative scholarship in the field of public international law. It publishes works on international law that are of a theoretical, historical, cross-disciplinary or doctrinal nature. The series also welcomes books providing insights from private international law, comparative law and transnational studies which inform international legal thought and practice more generally.

The series seeks to publish views from diverse legal traditions and perspectives, and of any geographical origin. In this respect it invites studies offering regional perspectives on core *problématiques* of international law, and in the same vein, it appreciates contrasts and debates between diverging approaches. Accordingly, books offering new or less orthodox perspectives are very much welcome. Works of a generalist character are greatly valued and the series is also open to studies on specific areas, institutions or problems. Translations of the most outstanding works published in other languages are also considered.

After seventy years, Cambridge Studies in International and Comparative Law sets the standard for international legal scholarship and will continue to define the discipline as it evolves in the years to come.

A list of books in the series can be found at the end of this volume.

INTERNATIONAL INVESTMENT LAW AND LEGAL THEORY

Expropriation and the Fragmentation of Sources

JÖRG KAMMERHOFER
University of Freiburg

CAMBRIDGE
UNIVERSITY PRESS

CAMBRIDGE
UNIVERSITY PRESS

University Printing House, Cambridge CB2 8BS, United Kingdom

One Liberty Plaza, 20th Floor, New York, NY 10006, USA

477 Williamstown Road, Port Melbourne, VIC 3207, Australia

314–321, 3rd Floor, Plot 3, Splendor Forum, Jasola District Centre, New Delhi – 110025, India

79 Anson Road, #06–04/06, Singapore 079906

Cambridge University Press is part of the University of Cambridge.

It furthers the University's mission by disseminating knowledge in the pursuit of education, learning, and research at the highest international levels of excellence.

www.cambridge.org
Information on this title: www.cambridge.org/9781108839174
DOI: 10.1017/9781108989428

First published 2021

A catalogue record for this publication is available from the British Library.

Library of Congress Cataloging-in-Publication Data
Names: Kammerhofer, Jörg, author.
Title: International investment law and legal theory : expropriation and the fragmentation of sources / Jörg Kammerhofer, University of Freiburg.
Description: Cambridge, United Kingdom ; New York, NY : Cambridge University Press, 2021. | Series: Cambridge studies in international and comparative law ; 158 | Includes bibliographical references and index.
Identifiers: LCCN 2021004906 (print) | LCCN 2021004907 (ebook) | ISBN 9781108839174 (hardback) | ISBN 9781108989428 (ebook)
Subjects: LCSH: Investments, Foreign (International law) | Investments, Foreign – Law and legislation.
Classification: LCC K3830 .K36 2021 (print) | LCC K3830 (ebook) | DDC 346/.092–dc23
LC record available at https://lccn.loc.gov/2021004906
LC ebook record available at https://lccn.loc.gov/2021004907

ISBN 978-1-108-83917-4 Hardback

DEM ANDENKEN MEINES VATERS

CONTENTS

FIGURES

PREFACE

It is common to lament that academic writing is a lonely business and it is slightly odd when those who are masters at networking tell us in their prefaces that their existence has been a solitary one during the writing process, usually just before they name a large number of people who have helped them with their enterprise. When I came to draft the preface to my first monograph, *Uncertainty in International Law*, I found that this was not true in my case – I had the benefit of many debates, of written and oral feedback and, generally, of many friends who supported me and my work. With regard to *this* book, I am grateful for the support and feedback that I have received, as well as for the friendships which have made this new book possible. However, for a variety of reasons, the years working on the manuscript to this book have indeed seen me treading a more solitary path. There were personal reasons and reasons related to the *genus loci*, which are not relevant here. There were, however, also substantive reasons, for I seem to excel at finding the space between stools.

My recent scholarship aims to combine two realms of knowledge: legal theory and international legal scholarship. This is not unprecedented – there is a vibrant community of international legal theorists – but the specific form and approach I have chosen seem to be. And as well suited as the Pure Theory of Law, on the theoretical side, and international investment law, on the doctrinal side, are to demonstrate what I have set out to do, they seem to be like oil and water. Rather, those with whom I talk about one tend to have limited patience for the other, which has contributed to the solitary nature of my endeavour. Another factor is that I have searched less for conventional sources of reaffirmation. While academic self-sufficiency may partly be what a second book is about, I must confess to a certain amount of smugness, which is a particularly serious offence for scholars. Mea culpa, particularly in failing to engage more deeply with the community of international investment lawyers. The feeble excuse is that this hermit-like existence has perhaps allowed a more coherent and bold argument to emerge than if I had, through constant feedback, micro-managed my text in order not to offend conventional sensibilities. A lonely book allows breathing-space for big new ideas.

As I have gained more experience as a scholar, I have found that my writings serve as a space in which to tighten the weave in the net of my larger theoretical argument. Ralf Dreier's encouragement to Alexander Somek that 'it is possible for a systematic theoretical programme to be conducted by way of a series of discrete [smaller] projects'[1] as well as Kelsen's late rethink of the problem of legal logic have helped to open my mind to the fact that no single project will be the last word, but every project is a chance to take at least one step further. Monographs are better suited to accomplishing this than any other genre of scholarly writings – the very Germanic process of the *Habilitation* supremely so. I have found the freedom to develop big ideas, which, in this format, is extraordinarily daunting but also extraordinarily liberating; being forced into and counselled towards this course of action has thus had the upside of allowing me to grow as a scholar.

Scholarship is not merely an exercise in making innovative arguments; in many aspects it is surprisingly close to a trade (*Handwerk*). Just as one learns to turn a piece of shafting on a lathe or to build a brick wall by watching those more senior and then trying oneself, so it is with some aspects of scholarship. There is an element of talent and creativity which one either has or has not, but there are many aspects where experience counts. This is where colleagues and teachers – both formal and informal – play a vital role. And this is how I would like the list of names which follows to be read: as thanking those from whom I have learnt one aspect or many, rather than as proof that I have associated with important people.

Erich Vranes has been my indispensable guide to the vagaries of this big project throughout as friend, colleague and *Habilitationsvater* – ever ready with in-depth comments, advice and practical suggestions, ever ready to fight in my corner when progress was threatened and ever ready to gently propel me forward when I was my own worst enemy. Once more, Matthias Jestaedt has held the dual role of *Meister* in the trade aspect and senior colleague in the academic aspect of our profession. In the former role, he exhibited a mastery in tradecraft which allowed me to learn despite my nonconformist inclinations; in the latter, we traded

[1] 'Ralf Dreier, der mir klar machte, daß sich ein systematisch angelegtes Theorieprogramm durchaus in der Form von Einzelprojekten durchführen läßt'; Alexander Somek, *Der Gegenstand der Rechtserkenntnis: Epitaph eines juristischen Problems* (Baden-Baden: Nomos 1996) 5. Unless otherwise noted, all translations in this book are mine.

many ideas and arguments which helped me, despite our partially divergent areas of interest, to sharpen and rally my arguments. In recent years Georg Lienbacher has remained a friend but has also become a pillar or brace for me, in many conversations which sometimes took on aspects of a confessional, and his guidance behind the scenes shall remain there.

As I have become ever more involved in the Hans Kelsen Institute in Vienna, my collaboration with its staff has increased and so have collegiality and friendship; Clemens Jabloner, Thomas Olechowski and Klaus Zeleny can be relied on to defend Kelsen – and Merkl – and to propagate their ideas and I am comforted that in advancing the cause of the Pure Theory, we stand shoulder-to-shoulder to face the onslaught. A number of people have been sounding-boards throughout, particularly Camilla Schiefler, David Freudenberg, Jean d'Aspremont, Stanley Paulson, Gleider Hernandez and Ewald Wiederin.

Two particularly memorable two-month periods helped to shape the basic argument of this book. Thanks to Armin von Bogdandy and Jochen von Bernstorff for conversations in November–December 2008 during my time at the Max Planck Institute for International Law in Heidelberg. I would like to thank Marc Weller, Marie-Claire Cordonnier Segger and Markus W Gehring as well as the permanent and visiting fellows at the Lauterpacht Centre for International Law in Cambridge and the fellows of Queens' College for hosting me during my Brandon Fellowship at the Centre and Distinguished Academic Visitorship at my college during Easter Term 2011.

I have had the opportunity to present chapters and sections of this book in varying stages of completion at a number of venues and would like to thank participants for their feedback and the following people for inviting me and/or for more in-depth conversations on these occasions, often over a leisurely meal: Curt Bradley, Michael Wood and Omri Sender for a Duke and Geneva Universities conference on customary international law in Geneva in July 2013, in particular for a memorable and challenging group dinner; Patrick Capps and Richard Collins for a conference on methodology in Bristol in January 2014; Julian Davis Mortenson for a short but very productive visit in Ann Arbor in June 2014; Marco Pertile, Lorenzo Gradoni, Emmanuel Voyiakis and Peter Hilpold for a conference on custom in Trento and Andrea Gattini for a guest lecture in Padua in November 2014; Stephan Schill, Rainer Hoffmann and Christian Tams for a workshop on investment law at the University of Frankfurt in March 2015; Oliver Digglemann and Tilmann Altwicker for a guest lecture at the University of Zurich in

September 2015; Andreas Kulick for a guest lecture in January 2016 at the University of Tubingen and for a wonderful and truly 'civilian' dinner with him and Johannes W Flume; Panos Merkouris for hosting and co-organising with me a conference on customary law in Groningen in May 2019 and for many discussions before, during and after; and Pauline Westermann, Kostiantyn Gorobets and Andreas Hadjigeorgiou for a workshop at the IVR World Congress in July 2019.

TABLE OF CASES

Investment Tribunals

Accession Mezzanine (2013): Accession Mezzanine Capital L.P. and Danubius Kereskedőház Vagyonkezelő Zrt *v.* Hungary, ICSID, ARB/12/3, Decision on Respondent's Objection under Arbitration Rule 41(5) of 16 January 2013

Achmea I (2012): Achmea B.V. (formerly Eureko B.V.) *v.* The Slovak Republic, UNCITRAL, PCA 2008–13, Final Award of 7 December 2012

ADC (2006): ADC Affiliate Limited and ADC & ADMC Management Limited *v.* Republic of Hungary, ICSID, ARB/03/16, Award of 2 October 2006

ADM (2007): Archer Daniels Midland Company and Tate & Lyle Ingredients Americas, Inc. *v.* United Mexican States, NAFTA-ICSID, ARB(AF)/04/05, Award of 21 November 2007

AES (2005): AES Corporation *v.* Argentine Republic, ICSID, ARB/02/17, Decision on Jurisdiction of 26 April 2005

AES (2010): AES Summit Generation Limited and AES-Tisza Erömü Kft. *v.* Republic of Hungary (II), ICSID, ARB/07/22, Award of 23 September 2010

AIG (2003): AIG Capital Partners Inc. and CJSC Tema Real Estate Company *v.* Republic of Kazakhstan, ICSID, ARB/01/6, Award of 7 October 2003

Allard (2016): Peter A Allard *v.* Government of Barbados, PCA 2012–06, Award of 27 June 2016

Alpha (2010): Alpha Projektholding GmbH *v.* Ukraine, ICSID, ARB/07/16, Award of 8 November 2010

Al Tamini (2015): Adel A Hamadi Al Tamimi *v.* Sultanate of Oman, ICSID, ARB/11/33, Award of 3 November 2015

Al-Warraq (2014): Hesham Talaat M. Al-Warraq *v.* Republic of Indonesia, UNCITRAL, Final Award of 15 December 2014

Ambiente Ufficio (2013): Ambiente Ufficio SPA and Others *v.* Argentine Republic, ICSID, ARB/08/9, Decision on Jurisdiction and Admissibility of 8 February 2013

Ampal (2017): Ampal-American Israel Corporation, EGI-Fund (08–10) Investors, LLC, EGI-Series Investments, LLC, and BSS-EMG Investors, LLC *v.* Arab Republic of Egypt, ICSID, ARB/21/11, Decision on Liability and Heads of Loss of 21 February 2017

Anglia Auto (2017): Anglia Auto Accessories Limited *v.* Czech Republic, SCC, V 2014/181, Final Award of 10 March 2017

Arif (2013): Franck Charles Arif *v.* Republic of Moldova, ICSID, ARB/11/23, Award of 8 April 2013

Aven (2018): David Aven et al. *v.* Costa Rica, UNCITRAL, UNCT/15/3, Final Award of 18 September 2018

Azurix (2006): Azurix *v.* Argentina, ICSID, ARB/01/12, Award of 14 July 2006

Azurix (2009): Azurix Corp. *v.* Argentine Republic, ICSID, ARB/01/12, Decision on the Application for Annulment of the Argentine Republic of 1 September 2009

A11Y (2018): A11Y Ltd. *v.* Czech Republic, ICSID–UNCITRAL, UNCT/15/1, Award of 29 June 2018

Bayindir (2005): Bayindir Insaat Turizm Ticaret Ve Sanayi A.S. *v.* Islamic Republic of Pakistan, ICSID, ARB/03/29, Decision on Jurisdiction, 14 November 2005

Bayindir (2009): Bayindir Insaat Turizm Ticaret Ve Sanayi A.S. *v.* Islamic Republic of Pakistan, ICSID, ARB/03/29, Award of 27 August 2009

BCB (2014): British Caribbean Bank Ltd. *v.* Government of Belize, UNCITRAL, PCA 2010–18, Award of 19 December 2014

Bear Creek (2017): Bear Creek Mining Corporation *v.* Republic of Peru, ICSID, ARB/14/21, Award of 30 November 2017

Belokon (2014): Valeri Belokon *v.* Kyrgyz Republic, UNCITRAL, Award of 24 October 2014

BG (2007): BG Group Plc. *v.* Republic of Argentina, UNCITRAL, Final Award of 24 December 2007

Binder (2011): Rupert Joseph Binder *v.* Czech Republic, UNCITRAL, Final Award of 15 July 2011

Biwater Gauff (2008): Biwater Gauff (Tanzania) Ltd. *v.* United Republic of Tanzania, ICSID, ARB/05/22, Award of 24 July 2008

Blusun (2016): Blusun S.A., Jean-Pierre Lecorcier and Michael Stein *v.* Italian Republic, ICSID, ARB/14/3, Award of 27 December 2016

Bogdanov I (2005): Iurii Bogdanov, Agurdino-Invest Ltd and Agurdino-Chimia JSC *v.* Republic of Moldova, SCC, Award of 22 September 2005

Bosh (2012): Bosh International, Inc. and B&P, LTD Foreign Investments Enterprise *v.* Ukraine, ICSID, ARB/08/11, 25 October 2012

Burlington (2012): Burlington Resources Inc. *v.* Republic of Ecuador, ICSID, ARB/08/5, Decision on Liability of 14 December 2012

Busta (2017): I.P. Busta & J.P. Busta *v.* Czech Republic, SCC, V 2015/014, Final Award of 10 March 2017

Cargill I (2008): Cargill, Incorporated *v.* Republic of Poland, ICSID-UNCITRAL, ARB (AF)/04/2, Award of 29 February 2008

Cargill II (2009): Cargill, Incorporated *v.* United Mexican States, NAFTA-ICSID, ARB (AF)/05/2, Award of 18 September 2009

Charanne (2016): Charanne B.V., Construction Investments S.A.R.L. *v.* Kingdom of Spain, SCC, 062/2012, Award of 21 January 2016

Chemtura (2010): Chemtura Corporation *v.* Government of Canada, NAFTA-UNCITRAL, Award of 2 August 2010

Chevron (2010): Chevron Corporation (USA) and Texaco Petroleum Company (USA) *v.* Republic of Ecuador, UNCITRAL, PCA 34877, Partial Award on the Merits of 30 March 2010

CME (2001): CME Czech Republic B.V. *v.* Czech Republic, UNCITRAL, Partial Award of 13 September 2001

CMS (2003): CMS Gas Transmission Company *v.* Argentine Republic, ICSID, ARB/01/8, Decision of the Tribunal on Objections to Jurisdiction of 17 July 2003

CMS (2005): CMS Gas Transmission Company *v.* Argentine Republic, ICSID, ARB/01/8, Award of 12 May 2005

ConocoPhillips (2013): ConocoPhillips Petrozuata B.V., ConocoPhillips Hamaca B.V., ConocoPhillips Gulf of Paria B.V. and ConocoPhillips Company *v.* Bolivarian Republic of Venezuela, ICSID, ARB/07/30, Decision on Jurisdiction and the Merits of 3 September 2013

Continental Casualty (2008): Continental Casualty Company *v.* Argentine Republic, ICSID, ARB/03/9, Award of 5 September 2008

Copper Mesa (2016): Copper Mesa Mining Corporation *v.* Republic of Ecuador, UNCITRAL, PCA 2012-2, Award of 15 March 2016

Corn Products (2008): Corn Products International, Inc. *v.* United Mexican States, NAFTA-ICSID, ARB(AF)/04/01, Decision on Responsibility of 15 January 2008

Crystallex (2016): Crystallex International Corporation *v.* Bolivarian Republic of Venezuela, ICSID, ARB(AF)/11/2, Award of 4 April 2016

Czescik (2017): Tomasz Częścik and Robert Aleksandrowicz *v.* Republic of Cyprus, SCC, V 2014/169, Award of 11 February 2017

Deutsche Bank (2012): Deutsche Bank AG *v.* Democratic Socialist Republic of Sri Lanka, ICSID, ARB/09/2, Award of 31 October 2012

Devas (2016): CC/Devas (Mauritius) Ltd., Devas Employees Mauritius Private Limited, and Telcom Devas Mauritius Limited *v.* Republic of India, UNCITRAL, PCA 2013-09, Award on Jurisdiction and Merits of 25 July 2016

ECE (2013): ECE Projektmanagement International GmbH and Kommanditgesellschaft PANTA Achtundsechzigste Grundstücksgesellschaft mbH & Co *v.* Czech Republic, UNCITRAL, PCA 2010-5, Award of 19 September 2013

EDF I (2012): EDF International S.A., SAUR International S.A. and León Participaciones Argentinas S.A. *v.* Argentine Republic, ICSID, ARB/03/23, Award of 11 June 2012

E energija (2017): UAB E energija (Lithuania) *v.* Republic of Latvia, ICSID, ARB/12/33, Award of 22 December 2017

Electrabel (2012): Electrabel S.A. *v.* Republic of Hungary, ICSID, ARB/07/19, Decision on Jurisdiction, Applicable Law and Liability of 30 November 2012

El Paso (2006): El Paso Energy International Company *v.* Argentine Republic, ICSID, ARB/03/15, Decision on Jurisdiction of 27 April 2006

El Paso (2011): El Paso Energy International Company *v.* Argentine Republic, ICSID, ARB/03/15, Award of 31 October 2011

Emmis (2013): Emmis International Holding, B.V., Emmis Radio Operating, B.V., Mem Magyar Electronic, Media Kereskedelmi és Szolgáltató Kft *v.* Hungary, ICSID, ARB/12/2, Decision on Respondent's Objection under ICSID Arbitration Rule 41(5) of 11 March 2013

Emmis (2014): Emmis International Holding, B.V., Emmis Radio Operating, B.V., Mem Magyar Electronic Media Kereskedelmi és Szolgáltató Kft. *v.* Hungary, ICSID, ARB/12/2, Award of 16 April 2014

EMV (2009): European Media Ventures *v.* Czech Republic, UNCITRAL, Partial Award on Liability of 8 July 2009

EnCana (2006): EnCana Corporation *v.* Republic of Ecuador, UNCITRAL, LCIA UN3481, Award of 3 February 2006

Enkev (2014): Enkev Beheer B.V. *v.* Republic of Poland, UNCITRAL, PCA 2013–01, First Partial Award of 29 April 2014

Enron (2007): Enron Corporation Ponderosa Assets LP *v.* Argentine Republic, ICSID, ARB/01/3, Award of 22 May 2007

Feldman (2002): Marvin Roy Feldman Karpa *v.* Mexico, NAFTA-ICSID, ARB(AF)/99/1, Award of 16 December 2002

Fireman's Fund (2006): Fireman's Fund Insurance Company *v.* United Mexican States, NAFTA-ICSID, ARB(AF)/02/1, Award of 17 July 2006

Flemingo (2016): Flemingo DutyFree Shop Private Limited *v.* Republic of Poland, UNCITRAL, PCA, Award of 12 August 2016

Foresight (2018): Foresight Luxembourg Solar 1 S.à.r.l., Foresight Luxembourg Solar 2 S.à.r.l., Greentech Energy System A/S, GWM Renewable Energy I S.p.A. and GWM Renewable Energy II S.p.A *v.* Kingdom of Spain, SCC, 2015/150, Award of 14 November 2018

Funnekotter (2009): Bernardus Henricus Funnekotter and others *v.* Republic of Zimbabwe, ICSID, ARB/05/6, Award of 22 April 2009

GAMI (2004): GAMI Investments, Inc. *v.* Government of the United Mexican States, NAFTA-UNCITRAL, Final Award of 15 November 2004

Gavrilović (2018): Georg Gavrilović and Gavrilović D.O.O. *v.* Republic of Croatia, ICSID, ARB/12/39, Award of 26 July 2018

Gemplus (2010): Gemplus S.A., SLP S.A., Gemplus Industrial S.A. de C.V. *v.* United Mexican States; Talsud S.A. v. United Mexican States, ICSID, ARB(AF)/04/3, ARB (AF)/04/4, Award of 16 June 2010

Generation Ukraine (2003): Generation Ukraine, Inc. *v.* Ukraine, ICSID, Award of 16 September 2003

Glamis Gold (2009): Glamis Gold, Ltd. *v.* United States of America, NAFTA-UNCITRAL, Final Award of 8 June 2009

Gold Reserve (2014): Gold Reserve Inc. *v.* Bolivarian Republic of Venezuela, ICSID, ARB(AF)/09/1, Award of 22 September 2014

Grand River (2011): Grand River Enterprises Six Nations, Ltd., et al. *v.* United States of America, NAFTA-UNCITRAL, Award of 12 January 2011

Guaracachi (2014): Guaracachi America, Inc. and Rurelec Plc *v.* Plurinational State of Bolivia, UNCITRAL, PCA 2011–17, Award of 31 January 2014

Houben (2016): Joseph Houben *v.* Republic of Burundi, ICSID, ARB/13/7, Award of 12 January 2016

Impregilo (2005): Impregilo SpA *v.* Islamic Republic of Pakistan, ICSID, ARB/03/3, Decision on Jurisdiction of 22 April 2005

Inmaris (2012): Inmaris Perestroika Sailing Maritime Services GmbH and others *v.* Ukraine, ICSID, ARB/08/8, Award of 1 March 2012

Invesmart (2009): Invesmart, B.V. *v.* Czech Republic, UNCITRAL, Award of 26 June 2009

Jan de Nul (2006): Jan de Nul N.V. and Dredging International N.V. *v.* Arab Republic of Egypt, ICSID, ARB/04/13, Decision on Jurisdiction of 16 June 2006

Kardassopoulos (2010): Ioannis Kardassopoulos and Ron Fuchs *v.* Republic of Georgia, ICSID, ARB/05/18 and ARB/07/15, Award of 3 March 2010

Karkey (2017): Karkey Karadeniz Elektrik Uretim A.S. *v.* Islamic Republic of Pakistan, ICSID, ARB/13/1, Award of 22 August 2017

Koch (2017): Koch Minerals Sàrl and Koch Nitrogen International Sàrl *v.* Bolivarian Republic of Venezuela, ICSID, ARB/11/19, Award of 30 October 2017

Lauder (2001): Ronald S. Lauder *v.* Czech Republic, UNCITRAL, Final Award of 3 September 2001

LG&E (2006): LG&E Energy Corp., LG&E Capital Corp. and LG&E International Inc. *v.* Argentine Republic, ICSID, ARB/02/1, Decision on Liability of 3 October 2006

Liman (2010): Liman Caspian Oil BV and NCL Dutch Investment BV *v.* Republic of Kazakhstan, ICSID, ARB/07/14, Award of 22 June 2010

Mamidoil (2015): Mamidoil Jetoil Greek Petroleum Products Société S.A. *v.* Republic of Albania, ICSID, ARB/11/24, Award of 30 March 2015

Marfin (2018): Marfin Investment Group Holdings S.A., Alexandros Bakatselos and others *v.* Republic of Cyprus, ICSID, ARB/13/27, Award of 26 July 2018

MCI (2007): M.C.I. Power Group L.C. and New Turbine Inc. *v.* Republic of Ecuador, ICSID, ARB/03/6, Award of 31 July 2007

Merrill & Ring (2010): Merrill & Ring Forestry L.P. *v.* Government of Canada, NAFTA-UNCITRAL, Award of 31 March 2010

Metalclad (2000): Metalclad Corporation *v.* United Mexican States, NAFTA-ICSID, ARB(AF)/97/1, Award of 30 August 2000

Metalpar (2008): Metalpar S.A. and Buen Aire S.A. *v.* Argentine Republic, ICSID, ARB/03/5, Award on the Merits of 6 June 2008

Methanex (2001): Methanex Corporation *v.* United States of America, NAFTA-UNCITRAL, Decision of the Tribunal on Petitions from Third Persons to Intervene as 'Amici Curiae' of 15 January 2001

Methanex (2005): Methanex Corporation *v.* United States of America, NAFTA-UNCITRAL, Award of 3 August 2005

Middle East Cement (2002): Middle East Cement Shipping and Handling Co. S.A. *v.* Arab Republic of Egypt, ICSID, ARB/99/6, Award of 12 April 2002

Mitchell (2004): Patrick Mitchell *v.* Democratic Republic of the Congo, ICSID, ARB/99/7, 9 February 2004

Mondev (2002): Mondev International Ltd. *v.* United States of America, NAFTA-ICSID, ARB(AF)/99/2, Award of 11 October 2002

National Grid (2008): National Grid plc *v.* The Argentine Republic, UNCITRAL, Award of 3 November 2008

Novenergia II (2018): Novenergia II – Energy & Environment (SCA) (Grand Duchy of Luxembourg), SICAR *v.* Kingdom of Spain, SCC 2015/063, Award of 15 February 2018

Nykomb (2003): Nykomb Synergetics Technology Holding AB *v.* Republic of Latvia, SCC, Award of 16 December 2003

Occidental I (2004): Occidental Exploration and Production Co. *v.* Ecuador, UNCITRAL, LCIA, UN3467, Award of 1 July 2004

Olguín (2001): Eudoro Armando Olguín *v.* Republic of Paraguay, ICSID, ARB/98/5, Award of 26 July 2001

Olin (2018): Olin Holdings Limited *v.* Libya, ICC, 20355/MCP, Final Award of 25 May 2018

Oxus Gold (2015): Oxus Gold Plc *v.* Republic of Uzbekistan, UNCITRAL, Award of 17 December 2015

Parkerings (2007): Parkerings-Compagniet AS *v.* Republic of Lithuania, ICSID, ARB/05/8, Award of 11 September 2007

Perenco (2014): Perenco Ecuador Limited *v.* Republic of Ecuador, ICSID, ARB/08/6, Decision on Remaining Issues of Jurisdiction and on Liability of 12 September 2014

Petrobart (2005): Petrobart Ltd. *v.* Kyrgyz Republic, SCC, 126/2003, Arbitral Award of 29 March 2005

Pezold (2015): Bernhard Friedrich Arnd Rüdiger von Pezold et al. *v.* Republic of Zimbabwe, ICSID, ARB/10/15, Award of 28 July 2015

Philip Morris (2016): Philip Morris Brands SÀRL, Philip Morris Products S.A. and Abal Hermanos S.A. *v.* Oriental Republic of Uruguay, ICSID, ARB/10/7, Award of 8 July 2016

Plama (2008): Plama Consortium Limited *v.* Republic of Bulgaria, ICSID, ARB/03/24, Award of 27 August 2008

Pope & Talbot (2000): Pope & Talbot Inc *v.* Government of Canada, NAFTA-UNCITRAL, Interim Award of 26 June 2000

PSEG (2007): PSEG Global Inc. and Konya Ilgin Elektrik Üretim ve Ticaret Limited Sirketi *v.* Republic of Turkey, ICSID, ARB/02/5, Award of 19 January 2007

Quiborax (2015): Quiborax S.A. and Non Metallic Minerals S.A. Claimants *v.* Plurinational State of Bolivia, ICSID, ARB/06/2, Award of 16 September 2015

RDC (2012): Railroad Development Corporation (RDC) *v.* Republic of Guatemala, ICSID, ARB/07/23, Award of 29 June 2012

RFCC (2003): Consortium RFCC *v.* Morocco, ICSID, ARB/00/6, Award of 22 December 2003

RosInvestCo (2010): RosInvestCo UK Ltd. *v.* The Russian Federation, SCC, V 079/2005, Final Award of 12 September 2010

Roussalis (2011): Spyridon Roussalis *v.* Romania, ICSID, ARB/06/1, Award of 7 December 2011

Rumeli (2008): Rumeli Telekom A.S. and Telsim Mobil Telekomunikasyon Hizmetleri A.S. *v.* Republic of Kazakhstan, ICSID, ARB/05/16, Award of 29 July 2008

Rusoro (2016): Rusoro Mining Limited *v.* Bolivarian Republic of Venezuela, ICSID, ARB(AF)/12/5, Award of 22 August 2016

Ryan (2015): Vincent J. Ryan, Schooner Capital LLC, and Atlantic Investment Partners LLC *v.* Republic of Poland, ICSID, ARB(AF)/11/3, Award of 24 November 2015

Saar Papier (1995): Saar Papier Vertriebs GmbH *v.* Republic of Poland, UNCITRAL, Final Award of 16 October 1995

Saint-Gobain (2016): Saint-Gobain Performance Plastics Europe *v.* Bolivarian Republic of Venezuela, ICSID, ARB/12/13, Award of 30 December 2016

Saipem (2007): Saipem S.p.A. *v.* People's Republic of Bangladesh, ICSID, ARB/05/7, Decision on Jurisdiction and Recommendation on Provisional Measures of 21 March 2007

Saipem (2009): Saipem S.p.A. *v.* People's Republic of Bangladesh, ICSID, ARB/05/7, Award of 30 June 2009

Saluka (2006): Saluka Investments *v.* Czech Republic, UNCITRAL, Partial Award of 17 March 2006

Santa Elena (2000): Compañia del Desarrollo de Santa Elena, S.A. *v.* Republic of Costa Rica, ICSID, ARB/96/1, Final Award of 17 February 2000

SAUR (2014): SAUR International *v.* Argentine Republic, ICSID, ARB/04/4, Award of 22 March 2014

SD Myers (2000): S.D. Myers, Inc. *v.* Government of Canada, NAFTA-UNCITRAL, Partial Award of 13 November 2000

Sedelmayer (1998): Franz Sedelmayer *v.* Russian Federation, SCC, Award of 7 July 1998

Sempra Energy (2005): Sempra Energy International *v.* Argentina, ICSID, ARB/02/16, Decision on Objections to Jurisdiction of 11 May 2005

Sempra Energy (2007): Sempra Energy International *v.* Argentine Republic, ICSID, ARB/02/16, Award of 28 September 2007

Servier (2012): Les Laboratoires Servier, S.A.S., Biofarma, S.A.S., Arts et Techniques du Progrès S.A.S. *v.* Republic of Poland, UNCITRAL, Final Award of 14 February 2012

SGS Philippines (2004): SGS Société Générale de Surveillance S.A. *v.* Republic of the Philippines, ICSID, ARB/02/6, Decision of the Tribunal on Objections to Jurisdiction of 29 January 2004

Siag (2009): Waguih Elie George Siag and Clorinda Vecchi *v.* Arab Republic of Egypt, ICSID, ARB/05/15, Award of 1 June 2009

Siemens (2007): Siemens A.G. *v.* Argentine Republic, ICSID, ARB/02/8, Award of 6 February 2007

SPP (1992): Southern Pacific Properties (Middle East) Limited *v.* Arab Republic of Egypt, ICSID, Award of 20 May 1992

Suez I (2010): Suez, Sociedad General de Aguas de Barcelona S.A. and InterAgua Servicios Integrales del Agua S.A. *v.* Argentine Republic, ICSID, ARB/03/17, Decision on Liability of 30 July 2010

Suez II (2010): Suez, Sociedad General de Aguas de Barcelona S.A. and Vivendi Universal S.A. *v.* Argentine Republic, ICSID, ARB/03/19 and AWG Group v. Argentine Republic, UNCITRAL, Decision on Liability of 30 July 2010

SwemBalt (2000): SwemBalt AB, Sweden *v.* The Republic of Latvia, UNCITRAL, SCC, Decision by the Court of Arbitration of 23 October 2000

Tecmed (2003): Técnicas Medioambientales Tecmed S.A. *v.* United Mexican States, ICSID, ARB(AF)/00/2, Award of 29 May 2003

Teinver (2017): Teinver S.A., Transportes de Cercanías S.A. and Autobuses Urbanos del Sur S.A. *v.* Argentine Republic, ICSID, ARB/09/1, Award of 21 July 2017

Telenor (2006): Telenor Mobile Communications A.S. *v.* Republic of Hungary, ICSID, ARB/04/15, Award of 13 September 2006 (Jurisdiction)

Thunderbird (2006): International Thunderbird Gaming Corporation *v.* United Mexican States, NAFTA-UNCITRAL, Award of 26 January 2006

Tidewater (2015): Tidewater Investment SRL and Tidewater Caribe, C.A. *v.* Bolivarian Republic of Venezuela, ICSID, ARB/10/5, Award of 13 March 2015

Tokios Tokelės (2007): Tokios Tokelės *v.* Ukraine, ICSID, ARB/02/18, Award of 26 July 2007

Total (2010): Total S.A. *v.* Argentine Republic, ICSID, ARB/04/1, Award of 27 December 2010

Toto (2009): Toto Costruzioni Generali S.p.A. *v.* Republic of Lebanon, ICSID, ARB/07/12, Decision on Jurisdiction of 11 September 2009

Tza Yap Shum (2011): Tza Yap Shum *v.* Republic of Peru, ICSID, ARB/07/6, Award of 7 July 2011

Unglaube (2012): Marion Unglaube and Reinhard Unglaube *v.* Republic of Costa Rica, ICSID, ARB/08/01 and ARB/09/20, Award of 16 May 2012

UPS (2002): United Parcel Service of America, Inc *v.* Canada, NAFTA-UNCITRAL, Award on Jurisdiction of 22 November 2002

UP and CD (2018): UP and C.D. Holding Internationale *v.* Hungary, ICSID, ARB/13/35, Award of 9 October 2018

Urbaser (2016): Urbaser S.A. and Consorcio de Aguas Bilbao Biskaia, Bilbao Biskaia Ur Partzuergoa *v.* Argentine Republic, ICSID, ARB/07/26, Award of 8 December 2016

Venezuela Holdings (2014): Venezuela Holdings, B.V., Mobil Cerro Negro Holding, Ltd., Mobil Venezolana de Petróleos Holdings, Inc., Mobil Cerro Negro, Ltd., Mobil Venezolana de Petróleos, Inc. *v.* Bolivarian Republic of Venezuela, ICSID, ARB/07/27, Award of 9 October 2014

Vestey (2016): Vestey Group Limited *v.* Bolivarian Republic of Venezuela, ICSID, ARB/06/4, Award of 15 April 2016

Veteran Petroleum (2014): Veteran Petroleum Limited *v.* Russian Federation, PCA AA 228, Final Award of 18 July 2014

Vivendi (2007): Compañia de Aguas Del Aconquija SA and Vivendi Universal SA *v.* Argentine Republic, ICSID, ARB/97/3, Award of 20 August 2007

Walter Bau (2009): Walter Bau AG *v.* Kingdom of Thailand, UNCITRAL, Award of 1 July 2009

Waste Management (2004): Waste Management Inc. *v.* United Mexican States, NAFTA-ICSID, ARB(AF)/00/3, Award of 30 April 2004

Wena (2000): Wena Hotels Limited *v.* Arab Republic of Egypt, ICSID, ARB/98/4, Award on the Merits of 8 December 2000

Wena (2005): Wena Hotels Limited *v.* Arab Republic of Egypt, ICSID, ARB/98/4, Decision on Interpretation, 31 October 2005

Windstream (2016): Windstream Energy LLC *v.* Canada, UNCITRAL, PCA, Award of 27 September 2016

WNC (2017): WNC Factoring Ltd (United Kingdom) *v.* Czech Republic, UNCITRAL, PCA 2014-34, Award of 22 February 2017

Yukos (2014): Yukos Universal Limited (Isle Of Man) *v.* Russian Federation, UNCITRAL, PCA AA 227, Final Award of 18 July 2014

Other Courts and Tribunals

AMINOIL (1982): Kuwait *v.* American Independent Oil Company (AMINOIL), Award of 24 March 1982, 21 ILM (1982) 976

Armed Activities (2005): Armed Activities on the Territory of the Congo (Democratic Republic of the Congo *v.* Uganda), Merits, Judgment of 19 December 2005, ICJ Reports (2005) 168

Barcelona Traction (1970): Barcelona Traction, Light and Power, Limited (New Application: 1962) (Belgium *v.* Spain), Second Phase, Judgment of 5 February 1970, ICJ Reports (1970) 3

Chorzów (1926): Certain German Interests in Polish Upper Silesia (Germany *v.* Poland), Judgment on the Merits of 25 May 1926, PCIJ Series A No 7 (1926)

Chorzów (1927): Factory at Chorzów (Claim for Indemnity) (Germany *v.* Poland), Judgment on Jurisdiction of 26 July 1927, PCIJ Series A No 9 (1927)

Chorzów (1928): Factory at Chorzów (Claim for Indemnity) (Germany *v.* Poland), Judgment on the Merits of 13 September 1928, PCIJ Series A No 17 (1928)

Diallo (2007): Ahmadou Sadio Diallo (Republic of Guinea *v.* Democratic Republic of the Congo), Preliminary Objections, Judgment of 24 May 2007, ICJ Reports (2007) 582

Diallo (2010): Ahmadou Sadio Diallo (Republic of Guinea *v.* Democratic Republic of the Congo), Judgment of 30 November 2010, ICJ Reports (2010) 639

ELSI (1989): Elettronica Sicula SpA (ELSI) (United States of America *v.* Italy), Judgment of 20 July 1989, ICJ Reports (1989) 15

Kosovo (2010): Accordance with International Law of the Unilateral Declaration of Independence in Respect of Kosovo, Advisory Opinion of 22 July 2010, ICJ Reports (2010) 403

Lotus (1927): S.S. 'Lotus' (France *v.* Turkey), Judgment of 7 September 1927, PCIJ Series A No 10 (1927)

Oil Platforms (2003): Oil Platforms (Islamic Republic of Iran *v.* United States of America), Merits, Judgment of 6 November 2003, ICJ Reports (2003) 161

Nicaragua (1984): Military and Paramilitary Activities in and Against Nicaragua (Nicaragua *v.* United States of America), Jurisdiction and Admissibility, Judgment of 26 November 1984, ICJ Reports (1984) 392

Nicaragua (1986): Military and Paramilitary Activities in and Against Nicaragua (Nicaragua *v.* United States of America), Merits, Judgment of 27 June 1986, ICJ Reports (1986) 14

Norwegian Shipowners (1922): Norwegian Shipowners' Claims (Norway *v.* United States of America), Permanent Court of Arbitration, Award of 13 October 1922, 1 RIAA (1948) 307

Nottebohm (1955): Nottebohm (Second Phase) (Liechtenstein *v.* Guatemala), Judgment of 6 April 1955, ICJ Reports (1955) 4

NSCS (1969): North Sea Continental Shelf (Federal Republic of Germany/Denmark; Federal Republic of Germany/Netherlands), Judgment of 20 February 1969, ICJ Reports (1969) 3

Phillips Petroleum (1989): Phillips Petroleum Company, Iran *v.* Islamic Republic of Iran, National Iranian Oil Company, Iran–USCT, Award 425-39-2 of 29 June 1989, 21 Iran–USCT Reports (1990) 79

Revere Copper (1978): Revere Copper and Brass, Inc. *v.* Overseas Private Investment Corporation, Award of 24 August 1978, 56 International Law Reports (1980) 258

Sedco (1987): Sedco Inc., Sedco International SA and Sediran Drilling Company *v.* National Iranian Oil Company and Islamic Republic of Iran, Iran–USCT, Award ITL 55-129-3 of 24 October 1985, 9 Iran–USCT Reports (1987) 248

Texaco (1978): Texaco Overseas Petroleum Co. *v.* Libyan Arab Republic, 1977, 17 ILM (1978) 1

Wall (2004): Legal Consequences of the Construction of a Wall in the Occupied Palestinian Territory, Advisory Opinion of 9 June 2004, ICJ Reports (2004) 136

1

Introduction

1. In (international) legal scholarship, theoretical and doctrinal arguments are inextricably linked and mutually dependent. Doing one without the other inevitably distorts our view of the law, so much so that it might not be entirely unreasonable to paraphrase Kant's famous aphorism: legal theory without legal doctrine is empty, legal doctrine without legal theory is blind.[1] This is what this book seeks to prove or, rather, seeks to demonstrate by way of a case-study. Purely theoretical speculation about the nature and value of theory is not only as empty as first-order theory which proceeds in this manner but there is greater didactic value in showing how theory 'works' with respect to specific legal rules and arguments on the law – and how theoretical and doctrinal arguments intermesh. Proceeding from substantive questions to structural analysis and from there to methodology and epistemology may engender a greater acceptance among those not normally inclined to spend their energy on theoretical deliberations. In other words, showing the theoretical dimension of 'ordinary' legal questions may be more convincing than scholastic exercises on the theoretical level. Accordingly, the theoretical approach adopted here is used in every chapter, rather than remaining confined to an introductory section.

There is hardly a topic better suited to serve as case-study than expropriation in international investment law, for it is hotly debated yet under-theorised. The arguments developed to support one or another position are suffused with theoretical significance, particularly regarding the structure of the expropriation norm. Yet at the same time, hardly anywhere in international law is theory treated with greater disregard – and

[1] See Immanuel Kant, *Kritik der reinen Vernunft* (Riga: Hartknoch 1781/1787) A 48, B 75: 'Ohne Sinnlichkeit würde uns kein Gegenstand gegeben, und ohne Verstand keiner gedacht werden. Gedanken ohne Inhalt sind leer, Anschauungen ohne Begriffe sind blind.' 'Without sensibility no object would be given to us, without understanding no object would be thought. Thoughts without content are empty, intuitions without concepts are blind.' (Translation Norman Kemp Smith 1929.)

sometimes open disdain – than here. Contributors to debates in investment law in general and expropriation law in particular find it particularly hard to separate their ideological inclinations from the analysis of the law, yet seem to believe strongly that their arguments relate to the law.

However, the proposed *modus operandi* – demonstration, rather than abstract argument – is itself fraught with problems. The book could be taken for an 'ordinary' monograph on expropriation law whose theoretical chapters are at best a superfluous growth and at worst contain a malignancy whose metastases threaten to destroy what is left of 'healthy' doctrinal arguments. If that were the case, a book of this type and scope at this moment in the development of international investment law would seem untimely, superfluous and both too narrow and too broad. One could say with some justification that the time for writing a monograph on expropriation in international investment law has passed. Both investment law as a whole and the protection of foreign investors specifically against indirect expropriation have passed their zenith. All judges, counsel, academics, state officials and other 'stakeholders' must now be active participants in a complete rethinking of the law governing foreign direct investment, rather than worry about the foundations for the 'old' view of expropriation law under the network of outdated International Investment Agreements (IIAs). At best, we should be looking for pragmatic ways to incorporate legitimate concerns from a variety of legal, political and ethical considerations into 'legacy' IIAs. We cannot be concerned with deconstruction and legal reconstruction in the manner proposed when we have, to use the colloquial phrase, bigger fish to fry.

From another perspective, this type of book on expropriation would go too far: we already have a number of excellent works portraying the law in the time-honoured tradition of international legal scholarship. We do not need another, particularly one which expends so much effort on sowing doubt about the foundations for our arguments while not providing comprehensive coverage of the topic. Therefore, if this book were simply aiming to describe 'expropriation', the execution would be problematic: it is not a critique of the law itself, but it is critical of the methods that lawyers use. It does not attempt to find an 'acceptable' view of the law – one commensurate with the politics of the moment which allows a 'balanced' view of investor and state interests. It is not a reference work for practitioners, yet it seeks to show what the 'positive law' on expropriation is, warts and all.

This weak-spot would be real enough if this were yet another monograph on expropriation law – but it is not. The book aims to demonstrate that our arguments about the (content of the) law are dependent on theoretical foundations, such as how norms are created and interact or how legal scholarship should work. It also argues that the reverse is true: theory must respond to the law and the way we talk about the law. Expropriation in international investment law is the example chosen and this book will approach the demonstration of inter-linkage in a twofold manner. The theoretical chapters show how theoretical questions find their expression in doctrine; the doctrinal chapters show how doctrine raises theoretical questions. The law (respectively, our construction of it) is portrayed to show theoretical relevance; theory is portrayed to show its relevance for doctrine. Such an enterprise, however, cannot be apologetic and must include a critique and a deconstruction of the aims and methods of both jurisprudence and academic writings on expropriation.

2. Expropriation in international investment law has been a pressing and hotly debated issue for some time. A large number of authors and arbitral awards have attempted to grapple with the problem of what it is and how to apply the unspecific prescriptions in the network of thousands of IIAs. Foundational critiques of protection against so-called 'regulatory' expropriation – general legislative and administrative measures which may negatively affect foreign investors and their investments – have flourished as has the attempt to reconstruct the law to account for this critique. A large body of thought has developed to overcome the fundamental fragmentation of the 'base layer' of the law. After all, there is no universal investment treaty and it largely consists of a collection of bilateral or plurilateral treaties with no systematic interconnectedness. While largely similar in content, they are separate entities in law. Also, while there is case-law, there is no standing court, only ad hoc arbitral tribunals, which are deliberately designed to deliver decisions valid only *inter partes*. Despite this, in recent decades it has become commonplace to argue both that similarity of text means cross-treaty equality of legal content and that 'de facto' precedential value accrues to investment awards.

Take a typical example: the phrase 'measures having effect equivalent to nationalisation or expropriation' in Article 5(1) of the Pakistan–Denmark Bilateral Investment Treaty (BIT) 1996 cannot be made more specific by a tribunal deciding on the basis of the France–Venezuela BIT 2001 that the taking-over, by a national oil company, of a fracking proppants plant, amounts to indirect expropriation.[2] In other words, even if Pakistan State Oil were to take over a Danish investor's fracking proppants plant in similar circumstances, 'the law' does not mandate a similar decision. On the evidence available, it can even be argued that the *factual likelihood* of a similar decision by a future tribunal is not particularly high.

3. While the past decade has seen a burgeoning of theoretical writings[3] on international investment law, most writings[4] tend to follow the 'orthodox' pattern of doctrinal international legal scholarship (*Rechtsdogmatik*). Orthodox international legal writings operate on the basis of 'default' legal positivism,[5] wanting to discover the law 'as it is', as opposed to a law based on perceived moral or political imperatives. However, it also tends to be non-theoretical and quasi-positivist, believing in received authorities, foremost international tribunals, without a sustained critique of their authority or correctness of their pronouncements. In investment law, this means trying to find specific rules in unspecific treaty provisions – and primarily using prior reasoning by arbitral tribunals. However, IIAs do not contain specific prescriptions: 'the law' applied by arbitral tribunals is 'coarse' and arbitral case-law does not change that fact. While IIAs typically prohibit uncompensated 'indirect expropriation', neither they themselves nor arbitral awards rendered on their basis determine (beyond the specific case) whether a tax of 99 per cent on oil production is an indirect expropriation – yet the orthodox approach (implicitly) argues that they do.

Both scholarship and practice employ a range of methods to unify and specify the law on expropriation. There is a great mass of literature and a large number of precedents. Yet as soon as we stop taking mainstream contentions at face-value, once we take a closer look at the foundation for their arguments, many of the methods employed to get to these

[2] *Saint-Gobain Performance Plastics Europe* v. *Bolivarian Republic of Venezuela*, ICSID, ARB/12/13, Award of 30 December 2016 para 477.

[3] Leading investment law theorists include Zachary Douglas, Stephan Schill, Kate Miles and Andreas Kulick.

[4] Leading general publications on international investment law adopting this pattern include: Rudolf Dolzer, Christoph Schreuer, *Principles of International Investment Law* (2nd edn, Oxford: Oxford University Press 2012); August Reinisch (ed.), *Standards of Investment Protection* (Oxford: Oxford University Press 2008); Campbell McLachlan, Laurence Shore, Matthew Weiniger, *International Investment Arbitration: Substantive Principles* (Oxford: Oxford University Press 2007).

[5] Jörg Kammerhofer, 'International Legal Positivist Research Methods' in Rossana Deplano, Nicholas Tsagourias (eds.), *Research Methods in International Law: A Handbook* (Cheltenham: Edward Elgar in press), available at: ssrn.com/abstract=3503295, section 2.

contentions can be shown to be deeply problematic; some are unsustainable. That is, they are not sustainable if we take seriously the idea of wishing to discover the positive law in force *only*, rather than our conscious or subconscious ideological, ethical or pragmatic wishes or positions.

Mainstream scholarship on expropriation suffers from a range of problems. For example, it is based on a narrow band of arguments to sustain its construction of the law. Almost exclusively, orthodox views on case-law are encyclopaedic-apologetic, rather than critical. In elucidating the concept of 'expropriation', these voices privilege a balancing approach – balancing investment protection against the right to regulate – which, although its reliance on a highly technical and complex proportionality analysis suggests legality, is really an exercise in diplomacy. Where writings are pragmatic, untheoretical (or outright anti-theoretical), they are in danger of misrepresenting the law, as the lack of reflection on the theoretical foundations will result in an obfuscation of the limits of the law. Lack of critical reflection of the legal method leads to a falsification of results. Many are beholden to the *horror vacui* – they cannot abide the possibility of the law not being specific, not being unified, not providing a solution. Legal scholarship's subconscious drive to provide 'solutions' also hinders its task of accurately portraying the law in force.

Why is this tendency so strong in those writing about international law? Among other causes, there is a lack of awareness for the interlinkage and mutual dependency of theory and doctrine. A partial answer to this lack of awareness is that international legal scholarship does not have a group of people common to public legal scholarship in national contexts: scholars of constitutional law. In the municipal realm, these are primarily concerned with the arrangements for organising the highest organs of the state; administrative scholars are charged with describing the content of administrative rules. However, the former also take particular parts of and changes to administrative law as opportunity to expound on the foundations of administrative-legal doctrine, to explain the structural-hierarchical relationships and to critique arguments made by doctrinal scholars. They discuss topics such as the sources of public law, interpretation, norm-conflict and derogation. Constitutional lawyers serve as intermediary, talking about administrative doctrine, constitutional doctrine as well as legal theory proper,[6] raising awareness of

[6] A very good example for this type of scholarship is Ewald Wiederin, *Bundesrecht und Landesrecht: Zugleich ein Beitrag zu Strukturproblemen der bundesstaatlichen Kompetenzverteilung in Österreich und Deutschland* (Vienna: Springer 1995).

theory among doctrinal scholars as well as spelling out how their theoretical arguments can be applied with respect to substantive law. Perhaps we are missing the constitutional lawyers of international law.[7]

In order to *apply* legal theory, a specific theoretical approach needs to be chosen. We will proceed on the basis of the normativist positivism of the Pure Theory of Law and of its founder, Hans Kelsen. The following is based on the premise that its basic tenets can be gainfully applied to the study of international law. The Pure Theory contains a theory of legal scholarship (*Rechtswissenschaftstheorie*), a theory of how cognition of law as norms is possible without admixing it with norms belonging to other normative orders (or even 'absolute' values) or reducing law to socio-psycho-linguistic facts. It avoids reducing legal scholarship to a form of sociology, political science, psychology or linguistics. Yet it is not, cannot and does not want to be an explanation of the totality of 'the law'.[8]

This approach recognises, for example, that written norms, couched in natural languages, are not determinate and that legal scholarship cannot give an 'interpretation' that gains in specificity. It realises that, as a matter of *social fact*, concrete (tribunal) decisions are an important factor influencing future behaviour. Stakeholders such as states, investors and professional jurists such as counsel and arbitrators are influenced by the great amount of investment arbitral awards or, rather, by the reasoning therein. Yet, the Pure Theory is adamant that this highly important set of facts cannot be called 'the law'. Decisions *as facts* neither replace general norms nor make decisions (i.e. individual norms) generally binding. Even their factual influence is contingent on a wide variety of factors.

4. This book's focus on the interlinkage of theory and doctrine engenders a number of limitations. First, we will focus only on the 'modern' investment law based on the large network of IIAs, not on traditional norms, including customary international law (except as relevant to IIAs) or on the law and jurisprudence of the Iran–US Claims Tribunal. Second, there will be no attempt to collect and cite *all* writings and jurisprudence on the topic; while this book attempts to be reasonably comprehensive with respect to its sources, only writings (and case-law) in English and German were systematically canvassed; texts and awards in other languages were used only sporadically. Third, only literature published and

[7] See Jörg Kammerhofer, *Uncertainty in International Law: A Kelsenian Perspective* (Abingdon: Routledge 2010) 196–7.

[8] See Jörg Kammerhofer, 'Positivistische Normbegründung' in Eric Hilgendorf, Jan C Joerden (eds.), *Handbuch Rechtsphilosophie* (Stuttgart: Metzler 2017) 200–8 at 205.

awards rendered before 1 January 2019 were canvassed. The linguistic and temporal limits are owing to pragmatic factors, such as the necessity to cut a significant part of the original manuscript before publication and my limited knowledge of other languages. A more encyclopaedic approach to sources was not necessary because this book focuses on theory: it is simply not necessary to provide all sources for a typical doctrinal argument – the theoretical critique attaches to the form of the argument, not to a specific number of treatments. Moreover, as far as I can ascertain, neither in scholarship published nor in awards rendered since 2019 have there been any arguments made which are so significantly different as to warrant a change in the points made in the following chapters.

5. How will the argument sketched out above be made in the remainder of this book? The first approach will be from a legal-theoretical vantage-point. The three 'theoretical' chapters will each discuss a significant type of doctrinal argument – customary international law, the authority of jurisprudence and the epistemic authority of interpretation – by which the universalisation, specification and greater certainty of expropriation are to be achieved. On the legal-theoretical framework adopted here, all three types of argument must face significant hurdles; none yields the benefit which modern investment doctrine expects.

Chapter 2 asks whether IIAs have generated or changed customary law. Investment scholarship's optimistic approach to the status of customary international law after the 'BIT movement'[9] must face four theoretical issues. First, there is a consistent failure to distinguish the elements of custom-creation (*usus* and *opinio iuris*) from their proofs; if we do so, however, IIAs help us rather less than expected to prove a modern customary expropriation norm. Second, IIAs counted as state practice are problematic because verbal acts as such are problematic. If customary norms get their content from a repetition of the behaviour to be prescribed, then verbal acts are no more than practice of *making* a verbal act, not of the content of that verbal act: an IIA prescribing that states ought to do 'x' is not the same as states actually doing 'x'. Third, IIAs counted as *opinio iuris* cannot supply the content of the resulting norm: customary norms are given their content by the repetition of behaviour, not of beliefs. Fourth, the idea that treaties are an *inter partes* opt-out from general international law means that IIAs are likely

[9] Andreas F Lowenfeld, 'Investment Agreements and International Law' 42 *Columbia Journal of Transnational Law* (2003) 123–30 at 129.

concluded to counter perceptions of custom and a fortiori not custom-building. Therefore, a customary international law on expropriation is unlikely to be shaped significantly by IIAs: IIAs are not instances of expropriation or non-expropriation, hence they cannot serve as state practice *sensu stricto*. Also, the treaty norm-formulation for expropriation without more does not tell us whether this is the *opinio iuris*. However, some evidence for *opinio iuris* can probably be gleamed from treaty-related texts or events. Further, even if IIAs did shape customary international law or if IIA expropriation clauses did incorporate a customary expropriation norm, the likely specificity of such a norm would be extraordinarily low.

Chapter 3 evaluates jurisprudence's precedential force. Orthodox approaches are marked by an agreement on a narrow set of arguments, namely that international law is not a common law and arbitral awards do not have *stare decisis* power, that jurisprudence is hugely important and tribunals rely on it and that there must therefore be a sort of de facto system of precedents in operation. In effect, 'factual importance' is fashioned into a source of legal authority. However, few arguments are given as to why this transfer from fact to law would occur and they do not provide a foundation for a general *legal* value for precedents. Yet the weight of arbitral jurisprudence is both too great to ignore and too helpful in discovering what 'expropriation' means in a pragmatic sense. Precedents are statements about general norms; outside the common law, judge-made law is merely an interpretation of a general norm in a judgment. Not even a constant tradition of decisions can turn such a statement into a norm.

Chapter 4 focuses on the claim that (tribunal) interpretation of IIAs is an epistemic 'authority' and that it is the integrative factor. Interpretation is, at once, the most promising, the most complex and the most problematic avenue, for there are two fundamentally different and to some extent irreconcilable meanings of interpretation: it can mean both the process of finding out what texts mean and guidance to the concretisation of abstract general norms in individual instances. In that second sense, interpretation is subconsciously used to narrow the freedom implicit in empowering an organ to decide and is therefore caught in the no-man's -land between decision and cognition. A range of interpretative tools is used to generate a quasi-formal unity of meaning across IIAs; systemic integration is the most used and most potent tool. It relies on two arguments: 'Reference' is based on the idea that systemic integration merely brings to the fore the intention of the treaty parties that wish their treaty to be interpreted in the light of other parts of international law. Yet treaties are not reducible to party intentions. 'Coherence' assumes that international law is a rational system and that treaties must be (made) coherent with the system. However, international law is not a rationally coherent whole.

If customary law supplies the content in the process of systemic integration, then how does a treaty as contracting-out from customary law square with bringing its content back by means of interpretation? What difference would remain between such a potent interpretative tool and a straight-up modification of the treaty? Systemic integration enjoins us to assume that meanings are identical but that assumption is baseless: taking into account external rules could just as easily be the basis for a divergence. However, these problems are not as urgent as they may seem: customary law is less certain and precise than assumed; from the perspective of peer-accepted reasoning-before-decision-making, the interpreter takes *meanings*, not external rules into account. Arbitral tribunals interpret IIAs in light not of a customary norm but of other investment tribunals' understanding of the meaning of *pari materia* treaties' norms on expropriation. This is a paradigm change because it negates the distinctions among systemic integration, *pari materia* interpretation and other interpretative tools. Interpretation cannot provide a legal process of universalisation of international investment law because it *does not change the law*. It is, however, a powerful *factual* universaliser.

Chapter 5 discusses what doctrinal investment law scholarship can be and thus introduces the three doctrinal chapters. Can a doctrinal scholarship which is based on the normativist-positivist framework espoused in this book do any better? Starting from a critique of certain hyper-systematising approaches, it introduces Kelsen's idea of legal scholarship properly so called, one devoid of external influences, because these make it impossible to correctly cognise the law. Reconstructed in this manner, doctrinal scholarship can provide a structural analysis of the law, both on the macro-level of system-coherence and on the micro-level as frame-determination. It can also give practical information on how awards have exercised their freedom within the frame of possible meanings.

Chapter 6 deconstructs the main argument of orthodox doctrinal scholarship on regulatory expropriation. It argues that the strong impetus of orthodox scholarship to solve problems leads both camps – those favouring strong investor protection and those arguing for a wide state freedom to regulate – to see the problem in virtually the same terms and to develop the same solution. The problem identified is that none of the two extremes is sustainable; the solution is that a balance has to be struck. Yet such a view is ideological, not legal, because it cannot contemplate and must deny a priori the possibility that IIA expropriation clauses are skewed in one direction or that the law does not provide for a balanced, proportional solution. Doctrinal scholarship, however, must analyse the law as it is, not as we may wish it to be.

Chapter 7 demonstrates the method of 'frame-determination' for IIA expropriation clauses and identifies three limits of the *actus reus* condition (the *Tatbestand*) of typical IIA expropriation clauses: First, on the macro-structural level – concerning the interaction of IIA clauses with the rest of international law – facile references to customary international law are shown to be problematic: 'expropriation' in IIAs does not refer to a customary norm of certain validity and great specificity. Second, on the micro-structural level, the necessity of treating direct and indirect expropriation as fully equivalent is structurally inherent in typical IIAs. Third, the other micro-structural argument is that all legality conditions are equal and cannot be doubled in the *Tatbestand* of indirect expropriation. The structure of typical IIA clauses does not support the majority of arguments based on 'police powers' or on a 'right to regulate'.

Chapter 8 turns to the frame of possible meanings, for there is ample room for tribunals to decide cases within that frame. It discusses tribunal arguments and holdings and by analysing and structuring extant jurisprudence for three topics: the 'substantial deprivation' standard, the preeminent measure of the intensity of measures in modern case-law; the controversy over the possibility of partial expropriation; and the distinction between compensation under IIAs and reparation under the law of state responsibility.

2

Customary International Law

2.1 Introduction: The Specialist Debate

If there is still doubt that the fragmentation of international law is very real, one need only take a look at the International Court of Justice's (ICJ) 2007 and 2010 judgments in *Ahmadou Sallo Diallo*.[1] In that case, the Court pointedly ignored the very closely interwoven customary international law on the protection of foreigners and their property abroad and the treaty-based investment law and arbitral case-law. In its 2007 judgment on preliminary objections, it 'note[d] that, in contemporary international law, the protection of the rights of companies ... [is] essentially governed by bilateral or multilateral agreements for the protection of foreign investments'.[2] Yet, given the usual open-mindedness of orthodox international lawyers towards the influence of treaties on customary international law-making,[3] the Court drew a surprisingly narrow conclusion from the recent developments:

> The Court, having carefully examined State practice and decisions of international courts and tribunals ... is of the opinion that these do not reveal – at least at the present time – an exception in customary international law ... The fact invoked by Guinea that various international agreements, such as agreements for the promotion and protection of foreign investments ... have established special legal régimes governing investment protection ... is *not sufficient to show that there has been a change in the customary rules of diplomatic protection; it could equally show the contrary.*[4]

[1] *Ahmadou Sadio Diallo (Republic of Guinea* v. *Democratic Republic of the Congo)*, Preliminary Objections, Judgment of 24 May 2007, ICJ Reports (2007) 582; *Ahmadou Sadio Diallo (Republic of Guinea* v. *Democratic Republic of the Congo)*, Judgment of 30 November 2010, ICJ Reports (2010) 639.

[2] *Diallo* (2007) note 1 at 614 (para 88).

[3] Not least by the Court itself, eg in *Nottebohm* (*Second Phase) (Liechtenstein* v. *Guatemala*), Judgment of 6 April 1955, ICJ Reports (1955) 4 at 22–3.

[4] *Diallo* (2007) note 1 at 615 (paras 89–90) (emphasis added).

This is not particularly surprising, given the Court's previous holdings on the relationship between the customary and treaty norms on the protection of foreign investments, for example in *Barcelona Traction*.[5] Contrast its holding to the position of investment tribunals, for example in *CMS*:

> Although it is true, as argued by the Republic of Argentina, that this is mostly the result of *lex specialis* and specific treaty arrangements that have so allowed, the fact is that *lex specialis* in this respect is so prevalent that it can now be considered the general rule, certainly in respect of foreign investments and increasingly in respect of other matters.[6]

Regarding the general argument relating to the influence of pre-existing treaty-law on the creation of customary international law, however, the Court ignored its own holdings in *Nicaragua*.[7] If the UN Charter has had an impact on the law on the use of force as the Court held there, the network of IIAs could arguably also have had a similar impact on the customary international investment law. Why then did the Court differentiate? Moreover, in *Diallo*, the Court accorded different treatment to the human rights and investment law regimes. It held that the recent developments in the treatment of foreign investments had no capacity to influence the customary law in this area.[8] The question of the possibility of a change of customary norms after the network of IIAs has been established can apparently be raised only for issues not covered by investment treaty norms, because, in contrast, the Court intimated a much closer relationship to human rights law. For example, it did not shy away from using the jurisprudence of the European and the Inter-American Courts of Human Rights.[9] This is in line with the Court's *jurisprudence constante* in readily holding that treaty-based human rights and humanitarian law norms have become customary international

[5] *Barcelona Traction, Light and Power, Limited (New Application: 1962) (Belgium* v. *Spain)*, Second Phase, Judgment of 5 February 1970, ICJ Reports (1970) 3 at 40, 47 (paras 61–3, 90).

[6] *CMS Gas Transmission Company* v. *Argentine Republic*, ICSID, ARB/01/8, Decision of the Tribunal on Objections to Jurisdiction of 17 July 2003, para 48.

[7] *Military and Paramilitary Activities in and Against Nicaragua (Nicaragua* v. *United States of America)*, Merits, Judgment of 27 June 1986, ICJ Reports (1986) 14 at 96–7 (para 181): 'However, so far from having constituted a marked departure from a customary international law which still exists unmodified, the Charter gave expression in this field to principles already present in customary international law, and that law has in the subsequent four decades developed under the influence of the Charter.'

[8] *Diallo* (2007) note 1 at 614–15 (para 88).

[9] *Diallo* (2010) note 1 at 664 (para 68).

law.[10] How can we reconcile the double standard employed by the Court? More importantly, what is the relationship between general (customary) international law and international investment treaty law beyond specific adjudicative *fora*?

This chapter discusses the structural problems of the claim to multilateralise international investment law via customary international law. We will look at legal-theoretical challenges, focusing on the impact of the network of investment treaties and on the process of customary law-making as a source for constructing a general norm on expropriation. The reverse influence of customary international law on IIAs is less central here, but the two avenues are interlocking: treaties may refer to custom and the existence of treaty rules might influence the development of customary law. Yet there is a question of whether a treaty norm that 'merely' incorporates customary international law norm can influence or change the same customary norm. A potential 'point of entry' for customary law, even in the treaty-based field of investment law, is that IIAs refer to or incorporate concepts from customary international (investment) law (Section 4.3). Jürgen Kurtz argues against

> a blunt claim ... that the investment treaty project was designed to exclude most if not all customary norms. The reality is far more complex. The treaty project was structured to offer a tailored system of legal regulation ... which incorporated select customary norms and also constructed new treaty norms with a different tenor and direction from the protections at customary international law.[11]

But, 'do BITs represent the "new" custom in this field?'[12] Whether IIAs have created customary international investment law has been hotly debated in academic literature, with a high-point reached in 2008–11. There is agreement in the specialist investment law debate that IIAs can in principle be the basis of customary international law norms; none of the writings canvassed for this chapter raise categorical

[10] Examples from recent jurisprudence include: *Legal Consequences of the Construction of a Wall in the Occupied Palestinian Territory*, Advisory Opinion of 9 June 2004, ICJ Reports (2004) 136 at 172 (para 89); *Armed Activities on the Territory of the Congo (Democratic Republic of the Congo* v. *Uganda)*, Merits, Judgment of 19 December 2005, ICJ Reports (2005) 168 at 229–30, 242, 244 (paras 172, 214, 219).

[11] Jürgen Kurtz, 'Adjudging the Exceptional at International Investment Law: Security, Public Order and Financial Crisis' 59 *International and Comparative Law Quarterly* (2010) 325–71 at 357.

[12] Patrick Dumberry, 'Are BITs Representing the "New" Customary International Law in International Investment Law?' 28 *Penn State International Law Review* (2010) 675–701 at 680.

problems[13] and even authors who deny that treaty rules have become custom do not raise fundamental concerns. Patrick Dumberry, for example, is sceptical about treaty influence on customary international law, yet he concedes that '[t]here is no doubt that the content of contemporary custom is "shaped" (or "reshaped") by these numerous BITs';[14] Tarcisio Gazzini believes that '[i]t is undisputed that multilateral treaties may generate customary rules'.[15] The unanimity of writers in this respect may be a result of their inclination to consider the jurisprudence of the ICJ as authoritative statements of the law (see Chapter 3 and Section 4.1). Therefore, the Court's view – customary law-creation from treaty provisions 'is a perfectly possible [process] and does from time to time occur: it constitutes indeed one or the recognized methods by which new rules or customary international law may be formed'[16] – adds decisive authority. Also, for the most part these treaties are regarded as 'evidence' of the elements for custom-creation or form some sort of influence,[17] rather than constituting state practice or *opinio iuris* themselves, although that view can also be found.[18]

[13] See eg Dumberry (2010) note 12 at 680–1; Tarcisio Gazzini, 'The Role of Customary International Law in the Field of Foreign Investment' 8 *Journal of World Investment & Trade* (2007) 691–716 at 698–703; Steffen Hindelang, 'Bilateral Investment Treaties, Custom and a Healthy Investment Climate: The Question of Whether BITs Influence Customary International Law Revisited' 5 *Journal of World Investment & Trade* (2004) 789–809 at 793–4; Bernard Kishoiyian, 'The Utility of Bilateral Investment Treaties in the Formulation of Customary International Law' 14 *Northwestern Journal of International Law & Business* (1994) 372–5 at 329, 340–1; Campbell McLachlan, 'Investment Treaties and General International Law' 57 *International and Comparative Law Quarterly* (2008) 361–401 at 392–3; Stephen M Schwebel, 'The Influence of Bilateral Investment Treaties on Customary International Law' 98 *American Society of International Law Proceedings* (2004) 27–30 at 27, 29–30; Muthucumaraswamy Sornarajah, *The International Law on Foreign Investment* (3rd edn, Cambridge: Cambridge University Press 2010) at 175–8.

[14] Dumberry (2010) note 12 at 681.

[15] Gazzini (2007) note 13 at 701.

[16] *North Sea Continental Shelf (Federal Republic of Germany/Denmark; Federal Republic of Germany/Netherlands)*, Judgment of 20 February 1969, ICJ Reports (1969) 3 at 41 (para 71).

[17] Dumberry (2010) note 12 at 685; Abdullah Al Faruque, 'Creating Customary International Law through Bilateral Investment Treaties: A Critical Appraisal' 44 *Indian Journal of International Law* (2004) 292–318 at 299; Hindelang (2004) note 13 at 792; Sornarajah (2010) note 13 at 176.

[18] Eg Gazzini (2007) note 13 at 692–3; Campbell McLachlan, Laurence Shore, Matthew Weiniger, *International Investment Arbitration: Substantive Principles* (Oxford: Oxford University Press 2007) 18; McLachlan (2008) note 13 at 392–3 (refers to the act of concluding treaties as state practice, though).

Yet there is reason to suspect that the assumption that treaty rules can become customary law is not as well-founded as these statements in the canvassed literature suggest. Broadly speaking, the argument is that state practice and *opinio iuris* (as expressed, even partially, in treaties) suffice to create customary law. As regards state practice, even cautious writers admit to the influence of the 'BIT movement'.[19] 'The repetitive enunciation of some of the standards of protection existing under BITs may be the starting point of State practice which will eventually become custom.'[20] At the very least, common principles or the lowest common denominator in the mass of IIAs 'evince the practice of States'.[21] *Opinio iuris*, in contrast, seems to flow by default from the conclusion of IIAs, unless specific countervailing reasons prevail. Steffen Hindelang suggests looking for a 'presumption . . . that would *bar* the acceptance of principles on foreign investment derived from BITs into customary international law'.[22] Campbell McLachlan, in contrast, argues that '[t]he mere prevalence of similarly worded treaty language, however numerous, will not, without more, give rise to a binding obligation in custom',[23] while model treaties are 'something more than a mere offer to treat' and a 'modern expression of a rule of custom', though not one that meets 'the classic test for the formation of a rule of custom in this area',[24] which does beg the question why these proto-rules should be part of international law.

Patrick Dumberry's critique of this argument is that 'BITs Are Missing the Two Necessary Elements of Custom'.[25] He argues that while a multitude of bilateral agreements *can* produce customary international law rules, this has not happened (yet) for IIAs. First, state practice is not consistent enough. IIAs inevitably vary in the formulations they use and in the protections they grant to investors, as they (mostly) are 'the result of bilateral negations'.[26] '[A]lthough there is a fair degree of uniformity of principles, wide inconsistency in detailed rules pervade[s] the BITs, which greatly diminish[es] their potential to give rise to precise rule on

[19] Andreas F Lowenfeld, 'Investment Agreements and International Law' 42 *Columbia Journal of Transnational Law* (2003) 123–30 at 129.

[20] Dumberry (2010) note 12 at 696.

[21] Kishoiyian (1994) note 13 at 374; Gazzini (2007) note 13 at 704; Hindelang (2004) note 13 at 799; Lowenfeld (2003) note 19 at 129–30.

[22] Hindelang (2004) note 13 at 805 (emphasis added).

[23] McLachlan (2008) note 13 at 400.

[24] McLachlan (2008) note 13 at 394.

[25] Dumberry (2010) note 12 at 684.

[26] Gazzini (2007) note 13 at 703; see Kishoiyian (1994) note 13 at 332–3.

[a] particular issue.'[27] Hence, 'there is no consistent State practice on [a number of] issues'.[28] Nor can it be said that the quantity of IIAs is decisive in this respect; 'no conclusion can be reached on the existence of any customary rule by simply adding up the number of treaties'.[29] Abdullah Al Faruque singles out other areas of international law where the presence of a large number of bilateral treaties has arguably not created customary rules, for example bilateral air navigation agreements.[30]

Second, the conclusion of a BIT is essentially an expression of contractual freedom and 'there is no indication that they reflect a general sense of obligation',[31] that is, that the rules in the treaty (also) reflect customary rules.[32] 'BITs are the result of a compromise between conflicting interests; they are not entered into by States based on any perceived legal obligation.'[33] With an eye perhaps on Richard R Baxter's path-breaking work,[34] Andrew T Guzman maintains that it would be most important for the treaty texts to include 'an explicit acknowledgment that the treaty merely codified rules of customary law; unfortunately, BITs do not contain such language'.[35] Equally, it seems to him just as 'plausible that BITs represent a permissible derogation from the existing rules of customary law'[36] (see Section 2.5), a sentiment echoed by the Court in *Diallo*.[37]

The voices within specialist scholarship are not as far apart as they may seem at first glance, mainly because they share the belief that treaties are able to shape the content of customary international law. While, for

27 Al Faruque (2004) note 17 at 310.

28 Dumberry (2010) note 12 at 687, citing Sornarajah (2010) note 13 at 176; Kishoyan (1994) note 13 at 372–3; McLachlan (2008) note 13 at 393; Al Faruque (2004) note 17 at 301, 304–10.

29 Dumberry (2010) note 12 at 682; see also McLachlan (2008) note 13 at 400; Al Faruque (2004) note 17 at 300.

30 Al Faruque (2004) note 17 at 301.

31 *United Parcel Service of America, Inc* v. *Canada*, NAFTA-UNCITRAL, Award on Jurisdiction of 22 November 2002, para 97.

32 Dumberry (2010) note 12 at 691–2; Andrew T Guzman, 'Why LDCs Sign Treaties that Hurt Them: Explaining the Popularity of Bilateral Investment Treaties' 38 *Virginia Journal of International Law* (1998) 639–88 at 687; Sornarajah (2010) note 13 at 184–5.

33 Dumberry (2010) note 12 at 692.

34 Richard R Baxter, 'Multilateral Treaties as Evidence of Customary International Law' 41 *British Year Book of International Law 1965–66* (1968) 275–300; Richard R Baxter, 'Treaties and Custom' 129 *Recueil des Cours 1970* (1971) 25–106.

35 Guzman (1998) note 32 at 686.

36 Guzman (1998) note 32 at 686.

37 *Diallo* (2007) note 1 at 615 (para 90).

Dumberry, 'the content of custom and the thousands of BITs are simply not the same',[38] this does not mean that they cannot be slightly different, as 'the "common law of investment protection" resulting from BITs will also contribute to the crystallisation of new rules of customary international law in the future'.[39] On the other side, Hindelang relativises the influence of IIAs, as '[o]n the one hand, they contain common principles on foreign investment which have passed into customary international law and, on the other hand, there are particular provisions [that] are applicable only between the parties'.[40] Very seldom do specialists venture into the field of theory, as the generalist debate on customary international law has tended to do.

2.2 The Evidence–Element Relationship

Sections 2.2–2.5 will apply elements of the generalist debate on the role of treaties in customary international law-making to the problem at hand, but we will also use legal theory and historiography to provide a structural analysis of this particular problem of international legal order. The following sections will highlight a number of problems that may hinder the content of IIAs from becoming customary international law. One, the two elements of custom-creation (*usus* and *opinio iuris*) need to be distinguished from the evidence for their presence. Confusion on this point is prevalent in international legal scholarship and leads to confusion about the exact role of treaties in customary law-making (Section 2.2). Two, using IIAs either as state practice or as *opinio iuris* is a highly problematic move; a transfer between treaty and customary law is assumed far too easily (Sections 2.3 and 2.4). Three, the interaction of the two main sources is problematic as well. Do treaties constitute an *inter partes* derogation? Are they *lex specialis conventionalis* (rather than a *ius dispositivum consuetudinalis*) or does the development of general customary legal norms on the basis of concordant treaties run parallel to these treaties (Section 2.5)?

Because it is generally assumed that customary international law and international treaty law are two separate and non-hierarchical sources of law,[41] a 'disconnect' operates between them. In other words: because

[38] Dumberry (2010) note 12 at 693.
[39] Dumberry (2010) note 12 at 695–6.
[40] Hindelang (2004) note 13 at 809.
[41] For a discussion of the possible architecture of sources in international law, see Jörg Kammerhofer, *Uncertainty in International Law: A Kelsenian Perspective* (Abingdon: Routledge 2010) 235–8.

custom and treaties are two sources rather than one,[42] they cannot easily and directly (as a matter of legal change) influence each other: the treaty norm itself does not create customary law.[43] However, an influence mediated through the realm of facts or through the conditions for customary international law-creation is possible. Is the distinction between the elements of customary law-making and their proofs or evidences relevant in this connection?[44] The subjective and objective elements are the *actus reus* conditions (*Tatbestand*) of a special sort of norm: a norm empowering the creation of norms of customary international law.[45]

The orthodox concept of customary international law[46] is composed both of the repetition of similar behaviour to form a pattern (which will form the content of the resultant norm) and of the accumulation of acts of will (becoming a collective will),[47] expressed as belief.[48] The presence of an actual act of will is the normative 'spark' which creates positive norms.[49] At least for a norm's immanent sense, the act of will is a sufficient condition. For its systemic sense – its membership in a specific normative order – it is a necessary, but most likely not a sufficient condition, as this depends on the content of positive empowerment norms.[50]

Even if state practice and *opinio iuris* (as *actus reus* conditions of customary international law-making) are made up of facts or states of mind, the elements of proof for their existence, particularly indirect ones such as treaties or jurisprudence, are not the elements themselves; they are not part of the law. 'Proofs' or 'evidences' are heuristic devices and are not identical with the object of proof – in a criminal case, for example,

[42] Bing-Bing Jia, 'The Relations between Treaties and Custom' 9 *Chinese Journal of International Law* (2010) 81–109 at 97.

[43] Jean d'Aspremont, 'International Customary Investment Law: Story of a Paradox' in Tarcisio Gazzini, Eric De Brabandere (eds.), *International Investment Law: The Sources of Rights and Obligations* (Leiden: Martinus Nijhoff 2012) 5–47 at 35. We will return to this question in Section 2.5.

[44] Hugh WA Thirlway, *International Customary Law and Codification: An Examination of the Continuing Role of Custom in the Present Period of Codification of International Law* (Leiden: AW Sijthoff 1972) 57.

[45] On the notion of empowerment norms, see eg Hans Kelsen, *Allgemeine Theorie der Normen* (Vienna: Manz 1979) 82–84.

[46] For a reconstruction of the orthodox concept, see Kammerhofer (2010d) note 41 at 59–86.

[47] Hans Kelsen, *Reine Rechtslehre* (2nd edn, Vienna: Deuticke 1960) 9.

[48] Kammerhofer (2010d) note 41 at 82–5.

[49] Kelsen (1979) note 45 at 4.

[50] On the distinction between immanent and systemic senses, see Rainer Lippold, *Recht und Ordnung: Statik und Dynamik der Rechtsordnung* (Vienna: Manz 2000) 288–9.

a conversation between the accused and a third person about motive may be evidence of *mens rea*, but it will not be seen as *mens rea* itself.

There are no formal 'rules of evidence' for customary international law-making, but it is generally accepted that treaties can play a role. Logic gives us a number of possible combinations of what treaties could be: instances of state practice, evidence of state practice, instances of *opinio iuris*, evidence of *opinio iuris*, instances of both state practice and *opinio iuris*, evidence of both state practice and *opinio iuris*, customary international law or evidence of the state of customary international law. It is not surprising that these options are not commonly distinguished; take, for example, the following argument by Gennady Danilenko: '[a]s treaties also reflect the acceptance of certain rules of conduct by the parties, they can be regarded as acts which are part of State practice'.[51] If treaties reflect the acceptance of rules, they point towards the presence of *opinio iuris*, not of state practice.[52] This quote could also be read to imply that treaties themselves are instances of state practice or that they are *evidence* of state practice.

A well-known passage in *North Sea Continental Shelf* is the springboard for claims that treaties alone can 'make' customary international law: 'it might be that, even without the passage of any considerable period of time, a very widespread and representative participation in the convention might suffice of itself'.[53] Danilenko's plea to read this passage in its context[54] is apt: at that stage, the Court had not yet considered state practice and *opinio iuris*. The state practice requirement in particular is described a paragraph later in different terms: 'an indispensable requirement would be that . . . State practice . . . should have been both extensive and virtually uniform'.[55] In the specific case, the Court felt that it 'must now consider whether State practice in the matter of continental shelf delimitation has . . . been of such a kind as to satisfy this requirement'. The Court considered 'some fifteen cases . . . in which continental shelf boundaries have been delimited according to the equidistance principle'[56] as instances of state practice. Indeed, it held that 'no inference

[51] Gennady M Danilenko, 'The Theory of International Customary Law' 31 *German Yearbook of International Law* (1988) 9–47 at 27.

[52] Although Danilenko holds the 'wide' concept of state practice, see Kammerhofer (2010d) note 41 at 66–7; Danilenko (1988) note 51 at 28.

[53] *NSCS* (1969) note 16 at 42 (para 73).

[54] Danilenko (1988) note 51 at 27–8.

[55] *NSCS* (1969) note 16 at 43 (para 74).

[56] *NSCS* (1969) note 16 at 43 (para 75). The fact that several of these delimitations were carried out by way of bilateral treaty does not mean that the Court saw the rule in question potentially

could legitimately be drawn as to the existence of a rule of customary international law'[57] from the fact of being a party to the convention. The Court in effect held that state practice and arguably also *opinio iuris* is manifested primarily by acts extraneous to the treaty.

What we seek to prove (*Beweisziel*) is decisive; the means to this end (*Beweismittel*) are secondary. We seek the two elements, certainly, but what do they mean? The lack of clarity about what 'state practice' and '*opinio iuris*' mean results in uncertainty about the evidentiary goal. We will therefore need to discuss the role of treaties (and IIAs in particular) as emanations of or evidence for state practice (Section 2.3) or *opinio iuris* (Section 2.4).

2.3 Treaties and State Practice: The 'Verbal Act' Problem

How can the claim made above – that treaty norms cannot directly become customary law – be squared with the generally accepted proposition that treaties are a form of state practice? Of course, what is generally accepted is not that the treaty norm, by virtue of being state practice, mutates into a customary norm. Rather, the *content*, the norm-formulation as text, is seen as practice – as if the content prescribed in the treaty had actually been practised in the real world. The claim in effect is that a bilateral treaty between A and B, which prescribes 'A and B ought to do x', is equivalent to A and/or B actually doing 'x'. While this version is no less problematic than the direct change argument, it is so for different reasons. If the content of treaties is to serve as a building block for a budding customary rule, then the classical debate on the nature of state practice is highly relevant. Are statements state practice? Can this be squared with the idea of law based on customs?[58] Of course, there are non-treaty-content verbal acts as well as treaty-related non-verbal acts. But the point at issue here is whether a customary norm can develop from a large number of similarly worded (mostly bilateral) treaties, which is widely claimed in scholarship and jurisprudence.

The classical generalist debate on the duality of acts and statements[59] was sparked, inter alia, by the ICJ's use of treaties, General Assembly

arising directly from these treaties. Some of the instances of state practice cited were unilateral declarations – the state practice was the delimitation, not the agreement as norm.

57 *NSCS* (1969) note 16 at 43 (para 76).

58 The following builds on the discussion in Kammerhofer (2010d) note 41 at 62–6.

59 Anthony A D'Amato, *The Concept of Custom in International Law* (Ithaca: Cornell University Press 1971); Michael Akehurst, 'Custom as a Source of International Law' 47

Resolutions and other texts as proofs for customary norms in *North Sea Continental Shelf* and *Nicaragua*.[60] While both sides of the argument found support,[61] the pragmatic tendencies in international legal scholarship[62] have meant that we are loath to exclude any information which might possibly be useful in finding out what the law says.[63] The debate has abated in recent decades and the side favouring admitting statements as practice for all intents and purposes has 'won',[64] with the International Law Commission's (ILC) rapporteur on customary international law, for example, stating that state practice 'may comprise both physical and verbal (written and oral) conduct: views to the contrary . . . are too restrictive'.[65] Equally, after the Court's pronouncements in *North Sea Continental Shelf* at the latest, treaties or their content have

British Year Book of International Law 1974–75 (1977) 1–53; Karol Wolfke, *Custom in Present International Law* (2nd edn, Dordrecht: Martinus Nijhoff 1993); Mark E Villiger, *Customary International Law and Treaties: A Manual on the Theory and Practice of the Interrelation of Sources* (2nd edn, The Hague: Kluwer Law International 1997).

60 *NSCS* (1969) note 16 at 41 (para 71); *Nicaragua* (1986) note 7 at 99–104 (paras 188–95).

61 In favour of counting statements, see eg Akehurst (1977a) note 59; Michael Byers, *Custom, Power and the Power of Rules: International Relations and Customary International Law* (Cambridge: Cambridge University Press 1999); Danilenko (1988) note 51; Maurice H Mendelson, 'The Formation of Customary International Law' 272 *Recueil des Cours 1998* (1999) 155–410; Rein Müllerson, 'The Interplay of Objective and Subjective Elements in Customary Law' in Karel Wellens (ed.), *International Law: Theory and Practice: Essays in Honour of Eric Suy* (The Hague: Martinus Nijhoff 1998) 161–78; Villiger (1997) note 59; Michael Wood, *Second Report on Identification of Customary International Law*, UN Doc A/CN.4/L.672, 22 May 2014; Karl Zemanek, 'What Is State Practice and Who Makes It?' in Ulrich Beyerlin et al. (eds.), *Recht zwischen Umbruch und Bewahrung: Völkerrecht, Europarecht, Staatsrecht: Festschrift für Rudolf Bernhardt* (Berlin: Springer 1995) 289–306; against eg Yoram Dinstein, 'The Interaction between Customary International Law and Treaties' 322 *Recueil des Cours 2006* (2007) 243–428; Thirlway (1972) note 44; Wolfke (1993) note 59.

62 This pragmatic tendency causes problems when it comes to conducting legal *scholarship*, see Jörg Kammerhofer, 'Orthodox Generalists and Political Activists in International Legal Scholarship' in Matthew Happold (ed.), *International Law in a Multipolar World* (Abingdon: Routledge 2011) 138–57 at 139–45.

63 See eg Maarten Bos, 'The Identification of Custom in International Law' 25 *German Yearbook of International Law* (1982) 9–53 at 23; Zemanek (1995) note 61 at 293.

64 Niels Petersen, 'Customary Law Without Custom? Rules, Principles, and the Role of State Practice in International Norm Creation' 32 *American University International Law Review* (2007) 275–310 at 278.

65 Wood (2014) note 61 at 19–20 (para 37). On the ILC project and the acceptance of treaties as state practice, see Jörg Kammerhofer, 'Between Pragmatism and Disenchantment: The Theory of Customary International Law after the ILC Project' in Panos Merkouris, Jörg Kammerhofer, Noora Arajärvi (eds.), *The Theory, Practice and Interpretation of Customary Law* (Cambridge: Cambridge University Press in press), available at: ssrn.com/abstract=3522535.

increasingly been seen as capable of being (or providing evidence of) state practice[66] and there is agreement regarding verbal practice as well.[67] Most writers' acceptance of treaties as state practice follows from their views on the relevance of verbal acts, even where this is not explicitly argued; Michael Akehurst, for example, 'has defined State practice in very wide terms, and has no difficulty in regarding treaties as State practice'.[68]

However, the treaty-as-state-practice debate is as problematic as the verbal-act-as-state-practice debate. The theoretical merits of the arguments are open to criticism, as 'default empiricism' often supplants epistemological reflection. This mindset, a vicious circle on a grand scale that permeates international legal doctrinal writings and is not limited to the question of verbal acts as state practice, could be summarised thus: we know that practice is relevant because practice tells us that practice is relevant.[69]

> [T]here is much merit in qualifying verbal acts as State practice. . . . [T]he above authorities [denying the validity of verbal acts] cannot support their views *on* State practice *with* State practice, or with recent judicial decisions. Indeed, this would hardly be possible, since States themselves as well as courts regard comments at conferences as constitutive of State practice.[70]

Less strictly a logical fallacy but question-begging nonetheless is the argument that '[i]nternational practice . . . recognizes that international custom is a broad concept that may cover any type of act or form of conduct of States'.[71] The thrust of the argument is that what actually

[66] In favour of counting treaties, see eg Akehurst (1977a) note 59; D'Amato (1971) note 59; Danilenko (1988) note 51; Mendelson (1999) note 61; Müllerson (1998) note 61; Ulrich Scheuner, 'Internationale Verträge als Elemente der Bildung von völkerrechtlichem Gewohnheitsrecht' in Werner Flume et al. (eds.), *Internationales Recht und Wirtschaftsordnung: Festschrift für FA Mann zum 70. Geburtstag am 11. August 1977* (Munich: CH Beck 1977) 409–38; Thirlway (1972) note 44; Villiger (1997) note 59; Arthur M Weisburd, 'Customary International Law: The Problem of Treaties' 21 *Vanderbilt Journal of Transnational Law* (1988) 1–46; Wood (2014) note 61; against Dinstein (2007); Karl Doehring, 'Gewohnheitsrecht aus Verträgen' 36 *Zeitschrift für ausländisches öffentliches Recht und Völkerrecht* (1976) 77–95, Herbert Günther, *Zur Entstehung von Völkergewohnheitsrecht* (Berlin: Duncker & Humblot 1970); Jia (2010) note 42; Wolfke (1993) note 59.

[67] *Pars pro toto*: Wood (2014) note 61 at 26 (para 41(h)).

[68] Akehurst (1977a) note 59 at 43; see also Mendelson (1999) note 61 at 324; Wood (2014) note 61 at 26 (para 41(h)).

[69] I have previously portrayed variants of this method in Kammerhofer (2010d) note 41 at eg 132, 200, 204.

[70] Villiger (1997) note 59 at 19–20.

[71] Danilenko (1988) note 51 at 24.

happens determines how law comes about[72] and its hidden premise is that regularities of behaviour are at least irrefutable proof, but more likely directly determine how law is created. On that view, all law is ultimately based on facts alone, a pragmatic variant of legal realism. Insofar as it claims that verbal practice confirms that verbal practice counts, it is a technical *petitio principii*, but even when it does not make that claim, it is not particular convincing on the legal level.

Much of the confusion in the debate is owing to a disconnect between a wide and a narrow understanding of state practice.[73] For a minority of scholars, the term 'state practice' has the status of a technical term diverging from ordinary usage of the term 'practice'. They see practice as *usus* in the technical sense, a regularity of (observable) behaviour; 'state practice' is defined as not being *opinio iuris*; the *usus* shapes the content of the budding norm, the 'prospective prescribed behaviour'. Most scholars do not subscribe to such 'scholastic punctuality'[74] and adhere to a wider understanding of state practice which combines *usus* and *opinio*. Because state activities in a wide sense also communicate opinions on the law, practice is inseparable from *opinio iuris*, at least when it comes to the evidentiary function of facts in the world. A passage from Mark Villiger's book highlights the 'significance [of the acceptance of a convention] *as State practice, namely as expression of* opinio juris'[75] – surely for someone adhering to the orthodox two-element theory of custom-formation, state practice's function cannot be exhausted by its expressing *opinio iuris*? This wide, informal view of state practice in this context is probably connected to default empiricism, for a thin empiricist-factualist account seems to dictate that facts alone make law and that law as a social phenomenon must by-and-large conform to social reality.

This thin empiricism cannot convince because it is circular. Moreover, it refuses to distinguish between the ordinary meaning of 'practice' (all that is done regularly) and the technical meaning of state practice as *actus reus* material. Yet only the latter concept is truly commensurate with the nature of the customary mode of norm-creation, whether in international law or other normative orders. Because the orthodox claim is that the text as norm-formulation is counted as if the content had been

72 Villiger (1997) note 59 at 21: 'a restricted view of State practice has not accommodated sufficiently the immense changes of the past 50 years in the State community'.

73 Kammerhofer (2010d) note 41 at 62–6.

74 'scholastische *Pünktlichkeit*' Immanuel Kant, *Metaphysik der Sitten* (Königsberg: Friedrich Nicolovius 1797) AA VI 206.

75 Villiger (1997) note 59 at 27 (emphasis added).

actualised, the heart of the debate is whether, either directly as text or mediated by ratification, etc., a treaty *text* can do double-duty as treaty rule and state practice.

In this context, the much-maligned views of Karol Wolfke are worth another look. He is on the right track and argues, against the majority position, that verbal acts (including treaties) cannot count as state practice for customary law-formation, because this 'neglects the very essence of every kind of custom, which for centuries has been based upon material deeds and not words'. For him, 'customs arise from acts of conduct and not from promises of such acts'.[76] Saying 'I will do x' is not the same as actually doing 'x'; accordingly, 'repeated verbal acts ... can give rise to international customs, but only to customs of making such declarations, etc., and not to customs of the conduct described in the content of the verbal acts'.[77] Treaties therefore, 'being strictly speaking only a promise of certain conduct, are by no means the practice described in their content[;] ... they constitute true custom-forming precedents only in the customary law of treaties'.[78]

While Wolfke's argument does not delve deeply into legal theory, he highlights certain foundational beliefs regarding customary law which at least civilian lawyers have long held and the incommensurability of the orthodox view on customary international law with those beliefs. The customary form of norm-creation is and has always been *predicated* on what actually happens being or becoming obligatory. Whatever else is uncertain about customary law, at least we agree that it should be *customary* law, law based on customs. Usage, practice, behaviour, custom, is the one crucial and defining characteristic of this form of norm-creation – no customary law without customs.[79] If we wish to take the notion of customary law seriously, there has to be a division of labour between the objective and subjective elements and *usus* must form the content of the norm.[80]

[76] Wolfke (1993) note 59 at 42.

[77] Wolfke (1993) note 59 at 42.

[78] Wolfke (1993) note 59 at 70.

[79] *Pars pro toto* Suárez: 'dicitur enim consuetudo, quia in communi est usu ... quomodo autem esse potest in usu communi sine actuum frequentia' 'for "custom" is so called because ... it is usage in common. But how can it be common usage except through a repetition of actions?' Francisco Suárez, *De legibus ac Deo legislatore* [1612] lib. 7 cap. 10, sect. 1 (translation by Gwladys L Williams, Ammi Brown, John Waldron, Henry Davis 1944 at 529–30).

[80] Bin Cheng is to be commended for no longer calling general international law 'customary' once he eliminates practice from the conditions for law-creation, eg Bin Cheng, 'Custom:

There is plenty of divergence in the rich and long civilian tradition on customary law from the *Corpus Iuris Civilis* to pre-codification *ius commune*; virtually everything about *consuetudo* as source of law is and has always been controversial, including the nature of *usus*. The most promising passage in the Digests for the claim made here shows both sides of the coin:

> But also those [rules], which have been approved/proven/confirmed through long usage and have been followed for [resp. reflected in the behaviour of] many years, just like a tacit agreement of citizens, are no less to be obeyed than written statutes.[81]

On the one hand, this passage expresses the argument to be made here very clearly: from post-classical Roman law onwards, there is broad agreement that only the behaviour that is (or is to become) the content of the norm – the 'practical exercise of the legal rule',[82] as Siegfried Brie puts it – can serve as the material element.[83] Again: only doing or abstaining from 'x', not talking about doing or abstaining from 'x', can be part of a customary law which specifies 'do/abstain from x'. On the other hand, however, even this short passage, important as it may be, can be read to confirm ideas – present throughout the history of customary law up to the early twentieth century – that clash with the classical theory of customary international law. This is the idea that usage merely expresses or is a manifestation of pre-existing norms, or that customary law is merely a tacit agreement and usage is either constitutive or expressive of it.

Moreover, there is also the very clear notion in some civilian historical sources that non-exercise can somehow form the *actus* (*frequens*) for customary law. Judgments, arbitral rulings and, most relevant for our discussion, terms of contract were variously admitted as forming the basis for customary law.[84] But there are complicating factors which help

The Future of General State Practice in a Divided World' in Ronald St John Macdonald, Douglas M Johnston (eds.), *The Structure and Process of International Law: Essays in Legal Philosophy Doctrine and Theory* (The Hague: Martinus Nijhoff 1983) 513–54 at 548.

[81] D.1.3.35: 'Sed et ea, quae longa consuetudine comprobata sunt ac per annos plurimos observata, velut tacita civium conventio non minus quam ea quae scripta sunt iura servantur.'

[82] 'Erfordernis der praktischen Uebung des Rechtssatzes' Siegfried Brie, *Die Lehre vom Gewohnheitsrecht: Eine historisch-dogmatische Untersuchung* (Breslau: Marcus 1899) 12.

[83] In connection with D.1.3.32.1: 'nam quid interest suffragio populus voluntatem suam declaret an rebus ipsis et factis?', the *Glossa Ordinaria* argues that: '*Factis*, id est consuetudine; quasi dicat, nihil interest' (Glossa *Factis* ad D.1.3.32.1).

[84] Eg Bartolus ad D.1.3.32, number 13: 'frequens actus in contractibus inducit consuetudinem'.

to explain the seeming contradiction between the free admission of (at least) judgments and contracts and the obviousness that only an exercise of the rule can form the *usus*. As Brie writes for the Commentators/Postglossators: 'acts . . . of a specific kind were . . . considered as custom-creative . . . only, because these acts evidenced the *consensus tacitus* in an adequate form'.[85] The idea of customary law as tacit agreement explains this countervailing trend – today, we would probably call this evidence of *opinio iuris*.

A possible interjection at this point is that the implications of linguistic philosophy for the problems of verbal acts were overlooked. One particular theory that, if accepted, might be used as a counter-argument to scepticism vis-à-vis verbal acts is the idea of 'speech acts'.[86] Speech may be more than descriptive in certain circumstances – 'I name this ship "Queen Victoria"'; 'I now pronounce you man and wife.' If that is so, why should not some utterances be acts in a substantive sense? While it is possible that there are customary norms whose *usus* is a series of speech acts, not all speech is speech acts and this cannot happen for all, or indeed, for most legal rules. For example, 'I am washing my hair' is not a speech act, as the actual washing of hair does not happen through the utterance, only if the hair is actually being washed. Accordingly, the *usus* would still only be of making a statement, not of washing hair. The counter-argument is not dependent on the acceptance or rejection of the theory of performative utterances, because the objective element needs to be an exercise of the resultant norm to qualify. While customary law is not restricted to norms containing behaviour expressed as facts, the argument here is that there is an identity of the acts forming practice with the content of the resultant norm. For norms which specify actual behaviour, none but actual behaviour will do as *usus*. The prohibition of torture, for example, is not constituted with respect to state practice solely by states *saying* that they will not torture, only by the actual omission of torture.

Thus, there are good reasons for preferring the view that the objective element of customary international law-creation must consist in the

[85] 'Handlungen . . . von einer gewissen Beschaffenheit galten . . . als erforderlich für Bildung eines Gewohnheitsrechts . . . nur deshalb, weil in ihnen der für Entstehung eines Gewohnheitsrechts erforderliche consensus tacitus in geeigneter Weise sich bekunde.' Brie (1899) note 82 at 142.

[86] Most famously John L Austin, *How to Do Things with Words: The William James Lectures Delivered at Harvard University in 1955* (Cambridge, MA: Harvard University Press 1962); John R Searle, *Speech Acts: An Essay in the Philosophy of Language* (Cambridge: Cambridge University Press 1969).

observance of the budding rule or in the exercise of the budding right. This observance/exercise can consist of verbal acts, treaties included, but a verbal act is an observance/exercise of making a verbal *act* (eg of making a statement), not of the content of that verbal act. We cannot equate A and B agreeing in a contract that A ought to give B 100 with A giving B 100.[87] Customary law is a primitive form of law-making and practice may not be able to translate the complexity of the content into an observance of the actions or abstention expressed therein.

Yet perhaps the force of treaties as *evidence* of state practice[88] is higher than as state practice itself. As proofs, treaties serve a categorically different role (Section 2.2), but this does not mean that this argument is unproblematic, merely that the problems are pragmatic, rather than conceptual, for example the possible confusion arising from using practice to prove *opinio* or vice versa, or the limits of proving behaviour from a mere promise. Over the years, a number of scholars have contended that treaties are evidence of 'state practice' or 'state belief', both understood in a wide sense.[89] This line of reasoning can mean that, just as the line between the element and its evidence collapses, the line between the two elements is also blurred. At some point, the treaty's 'A ought to do x' subconsciously becomes state practice's 'A *has* done x'. If we agree with Maurice Mendelson's idea that state practice implies the subjective element, then it is also reasonable to argue that '[w]hether we classify a particular verbal act as an instance of the subjective or of the objective element may depend on circumstances, but it probably does not matter much which category we put it into'.[90] However, as he also points out, we must avoid 'counting the same act as an instance of *both* the subjective and the objective element'.[91] It might otherwise be the case that customary international law could be made solely on the basis of the popularity

[87] Günther (1970) note 66 at 117–18.

[88] Eg Weisburd (1988) note 66 at 10; Wolfke (1993) note 59 at 70.

[89] Eg Zemanek (1995) note 61 at 292–3; José E Alvarez, 'A BIT on Custom' 42 *NYU Journal on International Law and Politics* (2009) 17–80 at 57–8; Joseph L Kunz, 'The Nature of Customary International Law' 47 *American Journal of International Law* (1953) 662–9 at 668.

[90] Mendelson (1999) note 61 at 206. Karl Zemanek is even more radical (and is echoed in this by Wood): '[D]istinctions between "constitutive acts" and "evidence of constitutive acts" are artificial and arbitrary because one may disguise the other. ... [S]eparating material recording "State practice" from material recording *opinio iuris*, though theoretically perhaps desirable, is practically impossible because the first may, through its language, evidence the second.' Zemanek (1995) note 61 at 292–3; Wood (2014) note 61 at 21 (para 38).

[91] Mendelson (1999) note 61 at 207.

of a particular treaty, thus obviating the distinction between the two sources.

Treaties are a promise of conduct, rather than actual behaviour. Why should they then be particularly relevant to proving state practice, based as it is on actual behaviour? Herbert Günther notes on this point:

> [I]t is not possible to see the text of a treaty as evidencing state practice, because the text cannot tell us . . . what states [parties] will make of it. . . . To take this announcement [of what they agree to do] as what they are doing merely because of its obligatory character is both methodologically impure and would be contrary to historical experience. . . . Behaviour would be required which is substantially in line with that which is contractually agreed.[92]

It may be possible that an important multilateral treaty or a network of bilateral treaties accurately reflects the behaviour of most states. Even so, we will still need more than the promise of future behaviour in order to prove that the behaviour prescribed in a treaty text is actually being practised.[93] Hence, even if one cannot dismiss treaty-content as evidence of state practice, the probative force of these texts is not as high as is commonly claimed. Treaties are starting or auxiliary, not decisive or sole evidence.

2.4 Treaties and *Opinio Iuris*: The 'Baxter Paradox'

The argument that treaties are or express a belief of 'the law' is less problematic than their relationship to state practice, at least if framed in this unspecific way. We will proceed on the working assumption, tentatively outlined in an earlier publication, that *opinio iuris* is a collective act of will, expressed as truth-independent belief that a specific behaviour is obligatory, prohibited or permitted.[94] Even if we make this contentious assumption and therefore commit to a specific doctrine of customary (international) law which is close to, but not identical with orthodoxy,

92 '[U]nzulässig ist es, einen Vertragstext schon als Nachweis der Staatenpraxis zu werten, denn über das, was die Staaten daraus machen, . . . vermag er keine Auskunft zu geben. . . . Diese Ankündigung aber nur ihres verpflichtenden Charakters wegen schon für die Tat zu nehmen, wäre methodisch unsauber und stände im Widerspruch zu allen historischen Erfahrungen. . . . Dazu bedürfte es vielmehr eines Gebarens, das jedenfalls materiell in der Realisierung des vertraglich geschuldeten Erfolges besteht.' Günther (1970) note 66 at 118.

93 One could ask whether perhaps this additional confirmation can come from arbitral jurisprudence, see Section 3.4.

94 Kammerhofer (2010d) note 41 at 76–85.

there are still major theoretical and practical problems with the idea that such a 'belief' is meaningfully connected to treaties.

1. The evidentiary problem is particularly acute for expropriation clauses in IIAs. The problem is that a norm-formulation in a treaty, without further information, is not particularly strong evidence of the subjective element for a parallel customary norm. How would the *opinio iuris* be expressed as text? On the working assumption used here, the subjects of law which evince an *opinio iuris* do so with respect to a specific regularity of behaviour: it is their belief that specific behaviour is obligated, prohibited, etc. The regularity to which *opinio iuris* refers can be recast as text and this is the case with treaty texts: in addition to serving as norm for the treaty (*lex scripta*), they can also serve as norm-formulation for purposes of creating a customary norm. The norm-formulation is not the norm itself[95] – customary law is *lex non scripta* – but the regularity of behaviour can be expressed as text.

On the theory of customary law applied here, the *opinio* cannot, however, supply the *actus reus* of the resultant norm. By definition, the content of a customary norm is determined by a behavioural regularity: the *custom*;[96] if that were not so, it would not be customary law. Hence, the norm-formulation used in treaties is not constitutive of the content of the resultant customary norm; it can only give a verbalised pointer to the behavioural regularity referred to by the *opinio iuris*. A treaty-based norm-formulation is not particularly effective as a building-block for a customary norm (Section 2.3), because it is a *treaty* norm. It is unlikely to be an accurate expression of *opinio iuris* for a parallel customary norm, as treaty law is by definition different from customary law. Without evidence going beyond the norm-formulation, it stands to reason that a *treaty* norm cannot be a particularly effective pointer to the customary norm.

What would turn a treaty into better evidence of *opinio iuris*? One factor would be to explicitly mention *opinio iuris* in the text, such as an expression in the treaty that the drafters believed that the treaty norm accurately reflects the content of (pre-existing) customary international laws. Another would be state behaviour extrinsic (and perhaps subsequent) to the treaty text, such as statements that a certain treaty clause (now) reflects customary international law. Both factors have often been described in scholarship,[97] but

95 Tentatively argued in Doehring (1976) note 66 at 80–1.

96 Thirlway (1972) note 44 at 91.

97 Eg Akehurst (1977a) note 59 at 44–52, 53 (point 5); Jonathan I Charney, 'International Agreements and the Development of Customary International Law' 61 *Washington Law Review* (1986) 971–96 at 992.

these elements are not just helpful, they are crucial in order to be able to identify *opinio iuris consuetudinalis* in this situation. Hence, we *need* to look for additional evidence, but that information is difficult to come by for IIA expropriation clauses.

2. Even if our search for *opinio iuris* is widened beyond the text, we are faced with the 'Baxter paradox':[98] the major problem confronting customary law-formation in today's treaty-dominated international law is that treaties can become too successful. It is 'the paradox that as the number of parties to a treaty increases, it becomes more difficult to demonstrate what is the state of customary international law *dehors* the treaty'.[99] *Mutatis mutandis* this also concerns successful networks of similarly worded treaties.

However, the paradox only arises if we accept the premise that *opinio iuris* properly so called (*opinio iuris consuetudinalis*) can be separated from treaty-related acts and statements which can be seen to express an *opinio iuris conventionalis*, directed at the treaty in its strict sense as treaty law.[100] If that is so, the treaty-parties – at least in their *inter partes* relations – can only generate *opinio iuris conventionalis* and their acts and statements are thus excluded from contributing a building block to the subjective side of a customary norm on the basis of that treaty. Generalist international legal scholarship, Baxter included, has taken this premise from *North Sea Continental Shelf*, where the Court restricted the utility of the state practice (in the untechnical sense) of states parties to the Geneva Convention on the Continental Shelf 1958, because they 'were therefore presumably ... acting actually or potentially in the application of the Convention. From their action no inference could legitimately be drawn as to the existence of a rule of customary international law.'[101] If we accept this argument and if the universal multilateral treaty or network of bilateral treaties in question covers potential relations between pairs of treaty parties to such a degree that hardly any are not 'touched' by the treaty, then independent proof of *opinio iuris consuetudinalis* – proof of belief in a customary norm that cannot be said to relate to the fulfilment of treaty obligations – is virtually impossible. In

[98] Eg James Crawford, *Brownlie's Principles of Public International Law* (8th edn, Oxford: Oxford University Press 2012) 32.

[99] Baxter (1971) note 34 at 64 (emphasis added).

[100] Robert Kolb, 'Selected Problems in the Theory of Customary International Law' 50 *Netherlands International Law Review* (2003) 119–50 at 145–6.

[101] *NSCS* (1969) note 16 at 43 (para 76).

other words, we will have to prove the theoretical contention and also show that the network of IIAs is 'too successful'. Only then can the paradox arise for a potential customary norm of expropriation derived from IIAs.

But do we have to accept this premise? Classical orthodox scholarship does,[102] but most deny the relevance of party *opinio*, for example by agreeing with the Court in *North Sea Continental Shelf* or by pointing to the possibility of *inter partes* abrogation of customary law (Section 2.5). The only interesting counter-move is to admit to the difficulties of making a theoretical distinction and to transfer it to the level of evidence:

> The Institut de droit international has taken the position that the practice of Contracting Parties should be taken into account ... Logically, this approach is not unsound. Empirically, though, proof of the specific conviction of Contracting Parties that their practice is required by custom – separately from, and independently of, the treaty – may be fraught with intractable difficulties.[103]

It is possible in principle to distinguish between the belief of states that the norm-formulation in a treaty expresses a norm of customary international law and their (obvious) belief that a clause in a treaty is treaty law. However, it is much less convincing to conclude that this distinction means that it is impossible for a treaty party to express an *opinio iuris consuetudinalis* with respect to a budding customary norm whose verbalised expression happens to coincide with a treaty norm of a treaty to which it is a party.[104] It is clear that separating *opinio iuris consuetudinalis* from *opinio iuris conventionalis* faces both practical and evidentiary difficulties which will not be easily surmounted. This is so unless special circumstances prevail or unless additional evidence points to *opinio iuris consuetudinalis* – such as statements to that effect in the treaty, statements or party behaviour connected with the treaty. IIAs, particularly their expropriation clauses, are not replete with such evidence. The *travaux préparatoires*, such as they are, are usually not published and expropriation clauses do not explicitly reference customary law. States do not usually make statements about whether the content of the IIAs they have concluded reflect customary law, at least outside litigation.

102 Eg Baxter (1971) note 34 at 64, 73; Danilenko (1988) note 51 at 38–9; Dinstein (2007) note 61 at 376–378; Doehring (1976) note 66 at 80–1; Thirlway (1972) note 44 at 91; Villiger (1997) note 59 at 27–8, 183–4.

103 Dinstein (2007) note 61 at 376–7; see also Danilenko (1988) note 51 at 39; Doehring (1976) note 66 at 80; Kolb (2003) note 100 at 146.

104 As argued eg by Danilenko (1988) note 51 at 38.

Baxter's paradox is not a legal-theoretical necessity; it is a major practical or evidentiary problem. If, then, the *opinio iuris* of parties is not in doubt in principle, but very much in practice, the second issue, namely that of an excessive 'success' of treaties, comes to the fore. If we do not have reliable evidence that the norm-formulation in IIAs is *also* an expression of the parties' *opinio iuris consuetudinalis*, the question becomes whether the reservoir of potential non-party practice is large enough to be able to form a general *opinio iuris* on the purported norm of customary international law on expropriation. While the number of IIAs has rapidly risen in recent decades (more than 3,000), the coverage of potential bilateral relations is only about 15 per cent. On the other hand, not many states are untouched by the IIA phenomenon, as 'almost all countries are parties to one or several IIAs'.[105] If we assume that most IIAs contain *approximately* the same rule on expropriation and if we analogise a network of bi- and plurilateral treaties with a roughly similar set of prescriptions to Baxter's 'very popular' multilateral treaty, only very few non-party states exist vis-à-vis the IIA-type expropriation rule and the Baxter paradox arises.

2.5 Changing General Customary Law or Sectoral *lex specialis*?

But can we analogise the network of IIAs to the paradigm case of a very successful multilateral treaty, eg the UN Charter? The Baxter problem was relevant in *Nicaragua*, where the status of customary law *dehors* the Charter, but *inter partes*, was much discussed. But what determines whether one (set of) treaties is custom-creative and another remains without such influence? The overarching theoretical problem is that we have two views of the relationship between international treaty law and customary international law and both have compelling plausibility, but seemingly cannot be reconciled without sacrificing theoretical consistency. On the one hand, there is the traditional civilian idea that treaties – like contracts in domestic law – can create *inter partes* norms which have the power to abrogate, as between the treaty parties, general customary law, at least the part classified as *ius dispositivum*. On that view, treaty-making in some sense involves turning one's back on customary law. On the other hand, it seems perfectly possible, as the Court pointed out in *Nicaragua*,[106] that a treaty norm and

105 United Nations Conference on Trade and Development, *World Investment Report 2014: Investing in the SGDs: A Plan for Action* (New York: United Nations 2014) 126.

106 *Military and Paramilitary Activities in and Against Nicaragua (Nicaragua* v. *United States of America)*, Jurisdiction and Admissibility, Judgment of 26 November 1984, ICJ Reports (1984) 392 at 424 (para 73); *Nicaragua* (1986) note 7 at 92–6 (paras 172–9).

a customary norm with the same content can exist in parallel. Treaty-making would not necessarily impinge on the validity or applicability of customary law; treaty-making would also not be barred from potentially contributing to customary international law-making. In this section, we will discuss the implications of these two models for the question of the emergence of a new general customary norm from a network of treaties.

2.5.1 *The* Ius Dispositivum *Model*

As discussed in Section 2.3, international lawyers have subconsciously been influenced by a number of foundational beliefs on customary law, as discussed over at least the past 200 years. In effect, many seem implicitly to have taken on board concepts and arguments of the nineteenth-century Pandectist tradition. One such transplant is the decidedly un-Roman[107] concept of *ius dispositivum*, which is usually mentioned only in passing, for example in *Oppenheim's International Law*: 'States may, by and within the limits of agreement between themselves, vary or even dispense altogether with most rules of international law.'[108] The idea is that the law (either the civil code or customary law) provides 'default' rules which come into force only if there is no private agreement on a specific point. A few passages in the *Corpus Iuris Civilis* could be read as expressing this concept, foremost: '[i]us publicum privatorum pactis mutari non potest',[109] which expresses the opposite side of the coin but has been taken to imply that there are parts of the law which *can* be abrogated by contracts.[110] There is ample scholarship proving that the dichotomy of *ius cogens* and *ius dispositivum* is not of Roman origin.[111] The true origin of this construct is nineteenth-century

[107] Max Kaser, '"Ius publicum" und "ius privatum"' 103 *Zeitschrift der Savigny-Stiftung für Rechtsgeschichte Romanistische Abteilung* (1986) 1–101 at 77.

[108] Robert Y Jennings, Arthur Watts (eds.), *Oppenheim's International Law, vol 1: Peace* (9th edn, London: Longman 1992) 7; see also Martti Koskenniemi, 'Fragmentation of International Law: Difficulties Arising from the Diversification and Expansion of International Law: Report of the Study Group of the International Law Commission' in *International Law Commission, Fifty-Eighth Session, Geneva, 1 May–9 June and 3 July–11 August 2006*, A/CN.4/L.682 (2006), para 108.

[109] D.2.14.38; see also D.50.17.45.1: 'Privatorum conventio iuri publico non derogat.' In contrast, C.2.3.29.1 may indirectly be a hint at what the Roman jurists felt to be dispositive law: 'regula est iuris antiqui omnes licentiam habere his quae pro se introducta sunt renuntiare'.

[110] Eg Paul Auerbach, *Dispositives Recht insbesondere des BGB* (Frankfurt: Mahlau & Waldschmidt 1900) 8.

[111] Max Kaser, Das Römische Privatrecht, vol 1: Das altrömische, das vorklassische und klassische Recht (Munich: CH Beck 1955) 175.

German civil law scholarship, most famously Carl von Savigny and Bernhard Windscheid – their efforts to reconstruct the sources of civil law introduced us to this idea. Windscheid, for example, argued in his 1861 *Lehrbuch des Pandektenrechts*: 'Some [laws] tolerate the ordering of legal relations by private regulation and are only applicable if there is no such ordering by private regulation.'[112]

How the Pandectist notion of *ius dispositivum* found its way into (parts of) orthodox international legal scholarship is unclear. Late nineteenth- and early twentieth-century German, French and Italian general works on international law seem largely to have proceeded from very different conceptions of the sources of international law and the typical situation of a treaty providing for different regulation *inter partes* in the face of a general customary norm could not arise under these.[113] A survey of this literature does not bear out the idea that this reading of civil law influenced them to any degree;[114] if anything, German public (international) law scholarship of the period is awash with warnings against taking licences with analogies from private law.[115] Yet, by the mid-twentieth century, we find that the view of customary international law as *ius dispositivum* is common, particularly in German, but also in English- and French-language works.[116] This shift

[112] 'Andere [Rechtssätze] lassen es sich gefallen, daß das betreffende Verhältniß durch Privatwillkühr anders geordnet werde, und kommen nur dann zur Anwendung, wenn eine Ordnung des Verhältnisses durch Privatwillkühr nicht vorliegt.' Bernhard Windscheid, *Lehrbuch des Pandektenrechts*, vol 1 (Dusseldorf: Julius Buddeus 1862) 65; see also Friedrich Carl von Savigny, *System des heutigen Römischen Rechts*, vol 1 (Berlin: Veit und Comp. 1840) 57–8 (§ 16).

[113] Eg Lassa Oppenheim, *International Law: A Treatise, vol 1: Peace* (London: Longmans, Green and Comp. 1905) 20–4.

[114] Eg Georg Jellinek, *Die rechtliche Natur der Staatenverträge: Ein Beitrag zur juristischen Construction des Völkerrechts* (Vienna: Alfred Hölder 1880) 64–5; Franz von Holtzendorff, 'Die Quellen des Völkerrechts' in Franz von Holtzendorff (ed.), *Handbuch des Völkerrechts: Auf Grundlage Europäischer Staatspraxis*, vol 1 (Berlin: Carl Habel 1885) 67–156 at 147–9. Though see eg Johann Caspar Bluntschli, *Das moderne Völkerrecht der civilisirten Staaten als Rechtsbuch dargestellt* (Nördlingen: CH Beck 1868) 59–60, (3rd edn, 1878) 65–6; Ernst Radnitzky, 'Dispositives Völkerrecht' 1 *Österreichische Zeitschrift für öffentliches Recht* (1914) 656–74; Alfred Verdross, *Die Verfassung der Völkerrechtsgemeinschaft* (Vienna: Springer 1926) 45; Alfred Verdross, *Völkerrecht* (Berlin: Springer 1937) 78.

[115] Most famously Jellinek (1880) note 114 at 50–1; Heinrich Triepel, *Völkerrecht und Landesrecht* (Leipzig: CL Hirschfeld 1899) 211–25; Georg Jellinek, *System der subjektiven öffentlichen Rechte* (Tubingen: Mohr 1905) 314–15; see on this point Hersch Lauterpacht, *Private Law Sources and Analogies of International Law (With Special Reference to International Arbitration)* (London: Longmans, Green and Co. 1927).

[116] Eg Günther Jaenicke, 'Völkerrechtsquellen' in Hans-Jürgen Schlochauer (ed.), *Wörterbuch des Völkerrechts, vol 3: Rapalo-Vertrag bis Zypern* (2nd edn, Berlin: Walter

could possibly be influenced by the drafting of Article 38 PCIJ/ICJ Statute,[117] but the idea of *ius dispositivum* was not overwhelmingly accepted in literature even before *Nicaragua*. There are two other reasons why even by the mid-twentieth century and despite using the phrase, international legal doctrine had not fully adopted the Pandectist concept of *ius dispositivum*.[118]

First, most general works of international law speak of customary and treaty law as equals, coupled with the *lex posterior* and *lex specialis* maxims,[119] for example Akehurst: 'Where the maxim *lex specialis derogat generali* provides no clear guidance . . . it seems that treaties and custom are of equal authority. The later in time prevails.'[120] This view of the relationship between equal sources is difficult to reconcile with the notion that almost all norms of customary international law are dispositive vis-à-vis *inter partes* treaty regulation. Arguing that customary and treaty law are *mutually* derogable is a more pragmatic solution, but neither does it work with the idea of *ius dispositivum* nor is it based on a particularly sustainable view of the structure of the international legal order.[121]

de Gruyter 1960) 766–75 at 773–4; Georg Dahm, *Völkerrecht*, vol 1 (Stuttgart: W Kohlhammer 1958) 16; Ernst Sauer, *Grundlehre des Völkerrechts* (Cologne: Balduin Pick 1948) 57–8; James L Brierly, *The Law of Nations: An Introduction to the International Law of Peace* (Oxford: Clarendon Press 1955) 58; Hersch Lauterpacht, 'International Law – the General Part' (unpublished ms.) in Eliuh Lauterpacht (ed.), *International Law: Being the Collected Papers of Hersch Lauterpacht*, vol 1: *The General Works* (Cambridge: Cambridge University Press 1970) 1–178 at 87; Hersch Lauterpacht, 'General Rules of the Law of Peace' (English ms. unpublished) in Eliuh Lauterpacht (ed.), *International Law: Being the Collected Papers of Hersch Lauterpacht*, vol 1: *The General Works* (Cambridge: Cambridge University Press 1970) 179–444 at 234; Jean L'Hullier, *Éléments de droit international public* (Paris: Rousseau 1950) 226; American Law Institute, *Restatement of the Law: The Foreign Relations Law of the United States*, vol 1 (St Paul: American Law Institute Publishers 1987) 27–8, 33; see also *NCSC* (1969) note 16 at 42 (para 72).

117 Permanent Court of International Justice Advisory Committee of Jurists, *Procès-verbaux of the Proceedings of the Committee June 16th–July 24th 1920 with Annexes* (The Hague: van Langenhuysen 1920) 323–7; reported, inter alia, in Verdross (1926) note 114 at 44–5.

118 Though see the possibility that the history of the common law may be slightly clearer with the non-civilian maxim *conventio vincit legem*: Bernhard Rudden, 'Ius cogens, ius dispositivum' 11 *Cambrian Law Review* (1980) 87–100 at 91.

119 Deconstructing the conflict avoidance maxims: Kammerhofer (2010d) note 41 at 146–71.

120 Michael Akehurst, 'The Hierarchy of the Sources of International Law' 47 *British Year Book of International Law 1974–1975* (1977) 273–85 at 275.

121 Kammerhofer (2010d) note 41 at 154, 177–8, 238 fn 204, referring to Wolfram Karl, *Vertrag und spätere Praxis im Völkerrecht: Zum Einfluß der Praxis auf Inhalt und Bestand völkerrechtlicher Verträge* (Berlin: Springer 1983) 86–110.

Second, the re-importation of *ius dispositivum* into international legal scholarship in the mid-twentieth century may be owing to a misunderstanding connected to the rise of the idea of *ius cogens* in the (non-civilian) international legal sense. At the ILC discussions on the law of treaties, the term was introduced tentatively and always in competition with terms like 'international public order'. The ILC's fourth rapporteur, Humphrey Waldock, 'had used the term *jus cogens*' only '[f]or lack of a better'.[122] It is therefore suggested that the idea of 'peremptory norms', as they later became, might not have originated not in the Pandectist *ius cogens–ius dispositivum* dichotomy; rather, it might have a different back story.[123] The one element of the Pandectist notion – abrogation *inter partes* is not permitted – is contained only incidentally in the international law notion, not by necessity. The difference can be seen in cases where the two conceptions of *ius cogens* diverge. Various parts of the law of treaties, such as fraud as grounds for the invalidity of a treaty, reservations contrary to the treaty's object and purpose or the *pacta tertiis* rule could probably not be abrogated in an agreement. These are *ius cogens* in the civilian sense, but would probably not be called *ius cogens* in the international law sense.

What might have happened with the re-importation of *ius dispositivum* in twentieth-century scholarship is that the use of the term *ius cogens* triggered a knee-jerk reaction with civilian-trained international lawyers. Subconsciously, they may have reasoned that if there is *ius cogens* in international law, then certainly other parts are *ius dispostivium*. However, as a matter of norm-structural analysis, it does not automatically follow that most parts of customary international law may be abrogated from the idea that certain parts may not be. This may also explain why, in the mid-twentieth-century writings canvassed here, *ius dispositivum* is mentioned without any historical-doctrinal embedding or references to literature.

Thus, the *ius dispositivum* model never existed on the terms we imagine. If we assume that it does and assume that treaties can 'impact'

[122] *Yearbook of the International Law Commission 1963*, vol 1: *Summary Records of the Fifteenth Session 6 May–12 July 1963*, UN Doc A/CN.4/SER.A/1963 (New York: United Nations) 62.

[123] The ample literature on international *ius cogens* seems to be united in accepting this, eg three arbitrarily selected books: Heinrich Bernhard Reimann, *Ius cogens im Völkerrecht: Eine quellenkritische Untersuchung* (Zurich: Schulthess 1971) 1–60; Stefan Kadelbach, *Zwingendes Völkerrecht* (Berlin: Duncker & Humblot 1992) 26–68; Alexander Orakhelashvili, *Peremptory Norms in International Law* (Oxford: Oxford University Press 2006).

dispositive customary international law norms for treaty parties, then the customary norm in question must have been changed. At least the personal sphere of validity is changed for the treaty parties vis-à-vis each other.[124] Therefore, the network of IIAs has an impact on pre-existing customary norms by excluding at least its application to treaty-covered relationships. For specific home state–host state relationships and within the terms of the IIA in question, customary norms would not apply, only the treaty norm. What, however, is the impact on *future* customary international law-making in the area covered by IIAs? As mentioned in Section 2.4, it would be less likely that the treaty parties would form an *opinio iuris consuetudinalis* with respect to areas covered by the treaty.

However, despite the abrogation in the personal sphere – the *inter partes* exclusion of customary law – it is theoretically possible that *ius dispositivum superveniens* is created.[125] This is owing to the fact that even if the *inter partes* action were to exclude customary law, it is possible that the treaty (or connected events or texts) would provide evidence for the presence of instances of state practice and *opinio iuris*. If we take the idea of *ius dispositivum* seriously, then even states which exclude customary international law norms for particular treaty relationships with other states are able to create customary international law outside the *ratione materiae*, *temporis* and *personae* confines of the treaty. It is therefore not theoretically excluded that a customary international law norm is created despite the validity of treaties which contain *inter se* regulation, including by way of practice and *opinio* contributed by treaty parties.

The question is then whether this later customary norm (*ius dispositivum superveniens*) is automatically abrogated by the previously concluded treaty which provided for *inter se* exceptions to the old customary norm. If the *ius dispositivum* view is valid, it seems unlikely that two states, concluding a treaty in 1980, were capable of excluding *inter partes* the validity of a customary norm which became valid only in 1990. Leaving this problem aside, the creation of new customary international law despite existing treaty networks is not impossible but much less easy

124 I will not discus the norm-theoretical implications of changes to spheres of validity here (though see Kammerhofer (2010d) note 41 at 149). However, contrary to the legal theoretical perspective developed here, the understanding of 'mutari' in Roman texts tends towards not denoting derogation (Auerbach (1900) note 110 at 9–10) but is more akin to the modern primacy of application (*Anwendungsvorrang*) claimed for European law.

125 With a different reasoning: Dinstein (2007) note 61 at 407.

to prove, because it is much less likely that *opinio iuris* is present. By abrogating customary international law through the treaty in question, states may even wish to express an *opinio non consuetudinalis* in the treaty or connected events or texts, but again this is a matter of evidence.

2.5.2 The Nicaragua *Model*

On the view espoused in *Nicaragua* (but not only there):

> The fact that ... principles, recognized as such, have been codified or embodied in multilateral conventions does not mean that they cease to exist and to apply as principles of customary law, even as regards countries that are parties to such conventions.[126]

This means, as the Court held in the judgment on the merits:

> [T]here are no grounds for holding that when customary international law is comprised of rules identical to those of treaty law, the latter 'supervenes' the former, so that the customary international law has no further existence of its own. ... It will therefore be clear that customary international law continues to exist and to apply, separately from international treaty law, even where the two categories of law have an identical content.[127]

This view also faces challenges, for example: are the two sources, if they exist concurrently, normatively connected and part of the same legal order? What, if any, norm-conflict rules exist to resolve a possible divergence of treaty and customary norms?[128] If customary law and treaty diverge in their prescription, do treaty parties persistently violate customary law? While these particular problems are not central to the argument about customary law from a network of treaties, if treaty-making does not result in *inter partes* abrogation, there is no direct impact on the customary norm. If treaty and customary norms are valid simultaneously even for two treaty parties in their mutual relations, the results laid out above for the *ius dispositivum* model and its impact on *opinio iuris* (Sections 2.5.1 and 2.4) apply a fortiori. Treaty-related behaviour by treaty parties would probably be relevant and the events surrounding treaty-making can in principle provide evidence for state practice and *opinio iuris*. However, its evidentiary value would probably

[126] *Nicaragua* (1984) note 106 at 424 (para 73); see also eg Jia (2010) note 42 at 83, 92.
[127] *Nicaragua* (1986) note 7 at 95, 96 (paras 177, 179).
[128] For a discussion of some aspects of this problem see Kammerhofer (2010d) note 41 at 137–94, 230–8.

not be high, because a treaty or actions connected to it concern treaty law, not customary law. An *opinio iuris conventionalis* is more likely to be expressed than an *opinio iuris consuetudinalis* on the topic of the treaty.

The theoretical points raised by *inter se* regulation are highly contentious, but, for the emergence of a customary norm in the circumstances relevant here, the results do not differ significantly for the two models. The question of whether treaty parties can abrogate customary law *inter se* does not determine whether it is possible in principle for customary law to change after the entry-into-force of the treaty. On both the *ius dispositivum* and the *Nicaragua* models, the mere presence of treaty norms, as well as the fact that more of the activities of the treaty parties will relate to the treaty, reduce the likelihood that the treaty can be used to evidence state practice and *opinio iuris*. This is so even though the reduction is probably less significant for the *Nicaragua* model. The two models do produce a different outcome in one area, however. On the *ius dispositivum* model, any emerging customary international law norm might have a reduced personal sphere of application *ex tunc* – if, that is, *inter se* abrogation entails the abrogation of later customary law as well, as discussed. In contrast, on the *Nicaragua* model, the emerging customary international law norm is in principle binding on all states, including the treaty parties.

2.6 Conclusion: A General Customary Rule on Expropriation?

It is commonplace to argue that the network of IIAs has created customary investment law which is indistinguishable from treaty law. Voices in legal theory and generalist international legal scholarship have tended to counter that assumption; they raise a principled set of objections to this idea. How likely is it, then, that IIAs have played a significant role in creating a norm of customary international law on the expropriation of investments which is similar to IIA expropriation clauses (see also Section 7.2)?

Sections 2.2 and 2.3 have shown that 'state practice' in a wide sense (all that states do or omit to do) is not identical with the objective element of customary law-creation. State practice in the technical sense is the observance of the rule or the exercise of the right, which alone forms the content of the budding norm. The majority opinion commingles these two meanings of state practice. Some also seem to assume that talking about doing 'x' is the same as doing 'x'. What sort of state practice (*usus*) is required to create a customary norm which would be similar to the IIA expropriation clauses? IIA expropriation clauses can be reconstructed as prohibitions: 'All parties are prohibited from doing *x*, unless they do *a*, *b*, *c* and *d*.' For a customary norm, the practice-forming regularity of behaviour would consist of states either not expropriating or expropriating only when the legality conditions are met. A third category of actions could also count as instances of state practice (*usus*): states expropriating without the conditions being met but with these actions typically being met with protest, sanctions, etc.[129]

Another question is whether a norm containing the term 'expropriation' – with all its connotation of transfer of property rights[130] – can be created using the customary method. An important insight of legal theory is that customary law, as law based on repetition of behaviour, is inherently limited in its forms and functions. It cannot create empowerment or derogating norms, because neither norm-functions can be adequately communicated via factual behavioural regularities.[131] Validity-creation that forms the content of an empowerment norm is not an act in reality which can be portrayed in behavioural regularities; these can only reflect outward manifestations, for example the signing of a piece of paper, not the norm-creation itself, in our case the ratification of the treaty. Direct expropriation at a minimum and to a large degree depends on the transfer of property rights. However, property and transfer of property as specifically normative concepts[132] are not exhausted by external behaviour forming *usus*. Hence, a possible customary norm on expropriation would not be able to reflect the formal transfer of property element, only the factual elements of 'taking' or 'restrictions of use' and so forth.

IIAs are instances neither of expropriation nor of non-expropriation. They are not instances of the behaviour prescribed by a possible expropriation norm. Hence, in the technical sense, they cannot serve as state practice (*usus*). At best, IIAs are state practice in a wide sense – all that states 'do'; they could be *expressions* or evidence of 'practice', for example expressing what states have done, are doing or intend to do. It is possible that the network of IIAs gives us clues as to what the behaviour of states was, is or will be, but such evidence is weak. Yet 'practice' in this wide sense may also express the 'opinions' and 'beliefs' of states. Therefore, the state practice (*usus*) of a customary norm on expropriation is unlikely to

[129] See, possibly, *Nicaragua* (1986) note 7 at 98 (para 186).
[130] See, however, Section 8.3.1.
[131] On this see Kammerhofer (2010d) note 41 at 72–4.
[132] As bundle of legal norms: Kelsen (1960) note 47 at 135–7.

be found in IIAs; one has to look to the actual behaviour of states in expropriating or not expropriating investments.

Do IIAs help us in finding *opinio iuris* on expropriation? Sections 2.4 and 2.5 have shown that the treaty norm-formulation for expropriation *itself* ('neither Party shall nationalize or expropriate') is a norm only as words in a treaty. It can give us a clue, in a verbalised form, as to what the content-forming behavioural regularity referred to by the *opinio iuris* would be. However, such a norm-formulation without more does not tell us whether this is what the states parties believe to be customary law. If the IIA expropriation clause were to include the phrase 'in accordance with customary international law', the words would not be part of the treaty norm in a strict sense. However, both the treaty text and the events surrounding it might give us indications as to the *opinio iuris* of the treaty parties. Are there such indications in IIAs or connected events/texts for a customary expropriation norm? Generally, articles on expropriation do not contain references to the state of customary international law. In order to prove *opinio iuris*, we would have to do more than assert that 'the definition commonly found in investment treaties has been . . . patently adopted from a formulation widely employed in customary international law'.[133] There are occasional indications, such as Annex B of the series of US Model BITs since 2004, where the parties express their agreement that the expropriation clause 'is intended to reflect customary international law'.[134] It is reasonable to presume that such statements in a treaty express the *opinio iuris* of the United States and of its treaty partners (see Section 7.5). There may also be occasional hints in texts or events connected to IIAs, such as *travaux préparatoires*, statements in connection with investment agreements or actions. The subjective element is not suppressed by the presence of treaty-law, but their evidentiary value is low. It is therefore reasonable to assume that some evidence for *opinio iuris* can be gleamed from treaty-related texts or events. However, it would be necessary to exhaustively analyse the raw material. IIAs may be a little more helpful in finding *opinio iuris* than state practice.

This chapter has not sifted all the available state practice and *opinio iuris* for and against a customary norm on expropriation. Yet, two major and overarching issues have reared their heads already in this chapter. The first is the difference between the creation of the law through the

133 McLachlan (2007) note 18 at 16.
134 US Model BIT 2012, Annex B, available at: www.state.gov/documents/organization/188371.pdf.

formal sources of law versus factual influences on our perception of the law. For example, it is palpable that the pronouncements of tribunals significantly influence our perception of customary international law, but it is much less clear what the exact *legal* relationship is between jurisprudence and custom. The other factor is the role of doctrinal legal scholarship's ordering, systematising and drawing conclusions from the materials.[135] This may seem a peculiarly Germanic preoccupation, but it goes to the heart of what legal scholarship can and should be and it determines what propositions of the law are. If the legal norms are fragmented, as seems to be the case for IIAs, is doctrinal scholarship allowed to construct an overarching narrative? More importantly: if it does, what is this scholarly narrative? Is it perhaps no more than a collection of social scientific probabilities that tribunals will decide thus in specified fact-situation and is thus legal scholarship no more than what legal realists imagined?

On a legal-theoretical approach, using treaties to create and identify customary law may be generally accepted, but it is highly problematic. As discussed in Chapters 3, 4 and 5, the other 'factors' – jurisprudence, scholarly writings and interpretation – are equally problematic. While it may be tempting to take all factors in combination, there is no reason to suppose that where arguments or legal sources fail individually, they will succeed together.

[135] Eg Matthias Jestaedt, 'Wissenschaft im Recht: Rechtsdogmatik im Wissenschaftsvergleich' 69 *JuristenZeitung* (2014) 1–12; Alexander Somek, 'Legal Science as a Source of Law: A Late Reply by Puchta to Kantorowicz' (working paper 2012), available at ssrn.com /abstract=2175235; Alexander Somek, 'The Spirit of Legal Positivism' 12 *German Law Journal* (2011) 729–56. See Section 5.1.

3

Investment Precedents

3.1 Introduction: Persistent Questions

No other factor seems to have greater practical influence on or relevance for our perception of international investment law, none is used as extensively or scrutinised more intensely than the awards of investment tribunals. Yet their unquestionable factual importance seems to obscure another dimension of this jurisprudence. Scholars and tribunals opining on the role of precedents seem mesmerised by that factual importance and are inclined to de-emphasise the distinction between the proper legal role of precedents and their factual influence.

In one sense or another, investment arbitral jurisprudence is used as means of generating general international investment law. Authors believe that we can create a general, non-fragmented international investment law through case-law. The usual analytical approach to investment arbitration is either to develop a theory of judicial or legal reasoning or decision-making, or to engage in a quasi-empirical study of the factual influence or impact of arbitration or arbitral awards on later decisions or on 'the law'. The role of precedents or of the arbitral process is analysed on an empirical, rational-decisional or (policy or moral) normative level. In line with the normativist-positivist methodology adopted here, this chapter will largely foreground structural analysis. Indeed, for an international legal scholarship that focuses on its *proprium* and does not extend into social sciences, two directions of inquiry are interesting. Is precedent a general (rather than individual) norm of international investment law or does it generate one – is it binding on other states and investors? Is precedent a decisional norm only binding on *arbitrators* but not on others – is it a norm added to the applicable law, influencing or modifying the law during the process of deciding a case?

This chapter takes seriously the exhortation in *Barcelona Traction* that 'the general arbitral jurisprudence which has accumulated in the last half-century . . . cannot therefore give rise to generalization going beyond the special circumstances of each case'.[1] We will not – as many commentators seem to do – seek to justify, defend, condemn or explain the actual behaviour of investment tribunals in citing, regarding, following or distinguishing prior decisions. Instead we will discuss whether general *norms* can follow, whether these are part of international (investment) law or whether their influence is limited to the realm of facts. This chapter will analyse the present debate on precedents in international investment law, which seems to focus on a small number of questions with limited heuristic value. Two beliefs are held simultaneously: on the one hand, international law is not a common law and *stare decisis* does not exist here; on the other hand, tribunals are 'somehow' required to respect prior awards (Section 3.2). The chapter will also discuss the role of precedents as a factor in the making of a customary international law norm of expropriation (Section 3.4).

The specialist, 'practice-friendly' debate on the role of precedent in investment arbitration reached a high-point in the years 2006–8[2] which has abated since then, as the writings in this sub-field have become less dominated by practitioners. The specialist debate also echoes generalist debates on the function of precedent for other tribunals, foremost the ICJ,[3] which are also marked by a narrow set of arguments and questions as well as by a narrowly bounded set of answers. However, while they generally have a more pragmatic ambit, more geared towards the needs of

[1] *Barcelona Traction, Light and Power, Limited (New Application: 1962) (Belgium* v. *Spain)*, Second Phase, Judgment of 5 February 1970, ICJ Reports (1970) 3 at 40 (para 63).

[2] Typical and oft-cited examples: Andrea K Bjorklund, 'Investment Treaty Arbitral Decisions as *Jurisprudence Constante*' in Colin B Picker, Isabella D Bunn, Douglas W Arner (eds.), *International Economic Law: The State and Future of the Discipline* (Oxford: Hart 2008) 265–80; Tai-Heng Cheng, 'Precedent and Control in Investment Treaty Arbitration' 30 *Fordham International Law Journal* (2007) 1014–49; Jeffery P Commission, 'Precedent in Investment Treaty Arbitration: A Citation Analysis of a Developing Jurisprudence' 24 *Journal of International Arbitration* (2007) 129–58; Christopher S Gibson, Christopher R Drahozal, 'Iran–United States Claims Tribunal Precedent in Investor-State Arbitration' 23 *Journal of International Arbitration* (2006) 521–46; Gabrielle Kaufmann-Kohler, 'Arbitral Precedent: Dream, Necessity or Excuse?' 23 *Arbitration International* (2007) 357–78; Martins Paparinskis, 'Investment Protection Law and Sources of Law: A Critical Look' 103 *ASIL Proceedings* (2010) 76–9; Jan Paulsson, 'The Role of Precedent in Investment Arbitration' in Katia Yannaca-Small (ed.), *Arbitration under International Investment Agreements: A Guide to the Key Issues* (Oxford: Oxford University Press 2010) 699–718; August Reinisch, 'The Role of Precedent in ICSID Arbitration' *Austrian Arbitration Yearbook* (2008) 495–510; Christoph Schreuer, Matthew Weininger, 'A Doctrine of Precedent?' in Peter Muchlinski, Federico Ortino, Christoph Schreuer (eds.), *The Oxford Handbook of International Investment Law* (Oxford: Oxford University Press 2008) 1188–1206.

[3] Eg Mohamed Shahabuddeen, *Precedent in the World Court* (Cambridge: Cambridge University Press 1996).

arbitrators and counsel, rather than an abstract elucidation of the value of precedent, they are worthy of study.

Three questions and answers keep reappearing in the manner described above. (1) International law, including international investment arbitration, does not have a common law-type system of formal precedents or *stare decisis*. As a matter of the 'formal sources of law', the awards only bind the parties to the arbitral proceedings. (2) Jurisprudence is nonetheless of major importance; tribunals rely on it to a large degree. Moreover, the specific points of law are determined largely by argument from precedent, for example on whether and which regulation can be indirect expropriation. (3) Therefore, *some* sort of system of precedents is in operation in international investment arbitration nonetheless. Explanations vary, particularly whether this is entirely factual or somehow connected to the law, but the tendency is to assert that the reliance is relevant and also relevant to the law. In the following, we will describe and critique each of these in turn.

3.2 Awards Are Not 'Formally Binding', but They Are Immensely Important

'International law does not recognize a binding force of precedents or the principle of *stare decisis*, nor is a Court decision ... a source of international law.'[4] This is Rudolf Bernhard's magisterial answer to the first question, followed by the inevitable reminder, vis-à-vis the second question, that '[t]his is correct in legal theory, but the reality is different',[5] that is, the 'real' importance of jurisprudence is much higher than theory suggests. In orthodox scholarship, these two are arguments nearly always found together; it is almost unanimously agreed that prior pronouncements do not bind, while it is at the same time held that this first statement, the 'strict', 'technical', 'formal' view, is not the 'reality on the ground'.[6]

Investment tribunals continuously opine that previous decisions do not have binding force beyond the individual decisions; tribunals certainly do not consider themselves bound or able to bind other tribunals.[7] The

[4] Rudolf Bernhardt, 'Article 59' in Andreas Zimmermann, Christian Tomuschat, Karin Oellers-Frahm (eds.), *The Statute of the International Court of Justice* (Oxford: Oxford University Press 2006) 1231–51 at 1244.

[5] Bernhardt (2006) note 4 at 1244.

[6] Both statements in one sentence, eg Commission (2007) note 2 at 132; Reinisch (2008d) note 2 at 498.

[7] *Methanex Corporation* v. *United States of America*, NAFTA-UNCITRAL, Decision of the Tribunal on Petitions from Third Persons to Intervene as 'Amici Curiae' of 15 January 2001, para 51; *SGS Société Générale de Surveillance S.A.* v. *Republic of the*

question is rarely explored in depth; as Marc Jacob puts it, 'even a cursory glance at Article 38 of the ICJ Statute will yield an undemanding "no"'.[8] When the reason for the absence of 'formal' bindingness is discussed, two sets of questions are interlinked in orthodox debate: are investment *arbitrators* bound by procedural law (or overarching systemic principles) to follow earlier awards; is there a system of *stare decisis* in international investment arbitration? Article 53(1) ICSID Convention 1965 and Article 57 ICJ Statute are invariably used and both are read as restricting the binding effect of judgments or awards to the parties to a dispute.[9] For the ICSID Convention, an *argumentum e contrario* is employed: 'Article 53(1) provides that "[t]he award shall be binding *on the parties*", thus implying that an ICSID award has no binding effect over other parties.'[10] Equally, and more generally, orthodox scholarship is united in opining that 'there is no doctrine of *stare decisis* or, put another way, no system of "binding precedent," in international law',[11] including international investment arbitration.[12] Sometimes this is justified by pointing to the lack of a hierarchy of courts, the

Philippines, ICSID, ARB/02/6, Decision of the Tribunal on Objections to Jurisdiction of 29 January 2004, para 97; *AES Corporation v. Argentine Republic*, ICSID, ARB/02/17, Decision on Jurisdiction of 26 April 2005, para 23; *El Paso Energy International Company* v. *Argentine Republic*, ICSID, ARB/03/15, Decision on Jurisdiction of 27 April 2006, para 39; *Jan de Nul N.V. and Dredging International N.V.* v. *Arab Republic of Egypt*, ICSID, ARB/04/13, Decision on Jurisdiction of 16 June 2006, para 64; *Saipem S.p.A.* v. *People's Republic of Bangladesh*, ICSID, ARB/05/07, Decision on Jurisdiction and Recommendation on Provisional Measures of 21 March 2007, para 67; *Glamis Gold, Ltd.* v. *United States of America*, NAFTA-UNCITRAL, Final Award of 8 June 2009, para 8; *Chevron Corporation (USA) and Texaco Petroleum Company (USA)* v. *Republic of Ecuador*, UNCITRAL, PCA 34877, Partial Award on the Merits of 30 March 2010, para 163; *Suez, Sociedad General de Aguas de Barcelona S.A. and Vivendi Universal S. A.* v. *Argentine Republic*, ICSID, ARB/03/19 and *AWG Group* v. *Argentine Republic*, UNCITRAL, Decision on Liability of 30 July 2010, para 189.

8 Marc Jacob, 'Precedents: Lawmaking through International Adjudication' 12 *German Law Journal* (2011) 1005–32 at 1008.

9 Commission (2007) note 2 at 134; Gibson (2006) note 2 at 525–6; Kaufmann-Kohler (2007) note 2 at 360–1; Paulsson (2010) note 2 at 702; Reinisch (2008d) note 2 at 498–500; Schreuer (2008) note 2 at 1190.

10 Florian Grisel, 'The Sources of Foreign Investment Law' in Zachary Douglas, Joost Pauwelyn, Jorge E Viñuales (eds.), *The Foundations of International Investment Law: Bringing Theory into Practice* (Oxford: Oxford University Press 2014) 213–33 at 224.

11 Gibson (2006) note 2 at 525.

12 John C Gardner, 'Judicial Precedent in the Making of International Public Law' 18 *Journal of Comparative Legislation and International Law* (1935) 251–9 at 254; Bjorklund (2008) note 2 at 265; Commission (2007) note 2 at 134; Grisel (2014) note 10 at 233; Kaufmann-Kohler (2007) note 2 at 357; D Brian King, Rahim Moloo, 'International Arbitrators as Lawmakers' 46 *New York University Journal of International Law and Politics* (2014) 875–910 at 884; Paulsson (2010) note 2 at 699; Shahabuddeen (1996) note 3 at 97.

decentralisation of international justice,[13] as if binding rules from judgments could exist only within a hierarchical system of courts.

In order to soften this rather categorical statement of law in preparation for its inevitable twin (that jurisprudence is nonetheless important), even those who remain within a reasonably orthodox understanding of the sources doctrine tend to fudge a bit on a doctrinal level. Article 53(1) ICSID Convention, for example, is said to be weaker than Article 59 ICJ Statute, as the former mentions binding force 'for the parties', whereas the latter is clear: decisions have 'no binding force except between the parties'.[14] Or this: 'nothing in the [ICSID] Convention's *travaux préparatoires* suggests that the doctrine of *stare decisis* should be applied, though nothing in the *travaux préparatoires* suggests that it should *not* be applied'.[15] Reading Article 59 ICJ Statute as denying precedential force to judgments is criticised. It is argued that the article deals with *chose jugée*, *res iudicata* or is directed at delimiting the legal position vis-à-vis intervenors.[16]

The other question commonly asked is whether awards or judgments are in any sense and with any form of legal effect a 'source' of international law; are the *subjects* of international law 'in general' bound by precedents (or norms contained therein)? Even if there is no *stare decisis* meta-rule applicable to arbitrators, previous awards could still be part of the law, if 'awards' (or norms therein) were one of the ways in which general or sectoral international law could be created. Of course, one could say that the second question is answered by the first, as the relevant statutes specify that they are a source of law, but only as an individual norm binding on the parties to the dispute.

Scholarship starts with a look at Article 38(1)(d) ICJ Statute, but takes its terms perhaps too seriously as a catalogue of the sources of law, which is a venerable tradition in international legal scholarship.[17] Scholars recognise[18] that, in Article 38, 'judicial decisions' are not only 'subject to the provisions of Article 59' but also 'subsidiary means for the

[13] Bjorklund (2008) note 2 at 265; Grisel (2014) note 10 at 224.

[14] Reinisch (2008d) note 2 at 499–500; Schreuer (2008) note 2 at 1190.

[15] Kaufmann-Kohler (2007) note 2 at 368.

[16] Shahabuddeen (1996) note 3 at 63–6; Hersch Lauterpacht, 'The So-Called Anglo-American and Continental Schools of Thought in International Law' 12 *British Year Book of International Law* (1931) 31–62 at 58; Hersch Lauterpacht, *The Development of International Law by the International Court* (London: Stevens & Sons 1958) 8.

[17] See Jörg Kammerhofer, *Uncertainty in International Law: A Kelsenian Perspective* (Abingdon: Routledge 2010) 208–10.

[18] Commission (2007) note 2 at 134; Kaufmann-Kohler (2007) note 2 at 361; Schreuer (2008) note 2 at 1189.

determination of rules of law'. Given the great factual impact of awards, it is not surprising that scholars are unhappy to consign them to being mere evidence:[19] 'awards cannot now be reasonably described as only a subsidiary source of international law'.[20]

At this point, having established that past awards are neither formal precedents nor formal sources, the reversal starts. But it bears asking whether the argument could not have been deepened. It should at least be emphasised that binding later tribunals to earlier decisions (*stare decisis*/formal precedent) and making such decisions binding on the subjects of law cannot come about by default – both require positive law. However, orthodox scholars do not usually argue that this is the law – being perhaps eager to highlight the factual impact of arbitral jurisprudence. Even those who disagree with the orthodox disavowal of a wider binding force of awards fail to present a legal case against this assertion. Returning to Jacob: 'this denial [of wider binding force] is as undemanding as it is limited in explanatory power. What follows is . . . a refutation . . . of the significance of the perspective it adopts.'[21] The question of *stare decisis*, however, is of lesser interest here, as we are not concerned with the position which investment arbitrators find themselves in. Rather than ask whether such a tribunal ought to take into account earlier jurisprudence, our focus here is whether (such a body of) jurisprudence can create general investment law.

As to the second assertion, scholarship is unanimous in diagnosing that the body of investment arbitral jurisprudence has great impact on a factual level. This argument is not often supported by empirical evidence. Four arguments typically prepare the way for the third argument (Section 3.3). First, tribunals frequently cite earlier awards.[22] Second, investment awards in their reasoning rely heavily on jurisprudence.[23] Moreover, they seek to 'decide disputes consistently with prior judicial decisions'.[24] Third, our perception of the law in this field is largely shaped by jurisprudence and more so than by the other sources of investment

[19] Though cf Lauterpacht (1958) note 16 at 14: 'evidence or, what is in fact the same, as a source of international law'. It bears questioning, though, whether a legal scholar should be more concerned whether 'x' is *in fact* the same as 'y' – or *in law*.

[20] Commission (2007) note 2 at 132.

[21] Jacob (2011) note 8 at 1008.

[22] For empirical citation analyses, see eg Commission (2007) note 2; Gibson (2006) note 2.

[23] Bjorklund (2008) note 2 at 266–7; Cheng (2007) note 2 at 1030; Commission (2007) note 2 at 131; Kaufmann-Kohler (2007) note 2 at 357; King (2014) note 12 at 883; Reinisch (2008d) note 2 at 499; Schreuer (2008) note 2 at 1189.

[24] Cheng (2007) note 2 at 1018.

law.[25] Fourth, the impact of award-following has strengthened over the past twenty-odd years.[26]

Rather than let the two arguments (no formal precedent or binding force but increasing factual importance) stand, scholars seek to reconcile theory and practice. The pressure is therefore on scholars to explain away this apparent contradiction, to harmonise our idea of the law with actual arbitral practice. Numerous authors have developed explanations of why and how this practice can nonetheless be precedential and how previous decisions are somehow relevant from a legal perspective. As Hersch Lauterpacht concisely put it in 1958: 'It is not suggested that in pursuing the practice of relying upon and following its previous decisions the Court has adopted the common law doctrine of judicial precedent. However, while not fettered by the rigidity of the formal doctrine of precedent, it has . . . largely adopted its substance.'[27]

3.3 The Orthodox De Facto Precedential System

The giving of some lesser 'force of law' to precedents is the third argument employed by investment law scholarship. An apposite example for this mindset is the following quotation:

> [W]axing over classifications of decided cases as formal sources of law or not is to a large extent a red herring. Adopting such a perspective to the exclusion of all others (deliberately) fails to see the larger picture. At the risk of sounding trite, it is suggested here that no matter what their exact jurisprudential providence may be, prior cases are crucial to adjudication, including dispute settlement in public international law.[28]

However, this classification is not irrelevant, as legal scholarship is not a study of perceptible phenomena alone. It would be equivalent to a zoologist arguing that a poisonous animal and a non-poisonous mimic are the same species because predators respond to both in the same manner. We need to look beyond phenomena to discover the fundamental *legal* difference between the binding force of precedents and the pragmatic effects of non-binding precedents.

25 Patrick M Norton, 'A Law of the Future or a Law of the Past? Modern Tribunals and the International Law of Expropriation' 85 *American Journal of International Law* (1991) 474–505 at 498; Stephan W Schill, *The Multilateralization of International Investment Law* (Cambridge: Cambridge University Press 2009).

26 Bjorklund (2008) note 2 at 266–7; Commission (2007) note 2 at 131; Grisel (2014) note 10 at 224; Kaufmann-Kohler (2007) note 2 at 357; King (2014) note 12 at 883.

27 Lauterpacht (1958) note 16 at 13–14.

28 Jacob (2011) note 8 at 1010.

If we turn this into a constructive argument, the omnipresence of arbitral jurisprudence is brought into the legal realm, albeit in a loose sense. Three main forms of argument can be found. The first is an acknowledgement that while single precedents do not have the power that they can have in common law systems, a line of decisions may come close to having this force; this is often equated with the civil law doctrine of *jurisprudence constante*. The second idea is that even when formal precedent is not applicable, prior reasoning will often convince other tribunals; here, the common law doctrine of persuasive precedent is used. Third are arguments that this factual importance has a quasi-legal binding effect, for example that precedents 'constrain' later tribunals.

The solution probably most congenial to those hailing from a continental legal background is some version of *jurisprudence constante*, because for the civilian tradition judgments merely discover the law and do not create general norms. Andrea Bjorklund aptly summarises this position:

> In the French tradition, the starting point for any analysis is the language of the code, but judicial decisions construing the code will have an influence on other courts as representing an accepted interpretation of the statute. . . . [P]recedent . . . [inter alia] refers to the decision of even a lower or equal court which, while not binding, can serve as a positive (or negative) model for the case under consideration. . . . [O]ne of the distinguishing features of *jurisprudence constante* is the development of doctrine through the accretion of a consistent line of cases, rather than the establishment of a rule by an individual case.[29]

If international investment arbitration is to have adopted that doctrine, one would expect arbitral argument to rely on lines of jurisprudence, or on leading cases as manifestations of such lines, rather than on single precedents.[30] One would also expect arguments on the basis of the reasonable interpretation of an IIA, as manifested in that line of cases, rather than on the basis of the *authority* of the line of decisions itself: 'a line of prior, consistent decisions may be persuasive evidence of the proper interpretation of the law'.[31] This civilian understanding, however, is not universally acknowledged and a certain bindingness is inferred. 'This would actually be a *stare decisis*

[29] Bjorklund (2008) note 2 at 272–3.

[30] See eg Michele Taruffo, Massimo La Torre, 'Precedent in Italy' in D Neil MacCormick, Robert S Summers (eds.), *Interpreting Precedents: A Comparative Study* (Aldershot: Ashgate 1997) 141–88 at 160–1.

[31] Mary Garvey Algero, 'The Sources of Law and the Value of Precedent: A Comparative and Empirical Study of a Civil Law State in a Common Law Nation' 65 *Louisiana Law Review* (2005) 775–822 at 783.

doctrine applied not to a single decision, but to a line of cases.'[32] Often, a certain compliance pull is associated with this notion; if *jurisprudence constante* is defined as 'the general sense of the way decisions *should be made*'.[33] It is difficult not to read this as inferring a legal relevance and authority to the line of cases in question: '[a] more cabined concept of lawmaking . . ., but nonetheless one that influences behavior'.[34] Another reading of *jurisprudence constante* is Thomas Wälde's in his separate opinion in *Thunderbird*:

> While individual arbitral awards by themselves do not as yet constitute a binding precedent, a consistent line of reasoning . . . should be respected; if an authoritative jurisprudence evolves, it will acquire the character of customary international law and must be respected. . . . An increasingly continuous, uncontested and consistent modern arbitral jurisprudence is part of the authoritative source of international law embodied in 'judicial decisions' . . . and will develop, with an even greater legally binding effect, into 'international custom . . .'.[35]

Gabrielle Kaufmann-Kohler elucidates this reading: '[i]t would imply not only a well established practice but also an *opinio juris*, namely, the belief . . . that . . . a tribunal must follow the solution arising from a consistent line of earlier cases'.[36] But this is far removed from the civilian tradition of the relationship between statutes and judgments, which is based on the idea that the court finds the law in the statute.[37] '*Jurisprudence constante* leaves an

[32] Kaufmann-Kohler (2007) note 2 at 377, see also 359–60; Gabrielle Kaufmann-Kohler, 'Is Consistency a Myth?' in Yas Banifatemi (ed.), *Precedent in International Arbitration: IAI Seminar Paris – December 14, 2007* (New York: Juris 2008) 137–47 at 146–7.

[33] James Crawford, 'Similarity of Issues in Disputes Arising under the Same or Similarly Drafted Investment Treaties' in Yas Banifatemi (ed.), *Precedent in International Arbitration: IAI Seminar Paris – December 14, 2007* (New York: Juris 2008) 97–103 at 102 (emphasis added).

[34] King (2014) note 12 at 883; see also Irene M Ten Cate, 'The Costs of Consistency: Precedent in Investment Treaty Arbitration' 51 *Columbia Journal of Transnational Law* (2013) 418–78 at 444: 'By demanding "compelling reasons" to justify departure from settled rules, *jurisprudence constante* places a significant decisional burden on adjudicators.'

[35] *International Thunderbird Gaming Corporation* v. *United Mexican States*, NAFTA-UNCITRAL, Award of 26 January 2006, Separate Opinion Thomas W Wälde, para 16; see also Thomas W Wälde, 'Specific Nature of Investment Arbitration' in Philippe Kahn, Thomas W Wälde (eds.), *New Aspects of International Investment Law* (Leiden: Brill 2007) 43–120 at 47. On the role of jurisprudence for customary law-creation, see Section 3.4.

[36] Kaufmann-Kohler (2007) note 2 at 377.

[37] For French law, see eg Michel Troper, 'Precedent in France' in D Neil MacCormick, Robert S Summers (eds.), *Interpreting Precedents: A Comparative Study* (Aldershot: Ashgate 1997) 103–40.

opening for adjudicators to deviate from earlier awards if the text of the code does not appear to support the interpretation.'[38] One could perhaps also read *SGS Philippines* in this light: '[i]t must . . . in the longer term [be] for the development of a common legal *opinion* or *jurisprudence constante*, to resolve the difficult legal questions'.[39]

The common lawyers' preferred option is probably *persuasive precedent*; while the underlying legal cultures are different, in effect it comes surprisingly close to *jurisprudence constante. Stare decisis* does not operate with respect to each and every prior decision, for example outside a given court's own hierarchy. Where binding precedent does not apply, decisions may be and are used as 'persuasive precedent'.[40] Some international lawyers proffering the *jurisprudence constante* analogy stress the persuasiveness of prior decisions[41] and one may be tempted to say that the only difference between them is between being persuaded by the reasoning in a *line* of cases and being persuaded by a single prior decision. However, persuasive precedent tends to be seen as having a creative effect, whereas *jurisprudence constante* is understood to merely discover the features of the law it interprets.

The doctrine of persuasive precedent is certainly popular with international lawyers wishing to explain the effect of investment jurisprudence.[42] Having found no legal bindingness, but being convinced that jurisprudence shapes the law[43] or provides 'consistency',[44] writers turn naturally to persuasiveness or perhaps to 'persuasive authority'[45] as an explanatory model. Prior decisions do not *have* to be followed as a matter of law; they may and will be followed if and 'to the extent that the prior opinion contains a convincing analysis of the

[38] Ten Cate (2013) note 34 at 444–5.

[39] *SGS Philippines* (2004) note 7 at para 97 (emphasis added).

[40] Eg Zenon Bankowski, D Neil MacCormick, 'Precedent in the United Kingdom' in D Neil MacCormick, Robert S Summers (eds.), *Interpreting Precedents: A Comparative Study* (Aldershot: Ashgate 1997) 315–54 at 323; Grant Lamond, 'Persuasive Authority in the Law' 17 *Philosophy of Law* (2010) 16–35 at 16.

[41] Bjorklund (2008) note 2 at 268.

[42] Commission (2007) note 2 at 135–6; Gibson (2006) note 2; Reinisch (2008d) note 2 at 498; Frédéric G Sourgens, 'Law's Laboratory: Developing International Law on Investment Protection as Common Law' 34 *Northwestern Journal of International Law & Business* (2014) 181–247; Frédéric G Sourgens, *A Nascent Common Law: The Process of Decisionmaking in International Legal Disputes Between States and Foreign Investors* (The Hague: Nijhoff 2015); Ten Cate (2013) note 34 at 441–3.

[43] See eg Paulsson (2010) note 2 at 703; Ten Cate (2013) note 34 at 423.

[44] Eg Gibson (2006) note 2 at 527.

[45] Eg Lamond (2010) note 40.

legal problem'.[46] Yet persuasive precedent is more than that: later tribunals can accept the prior decision as precedent either because they are persuaded or because the careful argument is entitled to a degree of authority and deference. Where the prior decision is on point and its reasoning is compelling, good countervailing reasons must be given why the later tribunal does not use this as precedent.[47] This 'persuasive authority' reading tends to cross the line to binding precedent. Grant Lamond sees this as a case of theoretical, rather than practical, authority, as giving reasons for believing, rather than reasons for action.[48] Frédéric Gilles Sourgens differentiates three reasons for the precedential effect of persuasive authority: 'precision, weight, and canonicity':[49]

> [1] A decision's persuasiveness is determined by the precision with which it analyzes a problem that is relevant to a subsequent case. A decision is particularly persuasive when it addresses the same problem or rejects a principal argument in the current case. A decision can also be highly persuasive if it makes a question in the current case less vague or ambiguous. . . . [2] Alternatively, a decision's persuasiveness may depend on its weight – . . . the frequency with which it bests other rival prescriptions. . . . [3] Persuasiveness more generally also can be aphoristic or canonical. . . . the anthologizing of decisional law that is not formally binding, for example in textbooks, can also be described as canonical.[50]

This may give the impression that what happens is more than one tribunal merely weighing the arguments of another tribunal, that is, that persuasive precedents are binding or can generate general norms. Perhaps this is due to the different stories that legal doctrine tells for code-based and common law systems. For civilian private law doctrine, the law (in a particularly narrow sense encompassing only statutes) is being interpreted and cognised. Leading cases, a *jurisprudence constante* or a *ständige Rechtsprechung*, are entitled to 'respect' largely because they

[46] Stefanie A Lindquist, Frank B Cross, 'Empirically Testing Dworkin's Chain Novel Theory: Studying the Path of Precedent' 80 *New York University Law Review* (2005) 1156–1206 at 1162; see also Sourgens (2014) note 42 at 241–2; Sourgens (2015) note 42 at 350.

[47] Norton (1991) note 25 at 501; Aleksander Peczenik, 'The Binding Force of Precedent' in D Neil MacCormick, Robert S Summers (eds.), *Interpreting Precedents: A Comparative Study* (Aldershot: Ashgate 1997) 461–479 at 467. This thinking is employed vis-à-vis *jurisprudence constante* as well (or for that alone): Taruffo (1997) note 30 at 160–1; Ten Cate (2013) note 34 at 444.

[48] Lamond (2010) note 40 at 20.

[49] Sourgens (2014) note 42 at 243; Sourgens (2015) note 42 at 352.

[50] Sourgens (2014) note 42 at 241–3; Sourgens (2015) note 42 at 350–1.

accord with the statute. This thinking does not obtain in the common law; applied to investment law, precedents are part of the law just as much as IIAs, perhaps even more so, because they are closer to the point of application, to the facts of the case and offer a more detailed regulation. The law as formed by the sum-total of judicial decisions is privileged even more than the abstract statutory norm is privileged in traditional civilian thinking. The unwillingness to consider IIAs the exclusive seat of the law is combined with a strong unwillingness for judgments to be merely the *bouche de la loi*. This leads directly to legal realism.

Quite independently of the specific doctrinal concept in which it is clothed, the claim is widespread that the body of investment jurisprudence *in fact* constrains arbitrators and in fact generates a more-or-less coherent body of 'law'. In other words, factual effects are seen as generative of at least some knowledge about how arbitral tribunals will decide future cases, a certainty that is all too easily translated into a certainty about what, for example, 'indirect expropriation' means in international investment law.[51] Despite this claim being rather vague, it generally uses the two arguments of decisional constraint and content-generation.

There are extreme opinions which tend to push both *jurisprudence constante* and persuasive precedent towards generating constraint for later decision-makers. Prior arguments and decisions deserve respect where and because they are well reasoned:[52] decisions which diverge require good reasons and more exhaustive reasoning; following (a line of) precedents less so. The body of investment jurisprudence is almost always considered, discussed and distinguished by later tribunals;[53] this fact is said to constrain them.[54] If everybody argues from precedent, one is under pressure to do so to even if one is not formally bound to follow or distinguish, even if one does so gladly or unthinkingly. There is a clear

[51] Reinisch (2008d) note 2 at 505–6: 'Indeed, the law of indirect expropriation has been a particularly promising field for the concretization of rather vague general standards through investment arbitration and . . . ". . . presents a situation where the common law method of case by case development is pre-eminently the best method, in fact probably the only method, of legal development"' citing GC Christie, 'What Constitutes a Taking of Property under International Law?' 38 *British Year Book of International Law 1962* (1964) 307–38 at 338.

[52] Ten Cate (2013) note 34 at 473: 'And it is unproblematic for tribunals to adopt solutions from earlier awards and decisions on the basis that they are convinced by the strength of the reasoning.'

[53] W Mark C Weidemaier, 'Toward a Theory of Precedent in Arbitration' 51 *William and Mary Law Review* (2010) 1895–1958 at 1938–40.

[54] King (2014) note 12 at 883.

tendency 'to decide disputes consistently with prior judicial decisions, except where new policy considerations strongly require a different result or where the prior decision was wrongly decided'.[55] This partially 'persuasive authority'[56] 'constrains arbitrators to account for prior published awards' and 'provid[es] reasons for following or departing from those awards'.[57] While failure to follow persuasive precedent is not sanctioned, writers argue that the coherence of the system is endangered by not doing so: 'not tak[ing] into account what earlier decisions have held ... would deprive ICSID dispute settlement of its predictability and, thus, of an important facet of legal certainty'.[58]

If decisional constraint is the negative side of this argument, the content-generative (or perhaps even system-generative)[59] function of precedent is its positive aspect. D Brian King and Rahim Moloo, for example, have connected the positive and negative aspects:

> Arbitrators regularly cite to prior awards, appear to consider themselves cabined by them to some extent, and demonstrate concern about the impact that the awards they render may have on the development of the law. ... whether they like it or not, arbitrators do in fact 'make law' in the sense of rendering decisions that are likely to influence the behavior of both future tribunals and economic actors.[60]

On that view, 'law' seems to be the likelihood of influencing future behaviour or, in slightly different terms, 'the development of normative rules that, while not binding, influence future awards, shape party expectations, and thereby affect the future behavior of both arbitral panels and economic actors'.[61] The body of arbitral jurisprudence is seen to create a 'system of arbitral case-law in which tribunals develop the details of ... investment standards'[62] and concretise the vague terms of IIA law.[63] There is no consensus among writers as to what, exactly, this 'content-generation' is; it could be (1) a series of similar interpretations of similar treaty clauses, (2) a form of authoritative 'interpretation' worthy of deference, (3) a tribunal-based gap-filling exercise, (4) a new multilateral

[55] Cheng (2007) note 2 at 1018.
[56] Reinisch (2008d) note 2 at 499; see also Schreuer (2008) note 2 at 1196.
[57] Cheng (2007) note 2 at 1016, 1044; cf Weidemaier (2010) note 53 at 1925–6.
[58] Reinisch (2008d) note 2 at 504.
[59] See Schill (2009) note 25 at 278–361; Stephan W Schill, 'System-Building in Investment Treaty Arbitration and Lawmaking' 12 *German Law Journal* (2011) 1083–1110.
[60] King (2014) note 12 at 877.
[61] King (2014) note 12 at 883.
[62] Bjorklund (2008) note 2 at 269.
[63] Reinisch (2008d) note 2 at 505–6.

or universal body of norms (law) in addition to IIAs, (5) an actual change in IIAs, (6) a move of 'the law in action' or 'real law' from IIAs to decisional law, (7) a mere factual change in arbitrator behaviour or (8) a combination of some of these factors.

As legal scholars, we must go beyond unsupported claims; we cannot consider the quest for the 'exact jurisprudential providence' of investment arbitration precedents to be 'a red herring' or '[t]heory [m]yopia'[64] which is said to be irrelevant for the larger picture. As scholars, rather than practitioners, we do need to explain the exact legal relevance of this phenomenon. If we did not, we would be reduced to making vague claims without committing ourselves as to whether this is part of general international law proper – rather than particular law merely binding the parties – and, if so, what part of the law it is and, crucially, why it is law. Is 'concretisation' through 'interpretation' a change of the law in IIAs, is it a mere heuristic tool, is it a norm or a mere hypothetical imperative ('if you want to be successful in your claim, you had better argue in line with established precedents')?

In addition to the orthodox argument about explanations of the force of a body of arbitral jurisprudence in international investment law, more-or-less heterodox, theory-affine approaches have flourished since 2008. The two approaches which are currently most favoured by academia are that international investment law is essentially a type of public law[65] as well as the legal-realist argument.[66] Both transcend the pragmatism of orthodox writings, provide theoretical arguments and seek to produce a general body of law from fragmented sources, but neither can convince if law is a collection of positive (human-made) norms. Considerations of space prohibit a more detailed analysis except to say that, to a certain extent, legal realism has a point. While an empirical analysis of decisions cannot yield 'the law' (whether 'in action' or not) and while law as a body

64 Jacob (2011) note 8 at 1010.

65 Eg Schill (2009) note 25; Stephan W Schill, 'International Investment Law and Comparative Public Law – An Introduction' in Stephan W Schill (ed.), *International Investment Law and Comparative Public Law* (Oxford: Oxford University Press 2010) 3–37; Schill (2011)note 59.

66 Eg Daniel Bodansky, 'Legal Realism and Its Discontents' 28 *Leiden Journal of International Law* (2015) 267–81; Andrew T Guzman, Timothy L Meyer, 'International Common Law: The Soft Law of International Tribunals' 9 *Chicago Journal of International Law* (2009) 515–35; Gregory Shaffer, The New Legal Realist Approach to International Law' 28 *Leiden Journal of International Law* (2015) 189–210; Sourgens (2014) note 42; Sourgens (2015) note 42.

of norms is not reducible to facts, the general direction is accurate. Specific decisions are important for the daily operation of international investment law and the expectations of actors are largely shaped by these. Hence, the idea of empirical research to determine the factual influence of jurisprudence is sound, but only as a social-scientific counterpart to legal-doctrinal analysis. If consistently legal scholarship comes to the conclusion that no general norms on expropriation are valid, then such a quasi-realist method might be able to discern *factual* patterns of decision-making, as discussed later in this book.

3.4 Arbitral Jurisprudence and Customary Law

What role does arbitral investment jurisprudence have to play in the possible formation of customary investment law norms? Investment jurisprudence or phenomena related to jurisprudential pronouncements, such as pleadings, could conceivably be counted as practice, *opinio iuris*, a customary norm itself, evidence for practice or *opinio* or evidence for the state of customary international law. As in Section 2.2, this classification is not reflected in writings and we will again focus on the choice between the element and evidence.

If generalist or specialist writings mention customary international law as 'outcome' (*sensu largo*) of tribunal 'activity', they largely accord it some kind of evidentiary function. Yoram Dinstein embodies generalist orthodoxy: 'international courts and tribunals are much better placed than domestic judicial bodies when it comes to appraising impartially and authoritatively whether an international custom actually exists and, if so, what its contours are'.[67] Investment scholarship largely echoes the generalist mainstream: 'judicial decisions and arbitral awards are not a formal source of international law'.[68] 'Strictly speaking, . . . they cannot be considered as State practice.'[69] Some writers go even further: 'Awards are the product of tribunals, not States. For this reason, awards simply cannot be considered as *evidence* of State practice. Similarly, what

[67] Yoram Dinstein, 'The Interaction between Customary International Law and Treaties' 322 *Recueil des Cours 2006* (2007) 243–428 at 316–17; see also eg Michael Wood, *Third Report on Identification of Customary International Law*, UN Doc A/CN.4/682, 27 March 2015, para 59; Shahabuddeen (1996) note 3 at 71, 76.

[68] Patrick Dumberry, *The Formation and Identification of Rules of Customary International Law in International Investment Law* (Cambridge: Cambridge University Press 2016) 42.

[69] Tarcisio Gazzini, 'The Role of Customary International Law in the Field of Foreign Investment' 8 *Journal of World Investment & Trade* (2007) 691–716 at 693.

matters is the *opinio juris* of States, not that of arbitrators.'[70] This is tempered with the inevitable bow towards the factual importance of arbitral jurisprudence and the inevitability of reliance on jurisprudence. '[E]ven if judges and arbitrators are clearly not law-makers (and have no formal role in the creation of customary rules), it is undeniable that they do in fact play an important role.'[71] This bowing to accepted authority – 'we all use "x", therefore "x" must be legally relevant' – finds different forms and outlets. Scholars and practitioners have sought different ways of explaining the proliferation of and almost exclusive reliance on arbitral awards in international investment law,[72] for example arbitral jurisprudence as customary law, as custom-building or as custom-evidencing.

If we uphold the idea of customary norms as norms *developed* by way of the acting out of the *actus reus* by those who are obligated by the norm and if neither treaties nor judicial pronouncements can constitute this usage (Section 2.3), this argument is inherently unstable. States not expropriating without compensation, etc. is the *actus reus* of a customary expropriation norm and this is the state practice required. Arbitral awards finding a violation of a treaty norm of expropriation is not and cannot be the acting out of the *actus reus* by those obligated. Hence, the argument largely is on the level of evidence, for if jurisprudence is no more than a 'subsidiary means for the determination of rules of law' (Article 38(1)(d) ICJ Statute), then we need not worry about legal relevance in a narrow sense. After all, we have left the realm of proper source theory and moved to the murky domain of proofs and evidences. However, even a general caution that the influence of a line of jurisprudence (or single instances) 'will depend' on a number of factors, for example 'the quality of the reasoning, the composition of the court or tribunal, and the size of the majority by which they were adopted',[73] can do little to dispel theoretical concerns.

Dumberry's argument proceeds in three steps. First, a 'statement by a tribunal on whether or not a rule exists may have a decisive influence on the very development of such a rule', either negatively: 'a . . . pronouncement by a court that one given State conduct is not part of custom can be fatal to its evolution' or positively: 'when a court convincingly enunciates . . . that a rule is custom, this will often provide sufficient

[70] Dumberry (2016) note 68 at 286–7 (some emphasis removed, emphasis added).

[71] Dumberry (2016) note 68 at 43.

[72] See eg José E Alvarez, 'A BIT on Custom' 42 *New York University Journal on International Law and Politics* (2009) 17–80 at 47.

[73] Wood (2015) note 67 at para 60; see also Dumberry (2016) note 68 at 43–4.

"proof" *in itself* to others that it is indeed the case'.[74] Second, such judgments or awards will influence future conduct: 'any decision containing a comprehensive and persuasive analysis of whether a customary rule exists will be considered as an inestimable guide for future tribunals having to address the same issue'; such decisions 'will also influence the subsequent practice of States'.[75] Third, the most obvious solution is that '[i]nternational decisions, in turn, are valuable insofar as they confirm the existence of customary rules and contribute to clarify their content'.[76]

Some go further in the role that investment jurisprudence plays for the state of customary investment law, for example connecting *jurisprudence constante* to customary law. Wälde argues:

> Judge-made law (here tribunal-made law) has a tentative, experimental character. If a rule developed does not work out and is rejected by the relevant professional communities, it can be given up and forgotten. If a rule developed works and finds support, it will be followed, with broadening support and acceptance. Eventually, when rules and principles are no longer seriously contested and adopted by tribunals as established truth, arbitral jurisprudence, as any judge-made law, will have become 'customary international law'.[77]

Kaufmann-Kohler explains how this would happen: 'It would imply not only a well established practice but also an *opinio juris*, namely, the belief among states, investors and arbitrators that, in the absence of compelling reasons to do otherwise, a tribunal must follow the solution arising from a consistent line of earlier cases.'[78]

This argument is based on a theory of customary law-making which ceases to rely exclusively on customs. Judicial practice is judicial opinion which is made into a judicial and then a general acceptance of presumptive norms. This acceptance is then transmorphed into 'customary international law'. Yet whereas Wälde explains judicial law-making as customary norm, Kaufmann-Kohler argues on the meta-level. By defining *opinio iuris* as the belief that tribunals 'must follow the solution

[74] Dumberry (2016) note 68 at 44–5.

[75] Dumberry (2016) note 68 at 45–7.

[76] Gazzini (2007) note 69 at 692–3, citing Robert Y Jennings, 'What Is International Law and How Do We Tell It When We See It?' 37 *Schweizerisches Jahrbuch für internationales Recht 1981* (1982) 59–88; Dumberry (2016) note 68 at 43–4, 287; see also Shahabuddeen (1996) note 3 at 76; Dinstein (2007) note 67 at 316–17.

[77] Wälde (2007) note 35 at 46–7, referring to Maurice H Mendelson, 'The Formation of Customary International Law' 272 *Recueil des Cours 1998* (1999) 155–410. See also Bjorklund (2008) note 2 at 278–88.

[78] Kaufmann-Kohler (2007) note 2 at 377.

arising from a consistent line of earlier cases',[79] she seems to be describing the *opinio iuris* for a customary rule of precedent-following, not for a customary rule prohibiting expropriation. Indeed, is it not more believable that an opinion arises about the binding quality of awards than about the customary nature of judicial determinations on expropriation? It is, if we leave aside the question of whether such opinions by legal professionals can count in any meaningful way as *opinio iuris* for a customary norm of either precedent-following (binding arbitrators) or expropriation (binding states).

From a Dworkinian vantage-point, in a 1991 article Patrick M Norton condemns the 'positivist' dogma on this question and puts forward a robust affirmation of judicial decisions on expropriation as customary law-making. For him, the question 'What do scholars mean when they say that . . . at some point customary "international law" required full compensation?' has this answer: '[T]hey mean that previous tribunals so held.'[80] He reaches this conclusion by way of a negative argument: 'They must mean this because there are *no* other authoritative sources from which such a rule can be derived – no applicable convention, no *opinio juris* of a state not controverted by the *opinio juris* of another state, no consistent view of "publicists" – *only* an accretion of judicial and arbitral precedents.'[81]

There are 'applicable conventions' now, of course, but the interjection must still be that to conclude from the absence of other sources that the one remaining potential source must determine the law is not convincing. If an examination of the legal sources has come up empty, a more sustainable answer is that there is *no* general law on the point. His next argument is equally problematic:

> [O]ne can reasonably argue that judicial and arbitral decisions are a kind of state practice. The decisions have their authority because states have agreed to submit the disputes in question to judicial or arbitral resolution and have generally abided by the results. Indeed, by expressly agreeing to have these disputes determined *by law*, states have arguably shown a much greater *opinio juris* than in most forms of state practice.[82]

On this view, the agreement to have a dispute settled, together with abiding by the settlement terms, is the same thing as a state actually

[79] Kaufmann-Kohler (2007) note 2 at 377.
[80] Norton (1991) note 25 at 504.
[81] Norton (1991) note 25 at 504.
[82] Norton (1991) note 25 at 504.

behaving in such a fashion that it accords with the norm generalised from the judgment or award. Equally, an agreement to arbitrate would be a 'belief' that *whatever* the tribunal decides is law. This is far removed from orthodox descriptions of state practice and *opinio iuris*. No wonder, then, that Sourgens opines that the proponents of this solution 'take... the side of new custom',[83] that is, privileging the subjective element over the objective element in customary law-making, particularly in areas like humanitarian and human rights law.[84] This approach has little to do with *customary* law as norms created by way of *customs*, *usus*, a regularity of behaviour. As Sourgens puts it, new custom 'operates deductively from a strong (moral) principle of protection of property'.[85] The question is, though, whether the modification of the meta-law on customary international law-making to respond to the perceived needs of the hour is legally *allowed*.[86]

Norton is correct to point out the weak position of regarding awards as 'best available evidence' of customary norms: 'this is doctrinal legerdemain. Even the earliest decisions in expropriation cases fail to cite actual state practice. They either assume full compensation as an a priori rule or invoke the authority of their predecessors.'[87] In other words, using 'x' as evidence or proof of 'y' depends on 'x' being capable of proving 'y'. It is generally accepted that neither the international judiciary[88] nor investment tribunals have ever conducted serious research into the existence of sufficient instances of state practice or *opinio iuris*; none have actually counted instances. At a maximum, tribunals either point to a line of jurisprudence which runs dry, because the first cases did not do the research either, or give other sources like ILC documents, which mostly get their information about the state of customary law from prior case-law. We cannot even begin to expect information on state practice and *opinio iuris* to be incorporated in jurisprudence if neither jurisprudence nor the sources it provides have ever actually done the required research.

83 Sourgens (2015) note 42 at 259.
84 Anthea Elizabeth Roberts, 'Traditional and Modern Approaches to Customary International Law' 95 *American Journal of International Law* (2001) 757–91.
85 Sourgens (2015) note 42 at 259.
86 See also Jörg Kammerhofer, 'Orthodox Generalists and Political Activists in International Legal Scholarship' in Matthew Happold (ed.), *International Law in a Multipolar World* (Abingdon: Routledge 2011) 138–57 at 146–53.
87 Norton (1991) note 25 at 504.
88 See eg Dinstein (2007) note 67 at 318; Stefan Talmon, 'Determining Customary International Law: The ICJ's Methodology between Induction, Deduction and Assertion' 26 *European Journal of International Law* (2015) 417–43.

If jurists in any other case were to find that the method of proof is utterly incapable of proving what they seek, they would cease to rely on it. They may acknowledge this dearth with respect to jurisprudence, but cannot find the courage to cease relying on it, because it is simply too important. Unless and except to the extent that investment tribunals actually research (or point to sources which do), scholarship, however, should disavow jurisprudence as good evidence of customary law or of its elements.[89]

Another legal-theoretical problem arising from using jurisprudence as custom-generative or custom-evidencing is the question of generality of the customary norms. This is a problem in two dimensions. *Ratione personae*, the question is whether arbitral investment jurisprudence can really generate (or evidence) a *general* customary international law, that is, one in principle binding on all states. Since the vast majority of such awards will be based on bilateral treaties, and based on behaviour of (either) one of the parties to that BIT, how could one expect this process to yield (evidence of) *general*, rather than bilateral, customary law? The behaviour judged was that of a specific subject; the '*opinio*' (if we treat it as such) expressed in the treaty and the agreement to arbitrate was directed at *bilateral* behaviour, at a bilateral norm.

Ratione materiae, the matter is slightly different: arbitral awards produce detailed case-law – specific decisions of specific disputes, subsumptions of a specific set of facts under rules.[90] It is unlikely that a series of judicial decisions would 'produce' a unified and unspecific customary norm. If one were to abstract a (*ratione personae*) general norm from judgments or awards, it would be very specific *ratione materiae*, for example 'punitive taxation is an indirect expropriation'[91] or 'requirements to refill open cast gold mines are not an indirect expropriation'.[92] The customary process overwhelmingly generates unspecific norms precisely because the many instances of *usus* that form the behavioural regularity will not be uniform in their 'prospective prescribed behaviour', the future *actus reus* element. Would such general *ratione personae* but specific *ratione materiae* norms typically exist in customary international

[89] See Dumberry (2016) note 68 at 44–7.

[90] See eg Sourgens (2015) note 42 at 334–7, reminding us that the common law is much more about sets of facts than about general norms.

[91] See *EnCana Corporation* v. *Republic of Ecuador*, UNCITRAL, LCIA UN 3481, Award of 3 February 2006, para 177.

[92] See *Glamis Gold* (2009) note 7 at paras 412–36, 534–6.

law? Could they even be created in the customary mode of norm-generation? Both are highly unlikely.

3.5 Conclusion: A General Norm of Expropriation from Jurisprudence?

The orthodox approach cannot work as advertised. Applying the legal-theoretical approach of the Pure Theory of Law, we will analyse the question of jurisprudence's role with respect to a general *norm* on expropriation in this section. The basic idea of the theory of the hierarchical ordering of norms (*Stufenbau* theory; see also Section 5.2)[93] is that the validity-relationship is the only necessary connection between norms. If law is norms and if a norm's 'existence' is its validity, then a norm cannot be valid without its validity being traced back to another norm.[94] The 'higher' norm[95] establishes the validity of the 'lower' norm; it is the 'source' which empowers law-creation.[96] This establishes a connection between norms (and the possibility of legal ordering) which is necessary in the sense that it is inherent in those norms' nature as norms. When tasked with finding out what the *legal* role of arbitral decisions is, what legal relevance jurisprudence has for international investment law, we must start by looking for 'empowerment norms', norms authorising the creation of norms.[97] 'Whether judge-made law is

93 On my reading of the *Stufenbau* theory, see in more detail Jörg Kammerhofer, 'Sources in Legal Positivist Theories: The Pure Theory's Structural Analysis of the Law' in Samantha Besson, Jean d'Aspremont (eds.), *The Oxford Handbook of the Sources of International Law* (Oxford: Oxford University Press 2017) 343–62 at 336–53.

94 Hans Kelsen, *Reine Rechtslehre* (2nd edn, Vienna: Deuticke 1960) 196.

95 Adolf Julius Merkl, 'Prolegomena einer Theorie des rechtlichen Stufenbaues' in Alfred Verdross (ed.), *Gesellschaft, Staat und Recht: Festschrift für Hans Kelsen zum 50. Geburtstag* (Vienna: Springer 1931) 252–94 at 275–6, reprinted in Hans Klecatsky, René Marcic, Herbert Schambeck (eds.), *Die Wiener rechtstheoretische Schule: Ausgewählte Schriften von Hans Kelsen, Adolf Julius Merkl, Alfred Verdross* (Vienna: Europa 1968) (abbreviated as: *WRS*) 1311–61 at 1339–40 and in Dorothea Mayer-Maly, Herbert Schambeck, Wolf-Dietrich Grussmann (eds.), *Adolf Julius Merkl: Gesammelte Schriften*, vol I/1 (Berlin: Duncker & Humblot 1993) (abbreviated as: *MerklGS*) 437–92 at 467–8.

96 Adolf Julius Merkl, *Die Lehre von der Rechtskraft, entwickelt aus dem Rechtsbegriff: Eine rechtstheoretische Untersuchung* (Leipzig: Deuticke 1923) 196, 216; Merkl (1931) note 95 at 273 (*WRS* 1336, I/1 *MerklGS* 464–5); Hans Kelsen, *Allgemeine Theorie der Normen* (Vienna: Manz 1979) 82; Rainer Lippold, *Recht und Ordnung: Statik und Dynamik der Rechtsordnung* (Vienna: Manz 2000) 382; Jürgen Behrend, *Untersuchungen zur Stufenbaulehre Adolf Merkls und Hans Kelsens* (Berlin: Duncker & Humblot 1977) 32.

97 Kelsen (1979) note 96 at 82–4.

a source of law is not a question of legal epistemology, but of the content of a positive legal order.'[98]

The Pure Theory argues that judgments are a central part of legal orders and most certainly part of the law.[99] It may be surprising to call judgments 'law', and it is probably not how orthodox scholarship would use the term, but from the Pure Theory's perspective it is accurate. Merkl describes continental European legal orders in the following manner:

> Judge-made law is not an exception, but part of every single judgment. It is not an accidental, but a necessary part of the law; it is not a secondary, but a primary source of law. . . . The uniquely complementary character of judge-made law . . . means, however, that there is a shift in our conception of the two sources of law. Statutes and judge-made law are not equal, as conventional wisdom has it, but are in a hierarchical relationship [ie statutes above judgments]. . . . Judge-made law retains its legitimacy and necessity, albeit on a different understanding of its nature. . . . In reality, judge-made law is indispensably part of any legal order because of the logical tension between abstract and usually general nature of statutes and the comparatively concrete and individual nature of judgments . . ..[100]

At least for domestic legal orders, judgments are a highly important individualisation of statutory norms. Legal orders regularly contain empowerment norms which enable the creation of judgments as binding decisions of specific disputes (as individual norms). Because their

[98] 'Ob Richterrecht als Rechtsquelle gilt, ist keine Frage rechtstheoretischer Erkenntnis, sondern Sache einer positiven Rechtsordnung.' Clemens Jabloner, 'Richterrecht als Rechtsquelle?' in Clemens Jabloner et al. (eds.), *Gedenkschrift Robert Walter* (Vienna: Manz 2013) 185–201 at 199.

[99] Although it is possible that there are legal orders which do not give judgments (awards) binding force.

[100] 'Das Richterrecht tritt nicht nur ausnahmsweise, sondern . . . ausnahmslos in jedem Richterspruche in Erscheinung. Es ist keine bloß zufällige, sondern eine notwendige Erscheinungsform des Rechtes. Es ist nicht eine bloß subsidiäre, sondern eine primäre Rechtsquelle. . . . Der eigentümlich komplementäre Charakter des Richterrechtes . . . bedingt aber auch eine Verschiebung des herkömmlicherweise vorgestellten Verhältnisses der beiden Rechtsquellen; nicht in Gleichordnung, sondern in Über- und Unterordnung stehen im modernen Staate Gesetzes- und Richterrecht einander gegenüber. . . . Trotz dem Gesetze behält das Richterrecht – inhaltlich freilich gewandelt – seine Daseinsberechtigung und Daseinsnotwendigkeit. . . . In Wirklichkeit erklärt sich die Unentbehrlichkeit des Richterrechtes für jedes Rechtssystem . . . aus der logischen Distanz zwischen der immer abstrakten und regelmäßig generellen Rechtsgestalt des Gesetzes und der verhältnismäßig konkreten und individuellen Gestalt des richterlichen Urteils . . . ' Adolf Julius Merkl, 'Gesetzesrecht und Richterrecht' 2 *Wissenschaftliche Vierteljahresschrift der Prager Juristischen Zeitschrift* (1922) 337–44 (*WRS* 1615–24, I/1 *MerklGS* 317–27) at *WRS* 1617, 1621, 1622, I/1 *MerklGS* 319, 324, 325 (emphasis removed; the original publication was not available).

creation is authorised by norms which are part of the legal order in question, these individual norms are themselves part of the law, just as administrative orders are. The legal order could also contain a norm empowering the creation of judgments which are both individual and general (or only general) norms.[101] The court can create general norms only if it is so empowered.

A clear analysis of this problem on the basis of the Pure Theory of Law has been advanced by Alfred Schramm. 'Precedents elucidate the [applicable] law and state it in a more precise manner; they are . . . applied until a new interpretation supersedes the old one.'[102] However, precedents thus understood are *not* the individual norm in a judgment; there is no identity between judgment and general prescription:

> Precedents . . . are general statements on the content of norms, *Rechtssätze*. They describe (interpret) norms, which are mostly general and abstract in scope, in general and abstract statements. They are interpretations which elucidate parts of specific norms applicable to a particular dispute in such a way that they [the interpretations] again take the form of general and abstract *Rechtssätze*. . . . Precedents . . . are not themselves norms nor individual nor specific. . . . A precedent is the description of the process of deduction, that is a description of how the delegating (empowerment) norm (or a part thereof) is to be understood. . . . This statement on the content of a norm (*Rechtssatz*) does not become yet another norm.[103]

On this approach, then, precedents *cannot ever become norms* on their own terms. They are statements about norms and not even a constant tradition of decisions can turn a statement into a norm.[104] Schramm's ideas are a solid basis for summarising the role of investment jurisprudence

[101] Kelsen (1960) note 94 at 255.

[102] 'Präjudizien erläutern, präzisieren den Normbestand, sie werden . . . angewendet, bis eine neue Interpretation die alte ablöst.' Alfred Schramm, '"Richterrecht" und Gesetzesrecht: Eine rechtsvergleichende Analyse anhand von Merkls Rechtsnormenlehre' 36 *Rechtstheorie* (2005) 185–208 at 197.

[103] 'Präjudizien . . . sind allgemein-abstrakte normative Aussagen, also Rechtssätze. Sie beschreiben (interpretieren) Normen, die zumeist allgemein-abstrakt sind, wiederum in allgemein-abstrakten Sätzen. Sie sind Interpretationen, die einzelne unklare Teile von gegebenen im konkreten Rechtsfall anzuwendenden Normen anhand verschiedener Interpretationsmethoden dahingehend erläutern, daß wiederum allgemein-abstrakte Rechtssätze entstehen. . . . Präjudizien . . . sind aber selbst weder Normen, noch individuell-konkret. . . . Das Präjudiz ist vielmehr die Beschreibung der Deduktionstätigkeit, und zwar dahingehend, wie die delegierende (ermächtigende) Norm (oder ein Teil dieser) verstanden wird. . . . Mit der Aussage über eine Norm (Rechtssatz) wird keine (weitere) Norm gebildet.' Schramm (2005) note 102 at 198–9 (emphasis removed).

[104] Schramm (2005) note 102 at 201.

in shaping a possible general norm of expropriation, but these thoughts require translation into the investment law idolect. Since jurisprudence does not make general norms, a norm or a set of general norms on expropriation in international investment law cannot be created by way of investment jurisprudence. This does not mean, however, that this is the end of the matter.

Each award contains an individual norm with a narrow scope of application both *ratione personae* (the parties) and *ratione materiae* (the *dispositif*). This much is not contended and we can accordingly restate the question: is there a *legal* basis for according the status of law to certain parts of single or a line of investment awards? We are thus looking for a norm which authorises investment tribunals – either individually or as a collective (for a line of jurisprudence) – to create either general norms binding on all states or general decisional norms applicable before and binding for all later investment tribunals. No such empowerment norm is apparent. But why do we need such an empowerment norm? We do because if we cannot find one, precedents (as general prescriptions) do not form part of the law and are *legally irrelevant.*

Once more we are left with an undisputedly important body of judicial pronouncements on the content of the prohibitions of expropriation in IIAs (and perhaps even in customary law) and their subsumption to specific sets of facts. But we are now in a position to evaluate and categorise this phenomenon. What exactly is that significant body of texts? They are best understood as statements on the content of the norm applied by the tribunal, 'a description of how the delegating (empowerment) norm (or a part thereof) is to be understood'.[105] In this case, a multitude of ad hoc tribunals have provided understandings of a multitude of treaty norms on expropriation, which happen to have similar wording. Their nature as statements of the law (rather than law themselves) and, in addition, the unbridgeable fragmentation into a multitude of IIAs mean that using these awards cannot be a matter for legal scholarship as norm-cognising scholarship. 'The connection in this case can only be causal, not normative. Cognising these phenomena on the basis of the law of causality is a matter for natural sciences, not of legal scholarship.'[106]

[105] 'Beschreibung ... wie die delegierende (ermächtigende) Norm (oder ein Teil dieser) verstanden wird.' Schramm (2005) note 102 at 198–9 (emphasis removed).'

[106] 'Hier kann keine normative Verbindung, sondern nur eine kausale vorliegen. Eine Deutung der Geschehnisse nach dem Kausalgesetz ist aber Sache der Naturwissenschaft, nicht der Jurisprudenz.' Robert Walter, 'Die Gewohnheit als rechtserzeugender Tatbestand' 18 *Österreichische Juristen-Zeitung* (1963) 225–32 at 232.

We can proceed on the basis of seeing this body of statements as a prognostic calculus.[107] The required empirical research, however, must still proceed in a scholarly, rather than anecdotal, manner. Legal realism may help in framing the possibilities and in developing the tools of such an empirical prognostication of future decision-making by way of this body of interpretations of general expropriation norms. Thus, investment jurisprudence is neither law qua norms nor 'law in action' and both normativist-positivist scholarship and legal sociology have a role to play.

[107] Heinz Schäffer, 'Rechtsquellen und Rechtsanwendung' in *Verhandlungen des fünften Österreichischen Juristentages Wien 1973*, vol I.1.B (Vienna: Manz 1973) 1–172 at 70.

4

Treaty Interpretation

4.1 Introduction

It is probably a significant understatement to say that a lot depends on what interpretation is. If interpretation is no more than a hermeneutic method, then it has little to tell us about the meaning of 'expropriation'. On a pragmatic level, it would be reduced to a prediction of what those we accept as authority tell us it is. If, however, interpretation is more than that, a range of tools, enshrined as law, which help to generate unity of 'correct' meaning, then 'expropriation' can be made to look like a coherent concept, owing to the guidance which the methods, tools and process of interpretation in this second sense provide. A choice needs to be made between these two views.

The usual throwaway *caveat* – approach interpretation with trepidation – should be taken significantly more seriously than it usually is. If interpretation is the touchstone for our 'understanding' of what expropriation means in international law and if almost all international lawyers insist on developing the tools for construing meaning of treaty texts by sole reference to the text of the Vienna Convention on the Law of Treaties (VCLT) rules, more trepidation is warranted than international investment lawyers have hitherto shown. The 'applicative construction of law's meaning', as this understanding of interpretation could be called, will have to be described and critiqued before the various ways by which this process arguably generates coherence and unity across the sources of expropriation law can be discussed in detail.

Why should interpretation serve as the lynchpin of a book critically evaluating the possibility of unity for international investment law? Given the fragmentation of its sources, interpretation is taken to be investment law's best hope for unity. If meaning across IIAs and ad hoc tribunal decisions can be constructed in a substantive sense using interpretative tools, then (so it could be argued) *unity of the law* would in effect be established, rather than factual more-or-less coherent tribunal decision-making. The great hope is that the rules or tools of interpretation elevate practice to law not by making arbitral awards binding or quasi-binding (see Chapter 3) but by allowing us to speak of a 'correct' interpretation and of establishing 'correct' meaning. This would allow us to distinguish between arbitral decisions which provide a 'correct' and those which provide an 'incorrect' interpretation (hence meaning) of the words 'direct or indirect expropriation'. It would admit as evidence only those which provide the former – as measured, so it might be argued, on their fealty to the Vienna Convention rules.

The method on which this concept of interpretation is based, how arguments made in support of these contentions can be justified or grounded – given that scientific certainty eludes us – can be called 'orthodoxy' or 'default empiricism'. It is, perhaps, a slightly tendentious reading of the word but, on balance, a fair one. Orthodox belief is not just not heterodox (it is the majority, not the minority), it is also characterised by respect for traditional, conventional authority. While this respect is not absolute and while even the ICJ may be criticised, the implicit idea is that the majority of 'authorities' (mostly courts and tribunals) cannot err over a long time and on a vital question.[1] Equally, it may be no more than a presumption that certain 'epistemic authorities' are presumed to give a good indication of what the law is. Yet it has the effect of hindering argument not based on these authorities from overriding the presumption, as *arguendo* there are no better indications.[2] However, the law is not created by such 'authorities'. Judicial pronouncements (and writings) at best accurately declare what the law is and they are declarative only if they happen to correctly portray the law: *Rechtserkenntnisquelle* (source of law-cognition), not *Rechtserzeugungsquelle* (source of law-creation). Positivism's exhortation to consider only the law actually created is perverted to the proposition that all generally held beliefs must be right. What interpretation is and how it works can, so it is argued, be gleamed from the various pronouncements that tribunals have made about interpretation. This can be likened to a modified version of Schrödinger's cat, where the 'authorities' paint picture after picture of whether they think the cat is dead or alive, without anyone able to open the box, even (and particularly) the authorities themselves.

1 For a similar argument see Jean d'Aspremont, 'If International Judges Say So, It Must Be True: Empiricism or Fetishism?' 4:9 *ESIL Reflections* (2015).

2 See eg Richard Gardiner, *Treaty Interpretation* (Oxford: Oxford University Press 2008) 11.

Section 4.2 will explore the split of interpretation into hermeneutic process and determination of content. This will allow us to critique, in Section 4.3, the various designs for interpretative tools, as proposed in international investment law discourse, to create unity of meaning, foremost 'systemic integration'.

4.2 Treaty Interpretation in International Law

The utility of interpretation for stabilising and unifying the law on expropriation is partially dependent on accepting as law the Vienna rules of interpretation. The orthodox position is, first, that Articles 31–3 VCLT or co-existing customary rules are applicable to any treaty (and even to customary law).[3] Second, this set of norms displaces general legal hermeneutics, as interpretation is to be exclusively done through and in observance of law. Third, interpretative tools – if correctly applied – allow interpreters to give norms concreteness, that is, meanings which are more detailed than the interpreted norms, yet to transcend the individual case, which in turn allows us to overcome the vagueness of general regulation. Most international lawyers seem to assume that there is a detailed body of law on the construction of treaties, prescribing the task of the tribunal which allows giving a treaty detailed meaning. Not only is the law quite detailed, but it is also shaped by tribunal practice. 'Interpretation' in this sense would then be central to successfully constructing a unified and detailed law of expropriation.

Since the rules of interpretation are key to orthodoxy's hidden stance on the theory of interpretation, we will proceed in a somewhat roundabout way and first ask whether they really are positive law (Section 4.2.1). The argument then changes tack to the theoretical level to discuss what interpretation can be (Section 4.2.2). Finally, the tools for construing meaning will be reassessed and the rules reconstructed from a theoretical perspective (Section 4.2.3).

4.2.1 *Rules of Interpretation as Norms of International Law?*

Recent contributions to treaty interpretation are agreed: Articles 31–3 VCLT are the sole binding law on interpretation and applicable both as treaty and as customary law.[4] This stance is not questioned in

[3] Panos Merkouris, *Article 31(3) VCLT and the Principle of Systemic Integration: Normative Shadows in Plato's Cave* (Leiden: Martinus Nijhoff 2015) 231–300.

[4] From the recent crop of generalist literature on interpretation, eg Christian Djeffal, *Static and Evolutive Treaty Interpretation: A Functional Reconstruction* (Cambridge: Cambridge

contributions to international investment law.[5] Thomas W Wälde sums it up memorably: '[T]he Vienna Rules are now the only "game in town".'[6] Dissent against this imperiously[7] held conviction is seldom voiced.[8] It is

University Press 2016) 3–4; Malgosia Fitzmaurice, Panos Merkouris, 'Canons of Treaty Interpretation: Selected Case Studies from the World Trade Organization and the North American Free Trade Agreement' in Malgosia Fitzmaurice, Olufemi Elias, Panos Merkouris (eds.), *Treaty Interpretation and the Vienna Convention on the Law of Treaties: 30 Years On* (Leiden: Martinus Nijhoff 2010) 153–237 at 153–4; Gardiner (2008) note 2 at 5, 12–19; Ulf Linderfalk, *On the Interpretation of Treaties: The Modern International Law as Expressed in the 1969 Vienna Convention on the Law of Treaties* (Dordrecht: Springer 2007) 3–7; Merkouris (2015) note 3 at 6, 10–11; Alexander Orakhelashvili, *The Interpretation of Acts and Rules in Public International Law* (Oxford: Oxford University Press 2008) 316.

5 Hervé Ascensio, 'Article 31 of the Vienna Conventions on the Law of Treaties and International Investment Law' 31 *ICSID Review* (2016) 366–87 at 367–8; John Gaffney, James Loftis, 'The "Effective Ordinary Meaning" of BITs and the Jurisdiction of Treaty-Based Tribunals to Hear Contract Claims' 8 *Journal of World Investment & Trade* (2007) 5–68 at 7–9; Tarcisio Gazzini, *Interpretation of International Investment Treaties* (Oxford: Hart 2016) 2–11, 56–7; Lars Markert, 'International Investment Law and Treaty Interpretation – Problems, Particularities and Possible Trends' in Rainer Hofmann, Christian Tams (eds.), *International Investment Law and General International Law: From Clinical Isolation to Systemic Integration?* (Baden-Baden: Nomos 2011) 53–69 at 57; Makane Moïse Mbengue, 'Rules of Interpretation (Article 32 of the Vienna Convention on the Law of Treaties)' 31 *ICSID Review* (2016) 388–412 at 388; Campbell McLachlan, Laurence Shore, Matthew Weiniger, *International Investment Arbitration: Substantive Principles* (Oxford: Oxford University Press 2007) 221; Campbell McLachlan, 'Investment Treaties and General International Law' 57 *International and Comparative Law Quarterly* (2008) 361–401 at 371; Martins Paparinskis, 'Investment Protection Law and Systemic Integration of Treaty and Custom', *SIEL Online Proceedings Working Paper 2010/21*, available at: ssrn.com /abstract=1632559 at 4; Martins Paparinskis, 'Investment Treaty Interpretation and Customary Investment Law: Preliminary Remarks' in Chester Brown, Kate Miles (eds.), *Evolution in Investment Treaty Law and Arbitration* (Cambridge: Cambridge University Press 2011) 65–96 at 70; August Reinisch, 'The Interpretation of International Investment Agreements' in Marc Bungenberg et al. (eds.), *International Investment Law: A Handbook* (Baden-Baden: Nomos 2015) 372–410 at 374–6; Andrea Saldarriaga, 'Investment Awards and the Rules of Interpretation of the Vienna Convention: Making Room for Improvement' 28 *ICSID Review* (2013) 197–217 at 198; Hai Yen Trinh, *The Interpretation of Investment Treaties* (Leiden: Martinus Nijhoff 2014) 36; Thomas W Wälde, 'Interpreting Investment Treaties: Experiences and Examples' in Christina Binder et al. (eds.), *International Investment Law for the 21st Century: Essays in Honour of Christoph Schreuer* (Oxford: Oxford University Press 2009) 724–81 at 725; J Romesh Weeramantry, *Treaty Interpretation in Investment Arbitration* (Oxford: Oxford University Press 2012) 5–8, 24–30; Todd Weiler, *The Interpretation of International Investment Law: Equality, Discrimination and Minimum Standards of Treatment in Historical Context* (Leiden: Martinus Nijhoff 2013) 34–5.

6 Wälde (2009) note 5 at 725.

7 This includes issuing threats of annulment of awards that do not reference the Vienna Convention rules: Gazzini (2016) note 5 at 58; Trinh (2014) note 5 at 98–9.

8 Eg Jörg Kammerhofer, *Uncertainty in International Law: A Kelsenian Perspective* (Abingdon: Routledge 2010) 92–6 (the present section takes its inspiration from that passage); Jan Klabbers, 'Virtuous Interpretation' in Malgosia Fitzmaurice, Olufemi Elias,

generally agreed by writers, the ICJ and other tribunals that these articles are *as such* part of customary international law. Yet are the Vienna rules of interpretation part of international law; is the majority position founded in law?[9]

The VCLT is an international treaty and has been in force since 27 January 1980. It applies *inter partes* (116 as of January 2018) and only to treaties concluded after the Vienna Convention's entry into force (Article 4 VCLT). Its Articles 31–3 are treaty law, whatever content those treaty norms actually have. These norms are claimed also to reflect customary law, but this claim is made in an undifferentiated manner and irrespective of the fact that customary law is unwritten law, meaning that customary norms do not consist of words. Yet customary law's content is not automatically identical[10] to the treaty norm whence it takes its inspiration; we also require proof of (state) practice and *opinio iuris*. Therefore, we will briefly query whether their presence has actually been proven, rather than asserted. As with so many cherished beliefs in international legal scholarship and practice, the more certain the proponents are, and the more widespread and widely accepted is the belief, the less likely it is that anyone has actually grounded it in a rigorous analysis of the law.

There is certainly plenty of *opinio iuris*, mostly of scholars and tribunals, but it is likely that states agree that the Vienna Convention rules are customary international law. However, *usus* is not an optional element in customary law-making. One interjection is that customary law, as law based on repetition of behaviour, is limited in its forms and functions (Sections 2.3 and 2.6). Custom-forming practice is a regularity of behaviour and provides the future norm's content, but whether 'interpretation' as an *actus reus* element can adequately be built up by repetition of behaviour is doubtful. Much depends on what exactly 'interpretation' means for the purposes of a customary rule. If it were no more than

Panos Merkouris (eds.), *Treaty Interpretation and the Vienna Convention on the Law of Treaties: 30 Years On* (Leiden: Martinus Nijhoff 2010) 17–37; hesitant criticism: Mark E Villiger, 'The Rules on Interpretation: Misgivings, Misunderstandings, Miscarriage? The "Crucible" Intended by the International Law Commission' in Enzo Cannizzaro (ed.), *The Law of Treaties Beyond the Vienna Convention* (Oxford: Oxford University Press 2011) 105–22.

9 Rudolf Bernhardt, *Die Auslegung völkerrechtlicher Verträge insbesondere in der neueren Rechtsprechung internationaler Gerichte* (Berlin: Duncker & Humblot 1963) 28.

10 See *Military and Paramilitary Activities in and Against Nicaragua (Nicaragua* v. *United States of America),* Merits, Judgment of 27 June 1986, ICJ Reports (1986) 14 at 93–4 (para 175).

a specific arrangement of words and sentences in written tribunal decisions (Section 4.2.3), then the repetition of certain text is easily subsumed as custom-forming practice. If it is the epistemic process of text-cognition, the *Verstehen* process occurring in every human being, the matter is less straightforward. The hermeneutic process is not 'behaviour' and cannot form the basis of a practice. In slightly different terms and with a slightly different emphasis, Jan Klabbers argues that 'the behaviour concerned must be ... of a "fundamentally norm-creating character", which suggests that, as an activity, interpretation can meaningfully be captured in terms of rules to begin with. This now is doubtful: it may very well be ... that interpretation is not a rule-governed activity.'[11] This depends, of course, on what 'interpretation' is; Klabbers concedes that it depends on whether rules of interpretation are rules of behaviour[12] or whether 'interpretation rules simply are of a different quality ... Instead of guiding behaviour, rules on interpretation are methodological devices, suggesting to judges and other decision-makers how relevant legal instruments may be read.'[13]

Assuming *arguendo* that 'interpretation practice' is in principle custom-forming, is there enough state practice of interpreting international law in line with the content of Articles 31–3 VCLT? We do not know; to my knowledge there is not a single case of anyone or any institution actually having counted instances of state practice. This is generally acknowledged, but the problem engendered by this failure is not taken seriously enough. Writers tend, instead, to point to tribunal practice recognising and applying the rules. Because the ICJ 'nowadays presents application of the rules as virtually axiomatic' and 'views the Vienna rules as general, or customary international law',[14] and because this view is virtually unanimously held across international courts and tribunals, it must be the law. The same reasoning is found in international investment scholarship.[15] This is a clear example of the deference in authorities, latching on to the fact that this view is held widely by authorities, not to the persuasiveness of the argument.

11 Klabbers (2010) note 8 at 24–5, referring to *North Sea Continental Shelf (Federal Republic of Germany/Denmark; Federal Republic of Germany/Netherlands),* Judgment of 20 February 1969, ICJ Reports (1969) 3 at 41–2 (para 72) and Jan Klabbers, 'On Rationalism in Politics: Interpretation of Treaties and the World Trade Organization' 74 *Nordic Journal of International Law* (2005) 405–28.

12 Klabbers (2010) note 8 at 29–30 fn 55.

13 Klabbers (2010) note 8 at 30–1.

14 Gardiner (2008) note 2 at 15, 16.

15 McLachlan (2008) note 5 at 371.

For a rigorous analysis of the customary law status of the Vienna Convention rules, we need to differentiate between the 'tribunal practice' as evidence of the objective element and as instances of the element itself (Section 2.2): tribunal pronouncements can serve as either practice or *opinio*, or as both – or as evidence of either state practice or *opinio*, or of both. If the argument is that tribunal pronouncements are evidence of the objective element (only), then it is only as good as tribunals' efforts to find state practice or to report good sources of state practice. Since tribunals do not conduct research into instances of state practice in the customary status of the Vienna Convention rules (or refer to a locus of such research), the evidentiary powers of this mass of tribunal pronouncements are low.

Something different entirely is tribunal practice 'interpreting' more-or-less consistently with the Vienna Convention rules and referring to them more-or-less constantly; the implicit claim here is that international courts and tribunals themselves can create instances of practice. Traditionally, of course, state practice in international law is the practice of states – the one organ empowered by international law to make general customary international law.[16] As a matter of legal theory, it is possible to argue that other behaviour could be relevant as well. If *usus* in customary law-formation has a foundational role to play in the sense that customs become the *actus reus* content (*Tatbestand*) of the emerging norm, then the practice of non-states could be relevant for a norm obligating non-state behaviour. On that view, the customary norm of the prohibition of piracy would primarily be constituted by the omission of acts of piracy by private individuals. This is not to deny that states are currently empowered by international law as customary international law-makers. On that view, state *opinio iuris* would still be a necessary element and *usus* would merely provide the content. A crude analogy is that ministry officials provide the content for many parliamentary statutes but are not empowered to create statutes themselves. Yet this argument is tenuous because customary law has always been held to be a 'community practices'-based method of law-creation, presupposing an identity among those who practise the budding rule, those who voice legal belief and those who are bound by it.

Ulf Linderfalk proposes to focus on 'the Vienna Convention in its capacity of a contribution to state practice. . . . Articles 31–33 . . . should

[16] Martins Paparinskis, 'Sources of Law and Arbitral Interpretations of *Pari Materia* Investment Protection Rules' in Ole Kristian Fauchald, André Nollkaemper (eds.), *The Practice of International and National Courts and the (De-)Fragmentation of International Law* (Oxford: Hart 2012) 87–116 at 102.

therefore be seen as evidence ... of the rules that apply according to customary international law.'[17] As discussed in Sections 2.2–2.5, using treaties is problematic: treaties neither are nor are they likely to be evidence of state practice, as they are not themselves instances of the behaviour prescribed, in this case 'interpreting treaties'. It is likely, however, that Linderfalk uses 'state practice' in the loose sense, encompassing elements as well as the evidence. Articles 31–3 could potentially serve as evidence of *opinio iuris*, but, as Villiger notes,[18] the customary status of the rules was not generally acknowledged among states, tribunals and scholars in 1969 as it is now. Hence, in 1969, the articles were probably not an expression of *opinio iuris*. A treaty as 'practice' must be measured primarily – if not exclusively – at the time of conclusion. If the belief of states in the customary nature of a treaty comes about at a later point, the treaty is not, without more, made evidence of this later *opinio iuris*.

If we were to accept – contrary to orthodoxy's other assumptions – tribunal interpretation practice (rather than pronouncements that interpretation rules are law) as relevant, there is plenty of well-researched practice. The question then becomes: is this tribunal practice commensurate with the terms of Articles 31–3 VCLT to such a degree that the claim of a word-for-word identity of treaty and custom is warranted? Is the practice consistent and identical with the Vienna Convention rules and does the customary rule have a word-like quality? Is it actually the words 'Treaties shall be interpreted in good faith ...'? As to the first question, to support the identity thesis, tribunal practice would have to conform, by-and-large, to the prescribed behaviour in Articles 31–3 VCLT. If it did not, the resultant customary norm would either not be valid (if *opinio iuris* does not support this diverging practice) or have a different content from the Vienna Convention rules (if *opinio iuris* supports it). Divergent practice could not, however, be ignored insofar as and because it did not conform to the Vienna Convention. Even breaches of a norm are not disqualified from serving as building-blocks of a divergent customary norm.[19]

There are a number of voices which aim to reconstruct the actual practice of tribunals, in particular its divergence from the author's own reading of Article 31–3 VCLT. J Romesh Weeramantry argues that 'a

[17] Linderfalk (2007) note 4 at 7.
[18] Villiger (2011) note 8 at 117–19.
[19] Kammerhofer (2010d) note 8 at 74–5.

number [of international investment tribunals] . . . have merely paid lip service to the Convention Rules or have failed to apply or otherwise comply with those Rules';[20] Hai Yen Trinh is even clearer: 'arbitral tribunals have disregarded all or the basic interpretive tools required under international law, overrelied on supplementary means of interpretation, judicial decisions and scholarly writings, and liberally found a solely pro-investor object and purpose'.[21] Mark Villiger, a generalist, puts the same point in a less categorical fashion: '[w]hile Article 31 envisages the equal and balanced consideration of all means of interpretation stated therein, the practice of courts and states discloses different approaches as to the relative position of these means'.[22] He is quite clear on what this means for customary law: 'the emerging customary rule does not appear to conform to the text of Articles 31 and 32'.[23] It is problematic to claim, on the one hand, that the identity of the customary rules on interpretation with Articles 31–3 VCLT makes any differentiation by way of an analysis redundant and, on the other hand, that tribunal interpretation practice does not conform to the content of Articles 31–3 VCLT. Either the practice does not diverge and the two norms are identical or it does and they are not.

The other problem concerns the alleged *word-for-word* identity of the two norms, which itself relies on the implicit claim that the customary rules on interpretation are words. To take but one example, in discussing the remit of 'systemic integration', many scholars focus on the meaning of the words and phrases used in Article 31(3)(c) VCLT. Daniel Rosentreter's monograph is in large part a discussion of the debates over phrases like 'relevant rules' or 'applicable in the relations between the parties'.[24] Orthodox voices sometimes obsess over wording,[25] while professing that '[o]f course the customary law equivalent of Article 31(3)(c), being customary, is unwritten'.[26] 'Unwritten' seems to denote only that a rule is not written down, not that it does not take the form of words, but customary law's status as *lex non scripta* refers to norms which are not

[20] Weeramantry (2012) note 5 at 157.

[21] Trinh (2014) note 5 at 4, with a detailed indictment vis-à-vis investment tribunals at 75–98.

[22] Villiger (2011) note 8 at 114–15.

[23] Villiger (2011) note 8 at 119.

[24] Daniel Rosentreter, *Article 31(3)(c) of the Vienna Convention on the Law of Treaties and the Principle of Systemic Integration in International Investment Law and Arbitration* (Baden-Baden: Nomos 2015) 95–217.

[25] Eg Gardiner (2008) note 2 at 250–98.

[26] Merkouris (2015) note 3 at 6 fn 24.

couched in words – *sine litteris.*[27] Francisco Suárez argues that customary law 'does not of its nature demand a written instrument, nor does it flow from written law . . . [;] it is introduced by usage, for this is embodied *not in writing nor in words, but in facts*'.[28] Another argument has already been made in Chapter 2: if customs become the *actus reus* content (*Tatbestand*) of the emerging norm, then the content is formed by the regularity of behaviour itself. It is not made by using language to *describe* that regularity (not even in verbal *opinio iuris*). Customary law does not 'exist' as words, as language. On that view, the customary rules of interpretation by definition cannot be identical to Articles 31–3 VCLT because they cannot have a content that is made up of words. Customary international law is wordless; only our (scholarly or judicial) *reconstruction* of its content is, can be and has to be.

The identity of a customary norm with the VCLT rules is neither inevitable nor necessary. A dispassionate legal analysis must on balance conclude that it is highly unlikely that these are valid customary rules or that we can prove their validity. Only arguments from operational necessity remain: international law would not 'work' if these rules were not universal, hence they are. Yet this is a type of argument that legal scholarship cannot entertain.

However, an argument can be made on a different level, irrespective of whether the rules of interpretation are custom, treaty or both. As mentioned above, Klabbers argues that interpretative 'practice' is not of a 'fundamentally norm-creating character' and that interpretation 'cannot meaningfully be subjected to rules'.[29] Indeed, norms on 'interpretation' are not about interpretation properly speaking.[30] Two considerations may lead one to reflect more deeply on that argument. First, we could ask how an obligation to interpret would work on the technical level, for example whether 'transgressions could be classified as wrongful acts'.[31] It

[27] Cicero, *De partitone oratoria* C.37: 'sed propria legis et ea, quae scripta sunt, et ea quae sine litteris, aut gentium jure aut majorum more, retinentur'; see also Inst 1.2.9; D.1.1.6.1; A Arthur Schiller, 'Custom in Classical Roman Law' 24 *Virginia Law Review* (1938) 268–82 at 270.

[28] 'nec per se scripturam requirit, nec etiam manat ex iure scripto . . . usu ipso introducitur, usus enim *non scripturis, aut verbis, sed in factis consistit.*' Francisco Suárez, *De legibus ac Deo legislatore* [1612] lib. 7 cap. 2, sect. 2 (emphasis added) (translation by Gwladys L Williams, Ammi Brown, John Waldron, Henry Davis 1944 at 451).

[29] Klabbers (2010) note 8 at 20.

[30] See eg Kammerhofer (2010d) note 8 at 94–5; Jörg Kammerhofer, 'Systemic Integration, Legal Theory and the ILC' 19 *Finnish Yearbook of International Law 2008* (2010) 157–82 at 167–8.

[31] Klabbers (2010) note 8 at 29.

does border on the absurd to argue that a 'violation' of such an obligation would be considered a breach of international law in its own right. More broadly, who is obligated by the rules of interpretation? If interpretation means finding 'the meaning' of a treaty term, does not everyone who comes across a treaty and seeks to understand it interpret? Is, then, *everyone* obligated by Articles 31–3 VCLT or the customary norms, including private citizens? Does international law really order a Belgian university professor to interpret 'measures tantamount to expropriation' in Article 6 of the Mexico–Kuwait BIT 2013 in a certain way? Orthodoxy's near-exclusive focus on states and international tribunals as subjects of the interpretation norm (Section 4.2.2) indicates that this is not assumed.

The second issue, leading to the same question, is raised by those who believe that the question of 'treaty interpretation' is exhaustively covered by a (meta-)interpretation of Articles 31–3 VCLT: the rules of interpretation shall be interpreted by means of Articles 31–3 VCLT *themselves* or by their word-for-word identical customary law equivalent.[32] 'As the Vienna rules are set out in a treaty, they are themselves to be interpreted by application of the very rules that they state.'[33] Gardiner claims that this circularity is benign; this 'may sound rather circular and formulaic: but the result need not be too artificial if the flexibility which the rules were intended to retain is respected'.[34] Even if this is a circular argument, the argument continues, it is resolved with the application of *customary* rules to the Vienna Convention. Christian Djeffal's critique is apt, for 'if there was a rule in customary law, this rule can be ambiguous and, therefore, subject to interpretation'.[35] Irrespective of whether we accept the view that customary law can be interpreted as a text, the claim that the customary rule on interpretation is identical to the Vienna Convention must involve the presupposition that the text of Articles 31–3 VCLT itself shapes customary law. The circle closes: if the meanings are identical because the text is, then the text needs to be interpreted – and the meaning is then *arguendo* found by reference to itself! Yet norms of interpretation also need to be interpreted; this is not a tautological statement.[36] 'Interpreting the rule of interpretation ... would be either circular or trivial: circular since there is an indefinite need to interpret the

[32] Eg Merkouris (2015) note 3 at 6, 9–10.
[33] Gardiner (2008) note 2 at 9.
[34] Gardiner (2008) note 2 at 9.
[35] Djeffal (2016) note 4 at 69.
[36] Jan Klabbers, 'International Legal Histories: The Declining Importance of *Travaux Préparatoires* in Treaty Interpretation?' 50 *Netherlands International Law Review*

rules; trivial because the only way out of this is an assertion without arguments.'[37] That these rules also need interpretation is not a question of whether the Vienna Convention rules are successfully applied, as Villiger claims in response to a point I have made elsewhere.[38] Rather, interpretation will always happen, despite and beyond specific rules of interpretation. Even if international law contains norms on 'interpretation', the cognitive process of interpretation is not replaced by these norms. Instead, another layer is created.

4.2.2 *Two Concepts of Interpretation*

We cannot tell what specific interpretative tools can achieve to clarify and unify expropriation before we discuss what interpretation means. There are two fundamentally different and largely inconsistent conceptions of interpretation at play here. The first reading is preferred in recent general legal-philosophical debate and is marked by the taking into account of influences from general philosophy, hermeneutics and linguistics. On that reading, interpretation is hermeneutics, the process of finding out what texts mean, of which legal texts are merely one particular genre ('interpretation$_A$'). While legal interpretation is certainly shaped to a considerable extent by the culture and education of jurists and legal methodology, it is no more than what humans (jurists) do when they understand a legal text. The second reading, generally accepted by international lawyers, if not often reflected, is perhaps closest in alignment with a legal tradition stretching back to the Historical Legal School in Germany. For them, interpretation is 'more' than text-cognition. It is not quite application, not quite reduction to a single possible meaning; it is some form of 'applicative construction of law's meaning' ('interpretation$_B$').[39] The problem is not only that these different conceptions use the same word to denote different things but that orthodox international lawyers tend to define it in a way that supports equivocation, that is, as 'giving of meaning to a text'[40] or as 'the process of

(2003) 267–88 at 270; Kammerhofer (2010d) note 8 at 95; Kammerhofer (2010b) note 30 at 167.

37 Djeffal (2016) note 4 at 70.

38 Villiger (2011) note 8 at 121.

39 Friedrich Müller, *Juristische Methodik* (5th edn, Berlin: Duncker & Humblot 1993) 20: 'das optimale Maß an Rationalität und Kontrollierbarkeit normtextorientierter Rechtsverwirklichung'; Ascensio (2016) note 5 at 367.

40 Gardiner (2008) note 2 at 27.

determining the meaning of a text'.[41] Few realise that there is an incommensurability vis-à-vis the legal-philosophical approach and a communications breakdown ensues.

The first approach (interpretation$_A$) will not be discussed at length because only if understood as interpretation$_B$ can it potentially serve as tool to 'do things' and achieve results in the legal sphere. Only this conception of interpretation contains tools that might deconflict, defragment and unify international law. The relative innocence of the term 'interpretation' – we are 'merely' interpreting the law and do not claim to change it, the message goes – allows us to circumnavigate the objection that interpretation cannot change the law. This section will explore the two approaches in turn, because the answers given by legal theorists (interpretation$_A$) and by international lawyers (interpretation$_B$) differ on a fundamental level. The orthodox understanding will be contrasted and critiqued on the basis of the Pure Theory's concept of interpretation. Its strong theory of legal structure may establish limits to what interpretation$_B$ can do, even if it is acknowledged that interpretation$_B$ is not entirely dependent on interpretation$_A$. In turn, we might find that the tools used in the modern debate on the 'interpretation' of investment law (as discussed in Section 4.3) may not work as advertised or even not at all.

1. *The orthodox understanding of the process of interpretation.* Interpretation$_B$ is perhaps best understood in the context of the debate, already discussed in Chapter 3, of how abstract general norms are (to be) concretised in individual decisions, for example tribunal judgments. This sounds counter-intuitive: is not interpreting categorically different from deciding? Is that not a point of agreement between orthodox international legal scholarship and jurisprudence?[42] International lawyers tend to define (treaty) interpretation as 'clarification of the meaning'.[43] Yet, interpretation$_B$ is more than 'meaning-ascertainment', even if that is not argued explicitly. Matthias Herdegen's *Max Planck Encyclopedia* article is a convenient entry-point:

[41] Harvard Law School, Codification of International Law: Part III Law of Treaties, printed in 29 *American Journal of International Law Supplement* (1935) 653–1226 at 938; see also Rudolf Bernhardt, 'Interpretation in International Law' in Rudolf Bernhardt (ed.), *Encyclopedia of Public International Law*, vol 2 (Amsterdam: Elsevier 1995) 1416–26 at 1417; Gazzini (2016) note 5 at 1; Orakhelashvili (2008) note 4 at 285–6; Wälde (2009) note 5 at 724; Weeramantry (2012) note 5 at 30.

[42] See eg Kammerhofer (2010d) note 8 at 105–6, 115–16; Kammerhofer (2010b) note 30 at 166–7.

[43] Orakhelashvili (2008) note 4 at 285.

> Interpretation in international law essentially refers to the process of assigning meaning to texts and other statements *for the purposes of establishing rights, obligations, and other consequences* relevant in a legal context. Interpretation is *both a cognitive and a creative process*. On the one hand, interpretation purports to establish a pre-existing meaning. On the other hand, the interpretative process has a creative dimension. Creative elements flow from the necessary interconnection and balancing of relevant criteria as well as from the selective focus on facts deemed relevant from the interpreter's point of view.[44]

The italicised passages point to the applicative and decisionist function of interpretation$_B$. One argument for this expanded notion comes from the debate on *in claris non fit interpretatio*:[45] 'Strictly speaking, when the meaning of the treaty is clear, it is "applied", not "interpreted". Interpretation is a secondary process which only comes into play when it is impossible to make sense of the plain terms of the treaty, or when they are susceptible of different meanings.'[46]

Arnold Mc Nair's adage is recast by Linderfalk as the difference between two understandings of interpretation. One, where we interpret 'each time we are faced with a text, to which we (consciously or unconsciously) attach a certain meaning'. Another, where '[t]he text of a treaty does not always have to be interpreted', because 'it is only when we have already read a text, and the text has shown to be unclear, that we can say that we then interpret it'. The latter 'is clearly the way the word is used in the 1969 Vienna Convention'.[47] In the *Fragmentation* report, the ILC denies that the Vienna Convention rules are 'meant as an actual description of a psychological process. . . . But it is an apt account of *competent public reasoning* by lawyers and tribunals.'[48] On this view, '[i]nterpretation is . . . legal *reasoning*',[49] rather than cognition of the law.

[44] Matthias Herdegen, 'Interpretation in International Law' in Rüdiger Wolfrum (ed.), *Max Planck Encyclopedia of Public International Law*, vol 6 (Oxford: Oxford University Press 2012) 260–73 at 260 MN 1 (emphasis added).

[45] See, however, already D.25.4.1.11: 'Quamvis sit manifestissimum edictum praetoris, attamen non est neglegenda interpretatio eius.'

[46] Arnold Duncan McNair, *The Law of Treaties* (Oxford: Clarendon Press 1961) 365 fn 1.

[47] Linderfalk (2007) note 4 at 10 (capitalisation removed).

[48] Martti Koskenniemi, 'Fragmentation of International Law: Difficulties Arising from the Diversification and Expansion of International Law: Report of the Study Group of the International Law Commission' in *International Law Commission, Fifty-Eighth Session, Geneva, 1 May–9 June and 3 July–11 August 2006*, A/CN.4/L.682 (2006) 234 (para 464) (emphasis added).

[49] Campbell McLachlan, 'The Principle of Systemic Integration and Article 31(3)(c) of the Vienna Convention' 54 *International and Comparative Law Quarterly* (2005) 279–320 at 310.

Interpretation$_B$ is the justification of a legal argument; it is not primarily about gaining knowledge of the text. The theory of rational law (*Vernunftrecht*) is often an unacknowledged backdrop to this conception of interpretation, for example in the following text:

> The term 'interpretation' is often used to designate two separate things: a process in which the interpreter understands the meaning of a rule; and a process in which the interpreter justifies why the legal system should recognize a particular meaning of a rule as authoritative. ... On the one hand ... canons and methods of interpretation have little bearing on the process of understanding the meaning of a rule. Understanding is not a rigid, rule-guided activity ... On the other hand, the justification of a particular interpretation is subject to methodological constraints. Each legal system has its own ground rules for what constitutes an appropriate, rationally justifiable reading of a legal text.[50]

Yet if one does not agree with legal rationalism, it is hard to imagine what this 'rational argumentative justification' – wedged between 'human understanding of legal texts' and 'judicial decision of a case' – could possibly be. Orthodoxy sees interpretation as justificatory and reason-giving, rather than concerned only with meaning-ascertainment; interpretation$_B$ provides guidance in the process of the concretisation of abstract general norms in individual instances: '[a]dditional objectivity is expected from interpretation, assuming that it is possible to flow from signs to meaning through an activity of knowledge'.[51] It is clear that the interpreter has a choice and that interpretation is expected to be a source of objectivity in making this kind of choice. In the following, two questions will elucidate how interpretation$_B$ works: who is the interpreter and what is the difference between application and interpretation?

a. *The interpreter.* The tribunal in *Sempra Energy*, while defending against the argument that a state's auto-interpretation is binding on tribunals, gave a glimpse into the broader mindset in holding that 'interpretation is not the exclusive task of States. It is also the duty of tribunals called upon to settle a dispute.'[52] Who in fact seeks to understand ('interpret') treaties seems less important than 'who or what authorities *may* interpret treaties and ... the legal effect of their decisions'.[53] The key to understanding this position is that

[50] Dirk Pulkowski, *The Law and Politics of International Regime Conflict* (Oxford: Oxford University Press 2014) 275–6.

[51] Ascensio (2016) note 5 at 369; see also Linderfalk (2007) note 4 at 12.

[52] *Sempra Energy International* v. *Argentina*, ICSID, ARB/02/16, Decision on Objections to Jurisdiction of 11 May 2005, para 147.

[53] Harvard (1935) note 41 at 973 (emphasis added).

interpretation$_B$, as a 'legal process',[54] needs to be authorised,[55] at least when it is a 'binding' interpretation. Linderfalk, echoing Hans Kelsen's dichotomy, introduces the concepts of 'operative' and 'doctrinal' interpretation:

> Operative interpretation is performed by . . . authorities empowered to decide on issues concerning the application of international agreements. Doctrinal interpretation is typically performed by the legal scholar . . . In this work, attention will be focused on operative interpretation of treaties. The idea is to make an attempt to create some assumedly greater certainty among the appliers of international law with regard to the content of the currently existing legal regime for the interpretation of treaties.[56]

Only operative interpretation is seen as relevant to the 'legal regime for the interpretation of treaties' and will provide 'greater certainty' regarding the law. Orthodoxy in effect excludes interpretation by anyone because it restricts interpretation to those where the outcome of their interpretation has some legal 'relevance'. The assumption is that international (treaty) law is unique in this respect, as the treaty parties are accorded primary competence to interpret[57] in distinction to domestic contract law.[58] Treaty parties, international courts, tribunals and other organs conduct interpretation$_B$ because they are authorised to interpret. Orthodoxy constructs a hierarchy of authorities: first the parties together, then organs authorised (by the parties or otherwise) to interpret, whether judicial or of a different kind, and last unilateral interpretations by a state party,[59] with the 'bindingness' of interpretation ranked accordingly. There is thus an intimate link between interpretation$_B$ and change or application of the law: '[w]henever . . . international courts and tribunals are empowered to decide disputes with binding effect, their interpretation of a relevant text is likewise binding'.[60] Is this a mistaken use of words? Is not the court's *application* to a case binding? That is unlikely,

54 'Rechtsvorgang' Heribert Franz Köck, *Vertragsinterpretation und Vertragsrechtskonvention: Zur Bedeutung der Artikel 31 und 32 der Wiener Vertragsrechtskonvention 1969* (Berlin: Duncker & Humblot 1976) 23.

55 Weeramantry (2012) note 5 at 31.

56 Linderfalk (2007) note 4 at 12.

57 Gardiner (2008) note 2 at 109.

58 See eg Bernhardt (1995) note 41 at 1417–18.

59 Eg Bernhardt (1995) note 41 at 1417–18; György Haraszti, *Some Fundamental Problems of the Law of Treaties* (Budapest: Akadémiai Kiadó 1973) 43–77; Harvard (1935) note 41 at 975–6; Orakhelashvili (2008) note 4 at 511.

60 Bernhardt (1995) note 41 at 1417.

because interpretation$_B$ is largely seen as a determination of norm-content; orthodoxy combines bindingness and cognition of meaning.

'Authentic' and 'authoritative' interpretation are perhaps the clearest examples where the interpreter's authority is claimed to lead to a binding effect for interpretation. 'Authentic interpretation comprises only such interpretation under which the interpretative outcome ... enjoys the same level of binding force as the pertinent interpreted provision',[61] writes Alexander Orakhelashvili. 'The parties could even derogate from the interpretation rendered by judicial and arbitral organs.'[62] This is an 'interpretation' where the norm-creator issues a second norm specifying the meaning of the first norm – this is not a cognitive process. Authoritative interpretation, in contrast, is performed by an organ empowered to create binding decisions and, allegedly, binding interpretations.[63] It is often argued that 'an authoritative interpretation must by definition relate to and interpret the pre-existing rules of the relevant treaty. It cannot create new rules.'[64] As pointed out above, this notion is very close to 'application', even as understood by traditional scholarship.

Interpretation$_B$ is different as it seems important who the interpreting agency is, not only because these processes seem to be relatively far removed from the hermeneutic process of cognising texts but also because these forms of interpretation allegedly have legal consequences (whereas others do not). Also, which role do scholars play as interpreters in the orthodox scheme?[65] Scholars have no business conducting interpretation$_B$ – they can only be re-creators of interpretations of the creators and appliers of law (states and tribunals). In the Harvard Research report's argument that '[t]he interpretation of treaties is essentially a judicial process',[66] we can clearly see that interpretation$_B$ is intimately connected to the application of law. On this view, scholars simply do not interpret: 'we should have to keep the systematic scientific processing of the legal material apart from treaty interpretation'.[67]

61 Orakhelashvili (2008) note 4 at 514.
62 Orakhelashvili (2008) note 4 at 514; see also Gardiner (2008) note 2 at 109.
63 Orakhelashvili (2008) note 4 at 515.
64 Orakhelashvili (2008) note 4 at 516.
65 Linderfalk (2007) note 4 at 12.
66 Harvard (1935) note 41 at 973.
67 Haraszti (1973) note 59 at 19; a far more conventional position emerges later in the text: Haraszti (1973) note 59 at 77–8.

b. *Application and interpretation.* The orthodox argument inevitably sees 'interpretation' and 'application' as separate and takes its cue from Ludwik Ehrlich's dissenting opinion in *Chorzów*: 'interpretation, is [the process] of determining the meaning of a rule, while ... application, is ... that of determining the consequences which the rule attaches to ... a given fact'.[68] Almost as inevitably, however, their close connection is emphasised: '[i]n practice, ... there is a good chance that the two (interpretation and application) might lapse into each other – such would seem well-nigh inevitable'.[69] This intimate connection is supported by the argument that interpretation is a necessary condition for application. 'Any application of a treaty ... presupposes ... a preceding conscious or subconscious interpretation of the treaty.'[70] The reason for this connection is said to lie in a 'natural sequence' in which 'interpretation ... is separate from application of the provision and, logically, must come before it'.[71] '[I]nterpretation constitutes the step before application – one cannot apply a law unless its precise meaning is known.'[72]

In this manner, the mainstream generalises a particular understanding of a particular situation, namely, that facing judges. Because professional jurists usually interpret before they apply the law, this must necessarily be so in order for application to occur. For Maarten Bos, 'it is simply impossible to divorce interpretation and application to a point where the outcome of the interpretation of a text would be nullified by the application given to it'.[73] This, in turn, presupposes the judicial setting, where procedural rules usually require tribunals to give reasons for their

68 *Factory at Chorzów (Claim for Indemnity) (Germany* v. *Poland)*, Judgment on Jurisdiction of 26 July 1927, PCIJ Series A No 9 (1927), dissenting opinion Ehrlich at 39. This is echoed by Bernhardt (1995) note 41 at 1417; Gardiner (2008) note 2 at 27–8; Harvard (1935) note 41 at 938; Haraszti (1973) note 59 at 18; Weeramantry (2012) note 5 at 30.

69 Jan Klabbers, 'Reluctant *Grundnormen*: Articles 31(3)(c) and 42 of the Vienna Convention on the Law of Treaties and the Fragmentation of International Law' in Matthew Craven, Malgosia Fitzmaurice, Maria Vogiatzi (eds.), *Time, History and International Law* (Leiden: Martinus Nijhoff 2007) 141–61 at 144; see also Bernhardt (1995) note 41 at 1417; Maarten Bos, 'Theory and Practice of Treaty Interpretation' 27 *Netherlands International Law Review* (1980) 3–38, 135–70 at 13; Haraszti (1973) note 59 at 16; Weeramantry (2012) note 5 at 30.

70 Georg Schwarzenberger, 'Myths and Realities of Treaty Interpretation: Articles 27–29 of the Vienna Draft Convention on the Law of Treaties' 22 *Current Legal Problems* (1969) 205–27 at 212.

71 Gardiner (2008) note 2 at 27.

72 Weeramantry (2012) note 5 at 30.

73 Bos (1980) note 69 at 13.

decision. Yet if any application necessarily implies a previous interpretation (i→a), does any interpretation necessarily imply application (a→i)? Are they co-dependent (i↔a)? This, however, is a more controversial proposition, as the Harvard Research points out:

> It is evident, therefore, that, even though interpretation may be essential to application, it is perfectly possible to have interpretation without application. ... In actual practice, however, the case involving solely a question of abstract interpretation is relatively rare. Differences as to the interpretation of a treaty practically always arise in connection with its application; disputes as to its application almost invariably involve a question of interpretation.[74]

In the judicial context, the inevitable intermingling *in fact* of cognition and decision hides their differences and leads to the muddled conclusion of the quote. The best test-case is scholarly interpretation: 'The critiques denying the difference between applying and interpreting would have to show that it is impossible to interpret a legal text without applying it. ... If one were to write a commentary or an encyclopaedic entry, is it strictly necessary to apply the text in any way?'[75] Does the application of law need any interpretation at all?[76] In the domestic context, when individuals conclude a contract of sale, they apply the law, but would we ever argue that the parties must necessarily have interpreted the law before they applied it?

A second argument is that abstract interpretation is not possible; in practice, 'it would be difficult to apply something without at the same time interpreting it, and to interpret a term without a context in which to apply it'.[77] The application of abstract terms (general norms) to specific terms (verbalised facts) seems to be split into the decision and the individualising part of 'interpretation'. Because we tend to take our cue from the judicial process, our concept of 'interpretation' includes elements of application. György Haraszi draws the inevitable consequences that flow from this focus:

> On the other hand, we should have to keep the systematic scientific processing of the legal material apart from treaty interpretation. Else, i.e. if we recognized the permissiveness of an abstract interpretation of a treaty, then interpretation would of necessity lay a claim to being

74 Harvard (1935) note 41 at 938–9; see also Linderfalk (2007) note 4 at 32–3.
75 Djeffal (2016) note 4 at 14; see also Schwarzenberger (1969) note 70 at 212.
76 Eg Haraszti (1973) note 59 at 17.
77 Klabbers (2007) note 69 at 144.

> normative for each case as may emerge in the future. This, of course, would imply the forfeiture of the nature of an interpretation, and instead interpretation would virtually become equivalent to the creation of a new legal norm.[78]

Another consequence of this position is that '[j]uridical interpretation, ... far from being a merely preliminary activity, an act of "cognition" only, is in actual fact a composite notion harbouring both "cognition" and "will"'.[79] This is yet more evidence that interpretation$_B$ is re-imagined as the *construction* of treaties[80] by tribunals; it is a regulation of the process of judicial reasoning. While judicial decisions are not preordained by interpretation, the process leading up to those decisions is somehow seen as determined nonetheless. Interpretation$_B$ seeks to narrow the freedom implicit in empowering an organ to decide. It does so by means of (the rules of) interpretation.[81]

From a sociological perspective, this attempt to keep international law working on the operational level is extraordinarily effective. In order to ensure a reasonable coherence of decision-making, legal sub-systems develop mechanisms to socialise relevant participants in order to ensure similar decisions in similar situations. Among domestic jurists, this is commonly achieved by means of legal education and the development of a legal culture and ethos. In international law, both a shared legal culture and a uniform education are missing and the rules of interpretation are probably subconsciously seen as necessary to ensure the operation of the international legal order. Reasonably consistent decision-making by tribunals is ensured by developing an ethos of 'interpretation'.

2. *The Pure Theory of Law as an alternative approach.* However, on the level of legal theoretical discourse, we will need to establish what the 'rules of interpretation' can be (Section 4.2.3) and what international investment lawyers are doing when they use interpretative tools to unify expropriation in investment law (Section 4.3). Confronting interpretation$_B$ with the theory of legal interpretation developed by the Pure Theory of Law,[82] we will find out what interpretation$_B$ is and what

[78] Haraszti (1973) note 59 at 19.

[79] Bos (1980) note 69 at 11, summarising Serge Sur, *L'interprétation en droit international public* (Paris: LGDJ 1974) 98–9.

[80] Harvard (1935) note 41 at 939.

[81] Djeffal (2016) note 4 at 9.

[82] In the following, I will use: Adolf Julius Merkl, 'Zum Interpretationsproblem' 42 [*Grünhutsche*] *Zeitschrift für das Privat- und öffentliche Recht der Gegenwart* (1916) 535–56, reprinted in Hans Klecatsky, René Marcic, Herbert Schambeck (eds.), *Die*

using the interpretative tool-box in international investment law means for (our understanding of) the law. The Pure Theory of Law can help us to distinguish between the cognition of law, on the one hand, and the process of (judicial) reasoning leading to a decision in a specific case, on the other. Scholars like Kelsen and Adolf Julius Merkl developed explanations of the relationship between interpretation and the hierarchy of legal orders (the *Stufenbau* theory)[83] and it is submitted that their writings help us make the distinction in a sustainable manner.

A large part of German-language domestic legal scholarship in the early twentieth century believed that judging is an act of cognition *only*. The judge cognises law and 'speaks' it: *Rechtsprechung*. Today's international legal orthodoxy does not agree with many of the positions that Kelsen's adversaries held. It does not believe that interpretation mechanically produces a specific outcome, that judgments are deduced by a quasi-logical operation, or that interpretation and the act of decision are one and the same. Therefore, in order to apply the Pure Theory's ideas to today's international legal writings, we will have to adjust our arguments slightly, and will not take Kelsen or Merkl at their words in every respect. However, once this is done, their arguments are powerful indeed:

> The act of application of the law by a legal organ combines the cognitive interpretation of the applicable law with an act of will; the latter is a choice by the law-applying organ between the possible meanings identified by cognitive interpretation. ... This act of will is the difference between a legal interpretation by the applying organ and any other [form of] interpretation, particularly the interpretation of the law by legal scholarship.[84]

Wiener rechtstheoretische Schule: Ausgewählte Schriften von Hans Kelsen, Adolf Julius Merkl, Alfred Verdross (Vienna: Europa 1968) (abbreviated as: *WRS*) 1059–77 and in Dorothea Mayer-Maly, Herbert Schambeck, Wolf-Dietrich Grussmann (eds.), *Adolf Julius Merkl: Gesammelte Schriften*, vol I/1 (Berlin: Duncker & Humblot 1993)(abbreviated as: *MerklGS*) 63–83; Adolf Julius Merkl, 'Das Recht im [Spiegel] Lichte seiner [Auslegung] Anwendung' [the title varies] 8 *Deutsche Richterzeitung* (1916) col 584–92, 9 *Deutsche Richterzeitung* (1917) col 162–76, 394–8, 443–50, 11 *Deutsche Richterzeitung* (1919) col 290–8 (*WRS* 1167–1201, I/1 *MerklGS* 85–146); Hans Kelsen, *Reine Rechtslehre* (2nd edn, Vienna: Deuticke 1960) 346–54; Hans Kelsen, *The Law of the United Nations: A Critical Analysis of its Fundamental Problems* (New York: Praeger 1950) xiii–xvi.

83 For a portrayal of the *Stufenbau* theory in international law, see eg Kammerhofer (2010d) note 8 at 180–5, 230–40; Jörg Kammerhofer, 'Sources in Legal Positivist Theories: The Pure Theory's Structural Analysis of the Law' in Samantha Besson, Jean d'Aspremont (eds.), *The Oxford Handbook of the Sources of International Law* (Oxford: Oxford University Press 2017) 343–62.

84 'In der Anwendung des Rechtes durch ein Rechtsorgan verbindet sich die erkenntnismäßige Interpretation des anzuwendenden Rechtes mit einem Willensakt, in

The 'act of will' makes all the difference; if we subtract it, interpretation is an exercise in cognition; it is the epistemic process of understanding texts. No decision is taken; no judgment is created. If, as described above, an act of application is missing that process of finding out what the law means, the court case is still decided and the judgment (or other outcome) is still valid.

> Legal practice thus uses . . . a different method of interpretation than legal theory. After all, practice creates new law, while legal theory only wishes to clarify or explain the law . . . thus created. The hermeneutic interpretation of law is limited to the legal material already in existence; legal practice is about adding new law, expanding the *lex lata* by inserting elements [hitherto] not part of the law, and is therefore legal production.[85]

Merkl's and Kelsen's *Stufenbau* theory describes the creation and destruction of norms; interpretation in a wide sense has a place in the dynamic structure of law. That theory, however, deconstructs the inevitability of a connection between hermeneutic process and norm-creation. A more sustainable concept can be constructed by re-evaluating the two issues discussed above on the basis of that theoretical perspective.

a. *The interpreter.* The question of who is authorised to interpret the law can arise only if and insofar as such an interpretation impinges on the law, but not if interpretation is understood as epistemic function: 'legal cognition . . . is not capable of acquiring for the law any element [previously] not part of the law; . . . Scholarship is reproduction and its products can never go beyond the object thus reproduced.'[86] The relevance of the epistemic function of interpretation is tested by both authentic and authoritative interpretation. In authentic interpretation, the organs

dem das rechtsanwendende Organ eine Wahl trifft zwischen den durch die erkenntnismäßige Interpretation aufgezeigten Möglichkeiten. . . . Durch diesen Willensakt unterscheidet sich die Rechtsinterpretation durch das rechtsanwendende Organ von jeder anderen Interpretation, insbesondere von der Interpretation des Rechts durch die Rechtswissenschaft.' Kelsen (1960) note 82 at 351.

85 'Die Rechtspraxis bedient sich also, . . . einer anderen Interpretationsmethode als die Rechtstheorie. Die Rechtspraxis zielt ja darauf ab, neues Recht zu schaffen, während die Rechtstheorie das jeweils . . . geschaffene Recht nur klären, erklären will. Die erkenntnismäßige Rechtsauslegung ist auf die gegebene Rechtsmaterie beschränkt; neue Rechtspartien anzugliedern, das gegebene Recht durch die Hereintragung bisher rechtsfremder Elemente zu erweitern ist der Zweck der Rechtspraxis, die zugleich Rechtsproduktion ist.' Merkl (1916–19) note 82 at col 174–5 (*WRS* 1184, I/1 *MerklGS* 114).

86 'Rechtserkenntnis . . . ist durch nichts in die Lage versetzt, Rechtsfremdes auf welche Weise immer dem Rechte zu akquirieren; . . . Wissenschaft ist Reproduktion und Reproduziertes kann in keiner Richtung über das zu Reproduzierende hinausragen.' Merkl (1916–19) note 82 at col 174 (*WRS* 1183, I/1 *MerklGS* 113–114) (emphasis removed).

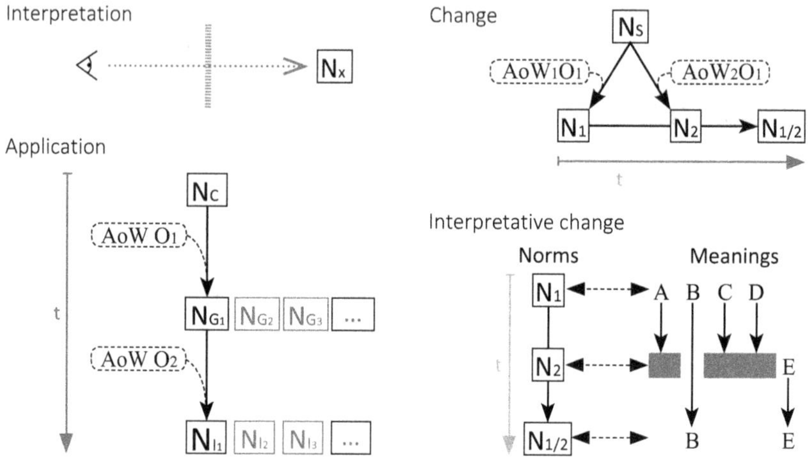

Figure 4.1 Interpretation, application, change and interpretative change[87]

authorised to change the norm to be interpreted proffer an 'interpretation' of that same norm. In our case, the states parties collectively decide on the meaning of a provision in that treaty. An authoritative interpretation can occur when an organ is authorised to decide specific cases and to create an individual norm based, inter alia, on that general norm. Authoritative interpretation occurs when an organ (incidentally) proffers an opinion on what the general norm means with respect to the pertinent set of facts to that case. For example, an arbitral tribunal is authorised to decide a dispute by way of an award binding on the parties to it. The tribunal bases its decision on an 'interpretation' of the meaning of a provision in the IIA at issue, which, it is claimed, concretises the meaning of that provision *in that case and for these parties.*

[87] *Interpretation*: humans (eye) cognise written norms (N_x) across the Is–Ought divide. *Application*: creating norms means that an organ (O) is authorised to apply a norm to create another; creation requires an act of will (AoW). Norms are applied at several points in the legal hierarchy: a constitution (N_C) may authorise one organ (O_1) to create general norms (N_{G1}, . . .), eg statutes. In creating these norms, the organ applies the constitution. Equally, N_{G1} may authorise another organ (O_2) to create individual norms (N_{I1}, . . .), eg judgments. *Change*: it is commonly assumed that norms are changed by way of the creation of successive norms over time (t) via two acts of will by the same organ. The later norm (N_2) can (but does not have to) change the earlier norm (N_1). The accumulation of the two norms is $N_{1/2}$. *Interpretative change*: this idea follows the same principle, but the focus here lies on N_2 being able to eliminate meanings from or to add new meanings to N_1.

Neither form of interpretation$_B$ can be performed by scholarship. Both forms produce legal effects that not only create law but also seem to make the process of 'interpretation' itself more potent than that performed by non-authorised persons. Interpretation$_B$ is a legal process or function and '[i]nterpretation as a legal function can be performed only by those whom the law authorises to interpret the law: the law-creating and law-applying organs'.[88] Most international lawyers would probably agree that authentic interpretation has little to do with interpretation proper. 'Authentic interpretation, whether general or individual, is a law-creating act',[89] Kelsen argues, but is any trace of meaning-ascertainment left in this process? How does change declared as such differ from an ostensible attempt to affix meanings to a norm by those authorised to create it? Should we believe an act's self-description as 'interpretation'? Take the following case: at time$_1$ parties A and B conclude treaty T_1, containing provision P_1. At time$_2$ A and B conclude T_2, which reads, 'P_1 (in T_1) shall be interpreted in the following manner . . .'. How does that differ from T_3, which reads, 'P_1 is hereby amended . . .' but is otherwise identical to T_2? They do not and, in this case, we cannot take T_2 at its words. A later treaty can completely change the earlier treaty norm,[90] including eliminating possible readings of the earlier norm or adding to them. It is then irrelevant whether the later norm claims that this is an interpretation – the law is changed, rather than interpreted.

Another scenario is far more likely: the states parties to T_1 do not use a second treaty for their authentic interpretation but publish an informal communique reading, 'We agree that P_1 (in T_1) shall be interpreted in the following manner . . .'. We tend to anthropomorphise the state as subject of international law. In this case, orthodoxy assumes that the power of authentic interpretation necessarily lies with the 'states parties' – as pre-legal entity – and that it does so irrespective of the form they select. '[I]nterpretation performed by all parties to the treaty jointly will in all events be binding on all',[91] whether 'in the form of joint declarations, agreed minutes, protocols, exchanges of notes, or any other suitable form'.[92] The exact scope of 'agreement' or 'practice'

88 Kelsen (1950) note 82 at xv–xvi.
89 Kelsen (1950) note 82 at xv.
90 As a matter of legal theory, however, 'change' of the law is a rather more complicated and problematic proposition, see Kammerhofer (2010d) note 8 at 139–94.
91 Haraszti (1973) note 59 at 43.
92 Gazzini (2016) note 5 at 337; see also Bernhardt (1995) note 41 at 1423; Herdegen (2012) note 44 at 266 MN 34.

under the Vienna Convention rules is not at issue in this section. Arguments of this kind show, however, that there is a strong belief that treaty-makers have a necessary or innate capacity to 'interpret' the treaty: *eius est interpretare cuius est condere.*[93]

Yet while those who are authorised to create a norm may usually later create another norm of the same kind – which, in turn, could seek to determine the 'interpretation' of the first norm – they may do so only if they observe the original conditions for law-creation. In more theoretical terms: it is the rules of legal change which constitute the change-inducing organ. There is no pre-legal entity 'states parties' which is able to interpret its own treaties with binding force irrespective of whether that interpretation is issued as treaty or as informal declaration, or is mere practice. The same is the case in contract law: parties do not have an a priori right to interpret their own contracts with binding force for the courts. The organ 'states acting jointly' is empowered by international law to conclude treaties – the organ is created only by that empowerment norm.[94] 'Authentic interpretations' issued outside the limits of that empowerment norm cannot legally change the (content of the) treaty. Explicit interpretation authorisations in treaties aside,[95] only a treaty with the same parties (Article 39 VCLT) can 'authentically interpret' the earlier treaty, because an authentic interpretation is a change of the law. While interpretation$_{B}$ in this extreme case has no hermeneutic function, it has every power to expand, restrict or modify the text or meanings of the first norm.

Authoritative interpretation is more limited because it is binding on the parties to a particular case and for that case only. However, the orthodox proposition includes the *interpretation*, the 'construction' of the treaty provision at issue, in the bindingness of the decision. This inclusion is based on an argument in four steps: (i) an organ is empowered to apply a treaty (ie to create an individual norm), (ii) a process of interpretation will usually precede the decision-making, (iii) interpretation is usually an important reason for the decision, and (iv) the resulting norm is binding on the parties. For the mainstream, authoritative interpretation by way of judgments in some way determines – or exercises some form of indirect influence on – the norm to be interpreted, blurring the border-line between application

[93] Gazzini (2016) note 5 at 337.

[94] Kelsen (1960) note 82 at 239–40, see also 154–62.

[95] Eg Article 1131(2) NAFTA.

and cognition of law. Yet even if tribunals are authorised to make binding decisions, are they thereby authorised to provide binding interpretations of the law they have applied?

> If [the judgment] thus carries one of several meanings ascribed to the statute, the statute is nonetheless not concretised by this move. The judgment does not impinge on the statute; it remains as indeterminate [not concretised] as the judgment is determinate [concrete]. . . . A statute cannot . . . be rid of its generality by application . . . by practice, which only manages to create a number of new individual norms, which are by definition separate entities vis-à-vis the statute.[96]

For interpretation-as-cognition (interpretation$_A$), the answer to the question, 'who may interpret?' cannot be states, courts, or even individuals (as subjects of law). No subjects of law, only physical human beings *can* cognise the law, because interpretation is an epistemic process which happens in reality, not within a legal order. Just as a state cannot blow its nose, legal organs cannot interpret.

b. *Application and interpretation.* If interpretation is what judges do before they apply the law and even if interpretation were to necessarily precede application, interpretation would still be separate from application. As discussed above, because interpretation$_B$ tends to take on elements of the process by which the specific case is aligned with general terms, orthodoxy is unwilling to separate them clearly. Kelsen's thoughts on the role of 'application' in the dynamic process of the creation of law in a hierarchy of norms may be helpful in this connection:

> A norm regulating the creation of another norm is applied in order to create the second norm in the manner prescribed by the first norm. To apply the law means to create it. . . . This is, because . . . [nearly] every legal act [is] at the same time the application of a higher norm as well as the creation of a lower norm, empowered by the higher norm. . . . The creation of general legal norms like statutes and customary law happens as application of the constitution. The creation of individual norms like

[96] 'Wird [das Urteil] nun zum Träger eines von mehreren dem Gesetze zugeschriebenen Sinnen – so wird das Gesetz dadurch nicht bestimmt. Denn das Urteil reicht an das Gesetz nicht heran. Das Gesetz bleibt unbestimmt, wie sehr das Urteil bestimmt sei. . . . Das Gesetz . . . kann . . . durch kein Mittel aus seiner Allgemeinheit gehoben werden, . . . durch die Praxis nicht, welche nur eine Anzahl neuer, in ihrem Wesen vom Gesetz verschiedener individueller Normen erzeugt.' Elisabeth Ephrussi, 'Interpretation und Analogie' 4 *Zeitschrift für öffentliches Recht* (1924) 132–59 at 141, 150.

judgments and administrative orders happens as application of these general norms.[97]

Courts *seem* almost certain to interpret (cognise) the law before they apply it – but not always and not necessarily. Far more fundamentally and as discussed above, the root of the problem lies in our tendency to anthropomorphise. Cognition is performed by humans, not by organs; from a legal perspective, law is created only by organs, not by physical human beings – even when the law requires, for law-creation, the attribution of only a single human being's behaviour. Even on a consistent reading of the mainstream, interpretation and application are not linked by necessity because there are valid cases where one happens without the other. The interpretation-before-application model holds true almost exclusively only in the case of judges. In a number of cases, application happens without prior interpretation, for example members of parliament not interpreting the constitution before they apply it in order to create a statute. The 'man or woman on the street' (even if they happened to be jurists) will certainly not interpret the civil code which they then apply to conclude a contract of sale in order to buy groceries. Both are bona fide cases of the application of law. Even states/state officials might on occasion omit to interpret the VCLT when they apply it to conclude treaties. 'The applier of the law . . . is correct [respectively, is in possession of the law], . . . not because of a piece of knowledge, but because of his powers, not because he knows better, but because he can do more.'[98] As Section 4.2.3 will show, even judges may not actually be required to cognise the law or be required to actually follow the mandated process in their own minds. They may merely need to write up their reasoning in a certain (*lege artis*) manner, a going through the motions. This is one of the issues arising from the focus of legal scholarship on the socio-psychological process of judicial reasoning.

[97] 'Eine Norm, die die Erzeugung einer anderen Norm bestimmt, wird in der von ihr bestimmten Erzeugung der anderen Norm angewendet. Rechtsanwendung ist zugleich Rechtserzeugung. . . . Denn . . . [nahezu] jeder Rechtsakt [ist] zugleich die Anwendung einer höheren Norm und die durch diese Norm bestimmte Erzeugung einer niederen Norm. . . . In Anwendung der Verfassung erfolgt die Erzeugung der generellen Rechtsnormen durch Gesetzgebung und Gewohnheit; und in Anwendung dieser generellen Normen erfolgt die Erzeugung der individuellen Normen durch richterliche Entscheidungen und Verwaltungsbescheide.' Kelsen (1960) note 82 at 240.

[98] 'Der Rechtsanwender, . . . hat Recht . . . nicht auf Grund eines Kennens, sondern eines Könnens, nicht weil er es besser weiß, sondern weil er es besser kann.' Merkl (1916–19) note 82 at col 449–50 (*WRS* 1200, I/1 *MerklGS* 132–3) (Merkl plays with two meanings of 'Recht haben', which can signify both 'being right' and 'having/possessing the law').

There are also a number of valid cases for interpretation without application, such as advisory opinions, but the prime example is legal scholarship. Judges will regularly find that interpretation does not result in a single solution; they will come to a point where several decisions are equally possible under the applicable law. '[I]t is thus necessary to speak of a subjective function of will (rather than mere cognition), which can be guided by subjective *fiat*, but also by other non-legal motives.'[99] Legal scholarship, in contrast, 'has to stop at the point where several interpretative results are possible and may not . . . construct a definite meaning which the positive law does not allow'.[100] Merkl argues in this connection that the opposite view is absurd: 'this is a bit like a specialist who undertakes to describe constitutional law . . . by telling us what the statutes that could be created on the basis of the constitution would say'.[101]

Therefore, the two functions – (1) interpretation as finding or creating 'meaning' from a given text and (2) application as creation of a norm – are *incidentally collocated.* Interpretation is therefore either meaning-ascertainment, but neither a legal process nor necessary for law-application, or a legal process which may sometimes be required by law before an application but which has little to do with the hermeneutic function. Not only can application happen without prior interpretation but interpretation is also independent of the success of acts of application. As long as the result of the act of application fits within the frame of possible meanings for the applied norm, it does not matter whether this result was based on an act of interpretation conducted by the applier. There are good reasons why states may create treaties only under certain conditions (eg Article 2(1)(a) VCLT).[102] However, states are not required to 'interpret' the VCLT before *applying the VCLT* to create treaties. States will

[99] 'ergibt sich die Notwendigkeit einer subjektiven Willens- (an Stelle einer bloßen Erkenntnis)funktion, welche wie von subjektiver Willkür so auch von anderen außerrechtlichen Motivationen . . . gelenkt sein kann' Merkl (1916) note 82 at 544 (*WRS* 1067, I/1 *MerklGS* 71–2).

[100] 'hat aber allenfalls auch beim mehrdeutigen Auslegungsergebnis halt zu machen und hat nicht . . . eine Eindeutigkeit des Auslegungsergebnisses herbeizuführen, die ihm de lege lata nicht zukommt.' Merkl (1916) note 82 at 545 (*WRS* 1067, I/1 *MerklGS* 72).

[101] '[das] kommt mir ungefähr so vor, wie jener Spezialist unter den Juristen, der bloß das Verfassungsrecht darzustellen unternimmt . . ., dies aber auf die Weise besorgt, daß er gleich bereits den Inhalt der auf Grund der Verfassung zu erlassenden Gesetze angibt.' Merkl (1916–19) note 82 at col 168 (*WRS* 1175, I/1 *MerklGS* 105) (emphasis removed).

[102] . . . notwithstanding a possible authorisation in international law to conclude treaties beyond the VCLT's remit.

successfully have created a treaty as long as the VCLT's conditions for treaty-creation are observed, whether or not they had conducted an interpretation of the VCLT beforehand.

4.2.3 The Vienna Convention Rules Reconstructed

The various strands of argument developed in Sections 4.2.1–4.2.2 can now be drawn together in order to reconstruct what the Vienna Convention rules on interpretation can be. In light of the overall aim to analyse the possible roles for interpretation to achieve unity in international investment law, it is possible to proceed on the basis of a suspension of our earlier legal critique of the Vienna Convention rules as customary international law. The crucial question for this chapter is what interpretation is as a process, because the current word-use suggests a legal process involving more potency than a hermeneutic process, while continuing to suggest that it is no more than meaning-ascertainment. If the rules of interpretation concern something other than the hermeneutic process, this changes what these rules can be. Having proven the categorical difference of the two meanings of interpretation and having spelt out the differences between interpretation$_A$ and interpretation$_B$, we can analyse four probable alternative constructions of rules of treaty interpretation. Merkl frames the core problem in his article 'Das Recht im Lichte seiner Anwendung':

> Interpretation is obviously a tool of legal cognition, hence it cannot be an object of cognition at the same time! [If it were an object of cognition,] how would we then cognise this particular object? We would again have to use interpretation. Yet this interpretation of ... legal interpretation cannot be juridical in nature. ... Admittedly, statutory rules of interpretation are part of the legal order. Because they are law, they are not just a tool, but also an object of legal cognition and thus an *interpretandum* ... Despite the peculiarity of statutory rules of interpretation simultaneously serving two functions, this does not invalidate the argument that rules of interpretation are not part of the law, more precisely: that certain rules of interpretation necessarily exist beyond the law.[103]

[103] 'Die Auslegung, der doch offenbar die Rolle eines Werkzeugs der Rechtserkenntnis zukommt, kann doch nicht gleichzeitig ein Gegenstand der Rechtserkenntnis sein! Mit welchem Werkzeuge würde man denn dieses besonderen rechtlichen Erkenntnisobjektes Herr werden? Doch wieder nur mit Auslegung. Doch diese Auslegung des rechtlichen Interpretationsproblems kann doch selbst nicht wieder juristischer Natur sein. ... Freilich, die gesetzlichen Auslegungsregeln sind ein Bestandteil des Rechtes und zufolge dieser ihrer Eigenschaft nicht bloß ein Werkzeug, sondern auch ein Gegenstand der Rechtserkenntnis

1. *A duty of motif-writing.* The first and most pragmatic approach is to see the rules of interpretation as a legal duty of writing the motifs of a judgment in a particular way or to provide cogent reasoning in a judgment or award (*Begründungspflicht*). A number of authors describe the rules of interpretation in this manner. Scholarship agrees that 'a number of [investment tribunals] have merely paid lip service to the Convention Rules or have failed to apply or otherwise comply with those Rules',[104] or 'do not refer to all the Article 31 and 32 criteria . . . [or] generally mention only those criteria they consider as relevant' (see Section 4.2.1).[105] On a pragmatic level, 'it would be inefficient and overly burdensome to require tribunals to apply explicitly and in detail every criterion of the Convention Rules for every interpretation it needs to perform'.[106] Djeffal argues that the rules are 'an obligation to decide based on legal arguments relating to the interpretative issue in the treaty. . . . [I]t obliges interpreters only to use a certain process of balancing.'[107]

> Th[is] could be termed context of discovery as opposed to context of justification or as hermeneutical as opposed to justificatory function: Both relate to a subject. The hermeneutical aspect relates to the influence of interpretative method on the actual understanding of the subject. The justificatory aspect stresses the fact that the interpreter is a decision-maker and prescribes the function of the rule on interpretation in this context.[108]

On this reading, the content of the rules-as-norms is therefore not much more than an obligation for tribunals to provide a specific reasoning for their decisions or a specific external form of reasoning. At a minimum, organs of international law ought to pay lip-service to the Vienna Convention rules when issuing a reasoned judgment or award. In this case, the rules of interpretation are part of the wider empowerment norm for international legal tribunals. Just as various procedural norms

und damit auch der Rechtsauslegung . . . Aber diese eigentümliche Doppelfunktion der gesetzlichen Auslegungsregeln entkräftet doch nicht unsere Behauptung von der außerrechtlichen Natur der Auslegungsregeln, richtiger, von der Notwendigkeit des Bestandes außerrechtlicher Auslegungsregeln.' Merkl (1916–19) note 82 at col 586 (I/1 *MerklGS* 87) (emphasis removed, translated in a liberal fashion).

104 Weeramantry (2012) note 5 at 157.

105 Weeramantry (2012) note 5 at 162; a finding equally applicable to the ICJ, see Klabbers (2005) note 11 at 426.

106 Weeramantry (2012) note 5 at 162.

107 Djeffal (2016) note 4 at 140 (emphasis removed); see also Weeramantry (2012) note 5 at 214; Wälde (2009) note 5 at 730.

108 Djeffal (2016) note 4 at 141 (emphasis removed).

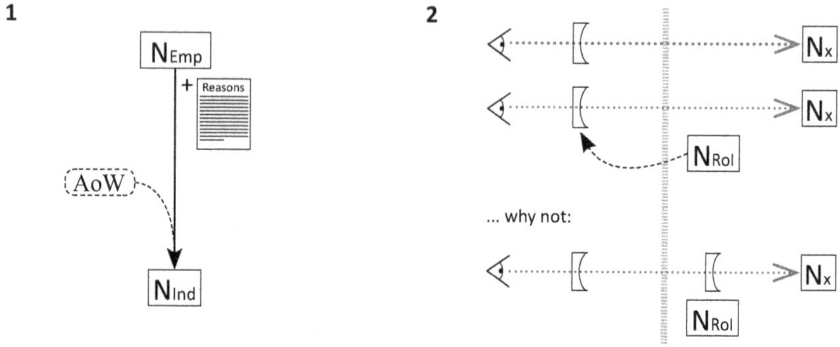

Figure 4.2 Reconstructing the rules of interpretation – Variants 1 and 2[109]

require tribunals to be constituted in a specific format or to decide on the basis of a specific substantive applicable law, the Vienna Convention rules would require the reasoning to take into account the various elements of Articles 31–3 VCLT. The legal consequences of adopting this view are clear: the law thus 'interpreted' is not changed or otherwise influenced one iota, whether in a 'binding' manner or not. The factual consequences, in contrast, are likely a mild convergence in both decisions and scholarly opinions.

2. *Replacing legal hermeneutics.* Perhaps the proper juridical techniques of interpretation of the legal world – '*lege artis* interpretation' – can be analogised to the proper methods, techniques, tools and instruments in the natural sciences and their cognition of the factual world? After all, scientists wanting to see bacteria cannot rely on the naked eye. Juridical hermeneutic methods, in particular the canons of interpretation, could then be just as necessary to find the meaning of law as a microscope is for bacteriology. These methods could be guided by norms of interpretation, for example the Vienna Convention rules. However, in legal orders without positive-legal rules of interpretation, the canons of interpretation

[109] 1. Rules as duty of *motif*-writing: within the dynamic process of law-creation, organs will have to comply with the empowerment norm (N_{Emp}) and apply the substantive norms (N_{Subs}) in order to create an individual norm. For courts, the empowerment norm will include a duty of writing up its reasoning in a specific way, which may, in turn, include a reference to rules of interpretation. An act of will (AoW) to create the norm is also required for the creation of positive norms. 2. Rules replace legal hermeneutics: human cognition of legal norms goes through the 'optics' of legal methods which reside in the realm of human consciousness, but perhaps rules of interpretation (N_{RoI}), in the realm of the ideal, supplant our in-built predispositions? Why would there then not be two sets of optics?

do not have the force of law. In these legal orders, they guide 'proper' legal cognition regardless of the specific content of the legal order at issue. Why, then, should 'proper juridical techniques of interpretation' not also operate in legal orders which *do* have statutory rules of interpretation? The hermeneutic function of interpretation will continue to exist and will continue to be influenced by ideals of what it means to interpret *lege artis*, whether or not statutory rules of interpretation happen to be applicable in a specific case.

Why should norms seeking to influence these techniques be capable of doing so? Is it not more likely that the norms reproduce some of these techniques as part of the legal order, rather than influence the cognitive function of human beings, even if they happen to be professional jurists? This type of influence on the process of cognition is implausible, because if rules of interpretation are norms, they have a personal sphere of application, yet is it really a fair reading of Article 31 VCLT (or an equivalent customary norm) that it applies to everyone – states, tribunals, scholars, even private individuals – alike? This reading is implausible if the rules obligate certain subjects of law (obligations *in personam*; *obligatorisch*). The consequences of adopting this view are roughly the same as for the first approach.

3. *Part of the applicable law.* The rules of interpretation can be reconstructed to take effect in the realm of norms, rather than changing cognitive processes. These rules work like some sort of 'optics' or filter for the interpreted norm. Again, we must ask for whom the rules of interpretation are binding; does everyone use the Vienna Convention rules? The problem, mentioned above, remains that norms obligate legal subjects, not physical entities. Legal scholarship can again serve as a useful counterpoint, for a scholar is physically able to ascertain treaty norms without the Vienna Convention rules; scholars are also not bound by these rules and can and may cognise treaty provisions without the Vienna Convention. Linderfalk's argument is that when interpreting a treaty, scholars, in order 'to be taken seriously', will have to accord with 'the legal framework, within which the agreement will have to be applied'.[110] This points in the right direction, for scholars are then free to disregard the Vienna Convention rules, unless they wish to re-create the situation of treaty-application by a tribunal.

This exemplifies the crucial shift in perspectives which modern international lawyers have made and which now makes them unique. Rules of

110 Linderfalk (2007) note 4 at 12.

interpretation as norms play little role in the epistemic process; rather, insofar as they are applicable, these rules are part of the dynamic process of individualisation and concretisation in the hierarchy of law (*Stufenbau*). They are part of the rule of law-creation (*Rechtserzeugungsregel*);[111] only if the conditions in the empowerment norm are fulfilled can an arbitral award be considered part of the international legal order.[112] The empowerment norm in a wide sense could potentially also regulate the process of application and this may indeed be what legal rules of interpretation are about. If they are obligations *in personam*, law-applying organs would have to apply the Vienna Convention rules in conjunction with the treaty norm.

However, we must avoid a different equivocation, for the word 'apply' is commonly used in two senses. Sometimes we assume that tribunals being under an obligation to *apply* law (the applicable law in the case) is the same as them being under an obligation to *observe* the law, that is, to conform to its terms. If, for example, the ICJ has to apply the Vienna Convention rules as applicable law, then it applies rules that oblige others. In this case, the rules oblige states to interpret; the judiciary adjudicates upon whether they have complied with their obligations. The Court subsumes state behaviour – in this case, states interpreting – under the rules of interpretation. Even if the Court is under a duty to apply the Vienna Convention rules, that does not mean that it must *observe* them, that is, interpret the law according to the Vienna Convention rules. A domestic criminal court is also authorised and duty-bound to apply the prohibition of murder, but the court is not required to refrain from committing murder. Courts are not bound by the prohibition of murder, only individual persons. Is it possible, then, that rules of interpretation are part of the procedural law, directly obligating tribunals or other organs of international law? Yes, but we need proof that either a customary norm or a general principle exists which obligates international tribunals to interpret in this manner,[113] which no one seems to claim.

On this reading, the rules of interpretation would potentially be capable of 'influencing' the meaning of that treaty norm *for and in the*

[111] Robert Walter, *Der Aufbau der Rechtsordnung: Eine rechtstheoretische Untersuchung auf Grundlage der Reinen Rechtslehre* (Graz: Leykam 1964) 61.

[112] See further Kammerhofer (2017b) note 83.

[113] Though cf. Article 3(2) [WTO] Understanding on rules and procedures governing the settlement of disputes 1994, which majority opinion interprets as obligating its decision-making organs to use the Vienna Convention rules.

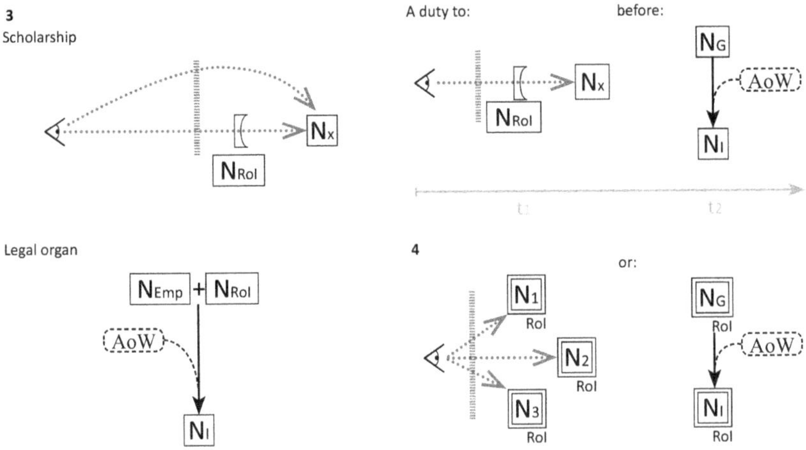

Figure 4.3 Reconstructing the rules of interpretation – Variants 3 and 4[114]

process of creating a judgment. The legal consequences of adopting this view are that the law 'interpreted' is not changed. However, because the rules of interpretation are part of the empowerment norm, the law regulating the creation of individual norms could be changed. The biggest potential factual consequence is that this inclusion has the capacity to consistently influence the outcome of arbitral awards.

4. *Rules of interpretation attach to norms.* Rules of interpretation can be constructed as attached to the treaty norms to be interpreted, rather than as obliging persons. We ask not who is obligated by the Vienna Convention rules but which norms are connected to the Vienna Convention rules. This special kind of norm[115] attaches itself to all treaty norms and potentially

[114] 3. Rules are part of the applicable law: while they are part of the realm of ideals, scholarship is free to disregard these rules and cognise the substantive norm only. Legal organs, however, in order to create individual norms, may have to apply the empowerment norm together with norms on interpretation. There may also be a duty (of the judge as subject of law) to cognise using the rules before the organ (the court) creates new law. 4. *In rem* reading: the rules of interpretation attach to norms and we can properly cognise only the combination of substantive and interpretation norms. Legal organs, however, would apply the general norm as combined with the rules of interpretation.

[115] This is somewhat similar to Klabbers' argument, mentioned in Section 4.2.1, that 'interpretation rules simply are of a different quality than ordinary norms of behaviour. Instead of guiding behaviour, rules on interpretation are methodological devices, suggesting to judges and other decision-makers how relevant legal instruments may be read.' Klabbers (2010) note 8 at 30–1, see also 29–30 fn 55.

determines their content. '[T]he legal norm [is] supplemented by the norm of interpretation',[116] the Vienna Convention rules apply on a truly *erga omnes* basis and the problem of the personal sphere of application cannot arise. One could compare this to the difference between obligations *in rem* (*dinglich*) and *in personam* (*obligatorisch*). Just as the civilian tradition sees property as not applicable to a (class of) legal person(s) or even *inter partes* but to the thing, the rules of interpretation would not depend on the Vienna Convention's contractual sphere of validity or on the subjects obligated by equivalent customary norms. The legal consequence of this view is even more potent than for the third variant: treaty-norms are (potentially) changed by combining them with rules of interpretation.

For legal theory, the *in rem–in personam* dichotomy is weak and not sustainable because the very idea of *in rem* is a didactic crutch:

> Every right to a thing is also a right vis-à-vis a person. If we . . . define the former as the right of an individual to have legal power over a certain thing, we fail to see that this right is nothing but the legal obligation by other individuals to tolerate these dispositions, ie not to hinder or impede them. The *ius in rem* is also a *ius in personam*. Of primary importance is the relationship between individuals, even in the case of the so-called law of property; it is the duty of specific behaviour vis-à-vis a specific other person. The relation to a thing is of secondary importance, because it only serves to clarify the primary relationship.[117]

This reification cannot eliminate the problem of the *ratione personae* dimension of rules of interpretation; Kelsen proposes to recast this dichotomy 'as distinction between relative and absolute reflexive rights. . . . If the behaviour refers to a specific thing, it is possible that all other individuals may have a duty to behave in a certain way vis-à-vis a certain other individual.'[118]

[116] 'dieser um die Auslegungsnorm ergänzte Rechtssatz' Merkl (1916) note 82 at 556 (*WRS* 1077, I/1 *MerklGS* 82).

[117] 'Auch das Recht an einer Sache ist ein Recht gegenüber Personen. Wenn man . . . jenes als das Recht eines Individuums definiert, über eine bestimmte Sache in irgendeiner Weise zu verfügen, so übersieht man, daß dieses Recht nur darin besteht, daß die anderen Individuen rechtlich verpflichtet sind, diese Verfügung zu dulden, das heißt: nicht zu hindern oder sonstwie zu beeinträchtigen; daß also das *jus in rem* zumindest auch ein *jus in personam* ist. Von primärer Bedeutung ist die Beziehung zwischen Menschen, die auch im Falle des sogenannten Sachenrechtes in der Pflicht zu einem bestimmten Verhalten gegenüber einem bestimmten anderen Menschen besteht. Die Beziehung zur Sache ist von sekundärer Bedeutung, da sie nur der näheren Bestimmung der primären Beziehung dient.' Kelsen (1960) note 82 at 135.

[118] 'als relative und absolute Reflexrechte unterschieden. . . . Wenn sich . . . das Verhalten auf eine bestimmte Sache bezieht, kann es die Pflicht aller anderen Individuen sein, sich

This concept also suffers from legal-doctrinal problems. Does the VCLT or an equivalent customary norm really establish an *in rem* duty? The Vienna Convention's restrictions on the personal sphere of application (Article 4: 'with regard to such States') and the phrase 'shall be interpreted' in Article 31(1) also hint at a personal obligation. Even if the Vienna Convention were to apply to treaties, the rules at issue prescribe a process to be followed (Article 31: 'a treaty shall be interpreted'), which again points to a duty to be performed by someone, not a particular status for the treaties at issue. While this is not an impossible reading of the Vienna Convention, it is highly improbable; one would probably expect more explicit regulation for a quasi *in rem* system.

We now have a clearer picture of what rules of interpretation can be. The 'applicative construction of law's meaning' is a duty of organs charged with applying the law, primarily of tribunals, in addition to their authorisation to decide cases. The idea is that before a tribunal takes a decision, there is a logically ordered, objective, rule-guided process called 'interpretation'. Interpretation in this sense is necessary for application and influences applicative decision-making. Because international lawyers are convinced that interpretation is determined by norms, it can no longer be about the understanding of texts.[119]

Is interpretation$_B$ a sustainable concept? Apart from the rather improbable *in rem* reading, neither the process nor the rules of interpretation can determine the meaning of treaties to be interpreted in an absolute sense. Each act of application is new and newly determinative for that case. Interpretation in its orthodox international legal sense, as conducted on the basis of the Vienna Convention rules, can potentially produce a substantive unification of acts of application and thus at least a semblance of unity in international investment law. 'Inasmuch as ... arbitral reasoning, if not binding, invites strong interpretive presumptions for subsequent interpretations, tribunals create the law by means of interpretation.'[120] On this view, systemic integration in Article 31(3)(c) VCLT as currently interpreted is the most potent tool (see Section 4.3).

One problem in particular assumes central importance. What the Vienna Convention rules require of us rather trivially depends on their

in bestimmter Weise gegenüber einem bestimmten Individuum zu verhalten.' Kelsen (1960) note 82 at 136–7.

[119] See also Linderfalk (2007) note 4 at 10.

[120] Catharine Titi, 'The Arbitrator as a Lawmaker: Jurisgenerative Processes in Investment Arbitration' 4 *Journal of World Investment & Trade* (2013) 829–51 at 831.

content. Orthodox scholarship believes that the Vienna Convention rules can be applied to their own interpretation. Yet this reasoning is circular: first, one cannot interpret the VCLT by applying the VCLT itself, which is not applicable to itself. Second, applying equivalent customary interpretation norms is problematic, because it is difficult to prove that they are applicable to the VCLT or what the content of customary law is. Finding out what the content of customary law is and finding the meaning of a legal text (hermeneutics) are categorically different enterprises.[121] Third, and crucially, rules of interpretation need to be interpreted too. This is not a trivial statement because, in order to cognise norms, the process of cognition must transcend the level of norms. 'Interpretation is obviously a tool of legal cognition, hence it cannot be an object of cognition at the same time.' Even when the law contains such rules, 'certain rules of interpretation necessarily exist beyond the law'.[122] At some point, the norms of interpretation *must* be ascertained: 'At the end of the day and despite all statutory rules of interpretation, statutes cannot ever prescribe how we should interpret a statute. Rather, this function is part of scholarship, which will always fashion even the most autocratic law into its own object [of cognition] and will thus subjugate this object . . ..'[123]

Yet another question is whether the Vienna Convention rules are as specific as claimed – or whether they really can produce more coherent or stable meanings for the treaty norms interpreted. Most would agree with Klabbers that 'seasoned members of [our] interpretive community can come to radically different interpretations of one and the same text and can do so by both relying on the rules on interpretation'; why do so few agree with his next statement that 'those rules themselves contribute little to any elucidation'?[124] The rules of interpretation do not restrict law-appliers but provide extraordinary freedom of decision-making.[125]

[121] *Pace* Merkouris (2015) note 3 at 165–300.

[122] 'Die Auslegung, der doch offenbar die Rolle eines Werkzeugs der Rechtserkenntnis zukommt, kann doch nicht gleichzeitig ein Gegenstand der Rechtserkenntnis sein'; '[die] Notwendigkeit des Bestandes außerrechtlicher Auslegungsregeln.' Merkl (1916–19) note 82 at col 586 (I/1 *MerklGS* 87) (emphasis removed).

[123] 'Wie ein Gesetz auszulegen sei, kann letzten Endes trotz allen gesetzlichen Auslegungsregeln nie das Gesetz selbst bestimmen, fällt vielmehr stets in die Kompetenz der das selbstherrlichste Recht zu ihrem Objekte wandelnden und damit dieses Objekt sich unterwerfenden . . . Wissenschaft.' Merkl (1916) note 82 at 556 (*WRS* 1077, I/1 *MerklGS* 82–3).

[124] Klabbers (2010) note 8 at 33.

[125] See Julius Stone, 'Fictitional Elements in Treaty Interpretation – A Study in the International Judicial Process' 1 *Sydney Law Review* (1953–5) 344–68 at 365.

4.3 Unity through Interpretation in Investment Law?

It is not surprising that writings on international investment law proceed on the basis of interpretation$_B$, the applicative construction of law's meaning. Equivocating 'understanding' with 'the process of adjudging' has changed our perception: 'all and sundry [insist] that articles 31 and 32 VCLT are to be applied'.[126] More importantly, however, many also believe that treaty interpretation is exclusively norm-governed and a legal process. After all, this seems to allow arbitral tribunals to give terms in IIAs such as 'indirect expropriation' concreteness and unity beyond the individual act of interpretation, without states having to amend their IIAs and without the law having to accord binding precedential status to arbitral awards. The residual innocence of the term 'interpretation', implying a mere process of understanding and shunning change, is (subconsciously) used to oversell the process and to hide attempts to change the law. Having established in Section 4.2 that international lawyers' ideas about and tools of treaty interpretation entail significant problems, this section will make the case that they persist when applied to investment law.

A range of interpretative tools, foremost 'systemic integration', has been used in writings on international investment law to construct this unity of meaning. In one sense, it is obvious that interpretation cannot fix the fragmentation of the sources of international investment law. Whatever 'interpretation' means, it cannot turn 3,300 IIAs into one. In another sense, however, the argument can be made that interpretative tools could cause arbitral decisions to become more predictable and unified. While, on the level of legal theory, the systemic integration of an IIA expropriation clause with customary expropriation law cannot create a detailed uniform content for the IIA provision, the phrase 'direct or indirect expropriation' could be seen as in fact multilateralised by its interpretation.[127]

This section will discuss the interpretative tools that may and have been or could be used to support a unification and concretisation of 'expropriation' in international investment law. This encompasses a whole range of qualifiers vis-à-vis a discussion of interpretation in investment law in general:[128]

[126] Klabbers (2010) note 8 at 33.

[127] Eg Stephan W Schill, *The Multilateralization of International Investment Law* (Cambridge: Cambridge University Press 2009) 278–361.

[128] Some important recent general works on the interpretation of international investment law are: Ascensio (2016) note 5; Gazzini (2016) note 5; Markert (2011) note 5; Mbengue

- We are looking at claims concerning interpretation, not concerning norm- or source-conflict. The conception of 'interpretation' at issue here is interpretation$_B$, as discussed in Section 4.2.
- While the ILC's 'crucible' approach,[129] where the various elements of interpretation work in concert and are inseparable, is generally accepted in doctrine, there is a tendency nonetheless to use some elements (for example systemic integration or *pari materia* interpretation) as separate tools or 'master-keys'.[130]
- This section is concerned with a description and critique of interpretative techniques which have been used as basis for claims to the construction of an overarching meaning from similar (but mostly non-identical) language in IIAs. The moniker 'unification or concretisation' can refer to a multitude of goals, such as a unity of norm-text (content), a unity of meaning, the predictability of (tribunal) concretisation of meaning or others.

Interpretative tools make sense only if we adopt what one could call the 'interpreter's perspective'. As discussed in Section 4.2, interpretation$_B$ generalises the situation of judges. The claim is that interpreters follow a rule-guided process to concretise general norms to give them meaning in the specific case. This process, in turn, is argued to be strictly and exclusively governed by the Vienna Convention rules; they tell us precisely which tools interpreters may employ and in which order. Hence the endless discussions about what 'the parties' in Article 31(3)(c) VCLT means; hence the uneasiness about *pari materia* interpretation, which seems so crucial to the interpretation of international investment law yet cannot be squared with the terms of Article 31 VCLT. However, as also discussed above, neither does the practice of interpreters conform to the Vienna Convention rules nor are deviations from the allegedly strict VCLT regime sanctioned.

(2016) note 5; Reinisch (2015) note 5; Rosentreter (2015) note 24; Trinh (2014) note 5; Weeramantry (2012) note 5.

129 International Law Commission, 'Draft Articles on the Law of Treaties with Commentaries' in International Law Commission, *Report of the International Law Commission on the Second Part of Its Seventeenth Session and on Its Eighteenth Session*, A/6309/Rev.1, 18 *Yearbook of the International Law Commission*, vol II (1966) 187–274 at 220.

130 Koskenniemi (2006) note 48 at 211 (para 420), referring to then-ILC member Xue Hanquin.

'The real issue', McLachlan reminds us, 'is in fact one of judicial method – namely how to go about deciding cases . . . This must be done largely through the process of interpretation.'[131] Yet even if interpretation$_B$ is guided by rules on legitimate argumentation, there are reasons to suspect that significant flexibility obtains which is incommensurable with another claim. From time to time, it is argued that the Vienna Convention rules are law which needs to be narrowly construed and used by all interpreters in the same way. International legal orthodoxy also indicates that there is no *numerus clausus* of tools, that the exact remit of the established tools is unclear and that the established law is not operable as absolute prescription of behaviour, only as convenient inspiration and *locus*, as a tool-box which interpreters may use in different ways. Even the ILC, advertising the tool of systemic integration in its 2006 *Fragmentation Report*, concedes that some 'matters must be left to the interpreter to decide in view of the situation. . . . when interpreting the treaties, the principle of integration should be borne in mind'.[132] The majority of international lawyers would probably agree that interpretation is 'an exercise in competent legal argument' which 'give[s] the text [to be interpreted] a justifiable meaning'.[133] In the final instance, are the tools really a matter of legal norms or are they not rather an 'apt account of competent public reasoning by lawyers and tribunals'?[134] This, in turn, makes the choice of tools a flexible issue of legitimacy for the interpretative process, rather than of legality.

It therefore looks like the real question is on a meta-level: how is it decided which tools are legitimate; what is the 'source' of the tools which are legitimately part of the interpretative tool-box? The formal sources of law alone cannot answer this question; we subconsciously measure the legitimacy of a tool in different terms. On the interpreter's perspective, the use of interpretative tools is determined by the answer to the question 'What sources can or may interpreters use in constructing meaning before deciding?' The criteria are thus not primarily legal: even if the

[131] Campbell McLachlan, 'Is There an Evolving Customary International Law on Investment?' 31 *ICSID Review* (2016) 257–69 at 264; see also Duncan French, 'Treaty Interpretation and the Incorporation of Extraneous Legal Rules' 55 *International and Comparative Law Quarterly* (2006) 281–314 at 286–7.

[132] Koskenniemi (2006) note 48 at 211 (para 419); see also Merkouris (2015) note 3 at 6.

[133] Koskenniemi (2006) note 48 at 234 (paras 465, 464).

[134] Koskenniemi (2006) note 48 at 233 (para 464).

Vienna Convention rules were to apply to all interpreters, the standard actually set by peers (scholars and practitioners) is more relevant in determining what is actually seen as good practice. This standard, however, is extraordinarily flexible; in contrast to recent attempts to lock in and strictly interpret the rules of interpretation in international (investment) law,[135] the connection of tools to the rules is rather looser than imagined.

> It is no surprise that . . . one can hear increasingly vocal affirmations of the general rules on interpretation as embodied in the Vienna Convention, and increasingly urgent admonitions that departures from those rules are not to be recommended. This suggests a deep paradox though: a quest for certainty in limits by invoking the very rules which allow for an unlimited variety of factors to be taken into account.[136]

Rather than interpreters being hemmed in by the Vienna Convention method, which gives a closed number of closely circumscribed tools, interpreters will actually use a wide range of tools at their disposal. Interpreters are not sanctioned when they do not comply with the Vienna Convention, but they are when they go beyond what is acceptable to their peers. Interpretation$_{B}$ in international law is not about specific prescribed behaviour by interpreters but about a framework of acceptable practices. On the interpreter's perspective, actors do not cognise meaning(s) using tools. Rather, *interpreters use a variety of sources which are acceptable to peers in order to 'justify' the interpreter's insertion of meaning into a treaty norm*. This happens relatively independently of any 'true' linguistic meaning-content of the treaty terms. It is also relatively unbounded by codified rules of interpretation – the sources and tools are accepted by peers. Consequently, the influence which interpretation$_{B}$ wields through these tools for the unification of international investment law is factual, and not in any sense determinative of the norms which are thus being interpreted.

Yet even if the sources or tools used are determined by a factual process, one limit does seem to be unavoidable: that the meaning(s) are somehow 'those of the norm' to be interpreted. Even if the interpreter 'constructs' or 'gives' meaning, rather than merely 'finding' it within the norm, interpretation will at the end of the day have to be in some way connected with the text; it will have to be 'of the text', rather than freely invented. For example, some warn us in connection with the systemic

[135] Eg Trinh (2014) note 5.
[136] Klabbers (2007) note 69 at 160–1.

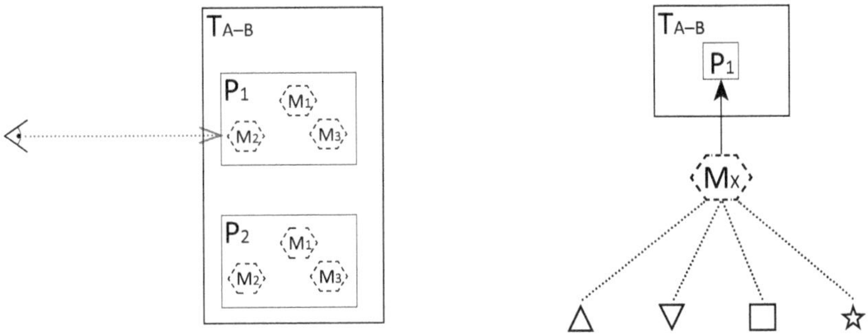

Figure 4.4 The interpreter's perspective[137]

integration debate: is not the point of treaty interpretation to interpret the treaty, not 'external factors'?[138] This one of the problems engendered by divorcing interpretation$_B$ from interpretation$_A$. The further the justificatory construction of law by interpreters is separated from the epistemic, hermeneutic and linguistic cognition of meaning-content, the more likely it is that this pragmatic function goes beyond the function of 'finding out what the treaty says'. Systemic integration and *pari materia* interpretation, the two tools which most promise to allow us to construct the concreteness and unity of international investment law, are also most likely to endanger the last remaining vestiges of the hermeneutic function in interpretation$_B$.

4.3.1 *The Theoretical Foundations of Systemic Integration*

A discussion of the tools, the sources of meaning-generation and of the specific technique in which these sources are used may help to clarify the theoretical problems which they engender. Foremost among these tools is systemic integration, allegedly expressed in Article 31(3)(c) VCLT, which has become popular among scholars and is possibly the interpretative tool with the greatest potency for unification.[139] Much has been written on systemic integration since the ICJ's 2003 judgment in *Oil*

[137] Interpretation could be seen as cognising meanings (M_{1-3}) in a provision (P_{1-2}) of a (eg bilateral) treaty (T_{A-B}). On the interpreter's perspective, however, the interpreter constructs a meaning (for the specific occasion/case), drawing on a range of sources, and projects it onto the treaty provision at issue.

[138] Rosentreter (2015) note 24 at 243; see also eg Gardiner (2008) note 2 at 252; Gazzini (2016) note 5 at 213–17.

[139] Philippe Sands, 'Treaty, Custom and the Cross-Fertilization of International Law' 1 *Yale Human Rights & Development Law Journal* (1999) 85–105 at 87.

Platforms, Campbell McLachlan's path-breaking 2005 article[140] and a central chapter of the *Fragmentation Report*.[141] It has super-charged the concept's advance as remedy to a serious ailment that seemed to have befallen international law: fragmentation. Klabbers felt able to conclude in 2007 that, with a new lease of life, Article 31(3)(c) VCLT could be used to 'keep the system intact' because 'fragmentation is now being fought not by closing off the system, but rather by radically opening it up. . . . [Article 31(3)(c)] embraces externalities wholeheartedly.'[142]

The two evergreen questions in systemic integration – 'the relevant rules' and 'the parties' – will not be discussed here because the language of Article 31(3)(c) VCLT is not relevant to us here. The principle of systemic integration is broader than the treaty norm; equally, even if the Vienna Convention rules are customary law, the customary norm will not be word-for-word identical to the treaty provisions (Section 4.2.1). The focus, instead, will be on a range of problems connected to concretisation and unification, transcending both the text of Article 31(3)(c) VCLT and the concept of systemic integration.

What is the general idea behind 'systemic integration'? McLachlan expresses a seemingly self-evident premise of treaty-making and treaty-interpretation: 'treaties . . . are predicated for their existence and operation on being part of the international law system. As such, they must be "applied and interpreted against the background of the general principles of international law".'[143] At the basis of this concept lies a notion of rational law (*Vernunftrecht*) which has been thoroughly decontextualised and thus robbed of its original philosophical foundation. It is expressed as presumption: 'international law is better understood as a normative system . . . rather than as rules'.[144] Law is seen as a rational unity, a conscious creation of interconnected argument and thought, poured into normative form, rather than an 'arbitrary' (*willkürlich*)[145] assemblage of norms united only by the

140 *Oil Platforms (Islamic Republic of Iran* v. *United States of America)*, Merits, Judgment of 6 November 2003, ICJ Reports (2003) 161 at 182 (para 41); McLachlan (2005) note 49.

141 Koskenniemi (2006) note 48 at 206–44 (paras 410–80).

142 Klabbers (2007) note 69 at 159.

143 McLachlan (2005) note 49 at 280 (emphasis removed), quoting McNair (1961) note 46 at 466; see also Sands (1999) note 139 at 95.

144 McLachlan (2005) note 49 at 282.

145 The etymology of the German word 'willkürlich' points to its original meaning, as 'Kür' is an act of choice or decision (or creation), whereas 'Wille' is will, ie creation by act of will. The English word 'arbitrary' has similar origins: an arbiter is the arbitrator or judge, one whose will is decisive; the Latin *arbitrium* is the judgment or decision more generally.

'happenstance' of human creation. Another foundational move is to employ an *e contrario* argument: 'investment treaties are not self-contained regimes. The meaning of their operative terms must therefore be informed by reference to the relevant rules.'[146] However, the denial of the idea of self-contained regimes does not imply acceptance of a coherent system of meaning;[147] it is not an exclusive disjunction. Neither argument is sustainable. The premise of the systemic integration argument engenders, McLachlan argues, two substantive consequences:

> [T]he principle of systemic integration ... may be articulated as a presumption with both positive and negative aspects: (a) negatively that, in entering into treaty obligations, the parties intend not to act inconsistently with generally recognised principles of international law or with previous treaty obligations towards third states; and, (b) positively that the parties are to taken 'to refer to general principles of international law for all questions which [the treaty] does not itself resolve in express terms or in a different way' ....[148]

Understood as presumptions, they are weak, for why should we presume international law to have this content? How could a 'presumption' possibly prevail over legal norms? Yet recast in terms of the rules of interpretation$_B$, the argument fits in well. In effect, systemic integration adds to the interpreter's duties: if no convincing contrary indications present themselves – and some believe that it is difficult to see how any could – interpreters have to interpret any treaty norm to conform to other law and to draw information for any vague term from general international law.[149] Three closely linked theoretical questions emerge at this point: how does systemic integration relate to internality of meaning versus external sources; how does the process of 'taking into account' work and how does it relate to customary law?

Systemic integration occurs in field-internal and external variants: the first takes into account elements outside the treaty but within its sub-field of international law; the second takes elements that are not only external to the treaty but hail from a different sub-field. In international investment law, a field-internal systemic integration uses other parts of

146 McLachlan (2007) note 5 at 15 (quotation mark removed).
147 Wälde (2009) note 5 at 770: 'Treaties are not a legal island cut off from everywhere else, but they are embedded in international law. But that does not allow us to deny that a treaty, bilateral or multilateral, creates a legal world of its own.'
148 McLachlan (2005) note 49 at 311(emphasis removed); see also Koskenniemi (2006) note 48 at 234 (para 465); McLachlan (2007) note 5 at 15; McLachlan (2008) note 5 at 372–4.
149 See Sands (1999) note 139 at 104.

investment law, yet, on a narrow construction of Article 31(3)(c) VCLT, other investment treaties are usually excluded. No matter how the phrase 'applicable in the relations between the parties' is understood, the (states) parties will typically only share one IIA. A reference to customary international investment law is preferred: 'light may be shed on the meaning of the terms used by reference to customary international law'.[150] 'In some core areas of investment law, like in the field of expropriation, tribunals may rely on general international law in order to interpret undefined IIA provisions that have a recognised meaning.'[151] This type of claim has featured in prominent arbitral awards,[152] for example in *Saluka* with respect to the right to regulate.[153] These claims presume that the IIA's use of a term implies a reference to a customary investment norm rather than non-connection or contracting out and that there is such a recognised meaning to refer to (see Sections 4.3.2–4.3.3).

The other variant uses external rules from sub-fields outside investment law, such as human rights or international economic law. In Wälde's acerbic words:

> The second role of Article 31(3)(c) is not conservative, but 'progressive'. It is used at present mainly by scholars to 'de-fragment' the various strands of international law by linking them through an interpretation that should create more 'harmony' where before more 'fragmentation' or chaos ruled. . . . It rests on the idea that 'fragmentation' in international law is bad and needs to be replaced with greater harmony.[154]

This distinction may seem crucial if we wish to distinguish true systemic integration – based on the idea that international law is a rational system of rules across various sub-fields – from the interpretative *renvoi* to customary law to clarify vague terms. But that is not the whole story, or, rather, the story actually does not depend on the internal–external distinction. Gazzini reformulates the question in a way which helps to guide our understanding in the right direction:

150 McLachlan (2007) note 5 at 222.

151 Reinisch (2015) note 5 at 389.

152 Eg *European Media Ventures* v. *Czech Republic*, UNCITRAL, Partial Award on Liability of 8 July 2009, para 47.

153 *Saluka Investments* v. *Czech Republic*, UNCITRAL, Partial Award of 17 March 2006, para 254; see also, echoing *Saluka*: *Marfin Investment Group Holdings S.A., Alexandros Bakatselos and others* v. *Republic of Cyprus*, ICSID, ARB/13/27, Award of 26 July 2018, para 827.

154 Wälde (2009) note 5 at 772–3.

> Article 31(3)(c) essentially performs two main functions in the interpretative process. The first function is to contribute to defining the meaning of any given term or provision. The interpreter has to take into account the relevant extraneous international rules in order (a) to clarify the meaning of a term or provision; (b) to inform a choice between two or more possible interpretations; or (c) to fill the gap in the treaty to be interpreted. … The second function … has systemic character. The interpreter is expected, indeed required, to ensure that the interpretation of any given provision is consistent with the international rights and obligations of the parties stemming from other sources …[155]

The two interpretative sub-functions are based on two qualitatively different arguments and perhaps also on two different types of connection between norms. They are best recast as *reference* and *coherence.* The first argument, reference, is based on the argument that a treaty already contains a connection of some sort to other norms or that we ought to interpret treaties as drawing on those other norms. The underlying assumption is that the norm to be interpreted has ceded ground to another norm: when an IIA uses an established and/or vague term ('expropriation'), *it* is giving over to customary law: Treaty $Norm_1$ is Customary $Norm_1$. Alternatively, the rules of $interpretation_B$ require or allow the interpreter to interpret TN_1 as ceding ground to CN_1. It is an explicative *renvoi*, an interpretation importing meaning from other norms, because these explicate the norm to be interpreted. But how does reference differ from a technical incorporation of customary law (Section 4.3.2)? Interpretative references of this sort are also very difficult to distinguish from an interpretation of generic terms, special meaning and even of 'ordinary' meaning (Section 4.3.4).

The second argument, coherence, is exactly the opposite, as it is based on the idea of non-reference. The norm to be interpreted is not explicated by and does not contain a reference to or incorporate the source-norms, but a substantive coherence between the different norms exists nonetheless. When an IIA uses a term like 'expropriation', this norm is taken not to be incoherent with the alleged customary right to regulate or with international environmental law. The rules of $interpretation_B$ require the interpreter to interpret the treaty norm as being in conformity with the external norm: an interpretation to achieve conformity. The norm is remade or is reinterpreted in such a fashion as not to contradict the external source. This is a well-known methodological ploy in

[155] Gazzini (2016) note 5 at 211–12; Gardiner (2008) note 2 at 284–5.

constitutional and European law: an interpretation conforming to the constitution, to European or to international law.[156]

Wälde's characterisation of the two *modi* as 'conservative' and 'progressive' is an important insight:

> The reference ... can be used in a 'conservative' way by arguing that treaties should in case of doubt be interpreted in light of earlier customary law ... ; [it] ... can also be used (as it seems to have been primarily intended) in a 'progressive' way by modernizing a treaty's meaning in light of subsequent, more modern terms of international law and other treaties. That would mean ... 'forwards interpretation' using, for example, subsequent investment treaties, customary law as it evolves under the impact of modern concurrent treaty practice, and developments in relevant but outside areas of international law, for example, trade, environment, climate change, and human rights.[157]

The justifications behind both are assailable and are assailable in such a symmetrical fashion that we are strongly reminded of Martti Koskenniemi's duality of apology and utopia.[158]

1. *Apology: Recourse to party intentions*. Many, but by no means all, of those who favour reference use the traditional apologists' argument: such a *renvoi* is true to the intentions of the parties and treaty interpretation is ultimately about finding party intentions. It was common in the traditional debate on treaty interpretation to simultaneously acknowledge the equality of the three 'schools of interpretation' and to argue that *in the last instance* all interpretation has the goal of finding the (common) intention of the treaty parties. Humphrey Waldock's 1964 *Third Report on the Law of Treaties* is a *locus classicus*. He admits that 'none of these approaches [textual, subjective and teleological] is exclusively the correct one',[159] only to argue in the next paragraph that 'doctrinal differences concerning the methods of interpretation have tended to weaken the significance of the text *as the expression of the will of the parties*'.[160] The

[156] See eg Clemens Höpfner, *Die systemkonforme Auslegung: Zur Auflösung einfachgesetzlicher, verfassungsrechtlicher und europarechtlicher Widersprüche im Recht* (Tubingen: Mohr 2008).

[157] Wälde (2009) note 5 at 748.

[158] Martti Koskenniemi, *From Apology to Utopia: The Structure of International Legal Argument* (1989, reissued: Cambridge: Cambridge University Press 2005) 59, on treaty interpretation in particular 333–45.

[159] Humphrey Waldock, 'Third Report on the Law of Treaties', A.CN.4/167, A.CN.4/167/Add.1-3, 16 *Yearbook of the International Law Commission*, vol II (1964), 5–65 at 54.

[160] Waldock (1964) note 159 at 54 (emphasis added).

proposed Article 70 'takes as the basic rule of treaty interpretation the primacy of the text *as evidence of the intentions of the parties*'. The famous passage immediately following – 'the text must be presumed to be the authentic expression of the intentions of the parties'[161] – is generally treated as proving the relative primacy of the text, but, in the end, it cements the absolute primacy of common party intent. If the ultimate goal of the interpretative exercise is to find the intention of the parties, it does not matter whether the text is the only authentic expression of this intention. This stance is prevalent in today's writings on international investment law: 'Such an 'objective' interpretative approach does not ask for the intent of the parties but seeks to uncover the intent of the provision. A reflection on the intent of the parties only takes place as a subsidiary means of interpretation because the true intent of the parties should find its expression in the text of the treaty itself.'[162]

The key lies in the difference between the proofs and the object of interpretation: the text is the best possible but not the only expression of party intent.[163] Arnold McNair summarises this viewpoint, namely that tribunals have a 'duty of giving effect to the expressed intention of the parties, that is, their intention as expressed in the words used by them in the light of the surrounding circumstances'.[164] The relevance of the party-intentions argument for systemic integration is twofold. Either it is the source of legitimacy for interpretative tools – 'the only reason why a tool is legitimate is because it helps us to find the party intentions' – or it is the proper or ultimate source of *renvoi*. The proper limit of systemic integration is uncovering party intentions, because that is the ultimate goal of all interpretation.

That 'the parties to a treaty ultimately control its interpretation'[165] has been called the 'juridically natural view'[166] which is generally accepted

[161] Waldock (1964) note 159 at 56 (emphasis added).

[162] Markert (2011) note 5 at 58; see also Villiger (2011) note 8 at 109; Andrew D Mitchell, James Munro, 'Someone Else's Deal: Interpreting International Investment Agreements in the Light of Third-Party Agreements' 28 *European Journal of International Law* (2017) 669–95 at 678–9.

[163] Eg Gardiner (2008) note 2 at 6, 8; ILC (1966) note 129 at 218, 220; McLachlan (2008) note 5 at 390–1.

[164] McNair (1961) note 46 at 365.

[165] Gardiner (2008) note 2 at 109.

[166] Gerald G Fitzmaurice, 'The Law and Procedure of the International Court of Justice: Treaty Interpretation and Certain Other Treaty Points' 28 *British Year Book of International Law 1951* (1952) 1–28 at 3.

and which 'no one seriously denies'.[167] A first objection to this concept[168] is about the nature of 'the intentions' of the parties. The treaty text is signed, its terms are agreed upon and the parties promise to abide by the text, not by shared intentions.[169] On many issues, agreement may not have gone beyond the text and no common intention may exist, for example where dilatory compromise formulas[170] were used. '[T]reaties . . . are often a political substitute for rather than a legal expression of the agreement of the parties',[171] yet, if '[a] treaty is a disagreement reduced to writing',[172] how can this fleeting, ephemeral, this very contingent element be the ultimate goal of treaty interpretation?

Even Hersch Lauterpacht, while acknowledging that 'common intention, if it can be ascertained, is the governing factor', argues that it may be possible that, 'in relation to the particular provision [to be interpreted], there is no such common intention'.[173] He warns against seeking to cut the Gordian knot by way of presumptions. (One is tempted to add: such as the ones claimed for systemic integration.) 'To presume – to imply – intention is to predicate that intention does not matter.'[174] For him, the absence of actual intentions is less important because the treaty is part of a system in the substantive rationalist sense: 'the treaty . . . is more than the expression of the intention of the parties. It is part of international law and must be interpreted against the general background of its rules and principles.'[175]

The second objection is that the treaty norm is the object to be interpreted and the (common) intention of the parties is not the norm. Agreement by the parties on (a common act of will concerning) more than the treaty text is not necessary to create treaty law. An IIA, for example, becomes law when agreement on words like 'expropriation' is reached. No common intentions going beyond the text are required.

167 Gerald G Fitzmaurice, 'The Law and Procedure of the International Court of Justice 1951–4: Treaty Interpretation and Other Treaty Points' 33 *British Year Book of International Law 1957* (1958) 203–93 at 204.

168 This argument is loosely based on Kammerhofer (2010d) note 8 at 88–92, 106–13.

169 Bernhardt (1963) note 9 at 31.

170 See Carl Schmitt, *Verfassungslehre* [1928] (9th edn, Berlin: Duncker & Humblot, 2003) 31–2.

171 Hersch Lauterpacht, 'Restrictive Interpretation and the Principle of Effectiveness in the Interpretation of Treaties' 26 *British Year Book of International Law* (1949) 48–85 at 82.

172 Philip Allott, 'The Concept of International Law' 10 *European Journal of International Law* (1999) 31–50 at 43.

173 Lauterpacht (1949) note 171 at 76.

174 Lauterpacht (1949) note 171 at 75.

175 Lauterpacht (1949) note 171 at 76.

Because positive norms are the sense of an act of will,[176] which for international treaty law could be transposed as 'common intentions', the aim of interpretation could be seen as directed at that will.[177] However, legislative will – in our case, the will of treaty-makers – is merely the impetus that allows positive norms to be created. An act of will (only) turns a norm into a positive norm:

> The sense of an act of will directed at the behaviour of another is the *meaning* of the expression of my act of will. . . . The person giving the order expects that the recipient understands the order, ie that he understands the sense of the statement of the person giving the order as an order, that he knows: 1. that he ought to behave in a certain way; and 2. how he ought to behave, what he should do or omit to do. The former is the sense, the latter is the content of the act of will constituting the order.[178]

Common party intention regarding possible content beyond the treaty text does not constitute the common act of will required to create the treaty. Even if the content of a treaty were to go beyond its text, the treaty to be interpreted is not the sum-total of party intentions. After all, orthodoxy insists that interpretation must not go beyond the boundaries of the treaty. 'The extent of the international law inquiry is confined to the context of the treaty provision, aiding its interpretation and, ultimately, its application.'[179]

2. *Utopia: International law as a coherent system.* The utopian counterpart may seem less pertinent to investment law, but that is not the case. Coherence by way of system-conformity does not respect subdisciplinary boundaries: it does not matter whether 'expropriation' is made coherent with the right to life or a right to regulate. For many proponents of systemic integration, its foundation is that international law is a 'system', whatever 'system' means. This idea is, inter alia, propagated by Koskenniemi in the 2005 postscript to *From Apology to Utopia*:

176 Hans Kelsen, *Allgemeine Theorie der Normen* (Vienna: Manz 1979) 4, 221 n 1: 'Sinn eines Willensaktes'.

177 Heinz Mayer, 'Die Interpretationstheorie der Reinen Rechtslehre' in Robert Walter (ed.), *Schwerpunkte der Reinen Rechtslehre* (Vienna: Manz 1992) 61–70 at 68.

178 'Der Sinn meines auf das Verhalten eines anderen gerichteten Willensaktes ist das, was ich mit dem Ausdruck meines Willensaktes meine. . . . Der Befehlsgeber erwartet, daß der Befehlsadressat den Befehl versteht, d.h., daß er den Sinn der Äußerung des Befehlsgebers als Befehl versteht, das heißt, daß er weiß: 1. daß er sich in bestimmter Weise verhalten soll; und 2. wie er sich verhalten soll, was er tun soll oder unterlassen soll. Das eine ist der Sinn, das andere der Inhalt des einen Befehl darstellenden Willensaktes.' Kelsen (1979) note 176 at 25–6.

179 Gardiner (2008) note 2 at 287, see also 266, 286.

'[the book] starts from the uncontroversial assumption that international law is not just some haphazard collection of rules and principles'. 'The sense that international law forms a "system" is . . . deeply embedded in legal thinking.'[180] When less theory-focused international lawyers propound the rational unity argument, it is, however, robbed of its philosophical grounding and lacks elaboration. Hence, we need to know what the concept of a 'legal system' does *not* properly denote before very briefly sketching its lineage and critiquing it.

The theoretical approach on which this book is premised, the Pure Theory of Law, provides a framework for the structural analysis of legal orders.[181] On that basis, it is crucial to distinguish between legal systems and legal orders, despite the widespread interchangeable use of these terms. When it is argued that international law is a system, not a haphazard assemblage of rules, and that the necessity for systemic interpretation arises from this foundation, it is a rationalist argument, even if unacknowledged or subconscious. In particular, it does not refer to system-building in the manner of HLA Hart or Kelsen.[182] The idea of a legal *system* in essentialist terms is that law is part of a grand plan, that it is a meaningful, sensible and rational construct or that it should be fashioned into one by the law's 'operators', such as judges. This does not merely run counter to the idea that law is source-based; it is antithetical to the nature of positive law. If international law is made up of norms created by human will, if it is positive law (*positus* – set/put into the world), then something can be valid as a norm ('exist') only by virtue of being traced back to a source-norm.[183] Because the 'source' empowers law-creation and empowerment is a necessary condition of the lower norm coming into 'being', a relationship between the source and its product is established.[184] There is only one necessary connection

[180] Koskenniemi (1989/2005) note 158 at 567, 567 fn 4. He is aware, of course, that 'systemic theories, too, are an aspect of international legal discourse, amenable to the play of utopia and apology'.

[181] See eg Kammerhofer (2017b) note 83.

[182] Though see Jean d'Aspremont, 'The International Court of Justice and the Irony of System-Design' 18 *Journal of International Dispute Settlement* (2017) 366–87 – his disavowal of an international legal 'system' seems to include both rationalist arguments as well as positivist analytical approaches.

[183] Kelsen (1960) note 82 at 196.

[184] Adolf Julius Merkl, *Die Lehre von der Rechtskraft, entwickelt aus dem Rechtsbegriff: Eine rechtstheoretische Untersuchung* (Leipzig: Deuticke 1923) 196, 216; Adolf Julius Merkl, 'Prolegomena einer Theorie des rechtlichen Stufenbaues' in Alfred Verdross (ed.), *Gesellschaft, Staat und Recht: Festschrift für Hans Kelsen zum 50. Geburtstag* (Vienna:

between norms, only one that is inherent in their nature as norms and without which they would not 'exist': the 'validity-relationship'. On orthodox terms: international law must heed the formal sources of law. In contradistinction to a legal *system*, a legal *order* is based on sources, not on rational-substantive coherence of content.[185]

It is important to distinguish between the essentialist concept of legal systems – the law *is* a system – and the idea that the analysis of the legal order by scholarship is a system reflecting their findings. Only the first assumption is relevant in this connection. Interpreters in the orthodox sense are not scholars committed to rational reconstruction. Rational reconstruction does not mean constructing a rationally ordered law but a commitment to rationally reconstructing the law in all its irrationality and arbitrariness – warts and all (see Chapter 5). This obtains despite the inevitable influence of method on our perception of the object.

Another distinction is between the solution of a norm-conflict and a postulate to interpret while avoiding conflictual outcomes. The issue here is not whether system-coherent interpretation results in the derogation of a norm;[186] actual system-coherence of the norms of a legal order does not need to be established. Interpretation$_B$ as rule-guided process to give general norms meaning in the specific case merely implies a duty to interpret *as if it were* coherent, which works irrespective of whether there is a coherence of norms and whether interpreters are empowered to create this coherence.

A reasonable assumption is that international lawyers do not directly rely on legal-philosophical approaches which provide 'system'-building with a rationalist or teleological foundation. One such tradition is civilian theory, remaining popular (in a similarly truncated fashion) in private law scholarship in the German-speaking countries.[187] It does not matter for our present purpose, however, to which of these rational-systemic traditions international legal writings are closest, whether, for example,

Springer 1931) 252–94 (*WRS* 1311–61, I/1 MerklGS 437–92) at 273 (*WRS* 1336, I/1 *MerklGS* 464–5); Kelsen (1979) note 176 at 82; Rainer Lippold, *Recht und Ordnung: Statik und Dynamik der Rechtsordnung* (Vienna: Manz 2000) 382; Jürgen Behrend, *Untersuchungen zur Stufenbaulehre Adolf Merkls und Hans Kelsens* (Berlin: Duncker & Humblot 1977) 32.

185 Kelsen (1960) note 82 at 228; Merkl (1931) note 184 at 256–7 (*WRS* 1316–17, I/1 *MerklGS* 443).

186 See Kammerhofer (2010d) note 8 at 87–138, 139–94, particularly 172–5 (criticising the intermingling of norm-conflict resolution and interpretation).

187 For an overview of the current German debate, focusing heavily on Karl Larenz, Claus-Wilhelm Canaris, Josef Esser and Bernd Rüthers, see Höpfner (2008) note 156.

the jurisprudence of interests (*Interessenjurisprudenz*) has won the day. It does not matter whether Claus-Wilhelm Canaris's reading of the *Rechtsidee* is truly determinative of the 'internal system of the law'. It does not matter whether a system emerges as a deductive cascade of concepts or as a result of inductive reasoning from the many *teloi* in specific rules. Or, rather, it would matter a great deal, but only if there were some meaningful connection left between these traditions and the modern international legal mainstream. Orthodox doctrinal writings often use popularised versions of legal theoretical arguments: yes, we are positivists, but not consistently so; we see international law as a system in order to demand systemic coherence in interpretation, but we want to make do without the rationalist superstructure. But this *Vulgata* cannot work: not accepting the consequences that follow from adopting a theory makes one extraordinarily vulnerable to charges of incoherence.

So it is here. As an expression of their 'default positivism',[188] orthodox lawyers insist that, whatever interpretation is, it should not go beyond the boundaries of the law interpreted. A true natural lawyer has little incentive to see the treaty(-text) as binding, because for this approach, the system alone counts and, where necessary, certain legal texts can be disregarded. The orthodoxy would probably not consciously go beyond the law because they do not adhere to the extreme rationalist position. Yet if one wants to achieve systemic coherence, one must be willing to disregard the positive law, for it is trivially true that the positive legal material is not coherent. Too many people have worked on it for too long a time. If we want to stay true to the positive law, however, systemic coherence is virtually impossible to achieve.

Both foundational strategies – party intent and law as a system – insist that the interpreted norms themselves conform to the rest of the system or that the parties intended them to refer to the other rules of international law. Both believe that interpretation is about the law and does not create or destroy the rules themselves. In both cases, the processes are not as simple as proponents make them out to be. Yet if interpretation$_B$ imparts meaning on norm-texts, rather than merely being an exercise in cognition, are limits of this nature relevant?[189] Further, if this exercise is

188 Jörg Kammerhofer, 'International Legal Positivist Research Methods' in Rossana Deplano, Nicholas Tsagourias (eds.), *Research Methods in International Law: A Handbook* (Cheltenham: Edward Elgar in press), available at: ssrn.com/abstract=3503295, section 2.

189 McLachlan (2016) note 131 at 268.

truly about interpretation$_B$ (as judicial reasoning), it is not relevant whether the norm 'contains' the meanings ascribed to it, only whether the method used is accepted by peers. Hearing the word 'interpretation', we may believe that all we are doing is finding out what the law says. Interpretation$_B$, in contrast, is conceived as importing meaning-content: the norm-text is not its meanings and meanings are generated. What difference does it then make where this external information comes from?

4.3.2 *Systemic Integration and Customary International Law*

It seems to be important from where and in what manner 'externalities' are incorporated in the interpretative process. The focus of the debate on systemic integration lies on the role and limits of customary international law; the modalities and problems of integrating custom certainly are the most talked-about. While this issue will be discussed here, it is not as central to the question of the legitimate sources of meaning-content in interpretation$_B$ as the vigorous debate suggests (see Section 4.3.3).

What does 'taking into account' mean, how does the process of systemic integration work and how does interpretation 'in light of' other rules differ from other mechanisms? International legal writings have focused on the (important) problems of differentiation and have largely ignored the crucial issue of process. The exact nature of the process of systemic integration as part of interpretation$_B$ is very much under-researched. One recurring *topos* is that it is an 'obligation to consider other rules'.[190] '[T]hat the customary norm "shall be taken into account" ... means that in interpreting the customary norm an adjudicatory body is not entitled to exercise discretion. It must "take account"'[191] of it. Another is that this process is part of the contextual sub-rule: 'what does this reference to "relevant rules of international law" mean? Every treaty provision must be read not only in its own context, but in the wider context of general international law.'[192] In this manner, systemic integration is itself integrated in the traditional theory of legal interpretation. The third point raised is that the phrase 'take account' in Article 38(3)(c) VCLT 'is stronger than "take into consideration" but weaker than "apply"'.[193] This is echoed in a much-cited passage of

[190] French (2006) note 131 at 301 (two sets of quotation marks removed).
[191] Sands (1999) note 139 at 103.
[192] Ian Sinclair, *The Vienna Convention on the Law of Treaties* (2nd edn, Manchester: Manchester University Press 1984) 139.
[193] Sands (1999) note 139 at 103.

Waldock's 1964 *Third Report*: 'The term "take account of" is used rather than "be subject to" or any similar term because, *if the rule is formulated as one of interpretation*, it seems better ... to use words that leave open the results of the interpretation.'[194]

These words invite speculation that the rule need not have been 'formulated as one of interpretation' and could potentially serve as a meta-rule of norm-conflict resolution as well. The tension between wishing to ensure the effectiveness of systemic integration, on the one hand, and the fact that nominally it is still part of interpretation as meaning-ascertainment, on the other, is palpable. The tension is usually eased by writers pointing out how weak the phrase 'take account of' is and that the result of interpretation is open. Modern writers, beginning with Sands, prefer to call it a presumption: 'the right approach is to apply a presumption that [eg] the WTO system ... is to be interpreted consistently with general international law'.[195] Other statements on the nature and functioning of 'taking into account' highlight the differences vis-à-vis other operations, such as Orakhelashvili for whom the goal is 'not to defer the provisions being interpreted to the scope and effect of those "relevant rules", but to clarify the content of the former by referring to the latter'.[196] Duncan French counters:

> However, 'clarification' is an amorphous term with various shades of meaning. ... in seeking clarification of a treaty provision through another rule of international law, a tribunal must necessarily 'clarify' what it considers to be the meaning of that second rule of law. Clarification through the use of other rules of international law is, therefore, clearly not an innocuous aspect of the 'ordinary' treaty interpretation process.[197]

This is echoed by Orakhelashvili: 'General rules of international law under Article 31(3)(c) are an interpretative tool to aid the interpretation of a treaty, as opposed to the interpretation of extraneous rules as such.'[198] The distinction is necessary because the residual innocuousness of interpretation as meaning-ascertainment is retained. Even systemic

[194] Waldock (1964) note 159 at 61 (emphasis added); see also Gazzini (2016) note 5 at 213–14.

[195] Sands (1999) note 139 at 104.

[196] Alexander Orakhelashvili, 'Restrictive Interpretation of Human Rights Treaties in the Recent Jurisprudence of the European Court of Human Rights' 14 *European Journal of International Law* (2003) 529–68 at 537; see also Gazzini (2016) note 5 at 213; French (2006) note 131 at 282.

[197] French (2006) note 131 at 282–3.

[198] Orakhelashvili (2008) note 4 at 366.

integration's proponents warn that its function is not 'to import into the treaty to be interpreted any legal elements from other treaties, and even less to alter the mandate of the tribunal';[199] 'there can be no question of the customary norm displacing the treaty norm, either partly or wholly'.[200] Systemic integration is not seen as applying or importing the extraneous norm, not about overruling, modifying or derogating from the treaty norm to be interpreted. It is not an operation on the level of norm-creation or destruction. Yet there is a wish, described at various points above, for interpretation to have the same effect, even if limited to the case at issue.

All these distinctions are, in short, motivated by the need to keep customary and treaty law separate, while still allowing for systemic coherence or the possibility of a treaty referring to other rules. But how do we distinguish between contracting out of customary law and bringing it back in by way of systemic integration? How can systemic integration by a tribunal be squared with restrictions flowing from the limits on the applicable law relevant to that tribunal? How does an interpretation while 'taking into account' differ from an incorporation of other law (eg customary international law) or from a straight-up modification of the treaty?

A partial answer is the difference between reference and coherence, described in Section 4.3.1. Interpretation connects the treaty norm (the target) to another norm (the source) in two modes. (a) The connection can be achieved by way of a *renvoi*, where it is argued that a technical or recognised term has an established meaning. The source and the target are, in the last instance, identical: 'expropriation' in IIA_A is or refers to 'expropriation' in customary international law. (b) It can also be an obligation to establish conformity through interpretation, where it is argued that the term in the target norm must be read in conformity with the source. The target is or contains something other than the source: 'expropriation' in IIA_A should be read in conformity with the duties under Environmental Treaty_B. For orthodox writers, the legitimacy of this interpretative tool depends on whether a form of 'normative connection' can be established. (Only) if 'expropriation' actually refers to customary law, (only) if the obligations of states *need to be coherent* as a matter of the constitution of international law would an interpretation in this sense be considered legitimate and necessary.

199 Gazzini (2016) note 5 at 215.

200 Sands (1999) note 139 at 102–3; see also Gazzini (2016) note 5 at 227–8.

Despite the rather liberal construction of interpretation$_B$ in the orthodox debate, the sources of law impose limits. Peers seem to require interpreters' arguments to demonstrate some form of 'link' between source and target norm. References to customary law are certainly the most important topic for source-based critique – and are motivated by the strictures imposed by the wording of Article 31(3)(c) VCLT. The underlying problems of inter-source mechanics are best suited to demonstrating the consequences that follow from widening the concept of interpretation, as international lawyers have done. Writers and tribunals have focused on three questions when discussing systemic integration of customary law. First, given the possibilities of systemic integration, how efficacious can contracting out be vis-à-vis customary regulation? Second, can applicable law clauses effectively constrain tribunal use of norms? Third, will the use of recognised wording eliminate the difference between incorporation and interpretative inspiration? Separating these issues 'might be over-concretizing what is often a much more fluid approach'.[201] Yet there is some merit in doing so, as they raise different theoretical issues.

1. *Contracting out.* It is generally assumed that treaty-making is a contracting out from the *ius dispositivum* part of customary law and either validly creates *inter se* regulation or at least creates parallel treaty norms which are not overridden by customary law (Section 2.5). Yet, if the first statement is true, why should interpretation create conformity of the content of the treaty and customary norm or, alternatively, why should we presume that customary law determines the content of the treaty? Would that not negate the distinction between treaty and customary law, blur the lines between the two sources or at least give interpreters more power than they should have? Even more orthodox voices would probably question equating the interpreted text with customary law if this means denying that a treaty can have an autonomous meaning – a well-recognised problem in both literature and case-law. For example, the Annulment Committee in *Azurix* held:

> The Committee accepts that a treaty may need to be interpreted against the general fabric of customary international law. However, except where norms of *ius cogens* are involved, a treaty is capable of modifying the rules of customary international law ... The purpose of investment protection treaties ... generally is to augment or modify the customary international law procedures for protection of foreign investors. Hence the starting

[201] French (2006) note 131 at 291.

> point in determining the effect of the treaty is the terms of the treaty itself, rather than the principles of customary international law that may or may not be displaced by the treaty provisions.[202]

There is some scepticism as to whether systemic integration can overcome the treaty–custom divide. 'The main risk of applying Article 31(3)(c)', Wälde argues, 'is to use general international law to override the special provisions of a treaty, a *lex specialis*, and thus to undermine the freedom to contract.'[203] Another argument is that 'treaties are structurally *lex specialis*'; using systemic integration in this manner means that 'the distinction between treaty and custom could be close to disappearing'.[204] Interpretation would trump source-based limits and 'an overly enthusiastic integrative argument could result in reintroduction of certain considerations as a matter of interpretation that were excluded as a matter of law-making'.[205]

The proponents of systemic integration are cautious in that they believe that a sustainable distinction between contracting out and using customary law in treaty interpretation can be drawn. McLachlan, for example, agrees that 'where the treaty itself resolves the matter in a different way [to customary law], it must prevail as *lex specialis*'.[206] However, the matter is not a 'black-and-white choice between complete discretion on the one hand, and the application of a conception of customary international law "frozen in amber" at some time in the past'.[207] Proponents believe that this is not an insoluble issue, merely one that requires an exercise in balancing and clarification:

> If the conclusion is reached that silence in a particular [treaty] equates to non-regulation, then the *lex specialis* principle does not come into play and the 'relevant rules' of general international law continue to govern the relevant area or question. If however, there is legal regulation under the treaty, either in express terms or by implication . . ., that regulation is applicable whatever the state of general international law. The latter law can however be relevant if the treaty regulation includes some concepts the essence of which may be defined and clarified by reference to general international law.[208]

[202] *Azurix Corp.* v. *Argentine Republic*, ICSID, ARB/01/12, Decision on the Application for Annulment of the Argentine Republic of 1 September 2009, para 90.
[203] Wälde (2009) note 5 at 769, see also 770.
[204] Paparinskis (2010b) note 5 at 6.
[205] Paparinskis (2010b) note 5 at 6.
[206] McLachlan (2007) note 5 at 17; see also Rosentreter (2015) note 24 at 289.
[207] McLachlan (2008) note 5 at 381.
[208] Orakhelashvili (2008) note 4 at 375–6.

The other avenue by which to avoid the contracting out problem is to reverse the presumption of parties contracting out by way of treaty-making: 'unless there is evidence that the parties intended to contract out', interpreters must assume that the treaty did not amount to a departure from 'the international rights and obligations of the parties stemming from other sources'.[209] This argument, made à propos interpretation but again extending to inter-source relationships, has been sharply criticised for turning the matter on its head. Interpreters, Wälde argues, have 'to start with the text of the treaty . . ., rather than start with a presumption that the treaty text more or less paraphrases international law . . . treat[ing] it . . . as if it were *ius cogens*'.[210] The question is which way such a presumption is shaped: 'does one expect the treaty text . . . to say clearly and explicitly that [it] *depart*[*s*] from customary law or does one require . . . the treaty to say clearly that it *refers* to customary law?'[211] Systemic integration in this sense needs 'to be distinguished from the frequent situation where the treaty drafters imported language, concepts, and mechanisms from previous and parallel treaty practice and treaty models',[212] to which we will turn later.

2. *Applicable law*. The second problem arises specifically in connection with interpretation by tribunals. The decision-making of tribunals is typically determined by applicable law clauses and by their jurisdictional basis.[213] There may be quite severe restrictions as to which parts of the law the organ may apply and – on the orthodox conception – which parts of the law it may interpret (Section 4.2.2). The problem is that if coherence or reference in systemic integration is taken too far, interpreters may end up interpreting and applying law which is not part of the applicable law for that organ. Again, a source-based restriction (this time in procedural law) is circumvented using an interpretative tool. This issue was raised by Judge Burgenthal in *Oil Platforms*:

> [T]he principles of customary international law and whatever other treaties . . . do not by virtue of Article 31, paragraph 3 (c), become subject to the Court's jurisdiction. . . . Whether one likes it or not, that is the

[209] Gazzini (2016) note 5 at 212; see also McLachlan (2008) note 5 at 390.

[210] Wälde (2009) note 5 at 776; see also Paparinskis (2010b) note 5 at 8.

[211] Wälde (2009) note 5 at 770 (emphasis added).

[212] Wälde (2009) note 5 at 770.

[213] Lorand Bartels, 'Jurisdiction and Applicable Law Clauses: Where Does a Tribunal Find the Principal Norms Applicable to the Case before It?' in Tomer Broude, Yuval Shani (eds.), *Multi-sourced Equivalent Norms in International Law* (Oxford: Hart 2011) 115–41.

> consequence of the fact that the Court's jurisdiction, in resolving disputes between the parties before it, is limited to those rules . . . with regard to which the parties have accepted the Court's jurisdiction.[214]

Similar complaints have been raised in international investment arbitration as well.[215] The 'distinction between using rules of international law as part of the apparatus of treaty interpretation and applying the rules of international law directly'[216] is made clear and the risk of 'blurring the distinction between applicable law and interpretation'[217] is acknowledged. Weeramantry construes a conundrum: if systemic integration 'is invoked, it may be seen to be deploying a rule in a manner that displaces the applicable law', yet if not, 'this may be viewed as a failure to apply relevant legal rules'.[218]

In legal theory, the distinction between an interpretative 'taking into account' by a tribunal and the limits imposed by the applicable law provisions for that tribunal is clear. The first is an exhortation to interpret the text in light of other norms of international law. The second is part of a specific tribunal's empowerment norm (Section 4.2.3). This juxtaposition is not regarded as producing an insurmountable problem: Gazzini, for example, argues that these 'are different exercises, but the distinction may not always be very neat' and 'it may be difficult for a tribunal to refrain from applying rule A as not falling within the applicable law while simultaneously "taking into account" . . . any relevant rule, including rule A'. He is not convinced that this is a problem: '[t]he distinction between systemic interpretation and applicable law tends to fade away entirely . . . customary law . . . becomes for all practical purposes the law applicable to the dispute'.[219] On that optimistic reading, the applicable law now *in effect* includes both the applicable treaty and other parts of international law.

3. *Incorporation.* Treaty-makers are free to incorporate norms of customary law into the treaty, both formally and informally (implicitly, by using technical terms of customary law). The customary law norm is made part of the treaty, a process called 'incorporation'. Yet one possible

214 *Oil Platforms* (2003) note 140, separate opinion Buergenthal 279 (para 22).

215 *Ambiente Ufficio SPA and Others* v. *Argentine Republic*, ICSID, ARB/08/9, Decision on Jurisdiction and Admissibility of 8 February 2013, dissenting opinion Torres Bernárdez, para 456.

216 Gardiner (2008) note 2 at 278.

217 Gazzini (2016) note 5 at 221.

218 Weeramantry (2012) note 5 at 95.

219 Gazzini (2016) note 5 at 225.

result of interpretation can be that the treaty provision shares a meaning with a norm of customary law. The proponents of systemic integration wish to enjoin interpreters to presume this to be the case, but it is doubtful whether one is allowed to make such a blanket presumption. The assumption that recognised terms share meanings across sources as a matter of course may not adequately reflect the treaty, even if no contrary indications are found. Orthodox voices probably overestimate the likelihood of this occurring. This issue is made even more vexed by the problem of distinguishing informal incorporation from *renvoi* to recognised meanings. McLachlan argues that reference can occur in three typical situations:

> (a) The treaty rule is unclear and the ambiguity is resolved by reference to a developed body of international law . . . (b) The terms used in the treaty have a well-recognised meaning in customary international law, to which the parties can therefore be taken to have intended to refer. . . . (c) The terms of the treaty are by their nature open-textured and reference to other sources of international law will assist in giving content to the rule.[220]

All three situations describe the reference argument in Section 4.3.1 – the idea that the source is an explanation of the target – rather than the coherence argument. Yet all three situations – unclear rules, open-textured rules or well-recognised meanings/technical terms – could be cases of incorporation just as well as examples of 'mere' interpretative *renvoi*. Take the following passage from *Emmis* as example: '[e]xpropriation and nationalization are terms that may also *properly refer to* the standards of customary international law'.[221] Do the italicised words denote identity of meaning or the incorporation of the customary norm?

It is important to distinguish these two processes. Norm-structurally, incorporation is the taking on board by the target treaty of the normative content of customary law. Incorporation clauses are a shorthand form of law-creation; in this manner, norms with the same content as the customary norm are created in the referring treaty. When a revolutionary

[220] McLachlan (2005) note 49 at 312; Koskenniemi (2006) at 235 (para 467).

[221] *Emmis International Holding, B.V., Emmis Radio Operating, B.V., Mem Magyar Electronic, Media Kereskedelmi és Szolgáltató Kft* v. *Hungary*, ICSID, ARB/12/2, Decision on Respondent's Objection under ICSID Arbitration Rule 41(5) of 11 March 2013, para 82 (emphasis added); see also *Accession Mezzanine Capital L. P. and Danubius Kereskedőház Vagyonkezelő Zrt* v. *Hungary*, ICSID, ARB/12/3, Decision on Respondent's Objection under Arbitration Rule 41(5) of 16 January 2013, paras 67–9.

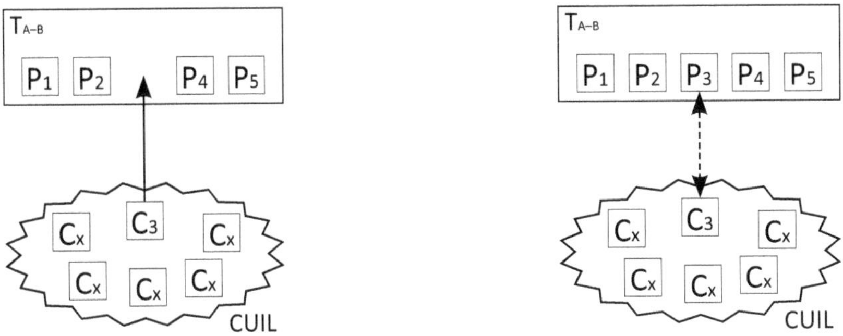

Figure 4.5 Incorporation and interpretative reference[222]

constitution incorporates law from the old regime, it may simply stipulate that the old civil code 'remains in force'. Norm-theoretically, this is exactly the same as enacting a new civil code, except that the content is not spelled out in the same manner. The content of the old civil code is taken and enacted by way of the incorporation clause: in this case, 'remains in force' means 'a new civil code with the same content as the old code is hereby created'. On the orthodox reading, however, the incorporating norm creates a connection to the source and thus becomes part of the target norm. Source and target norm are connected by the incorporating norm. On that view, the norm is merely a signpost to the external norm: 'I will not regulate this, please refer to customary law on the matter.' Merkouris draws the inevitable consequence from the orthodox concept; incorporated rules 'are exactly that part of the corpus of the treaty being interpreted. They do not help in interpreting the text. They are the text.'[223]

However, in actual treaty-making, the matter is usually less clear. While 'the very language of investment treaties often makes express reference to custom',[224] an implied incorporation is often assumed, both in domestic and in international law. The most common argument is that 'treaty language only explains the concept in treaty law terms without expressly confirming (or excluding) the reference to customary law', which generally involves using 'a term generally recognised as referring to customary law'.[225] The idea of 'provisions that have

[222] The orthodox understanding of incorporation is that a treaty provision (P_3) is merely the signpost which integrates a customary norm (C_3) into the treaty. On an interpretative equivalence by reference, interpreters establish that P_3 is equivalent in content to C_3.

[223] Merkouris (2015) note 3 at 69.

[224] McLachlan (2016) note 131 at 262; see also French (2006) note 131 at 292; Paparinskis (2010b) note 5 at 18.

[225] Paparinskis (2010b) note 5 at 18.

a recognised meaning'[226] is popular in orthodox writings and expropriation in IIAs is seen as a good example: 'the definition commonly found in investment treaties has been so patently adopted from a formulation widely employed in customary international law that it invites reference to the general authorities on its meaning'.[227]

The other concept is the assumption that certain 'well-recognised' treaty terms have the same content as certain customary norms: 'whenever the treaty parties apply terms which have a certain connotation in international law it is assumed that the parties have chosen this meaning'.[228] While the argument is not that it inevitably results in equivalence, the method has found favour with writers, particularly in investment law. The treaty norm does not incorporate the customary norm as norm; only the attributed meanings are duplicated. The claim is that 'customary international law may be used to interpret the scope of the treaty standard'[229] and it 'elucidate[s] undefined treaty terms'.[230]

A clear distinction between these two processes is seldom made. Rosentreter, for example, speaks of 'the standards contained in investment treaties [as] simply a *conventional codification of or at least very similar* to standards and principles that have long existed in customary international law'.[231] Reinisch sees the '"importation" of customary international law concepts' as 'additional criterion for interpretation in the sense of Article 31(3)(c)'.[232] This argument makes an interpretative method (an operation of decision-making by organs) into an issue of treaty-making (a norm-systemic operation). Does a treaty term *referring* to or being interpreted as referring to customary law differ significantly from a treaty term being interpreted while taking recourse to customary law? Unless, as in the orthodox conception of incorporation, it puts into place the norm of another legal order, the difference may be negligible,

226 Reinisch (2015) note 5 at 389; see also Paparinskis (2010b) note 5 at 8, 18; Paparinskis (2012) note 16 at 107.

227 McLachlan (2007) note 5 at 16; see also McLachlan (2008) note 5 at 399; McLachlan (2016) note 131 at 262; Orakhelashvili (2008) note 4 at 371; Paparinskis (2010b) note 5 at 18; Paparinskis (2012) note 16 at 104; Kate Parlett, 'Claims under Customary International Law in ICSID Arbitration' 31 *ICSID Review* (2016) 434–56 at 454; Reinisch (2015) note 5 at 389–90.

228 Rosentreter (2015) note 24 at 287.

229 Parlett (2016) note 227 at 454.

230 Rosentreter (2015) note 24 at 284.

231 Rosentreter (2015) note 24 at 80 (emphasis added).

232 Reinisch (2015) note 5 at 391; see also McLachlan (2008) note 5 at 399; Paparinskis (2010b) note 5 at 18; Parlett (2016) note 227 at 454; Weeramantry (2012) note 5 at 56.

but it is conceptually given nonetheless.[233] Interpreting a treaty provision by incorporating customary law involves finding out what customary international law says just as much as an interpretation 'taking account of' a customary norm. Merkouris's exhortation to differentiate may seem less urgent:

> Article 31(3)(c) . . . refers to extraneous rules . . . that are not included in the text of the treaty but that may shed light in deciphering its meaning. Rules that have been incorporated in a treaty text, either directly by reproducing the relevant provisions verbatim in the treaty being interpreted or simply by referring to those rules, are part of the body of the treaty. It is them that are being applied . . ., not them helping in interpreting the treaty.[234]

However, his argument clarifies the scepticism about whether we can and should *presume* identity, rather than autonomy; it indirectly also clarifies whether reference is a proper application for systemic integration. When 'a treaty term has a "recognised meaning" in customary law, would not it be more natural to say that reference to customary law *is* the "ordinary meaning" or "special meaning" of the particular term'[235] and thus not systemic integration? Why should we *assume* that treaty and customary concepts are identical? 'The fact that particular matters are not expressly dealt with in a treaty could simply suggest that they do not fall within the intended scope of treaty.'[236] Does this not also mean that interpretation could take into account some other rule and find that they contrast?[237] For example: treaty provision A is interpreted while taking into account customary rule B. B has the content *Op*. In light of this and perhaps other considerations, the result of interpretation could be that A has the content $O\neg p$ (or *Oq*, etc.), because this provision is *not* meant to be in accordance with customary law. The argument from international law as a coherent system (Section 4.3.1) militates against such an outcome, but this is not accepted in tribunal practice: 'some Tribunals have examined treaty practice of particular parties, suggesting that an express reference to customary law in some treaties may be employed *a contrario* in relation to other treaties'.[238]

233 See Zachary Douglas, 'The MFN Clause in Investment Arbitration: Treaty Interpretation Off the Rails' 2 *Journal of International Dispute Settlement* (2010) 97–113 at 106: 'the "incorporation by reference" analogy is inapposite and is liable to mislead'.
234 Merkouris (2015) note 3 at 69.
235 Paparinskis (2012) note 16 at 107.
236 Paparinskis (2012) note 16 at 107.
237 Paparinskis (2010b) note 5 at 19.
238 Paparinskis (2010b) note 5 at 19; see also McLachlan (2008) note 5 at 385.

4.3.3 *Renvoi* to Meanings, Rather than to Norms

The discussion regarding contracting out, applicable law provisions and incorporation is a mock battle. This is a surprising result; it is partially explained by the status of customary law. McLachlan cautions against too easily assuming the content of the referred customary investment law. The 'essentially contested nature of so many of the rights in customary international law'[239] means that the source of the reference, that is, the content of customary law, is likely not precise enough. Equally, for Reinisch customary law may be used 'for interpretation in the sense of Article 31(3)(c)', but he cautions against 'reliance on customary international law *arguably containing more precise definitions* of the notions of indirect expropriation left undefined in the applicable IIAs',[240] because it is possible that the customary norm on expropriation is less specific than the target treaty norm. Is there, then, any customary international law to refer to and is customary international law more detailed than IIAs so that 'taking into account' can provide more information on the content of the IIA? We will turn to this in Section 7.2.2.

We are now in a position to discuss what 'taking into account' can be. We need to discuss the process itself (what is the *renvoi*) as well as what content this process imports. On the interpreter's perspective, systemic integration is not an incorporation of customary *norms* into the treaty but a method of reasoning by the interpreter which provides a concretisation of content/meaning. As mentioned in Section 4.2.2, interpretation$_B$ claims that by interpreting, interpreters are put in a position to extract additional information from the treaty text. This might be no more than making the decision taken after interpretation defensible vis-à-vis peers. But we need to analyse where this additional information about the text comes from – rather than the word 'expropriation', we now have 'general non-discriminatory regulation is not an indirect expropriation'. In orthodox parlance, when interpreters are 'taking other rules into account', they are importing not target *norms* but *meanings*. The *renvoi*, such as it is, is to meanings, not norms, norm-content or norm-texts.

In terms of interpretation$_A$, we would have to ask whether 'taking into account' has any basis in theories of modern linguistics. We would have to ask whether this specific and directed contextualisation from one or a closed group of a particular source of context can properly be called

[239] McLachlan (2007) note 5 at 17.
[240] Reinisch (2015) note 5 at 391 (emphasis added).

interpretation. We would start from the observation that there is a qualitative difference between getting 'meaning' from within the treaty text and the context (in the linguistic sense) for legal interpretation. While, as a matter of understanding a legal text, context plays an important role, one could argue that meaning-construction is different for norm-texts than for other texts. If norm-texts are norms, they may not differ from other texts in their relative linguistic indeterminacy, but, as norms, may be relatively static as a matter of norm-theory. Kelsen's 'frame of possible meanings'[241] is not a linguistic theory but a result of the structural theory of normative orders which can provide a firmer structure of meaning vis-à-vis 'normal' texts. This is so because norms 'exist' in a normative order and because this structure provides a special kind of context which is primarily determined as a matter not of language but of law. In other words, it could be argued that norms as texts are not like 'normal' text – they have a different ontic status, have no 'speaker' or author in the linguistic sense and thus restrict the freedom of the interpreter.

Following this line of argument, we can say that, because the source of context in systemic integration is another norm (from another source), particular care should be taken as a matter both of linguistics and of the structural analysis of norms. Linguistically, it would be difficult, but by no means impossible, to argue that a different text means the same. Legally, we need good legal-structural reasons to assume identity of content with separateness of source. This is a very strong norm-ontological thesis which can mean arguing for the creation (change) of norms through interpretation (see Section 4.3.2). Alternatively, it would mean arguing that processes of cognition have strong norm-ontic effects and that language has priority over norm-creation.[242] For interpretation$_A$, content-generation

241 Kelsen (1960) note 82 at 348–9, though cf Dietrich Busse, *Juristische Semantik: Grundfragen der juristischen Interpretationstheorie in sprachwissenschaftlicher Sicht* (Berlin: Duncker & Humblot 1993) 191.

242 Take Jeand'Heur's theory as example (Bernd Jeand'Heur, *Sprachliches Referenzverhalten bei der juristischen Entscheidungstätigkeit* (Berlin: Duncker & Humblot 1989) 55–6): If the use of words by 'legal workers' (*Rechtsarbeiter*), ie judges or any practitioner, produces the 'meaning' of law, then legal scholarship neither is nor can be a cognition of law (of the legal order) independent of the practice of the application of law (jurisprudence). In that case, legal scholarship's interpretation of the law would no longer be 'equal' to the interpretation (as cognition) by appliers. Legal scholarship would be reduced to an analysis of the language used by 'legal workers' and an interpretation of the law by third parties (particularly scholarship) would not exist, only scholarly cognition of language use by 'legal workers'.

in this manner is possible as part of the context in the linguistic sense, but not very probable.[243]

Yet the debate on systemic integration is based on interpretation$_B$ where the idea of a *renvoi* to meanings has led us on a search for the source of the additional information. Within interpretation$_B$, we are not bound by the niceties of source-relationships and structural constraints. There is thus no limit on the sources of information for systemic integration. What is to hinder us from taking international lawyers' *perception* (expressed in case-law) of the content as valid source of the Article 31(3)(c) VCLT *renvoi*? After all, this is what actually happens and this is what orthodox writers try to avoid saying explicitly.[244] Given that *stare decisis* or a system of legal precedent (Chapter 3) does not exist and given the conceptual, theoretical and evidentiary problems of customary law (Chapter 2), 'systemic integration' is one reason among others to nonetheless regard treaty provisions determined by the way 'we all see it'. By arguing that IIA provisions are evidence of what customary law or *pari materia* treaties mean, and by claiming that interpreters are to be inspired by this, we seem to observe legal strictures while in fact constructing meaning not from law but from the opinions of professional jurists.

Tribunals interpret 'their' IIA in light of *interpretations* or *concretisations* by other interpreters, mostly of other tribunals. They do not interpret in light of other IIAs or customary law. They do so because they wish to generate or extract more detailed content from this process. In the case of expropriation, customary international law contains a norm on expropriation, to which IIA expropriation clauses allegedly refer.[245] However, if a tribunal, in wishing to interpret IIA$_A$, recurs to the interpretation by another tribunal, it recurs to an interpretation not of custom but of (eg) IIA$_B$. Interpreters of international investment law do not interpret IIAs in light of customary law but in light of investment tribunals' *understanding* of *pari materia* treaties. They do so because systemic interpretation is claimed to be an interpretation not of the source norm (customary international law) but of the target norm (IIA$_A$) and because few

[243] This is what I have tried to convey in earlier texts: Kammerhofer (2010b) note 30 at 170; Jörg Kammerhofer 'Law-Making by Scholarship? The Dark Side of 21st Century International Legal "Methodology"' in James Crawford, Sarah Nouwen (eds.), *Select Proceedings of the European Society of International Law: Third Volume: International Law 1989–2010: A Performance Appraisal. Cambridge, 2–4 September 2010* (Oxford: Hart 2012) 115–26 at 123.

[244] Eg McLachlan (2008) note 5 at 381.

[245] Reinisch (2015) note 5 at 389–91.

tribunals primarily apply the customary expropriation norm. From a more orthodox vantage point, Paparinskis comes to the same conclusion:

> The adjudicatory explanation of one treaty rule is at least in the first instance not relevant for other *pari materia* rules binding other parties. It is in this context that the interpretative question has to be asked: how and to what extent can the interpreter of investment treaties *incorporate the reasoning of tribunals* interpreting broadly similar rules that for the reason of historical developments are set out in different treaties and are binding on different parties?[246]

Two counter-arguments could be rallied, but they are not particularly convincing. First, could not the source of systemic integration nonetheless be part of customary law as a sort of 'custom *praeter legem*'[247] or interstitial law: customary norms which fill the 'gaps' left by general norms? As discussed in Chapter 2, this is possible but highly unlikely. Second, could the *renvoi* nonetheless be to the text itself and not to meanings expressed by arbitral tribunals?[248] On that view, the reference to jurisprudence would merely express the interpreter's support of the tribunal's opinion:

> To the extent that the investment protection rules can be demonstrated as having made explicit or implicit references to custom, the reliance on case law interpreting third-party treaties would become acceptable. While starting the interpretative process from different treaty rules set out in their respective treaties, all the tribunals would conclude the process by drawing upon the same rule of customary law . . . the question would still remain about whether the interpretation of customary law is persuasive, but different awards . . . purport. . . to explain the same legal rule.[249]

Yet, is it not more likely that the norms referred to do not contain the additional information but that the opinions of other (foremost judicial) interpreters simply masquerade as content *of the law* – a fiction which even orthodox writers acknowledge?[250]

[246] Paparinskis (2012) note 16 at 95–6 (emphasis added).

[247] Eg Hugh Thirlway, *International Customary Law and Codification* (Leiden: Sijthoff 1972) 97–8; GJH van Hoof, *Rethinking the Sources of International Law* (Deventer: Kluwer 1983) 277–8; Albert Bleckmann, 'Völkergewohnheitsrecht trotz widersprüchlicher Praxis?' 36 *Zeitschrift für ausländisches öffentliches Recht und Völkerrecht* (1976) 374–405 at 383.

[248] See McLachlan (2005) note 49 at 290; Schill (2009) note 127 at 319.

[249] Paparinskis (2012) note 16 at 104.

[250] Eg Weeramantry (2012) note 5 at 56.

4.3.4 *Differences vis-à-vis Other Tools of Interpretation*

The preceding sections have relativised the distinction between the different tools of interpretation. If, first, the rules of interpretation$_B$ are not about a specific set of prescriptions for interpretative practice, but only about a framework of practices acceptable to peers, then the 'tools' mentioned in Article 31 VCLT neither exhaust the proper ('legitimate') practice of interpretation$_B$ nor, through their exact wording, determine it. If, second, an analysis of systemic integration shows that meaning-ascertainment, meaning-creation and meaning-ascription by interpretative organs do not depend on the norm-structural relationship of the interpreted treaty to the source of meaning, then differences between and concerns about source–target relationships fall away (Section 4.3.2). If, third, interpretative *renvoi* is not established to other norms but to meaning-content created by other interpreters, irrespective of whether the ostensible source of the *renvoi* is customary international law or *pari materia* treaties (Section 4.3.3), the difference between the various tools or methods of interpretation$_B$ will fall away as well. In the present section, we will show how *pari materia* interpretation, the 'ordinary–special meaning' complex and subsequent practice – the other interpretative tools most relevant to international investment law – compare with systemic integration.

1. Pari materia *interpretation.* 'As a matter of empirical fact,' tribunals, particularly in investment law, 'quite often take into account the formulation of third country treaties in order to confirm or to contrast the interpretation of the treaty rules they have to apply'.[251] They rely for interpretative guidance on other treaties. A particularly salient tool, particularly in areas where a large number of similarly worded treaties exists, such as investment law, is *pari materia* interpretation, whereby interpretative '[r]eference [is made] to instruments of the same subject-matter for interpretative purposes'.[252] The label is adapted from domestic legal usage in common law countries, but the issue is not unique to that tradition. They can also be called '"common form treaties" . . . [ie] treaties that constitute a group, resembling one another in form and content through their derivation from a common model, or covering the same subject matter in similar provisions'.[253]

[251] Reinisch (2015) note 5 at 386.
[252] Merkouris (2015) note 3 at 76; see also Schill (2009) note 127 at 293–4.
[253] Gardiner (2008) note 2 at 282.

This tool is popular but controversial, primarily because it is difficult to fit within the scheme of the Vienna Convention rules on interpretation. The difficulties in fitting it into the strictures of Article 31(3)(c) VCLT are obvious: taking a treaty between C and D into account while interpreting a treaty between A and B is not covered by 'rules … applicable in the relations between the parties'.[254] However, writers are also reluctant to classify it as an example of supplementary means of interpretation (Article 32 VCLT),[255] for similar reasons. The terms of the Vienna Convention restrict the use of supplementary means, and *pari materia* interpretation as envisaged by its proponents does not fit the bill.[256] However, on the orthodox understanding, whether *pari materia* interpretation is part of the Vienna Convention rules is relatively insignificant, because *pari materia* could always be part of the customary international legal rules of interpretation. At any rate, it is recognised in tribunal practice.[257]

> Either *in pari materia* interpretation has become customary international law, or it has not. In the first scenario, [it] would fall under Article 31(3)(c). … As customary law, not only would it be a 'rule', but it would be binding on all States … all the *in pari materia* treaties would fall indirectly under Article 31(3)(c) by virtue of the customary rule of *in pari materia* interpretation. If, however, *in pari materia* interpretation is not considered to reflect customary international law then the *in pari materia* treaties … would each have to be categorised in and of themselves, to see if they come under any of the provisions of Articles 31 and 32, or are irrelevant for interpretative purposes.[258]

The strength of this argument is, however, also a source of weakness. If we assume that customary law contains such a rule, then, arguably, the (word-for-word) identity of VCLT and customary rules of interpretation (see Section 4.2.1) is shattered. The necessary-identity argument cannot accept the possibility of divergence of treaty and customary rules of

[254] Gazzini (2016) note 5 at 228; Mitchell (2017) note 162 at 689; Merkouris (2015) note 3 at 100.
[255] Eg Paparinskis (2012) note 16 at 101–3; Mitchell (2017) note 162 at 690–4; Merkouris (2015) note 3 at 78, 83, yet see 100.
[256] One set of counter-arguments is supplied by Merkouris (2015) note 3 at 52–3 fn 225.
[257] Gardiner (2008) note 2 at 281–2: 'Courts and tribunals, national and international, appear to have no hesitation over using provisions in treaties other than the one being applied as aids to interpretation … This is such an accepted and established practice that it is hard to find any situation in which justification in terms of the Vienna rules has been presented'; see also Schill (2009) note 127 at 305.
[258] Merkouris (2015) note 3 at 78.

interpretation. Another interjection is based on the principle of consent or the *pacta tertiis* rule. Gazzini, for example, argues that this 'is hardly compatible with the VCLT rules on interpretation since each treaty is and remains *res inter alios acta*'.[259] Referring to *Maffezini*, he makes the point that, '[e]ven assuming that the texts of all treaties concluded by Spain clearly point to any given interpretation, they have no relevance as such on the interpretation of the BIT between Argentina and Spain'[260] – a point one can make with even more force for third-party treaties (C–D *v.* A–B).

As many writers recognise, there are difficulties delimiting *pari materia* interpretation from other, more established methods, such as ordinary meaning, generic terms, special meanings (Article 31(4) VCLT), the incorporation of customary law and systemic integration *stricto sensu.*[261] *Pari materia* treaties may also 'sometimes be considered a part of "the context" [or] ... of "the circumstances of [the interpreted treaty's] conclusion"'.[262] 'The meaning is thus established through the examination of materials extrinsic to particular treaty(-making) but reflecting the generally accepted meaning of the term, somewhat similarly to dictionary definitions.'[263] Whether *pari materia* interpretation can be reduced to these methods is hotly contested, but, in light of the 'relativity' of the source for interpretative content, the difference between *pari materia* interpretation and systemic integration vanishes, which is recognised by some.[264]

Schill puts an optimistic spin on the question: 'Investment tribunals not only use third-country BITs as an interpretative tool, they also generate largely coherent decisions based on different BITs.' If that is the case, then specific meaning-content in international investment law is created through interpretation$_B$ (by arbitral tribunals), relying on various accepted methods, which need not be used in a distinct and precise manner for the result to be accepted. Ironically, meaning-content generation is largely independent of the interpreted treaty – the treaty is not specific enough. It also does not depend on an exact

259 Gazzini (2016) note 5 at 230.

260 Gazzini (2016) note 5 at 230; see also Merkouris (2015) note 3 at 77; Mitchell (2017) note 162 at 676–7; Schill (2009) note 127 at 295.

261 Gardiner (2008) note 2 at 282; see also Paparinskis (2012) note 16 at 96–7; Schill (2009) note 127 at 319.

262 Linderfalk (2007) note 4 at 255.

263 Paparinskis (2012) note 16 at 97.

264 Paparinskis (2012) note 16 at 104.

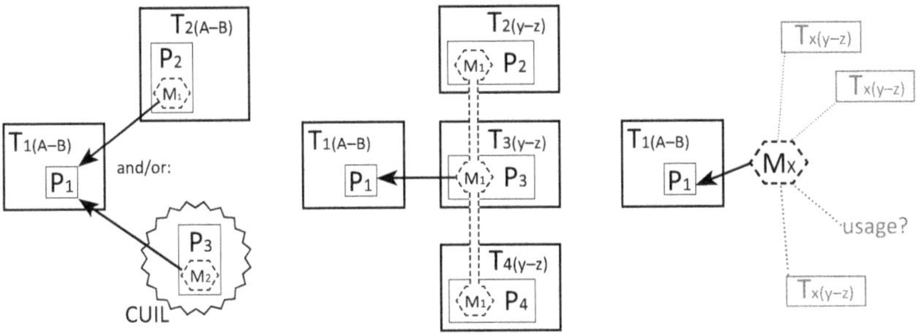

Figure 4.6 Systemic integration, *pari materia* interpretation and generic terms[265]

(exacting) set of rules of interpretation, as the process of acceptance of tribunals' interpretative methods is as factual as the meaning is external to the interpreted treaty.

2. *Ordinary and special meaning, generic terms.* The same holds true for some of the 'core' methods of interpretation of the Vienna Convention canon. Not only can both systemic integration and *pari materia* interpretation often be recast as an exercise in aiding textual interpretation (in whatever form and based on both objectivist and subjectivist theoretical foundations), but, on the interpreter's perspective (interpretation$_B$), the additional specificity required of a treaty provision in the process of ascertaining concrete meaning cannot come from the text itself. Hence any meaning – whether 'dictionary', 'ordinary', 'special' or 'generic' – is, as a matter of fact, imported. This is acknowledged even within the orthodox framework. For example, we find Weeramantry arguing that '[t]he determination of the ordinary meaning of a treaty text must avoid arriving at a literal meaning'. Since investment tribunals 'have been unwilling to be semantic',[266] it stands to reason that interpretation$_B$ means importing meaning-content into the norms interpreted: 'interpretations or applications of [substantive investment provisions] are usually influenced not by their "ordinary meaning" but by the accumulated body of relevant

265 Left: Article 31(3)(c) VCLT interpretation on the orthodox perspective; meanings in provisions in treaties 'between the parties' and/or customary norms. Middle: *Pari materia* interpretation on the orthodox perspective; a meaning shared by many treaties – irrespective of whether they share parties with the treaty at issue – are interpreted into the latter. Right: Generic terms; informed by use in treaties or by usage by the general public or (international) lawyers develops into a self-standing meaning as generic or technical term.

266 Weeramantry (2012) note 5 at 53 (emphasis removed); see also Wälde (2009) note 5 at 753.

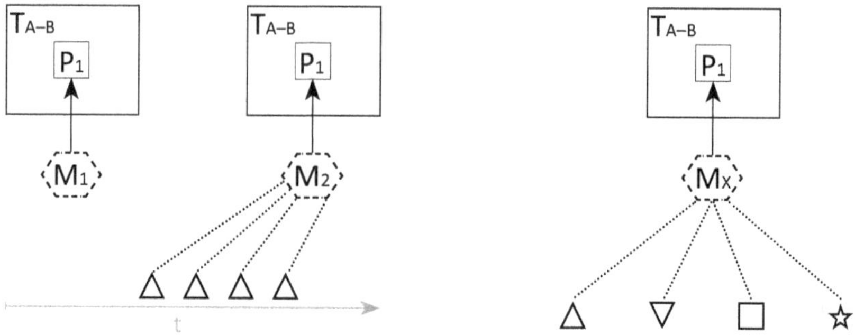

Figure 4.7 Subsequent practice and the interpreter's perspective[267]

international case law and commentary on those terms'.[268] Wälde shows how special meanings are, in effect, ordinary meanings: 'That approach, though made explicit in Article 31(4), is the normal approach of interpretation. That words are interpreted in the technical and professional meaning they have in the particularly relevant community of word-users.'[269]

3. *Subsequent practice.* This tool has received a great deal of attention in recent years, sparked by the ILC's work on the topic.[270] The unification of meaning across IIAs by way of interpretation could potentially be achieved by treating other IIAs (and other sources) as 'subsequent practice' (Article 31(3)(b) VCLT). Treaties thus serve as 'practice', particularly where one of the parties has managed to conclude multiple IIAs with

[267] On the orthodox understanding, instances of practice accumulate over time to inform a meaning of the same treaty provision that can be markedly different from a meaning established earlier. The same mechanism applies if jurisprudence is used as source of content in interpretation. On the interpreter's perspective, however, meanings are external to both the source and the target of interpretation, but 'informed' by a wide variety of acceptable sources, whether external norms, jurisprudence, practice or others.

[268] Weeramantry (2012) note 5 at 97.

[269] Wälde (2009) note 5 at 771.

[270] Eg Georg Nolte, 'First Report on Subsequent Agreements and Subsequent Practice in Relation to Treaty Interpretation', *International Law Commission, Sixty-Fifth Session, Geneva, 6 May–7 June and 8 July–9 August 2013*, A/CN.4/660 (2013); Georg Nolte, 'Second Report on Subsequent Agreements and Subsequent Practice in Relation to the Interpretation of Treaties', *International Law Commission, Sixty-Sixth Session, Geneva, 5 May–6 June and 7 July–8 August 2014*, A/CN.4/671 (2014); Georg Nolte, 'Third Report on Subsequent Agreements and Subsequent Practice in Relation to the Interpretation of Treaties', *International Law Commission, Sixty-Seventh Session, Geneva, 4 May–5 June and 6 July–7 August 2015*, A/CN.4/683 (2015); Georg Nolte, 'Fourth Report on Subsequent Agreements and Subsequent Practice in Relation to the Interpretation of Treaties', *International Law Commission, Sixty-Eighth Session, Geneva, 2 May–10 June and 4 July–12 August 2016*, A/CN.4/694 (2016).

an identical clause, perhaps through a model treaty. One could also argue that other treaties using identical clauses, with partially identical treaty parties, in conjunction (perhaps) with earlier jurisprudence on the meaning of this clause, can count as 'subsequent practice'. Third, the reaction of parties to jurisprudence in later (model) treaties (for example the exclusion of regulatory measures in recent treaty practice) could be treated as a disavowal of an earlier established meaning through subsequent practice, a recognition that the meaning or generality can be created that way and even a recognition that the earlier meaning was already established.[271]

This tool again does not differ in any major respect from the other tools of interpretation$_B$. Admittedly, if the integration of subsequent practice were a matter of the structure of norms, the topic would be highly problematic: practice alone does not change the law and, even if recast as customary law, its influence over treaty norms is highly doubtful. A critique could also be mounted against subsequent practice as interpretation, if 'interpretation' is understood as a hermeneutic process (interpretation$_A$).[272] Temporal dynamics as such are probably not relevant, but the temporal dimension can be an expression of language-use by relevant speakers. Therefore, as submitted by some, practice can serve as a pragmatic clarification (in the linguistic sense) of semantic vagueness.[273] Yet, from the vantage-point of orthodox scholarship, such a practice would primarily be that of tribunals.

4.4 Conclusion

This chapter has shown both the importance of interpretation for international lawyers as well as the futility of trying to make interpretation fulfil the promise which we think the law itself cannot keep. Interpretation is crucial for international investment law. Over the past decades, international legal orthodoxy has developed a complex doctrine – the 'Vienna Convention consensus'. This development, in turn, has probably fostered

[271] See eg Wälde (2009) note 5 at 767, 772.

[272] I have criticised subsequent practice as a tool for the interpretation (as interpretation$_A$) or modification of law along these lines, though before the ILC took up the topic: Kammerhofer (2010d) note 8 at 125–38.

[273] Stefan Griller, Michael Potacs, 'Zur Unterscheidung von Pragmatik und Semantik in der juristischen Hermeneutik' in Helmuth Vetter, Michael Potacs (eds.), *Beiträge zur juristischen Hermeneutik* (Vienna: Literas 1990) 66–105; Michael Potacs, *Rechtstheorie* (Vienna: facultas 2015) 134–9.

greater stability and more predictable outcomes of decisions made by organs who interpreted according to this set of rules. This last claim, of course, is empirical and subject to being tested as empirical hypothesis.

Framing the issue in this manner also elucidates the other major strain of argument in this chapter, namely that, in a specific sense, interpretation is not a properly legal function. It is not determinative of the law in any sense: treaties are neither narrowed nor concretised in their linguistic or normative content by interpretation; treaty interpretation does not change the law, whether based on ordinary meaning, systemic integration or subsequent practice. Yet the longing for concreteness, unity or certainty is so strong that one would rather be inconsistent and imagine some form of unsustainable law-creative and determinative power for interpretation than admit that the law might just not be concrete, unified or certain. Coherent interpretative outcomes may exist; we need to test them and will do so in Chapter 8. Yet a factual coherence of behaviour is at the basis of such outcomes, not legal norms of great specificity.

Two points which have particular import for the next chapters deserve to be highlighted again. The first is the consequences arising from the great freedom of interpreters. Whether the Vienna Convention rules are reconstructed as norms or not, interpreters have greater freedom than is commonly assumed. They are relatively free to decide from where they source the meaning of the provision(s) interpreted, what method or tool they use and what the result should be. While interpretation$_B$ is not a free-for-all, those who want to construct a rigid and strict corset of legal strictures mistake what interpretation is about. Such restrictions as exist will rather be a matter of (international legal) culture and tradition; a tribunal's interpretation is legitimate if the methods it uses are accepted by peers, not because of a strict and detailed law on treaty interpretation or because of absolute boundaries of language. What, then, is the 'net effect' of interpretative tools; what do they actually achieve? It is submitted that interpretation achieves less than is commonly assumed, because it is neither determinative of the law nor a de facto precedent, nor does it contribute to the creation of customary law. It can be *factually* important, although this is not necessarily the case. Even if the employment of the Vienna Convention consensus results in greater coherence and unification, what is the nature of such a unification or coherence? It is a matter of fact: consistent interpreting may provide some reassurance and a certain expectation of similar behaviour in the future. *If* it is there, this is a form of determination not of the law or even of its meanings but of behaviour, that is, of socio-psychologically relevant sets of facts.

The second overarching issue is the crucial de facto role of jurisprudence in interpretation. In the interpretation of international investment law by arbitral tribunals, much of the specific information which neither treaty norms nor customary law can provide on their own terms will come from other arbitral awards (though scholarly commentary will also play a role).[274] While Chapter 3 has shown that such precedents are not, in any sense, part of the law or binding, their *factual* importance cannot be understated. Case-law is the major provider of content which will – and may legitimately – be used by deciders. Yet orthodoxy's fudging of exactly why (on the basis of which theoretical grounds) jurisprudence is important hinders rather than helps us in the scholarly task of cognising the law. Portraying investment jurisprudence therefore requires another approach, if the information contained there is not to be discarded as not being part of 'the law', that is, the sum-total of *general* international legal norms, and thus not part of legal scholarship's task of describing the positive law in force, which Chapters 6–8 will attempt to do.

[274] On the role of scholarship: Jörg Kammerhofer, 'Lawmaking by Scholars' in Catherine Brölmann, Yannick Radi (eds.), *Handbook on the Theory and Practice of International Lawmaking* (Cheltenham: Edward Elgar 2016) 305–25.

5

Doctrinal Scholarship

5.1 Introduction: What Is Doctrinal Scholarship?

This chapter will analyse what international legal scholarship can say about the law of expropriation. Informed by the theoretical discussion in the first chapters, it will test international investment legal scholarship, for a legal scholarship which operates on the basis of inconsistent arguments is not scholarship. In contrast, case-law which does the same loses its persuasive authority, but this does not rob awards of their status as individual norms. As detailed in later chapters, we may find that the structure of IIAs invalidates certain arguments. Certain 'statements about the law', whether made by academics, by practitioners or by political stakeholders, may therefore not actually be *on the law*, do not correctly represent the law, even if they are popular or even when they are accepted by most.

However, in a very specific sense, the next chapters are also a test of the normativist-positivist approach to (international) legal scholarship. Can it provide a convincing critique of scholarly methods; is it a real alternative to what has been done before? Can it become 'a third way . . . beyond the stark choice of apology and utopia . . . focus[ing] exclusively on the analysis of the positive international law in force'?[1] And how does it deal with the undeniable reality of arbitral jurisprudence and its pull to a 'default legal realism', as mentioned in Chapters 3 and 4? This chapter is primarily a reflection on *how* to provide knowledge about the law. We will turn to a discussion of the methodology behind the analysis of the law. The idea and possible shape of legal-doctrinal scholarship (*Rechtsdogmatik*) will be discussed and the various methods used will be introduced and delimited from others.

[1] Jörg Kammerhofer, 'Orthodox Generalists and Political Activists in International Legal Scholarship' in Matthew Happold (ed.), *International Law in a Multipolar World* (Abingdon: Routledge 2011) 138–57 at 155.

The preceding chapters have sought to demonstrate that the orthodox method of finding out what the law says is not sustainable; the closer one looks, the more palpable is the disenchantment with doctrine as commonly practised. Theoretical analysis thus becomes the groundwork for a different perspective. Are doctrinal investment lawyers then reduced to attempting an exercise in social scientific award prediction? Given that the all-important case-law actually does follow prior awards (and to a minor extent doctrinal writings), should we not primarily discuss them as factual determinants of and as predictive tools to determine future arbitral awards? Should we not concentrate on coming to a workable predictive framework of how arbitral tribunals will in all likelihood decide on specific issues, such as 'regulatory expropriation'? Are we thus reduced to an exercise in reading tea leaves?

No doubt such an exercise is valuable, but it would not be *legal* scholarship in a strict sense. While there are certain things we can say in general about expropriation, they are not of a legal nature and not discovered by legal analysis. It seems that when we do use legal scholarship, we cannot produce general statements about the law, as it is fragmented. Yet, this assessment should be restated in a more nuanced fashion; we will explore how methods can be developed which will be able to say something meaningful about expropriation in international investment law while remaining within the bounds of legal scholarship proper.

While we have already discussed the possible role and limits of legal scholarship at several points, we have done so mostly in a critical and deconstructive mode. The next chapters will analyse the content of the law, which means that we need a positive idea of how to perform this legal-scholarly task. Legal scholarship's (*Rechtswissenschaft*) most important task is doctrinal scholarship (*Rechtsdogmatik*). Given the theoretical strictures discussed above, how (using which methods) can doctrinal international investment law scholarship operate? The idea of doctrinal scholarship is, of course, not German, but nineteenth-century German private law scholarship has had an undeniable influence on international legal scholarship (Section 2.5.1) – including subconsciously shaping our ideas of what is proper doctrinal scholarship. *Rechtsdogmatik* is an untranslatably German term; the idea is (culturally) German and highly controversial there.[2] However, the problems of *Rechtsdogmatik* tend to

[2] See Matthias Jestaedt, 'Wissenschaftliches Recht: Rechtsdogmatik als gemeinsames Kommunikationsformat von Rechtswissenschaft und Rechtspraxis' in Clemens Jabloner et al. (eds.), *Vom praktischen Wert der Methode: Festschrift Heinz Mayer zum 65. Geburtstag* (Vienna: Manz 2011) 169–87.

find their way into modern debates on international law. For example, Stephan Schill's idea of investment law as public law[3] is based on the idea of *Wissenschaftliches Recht*, of jurists making law by 'interpreting' it, which is an important element in the classical idea of *Rechtsdogmatik*. Also, the problems of orthodox international legal scholarship sometimes mirror problems of *Rechtsdogmatik*, even where the German concept was not taken on board. Matthias Jestaedt warns us against the dangers of transmuting[4] the rationality of scholarship into a 'rationality' of the law itself (see Section 4.3). 'The law is subjected to the doctrinal system: [legal phenomena] which do not fit in [the juridical] system are either re-interpreted or discarded.'[5] In this manner, the systematic construction created by *Dogmatik* is equated with 'the more or less coherent and contingent aims and goals of the human creators of a legal order'.[6] Integralist thought reigns supreme: '*Dogmatik* does not (or not seriously) distinguish the cognition of law from its creation and it does not distinguish *de lege ferenda* proposals and ... authorisations to create law [eg judgments].'[7] It may seem as if the very idea of *Rechtsdogmatik* is to obfuscate the distinction between thought and will, between method and legal authority. The term 'doctrinal scholarship' will merely serve as a convenient label; the German debate will not be analysed here. Yet, because our idea of what legal scholarship ought to do owes much to the debate about *Rechtsdogmatik*, we will recur to that tradition where applicable.

5.2 Theoretical Foundations for Doctrine

In order to develop a workable 'new' doctrinal scholarship based on normativist positivism, we first have to briefly discuss the Pure Theory of Law's

[3] Eg Stephan W Schill, *The Multilateralization of International Investment Law* (Cambridge: Cambridge University Press 2009); Stephan W Schill, 'System-Building in Investment Treaty Arbitration and Lawmaking' 12 *German Law Journal* (2011) 1083–1110.

[4] Jestaedt (2011) note 2 at 175: 'transmutatio dogmatica'.

[5] 'Das Recht untersteht hier dem dogmatischen System: was nicht ins System passt, wird entweder "passend" gemacht oder aber als systemwidrig verworfen.' Jestaedt (2011) note 2 at 184.

[6] 'die mehr oder minder (in)konsistenten und kontingenten Ordnungsvorstellungen seiner heterogenen Schöpfer' Jestaedt (2011) note 2 at 185.

[7] 'Es wird also in den Kategorien der Dogmatik nicht (oder doch nicht ernsthaft) unterschieden zwischen Rechtserkenntnis und Rechtserzeugung, auch nicht zwischen rechtswissenschaftlichen Rechtsetzungsvorschlägen und ... Rechtsetzungsermächtigungen.' Jestaedt (2011) note 2 at 185.

largely implicit theory of legal scholarship (*Rechtswissenschaftstheorie*).[8] It attempts to construct a framework for a true 'science' (*Wissenschaft*)[9] of law. This commitment primarily entails that legal scholarship 'is being kept free from all the elements foreign to the specific method of a science whose only purpose is the cognition of law'.[10] Constructively, this means that legal scholarship is about finding 'the truth' (even though it is a problematic concept), that is, establishing a correspondence of valid legal norms and legal cognition. Hence, doctrinal legal scholarship's aim should be to apprehend the law in a methodologically stringent manner.[11] Law as norms, as ought (*Sollen*),[12] has a specific form of 'existence' which can be perceived. The Pure Theory of Law is a normativist-positivist approach because it seeks to unite law's ideal quality – you *ought* to do something – with the reality of human creation: law is made, not given by a divine being or reason. 'The positivity of morals and law lies . . . in this act of creation by human acts. . . . [T]he Is-Fact . . . of Being-Enacted [is a] condition . . . for the validity of a norm, but not validity itself.'[13]

The Pure Theory of Law as a legal-theoretical approach is founded on and follows from this conception of scholarship.[14] Two elements of this

[8] This is Jestaedt's apt German compound word, eg in Matthias Jestaedt, 'Perspektiven einer Rechtswissenschaftstheorie' in Matthias Jestaedt, Oliver Lepsius (eds.), *Rechtswissenschaftstheorie* (Tubingen: Mohr 2008) 185–205; Horst Dreier speaks of Kelsen's '*Wissenschaftsprogramm*', his 'programme for [legal] scholarship' (Horst Dreier, 'Hans Kelsens Wissenschaftsprogramm' in Helmuth Schulze-Fielitz (ed.), *Staatsrechtslehre als Wissenschaft* (Berlin: Duncker & Humblot 2007) 81–114). The following paragraphs draw on an earlier publication: Jörg Kammerhofer, 'Hans Kelsen in Today's International Legal Scholarship' in Jörg Kammerhofer, Jean d'Aspremont (eds.), *International Legal Positivism in a Post-Modern World* (Cambridge: Cambridge University Press 2014) 81–113 at 83–7.

[9] The term 'science' is not used by Kelsen in the common English meaning but rather in the sense of 'proper scholarship'. 'The reality . . . at which a science of law is directed, is not the reality of nature which constitutes the object of natural science.' Hans Kelsen, *General Theory of Law and State* (Harvard: Harvard University Press 1945) xiv.

[10] Kelsen (1945) note 9 at xiv.

[11] Julius Binder, 'Der Wissenschaftscharakter der Rechtswissenschaft' 25 *Kant-Studien* (1920) 321–65 at 340; Hans Kelsen, *Das Problem der Souveränität und die Theorie des Völkerrechts: Beitrag zu einer reinen Rechtslehre* (Tubingen: Mohr 1920) iv (4 *HKW* 256); Hans Kelsen, *Reine Rechtslehre* (2nd edn, Vienna: Deuticke 1960) iii–iv, 72–8; Franz Weyr, 'Rechtsphilosophie und Rechtswissenschaft' 2 *Zeitschrift für öffentliches Recht* (1922) 671–82 at 672, 678.

[12] Kelsen (1960) note 11 at iii.

[13] 'In diesem – durch menschliche Akte – Gesetzt-Sein . . . liegt die *Positivität der Moral und des Rechts*. . . . die Seins-Tatsache . . . des Gesetzt-Werdens [ist eine] Bedingung . . . der Geltung einer Norm, aber nicht diese Geltung selbst.' Kelsen (1960) note 11 at 114.

[14] Though see Stanley L Paulson, 'The Purity Thesis' 31 *Ratio Juris* (2018) 276–306.

theory which we have already discussed in previous chapters are important for doctrinal scholarship: the *Stufenbau* theory of the hierarchy of law and the theory of interpretation as a frame of possible meanings.

1. *Structural analysis.*[15] Kelsen argues that 'theory ... is directed at a structural analysis [*Strukturanalyse*] of positive law';[16] it is central to the enterprise of doctrinal legal scholarship because legal orders are formally structured. The *Stufenbau* theory is based on the idea that it makes sense to metaphorically represent specific relationships between norms – that type of relationship which makes them part of one legal order rather than an assemblage of norms – as a hierarchical 'step pyramid'. However, the 'pyramid' is merely a heuristic tool to describe and represent inter-norm relationships in legal orders; it is a tool to analyse the structure of legal orders and cannot itself change the structure. Analysing an actual legal order, we will probably find that a simple pyramidal structure is inaccurate. It may look, for example, more like a network of norms.[17] Yet the metaphor cannot invalidate the doctrinal result[18] because it follows the theoretical insight into the dynamic nature of norms, not vice versa.

The *Stufenbau* theory describes those 'systemic connections which are ... a necessary corollary of the concept of law'[19] – the validity relationship

[15] See my previous writings on the *Stufenbau* theory, eg: Jörg Kammerhofer, *Uncertainty in International Law: A Kelsenian Perspective* (Abingdon: Routledge 2010) 180–5, 230–8; Jörg Kammerhofer, 'Sources in Legal Positivist Theories: The Pure Theory's Structural Analysis of the Law' in Samantha Besson, Jean d'Aspremont (eds.), *The Oxford Handbook of the Sources of International Law* (Oxford: Oxford University Press 2017) 343–62; Jörg Kammerhofer, 'Der Stufenbau des Völkerrechts: Strukturanalyse statt Quellenmystik' in Clemens Jabloner, Jan Kuklik, Thomas Olechowski (eds.), *Hans Kelsen in der tschechischen und internationalen Rechtslehre* (Vienna: Manz 2018) 173–90.

[16] Kelsen (1945) note 9 at xiv.

[17] Theo Öhlinger, *Der Stufenbau der Rechtsordnung: Rechtstheoretische und ideologische Aspekte* (Vienna: Manz 1975) 17.

[18] Adolf Julius Merkl, 'Prolegomena einer Theorie des rechtlichen Stufenbaues' in Alfred Verdross (ed.), *Gesellschaft, Staat und Recht: Festschrift für Hans Kelsen zum 50. Geburtstag* (Vienna: Springer 1931) 252–94 at 284, reprinted in Hans Klecatsky, René Marcic, Herbert Schambeck (eds.), *Die Wiener rechtstheoretische Schule: Ausgewählte Schriften von Hans Kelsen, Adolf Julius Merkl, Alfred Verdross* (Vienna: Europa 1968) (abbreviated as: *WRS*) 1311–61 at 1350 and in Dorothea Mayer-Maly, Herbert Schambeck, Wolf-Dietrich Grussmann (eds.), *Adolf Julius Merkl: Gesammelte Schriften*, vol I/1 (Berlin: Duncker & Humblot 1993) (abbreviated as: *MerklGS*) 437–92 at 479–80; Rainer Lippold, *Recht und Ordnung: Statik und Dynamik der Rechtsordnung* (Vienna: Manz 2000) 386.

[19] 'systematischen Zusammenhänge, die ... rechtswesenhaften Charakter aufweisen' Jürgen Behrend, *Untersuchungen zur Stufenbaulehre Adolf Merkls und Hans Kelsens* (Berlin: Duncker & Humblot 1977) 11.

(*Geltungsbeziehung*) between norms. The positivist validity-*regressus* – a norm must be based on another norm in order to be valid[20] – implies that the two norms are in a relationship because the source establishes the validity[21] of those norms created under it. This is the one and only type of relationship between norms inherent in their normativity (see Section 3.5): if they are not created, they cannot exist to prescribe behaviour. Legal scholarship can (and must) therefore be concerned with the analysis of the structure of that order,[22] both on a macro and on a micro level. That structural analysis[23] is the task not of legal theory but of doctrinal scholarship: portraying the structure which the law itself provides but which is most likely neither fully coherent nor fully rational. This is the doctrinal method most in tune with the idea of a 'legal science': analysing more-or-less complex and more-or-less coherent legal orders, finding out exactly how their component parts interrelate and interact. This task is neither banal nor trivial nor easy and it is far removed from the realist caricature of positivists as mere accountants or ledger-keepers of rules.

2. *Doctrinal interpretation as frame-determination.*[24] The other important tool for doctrinal scholarship, intimately connected to the structural analysis of the hierarchy,[25] perhaps best described as structural analysis on a micro-level, is the determination of the frame of possible meanings of the law studied. Interpretation as cognition (interpretation$_{A}$), rather than 'interpretation' as guiding judges (interpretation$_{B}$), is one of the proper functions of legal scholarship (see Chapter 4). '[T]he interpretation of law by legal scholarship must be sharply distinguished ... from the interpretation by legal organs. [Scholarly interpretation] is the cognition of the meaning of legal norms, not the creation of law.'[26] The scholarly cognition of the law,

[20] Kelsen (1960) note 11 at 196.

[21] Merkl (1931) note 18 at 275–6 (*WRS* 1339–40, I/1 *MerklGS* 467–8).

[22] Adolf Julius Merkl, *Die Lehre von der Rechtskraft, entwickelt aus dem Rechtsbegriff: Eine rechtstheoretische Untersuchung* (Leipzig: Deuticke 1923) 210.

[23] Merkl (1931) note 18 at 252 (*WRS* 1311, I/1 *MerklGS* 437); Lippold (2000) note 18 at 394.

[24] See Kammerhofer (2010d) note 15 at 104–17.

[25] Robert Walter, 'Das Auslegungsproblem im Lichte der Reinen Rechtslehre' in Günther Kohlmann (ed.), *Festschrift für Ulrich Klug zum 70. Geburtstag* (Cologne: Peter Deubner 1983) 187–97 at 188.

[26] '... muß die Interpretation des Rechtes durch die Rechtswissenschaft von der Interpretation durch Rechtsorgane ... auf das schärfste unterschieden werden. Sie ist rein erkenntnismäßige Feststellung des Sinnes von Rechtsnormen. Sie ist, zum Unterschied von der Interpretation durch Rechtsorgane, keine Rechtserzeugung.' Kelsen (1960) note 11 at 352.

establishing the 'meaning-content'[27] of norms, is bounded both by the use of natural language as a medium of law and by the essential constitutive freedom of legal organs to decide. The norms serving as basis for the creation of 'lower' norms cannot fully determine the latter's content; this lack of determination is inherent because they are relatively indeterminate norms. Intentional and unintentional indeterminacy means that multiple meanings are possible; a number of decisions are legally allowed. Norms are not univocal, not even vis-à-vis a specific set of factual circumstances.

> [T]he law to be applied merely provides a frame, within which there is more than one possibility of application. Any act that stays within this margin and gives the frame a possible sense is legal. . . . If 'interpretation' is to be understood as epistemic ascertainment of the meaning of the object to be interpreted, the result of a legal interpretation can only be the ascertainment of a frame (which is the law to be interpreted) and thus the cognisance of multiple possibilities [of meaning], which are possible within the frame.[28]

Doctrinal legal scholarship is limited in what it can say.[29] It defines the frame of possible meanings but does not determine them.[30] It describes the limits to the norm which are immanent in the validity (existence) of the norm interpreted. Doctrinal scholarship does not conduct interpretation$_B$, as cognition will probably almost never produce a single answer. The choice of natural languages in legal regulation alone makes this very unlikely. Orthodoxy's tendency to expect *one* answer from doctrinal interpretation, of interpretation producing

27 Riccardo Guastini, 'Kelsen on Legal Knowledge and Scientific Interpretation' in Letizia Gianformaggio, Stanley L Paulson (eds.), *Cognition and Interpretation of Law* (Milan: G Giappichelli 1995) 107–15 at 108.

28 'Das anzuwendende Recht bildet . . . nur einen Rahmen, innerhalb dessen mehrere Möglichkeiten der Anwendung gegeben sind, wobei jeder Akt rechtmäßig ist, der sich innerhalb dieses Rahmens hält, den Rahmen in irgendeinem möglichen Sinn ausfüllt. . . . Versteht man unter "Interpretation" die erkenntnismäßige Feststellung des Sinnes des zu interpretierenden Objektes, so kann das Ergebnis einer Rechtsinterpretation nur die Feststellung eines Rahmens sein, den das zu interpretierende Recht darstellt, und damit die Erkenntnis mehrerer Möglichkeiten, die innerhalb dieses Rahmens gegeben sind.' Kelsen (1960) note 11 at 348–9.

29 See Heinz Mayer, 'Die Interpretationstheorie der Reinen Rechtslehre' in Robert Walter (ed.), *Schwerpunkte der Reinen Rechtslehre* (Vienna: Manz 1992) 61–70 at 62.

30 Eg Michel Thaler, Mehrdeutigkeit und juristische Auslegung (Vienna: Springer 1982) 17 fn 35; Günther Winkler, *Rechtstheorie und Erkenntnislehre: Kritische Anmerkungen zum Dilemma von Sein und Sollen in der Reinen Rechtslehre aus geistesgeschichtlicher und erkenntnistheoretischer Sicht* (Vienna: Springer 1990) 213.

solutions, means asking scholarship to engage in a more-or-less subconscious effort at law-making.[31] The new doctrinal scholarship on the normativist-positivist approach cannot deliver that:

> We cannot deny that this fiction of legal norms having one determined meaning may be advantageous from some political point of view. However, such a political advantage cannot justify using this fiction in a scholarly work of the positive law by presenting one interpretation (desirable as it may be from a subjective political point of view) as being the only possible one from an objective scholarly vantage-point, where another interpretation is logically equally possible.[32]

The advantages of the new doctrine are that it will restrict itself to an effort at cognising the law in force, that it will be able to say something meaningful about the law beyond an uncritical apology for what states do or what tribunals say and that it will avoid merely reflecting what the scholar feels the law should be:

> [A] scholarly interpretation *stricto sensu* . . . can be of practical use [as well], one which far outweighs the political gain of clinging to the fiction that the law is unambiguous. A scholarly interpretation can show the law-creating authority how flawed its work is vis-à-vis the technical postulate of formulating provisions in an as unequivocal manner as possible, or at least in a manner that minimises the unavoidable ambiguity [of using language.][33]

[31] See Jörg Kammerhofer, 'Systemic Integration, Legal Theory and the ILC' 19 *Finnish Yearbook of International Law 2008* (2010) 157–82; Jörg Kammerhofer, 'Law-Making by Scholarship? The Dark Side of 21st Century International Legal "Methodology"' in James Crawford, Sarah Nouwen (eds.), *Select Proceedings of the European Society of International Law: Third Volume: International Law 1989–2010: A Performance Appraisal. Cambridge, 2–4 September 2010* (Oxford: Hart 2012) 115–26.

[32] 'Es soll nicht geleugnet werden, daß diese Fiktion der Eindeutigkeit der Rechtsnormen, von irgendeinem politischen Standpunkt aus gesehen, große Vorteile haben mag. Aber kein politischer Vorteil kann rechtfertigen, daß von dieser Fiktion in einer wissenschaftlichen Darstellung positiven Rechts Gebrauch gemacht wird, indem eine Interpretation, die von einem subjektiv-politischen Standpunkt aus erwünschter ist als eine andere, logisch ebenso mögliche Interpretation, als die von einem objektiv wissenschaftlichen Standpunkt aus allein richtige proklamiert wird.' Kelsen (1960) note 11 at 353.

[33] '[D]ie streng wissenschaftliche Interpretation . . . kann eine praktische Wirkung haben, die den politischen Vorteil der Eindeutigkeitsfiktion bei weitem aufwiegt: Eine solche wissenschaftliche Interpretation kann der rechtsetzenden Autorität zeigen, wie weit ihr Werk hinter der rechtstechnischen Forderung bleibt, Rechtsnormen möglichst eindeutig oder doch so zu formulieren, daß die unvermeidliche Vieldeutigkeit auf ein Minimum beschränkt bleibt . . ..' Kelsen (1960) note 11 at 353–4.

5.3 A New Doctrine of Investment Law

These two building-blocks come together to create a new style of doctrinal legal scholarship: international investment law is cognised in a structural sense, irrespective of politico-ethical strictures, irrespective of a perceived need to provide an apology for arbitral jurisprudence or to solve problems. This is the basis for a doctrinal analysis of expropriation law which takes account of the 'realities' of the field while reacting to three problems:

The problem of fragmentation. There are no universal norms (*ratione personae*) on expropriation, only a conglomerate of bi- and plurilateral treaty provisions. There are no specific norms (*ratione materiae*) on expropriation. Arbitral awards contain individual norms and some of their *reasoning* leading to the decision might be part of the individual norm that is the award. Yet not even as precedents will they be general norms. Are there things we *can* say about the law 'in general'?

The problem of boundless concretising and universalising. Orthodox scholarship tends to see the law as providing specific answers for each case (*Fallnorm*); they thus tend to restrict the possible decisions under an IIA clause. These solutions also sometimes transcend the frame of possible meanings under the norm to be studied or applied. In both cases, orthodox doctrinal scholarship supplants its own value-judgments for the content of the law – both when the law is incommensurable and when it is silent on the issue discussed.

The reality of jurisprudence. The 'authority' of jurisprudence is limited and the arguments made by arbitrators in their reasoning are not an a priori better analysis of the law than others. Tribunal members do not have a stronger 'epistemic authority'. Awards can go and have gone beyond the frame of possible meanings of IIA expropriation clauses and have done so more often than is commonly assumed. The new doctrinal scholarship must act as a critic of jurisprudence where it does so and cannot be apologist-in-chief for a jurisprudential consensus. However, no doctrinal scholarship can ignore the 'brute fact' of jurisprudential material; it must be taken into account and taken seriously for what it is.

Given these problems, the methods for a new doctrinal scholarship may not seem far removed from orthodox scholarship. Indeed, the new doctrinal scholarship under the auspices of the Pure Theory of Law is no more than legal common sense, albeit 'a common sense tweaked'.[34] And these 'tweaks' are of vital importance if legal scholarship is to cognise the law in force,

[34] Kammerhofer (2017b) note 15 at 343; see also Kammerhofer (2011d) note 1 at 154–7; Kammerhofer (2012) note 31 at 125–6.

rather than impose its own ideology upon its and our view of the law. Doctrinal legal scholarship of international investment law might employ a number of methods:

1. *Structural analysis*. This structural analysis of international investment law on the micro-level is a frame determination of the possible meanings of (for example) 'expropriation', based on the structure which the IIA provisions typically create. While this may look like orthodox systematic interpretation, it is subtly different. The contention in Chapter 7 is that, in contrast to the orthodox view, the structural equality of direct and indirect expropriation as well as the specific way in which the *Tatbestand* ('shall directly or indirectly expropriate') is connected to the four legality conditions ('unless') *structurally exclude* the majority's reading of what (indirect) expropriation typically means.

2. *Distillation of 'principles'*. This is a special form of macro-level structural analysis, adapted for the particularities of international investment law. In complex domestic legal orders, macro-level analysis will look at the connection between various *strata* of norms, analysing the complex interrelationships among constitution, statutes and other parts. Regarding investment law, however, an analysis of structurally similar but not legally connected provisions in IIAs is made. The fragmentation problem is taken up, but not by seeking to unify the law, and while it is also similar to orthodox portrayals, it is both based on a different theoretical basis and will come to different results.

New doctrinal scholarship does not try to overcome fragmentation by distilling overarching 'paradigms for understanding the system's nature';[35] it avoids the trap of inadvertently falsifying cognition by trying to fit into a preconceived mould what is *sui generis*. It can potentially generate general propositions for international investment law. This could be described as scholarship portraying the principles of expropriation law,[36] but 'principles' of a special kind. These are not part of a dichotomy of rule or principle; they are the result of a process of 'analysing and comparing the legal norms created by legal authorities'.[37] 'Legal scholarship contains propositions

[35] Anthea Elizabeth Roberts, 'Clash of Paradigms: Actors and Analogies Shaping the Investment Treaty System' 107 *American Journal of International Law* (2013) 45–94 at 75.

[36] This is inspired by works like Rudolf Dolzer, Christoph Schreuer, *Principles of International Investment Law* (2nd edn, Oxford: Oxford University Press 2012).

[37] 'im Wege von Analyse und Vergleichung der von der Rechtsautorität gesetzten Rechtsnormen festgestellt' Hans Kelsen, *Allgemeine Theorie der Normen* (Vienna: Manz 1979) 94.

which are statements *about* legal norms. It portrays legal norms, it describes them. These propositions themselves are not norms, but statements about norms.'[38] Legal scholarship can reconstruct an overarching statement, but this does not mean that 'expropriation' is thus made *one* norm, merely that it is the general outline of the mass of IIA expropriation norms. It is a portrayal of commonalities in the law and of its limits: a form of micro-level comparatist scholarship.

Writing about the possible functions of doctrinal constitutional law scholarship, Adolf Julius Merkl argues that scholars often limit themselves to portraying one *stratum* only, that of statutory law:

> One tends to forget ... that the[ir] epistemic object is not the law as a whole, but merely statutes, which are an unfinished transitory state of development of the law. ... I do not mind this self-restraint of legal scholarship, as long as it is coupled with self-restraint regarding the results of the act of cognition. ... The knowledge created by this legal scholarship looking at statutes are conditional on the law-appliers' actual acts of individual decision and determination. ... Legal scholars usurp the role which the law has given to another [organ] if they portray the law as if it were utterly concretised and determined for a specific case.[39]

We must guard against presuming to replace the individual decision with a scholarly determination of how a specific set of facts *ought* to be decided. However, doctrinal scholarship can – and our knowledge of the law will benefit from – seek(ing) to portray a specific legal *stratum*, for example IIA expropriation clauses. It can also portray arbitral awards as a more concrete and individualised *stratum*, as long as it is aware of the

[38] 'Die Rechtswissenschaft enthält Sätze, die Aussagen *über* Rechtsnormen sind. Sie stellt Rechtsnormen dar, beschreibt Rechtsnormen. Diese Sätze sind selbst keine Normen, sondern Aussagen über Normen.' Kelsen (1979) at 123; see also Kelsen (1960) note 11 at 57–8.

[39] 'Man vergißt eben ... daß nicht das Recht schlechthin, sondern bloß das unfertige Entwicklungs-, das Durchgangsstadium des Rechtes, als das sich uns das Gesetz herausgestellt hat, Gegenstand der Erkenntnis ist. ... Ich habe nichts gegen diese Selbstbeschränkung der Rechtswissenschaft, wenn sie mit der entsprechenden Selbstbescheidung hinsichtlich der Erkenntnisresultate gepaart ist. ... Die Erkenntnisse dieser auf das Gesetz abgestellten Rechtswissenschaft gelten gewissermaßen unpräjudizierlich der vom Rechtsanwender getroffenen Einzelentscheidung und Einzelverfügung. ... Der Rechtswissenschafter maßt sich selbst diese im Sinne des ... Gesetzes einem anderen zugedachte Rolle an, wenn er Rechtserkenntnisse für den Einzelfall in restloser Konkretisierung zum besten gibt.' Adolf Julius Merkl, 'Das Recht im [Spiegel] Lichte seiner [Auslegung] Anwendung' [the title varies] 8 *Deutsche Richterzeitung* (1916) col 584–92, 9 *Deutsche Richterzeitung* (1917) col 162–76, 394–8, 443–50, 11 *Deutsche Richterzeitung* (1919) col 290–8 (*WRS* 1167–1201, I/1 *MerklGS* 85–146) at col 169 (*WRS* 1176–7, I/1 *MerklGS* 106).

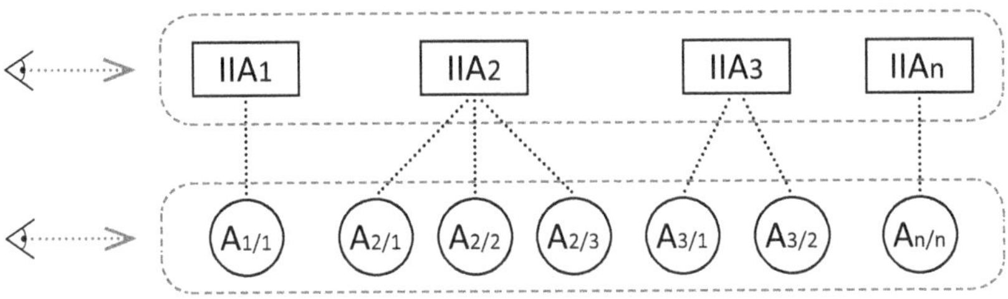

Figure 5.1 *Stratum* analysis[40]

limitations of doing so. Orthodox scholarship tends to commingle both levels (Chapter 4). We cannot validly conclude from an analysis of the 'lower' level of case-law that the 'higher' level of IIAs contains more specific prescriptions than its terms. We may not deduce from the general norm an individual decision which has not (yet) been rendered.[41] Also, Award_1, based on IIA_1, even if it could add specificity to IIA_1's content, certainly cannot do so for other IIAs. However, it is possible to systematically portray the level of arbitral awards without seeking to insert their content into (all) IIAs. Legal scholarship thus systematically portrays one particular legal *stratum*, summarises and condenses the results of the process of concretisation. It is able to do so without claiming that arbitral awards are (an expression of) a unified, multilateralised or general norm and without thus drawing generalising conclusions as to the content of (all) IIAs.

3. *Doctrine for practical use.* Legal scholarship eagerly participates in the production of what could be termed 'writings for practitioner use' (*Praktikerliteratur*) with the most important category being commentaries on civil codes. This trend has taken root in international legal scholarship as well, with a large number of commentaries on important codifications. This type of writing serves an important function for several categories of stakeholders, foremost state representatives, counsel and judges both in litigation and in their daily non-contentious work. They primarily give an overview of what realists would term 'the law in action' in the sense of providing predictability of potential future decision-making and acceptable stances by reflecting on past decision-making.[42] This is an aim which doctrinal legal scholarship can take on board even under the normativist-positivist approach. For the new doctrinal scholarship, this practitioner-oriented

40 Doctrinal scholarship (eye) can isolate its epistemic effort on cognising either the level of IIAs or that of arbitral awards ($A_{n/n}$) and thus overcome *some* aspects of fragmentation.
41 Merkl (1916–19) note 39 at col 168 (*WRS* 1175–6, I/1 *MerklGS* 105).
42 Alexander Somek, *Wissen des Rechts* (Tubingen: Mohr 2018) at 50–2.

taking-into-account of arbitral jurisprudence serves an important function, but it is pragmatic and empirical, a 'precept of prudence' (*Klugheitsregel*).[43] This does not invalidate its importance, but it is dangerous to conflate this prediction of future decisions with knowledge of the law.

5.4 Trends in Case-Law

Yet how can new doctrinal scholarship on a normativist-positivist basis be squared with a focus on actual decisions and future decisional trends? The key question for all legal scholars is how to cope with the pressing flood of judicial decisions. Almost irrespective of which approach is chosen, most legal scholarship tends to answer the siren call of jurisprudence, submit willingly to its yoke and become its servant.[44] Orthodox doctrinal scholarship[45] does so despite the insistence that in the final consequence it is portraying the general law: 'some type of mechanism of sorting, evaluating and weighing the different strands of arbitral case law is an essential component of any comprehensive text addressing this fast-moving field'.[46] On the other hand, legal realism in its many guises is geared towards the ultimate decision as a matter of principle and even 'lexicographers', those studying the legal profession's vocabulary, rather than abstract 'norms', cannot go far beyond the language-use of tribunals.

We have developed a possible path to a new doctrinal legal scholarship; that part of the new doctrine which produces practitioner-oriented statements seems certain to share some of its methods with legal realists. On the basis of normativist-positivist scholarship in the strict sense, we cannot hope to produce a prediction matrix, but if we are to generate prediction, we would need to see whether some form of empirical study of past jurisprudence can or is likely to predict future decisions.

[43] Immanuel Kant, *Grundlegung zur Metaphysik der Sitten* (2nd edn, Riga: Hartknoch 1786) AA IV 416.

[44] Somek (2018) note 42 at 49.

[45] For an interesting parallel to German constitutional law scholarship, see Bernhard Schlink, 'Die Entthronung der Staatsrechtswissenschaft durch die Verfassungsgerichtsbarkeit' 28 *Der Staat* (1989) 161–72.

[46] Jürgen Kurtz, 'Review Essay: The Shifting Landscape of International Investment Law and Its Commentary' 106 *American Journal of International Law* (2012) 686–94 at 691; see also Roberts (2013) note 35 at 91.

Three well-known arguments militate against a simple counting of past decisions and predicting future decisions from precedents: First, as many legal realists have realised, the prediction of future behaviour is unscientific, as past behaviour only gives anecdotal, 'pragmatic' indications, not predictability which can satisfy social-scientific standards. Second, the lines of past decision-making in several areas, particularly on the key question of regulatory expropriation, are simply not coherent enough to be able to extrapolate trends. Third, even a method accepted by social scientists, such as a citation-tree of arbitral awards restricted to statements on expropriation, would be confronted by several difficulties. Would we need to exclude pure references to party-cited jurisprudence by the arbitral tribunal, or at least put this in a different category?[47] Would we need to differentiate between different 'strengths' of citation, like a simple reference, a positive/negative connotation ('citing with approval'), whether the tribunal actually quotes a precedent or provides a substantive analysis of that case? Non-mechanical qualitative citation analysis faces the problem that the 'cleverer' and less mechanical it is, the more subjective it becomes and the more it approaches the orthodox method. Selecting, rationally ordering and commenting on jurisprudence is what mainstream doctrinal scholarship does best, but it must face the objection that both subjective value-judgement and an unwarranted belief in rationality are imported by the back-door.

An alternative may be the idea of a 'professional vocabulary', seeing 'expropriation' as bounded by a socio-linguistic community of understanding. This is part of Jean d'Aspremont's earlier writings, linking Hart's social thesis to the idea of 'communitarian semantics',[48] as well as Martti Koskenniemi's discursive understanding of international law as a 'professional vocabulary'.[49] For these approaches, meaning and thus legal content is created by playing the language-game well. Scholars and practitioners manoeuvre within their vocabulary to

[47] Frédéric G Sourgens, 'Law's Laboratory: Developing International Law on Investment Protection as Common Law' 34 *Northwestern Journal of International Law & Business* (2014) 181–247; Frédéric G Sourgens, *A Nascent Common Law: The Process of Decisionmaking in International Legal Disputes Between States and Foreign Investors* (The Hague: Nijhoff 2015).

[48] Jean d'Aspremont, *Formalism and the Sources of International Law: A Theory of the Ascertainment of Legal Rules* (Oxford: Oxford University Press 2011), critiqued in Jörg Kammerhofer, 'International Legal Positivism' in Florian Hoffmann, Anne Orford (eds.), *The Oxford Handbook of the Theory of International Law* (Oxford: Oxford University Press 2016) 407–26.

[49] Martti Koskenniemi, *From Apology to Utopia: The Structure of International Legal Argument* (1989, reissued: Cambridge: Cambridge University Press 2005) 589 (epilogue).

'determine' the law (in a socio-psychological sense). One could perhaps envisage a reconstructive effort proposed by Christian Djeffal for interpretation[50] of the vocabulary of influential actors in the practice of international law.

However, how would these two modes differ? Could we do away with the belief that we are using 'juristic methodology' and 'subsuming as deduction' when creating the meaning of expropriation clauses? Could we do that while still adhering to the idea that there are norms and maintaining the distinction between 'true' legal-scholarly analysis of the norms and a socio-linguistic analysis of the social practices (or vocabulary-building) which shape detailed understanding of 'expropriation law'? The same problems obtain. Semantic, pragmatic and social meanings are probably not sufficiently coherent and are instable; they may also be inherently incapable of providing even some stability and safety of meaning-content. While there is a theoretical difference between the socio-linguistic and the realist methods, the results will be similar. One difference is that scholars and state representatives would count for little on a realist analysis, whereas they are crucial to developing a professional vocabulary.[51]

Socio-empirical modes of analysis find their place, but in the following we will foreground the *stratum* analysis described above. Arbitral jurisprudence as in fact providing greater specificity will be analysed and used irrespective of the conventional need to deliver unity, coherence, meaningfulness and rationality.[52] At least part of Chapter 8 is a portrayal of the pragmatic features of expropriation as a practice-heavy area of law and of the consequences flowing from these features. The basic framework will remain legal-scholarly, including its attendant restrictions: the new doctrine practised

[50] Christian Djeffal, *Static and Evolutive Treaty Interpretation: A Functional Reconstruction* (Cambridge: Cambridge University Press 2016) 71–6.

[51] See eg John Dugard, 'The Future of International Law: A Human Rights Perspective – With Some Comments on the Leiden School of International Law' 20 *Leiden Journal of International Law* (2007) 729–39 at 731: 'As academic international lawyers outnumber international law practitioners, unlike the situation with any branch of national law, the opinions of academic lawyers become the law – at least as far as many academic lawyers are concerned.'

[52] Coming from a different theoretical direction, this is perhaps, to some extent, similar to Gregory Shaffer's ecumenical conception of a New Legal Realism: Gregory Shaffer, 'The New Legal Realist Approach to International Law' 28 *Leiden Journal of International Law* (2015) 189–210.

below cannot provide 'one right answer', cannot make scholarship norm-giving, must practice 'pluridisciplinarity'[53] and not commingle its results.[54]

5.5 Conclusion

The next chapters will portray the international investment law on expropriation, but will do so commensurate with the theoretical approach adopted here. This may engender large gaps in coverage: this book will discuss a small number of significant questions which are necessary for the two main points. The first point is the production of legal-scholarly knowledge about expropriation law which is true to the law and commensurate with all the constraints on doctrinal legal scholarship. The second point is that following this path of scholarship inevitably means disagreeing with the majority opinion on central points of expropriation law (Chapter 6). This is done not out of a desire to play the role of dissident at any cost but because the majority has constructed a narrative incommensurable with the law. For example, the point of my scepticism regarding the police powers doctrine and the resistance against an indisputable trend in international legal scholarship and jurisprudence (Chapter 7) is the view that mainstream doctrines on regulatory expropriation are not 'the law'. That is, the particular elements, stages, steps, priorities espoused are not what the law requires. The law is shaped in a different way; it contains other elements or it does not contain these elements. The doctrines and arguments are also not part of a relevant source – they are, for example, 'policy' reasons not relevant to the cognition of law as norms.

However, as mentioned in Section 5.2, we must highlight the essential difference between, on the one hand, micro-level structural analysis of IIA provisions and, on the other hand, the interpretation$_B$ of those provisions. As detailed above, at least classical IIA expropriation clauses are structured so as to restrict the possible meanings, including those that differentiate between direct and indirect expropriation or those which differentiate between the process conditions, on the one hand, and the

[53] Otto Pfersmann, 'Hans Kelsens Rolle in der gegenwärtigen Rechtswissenschaft' in Robert Walter, Werner Ogris, Thomas Olechowski (eds.), *Hans Kelsen: Leben–Werk–Wirksamkeit. Ergebnisse einer Internationalen Tagung, veranstaltet von der Kommission für Rechtsgeschichte Österreichs und dem Hans Kelsen-Institut (19.–21. April 2009)* (Vienna: Manz 2009) 367–87 at 378.

[54] Jörg Kammerhofer, 'The Challenges of History in International Investment Law: A View from Legal Theory' in Stephan W Schill, Christian J Tams, Rainer Hofmann (eds.), *International Investment Law and History* (Cheltenham: Edward Elgar 2018) 164–76 at 169.

compensation condition, on the other. This is the structure and stricture of IIAs. It is a result neither of the process of application by arbitral tribunals nor of orthodox interpretation (interpretation$_B$). Most other further determinations and specifications of the general norms, such as which acts breach a due process condition, may rightfully be the core issue before arbitrators, but they are not part of the (general) law. Any concretisation through judicial decisions is individually binding, no more, and does not *legally* determine the content of the IIA. Both jurisprudence and writings are extraordinarily important, so important as to lead to the claim that international law is an argumentative practice.[55] They are important determinants, *in fact*, of the socially pervasive and accepted understanding of law, not of the law and its (correct) scholarly cognition. New doctrinal scholarship can both engage in doctrinal legal scholarship (structural analysis) and also provide data-collection on the more pragmatic level (Section 5.3).

We will also need to clarify the terminology employed to describe the various elements of the 'typical', 'classical'[56] or 'traditional' IIA expropriation clause, which we will call 'Type A IIA expropriation clause'; see also Section 7.5. A random example is Article 7(1) of the Australia–Mexico BIT 2005:

> Neither Contracting Party shall expropriate or nationalise an investment either directly or indirectly through measures tantamount to expropriation or nationalisation (hereinafter referred to as "expropriation"), except:
>
> (a) for a public purpose;
> (b) on a non-discriminatory basis;
> (c) in accordance with due process of law; and
> (d) accompanied by payment of compensation in accordance with paragraphs 2, 3 and 4 below.[57]

This is a well-used and well-known formula; it consists of several component parts which we shall name as follows:

– *Tatbestand*. In previous chapters, this has been called the *actus reus* condition of expropriation, but the German technical term *Tatbestand*

[55] See Jean d'Aspremont, *International Law as a Belief System* (Cambridge: Cambridge University Press 2018) 27 fn 117: 'Nowadays it is common to think of international law as an argumentative practice.'

[56] *Tomasz Częścik and Robert Aleksandrowicz* v. *Republic of Cyprus*, SCC, V 2014/169, Award of 11 February 2017, para 210.

[57] Agreement between the Government of Australia and the Government of the United Mexican States on the Promotion and Reciprocal Protection of Investments, signed 23 August 2005, entry into force 21 July 2007, 2483 UNTS 247.

is more accurate because it includes *mens rea*.[58] *Tatbestand* is the behaviour which is prohibited: direct or indirect expropriation. It is not accurate to call it the 'threshold question',[59] as it certainly is not a minimum and prejudicial threshold but the core of the whole provision.

- *Legality conditions*. Expropriation, the prohibited act, is justified if all conditions are met, that is, an act (omission) which is an expropriation can be allowed under the IIA if it is for a public purpose, . . . and compensation is paid. All necessary conditions together will be called 'legality conditions'.
- *Process conditions*. IIAs typically prescribe two or three conditions which do not involve the payment of compensation. They are concerned with process, bona fides, or the rule of law. These will be called 'process conditions' in order to distinguish them from the final condition below.
- *Compensation condition*. The final condition typically is the payment (or the making of provision for the payment) of compensation.[60]

[58] It has the added advantage of not generating false preconceived notions among jurists who were not trained in German-speaking legal systems and of being the correct trigger for those who have.

[59] Sebastián López Escarcena, *Indirect Expropriation in International Law* (Cheltenham: Edward Elgar 2014) 39.

[60] Stephen R Ratner, 'Compensation for Expropriations in a World of Investment Treaties: Beyond the Lawful/Unlawful Distinction' 111 *American Journal of International Law* (2017) 7–56 at 7: 'process conditions' and 'payment condition'; Audley Sheppard, 'The Distinction between Lawful and Unlawful Expropriation' in Clarisse Ribeiro (ed.), *Investment Arbitration and the Energy Charter Treaty* (New York: JurisNet 2006) 169–99 at 170: 'conduct requirements' and 'compensation requirement'.

6

The Regulatory Expropriation Conundrum

6.1 Introduction: The Set-Up

Which actions constitute compensable expropriation?[1] This question is at the heart of the current legal debate on expropriation. Few topics have fired up experts, stakeholders and the interested public as much as whether measures such as taxation, packaging regulation of tobacco products[2] or Germany's exit from nuclear energy production indirectly expropriate foreign investors. Almost all IIAs provide an expropriation clause; in classical treaties, the *Tatbestand* (*actus reus*) is not defined: which actions does the law prohibit, which state behaviour can indirectly expropriate an investor? In Chapter 7, we will engage in a micro- and macro-structural analysis of typical IIA expropriation clauses. However, in order to counter predictable criticism, given the likely direction of my analysis, we will first have to deconstruct the regulatory expropriation puzzle. Regulatory expropriation means a host state's general regulatory measures potentially being found to constitute indirect expropriation under IIAs. This is the most-discussed area where a significant impact on state behaviour (investor treatment) can be expected. It is not just a convenient test-case for the theoretical assumptions made in previous chapters. Rather, both the analysis and the solution proposed are symptoms for a larger theoretical problem with the orthodox method. It is precisely on this question where the temptation to diverge from the path of accurate cognition of legal norms is greatest, and this is so precisely because of the fundamental flaw at the heart of orthodox scholarship.

Because of the particular way in which the problem is generally framed, the solutions proposed are also virtually indistinguishable. This

[1] Eg Stephen R Ratner, 'Regulatory Takings in Institutional Context: Beyond the Fear of Fragmented International Law' 102 *American Journal of International Law* (2008) 475–528 at 475.

[2] Eg *Philip Morris Brands SÀRL, Philip Morris Products S.A. and Abal Hermanos S. A. v. Oriental Republic of Uruguay*, ICSID, ARB/10/7, Award of 8 July 2016.

is a counter-intuitive proposition. As Section 6.1 demonstrates, doctrinal positions on regulatory expropriation are usually classified into those promoting state freedom and those prioritising investor protection. This way of framing the problem hinders, rather than helps in finding out what IIA expropriation clauses say. Because the conundrum is framed as it is, this leads to a single solution (Section 6.2), even where different results are achieved, and the solution is tainted by the set-up. This point is made by analysing four typical views representing a range of approaches (Section 6.3). The focus of the present chapter is a retelling of the story that has framed post-2000 regulatory expropriation analysis. In the end, however, it is a political conundrum and adopting political solutions seems inevitable.

Virtually all writings and a good number of arbitral awards set up the issue of regulatory expropriation as a conundrum, puzzle or dilemma.[3] The argument starts with the statement that 'most investment treaties ... do not provide a definition of "expropriation"'[4] – most IIAs, that is, bar the trend started by the United States and Canada in 2004 to provide at least elements of such a definition in their fight to contain the negative effects of a perceived expansive jurisprudence vis-à-vis regulatory expropriation (Section 7.5).[5] It is also generally agreed that states are

[3] Eg Ursula Kriebaum, 'Regulatory Takings: Balancing the Interests of the Investor and the State' 8 *Journal of World Investment & Trade* (2007) 717–44 at 720.

[4] L Yves Fortier, Stephen L Drymer, 'Indirect Expropriation in the Law of International Investment: I Know It When I See It, or *Caveat Investor*' 19 *ICSID Review – Foreign Investment law Journal* (2004) 293–327 at 296; see also eg Barry Appleton, 'Regulatory Takings: The International Law Perspective' 11 *New York University Environmental Law Journal* (2002–3) 35–48 at 40; Maurizio Brunetti, 'Introduction [Indirect Expropriation in International Law]' 5 *International Law Forum* (2003) 150–4 at 153–4; A Devin Bray, 'Non-compensatory versus Compensatory Takings under NAFTA' 9:7 *Transnational Dispute Management* (2012) 18; Rudolf Dolzer, Margrete Stevens, *Bilateral Investment Treaties* (The Hague: Martinus Nijhoff 1995) 99; Meg N Kinnear, Andrea K Bjorklund, John FG Hannaford, *Investment Disputes under NAFTA: An Annotated Guide to NAFTA Chapter 11* (Alphen aan den Rijn: Kluwer 2006), esp. 1110-1–1110-63 at 1110-13; Kriebaum (2007b) note 3 at 722; Ursula Kriebaum, *Eigentumsschutz im Völkerrecht: Eine vergleichende Untersuchung zum internationalen Investitionsrecht sowie zum Menschenrechtsschutz* (Berlin: Duncker & Humblot 2008) 261–2; Céline Lévesque, 'Distinguishing Expropriation and Regulation under NAFTA Chapter 11: Making Explicit the Link to Property' in Kevin C Kennedy (ed.), *The First Decade of NAFTA: The Future of Free Trade in North America* (Ardsley: Transnational 2004) 293–324 at 294, 299; Brigitte Stern, 'In Search of the Frontiers of Indirect Expropriation' in Arthur W Rovine (ed.), *Contemporary Issues in International Arbitration and Mediation: The Fordham Papers 2007* (Leiden: Nijhoff 2008) 29–51 at 30.

[5] Annex B of the US Model BIT 2004, available at: www.state.gov/documents/organization/117601.pdf; Annex B.13(1) of the Canada Model FIPA 2004, available at: www.italaw.com/documents/Canadian2004-FIPA-model-en.pdf.

'permitted' or 'have a right' to expropriate,[6] but whether this 'freedom' is a permissive norm, a subjective right or a 'negative permission'[7] is not uniformly answered. Pleading for a right, Rudolf Dolzer and Christoph Schreuer write that 'the classical rules of international law have accepted the host state's right to expropriate alien property in principle'.[8] Ursula Kriebaum, in contrast, argues that '[t]he expropriation of foreign property *was never prohibited*',[9] possibly pointing to a negative freedom as absence of prohibitory norm. Catherine Titi seems to combine these two views when she speaks of 'a *rule* of customary international law that states *are allowed* to expropriate the assets of foreign investors *without incurring* international *liability*'.[10] If it is seen as a norm of international law, it is mostly held to be customary international law.[11] This may seem like nit-picking, but it is a very interesting question in light of the discussion regarding the right to regulate and the police powers doctrine. The exact deontic status of the freedom does change the calculus. It does so not only regarding the questions of how and in which respects IIAs contain a *renvoi* to customary international law but particularly regarding the

6 Eg Appleton (2002–3) note 4 at 42; Bray (2012) note 4 at 3; Dolzer (1995) note 4 at 97; Rudolf Dolzer, Christoph Schreuer, *Principles of International Investment Law* (2nd edn, Oxford: Oxford University Press 2012) 98; Fortier (2004) note 4 at 295; Ursula Kriebaum, 'Expropriation' in Marc Bungenberg et al. (eds.), *International Investment Law* (Baden-Baden: Nomos 2015) 959–1030 at 962; Lévesque (2004) note 4 at 298–9; Organisation for Economic Co-operation and Development (OECD), 'Draft Convention on the Protection of Foreign Property' reprinted in 7 *International Legal Materials* (1968) 117–43 at 124; Ratner (2008) note 1 at 481; Giorgio Sacerdoti, 'Bilateral Treaties and Multilateral Instruments on Investment Protection' 269 *Recueil des Cours 1997* (1998) 251–460 at 380; Jeswald W Salacuse, *The Law of International Investment Treaties* (Oxford: Oxford University Press 2010) 288; Esmé Shirlow, 'Deference and Indirect Expropriation Analysis in International Investment Law: Observations on Current Approaches and Frameworks for Future Analysis' 29 *ICSID Review* (2014) 595–626 at 596; Sūrya Prasāda Subedī, *International Investment Law: Reconciling Policy and Principle* (3rd edn, Oxford: Hart 2016) 152; Aikaterini Titi, *The Right to Regulate in International Investment Law* (Baden-Baden: Nomos 2014) 148–9; Catherine Yannaca-Small, '"Indirect Expropriation" and the "Right to Regulate" in International Investment Law' in OECD (ed.), *International Investment Law: A Changing Landscape: A Companion Volume to International Investment Perspectives* (Paris: OECD 2005) 43–72 at 45; Christian Zielonka, *Der Ausgleich zwischen Investorenschutz- und Regulierungsinteressen in internationalen Investitionsschutzabkommen* (Berlin: Duncker & Humblot 2017) 88–9.

7 See on this question Jörg Kammerhofer, 'Gaps, the *Nuclear Weapons* Advisory Opinion and the Structure of International Legal Argument between Theory and Practice' 80 *British Year Book of International Law 2009* (2010) 333–60.

8 Dolzer (2012) note 6 at 98.

9 Kriebaum (2015) note 6 at 962 (emphasis added).

10 Titi (2014) note 6 at 148 (emphasis added).

11 Eg Fortier (2004) note 4 at 295; Lévesque (2004) note 4 at 298.

potential conflict of norms. Almost across the board, authors acknowledge that this right or freedom to expropriate exists only 'provided certain conditions are met, namely that the taking of the investments is done for a public purpose, in accordance with the law and against compensation',[12] the typical legality conditions in IIAs. The conditionality of the freedom to expropriate is seen as strengthened by the wave of IIAs in the second half of the twentieth century.[13] As a corollary, it is sometimes claimed that customary international law actually defines expropriation,[14] an issue discussed in more detail in Section 7.2.

Inevitably, however, after dismissing direct expropriation as easily defined or as the question having been 'settled',[15] almost all treatments of the subject find that the problem is defining indirect expropriation. 'Controversy here lies in where to draw the line between non-compensable regulatory and other governmental activity and measures amounting to indirect, compensable expropriation.'[16] Generally speaking, it is realised that there are 'various forms of administrative and regulatory actions that leave investors in possession of investment assets but diminish their freedom to control, manage, and derive benefits from them' and 'whether and to what extent such provisions protect covered assets'.[17] This could be extrapolated to the point where 'almost any

[12] Dolzer (1995) note 4 at 97; see also Sacerdoti (1988) note 6 at 380: 'BITs do not deny this right but aim at subjecting expropriation to the full respect of substantive and procedural requirements prescribed by international law.'

[13] Dolzer (2012) note 6 at 98; Zielonka (2017) note 6 at 88–9.

[14] Eg Appleton (2002–3) note 4 at 40; Lévesque (2004) note 4 at 299; Martins Paparinskis, 'Regulatory Expropriation and Sustainable Development' in Marie-Claire Cordonier Segger, Markus W Gehring, Andrew Newcombe (eds.), *Sustainable Development in World Investment Law* (Alphen aan den Rijn: Wolters Kluwer 2011) 299–327 at 303 (unclear).

[15] Sūrya Prasāda Subedī, 'The Challenge of Reconciling the Competing Principles within the Law of Foreign Investment with Special Reference to the Recent Trend in the Interpretation of the Term "Expropriation"' 40 *International Lawyer* (2006) 121–41 at 124.

[16] Energy Charter Secretariat, *Expropriation Regime under the Energy Charter Treaty* (Brussels: Energy Charter Secretariat 2012) 12; see also Appleton (2002–3) note 4 at 42; Dolzer (2012) note 6 at 102, 120; Fortier (2004) note 4 at 293, 296; Kriebaum (2007b) note 3 at 718; Ratner (2008) note 1 at 478; August Reinisch, 'Expropriation' in Peter Muchlinski, Federico Ortino, Christoph Schreuer (eds.), *The Oxford Handbook of International Investment Law* (Oxford: Oxford University Press 2008) 407–58 at 432; Salacuse (2010) note 6 at 287, 297; Subedī (2006) note 15 at 124; Subedī (2016) note 6 at 100, 197; Stern (2008) note 4; Titi (2014) note 6 at 148; United Nations Conference on Trade and Development, *Taking of Property* [UNCTAD/ITE/IIT/15] (2000) note 16 at 6, 14; Yannaca-Small (2005) note 6 at 44–5; Zielonka (2017) note 6 at 91.

[17] Salacuse (2010) note 6 at 287.

governmental measure could be construed as an act of interference in the business of a foreign investor'.[18] '[T]he power of government to regulate economic activity'[19] and the protection against indirect expropriation are seen as 'two, theoretically distinct, concepts'.[20]

> [T]here is increasing concern that concepts such as indirect expropriation may be applicable to regulatory measures aimed at protecting the environment, health and other welfare interests of society. The question that arises is to what extent a government may affect the value of property by regulation, either general in nature or by specific actions in the context of general regulations, for a legitimate public purpose without effecting a 'taking' and having to compensate for this act.[21]

At this point, the second universally consented rule of customary international law[22] makes an appearance, even though, for all the agreement it engenders, it is not well-proven: the right to regulate or to exercise a state's 'inherent' police power(s).[23] 'Under classic international law, normal regulatory measures to protect the public welfare . . . have fallen under the so-called police powers rule, and were excluded from consideration as an expropriatory measure.'[24] This is usually discussed twice: first, briefly, when the problem is set up and independent of the position adopted to solve the puzzle. The second discussion happens in a more nuanced fashion during the development of the solution (Sections 6.3 and 7.2). However, there is a difference in emphasis between (mostly) older sources mentioning police powers in a very narrow sense[25] and

[18] UNCTAD (2000) note 16 at 6.
[19] Ratner (2008) note 1 at 481.
[20] Reinisch (2008a) note 16 at 432.
[21] Yannaca-Small (2005) note 6 at 44–5.
[22] Yannaca-Small (2005) note 6 at 47 fn 10.
[23] I have chosen the plural form for consistency and convenience: 'police powers', rather than 'police power' and 'sole effects', rather than 'sole effect'. No particular substantive position should be inferred from this.
[24] ECS (2012) note 16 at 12; see also Appleton (2002–3) note 4 at 42; Fortier (2004) note 4 at 298; Francisco Orrego Vicuña, 'Regulatory Authority and Legitimate Expectations: Balancing the Rights of the State and the Individual under International Law in a Global Society' 5 *International Law Forum* (2003) 188–97 at 190; Salacuse (2010) note 6 at 298; Muthucumaraswamy Sornarajah, *The International Law on Foreign Investment* (3rd edn, Cambridge: Cambridge University Press 2010) 374, 388; Subedī (2016) note 6 at 262; Titi (2014) note 6 at 32–3; UNCTAD (2000) note 16 at 14; Yannaca-Small (2005) note 6 at 47 fn 10.
[25] Eg Rudolf L Bindschedler, *Verstaatlichungsmaßnahmen und Entschädigungspflicht nach Völkerrecht: unter besonderer Berücksichtigung der schweizerischen Praxis über den Schutz schweizerischer Vermögenswerte im Ausland* (Zurich: Polygraphischer Verlag 1950) 25; Samy Friedman, *Expropriation in International Law* (London: Stevens & Sons 1953) 1;

newer, wider readings.[26] Also, a difference is sometimes made between the 'police powers' exception to the *Tatbestand* of expropriation and a customary legal 'right to regulate' – a wide 'freedom to engage in political, economic, legislative and other regulatory activity as the state sees fit'.[27]

The conundrum is thus born of a dual dichotomy. As a minor factor, the strong and strongly conditional customary and conventional law norms attaching the legality conditions to expropriation conflicts with a strongly held belief in a robust police powers exception/right to regulate.[28] The far more prominent dilemma is an *argumentum ab inconvenienti*: granting either full investment protection or full state freedom of action is inacceptable:

> The following dilemma exists as regards regulatory interferences: [on the one hand,] it is established in international law that not every regulatory interference with property rights that has negative effects, is an expropriation requiring compensation. To question the State's regulatory power would make the exercise of many State functions impossible. On the other hand, doctrine as well as arbitral decision support the view that regulation can amount to expropriation.[29]

L Yves Fortier and Stephen Drymer are clear as to the policy considerations: 'the community cannot reasonably be required to bear the normal commercial risks associated with foreign investments'; but it is also clear that 'investors cannot be asked to endure unreasonable regulation without compensation, and they should not be asked to pay'.[30] If we follow

Werner Veith, Karl-Heinz Böckstiegel, *Der Schutz von ausländischen Vermögen im Völkerrecht* (Baden-Baden: Lutzeyer 1962) 172; Benjamin Alexander Wortley, *Expropriation in Public International Law* (Cambridge: Cambridge University Press 1959).

[26] Subedī (2016) note 6 at 191, who differentiates thus: 'Traditional international law admits the existence of (i) the "police power" of states and (ii) regulatory expropriations that could attract … no compensation'; United Nations Conference on Trade and Development, *Expropriation* [UNCTAD/DIAE/IA/2011/7] (2012) 79.

[27] Titi (2014) note 6 at 32.

[28] See Andrew Newcombe, Lluís Paradell, *Law and Practice of Investment Treaties: Standards of Treatment* (Alphen aan den Rijn: Kluwer 2009) 321: 'International expropriation law mediates between two general principles of international law: (i) that states exercise permanent sovereignty over their territories and natural resources; and (ii) that states must respect the acquired rights of foreigners.'

[29] Kriebaum (2007b) note 3 at 720–1; see also Kriebaum (2015) note 6 at 1000; Lévesque (2004) note 4 at 305; Vaughan Lowe, 'Regulation or Expropriation?' 55 *Current Legal Problems 2002* (2003) 447–66 at 447; Reinisch (2008a) note 16 at 433; Titi (2014) note 6 at 148.

[30] Fortier (2004) note 4 at 298; see also Lévesque (2004) note 4 at 296.

the majority in setting up the problem in this manner, the dilemma is inescapable: both extremes of consistent investor protection or state freedom are unacceptable. If we set ourselves up to fail in this manner, international law cannot follow either course, because giving in to one side means abandoning the other.

6.2 The Single Solution

At this point, we inevitably arrive at the solution most congenial to any international lawyer's heart: the middle ground. If we believe in the description of the problem as given above, we are inevitably guided towards a middle-of-the-road solution of balancing and proportionality. Céline Lévesque asserts that 'the concept of expropriation itself implies balance'.[31] This is the preferred approach of scholarship as well as arbitral case-law. What is more, this approach is followed almost independently of whether one favours state freedom or investor protection.

1. *Semantics.* Sometimes, traces of a reliance on semantic (lexical) definitions are visible in the writings canvassed here (see also Section 8.3.1). For A Devin Bray, for example, it can be '[g]enerally stated' that 'the term "expropriation" means "dispossession," "taking," "deprivation," or "privation."'[32] Lévesque argues that 'the etymology of the word "expropriation" reveals that it presupposes private property'[33] and draws certain inferences about the shape of the law from this. Burns Weston links this semantic foundation with the 'ordinary meaning' and word-use theories:

> Consider . . . the civil law term 'expropriation.' As every ordinary person might rightly suppose, these words can be understood to mean an act of sovereign power which, with or without compensation, results in an actual divestment of all or part of one's property. As every lawyer knows, however, they can refer also to the exercise of a special kind of sovereign power . . . .[34]

Most commonly, the semantic foundation is framed as a definitory exercise, such as this: '[i]n simple terms, "expropriation" means the taking of

31 Lévesque (2004) note 4 at 295.

32 Bray (2012) note 4 at 5.

33 Lévesque (2004) note 4 at 294; see also Thomas Rieger, *Grundsätze der Unternehmensenteignung in der Rechtsprechung des Iran–United States Claims Tribunal* (Cologne: Heymans 1997) 16; Wortley (1959) note 25 at 39.

34 Burns H Weston, '"Constructive Takings" under International Law: A Modest Foray into the Problem of "Creeping Expropriation"' 16 *Virginia Journal of International Law* (1975) 103–75 at 111.

the assets of foreign company or investors by a host state'.[35] The *Emmis* tribunal used a dictionary definition: 'The Oxford English Dictionary defines "expropriate" as "(of the state or an authority) take (property) from its owner for public use or benefit"/"dispossess (someone) of property".'[36] Sometimes, a mere working definition is proposed, particularly in writings penned before the explosion of IIAs and arbitral awards.[37] Given that the current debate has shifted to the question of the *Tatbestand* of indirect vis-à-vis direct expropriation, the semantic foundation is often employed to quickly dispense with the direct expropriation issue, as it is considered to be reasonably unproblematic. 'A direct expropriation ... occurs when an owner is required to relinquish both title and physical possession ... An indirect expropriation is more difficult to define.'[38] Indirect expropriation has also been defined as 'interference by a government towards a particular property ... for a long time, so that it could reasonably be inferred that the owner is perpetually deprived of the use, enjoyment or disposal of his property'.[39] However, where the semantic argument appears, it is not usually connected to the single solution to the regulatory expropriation conundrum.

2. *Jurisprudence.* All modern writings on expropriation in international investment law base their view at least partially on arguments and definitions in awards.[40] It is reasonably clear that jurisprudence is accorded

[35] Subedī (2016) note 6 at 150; see also Appleton (2002–3) note 4 at 40; ECS (2012) note 16 at 9; Sebastián López Escarcena, *Indirect Expropriation in International Law* (Cheltenham: Edward Elgar 2014) 3; Campbell McLachlan, Laurence Shore, Matthew Weiniger, *International Investment Arbitration: Substantive Principles* (Oxford: Oxford University Press 2007) 266; Sacerdoti (1998) note 6 at 379.

[36] *Emmis International Holding, B.V., Emmis Radio Operating, B.V., Mem Magyar Electronic Media Kereskedelmi és Szolgáltató Kft. v. Hungary*, ICSID, ARB/12/2, Award of 16 April 2014, para 159 (emphasis removed).

[37] Matti Pellonpää, Malgosia Fitzmaurice, 'Taking of Property in the Practice of the Iran–United States Claims Tribunal' 19 *Netherlands Yearbook of International Law 1988* (1989) 53–178 at 55; see also Wil D Verwey, Nico Schrijver, 'The Taking of Foreign Property under International Law: A New Legal Perspective?' 15 *Netherlands Yearbook of International Law* (1984) 3–96 at 5.

[38] Joseph A Strazzeri, 'A *Lucas* Analysis of Regulatory Expropriations under NAFTA Chapter Eleven' 14 *Georgetown International Environmental Law Review* (2001–2) 837–59 at 841; see also Salacuse (2010) note 6 at 294.

[39] Hossein Piran, 'Indirect Expropriation in the Case Law of the Iran–United States Claims Tribunal' 6 *Finnish Yearbook of International Law* (1995) 140–247 at 146; see also Salacuse (2010) note 6 at 297.

[40] Eg John A Westberg, 'Applicable Law, Expropriatory Takings and Compensation in Cases of Expropriation; ICSID and Iran–United States Claims Tribunal Case Law Compared' 8 *ICSID Review – Foreign Investment Law Journal* (1993) 1–28 at 13.

the function of a foundation or justification of the legal argument. Chapter 3, in particular, has discussed and problematised this reliance as precedent; Chapter 4 has done so with respect to its use as aid in interpretation. A particular case is the use of the jurisprudence of constitutional and human rights courts, typically adjudicating on rights to property to which we will return in Section 6.3.

Investment case-law from the year 2000 onwards is a particularly important source of arguments for the single solution to the regulatory expropriation conundrum, as it is widely assumed that two (or three) lines of jurisprudence have developed since the leading award in *Metalclad*.[41] Bjørn Kunoy, writing in 2005, frames the issue in these terms:

> In ICSID case law, there are . . . two different lines of cases. In accordance with [the *Metalclad*] approach, solely the effects of the contested measures are taken into account when determining if the investor has been subject to an indirect expropriation. No concerns are given to whether or not the contested act was a *bona fide* measure. This approach can be contrasted with that adopted by the ICSID Tribunal in *Tecmed*. . . . The Tribunal seems to have adopted a more traditional approach and implicitly recognized that bona fide measures depriving the investor of the main patrimonial attributes of an investment need not be qualified as indirect expropriation if the purpose of the act is legitimate.[42]

However, there is a difference between scholarship framing the problem and its solution as described above while using case-law as foundation for its argument, on the one hand, and awards themselves framing the regulatory expropriation conundrum and providing a solution to it, on the other. Case-law is not a legal authority beyond the individual case; it can serve as an expression of non-scholarly legal argument, but it is not privileged as 'epistemic authority' vis-à-vis scholarly opinion (see Chapter 4). In this study, jurisprudence is primarily of interest as the raw material for the doctrinal enterprise attempted in Chapter 8 and will be discussed there.

3. *Customary international law*. A reference to customary international law is another ubiquitous foundational move in developing the solution

[41] *Metalclad Corporation* v. *United Mexican States*, NAFTA-ICSID, ARB(AF)/97/1, Award of 30 August 2000.

[42] Bjørn Kunoy, 'Developments in Indirect Expropriation Case Law in ICSID Transnational Arbitration' 6 *Journal of World Investment & Trade* (2005) 467–91 at 471–2; see also eg Kriebaum (2015) note 6 at 1005–6; Allen S Weiner, 'Indirect Expropriations: The Need for a Taxonomy of "Legitimate" Regulatory Purposes' 5 *International Law Forum* (2003) 166–75 at 166–7.

to the regulatory expropriation conundrum (Chapter 2 and Section 4.3.2). As briefly discussed above, the regulatory expropriation solution depends on the idea of the existence, relevance and relative weight of two conflicting sets of norms: the treaty and/or a customary prohibition of expropriation, on the one hand, and a customary police powers exception and/or a right to regulate, on the other. W Michael Reisman, for example, integrates the customary police powers exception in the treaty itself. 'Consistent with customary international law, BITs do not prohibit expropriation per se. In the exercise of their sovereignty over natural resources or police powers, states remain entitled to expropriate foreign property.'[43] A number of arguments from customary international law are possible, for example a *renvoi* of the IIA expropriation clause to the controlling customary international law norm which itself integrates the police powers exception. However, as we will see in Section 7.2, one result of the macro-structural analysis is that a reference to customary international law can achieve relatively little.

4. *Telos and policy.* A fourth foundational move is a reference to what could charitably be described as teleological or policy-oriented arguments. The regulatory expropriation conundrum, as set up, is inherently political and it is no surprise to see it argued in this manner. The argument is that because either extreme has negative consequences (is undesirable in the writer's mind), both are excluded; the single solution is the law, because it is preferable from a practical/teleological standpoint. Andrew Newcombe, for example, in 'develop[ing] a framework for how international law should treat claims of regulatory expropriation', argues that '*the level of investment protection* in international law for foreign investment *should be based on a policy of promoting investment flows* that are welfare maximizing for both host states and foreign investors'.[44] In other words, international law should be and therefore is shaped according to a particular politico-ideological norm. A similar move is made by Max Gutbrod and Steffen Hindelang: 'determining indirect expropriation only by diminution in property value might reduce national policy space to zero . . . therefore . . . the impact of the State measure is a central but not the sole factor'.[45] The foundation for their legal argument – even

[43] W Michael Reisman, Robert D Sloane, 'Indirect Expropriation and Its Valuation in the BIT Generation' 74 *British Year Book of International Law 2003* (2004) 115–50 at 134; see also Strazzeri (2001–2) note 38 at 844, 852.

[44] Newcombe (2009) note 28 at 87 (emphasis added).

[45] Max Gutbrod, Steffen Hindelang, 'Externalization of Effective Legal Protection against Indirect Expropriation: Can the Legal Order of Developing Countries Live Up to

if ostensibly only on the 'interstitial' decision-making by arbitral panels in adjudicating indirect expropriation claims (see Sections 4.3.4) – is whether the substantial deprivation standard alone has negative practical effects on national policy-making. The opposite can and has also been argued: that the extreme police powers doctrine cannot be the law because it *practically* negates investor protection.

6.3 Four Approaches

At this point, it would probably be possible to undertake a classification of the various approaches to regulatory expropriation. We could then assume that classical writings argue for robust investor protection and apply orthodox methods of Articles 31–3 VCLT interpretation and precedent-following. We could then attempt to classify writers and even case-law as following one approach. This is a plausible, if complex, undertaking. However, for the purposes of this chapter the analysis of select examples is preferable. The point is to show that in the final analysis, whatever the differences in approach, they all operate on the basis of the same *problematique* and adopt the same solution to the regulatory expropriation conundrum. In the following, four representative English-language writings from 2008 to 2018 on regulatory expropriation will be analysed:

- August Reinisch's chapter on expropriation in the 2008 *Oxford Handbook of International Investment Law*,[46] typical of the new mainstream;
- Caroline Henckels' 2012 article on indirect expropriation and the right to regulate[47] as an example of a comparatist approach with proportionality analysis;
- Ben Mostafa's 2008 investor-protection-driven liberal defence of the sole effects doctrine;[48] and

Standards Required by International Investment Agreements? A Disenchanting Comparative Analysis' 7 *Journal of World Investment & Trade* (2006) 59–83 at 64; see also eg *Rupert Joseph Binder* v. *Czech Republic*, UNCITRAL, Final Award of 15 July 2011, para 480.

46 Reinisch (2008a) note 16.

47 Caroline Henckels, 'Indirect Expropriation and the Right to Regulate: Revisiting Proportionality Analysis and the Standard of Review in Investor-State Arbitration' 15 *Journal of International Economic Law* (2012) 223–55; see also Caroline Henckels, *Proportionality and Deference in Investor–State Arbitration* (Cambridge: Cambridge University Press 2015).

48 Ben Mostafa, 'The Sole Effects Doctrine, Police Powers and Indirect Expropriation under International Law' 15 *Australian International Law Journal* (2008) 267–96.

- the 2012 UNCTAD study on expropriation[49] as an example of a strongly sovereigntist reading of the law.

This section will eke out the underlying argumentative structures; we will return to the vast body of literature in Chapter 7, but we will work with it in different ways. Here, we will analyse the arguments of representative writers, while maintaining their own narrative, while in Chapter 7, the arguments will be critiqued regarding the three structural limits of IIAs.

6.3.1 *Reinisch: The New Orthodoxy*

Reinisch sets up the problem as described in Section 6.1. He sees 'the concept of indirect expropriation [as] generally accepted . . . as is the idea of legitimate regulatory action which does not give rise to claims of compensation'. The main problem is that 'the precise delimitation . . . is hard to establish' and the goal of such a distinction lies 'in establishing the exact borderline between an indirect expropriation and a regulatory measure'.[50] Relying heavily on case-law, the conundrum is established because of antagonistic 'assertions that . . . legitimate regulatory measures are outside the scope of indirect expropriation and . . . that any substantial deprivation of value regardless of its purposes should be considered expropriatory'.[51]

Reinisch does not foreground the question of whether such a carve-out for regulatory measures is part of the law. It is sufficient that 'there is a widespread consensus that regulatory measures pursued for legitimate objectives cannot be regarded as indirect expropriation'. This is so particularly since it 'has been endorsed by the Iran–US Claims Tribunal as well as by NAFTA panels . . . [and] in a number of recent investment awards', with a neutral reference to *Saluka*[52] in support of the contention that some 'have characterized the principle that legitimate regulatory action cannot be regarded as compensable "expropriation" as a firmly established rule of customary international law'.[53]

The foundation for this widely held belief is not discussed; hence, the exact status of a (customary) legal police powers exception or of a right to

[49] UNCTAD (2012) note 26.
[50] Reinisch (2008a) note 16 at 432.
[51] Reinisch (2008a) note 16 at 433.
[52] *Saluka Investments* v. *Czech Republic*, UNCITRAL, Partial Award of 17 March 2006, para 255.
[53] Reinisch (2008a) note 16 at 433.

regulate is not discussed in depth, nor is the question of the relationship of such a norm to the IIA. For the mainstream, whether a claimed norm is actually part of customary international law is not a particularly interesting question, as long as it finds widespread support in jurisprudence and scholarship, because 'authorities' cannot err over a long time and regarding an important issue. Far more central to Reinisch's analysis is 'the identification of legitimate purposes of regulatory measures'.[54] Orthodoxy embraces a balancing approach and the only relevant question is the respective weight to be given to investor protection vis-à-vis state regulatory freedom. In this case, however, the weighting is accomplished on the basis of selecting a specific range of police powers which negatively define indirect (but, presumably, not direct) expropriation: 'there appears to be an emerging consensus that certain types of state measures are considered legitimate'.[55]

Reinisch does not indulge in consequentialist phantasies – the solution is to be found in what is generally accepted, not in the consistent pursuance of either state regulatory freedom or investor protection. A range of areas of state regulation are judged on whether they serve 'legitimate regulator purposes' by looking at whether there is majority support in case-law. For example, '[i]nvestment arbitration practice has ... recognized taxation and environmental concerns as legitimate purposes. ICSID practice shows that the protection of cultural property may also be considered a legitimate regulatory purpose.'[56] However, '[a]lthough it is sometimes asserted that "bona fide general taxation" belongs to the category of non-compensable regulatory measures, this does not mean that taxation is entirely insulated from expropriation claims'.[57]

For those who embrace the regulatory expropriation conundrum, environmental regulation is the most vexing case because it is perceived as such a noble cause when contrasted with investor protection. Accordingly, Reinisch limits himself to portraying the leading cases of a diverging jurisprudence and argues that '[a]t one extreme, arbitral tribunals may totally disregard the intention of national legislators and look only at the effect of environmental measures', citing *Santa Elena* and *Tecmed*[58] for support; '[a]t the other end of the spectrum lie decisions ... which

[54] Reinisch (2008a) note 16 at 434.
[55] Reinisch (2008a) note 16 at 434.
[56] Reinisch (2008a) note 16 at 435.
[57] Reinisch (2008a) note 16 at 436.
[58] *Compañia del Desarrollo de Santa Elena, S.A.* v. *Republic of Costa Rica*, ICSID, ARB/96/1, Final Award of 17 February 2000, para 72; *Técnicas Medioambientales Tecmed S. A.* v. *United Mexican States*, ICSID, ARB(AF)/00/2, Award of 29 May 2003, para 121.

generally exclude non-discriminatory, regulatory measures from the scope of indirect expropriations',[59] including both *Methanex* and *Saluka*.[60] In his opinion, both extremes go too far and the middle ground is to be preferred. In particular, the extreme police powers doctrine which allegedly manifests itself in the *Methanex–Saluka* line of precedents is to be avoided:

> The broad implications of [this] approach, more or less removing any non-discriminatory regulatory action for a public purpose from the scope of compensable regulatory takings, has given rise to an intense debate. . . . It should be noted, however, that some investment tribunals have voiced concern over the appropriateness of a public purpose as a (sole) criterion to remove government action from the scope of indirect expropriation.[61]

The solution is inevitable: a 'case-by-case analysis' which does not operate 'through abstract legal principles'.[62] The orthodox balancing of public purpose takes into account a number of factors, such as the effect, public purpose, proportionality, non-discrimination or the protection of legitimate investor expectations[63] and weighs them in unique ways for each specific case in order to come to an equitable solution.

6.3.2 *Henckels: Comparatist Proportionality Analysis*

Henckels, in contrast, takes this sliding scale of factors as the starting point for her analysis. Her focus is not on the abstract law but on how arbitral tribunals should go about reviewing state measures in the case before them. For her, the 'standard of review' is crucial; in pure public law comparatism applied to international investment law, the key metric is the degree of judicial 'deference' vis-à-vis the state's measures at issue before the tribunal. 'This article argues that investment tribunals determining indirect expropriation claims should employ proportionality analysis, but do so in a way that is more deferential to host states.'[64] Henckels first restates a relatively orthodox position: 'Customary international law recognizes host states' right to regulate or take other measures significantly affecting foreign investors' property interests without

[59] Reinisch (2008a) note 16 at 437.
[60] *Methanex Corporation* v. *United States of America*, NAFTA-UNCITRAL, Award of 3 August 2005, para IV.7.7; *Saluka* (2006) note 52 at para 262.
[61] Reinisch (2008a) note 16 at 437–8, referring to *Azurix* v. *Argentina*, ICSID, ARB/01/12, Award of 14 July 2006, paras 310, 312.
[62] Reinisch (2008a) note 16 at 438.
[63] See Reinisch (2008a) note 16 at 438–51.
[64] Henckels (2012) note 47 at 224.

a finding of compensable expropriation in certain circumstances.' However, as she explains in a footnote, 'the treatment of police powers as an exception from expropriation ... conflates the concept of lawful expropriation with police powers'.[65]

Henckels argues that proportionality analysis is relevant and that it should be adopted, although it remains unclear what the basis for this norm is. Proportionality analysis is 'a discursive judicial technique or analytical structure for adjudicating disputes concerning measures intruding on protected rights or interests but pursuing a public objective or communal aim'.[66] As we have seen in Chapter 4, this is based on the idea that we can somehow regulate the process of the creation of arbitral awards through a doctrinalisation of juridical techniques.[67] Proportionality as a 'judicial technique' is a German phenomenon, as Henckels acknowledges: '[o]riginating in German administrative law, it is now employed by many international and supranational courts and tribunals in a variety of contexts'. This is an import (one is tempted to interject: of convenience) which, she claims, 'is evolving as the dominant judicial technique for mediating between the competing values of rights protection ... and the public interest pursued by government policy, and may be emerging as a general principle of international law'.[68] This is one face of the public law analogy theory: German public law is permeated with the idea of the effective protection of basic rights vis-à-vis all acts of public force (*öffentliche Gewalt*). Judicial review of public acts will also take into account public interests; hence proportionality is convenient; it has become an article of faith in German public law scholarship and its believers have tried to proselytise this faith for international law. Behind this transfer, this analogy on the grand scale, lies the idea that there is an inherently public law character to international (investment) law.[69] Investor–state dispute settlement is a form of administrative review: '[A]dministrative review means the review of the exercise of public authority vis-a-vis a private entity, which entails enforceable public law remedies against the State. ... [I]nternational investment law provides

65 Henckels (2012) note 47 at 225, 225 fn 5.

66 Henckels (2012) note 47 at 226.

67 For a description and critique, see Horst Dreier, 'Hans Kelsens Wissenschaftsprogramm' in Helmuth Schulze-Fielitz (ed.), *Staatsrechtslehre als Wissenschaft* (Berlin: Duncker & Humblot 2007) 81–114 at 106–13.

68 Henckels (2012) note 47 at 226.

69 See Gus Van Harten, Martin Loughlin, 'Investment Treaty Arbitration as a Species of Global Administrative Law' 17 *European Journal of International Law* (2006) 121–50.

for the protection of investors' rights against violative domestic regulation by the host State ... [I]nternational investment law displays all the characteristics of public law.'[70]

Henckels, like others in this tradition, turns the quasi-empirical classification of investment law as administrative law into the application of popular *domestic* and quasi-domestic (European Court of Human Rights (ECtHR) and European Court of Justice (ECJ)) administrative law doctrines (proportionality analysis and deference to public authority) to this sub-field of international law.[71] Another shift is from it being a judicial technique adjudged to be a good idea to being a prescribed step in arbitral award-making on indirect expropriation. Henckel makes this shift by first highlighting the advantages of proportionality analysis: 'it provides a much more transparent analytical structure for decision-making engaging competing public and private interests. ... [It] is a more methodologically robust approach to legal reasoning.'[72] The middle ground is sought once more, as it 'may be used to restrict the invocation of police powers to measures taken in good faith and in pursuit of legitimate regulatory objectives'.[73] However, the tenor later shifts to the normative:

> [*Tecmed's*] attempt to reconcile host state and investor interests through proportionality analysis nevertheless shows potential for the technique to be used to assist in delimiting non-compensable measures from indirect expropriations. These decisions are an important first step towards the development of a jurisprudence of indirect expropriation that gives broader scope for justifying measures interfering with investment without a requirement to pay compensation, where such measures reflect sound public policy objectives.[74]

But why should jurisprudence 'give... broader scope for justifying measures ... where [they] reflect sound public policy'? Where does this norm come from; is it to be found in IIAs? Is it an extra-legal imperative? Does reason command arbitrators to follow this path? She does not elaborate on the foundation for this claim.

Henckels constructs complex requirements for arbitral reasoning. The standard of review, that is, 'the degree of scrutiny or level of deference afforded by a court or tribunal to the primary decision-maker',[75] is

[70] Andreas Kulick, *Global Public Interest in International Investment Law* (Cambridge: Cambridge University Press 2012) 82–3.
[71] López (2014) note 35 at 192.
[72] Henckels (2012) note 47 at 228–9.
[73] Henckels (2012) note 47 at 228.
[74] Henckels (2012) note 47 at 235–6.
[75] Henckels (2012) note 47 at 238.

another highly relevant factor for how an arbitral decision should be made. 'Determining the appropriate standard of review'[76] on the regulatory expropriation question is based on a range of normative considerations which are explored but which are again unfounded. She concludes by staking out a wide-ranging and seemingly extreme position:

> Investment tribunals should apply a standard of review in proportionality analysis that reflects their role as international adjudicators of disputes engaging matters of public law . . . This approach should be manifested by a deferential approach to whether a measure's objective falls within the host state's police powers, . . . Such an approach would provide greater space for host states to promulgate bona fide measures in the interest of their populations, without being liable to compensate foreign investors for a finding of indirect expropriation.[77]

For all its stringency and apparent neglect of investor protection, the comparative public law approach, particularly with its emphasis on proportionality, adopts essentially the same solution as orthodox scholars, even though it has a different point of departure. What else is proportionality analysis but the demand for investment tribunals to formalise what they have been doing for years: balancing investor protection with state regulatory freedom?[78] For the critique in Chapter 7, it is not important whether this is an ad hoc balancing or a German-style proportionality analysis on the basis of a standard of review calibrated through policy reasoning. The *problematique* is identical and, in all respects that count, the solution is too.

6.3.3 *Mostafa: Classic Liberalism*

On first glance, Mostafa's defence of the sole effects doctrine looks like the polar opposite to the other approaches, but a closer analysis reveals that it is not. He argues 'that the sole effects approach should be preferred', inter alia, because it 'appropriately balances investor and State rights'[79] – expressing the very same sentiment as all other approaches. The formulation of the regulatory expropriation conundrum is classical;

[76] Henckels (2012) note 47 at 241.
[77] Henckels (2012) note 47 at 255.
[78] Alessandra Asteriti, 'Regulatory Expropriation Claims in International Investment Arbitrations: A Bridge too Far?' in Andrea K Bjorklund (ed.), *Yearbook on International Investment Law and Policy 2012–2013* (Oxford: Oxford University Press 2014) 451–73 at 468.
[79] Mostafa (2008) note 48 at 267.

Mostafa acknowledges a right to regulate which 'stems from principles of sovereignty and the territoriality principle' and which, if used, 'will not normally require any compensation to be paid to persons whose property is affected'.[80] There is thus a 'rising tension between indirect expropriation and the right to regulate'.[81]

The problem with the police powers doctrine, Mostafa insists, is that its adherents 'fail to provide a principled approach to determining when an indirect expropriation has occurred, and, to an extent, appear to conflict with certain established notions in international investment law'.[82] For one, he believes that the common definition of police powers as 'any regulation which is bona fide, non-discriminatory and in the interests of public health, safety, morals or welfare' does 'not in fact limit the application of the exception at all; rather, under this definition any indirect expropriation would be within the State's police power'.[83] The 'double counting' of 'public purpose' (Section 7.4) is also seen as counter-productive.[84]

Even the moderate police powers doctrine, limiting non-compensable measures to those related to 'tax, crime and "the maintenance of public order"' or, more broadly, related to 'health, safety or even morality',[85] is seen as problematic. Following a survey of cases, Mostafa concludes that 'international investment law has long held the view that States should be accorded the utmost discretion in defining their own public interest'.[86] Therefore, 'there is no recognisable distinction in international investment law . . . between acceptable and unacceptable public purposes'.[87] Rather than supporting the police powers doctrine, however, he believes that this fact invalidates it, because 'the public utility rule is irrelevant when determining the legality of an expropriation'.[88] If that thinking applies to the legal–illegal distinction, why then should it not apply to the definition of indirect expropriation?

> The difficulties that [these cases] demonstrate in delimiting acceptable public purposes equally apply to the views of the police powers doctrine,

[80] Mostafa (2008) note 48 at 269.
[81] Mostafa (2008) note 48 at 270.
[82] Mostafa (2008) note 48 at 268.
[83] Mostafa (2008) note 48 at 273–4.
[84] Mostafa (2008) note 48 at 274.
[85] Mostafa (2008) note 48 at 274.
[86] Mostafa (2008) note 48 at 275.
[87] Mostafa (2008) note 48 at 277.
[88] Mostafa (2008) note 48 at 277.

> which depend upon distinguishing between purposes pursued by States. ... [T]he fact that a purpose is pursued by the great majority of States does not automatically mean that measures in pursuance of this purpose are not subject to expropriation law.[89]

On this basis, Mostafa rejects the police powers doctrine and turns to the sole effects doctrine, the latter finding significant support in case-law.[90] However, he notes that '[t]he scope of the doctrine . . . is not broad. Measures which interfere with property significantly, but not to the extent that the property may as well have been directly expropriated, cannot be regarded as expropriatory.'[91]

And this is where balancing comes in. While the sole effects doctrine is regarded as part of the law, this must be reconciled with the right to regulate. This, in turn, is achieved in a roundabout manner: 'the high level of interference with property required under the sole effects approach means that the great majority of regulation cannot constitute an expropriation'. The 'substantial interference' test for indirect expropriation is simply seen as setting a 'very high threshold'[92] which most regulation will not reach. A number of secondary limitations are placed on the sole effects doctrine to make it more palatable, such as limiting the scope of expropriable rights, of (legitimate) expectations and by in effect punishing investors who abuse their position under domestic law by the non-compensability of measures affecting their investment.[93] This, once more, is the single solution: while police powers are not an exception to the compensation requirement for indirect expropriation, indirect expropriation requires such a level of interference that most regulation under police powers is de facto excluded. This requires a balancing of investor rights and state regulatory freedom, even if tilted in favour of the investor.

6.3.4 UNCTAD: Sovereigntist Activism

The second edition of the UNCTAD study on *Expropriation* of 2012 clarified the organisation's sovereigntist[94] position on expropriation, for

89 Mostafa (2008) note 48 at 277–8.
90 Mostafa (2008) note 48 at 279–87.
91 Mostafa (2008) note 48 at 287.
92 Mostafa (2008) note 48 at 288.
93 Mostafa (2008) note 48 at 288–91.
94 On sovereigntism as a position in international legal writings, see eg Richard Collins, 'Classical Legal Positivism in International Law Revisited' in Jörg Kammerhofer, Jean d'Aspremont (eds.), *International Legal Positivism in a Post-Modern World* (Cambridge: Cambridge University Press 2014) 23–49.

it is a clear-cut avowal of the strongest possible police powers doctrine. For example, the study clearly supports two arguments which we will later criticise as going beyond the limits of Type A IIA expropriation clauses. First, 'the conditions that determine the lawfulness of an expropriation' should not influence 'the question whether the expropriation has actually occurred': '[i]t is important not to confuse the question whether there has been an expropriation with that of whether the conditions have been satisfied'[95] (see Section 7.4). Second, the study asserts that direct and indirect expropriation need to be treated differently: '[e]ven though pursued for a public purpose, the direct expropriation, in order to be lawful under international law, must be accompanied by compensation', whereas 'when dealing with an allegation of an indirect (regulatory) expropriation, a broader assessment of the nature of the measure (which includes, but is not limited to, the public purpose) is essential'[96] (see Section 7.3). Even some of its factual assertions are tendentious. In categorical language, it asserts that '[m]ost provisions on indirect expropriation found in recent FTAs and BITs are based on the United States and Canadian BIT models of 2004',[97] a claim which a recent empirical study by Alec Stone Sweet and others on the basis of a large dataset has debunked: new style expropriation clauses are still the minority among newly concluded IIAs.[98]

While, given this activist statist position, it may seem that the UNCTAD study is too radical to partake of the singular solution, an argument can be made that it does – in terms of the *structure of its argument*. The *problematique* is presented in the classical form: '[t]he question ... arises how to distinguish between an expropriatory measure and a normal (and thus non-compensable) regulatory act of State'.[99] Yet, in contradistinction to the other writings analysed in this section, a venerable tradition is claimed not merely for an unspecific right to regulate but for the police powers exception *tout court*, irrespective of what IIA investor protection may do to it. 'It has long been accepted in international law that State acts *are in principle not subject to compensation* when they are an expression of the police powers of the State.'[100] This

[95] UNCTAD (2012) note 26 at 27, see also 95.
[96] UNCTAD (2012) note 26 at 31.
[97] UNCTAD (2012) note 26 at 31.
[98] Alec Stone Sweet, Michael Yunsuck Chung, Adam Saltzman, 'Arbitral Lawmaking and State Power: An Empirical Analysis of Investor–State Arbitration' 8 *Journal of International Dispute Settlement* (2017) 579–609 at 603.
[99] UNCTAD (2012) note 26 at 13.
[100] UNCTAD (2012) note 26 at 78 (emphasis added).

is an instance of 'moving the goalposts' where the constant repetition of a hitherto controversial position succeeds in changing the framework of the debate so that this is accepted as uncontroversial. In the 2004 High-Level Panel Report on Threats, Challenges and Change, a member of the panel inserted language incorrectly suggesting that anticipatory self-defence according to the *Caroline* criteria had long been recognised.[101] While the majority opinion was arguably in a process of change towards a more permissive reading,[102] anticipatory self-defence on the *Caroline* terms was certainly not long-established and was hotly contested even as the Report was being written. However, by moving the goalpost, the whole debate following the Report was shifted and so it is here.

The UNCTAD study assumes that the police powers *exception* to the customary prohibition of indirect expropriation, rather than a mere right of states to regulate domestic affairs which may face a customary or treaty-based prohibition of expropriation, has long been established. Under the mechanism described above, the debate can now shift from *whether* the police powers doctrine reflects the law to *how* the police powers exception is shaped: '[t]he police powers doctrine *in its contemporary meaning*'.[103] And this meaning is taken in a wide sense:

> [I]n a narrow sense, his doctrine covers State acts such as (a) forfeiture or a fine to punish or suppress crime; (b) seizure of property by way of taxation; (c) legislation restricting the use of property . . .; and (d) defence against external threats . . . In present times, the police powers must be understood as encompassing a State's full regulatory dimension. . . . [T]he right of States to engage in regulatory activity . . . should not be undermined or restricted by investment treaties.[104]

The study concludes that 'the support for the police powers doctrine appears to be *overwhelming*',[105] after a rather selective overview of authorities. Given the many sceptical arguments even of those sympathetic to the idea of state regulatory freedom, the study must probably be classified as a piece of advocacy, rather than legal scholarship.

101 *A More Secure World: Our Shared Responsibility: Report of the High-level Panel on Threats, Challenges and Change* [A/59/565] (2004) para 188.

102 Jörg Kammerhofer, 'The Resilience of the Restrictive Rules of Self-Defence' in Marc Weller (ed.), *The Oxford Handbook of the Use of Force in International Law* (Oxford: Oxford University Press 2015) 627–48.

103 UNCTAD (2012) note 26 at 79 (emphasis added).

104 UNCTAD (2012) note 26 at 79–80.

105 UNCTAD (2012) note 26 at 85 (emphasis added).

Yet from this point onwards, the balancing starts, just as with the other examples given above. The UNCTAD study employs the 'multiple factors' tactic: '[t]o assess a particular measure . . . it is necessary to undertake a broad examination of its nature, purpose and character'.[106] While the study posits a presumption of 'validity' regarding general regulatory acts and while the burden of proof is squarely on investors, there is a large 'list of . . . indicators that point to the abnormal or irregular nature of a measure' which could yet qualify a regulatory measure as expropriatory. For example, '[i]t includes the lack of genuine public purpose, of due process, of proportionality, and of fair and equitable treatment; discrimination, abuse of rights and direct benefit to the State'.[107] The balancing act between investor protection and state regulatory freedom is accomplished by the 'global assessment'[108] which the study regards as necessary to decide upon claims of regulatory expropriation:

> [O]ne would need to ask the following questions: Does the measure contain the characteristics of a bona fide exercise of police powers by the host State? Is it taken in pursuance of a genuine public purpose, in a non-discriminatory manner and in accordance with the due process of law? Was there a transfer of benefit of the investment of the State or any private party? Is there a manifest disproportionality between the aims pursued and the harm inflicted on the investor?[109]

Therefore, on the basis of the same analysis of the problem, even this clear example of a state-friendly approach to regulatory expropriation proceeds to develop virtually the same solution: because we cannot accept A and we cannot accept non-A, we need to find a balance between these extremes. The *argumentum ab inconvenienti* trumps legal analysis; a reasonable solution is more important than an analysis of the law. The necessity for a *sound* reading of the law invalidates the possibility that the law could be shaped in an unbalanced, disharmonic way.

6.4 Conclusion: Abandon the Conundrum

Most writings on the regulatory expropriation problem in international investment law come to the conclusion that there is no general solution

[106] UNCTAD (2012) note 26 at 92.
[107] UNCTAD (2012) note 26 at 94.
[108] UNCTAD (2012) note 26 at 94.
[109] UNCTAD (2012) note 26 at 105.

and that a case-by-case analysis on the basis of a weighing of multiple factors, including some form of proportionality analysis, is required. While, as we have seen, there are different approaches and while there are those who prefer an investor-friendly outcome and those who prefer a state-centric outcome (with the weight of the majority having shifted from the former to the latter in recent years), the problem and the solution are the same.

To see the regulatory expropriation problem as a sailing-trip between *Scylla* and *Charybdis* is entirely understandable; the pragmatic wish to solve this problem and to try to do so by finding a middle path between the extremes is a very good idea. However, this is an inherently *political* view and not one that legal scholars should adopt, because the conundrum is not one of the law. It is possible, even probable, that IIA provisions on expropriation require compensation even for measures which serve morally worthy goals such as human rights or the protection of the environment. It is probable that the relationship between a right to regulate and the IIA provision is such that, on the basis of a *legal* analysis of the treaty law, the duty of compensation prevails. The solutions developed are not legal enough; as we will show in detail in Chapter 7, the reasoning in favour of one or the other outcome is political as well and the doctrinal argument is suffused with politico-moral elements. Take as an example Ursula Kriebaum's 2008 book, which in all other respects remains very consistent in distinguishing between discussions *de lege lata* and *de lege ferenda*: 'applying the methods of the protection of property in human rights law to investment law allows us to better balance the interests of the state in regulation vis-à-vis those of the individuals in the protection of property'[110] – such a balance of interests can only be a political one.

The majority method of analysing the regulatory expropriation problem is flawed and this is symptomatic for the whole topic of expropriation in international investment law. In contrast, a truly legal-scholarly argument on the basis of a structural analysis of IIA expropriation clauses will discover a range of limitations on what arguments are possible. Put in positive terms, the new doctrinal scholarship proposed in Chapter 5 is a chance for a new beginning. It will not be able to 'solve' the problem because it does not set out to solve the political problem. However,

[110] 'eine Übernahme von Methoden aus dem menschenrechtlichen Eigentumsschutz im Investitionsschutz einen besseren Interessenausgleich zwischen staatlichem Regelungsinteresse und dem Interesse der Individuen am Eigentumsschutz ermöglichen' Kriebaum (2008a) note 4 at 39.

through structural analysis, it is in a position to find the frame of possible meanings of IIA expropriation clauses. The task of a genuine *Rechtswissenschaft* is not to solve problems or to decide cases but to find out what the law says and what it cannot tell us. This, in turn, also gives us the freedom to provide truly practical information in Chapter 8 on the basis of developments and trends in case-law. It is unshackled from the idea that the IIA norm actually needs to provide specific information on specific factual constellations, but it is simultaneously unburdened by the legal realist idea that the decisions of cases are the only 'law' we have and that there are no (abstract) norms. We can show the legal limits, such as they are, with attendant freedom for constitutive decision-making as well as the factual predetermination of later decisions by opinion and precedent.

7

Expropriation: A New Beginning

7.1 Introduction: Three Structural Limits

If this book has a core, a 'unique selling point', this is it. On the basis of the theoretical framework discussed in the previous chapters, I propose a bold argument – an argument that has been made before, but never on this basis and with this consistency. It is this: a sizeable chunk of the current academic debate on expropriation in international investment law, as well as some arguments made in arbitral awards, goes beyond what 'the law' allows. Polemically speaking: the vast majority of the arguments on the police powers doctrine needs to be excluded from discussions of what 'expropriation' means in (at least Type A) IIA expropriation clauses. Scholarly debates on international expropriation law need a reset: we have to rethink expropriation by focusing on the law, rather than on politics and feasibility. For all their vagueness, IIA expropriation clauses impose specific limits on what expropriation can be. These limits exclude certain arguments and positions, but the remaining freedom of tribunals to decide is still significant.

Chapter 8 will show, on a range of topics such as the intensity requirement, how wide the limits imposed by IIAs typically are. This chapter, in contrast, will explain (1) why there are limits, (2) how these limits work, (3) which arguments are excluded or limited and (4) what the 'shape' of (Type A) IIA clauses is. While the position espoused below may look like the sole effects doctrine, that is not the case, even if some of the arguments and results are similar. The macro- and micro-structural limits in this chapter are developed on the basis of the legal-theoretical groundwork discussed in the previous chapters and not on considerations of practicality or ideology as, in effect, are both the police powers and the sole effects doctrines (Chapter 6). The argument below is about finding the structure of IIA clauses, irrespective of whether these limits may be politically in tune with the times or in accordance with considerations of justice or morality.

The structure of the typical clause is shaped by three important limits: the complexity of the argument from customary law and general principles, the equivalence of direct and indirect expropriation and the strict conditionality of the four legality conditions. It will be remembered that (Section 5.2), in line with the Pure Theory of Law, norms – whatever the (considerable) vagueness and multivalence of language – have limits and that it is legal scholarship's task to find them. The three limits are part of that frame. Legal scholarship, as envisaged in Chapter 5, in exercising its task of a structural analysis of the law, can tell us what the limits of the law are.

We will set out a path to a reconceptualisation of the debate on expropriation by showing that the limits of the law require the abandonment of many arguments. The regulatory expropriation conundrum is of our own making, not the law's; the common solution is political and also not based on the law, as Chapter 6 has demonstrated. Also, in discussing (Type A) IIA expropriation clauses, we should actually heed their structural limits, rather than pretending that there is a continuum of possibilities from the extreme police powers doctrine to the sole effects doctrine. The argument here is based on three important assumptions: there are several types of IIA expropriation clause (and the argument applies fully only to Type A, as defined in Sections 5.5 and 7.5); their frame is restricted threefold; and non-legal arguments are not sufficiently qualified to serve as reasoning in legal(-scholarly) debates. The first two preconditions will be discussed in this chapter, but the last precondition, developed at several points already (including in Chapter 6), may require a brief recap here.

One example for a non-legal argument is the contention that a wide understanding of indirect expropriation would engender 'regulatory chill' – and, correspondingly, that a narrow understanding entails 'investment chill'. Martins Paparinskis, for example, argues that:

> From the perspective of sustainable development, the *Methanex–Saluka* and *Tecmed* approaches seem to be positive. Both approaches state expressly the importance of the legitimate regulatory purposes that may have been insufficiently articulated in the recent case law. Both approaches reduce the possibility of a regulatory chill caused by the mere effect of the measures, suggesting that the nature and character of the measures also have to be taken into account in the analysis. Finally, . . . the imposition of restrictions 'by law' in its qualitative sense in the latter approach, imposes a standard of regulatory conduct that States have to embrace.[1]

[1] Martins Paparinskis, 'Regulatory Expropriation and Sustainable Development' in Marie-Claire Cordonier Segger, Markus W Gehring, Andrew Newcombe (eds.), *Sustainable*

While 'the potential added cost occasioned by expropriation claims will inhibit or deter governments from taking measures to enhance the quality of life for the greatest number of their citizens', as Jack Coe and Noah Rubins define 'regulatory chill', is not explicitly an 'argument for *excusing* regulatory takings',[2] Paparinskis subconsciously moves out of the realm of legal argument by these considerations. The same applies to investment chill – 'where investment flows to countries perceived to impose an excessive regulatory burden are reduced'.[3] Caroline Henckels' argument for a 'need for international investment law to accommodate greater space for host states to regulate in pursuit of the public interest'[4] is not a legal argument. Neither is Céline Lévesque's *argumentum ab inconvenienti*, where '[t]he necessity for a category of measures that may affect property rights without giving rise to a duty of compensation' is regarded as 'obvious', because '[g]overning would be inconceivable if the state had such a duty'.[5] Without more, the law is not changed by a politico-economic need to pursue state interests nor is it changed by the perceived impossibility of governing. They may carry weight as political arguments, but they are not legal arguments without the law itself making these factors a condition for the change of the law. Even in terms of the 'assessment' of regulatory measures, policy considerations do not become relevant to the law by their nature as politico-ideological 'public welfare purposes'. Allen Weiner suggests the following: '[A] key factor in assessing regulatory measures is the specific *public welfare purpose* served by a challenged regulation. . . . What is needed . . .

Development in World Investment Law (Alphen aan den Rijn: Wolters Kluwer 2011) 299–327 at 322; see also Lauren E Godshall, 'In the Cold Shadow of Metalclad: The Potential for Change to NAFTA's Chapter Eleven' 11 *New York University Environmental Law Journal* (2002–3) 264–316.

2 Jack Coe, Jr, Noah Rubins, 'Regulatory Expropriation and the *Tecmed* Case: Context and Contributions' in Todd Weiler (ed.), *International Investment Law and Arbitration: Leading Cases from the ICSID, NAFTA, Bilateral Treaties and Customary International Law* (London: Cameron May 2005) 597–667 at 599 (emphasis added).

3 Alessandra Asteriti, 'Regulatory Expropriation Claims in International Investment Arbitrations: A Bridge too Far?' in Andrea K Bjorklund (ed.), *Yearbook on International Investment Law and Policy 2012–2013* (Oxford: Oxford University Press 2014) 451–73 at 452.

4 Caroline Henckels, 'Indirect Expropriation and the Right to Regulate: Revisiting Proportionality Analysis and the Standard of Review in Investor-State Arbitration' 15 *Journal of International Economic Law* (2012) 223–55 at 255.

5 Céline Lévesque, 'Distinguishing Expropriation and Regulation under NAFTA Chapter 11: Making Explicit the Link to Property' in Kevin C Kennedy (ed.), *The First Decade of NAFTA: The Future of Free Trade in North America* (Ardsley: Transnational 2004) 293–324 at 305.

are guidelines that elaborate which particular classes or categories of public welfare purposes are accepted … as purposes in furtherance of which states may regulate without having to compensate property owners for resulting losses.'[6]

On a legal view – and it is strongly suggested that *for legal scholars conducting legal scholarship*, this should be the only legitimate view – legal considerations can be the only sufficiently qualified reasons. For the law, from a legal viewpoint it is not a relevant criterion whether 'a world public order' is advanced.[7] Despite the virtually irresistible pull to politics,[8] legal scholars *must* restrict themselves to legal arguments.

On the basis of the preconditions outlined so far, this chapter will discuss three limits: (1) The relationship of IIAs to customary international law is not as facile and 'successful' as imagined. This is a *macro-structural* limit regarding the interaction of IIA clauses with a potential customary right to regulate or a police powers exception (Section 7.2). (2) Direct and indirect expropriation are truly equivalent in (virtually all) IIAs, despite their different natures. This is a *micro-structural* limit which disallows open or hidden arguments from a dis-equivalence, that is, readings/meanings which postulate less stringent conditions for states parties' indirect expropriation measures than for their direct expropriation measures. Thus, readings which define indirect expropriation less stringently than direct expropriation are not in accordance with the law (Section 7.3). (3) All conditions of legality are equal; none may be used to avoid the duty of compensation, as their co-equality means that they have all been taken into consideration by the states parties. In particular, they should not be doubled in elucidating the *Tatbestand*. This is a *micro-structural* limit which disallows breaking the conditionality (Section 7.4). As will be shown in the rest of this chapter, these are three separate limits which are nonetheless intimately linked.

Arguments similar to these three limits have been made before. A shrinking minority of scholars share elements of the approach

[6] Allen S Weiner, 'Indirect Expropriations: The Need for a Taxonomy of "Legitimate" Regulatory Purposes' 5 *International Law Forum* (2003) 166–75 at 166–7 (emphasis added).

[7] Burns H Weston, '"Constructive Takings" under International Law: A Modest Foray into the Problem of "Creeping Expropriation"' 16 *Virginia Journal of International Law* (1975) 103–75 at 123.

[8] See eg Jörg Kammerhofer, 'Orthodox Generalists and Political Activists in International Legal Scholarship' in Matthew Happold (ed.), *International Law in a Multipolar World* (Abingdon: Routledge 2011) 138–57.

espoused here, particularly on the second and third limits.[9] However, sharing the same interpretative result or even the same argument is not necessarily indicative of a shared (theoretical) approach. Orthodox approaches tend to differ in the way they use such arguments and in the theoretical foundation provided (or by way of a theory-averse non-foundation). It is submitted that the approach espoused here is more consistent in the application of these limits – they are absolute limits to the law and not factors to be considered and given weight within a larger balancing exercise. As a result, the limits developed below 'cut deeper' than similar orthodox arguments; they need to be taken much more seriously and to be applied more consistently. For example, if direct and indirect expropriation are equals, there is no conceivable argument

[9] See eg A Devin Bray, 'Non-compensatory versus Compensatory Takings under NAFTA' 9:7 *Transnational Dispute Management* (2012); Coe (2005) note 2; Joshua Elcombe, 'Regulatory Powers vs. Investment Protection under NAFTA's Chapter 1110: *Metalclad, Methanex*, and *Glamis Gold*' 68 *University of Toronto Faculty of Law Review* (2010) 71–98; Rosalyn Higgins, 'The Taking of Property by the State: Recent Developments in International Law' 176 *Recueil des Cours 1982* (1983) 259–391; Anne K Hoffmann, 'Indirect Expropriation' in August Reinisch (ed.), *Standards of Investment Protection* (Oxford: Oxford University Press 2008) 151–70; David Khachvani, 'Compensation for Unlawful Expropriation: Targeting the Illegality' 32 *ICSID Review* (2017) 385–403; Ursula Kriebaum, *Eigentumsschutz im Völkerrecht: Eine vergleichende Untersuchung zum internationalen Investitionsrecht sowie zum Menschenrechtsschutz* (Berlin: Duncker & Humblot 2008); Ursula Kriebaum, 'Expropriation' in Marc Bungenberg et al. (eds.), *International Investment Law* (Baden-Baden: Nomos 2015) 959–1030; Bjørn Kunoy, 'Developments in Indirect Expropriation Case Law in ICSID Transnational Arbitration' 6 *Journal of World Investment & Trade* (2005) 467–91; Sebastián López Escarcena, *Indirect Expropriation in International Law* (Cheltenham: Edward Elgar 2014); Justin R Marlles, 'Public Purpose, Private Losses: Regulatory Expropriation and Environmental Regulation in International Investment Law' 16 *Journal of Transnational Law and Policy* (2006–7) 275–336; Ben Mostafa, 'The Sole Effects Doctrine, Police Powers and Indirect Expropriation under International Law' 15 *Australian International Law Journal* (2008) 267–96; W Michael Reisman, Robert D Sloane, 'Indirect Expropriation and Its Valuation in the BIT Generation' 74 *British Year Book of International Law 2003* (2004) 115–50; Christoph Schreuer, 'The Concept of Expropriation under the ETC and Other Investment Protection Treaties' in Clarisse Ribeiro (ed.), *Investment Arbitration and the Energy Charter Treaty* (New York: JurisNet 2006) 108–59; Joseph A Strazzeri, 'A *Lucas* Analysis of Regulatory Expropriations under NAFTA Chapter Eleven' 14 *Georgetown International Environmental Law Review* (2001–2) 837–59; Aikaterini Titi, *The Right to Regulate in International Investment Law* (Baden-Baden: Nomos 2014); Todd Weiler, '*Methanex Corp. v. USA*: Turning the Page on NAFTA Chapter Eleven?' 6 *Journal of World Investment & Trade* (2005) 903–20; Christian Zielonka, *Der Ausgleich zwischen Investorenschutz- und Regulierungsinteressen in internationalen Investitionsschutzabkommen* (Berlin: Duncker & Humblot 2017). However, the degree to which these writers' arguments overlap with the ones presented here varies widely.

that could justify treating the legality conditions differently for indirect expropriation than for direct expropriation.

The limits for Type A IIA expropriation clauses may differ for other types of IIA. The potential influence of the different wording on the limits will be explored in Section 7.5. It is argued there, in line with the idea that doctrinal international legal scholarship can distil 'principles' by portraying a specific legal *stratum* (Section 5.3), that – while this process cannot result in the creation of a unified norm – differences in the wording of norms should not be ignored. Accordingly, potentially, the different types of expropriation clause can be radically different law, even to the point of eliminating the protection against indirect expropriation. The chapter will in a sense reconstruct the boundaries of IIA expropriation clauses, showing which arguments remain, which uncertainties cannot be eliminated by legal scholarship and where arbitral tribunals retain a considerable freedom to choose within the frame of possible meanings. Chapter 7 prepares the ground for Chapter 8, where this uncertainty and the remaining freedom will be explored for a range of topics.

7.2 The Argument from General Law

The argument from customary international law and to a lesser degree also from general principles of law is as widely used as it is problematic, both in international legal scholarship in general and in investment law scholarship in particular. This argument is of central importance and this is reflected in the weight given to it in writings, including the present book. All theoretical chapters either have been specifically concerned with customary international law (Chapter 2) or have had important sections devoted to it (Sections 3.4 and 4.3.2). We can therefore draw on these chapters in order to bring focus to the application in this chapter. The other factor allowing for a more focused discussion is that there are two stages to proving the integration of customary law (general principles) into IIA expropriation clauses: proponents first have to prove what the mechanics of integration are. In these chapters, we have had occasion to discuss several, such as incorporation, *renvoi* and systemic integration. These 'transmission mechanisms', to borrow a phrase from monetary policy, are much less permissive than the majority opinion avers. Because of these problems, the second stage – the duty of proponents to prove the exact content of the law to be integrated – is starkly reduced in scope and urgency. We will first look at the feasibility of the various claimed transmission mechanisms (Section 7.2.1); only then will we look at the content of the law, particularly with respect to a police powers exception and/or a (separate) right to regulate (Section 7.2.2).

We all suffer from confirmation bias: the more often an idea is repeated, the more convinced we are of its truth, irrespective of its merits. In the debate on expropriation in international investment law, this manifests itself in the argument favouring a recourse to customary law (and general principles). The claim that we can draw on general law is ubiquitous, but detailed argument – not to mention proof of state practice and *opinio iuris* – is scarce. For example, the *AIG* award held that 'Article III incorporates into the BIT international law standards for "expropriation" and "nationalisation"'.[10] The UNCTAD study feels confident in stating that 'State practice as well as arbitral awards and academic literature all acknowledge the right of States to engage in regulatory activity, which should not be undermined or restricted by investment treaties' so that an 'exemption of good faith non-discriminatory regulatory measures exists in general customary international law'.[11]

7.2.1 Transmission Mechanisms

An international legal scholarship which serves the goal of finding out what the law is, rather than that of pragmatically solving problems, can in many cases achieve sufficient clarity of analysis only if and where it clearly distinguishes among phenomena which would take the law in a different direction. So it is here: it is relevant whether this is a claim that an IIA expropriation clause needs to be *interpreted* in conformity with a customary right to regulate or a claim that this clause *incorporates* general customary law rule on expropriation which contains a police powers exception. With respect to the mechanisms of 'transmitting' general law to IIAs, it is possible and therefore necessary to distinguish in a more granular manner. A first distinction can be made between an analysis focusing on the kind of norms which interact ('element-centric view') and one focusing on the way in which the norms interact ('relationship-centric view'). A second distinction focuses on the kinds of relationship within the relationship-centric view – the *form* of the

[10] *AIG Capital Partners Inc. and CJSC Tema Real Estate Company* v. *Republic of Kazakhstan*, ICSID, ARB/01/6, Award of 7 October 2003, para 55.

[11] United Nations Conference on Trade and Development, *Expropriation* [UNCTAD/DIAE/IA/2011/7] (2012) 80, 88.

claimed 'interaction' or 'relationship'. What sort of relationship is claimed: interpretation or direct norm interaction?

1. *The element-centric view.* Looking at the building-blocks of the IIA–general law relationship, a primary and a secondary constellation emerge. The primary constellation (a.x) is between an IIA expropriation clause, on the one hand, and a norm of general law, on the other hand. This other norm is usually claimed to be a customary international legal norm, but sometimes it is also styled as a general principle of law in the sense of Article 38(1)(c) ICJ Statute or as a 'general principle of international law'.[12] At least four sub-variants can be construed, although not all have been proposed: (a.1) the IIA clause is mirrored, without more, in customary international law; (a.2) it is mirrored by an integrated customary expropriation norm which contains a police powers exception; (a.3) it is confronted by a separate customary norm containing a police powers exception; and (a.4) it is confronted by a separate subjective right to regulate. A secondary constellation (b.x) comes into consideration if we proceed from the assumption that the IIA expropriation norm is identical to a customary international law expropriation norm. Then, other (customary law) norms within the wider purview could potentially also relate to the customary law expropriation norm, rather than the IIA expropriation norm. In this case, at least two sub-variants can be construed: (b.1) the mirrored customary expropriation norm (without more) is confronted by a separate customary police powers exception; and (b.2) it is confronted by a separate customary right to regulate.

References to general international law are abundant in writings and case-law, given that Type A IIA expropriation clauses do not elaborate on their *Tatbestand*. However, given the tendency to pile on argument after argument in the hope that more will be more effective in making one's case, the distinctions made here are not usually found in neat separation. However, we can find hints in the material canvassed for this section for the primary constellations.

[12] I have voiced doubts before about the viability of this source outside the narrow confines of Article 38 ICJ Statute, see eg Jörg Kammerhofer, 'Hans Kelsen in Today's International Legal Scholarship' in Jörg Kammerhofer, Jean d'Aspremont (eds.), *International Legal Positivism in a Post-Modern World* (Cambridge: Cambridge University Press 2014) 81–113 at 105–12; Jörg Kammerhofer, 'Die Reine Rechtslehre und die allgemeinen Rechtsprinzipien des Völkerrechts' in Nikitas Aliprantis, Thomas Olechowski (eds.), *Hans Kelsen: Die Aktualität eines großen Rechtswissenschaftlers und Soziologen des 20. Jahrhunderts* (Vienna: Manz 2014) 25–35.

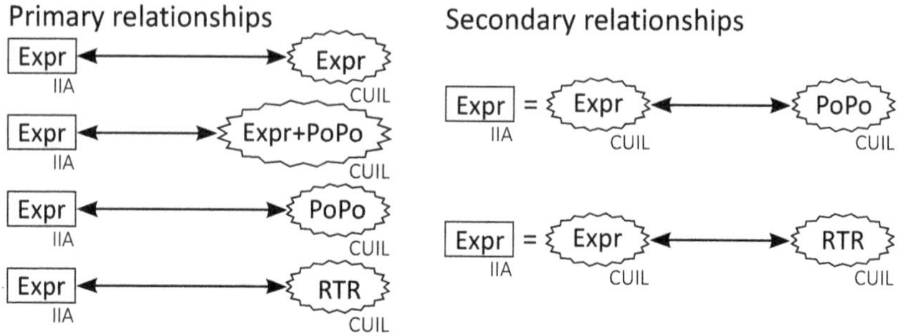

Figure 7.1 Primary and secondary relationships[13]

(a.1) Case-law frequently contains unspecific claims such as that an IIA, 'in using the terms "expropriation" and "tantamount to expropriation", incorporates this customary law of expropriation'[14] or that because 'the concept of "expropriation" is not defined in the Treaty . . . [i]t is appropriate . . . to look to general international law'.[15] Sometimes, the source is 'general principles of law', such as in *SwemBalt*.[16] This relationship is acknowledged in a wide range of writings on all points of the spectrum. Andrew Newcombe, for example, argues that 'in my view there is little evidence that BIT treaty drafters intended to broaden the scope of expropriation beyond its scope in customary international law';[17] 'States generally seek to incorporate in their BITs the "customary

[13] Primary relationships between IIA and: (a.1) a customary international law (CUIL) expropriation norm (Expr); (a.2) a CUIL expropriation norm which includes a police powers exception (Expr+PoPo); (a.3) a separate CUIL police powers exception norm (PoPo); (a.4) a CUIL right to regulate norm (RTR). Secondary relationships between the IIA which is identical with a CUIL expropriation norm and: (b.1) a separate CUIL PoPo exception norm; (b.2) a CUIL RTR norm.

[14] *Cargill, Incorporated* v. *United Mexican States*, NAFTA-ICSID, ARB(AF)/05/2, Award of 18 September 2009, para 372; see also *AIG* (2003) note 10 at para 55; *S.D. Myers, Inc.* v. *Government of Canada*, NAFTA-UNCITRAL, Partial Award of 13 November 2000, separate opinion Schwartz at para 78; *Saluka Investments* v. *Czech Republic*, UNCITRAL, Partial Award of 17 March 2006 at para 261.

[15] *European Media Ventures* v. *Czech Republic*, UNCITRAL, Partial Award on Liability of 8 July 2009, para 46.

[16] *SwemBalt AB, Sweden* v. *The Republic of Latvia*, UNCITRAL, SCC, Decision by the Court of Arbitration of 23 October 2000, para 38; see also *Eudoro Armando Olguín* v. *Republic of Paraguay*, ICSID, ARB/98/5, Award of 26 July 2001, para 65.

[17] Andrew Newcombe, 'The Boundaries of Regulatory Expropriation in International Law' 20 *ICSID Review – Foreign Investment Law Journal* (2005) 1–57 at 23; Andrew Newcombe, Lluís Paradell, *Law and Practice of Investment Treaties: Standards of Treatment* (Alphen aan den Rijn: Kluwer 2009) 339.

international law standards for expropriation".'[18] The same goes for interpretative relationships to customary law: 'NAFTA does not define what constitutes "expropriation" . . . The terms must therefore be interpreted consistently with international law and in light of their context.'[19]

(a.2) One element which is brought into a relationship with the IIA expropriation clause is a 'complex' customary international law expropriation clause which contains an exception or carve-out for various police powers. The *Saluka* tribunal famously held:

> However, in using the concept of deprivation, Article 5 imports into the Treaty the customary international law notion that a deprivation can be justified if it results from the exercise of regulatory actions aimed at the maintenance of public order. . . . [T]he principle that a State does not commit an expropriation when it adopts general regulations that are "commonly accepted as within the police power of States" forms part of customary international law today.[20]

This view is widely shared in case-law today,[21] and finds support in writings as well. Stephan Schill, for example, argues 'that international investment treaties do not only recognize a state's power of eminent domain . . . but furthermore acknowledge a police power exception in

[18] Campbell McLachlan, Laurence Shore, Matthew Weiniger, *International Investment Arbitration: Substantive Principles* (Oxford: Oxford University Press 2007) 275; see also Barry Appleton, 'Regulatory Takings: The International Law Perspective' 11 *New York University Environmental Law Journal* (2002–3) 35–48 at 40; Energy Charter Secretariat, *Expropriation Regime under the Energy Charter Treaty* (Brussels: Energy Charter Secretariat 2012) 10; Caroline Henckels, *Proportionality and Deference in Investor–State Arbitration* (Cambridge: Cambridge University Press 2015) 75; Weiler (2005) note 9 at 919.

[19] J Martin Wagner, 'International Investment, Expropriation and Environmental Protection' 29 *Golden Gate University Law Review* (1999) 465–538 at 527; see also Coe (2005) note 2 at 600–1; Paparinskis (2011b) note 1 at 303. Meg Kinnear, Andrea Bjorklund and John Hannaford use a peculiar double reference to both custom and principles: '[Article 1110 NAFTA] reflects customary international law . . . The key terms in Article 1110 . . . are not defined by NAFTA. As a result, treaty interpreters *must refer to general principles of international law* to define these terms.' Meg N Kinnear, Andrea K Bjorklund, John FG Hannaford, *Investment Disputes under NAFTA: An Annotated Guide to NAFTA Chapter 11* (Alphen aan den Rijn: Kluwer 2006) 1110-13 (emphasis added).

[20] *Saluka* (2006) note 14 at paras 254, 262.

[21] Eg *Glamis Gold, Ltd.* v. *United States of America*, NAFTA-UNCITRAL, Award of 8 June 2009, para 354; *Invesmart, B.V.* v. *Czech Republic*, UNCITRAL, Award of 26 June 2009, para 498; *Philip Morris Brands SÀRL, Philip Morris Products S.A. and Abal Hermanos S.A.* v. *Oriental Republic of Uruguay*, ICSID, ARB/10/7, Award of 8 July 2016, paras 291, 295, 301.

order to interfere with property rights'.[22] Others speak of 'customary international law, which recognizes that certain measures exist which interfere … with property or investment rights and yet cannot be considered expropriation'.[23] However, a clear distinction is difficult to draw vis-à-vis the other constellations. For example, in the *Suez I* award, the tribunal opined that 'it is important to recognize a State's legitimate right to regulate and to exercise its police power in the interests of public welfare and not to confuse measures of that nature with expropriation',[24] which could be seen as pointing to an integrated rule or to a separate subjective right. Schill, in the paper cited above, speaks of 'the police power exception' which 'has not been overridden by international investment treaties'[25] which, in turn, could be read as pitting an autonomous police powers norm directly against the IIA.

(a.3) It is difficult to find clear claims for a separate police powers exception. For example, the *Quiborax* tribunal held that '[i]nternational law has generally understood that regulatory activity exercised under the so-called "police powers" of the State is not compensable',[26] which might indicate a separate police powers exception, as might a passage in the *Burlington* award: '[G]eneral taxation is the result of a State's *permissible* exercise of regulatory powers. It is not an expropriation.'[27] Some passages in scholarly literature also point to this variant: 'Customary international law, however, has allowed an exception to the standard rule. … The exception stems from the police power of states.'[28] Two texts which

[22] Stephan W Schill, 'Revisiting a Landmark: Indirect Expropriation and Fair and Equitable Treatment in the ICSID Case Tecmed' 3:2 *Transnational Dispute Management* (2006) 2.

[23] Kinnear (2006) note 19 at 1110-50; see also Bashayer Al-Mukhaizeem, 'The Dilemma of Indirect Expropriation of Host States and the Right to Regulate in the International Investment Sphere' 4:2 *Legal Issues Journal* (2016) 1–23 at 7; Lévesque (2004) note 5 at 305; UNCTAD (2012) note 11 at 79.

[24] *Suez, Sociedad General de Aguas de Barcelona S.A. and InterAgua Servicios Integrales del Agua S.A.* v. *Argentine Republic*, ICSID, ARB/03/17, Decision on Liability of 30 July 2010, para 128.

[25] Schill (2006) note 22 at 2; see also Newcombe (2005) note 17 at 37; Sūrya Prasāda Subedī, *International Investment Law: Reconciling Policy and Principle* (3rd edn, Oxford: Hart 2016) 262.

[26] *Quiborax S.A. and Non Metallic Minerals S.A. Claimants* v. *Plurinational State of Bolivia*, ICSID, ARB/06/2, Award of 16 September 2015, para 202; possibly also *Marvin Roy Feldman Karpa* v. *Mexico*, NAFTA-ICSID ARB(AF)/99/1, Award of 16 December 2002, paras 103, 105; *Valeri Belokon* v. *Kyrgyz Republic*, UNCITRAL, Award of 24 October 2014, para 198.

[27] *Burlington Resources Inc.* v. *Republic of Ecuador*, ICSID, ARB/08/5, Decision on Liability of 14 December 2012, para 391 (emphasis added).

[28] Strazzeri (2001–2) note 9 at 844.

clearly distinguish a customary exception are sharply critical of the idea. A Devin Bray argues that 'the ... customary police powers doctrine should not eclipse NAFTA's prohibition against indirect expropriation';[29] Jack Coe writes that 'even if custom had produced a general "police powers" exception it would have to be applied in light of – and confined by – the *lex specialis* of any applicable investment treaty'.[30]

(a.4) Claims to the existence of a separate customary subjective right to regulate are easier to find, but such a 'right' can also be interpreted as a mere residual freedom to act. One question is whether, as Ben Mostafa puts it, '[t]he police powers doctrine should be seen merely as an expression of the general rule that international law allows States to act as they wish unless there is some rule proscribing such action'.[31] In that case, the police powers of a state would merely be the general right to regulate, without thereby indicating that there is a specific *justificatory* rule. Certainly, an argument by Francisco Orrego Vicuña is clearer if we make this assumption: 'the right of the State to adopt regulatory measures ..., generally brought under the vague concept of police powers'.[32] Catherine Titi wishes to distinguish between two 'rights':

> After assuming an international obligation, a state retains its ability to regulate, to terminate a treaty, or simply to renege on its international obligations. This capacity, or general state freedom to regulate, assumes a *de facto* existence and coincides with a *lato sensu* right to regulate. ... The right to regulate as a nascent concept in the field of international investment law is a technical term, one that is much narrower in meaning and which should not be confused with the general regulatory capacity ... the right to regulate denotes the legal right exceptionally permitting the host state to regulate in derogation of international commitments it has undertaken by means of an investment agreement without incurring a duty to compensate.[33]

2. *The relationship-centric view.* Most investment lawyers who are in favour of integrating external 'content' argue that this integration is achieved by way of 'interpretation'. This integrative interpretation

[29] Bray (2012) note 9 at 20.
[30] Coe (2005) note 2 at 639–40.
[31] Mostafa (2008) note 9 at 279; see also Zielonka (2017) note 9 at 121.
[32] Francisco Orrego Vicuña, 'Regulatory Authority and Legitimate Expectations: Balancing the Rights of the State and the Individual under International Law in a Global Society' 5 *International Law Forum* (2003) 188–97 at 190.
[33] Titi (2014) note 9 at 32–3; see also UNCTAD (2012) note 11 at 80–1.

(Section 4.3) in its application to the specific problem of regulatory expropriation will be discussed later. However, there are also claims to solve the problem by other, more direct norm–norm interactions, such as incorporation, contracting out and norm conflict. For both *modi* we will be guided by claims in literature and case-law, while sometimes departing from them where it is necessary to make the wider point that *all* claims from general law come up sharply against relatively immutable limits born of the structure of international law.

One preliminary issue is what to do in the face of the 'paucity of sources'.[34] The narrower issue was noted earlier: when it is argued that 'a state retains its ability to regulate . . .[, t]his capacity, or general state freedom to regulate', rather than being a 'well-entrenched [rule] in customary international law',[35] is much more akin to the 'residual negative principle',[36] allegedly expressed in the famous sentence in *Lotus*: 'Restrictions upon the independence of States cannot therefore be presumed.'[37] Admittedly, even those who use language to suggest that the right to regulate is an expression of a freedom to act insist that this is part of customary law. 'Under customary international law, States have a "clear right to regulate commercial and business activities" within their territory. . . . The power to take these actions stems from principles of sovereignty and the territoriality principle.'[38] Yet, the idea 'that international law allows States to act as they wish unless there is some rule proscribing such action'[39] is not a norm of international law. At its worst, it is an expression of what Judge Simma in *Kosovo* described as an 'anachronistic, extremely consensualist vision of international law',[40] a state-centred natural law obsession with an absolutist concept of sovereignty. In terms of legal theory, however, it can be reconstructed as 'negative legal regulation' or 'negative permission'. On that view, there

[34] Andrew Newcombe, *Regulatory Expropriation, Investment Protection and International Law: When Is Government Regulation Expropriatory and When Should Compensation Be Paid?* (LL.M. thesis, University of Toronto 1999) 4.

[35] Titi (2014) note 9 at 32.

[36] Julius Stone, '*Non liquet* and the Function of Law in the International Community' 35 *British Year Book of International Law 1959* (1960) 124–61 at 136.

[37] *S.S. 'Lotus' (France* v. *Turkey)*, Judgment of 7 September 1927, PCIJ Series A No 10 (1927) at 18.

[38] Mostafa (2008) note 9 at 269; see also Bray (2012) note 9 at 10.

[39] Mostafa (2008) note 9 at 279.

[40] *Accordance with International Law of the Unilateral Declaration of Independence in Respect of Kosovo*, Advisory Opinion of 22 July 2010, ICJ Reports (2010) 403 at 479 (Declaration Simma).

can be 'behaviour which is negatively permitted. This behaviour is not the object of a legal norm, because a legal norm neither obligates nor prohibits it.'[41] It would be wrong to follow the traditional reading of the *Lotus* principle by 'equat[ing] the absence of a prohibition with the existence of a permissive rule'[42] or, more generally, by confusing the absence of a norm with presence of subjective right: '[T]he concept of "negative legal regulation" is not a norm of the normative order . . . but only a statement of the fact that positive norms are absent where they are not present. Where there are norms, there are norms; where there are no norms, there are no norms.'[43]

This is also a better reading of the 'right' to regulate. If state freedom to act is simply a result of non-regulation, such a 'right' does not (need to) exist as customary norm. Yet, when a negative freedom to act encounters legal regulation, eg IIAs, the freedom cannot conflict or influence the treaty regulation and must of necessity 'yield', as is the case everywhere else. As formerly unregulated behaviour[44] is regulated, the factual – and only in this sense 'residual' – freedom to engage in behaviour is narrowed.

Yet that particular problem is merely the expression of a more general phenomenon of all normative orders: how to proceed when the law is 'sparse'? What is the 'default' position when there is little in the way of proven or provable law? For expropriation, Andrew Newcombe puts this problem as follows:

> The paucity of sources demonstrates that international law has failed to develop clear rules to determine what government measures amount to expropriation. Customary international law is unclear and BITs and other international treaties typically refer to an uncertain and vague international law to determine what amounts to an expropriation. Rather than clarifying the scope of expropriation under international law, international investment instruments incorporate vague standards to be applied by investor-state arbitration tribunals.[45]

41 'negatives Erlauben eines Verhaltens . . ., das keinen Gegenstand einer Rechtsnorm, weil von einer Rechtsnorm weder geboten noch verboten ist' Hans Kelsen, *Allgemeine Theorie der Normen* (Vienna: Manz 1979) 106.

42 *Kosovo* (2010) note 40 at 479 (Declaration Simma).

43 Jörg Kammerhofer, 'Gaps, the *Nuclear Weapons* Advisory Opinion and the Structure of International Legal Argument between Theory and Practice' 80 *British Year Book of International Law 2009* (2010) 333–60 at 357.

44 This is so *ceteris paribus* – the situation will be far more complex in real legal orders, given a complex system of norms of varying generality and hierarchical position.

45 Newcombe (1999) note 34 at 4.

When we cannot prove specific restrictions in international law because there are no norms, the default position is the *negative* freedom of states to regulate and thus also expropriate without compensation. However, IIAs are valid parts of international law. In light of this, the default position is that exceptions to the compensation requirement in these treaties need to be proven. In the face of the regulation in IIAs, a right to regulate or a police powers exception cannot be included by default. This is a similar situation to novel claims to exceptions to the prohibition on the use of force (like unilateral humanitarian intervention) which also need to be proven in light of the blanket prohibition.

The default argument also applies to the incorporation of customary international law, including the importation of pre-IIA content or the *non*-contracting-out by IIAs from customary international law. Arguing that 'in the absence of clear state practice ... the [IIA] expropriation provisions ... represent state parties' restatements ... of the customary international law position'[46] means assuming regulation which would have required proof. This is also part of the macro-structural limits of the law. The *assumption* that expropriation clauses incorporate customary law may make our life easier, for it means that we do not have to prove that the incorporation is required by law. It may also help us to solve a real and practical problem. Yet that this course is more convenient does not mean that the law actually is shaped in that way.

a. *Integration through interpretation.* Claims to concretise and unify international investment law through interpretation have particular relevance for indirect expropriation. For example, in *Saluka* the tribunal held that '[*i*]*n interpreting a treaty*, account has to be taken of ... relevant rules of general customary international law'.[47] J Martin Wagner argues that 'the general rules of international law should *inform the interpretation* of [expropriation]'.[48] In the following, we will rely heavily on the discussion of integrative interpretation in Section 4.3.2. The most pressing issue – as pressing theoretically as it is irrelevant on the pragmatic level – is how to differentiate between interpretative *renvoi* and the incorporation of norms. Orthodoxy's impatience in the face of a lack of practical relevance

[46] Newcombe (2009) note 17 at 339.

[47] *Saluka* (2006) note 14 at para 254 (emphasis added); see also *Philip Morris* (2016) note 21 at para 290.

[48] Wagner (1999) note 19 at 473 (emphasis added); see also Newcombe (1999) note 34 at 126; Paparinskis (2011b) note 1 at 303.

is palpable and finds its expression in texts conflating the two issues. A case in point is this passage: '[T]reaty provisions governing expropriation are generally interpreted on the basis of those principles. Rather than setting forth a definition for "expropriation," investment protection treaties leave the specific contours . . . to customary international law.'[49]

Do IIAs *surrender* the definition of expropriation to customary law or do we 'merely' have to *interpret* the word 'expropriation' in light of customary law? Practically, it does not matter whether a tribunal's reading of an IIA clause is informed by the clause's formal incorporation of customary law or by an informal equivalence of meaning with customary international law.[50] Theoretically and in terms of the structural limits of the possible content of the IIA norm, this difference is crucial. The pragmatic approach is instrumentalist and those who follow this method wish to integrate a certain set of information. Doing so has two significant disadvantages: not only might one well go beyond what the law can bear, but it is also impossible to discern whether that line was crossed, as the pragmatic viewpoint inevitably obfuscates our cognition of the law.

Interpretative integration via a *renvoi* to general law is difficult to delimit from its formal incorporation (see Section 4.3.2). Is there a 'real' difference between a treaty term referring to customary law and a treaty term being interpreted while taking recourse to customary law? Incorporation is a shorthand form of law-creation, a taking on board by the treaty of the same content as customary law. In contrast, interpretative integration is part of interpretation$_B$: certain treaty terms are presumed to have the same content as certain customary norms. The difference is one of kind; while interpretative *renvoi* is an external admonition that interpreters should interpret the law in this fashion, in incorporation, *the law itself* is changed (and is yet to be interpreted). Doubts whether the Vienna Convention rules do and can work in this manner remain (Section 4.2) and neither within the VCLT nor with respect to other claims do we need to take the word 'interpretation' literally.

Another important difference, also discussed in Section 4.3 is that between autonomous or 'subjective' integrative interpretation and heteronomous or 'objective' integrative interpretation. Autonomous integration is the call to heed the states parties' intentions when they wish to refer to external sources. Bray indirectly supports this reading: 'NAFTA

[49] Coe (2005) note 2 at 600–1.
[50] See Section 4.3.3 for a discussion of one aspect.

is a regional investment treaty subject to the customary international rules of interpretation . . .. Unless the treaty expressly requires the interpreter to consider the police powers doctrine, one could presume that the treaty drafters' intent was to codify a special law that trumps the more general customary international law, which arguably is the case with NAFTA.'[51]

The claim in this quote is that IIA provisions (eg on expropriation) are intended to refer to customary international law, specifically that the state parties to the IIA have specifically willed such a reference, which is connected to the reference argument in Section 4.3. At its core, this is the contention that the treaty itself is connected to customary law and that, accordingly, we should interpret it in accordance with the customary norm. Therefore, explicative *renvoi* of this type (importing meaning from other norms) is very close to the incorporation of customary law.

In contrast, it could be argued that heteronomous integration is founded on the 'constitutional norm'[52] of systemic integration which is applicable to all treaties by dint of its constitutional status. This reading may be at the root of the argument that '[t]he key terms in Article 1110 . . . are not defined by NAFTA. As a result, treaty interpreters must refer to general principles of international law to define these terms.'[53] It can also be found in the *Philip Morris* award: 'Article 5(1) of the BIT must be interpreted in accordance with Article 31(3)(c) of the VCLT . . . [which] directs the Tribunal to refer to the rules of customary international law as they have evolved.'[54] On that reading, if there are no contrary indications, the principle of systemic integration requires that *all* norms are to be interpreted in accordance with customary international law and that only if there are very good reasons may an interpretation depart from the general law. Similarly, the coherence argument rests on the idea that international law is a system in the substantive sense, a meaningful and rational construct – at least it should be constructed as if it were coherent. In our case, when an IIA uses a term, there is a requirement, a constitutional 'norm', to interpret the treaty norm in conformity with the system and a prohibition to produce incoherent interpretative results.

[51] Bray (2012) note 9 at 17.

[52] Campbell McLachlan, 'The Principle of Systemic Integration and Article 31(3)(c) of the Vienna Convention' 54 *International and Comparative Law Quarterly* (2005) 279–320 at 280.

[53] Kinnear (2006) note 19 at 1110-13.

[54] *Philip Morris* (2016) note 21 at para 290.

Section 4.3 has discussed the problems of both readings of systemic integration and the problems persist for a systemic integration of IIA expropriation clauses.[55] As argued in Section 7.4, interpreting 'indirect expropriation' to exclude legitimate regulation means ignoring the equality of the legality conditions. Even on an orthodox reading, this would be a problem, as Article 31(3)(c) would trump Article 31(1) VCLT. A boundless and ill-defined secondary interpretative tool would thus prevail not only over the text but also over a more traditional systematic interpretation – 'the ordinary meaning to be given to the terms of the treaty in *their* context'.

Interpretation$_B$ is understood by a significant section of both scholarship and practice as the way judicial bodies ought to argue. They seek to impose on or suggest to tribunals a particular *modus operandi* (a particular judicial 'test') when they decide upon indirect expropriation claims. It is not a question of applying traditional methods of interpretation but more a schematism of deciding and a series of steps and factors. It is an attempt (largely in scholarship)[56] to impose criteria of specific (arbitral) reasoning which seek to guide or co-determine arbitral decision-making. Yet these authors are reticent to explain *why* – for which *legal* reasons, rather than reasons of political legitimacy or practical expediency – either their preferred or indeed any mode of reasoning is required.

Claims relying on general principles of law, the analogy from domestic legal orders and comparative constitutional scholarship, are best understood as referring to interpretation, rather than norm-operations such as incorporation. A number of authors view expropriation as basically a human and/or constitutional rights issue. In 2001, for example, before international investment law had been 'narrowed down by precedent',[57] Thomas Wälde and Abba Kolo saw '[c]omparative constitutional law' as 'the most suitable analogy and precedent since treaties in effect set up a similar system of higher-ranked controls over domestic law-making'.[58] '[T]he constitutional law character of these [ECtHR and ECJ] cases makes them particularly apposite to serve as a laboratory – but also as a relative precedent – for the interpretative challenges in multilateral

[55] See Paparinskis (2011b) note 1 at 301–3.

[56] Eg Henckels (2012) note 4 at 228–9.

[57] Thomas W Wälde, Abba Kolo, 'Environmental Regulation, Investment Protection and Regulatory Taking in International Law' 50 *International and Comparative Law Quarterly* (2001) 811–48 at 818.

[58] Wälde (2001) note 57 at 822.

treaties [NAFTA] now arising.'[59] Equally, for Todd Weiler, 'a sharp divide exists between these two areas of legal practice – international human rights law and international investment law – which should not exist', because 'both IIL and IHRL address the relationship between the sovereign State and the individual … they are founded on the same premises' and because 'they share the same historical roots'.[60]

If that is the case, then one will, like Rudolf Dolzer, also likely argue that a comparative analysis of domestic legal orders and their provisions of the protection of property and thus a *renvoi* to general principles of law (Article 38(1)(c) ICJ Statute) is apposite.[61] Quite apart from theoretical doubts about the viability of general principles as a source of international law, the issue is that, at least within IIAs, any analogy to constitutional property protection is fraught with problems, as Jan Paulsson points out: 'While it is tempting to import notions from the international law of human rights dealing with deprivations of property and violations of due process, there can be no assumptions about the perfect correspondence between instruments devised for quite different purposes.'[62]

But perhaps the most far-reaching argument to limit integration by interpretation lies in the nature of interpretation itself. Whether we use interpretation$_A$ or interpretation$_B$, it must still remain an 'interpretation' – something which *by definition* is not a change of the law. Section 4.3 argued that the distinctions between the different tools of interpretative integration are relative, because interpretation$_B$ is a framework of practices acceptable to peers. Meaning-ascription by interpretative organs does not depend on the relationship of the IIA to customary law (or general principles). Interpretative *renvoi* is not established vis-à-vis norms but vis-à-vis meanings ascribed by other interpreters. There is no difference between the various tools or methods of

[59] Wälde (2001) note 57 at 847, although they warn that 'such national experience cannot be automatically transposed into the process of treaty interpretation'.

[60] Todd Weiler, 'International Investment Law and International Human Rights Law: Reuniting Two Long Lost Siblings (Speaking Notes)' 15 *Transnational Dispute Management* (2018) 1.

[61] Rudolf Dolzer, 'Indirect Expropriation of Alien Property' 1 *ICSID Review – Foreign Investment Law Journal* (1986) 41–65 at 59; see also Rudolf Dolzer, 'Indirect Expropriations: New Developments?' 11 *New York University Environment Law Journal* (2002–3) 64–92 at 76; Rudolf Dolzer, Christoph Schreuer, *Principles of International Investment Law* (2nd edn, Oxford: Oxford University Press 2012) 104.

[62] Jan Paulsson, 'Indirect Expropriation: Is the Right to Regulate at Risk?' 3:2 *Transnational Dispute Management* (2006) 7–8.

interpretation$_B$ and 'interpreters' in this sense are not bound by source-relationships.

With this insight comes, however, a heightened awareness of the utter impotence of interpretation (in both senses) to modify the sum-totality of norms in a normative order. Crucially, interpretation cannot be a *legal function*: it does not change or determine the law. Treaties, for example, are not concretised by the process of interpretation, whether or not this is designated as 'systemic integration'. Legally speaking, integration by interpretation achieves much less than far-reaching claims suggest. It may be important on the pragmatic level, but this is a form of the socio-psychology of judicial decision-making.

b. *Norm interaction.* Inasmuch as orthodox writings distinguish between the integration of general law into IIAs via interpretation and integration by norm interaction and insofar as the second variant is chosen, three arguments are made. First, it is argued that IIA expropriation clauses 'refer' to general (mostly customary) law in the sense that general law is formally incorporated into the treaty clause. Second, whether and to what extent IIAs constitute a contracting out remains unclear. If IIAs are *inter se* regulations which exist precisely in order *not* to be general international law, they would also not incorporate general law's content. Third, the relationship between IIAs and general law can also be seen as norm conflict without a presumption of substantive coherence.

Campbell McLachlan, Laurence Shore and Matthew Weiniger concisely express the widespread acceptance of a diffuse incorporation argument: 'States generally seek to incorporate in their BITs the "customary international law standards for expropriation". Thus, States have frequently relied on the language and standards commonly thought to express the international law of expropriation.'[63] Variations on this theme abound. 'The vast majority of investment treaties', it is argued, 'contain provisions reflecting customary international law of expropriation.'[64] This happens, even though 'international law has failed to develop clear rules to determine what government measures amount

[63] McLachlan (2007) note 18 at 275; see also Joel C Beauvais, 'Regulatory Expropriations under NAFTA: Emerging Principles and Lingering Doubts' 10 *New York University Environmental Law Journal* (2001–2) 245–96 at 278 (unclear); ECS (2012) at 10; Paparinskis (2011b) at 324 (unclear); Weiler (2005) note 9 at 919; *Generation Ukraine, Inc.* v. *Ukraine*, ICSID, Award of 16 September 2003, para 11.3.

[64] Henckels (2015) note 18 at 75.

to expropriation'; 'BITs and other international treaties typically refer to an uncertain and vague international law to determine what amounts to an expropriation.'[65] However, the most important move of the incorporation argument is the claim that this happens by default. The absence of evidence justifying incorporation does not hinder it from happening:

> [I]n the absence of clear state practice supporting this interpretation, the better view is that the expropriation provisions that appear in the vast majority of IIAs, represent state parties' restatements, of varying brevity, of the customary international law position . . . [T]here is no evidence in state practice that states intended to expand the meaning of expropriation beyond that ascribed to it under customary international law.[66]

That is, if the IIA 'does not expressly address the distinction between regulation and expropriation . . ., the issue is governed by customary international law',[67] unless there are good reasons to assume otherwise. This shifts the burden of proof to those who argue that IIAs are separate legal entities.

We can draw on our discussion of the mechanics of incorporation in Section 4.3.2 for the following. Treaty-makers are capable of incorporating norms of customary law into their treaty. The common understanding of incorporation is that the target customary law norm is made part of the treaty. However, as a matter of the macro-structure of legal orders, this operation is best reconstructed as taking the *content* of the target norm on board, not the norm itself. Incorporation is law-making by shorthand, for the treaty reference creates a norm with the same content as the target.[68]

On the level of norm interaction, the antipode to incorporation is contracting out of customary law through treaty-making. These arguments are made less often than those regarding incorporation. Treaty parties may contract out of both a parallel customary expropriation norm as well as other customary norms, such as an autonomous police powers exception or a right to regulate. Joshua Elcombe, in critiquing the *Methanex* award, points out that the award had 'conflat[ed] the meaning of "expropriation" in Chapter 11 with a typical definition from

65 Newcombe (1999) note 34 at 45, 4.
66 Newcombe (2009) note 17 at 339.
67 Kinnear (2006) note 19 at 1110-50.
68 For present purposes, we will ignore a further theoretical problem which arises when we wish to declare as identical the content of a *lex scripta* (treaty), on the one hand, and of a *lex non scripta* (customary law), on the other hand, see Sections 2.4 and 4.2.1.

international law, despite the fact that the NAFTA parties *have contracted out* of the customary international law approach'.[69] (This argument is sometimes most strongly made with respect to the distinction between the compensation condition and reparation under state responsibility; see Section 8.4.)[70] As discussed in Sections 2.5 and 4.3.2, the incorporation argument clashes with the orthodox assumption that treaty-making is a contracting out from customary law and creates *inter se* regulation. Why then should treaty and customary law be treated as one and why would customary law determine the content of treaty law? Would that not negate the very possibility of international treaty law as a source of international law? Surely, if *lex specialis* is to be conceptually possible, contracting out must not be made virtually impossible?

Perhaps presumptions are the key to resolving the dilemma of incorporation and contracting out? Section 4.3.2 demonstrated that a presumption in favour of autonomy is more adequate than one for identity of meaning; a fortiori, this is true for norm interaction. Wälde's question remains pertinent here: 'does one expect the treaty text . . . to say clearly and explicitly that [it] depart[s] from customary law or does one require . . . the treaty to say clearly that it *refers* to customary law?'[71] The orthodox discourse is correct in identifying the clash of two presumptions, but its choice in favour of 'systemic coherence' is problematic. Orthodoxy juxtaposes a *by default* incorporation to a *by default* contracting out, but on a macro-structural analysis neither incorporation nor a contracting out – in the sense that customary law ceases to be applicable for a particular relationship – should be assumed. As discussed in Section 2.5, all norms stipulate an Ought, because the Ought is a norm's validity and 'existence' as a norm. Anyone claiming a carve-out for treaty-parties needs to prove a change of the customary norm itself, because *inter se* regulation is a change of the personal sphere of application of the

[69] Elcombe (2010) note 9 at 74 (emphasis added); see also Coe (2005) note 2 at 639–40; Bray (2012) note 9 at 17–18 (unclear).

[70] Vicki Been, Joel C Beauvais, 'The Global Fifth Amendment? NAFTA's Investment Protections and the Misguided Quest for an International "Regulatory Takings" Doctrine' 78 *New York University Law Review* (2003) 30–143 at 53; Audley Sheppard, 'The Distinction between Lawful and Unlawful Expropriation' in Clarisse Ribeiro (ed.), *Investment Arbitration and the Energy Charter Treaty* (New York: JurisNet 2006) 169–99 at 196.

[71] Thomas W Wälde, 'Interpreting Investment Treaties: Experiences and Examples' in Christina Binder et al. (eds.), *International Investment Law for the 21st Century: Essays in Honour of Christoph Schreuer* (Oxford: Oxford University Press 2009) 724–81 at 770 (emphasis added).

customary norm.[72] This is difficult to reconcile with the mainstream theory of *ius dispositivum*.

There are reasons to err on the side of non-incorporation even on a more orthodox basis. That customary law (plus police powers) is incorporated in IIA expropriation clauses is made less likely by the fact that IIA expropriation clauses contain two *other* limits – the equivalence of direct and indirect expropriation as well as the strict conditionality of *all* legality conditions (Sections 7.3–7.4). These establish limits as to what IIAs mean by 'indirect expropriation' and therefore limit any incorporation which would go counter to these limits, as Bray points out: 'The prohibition against an unlawful indirect expropriation as a treaty norm is a specific law, consented to by the parties of the treaty. Unless the treaty expressly requires the interpreter to consider the police powers doctrine, one could presume that the treaty drafters' intent was to codify a special law that trumps the more general customary international law'.[73]

The question of norm interaction is therefore better framed in terms of norm conflict and inter-source relationships.[74] As shown above, there are a whole host of possible combinations, but there are significantly fewer variations in terms of norm conflict. The substantive content, for example, is much less relevant than the normative *modus* (permission, prohibition, derogation, etc.)[75] – or whether it is a conflict within a source or between two sources. Also, is the situation where two norms require such behaviour that we cannot observe both at the same time a true norm conflict?[76] This situation may very well be a problem for the human being faced with two incompatible claims, but this is a factual incompatibility, not a conflict of the norms themselves.[77] In the present case, states are usually faced with an incompatibility of behaviour, rather than a norm conflict in the strict sense. For example, a customary right to

[72] Kelsen (1979) note 41 at 90: '[Eine] Einschränkung oder Ausdehnung des Geltungsbereiches einer Norm ist eine *Änderung ihres Inhaltes*.' '[A] narrowing or widening of the sphere of validity of a norm is a *change of its content*.'

[73] Bray (2012) note 9 at 18.

[74] See Jörg Kammerhofer, 'The Theory of Norm Conflict Solutions in International Investment Law' in Markus Gehring, Andrew Newcombe, Marie-Claire Cordonier Segger (eds.), *Sustainable Development in International Investment Law* (Alphen aan den Rijn: Wolters Kluwer 2010) 83–98.

[75] Kelsen (1979) note 41 at 76–92.

[76] Kelsen (1979) note 41 at 99.

[77] See Jörg Kammerhofer, *Uncertainty in International Law: A Kelsenian Perspective* (Abingdon: Routledge 2010) 141–6, 193–4; Jörg Kammerhofer, '*Robert Walter*, die Normkonflikte und der zweite Stufenbau des Rechts' in Clemens Jabloner et al. (eds.), *Gedenkschrift Robert Walter* (Vienna: Manz 2013) 237–56 at 248–51.

regulate is a positive permissive norm of one source which does not purport to modify the IIA norm (a prohibitive norm of another source) but exists alongside it, potentially creating incompatibilities.

And this is the key to the problem: finding incompatibility and even conflict between two norms does not mean that it is solved, and a fortiori does not solve it in a particular manner.[78] The structure of the international legal order is such that the resolution of norm conflicts (in a wide sense) is not as easy as the majority opinion would have it. The likelihood of incorporation, of customary international law trumping over the terms of a treaty or even of the *ius dispositivum* solution 'working' is very low – it is much more likely that customary law norms and treaty norms are and remain valid alongside each other. As discussed in Section 2.5.2, treaty and customary norms are valid simultaneously even for treaty parties and even if the *ius dispositivum* model is applied. Two valid norms remain separate, simply because both norms retain their validity and neither norm can be changed or destroyed by declaring a conflict.

The larger point is that the fragmentation of international investment law cannot be avoided, because fragmentation is systemic. The possibility of different treaties, 'regimes' and even norms within the same 'regime' not being fully coherent cannot be ignored, because *on a legal view* (a view focusing solely on the norms, not political or moral precepts) separate norms necessarily *remain separate* and cannot be made coherent unless by a change in the law. Legal scholarship does not have to follow a precept to interpret with the goal of systemic coherence, nor are the norms themselves coherent. There is merit in particularity and if the law is not coherent, legal scholarship should say so. However, we must distinguish two kinds of fragmentation: the fragmentation of substantive law against the fragmentation of method, theory and the sources of law. While universalising the law without respect for boundaries is a misrepresentation, unifying the methods of scholarship is worse: approaches praising a 'cross-fertilisation'[79] are actually advocating 'cross-pollution'. There is no *legal* need and no *legal* possibility to do so, only political needs and pragmatic possibilities.[80]

[78] Ewald Wiederin, 'Was ist und welche Konsequenzen hat ein Normkonflikt?' 21 *Rechtstheorie* (1990) 311–33 at 328–9.

[79] Henckels (2012) note 4 at 233.

[80] See on this question – on the basis of a fundamentally different theoretical approach – Stephen R Ratner, 'Regulatory Takings in Institutional Context: Beyond the Fear of Fragmented International Law' 102 *American Journal of International Law* (2008) 475–528 at 521–5, eg 524: 'The participants in these regimes should not be denied the

7.2.2 *Content of General Law*

The second part of the limit of the argument from general law is that it is uncertain whether the claimed general norms exist and what their content is, particularly whether customary norms are as specific as claimed. As mentioned, it is possible that general law differs significantly from the law in IIAs. One particularly promising avenue to analyse general expropriation law seems to be a legal-historical inquiry. On the face of it, a lot seems to ride on the state and development of customary international law before the content of IIAs was concretised by investment arbitration, that is approximately 1945–2000. Questions include the following: was a customary norm which prohibits expropriation extant in 1945 – with or without some form of compensation requirement? Did the upheaval connected to the New International Economic Order (NIEO) destroy or modify such a norm or did it endure (was it still extant after 1974)? Has it been newly created or revitalised during the process of the 'BIT revolution'[81] and the expansion in ISDS? Regarding the *Tatbestand* of expropriation, has the prohibition of *indirect* expropriation been impacted by the 'old' debates on the measure of compensation, does the traditional law concern only *direct* expropriation and was the exercise of the right to regulate or were police powers always excepted from the *Tatbestand* and to which extent?

A lot of ink has been spilt over the years on these questions, but the argument in Section 7.2 is that recourse to customary law is not as unproblematic as is commonly assumed – it is an underestimated, but highly potent macro-structural limit on what the international (treaty) law on expropriation can be. These considerations will limit doctrinal arguments pro and contra constructs such as the sole effects or police powers doctrines or vis-à-vis analogies from other areas of international or domestic law. Some of the legal-theoretical arguments discussed in earlier chapters relate specifically to the development of customary law on expropriation. In the following, we will combine them with the legal-historical arguments.

opportunity to create law on regulatory takings to advance their policies. If one regime claims that international law allows the government to undertake policy X without compensating an affected property owner and another claims that international law requires the government undertaking that same policy to compensate for an expropriation, those choices should be respected.'

81 Beauvais (2001–2) note 63 at 253.

1. *Traditional police powers.* The traditional police powers exception was very specific and narrow (see Section 6.1).[82] 'Under customary international law, the police powers exception has a very limited ambit. The exception would cover forfeiture for crime, bona fide general taxation or measures necessary for the maintenance of public order.'[83] Ben Wortley, writing in 1959, distinguishes expropriation from 'confiscation in the public interest':

> Confiscation is the deliberate seizure of property, by a State, without provision for adequate compensation ... In certain exceptional cases, confiscatory and similar actions are proper exercises of State-power, and may be regarded as a defence to any claims for restitution or damages. These cases, it is submitted, fall into three classes: (1) When there is a forfeiture or a fine to punish or suppress crime; (2) When property is seized by way of taxation; (3) When loss is indirectly caused by the territorial State imposing legislation restricting the use of property, thereby confiscating or limiting rights normally enjoyed by an owner.[84]

Equally, Louis B Sohn and Richard R Baxter explain the famous formulation of the police powers exception in Article 10(5) of the Harvard Draft 1961 – measures 'otherwise incidental to the normal operation of the laws of the State shall not be considered wrongful' – in narrow terms: '[b]y a taking or deprivation of property which is "otherwise incidental to the normal operation of the laws of the State" is meant the carrying out of a judgment of a court in a civil case or a fine or penalty in criminal proceedings'.[85] See also Rudolf Bindschedler, writing in 1950: 'It is unanimously agreed that ... neither property taxes nor penalties nor restrictions on the use of property for police [administrative-legal] reasons nor the confiscation of items which public order requires to be

[82] See already *Norwegian Shipowners' Claims (Norway* v. *United States of America)*, Permanent Court of Arbitration, Award of 13 October 1922, 1 *RIAA* (1948) 307 at 332: 'The inviolability of the private property of a foreign citizen is a question of public policy, ... and the "power of eminent domain", as is called in the United States the power of a sovereign state to expropriate, take or authorize the taking of any property within its jurisdiction which may be required for the "public good" or for the "general welfare". The Courts in such cases have to settle three questions: 1. Whether this is a case of private property being appropriated or taken? ... 2. Whether the "taking" is justified by public needs? ... 3. Whether just compensation has been offered or paid in due time?'

[83] Simon Baughen, 'Expropriation and Environmental Regulation: The Lessons of NAFTA Chapter 11' 18 *Journal of Environmental Law* (2006) 207–28 at 211.

[84] Benjamin Alexander Wortley, *Expropriation in Public International Law* (Cambridge: Cambridge University Press 1959) 39.

[85] Louis B Sohn, Richard R Baxter, 'Responsibility of States for Injuries to the Economic Interests of Aliens' 55 *American Journal of International Law* (1961) 545–84 at 554, 561.

destroyed, are prohibited. ... These restrictions, however, must have a purpose genuinely connected to fiscal, police [administrative-legal] or criminal justice-related reasons.'[86]

But why it this discussion relevant? Proponents of police powers argue that such an exception is inherent in IIA expropriation clauses precisely because the police powers exception has always been recognised in customary international law. Yet if the police powers exception was interpreted narrowly back then, it is more likely that – if the exception was integrated in IIAs – only the traditional, narrow exception is now contained in IIAs. The likelihood that this exception is as wide as claimed is significantly decreased. Maybe later writers have turned two features into one.[87] One is the narrow traditional exception to expropriation, police measures in the narrowest possible sense. This venerable concept ironically refers to a more modern meaning of 'police': the averting of immediate dangers to public safety and security (*öffentliche Sicherheit und Ordnung*). The second and a wide modern idea of police powers as a taking with a public purpose. It, in turn, recurs to the sixteenth–nineteenth-century notion of 'police' as public administration in general (*Policey*). Alessandra Asteriti describes the tensions this view can create particularly when treaty-makers purport to recur to customary law themselves in this respect (see Section 7.5):

> [C]ustomary international law already recognizes that certain governmental measures, such as confiscation, forfeiture, or seizure for recovery of taxation or other fiscal duties, or health emergencies, are immune from the

86 'Es besteht Einigkeit darüber, daß ... weder Vermögenssteuern noch Vermögensstrafen noch Vermögensbeschränkungen aus polizeilichen Gründen noch die Einziehung von Gegenständen, deren Vernichtung durch die öffentliche Ordnung dringend geboten ist, verb[oten sind.] ... Es muß sich jedoch wirklich um Vermögenseingriffe aus fiskalischen, polizeilichen oder strafrechtlichen Gründen handeln.' Rudolf L Bindschedler, *Verstaatlichungsmaßnahmen und Entschädigungspflicht nach Völkerrecht unter besonderer Berücksichtigung der schweizerischen Praxis über den Schutz schweizerischer Vermögenswerte im Ausland* (Zurich: Polygraphischer Verlag 1950) 25–6; see also Samy Friedman, *Expropriation in International Law* (London: Stevens & Sons 1953) 1; Wolfgang Birke, *Die Konfiskation ausländischen Privatvermögens im Hoheitsbereich des konfiszierenden Staates nach Friedensvölkerrecht* (PhD thesis,University of Cologne 1960) 7–10; Werner Veith, Karl-Heinz Böckstiegel, *Der Schutz von ausländischen Vermögen im Völkerrecht* (Baden-Baden: Lutzeyer 1962) 172.

87 See Wortley (1959) note 84 at 33–4: 'The United Kingdom Memorial in the *Anglo-Iranian Oil Company Case* reaffirmed the traditional view that the acceptance of the international lawfulness of the expropriation of foreigners is conditional upon the obligation to make "adequate, effective and prompt compensation" .... The onus is upon the State which seeks by its legislation or otherwise to expropriate without adequate compensation to affirm the international legality of its act, for example, by showing that it seized property by way of taxation or as confiscation for a recognized crime.'

> duty to compensate the affected parties. If treaty law reflects customary international law in this regard, the only argument that remains is if the taxonomy of legitimate purposes can include general bona fide exercises of regulatory authority that have an expropriatory effect or if it is to remain confined to the traditionally accepted exceptions.[88]

Some proponents of a wide reading are fully aware of this problem and claim that the notion has changed: 'In present times, the police powers must be understood as encompassing a State's full regulatory dimension. Modern States go well beyond the fundamental functions of custody, security and protection.'[89] Yet this is a minor point and neither side has a knock-down argument; the older conception of the police powers exception is merely an indication that the status of customary law is not as settled as those wishing to integrate it in IIAs imply it is.

2. *The Hull formula.* Another indication is based on the fact that, in the crucial period before IIAs allegedly took the customary law norm on expropriation on board, the debates focused almost exclusively on the measure of compensation. Patrick M Norton opens a 1991 article by arguing that 'in recent years international tribunals have repeatedly held that international law requires full compensation for expropriations of foreign property'.[90] 'The Great Ideological Debate'[91] was fought over the compensation standard and the (continued) applicability of the Hull formula, not the expropriation *Tatbestand*: 'the post-World War II focus on the rules on compensation almost entirely ignored the content of the primary rule'.[92] The debate largely ignored the direct expropriation *Tatbestand* and completely ignored indirect and regulatory expropriation, which can be gleamed in Dolzer's lament in 1986 that 'one cannot but admit at this stage that the law of indirect expropriation can be established, at this moment, on the basis of primary sources of international law, only in a very sketchy and rough manner'.[93] This raises the question of whether customary international law, as of the 1970s, contained norms on indirect expropriation at all, which implies that the

[88] Asteriti (2014) note 3 at 459–60.

[89] UNCTAD (2012) note 11 at 79.

[90] Patrick M Norton, 'A Law of the Future or a Law of the Past? Modern Tribunals and the International Law of Expropriation' 85 *American Journal of International Law* (1991) 474–505 at 475.

[91] Norton (1991) note 90 at 478.

[92] Paparinskis (2011b) note 1 at 303.

[93] Dolzer (1986) note 61 at 59; see also Rudolf Dolzer, *Eigentum, Enteignung und Entschädigung im geltenden Völkerrecht* (Berlin: Springer 1985) 214.

NIEO disruption could not have had much of an impact – in one way or another – on a non-existing part of the expropriation rule.

3. *The NIEO disruption.* The impact of the NIEO on customary international investment law is disputed; the whole political process is not generally seen as having been successful in creating new customary law. Wil Verwey and Nico Schrijver argue in 1984 that 'the arbitral tribunals in the [then] leading *Texaco* and *Aminoil* cases found that the resolutions adopted after 1962 … proclaim political rather than valid legal principles' and do not 'represent *opinio juris communis*'.[94] Dumberry puts it succinctly: 'the Charter of Economic Rights and Duties of States could hardly be considered as a reflection of existing international law at the time. In other words, the Charter did not create a new rule of customary international law.'[95] If the NIEO process was not able to create *new* law, did it disrupt the 'traditional' rules of customary international law on expropriation? 'A number of writers believe this is the case. … The more established position … is that some customary rules *already existed* at the time when developing States started opposing them.'[96] Dolzer, for example, concludes that 'the radical efforts against international legal rules covering foreign investment … must by now [1986] be deemed to have failed … the international law of expropriation has, in principle, remained intact'.[97] For Dumberry, there is a difference to be made between the NIEO's impact on the Hull rule on compensation and on other areas, including the *Tatbestand* of expropriation: 'the conditions for lawful expropriation and the requirement for States to provide

[94] Wil D Verwey, Nico Schrijver, 'The Taking of Foreign Property under International Law: A New Legal Perspective?' 15 *Netherlands Yearbook of International Law* (1984) 3–96 at 79, 80; referring to *Texaco Overseas Petroleum Co.* v. *Libyan Arab Republic*, 1977, 17 ILM (1978) 1; *Kuwait* v. *American Independent Oil Company (AMINOIL)*, Award of 24 March 1982, 21 ILM (1982) 976.

[95] Patrick Dumberry, *The Formation and Identification of Rules of Customary International Law in International Investment Law* (Cambridge: Cambridge University Press 2016) 74; see also Yoram Dinstein, 'Deprivation of Property of Foreigners under International Law' in Nisuke Ando, Edward McWhinney, Rüdiger Wolfrum (eds.), *Liber Amicorum Judge Shigeru Oda*, vol 2 (The Hague: Kluwer 2002) 849–69 at 851; F Prugger, 'A Source Problem of International Law in the Field of Expropriation of Alien Property' 16 *Thesaurus Acroasium* (1990) 869–81 at 876–7; August Reinisch, 'Legality of Expropriations' in August Reinisch (ed.), *Standards of Investment Protection* (Oxford: Oxford University Press 2008) 171–204 at 175; Stephen M Schwebel, 'The United States 2004 Model Bilateral Investment Treaty: An Exercise in the Regressive Development of International Law' in Stephen M Schwebel, *Justice in International Law: Further Selected Writings* (Cambridge: Cambridge University Press 2011) 152–60 at 154.

[96] Dumberry (2016) note 95 at 75.

[97] Dolzer (1986) note 61 at 42; see also Kriebaum (2008a) note 9 at 27–8.

investors with some sort of "adequate" compensation . . . have generally survived the attack launched by Newly Independent States'.[98] This is not true of the Hull formula: 'because a large majority of countries made it clear that they felt no legal obligation to follow the Hull Rule, the resolutions demonstrated that "prompt, adequate, and effective" was no longer a rule of customary international law'.[99]

Yet there are doubts as to whether there were customary rules on expropriation in the first place which the NIEO process could have 'destroyed'.[100] One of *Barcelona Traction*'s better-known *dicta* is pertinent in this respect:

> [I]t may at first sight appear surprising that the evolution of [customary investment] law has not gone further and that no generally accepted rules in the matter have crystallized on the international plane. Nevertheless, a more thorough examination of the facts shows that the law on the subject has been formed in a period characterized by an intense conflict of systems and interests. It is essentially bilateral relations which have been concerned . . . The difficulties encountered have been reflected in the evolution of the law on the subject.[101]

Again, neither side has knock-down arguments: there is some pre-NIEO case-law (and some post-NIEO case-law looking at this period) which suggests that before the upheaval a norm of customary international law on expropriation was extant,[102] but neither is this evidence unchallenged nor does it appear that the customary norm, if it existed, would be of sufficient specificity. While 'the [NIEO] resolutions may have cast doubt on the traditional expropriation standard, . . . they have not created new customary international law'.[103] A theoretical question in this connection is whether *desuetudo* is the ebbing of the continued support by a constant accumulation of instances of state practice and

98 Dumberry (2016) note 95 at 76.

99 Andrew T Guzman, 'Why LDCs Sign Treaties that Hurt them: Explaining the Popularity of Bilateral Investment Treaties' 38 *Virginia Journal of International Law* (1998) 639–88 at 651; see also Dumberry (2016) note 95 at 76–9; Kenneth J Vandevelde, 'U.S. Bilateral Investment Treaties: The Second Wave' 14 *Michigan Journal of International Law* (1993) 621–704 at 625.

100 Muthucumaraswamy Sornarajah, *The International Law on Foreign Investment* (3rd edn, Cambridge: Cambridge University Press 2010) 366.

101 *Barcelona Traction, Light and Power, Limited (New Application: 1962) (Belgium* v. *Spain)*, Second Phase, Judgment of 5 February 1970, ICJ Reports (1970) 3 at 47 (para 89), partially quoted by Dumberry (2016) note 95 at 77.

102 See Paparinskis (2011b) note 1, for a concise overview.

103 Reinisch (2008b) note 95 at 175.

opinio iuris even after the customary norm has become valid, or whether changes to a customary norm can be accomplished only if the initial creation threshold is again reached. On the second view, '[a] norm no longer supported by any practice or *opinio iuris* remains valid unless there is practice and *opinio iuris* sufficient to create a norm to supersede it'.[104] Once more, the question is: what is the default position? What if we cannot definitively prove a complete derogation of the pre-NIEO customary rule, but can prove a disruption of mostly political import? The conclusion which the majority seems to have reached with hindsight – particularly because their hindsight is coloured by many IIAs and arbitral awards since then – is that the NIEO movement was not enough and that, in any case, later developments have confirmed this direction. While norm-theoretically one can agree with the first part of such a statement – customary law is not destroyed by a lack of state practice and *opinio iuris* once it is established – the unquestioned acceptance of the influence of treaties and awards is problematic.

4. *Emerging customary law.* Has the growing number of IIAs and investment awards had an impact on the customary law of expropriation? Has this customary law (as potentially changed) had an impact on treaty norms on expropriation? These questions have become more pressing as a large number of treaties and case-law has accrued and this is the reason why Chapter 2 and Section 3.4 have discussed them at length. The majority opinion is that this vast body of treaties and case-law has significantly influenced the modern content of customary investment law, particularly regarding expropriation. For example, take Mostafa's claim that tribunals 'rely heavily on customary international law to delimit indirect expropriation claims. … This … is likely to have the ultimate effect of assisting with the development of customary international law itself.'[105] W Michael Reisman and Robert D Sloane argue that '[t]he nearly 2,200 BITs in existence today … suggest… that the broader conception of expropriation embodied by BITs to some extent has become … customary international law'.[106] This process is seen to have occurred 'even if custom had produced a general "police powers" exception', in which case it, the exception, would 'have its modern content assessed in light of the considerable state practice embodied in the over 2000 BITs now in force'.[107]

[104] Kammerhofer (2010d) note 77 at 85.
[105] Mostafa (2008) note 9 at 271.
[106] Reisman (2004) note 9 at 150 fn 158.
[107] Coe (2005) note 2 at 639–40.

However, there are also critical voices. One group are those sympathetic to the aims of the NIEO, such as Sūrya Subedī. While 'customary international law is constantly evolving and new examples of state practice are liable to change the existing rules', as of 2006 he expresses scepticism that '[t]he law developed by NAFTA is not ipso facto capable of altering the meaning, nature, and scope of general customary international law'.[108] As late as 2016, his doubts have not receded, even though they are expressed on the basis of an orthodox sources theory, which generally argues in favour of treaties and jurisprudence being able to influence customary international law:

> Regardless of the number of BITs embodying the same and similar provisions, such provisions cannot necessarily be regarded to have crystallised into rules of international law. . . . Many of the provisions of BITs may not meet the test of *opinio juris* needed to constitute custom. Until it can be established that the central tenets have been modified by new state practice, traditional customary international law ... seem[s] to remain valid.[109]

This type of critique can also be applied to those who argue that the *Tatbestand* of expropriation includes a police powers exception because of new developments like the inclusion of such an exception in Type B clauses (Section 7.5), which allegedly reflect customary law. If the 2004 US model BIT 'codifies the right to regulate in Annex B . . ., its inclusion in the 2004 Model ... suggests that previous indirect expropriation provisions do *not* expressly account for the police powers doctrine'.[110] Surely the comparatively few Type B clauses are even less likely to modify 'the central tenets' of expropriation law than the vast majority of Type A IIA expropriation clauses?[111]

Chapters 2–4 have discussed doubts regarding claims to create a general law on expropriation or a universalised form of applying it and these doubts apply with full force to the specific problem discussed. Customary (international) law is far too problematic, is too difficult to establish, too slow-moving and too limited in what one can do with it to serve as the foundation for the claims to a general norm of expropriation.

[108] Sūrya Prasāda Subedī, 'The Challenge of Reconciling the Competing Principles within the Law of Foreign Investment with Special Reference to the Recent Trend in the Interpretation of the Term "Expropriation"' 40 *International Lawyer* (2006) 121–41 at 132.

[109] Subedī (2016) note 25 at 178–9.

[110] Bray (2012) note 9 at 18–19 (emphasis added).

[111] See Kriebaum (2008a) note 9 at 269.

One could paraphrase Carl Schmitt: whoever invokes customary international law wants to deceive.[112] All of the considerations above militate in favour of the claim from customary law being subject to very powerful restrictions. Sourgens expresses this idea exceptionally well:

> The claim that IIAs would create new custom is not without irony. Champions of IIAs as custom typically deny that UN General Assembly Resolutions purporting to limit the scope of international law with regard to the rights of aliens . . . created custom; their justification is that the rules contained in these resolutions failed the traditional definition of custom. Their own invocation of the new customary theory in the current, changed climate thus seems at best opportunistic and, at worst, hypocritical. Even admitting that the champions of IIAs as new custom had it right, custom would swing between extremes at an alarming rate. In twenty years, new custom would swing from strong investment protection at the end of World War II to a significant limitation of investment protection in the 1960s and 1970s. In another twenty years, it would swing back again to strong investment protection through the adoption of IIAs. The perceived backlash against IIAs could be used by IIA opponents as evidence of yet another sea change, swinging the pendulum of new custom back to the 1970s.[113]

5. *General principles of law*. Does the introduction of arguments based on general principles of law change this outcome? Some authors argue in favour of a general principle of expropriation, like Dolzer in his early writings: we should recur to general principles of law, to be 'established on the basis of parallel notions and rules in domestic legal orders'.[114] He queries 'whether . . . general principles of law can be established for the field of indirect expropriation [as can] be drawn from national orders of all the major legal systems and cultures'[115] and comes to a nuanced but broadly positive result.[116] Kinnear links this result to IIAs: '"nationalization," "expropriation," and "measures tantamount thereto" . . . are not defined by NAFTA. As a result, treaty interpreters must refer to general

[112] The original quote is 'Wer Menschheit sagt, will betrügen.' 'Whoever invokes humanity wants to deceive.' Carl Schmitt, *Der Begriff des Politischen* [1932] (7th edn, Duncker & Humblot, Berlin 1991) 55.

[113] Frédéric G Sourgens, *A Nascent Common Law: The Process of Decisionmaking in International Legal Disputes Between States and Foreign Investors* (The Hague: Nijhoff 2015) 261.

[114] Dolzer (1986) note 61 at 59; see also Dolzer (1985) note 93.

[115] Dolzer (1986) note 61 at 60.

[116] Dolzer (1986) note 61 at 60–4; see also Henckels (2012) note 4 at 226; Lévesque (2004) note 5 at 306; Schill (2006) note 22 at 13.

principles of international law to define these terms.'[117] In contrast, Paparinskis echoes earlier pessimism about the results that could be obtained on the basis of a comparatist exercise:

> Regarding general principles, after a thorough examination of different domestic approaches, Bullington concluded that 'the variations in practice ... render worse than useless the attempt to impose any one system of law as the standard for international comparison'. More generally, the perception that developed States were 'internationalizing' peculiar domestic concepts led to scepticism about the whole framework of treatment of aliens.[118]

Basing one's argument on general principles of law does not avoid the problems of the transmission mechanism between general international law and treaty law mentioned in Section 7.2.1. Establishing the content of general principles in a manner that does not rely on assertion is more difficult than counting state practice and *opinio iuris*. Domestic constitutional law and human rights law on the protection of property vary greatly, as a very telling argument demonstrates. For Wälde and Kolo, one 'criterion that emerges in particular from comparative constitutional law is the concept of the "Sonderopfer" ... [which] constitutes the core of German expropriation law; but it is also reflected in pertinent US Supreme Court practice'.[119] That may be the case, but on a truly representative comparative analysis of the protection of property throughout the world, it will most likely not be found to be as *general* a principle as they make out.

The character of the prohibition of expropriation in IIAs is not that of basic, constitutional or human rights law on the protection of property and cannot be analogised nor taken as source of a comparatist effort. In addition, general principles of law as a potential source of international law suffer from grave theoretical problems:[120] theoretically speaking, general principles are unlikely to be anything more than a gap-filler for the International Court of Justice. Article 38(1)(c) ICJ Statute is likely no more than the authorisation to the Court to make up ad hoc norms which it calls 'general principles' and to apply them.

[117] Kinnear (2006) note 19 at 1110-13.

[118] Paparinskis (2011b) note 1 at 314, citing John P Bullington, 'Problems of International Law in the Mexican Constitution of 1917' 21 *American Journal of International Law* (1927) 685–705 at 694; see also FA Mann, 'State Contracts and State Responsibility' 54 *American Journal of International Law* (1960) 572–91 at 583.

[119] Wälde (2001) note 57 at 845.

[120] Kammerhofer (2014a) note 12; Kammerhofer (2014b) note 12.

6. *Conclusion on general law.* The macro-structural limit established by the relationship of IIA expropriation clauses to general international law is complex. It does not provide as clear an answer regarding the *Tatbestand* of (indirect) expropriation as the two micro-structural limits in Sections 7.3 and 7.4. Yet, it is clear that the structure and the interaction of international legal norms hailing from different sources do not make it feasible to maintain simple assumptions about these relationships.

Without more, we cannot assume that IIAs 'refer to', 'incorporate' or 'are to be interpreted while taking into account' general law. Interpretation is not an adequate tool to achieve coherence of content as between customary law and treaties. Nor should we assume that treaties are (to be made) coherent with general international law. It is extremely unlikely that IIA expropriation clauses incorporate or otherwise refer to a customary expropriation norm. It is even less certain what the exact content of general law on expropriation is. Even among orthodox international legal scholars, there is significant scepticism that modern customary international law or general principles contain (significantly specific) norms on expropriation: 'international law has failed to develop clear rules to determine what government measures amount to expropriation. Customary international law is unclear'.[121] It is highly doubtful whether, indeed, any customary rule would be sufficiently specific (Section 4.3.3) to decide the questions of the *Tatbestand* of indirect expropriation, a police powers exception or the right to regulate. It is understandable that, in the face of vague treaty standards, we look to customary law (or case-law) for a clarification, but, by their very structure, both customary law and general principles of law are bound to be less precise than treaties: IIAs at least have a text, at least have language, however vague, whereas custom and principles lack even that.

Yet another reason militating against the assumption of coherence of IIAs and general law is this: IIA expropriation clauses contain two *other* limits, the equivalence of direct and indirect expropriation and the co-equality of all legality conditions (Sections 7.3 and 7.4). These establish limits as to what IIAs mean by 'indirect expropriation' which contradict the police powers friendly reading. Any influence which Type A IIAs might have had on customary international law would therefore rather point to the fact that custom is commensurate with the limits first

[121] Newcombe (1999) note 34 at 4.

established in IIAs.[122] The results of this section can be summarised as follows:

- The transmission, whether by way of interpretation or norm interaction, of legal content from general law to international treaty law is much less likely and less effective than is commonly assumed.
- The creation and change of customary law are much slower and much more difficult than is commonly assumed. In particular, neither the NIEO disruption nor IIAs nor arbitral jurisprudence could have had the impact claimed.
- In our specific case, if the traditional customary expropriation norm contained a police powers exception, that exception is likely to have been the narrow, traditional type.
- Customary law in general, and any customary norm on expropriation that has emerged in particular, is not as specific or detailed as we make out. It is certainly not more specific than the IIA expropriation clauses.

7.3 Equivalence of Direct and Indirect Expropriation

The second limit is reasonably straightforward, but not much discussed: in Type A IIA clauses, direct and indirect expropriation are to be treated the same; both operate on the basis of the same structure of prohibition and exception. The micro-structure of these IIA expropriation clauses is that the law cannot support arguments which result in indirect expropriation being subject to different conditions than direct expropriation. This argument is often made implicitly and is the basis for the police powers doctrine.

The mainstream discourages reliance on the award in *Santa Elena* of 17 February 2000 as precedent, despite it being a particularly important piece of case-law. Given the strong belief in the power of arbitral decisions, this may seem somewhat surprising argument, but on closer inspection it is not. *Santa Elena* runs counter to the *Zeitgeist*, for its consequentialist reasoning does not work well with orthodoxy's impetus to balance extremes and find a compromise solution (Chapter 6). It held that:

[122] *Waguih Elie George Siag and Clorinda Vecchi* v. *Arab Republic of Egypt*, ICSID, ARB/05/15, Award of 1 June 2009, para 428: 'It is equally well accepted, however, that an expropriation is only lawful if certain conditions are met. *Several of these requirements have become part of customary international law*' (emphasis added).

> While an expropriation or taking for environmental reasons may be classified as a taking for a public purpose, and thus may be legitimate, the fact that the Property was taken for this reason does not affect either the nature or the measure of the compensation to be paid for the taking. That is, the purpose of protecting the environment for which the Property was taken does not alter the legal character of the taking for which adequate compensation must be paid. The international source of the obligation to protect the environment makes no difference.[123]

This holding has been interpreted as a requirement under international investment law that compensation must be paid even for measures legitimately aiming to protect the environment and is thus seen as significant precedent in favour of the sole effects doctrine. An obvious solution when one wishes not to be bound by a clear precedent is to distinguish it and so it is here. Paparinskis, for example, notes that '*Santa Elena* has often been cited to support the irrelevance of environmental considerations for defining expropriation'. However, he believes that 'in fact the text and context of the particular paragraph clearly show that the Tribunal was talking only about compensation for direct expropriation.'[124] This argument is used by Asteriti as well; she believes that the award 'needs to be qualified and put into context: ... the tribunal was faced with a case of direct expropriation'.[125] However, this distinguishing is not universally accepted. Jan Dalhuisen and Andrew Guzman note that '[t]he *Santa Elena* reasoning ... was extended to regulatory takings in *Tecmed v Mexico*'.[126] Titi believes that this precedent is relevant for a more substantive reason: 'Although the dispute concerned a direct expropriation for conservation purposes and the issue was not the existence of a requirement to compensate but the amount of such compensation, the award uses the sole effects doctrine. In this sense, *its reasoning is also pertinent in the case of an indirect expropriation.*'[127]

[123] *Compañia del Desarrollo de Santa Elena, S.A.* v. *Republic of Costa Rica*, ICSID, ARB/96/1, Final Award of 17 February 2000, para 71; see also *Marion Unglaube and Reinhard Unglaube* v. *Republic of Costa Rica*, ICSID, ARB/08/01 and ARB/09/20, Award of 16 May 2012.

[124] Paparinskis (2011b) note 1 at 310; see also Catharine Titi, 'Refining the Expropriation Clause: What Role for Proportionality?' in Julien Chaisse (ed.), *China–European Union Investment Relationships: Towards a New Leadership in Global Investment Governance?* (Cheltenham: Edward Elgar 2018), available at and cited from: ssrn.com/abstract=2978530 (2017) at 12.

[125] Asteriti (2014) note 3 at 460.

[126] Jan H Hendrik Dalhuisen, Andrew T Guzman, 'Expropriatory and Non-expropriatory Takings under International Investment Law' 10:4 *Transnational Dispute Management* (2013) 10 fn 21.

[127] Titi (2014) note 9 at 285 (emphasis added).

The systemic equality of direct and indirect expropriation is seldom doubted directly. It is rather an under-estimation of this argument which manifests itself by heightening the 'special' nature of indirect (regulatory) expropriation.[128] In describing the limits of proportionality analysis, Henckels mentions that in customary international law, 'whether a direct expropriation has been effected for a public purpose is only relevant insofar as it affects the issue of whether an expropriation is lawful or unlawful, and not the issue of whether an expropriation has taken place'. This implies that for *indirect* expropriation – whether or not it is 'explicitly mandated by the ... treaty'[129] – a balancing operation takes place which brings public purpose analysis into the *Tatbestand.* Anne Hoffmann asks why 'modern bilateral and multilateral investment treaties' still use phrases like 'measures having an effect equivalent or tantamount to expropriation' and are reluctant 'to give up a paradigm of law that was developed in the context of direct expropriations, despite the fact that their legal form has meanwhile undergone a change'.[130] Arbitral case-law does this as well.[131]

The 2012 UNCTAD study is an example of a straightforward disavowal of the equivalence of direct and indirect expropriation. Whereas 'direct expropriation, in order to be lawful under international law, must be accompanied by compensation', even if 'pursued for a public purpose', this is not the case for 'an allegation of an indirect (regulatory) expropriation'. There, 'a broader assessment of the nature of the measure ... is essential in order to distinguish an indirect expropriation from the ordinary and legitimate regulatory conduct of the State, which is noncompensable':[132] As a result of this unequal treatment, the legality conditions are doubled (Section 7.4): 'Public purpose, non-discrimination and due process also serve as conditions for the legality of an expropriation. However, in that context, *they were designed for cases*

[128] See Coe (2005) note 2 at 632: 'Commentators and tribunals have occasionally referred to claims of regulatory taking as if they occupied a separate class of expropriation, perhaps implying that they require different handling.'

[129] Henckels (2015) note 18 at 173.

[130] Hoffmann (2008) note 9 at 151–2. Other variants of implicit distinctions can be found eg in: L Yves Fortier, Stephen L Drymer, 'Indirect Expropriation in the Law of International Investment: I Know It When I See It, or *Caveat Investor*' 19 *ICSID Review – Foreign Investment law Journal* (2004) 293–327 at 319; Kinnear (2006) note 19 at 1110-16; McLachlan (2007) note 18 at 290; Ratner (2008) note 80 at 482–3; Titi (2014) note 9 at 181.

[131] *Quiborax* (2015) note 26 at para 200.

[132] UNCTAD (2012) note 11 at 31.

of direct expropriation where the taking itself is self-evident. For cases involving alleged regulatory expropriations, the same requirements serve to distinguish compensable expropriation from noncompensable regulation'.[133]

A connection exists between the direct–indirect expropriation equivalence and two other dimensions of the expropriation question. First, since expropriation provisions are not a protection of property in the sense of human or constitutional rights provisions, but rules whose object are investments, could 'direct' expropriation not be seen as wider than assumed? It certainly could be wider than the formal taking of *property* by the state, for if 'investment' encompasses objects other than property – which cannot be expropriated in the formal sense – three variants are possible: (1) large parts of 'investments' can only be indirectly expropriated, (2) 'direct expropriation' takes a different form for parts of an investment which are not property or (3) a direct expropriation of an investment is something other than the formal taking of title to property. There is a hint of this line of argument in Epaminontas Triantafilou's case note on *EnCana*:[134] '[i]n support of its *direct* expropriation claim, EnCana contended that it was entitled to VAT refunds . . . The preliminary question that arose was whether these tax refunds were . . . a protected "investment."'[135]

The second connection is to partial expropriation (Section 8.3). If any amount would unequivocally be expropriation if taken directly, why do we discuss whether partial expropriation is an expropriation in the relevant sense of the IIAs? 'No one will question that an expropriation has occurred if someone is deprived of five of ten hectares of land.'[136] This is an implicit disaggregation of direct as against indirect expropriation:

> While a government will typically compensate property owners for a direct expropriation of an insubstantial piece of property, such as a sliver of a half acre lot required to widen a municipal road, it is unusual for a government to explicitly compensate property owners for significant

[133] UNCTAD (2012) note 11 at 95 (emphasis added).

[134] *EnCana Corporation* v. *Republic of Ecuador*, UNCITRAL, LCIA UN3481, Award of 3 February 2006.

[135] Epaminontas E Triantafilou, 'Taxation as Expropriation: Some Observations on *EnCana v. Ecuador*' 3:5 *Transnational Dispute Management* (2006) 4 (emphasis added).

[136] Ursula Kriebaum, 'Partial Expropriation' 8 *Journal of World Investment & Trade* (2007) 69–84 at 83.

reductions in property value resulting from common types of regulatory changes, such as land use zoning.[137]

Two grounds are advanced for reading IIA expropriation clauses as not requiring a total equivalence of the two forms of expropriation. The first is to highlight that, in fact, direct expropriation *is* different from indirect expropriation (D≠I): measures of direct expropriation are widely acknowledged to have a different nature than (particularly) general regulatory measures. While everyone would recognise a formal deprivation of property by legislative, administrative or judicial measure, surely this cannot, in fact, be the same type of measure as a plain packaging regulation for tobacco products or conditions for the operation of an open-cast mine? Hence there is neither a need nor the possibility to treat the two forms of expropriation as exact equals.

This line of reasoning is implicitly, rather than openly, made, for example in *Oxus Gold*. 'Contrary to what happens with a direct expropriation, where the goal of the legal act performing the expropriation is precisely to take a property,' it held, 'in case of indirect expropriation, there is a State law or regulation, or sometimes some behaviour, – the purpose of which was not to take the property'.[138] Paparinskis argues that '[i]f indirect expropriation is viewed through the lens of direct expropriation, it is natural to look at the effect of States' conduct'.[139] While this is directed at the question of the sole effects doctrine, it could also be read as an assertion that indirect expropriation is, in fact, significantly different and should thus be treated differently.

The award in *Electrabel* was sceptical of the D≠I thesis; it did 'not accept that these decisions and other materials cited by Electrabel reflect ... a different standard for direct and indirect expropriation'. These materials 'describe for both direct and indirect expropriation, consistently albeit in different terms, the requirement under international law [including the ECT] ... the ... fundamental deprivation of its rights [etc.]'.[140] Mostafa echoes the *Electrabel* critique when he counters critics of the sole effects doctrine who argue that the doctrine

137 Newcombe (1999) note 34 at 8.

138 *Oxus Gold Plc* v. *Republic of Uzbekistan*, UNCITRAL, Award of 17 December 2015, para 740.

139 Paparinskis (2011b) note 1 at 300; see also *Sedco Inc., Sedco International SA and Sediran Drilling Company* v. *National Iranian Oil Company and Islamic Republic of Iran*, Iran–USCT, Award ITL 55-129-3 of 24 October 1985, 9 *Iran–USCT Reports* (1987) 248 at 275.

140 *Electrabel S.A.* v. *Republic of Hungary*, ICSID, ARB/07/19, Decision on Jurisdiction, Applicable Law and Liability of 30 November 2012, paras 6.60, 6.62.

'should not apply in indirect expropriation cases'; this 'would suggest that there should be a significant cleavage between the two forms of expropriation'. For him, 'direct and indirect expropriation are merely two different manifestations of the same concept: expropriation as a whole'.[141] The cinching argument with respect to traditional (Type A) IIA expropriation clauses is that the law itself has formally made the two forms equivalent, hence it is *legally* irrelevant whether measures of direct expropriation are *factually* different from those of indirect expropriation. IIAs prescribe that the treatment of the two forms of expropriation should be identical.[142]

The second, closely related counter-argument is that it is irrelevant whether direct and indirect expropriation are in some sense equivalents, because the *Tatbestand* of (at least) indirect expropriation itself contains a police powers exception or a right to regulate. This is a core argument of the police powers doctrine and many would probably agree with this sentiment. In seeking to promote an interpretation of NAFTA in this sense, Daniel Clough argues that the *Tatbestand* of indirect expropriation is limited: '[t]here can be no expropriation because there has been no taking of property as a matter of law; the property has merely been regulated'.[143] In *EMV*, the tribunal, after distinguishing 'expropriation' from 'other measures of dispossession, direct or indirect, total or partial, having a similar effect'[144] in Article 3(1) of the BLEU–Czech Republic BIT 1989, held that 'international law treat[s] takings of property which are for a public purpose, in accordance with law, non-discriminatory and accompanied by proper provision for compensation as falling outside the scope of expropriation'.[145]

Once more, the structure of typical IIA clauses speaks against the inequality thesis. As the 2012 ECS study highlights, '[t]he guarantee in international investment treaties typically provides that when there is an expropriation, *whether direct or indirect*, it must be accompanied by compensation';[146] Dolzer and Christoph Schreuer's words are even

[141] Mostafa (2008) note 9 at 282.

[142] Schreuer goes a step further; he extends this equivalence to pre-IIA revolution customary law: 'Even before the introduction of pertinent treaty provisions, international courts and tribunals have treated indirect takings and equivalent measures in the same way as direct expropriations.' Schreuer (2006) note 9 at 115.

[143] Daniel Clough, 'Regulatory Expropriations and Competition under NAFTA' 6 *Journal of World Investment & Trade* (2005) 553–84 at 554.

[144] 'autres mesures de dépossession directe ou indirecte, totale ou partielle, ayant un effet similaire.'

[145] *EMV* (2009) note 15 at para 48.

[146] ECS (2012) note 18 at 35 (emphasis added).

more salient: 'General regulatory rules and the measures based on them are subject to the same standards of protection that have been developed for all other instances.'[147]

Even if we were *arguendo* to extend the police powers exception to direct expropriation,[148] thereby avoiding the charge of inequality, the systemic connection to the legality conditions has shaped the *Tatbestand* and will make it very unlikely that such an inclusion has taken place, as argued in Sections 7.2 and 7.4. A cross-check would be to ask about the possibility of regulatory *direct* expropriation. What about two measures that are enacted for exactly the same reasons, such as valid public policy objectives – does a formal taking for environmental reasons need to be compensated whereas a regulatory measure with the same effect does not? This might be what the tribunal in *Copper Mesa* had in mind when it held: 'As regards a measure amounting to a *direct* expropriation under the Treaty, the Tribunal considers that its constituent legal parts requires: ... (ii) that the resulting deprivation finds no justification as the legitimate exercise of the Respondent's police or regulatory powers'.[149]

For Type A IIA expropriation clauses, whatever is the law for direct expropriation is the law for indirect expropriation. The police powers doctrine implicitly carries with it 'a fragmentation within investment law between direct and indirect expropriations'.[150] Christian Zielonka, in picking up an argument first made in a systematic fashion by Kriebaum (to be discussed further in Section 7.4), writes: 'Because indirect expropriation is described by contrasting it with direct expropriation ..., controversies about the criteria for indirect expropriation are caused by the question in how far an indirect expropriation must conform to the direct expropriation model.'[151]

[147] Dolzer (2012) note 61 at 121–2; see also Kriebaum (2008a) note 9 at 271; *Suez I* (2010) note 24 at para 121.

[148] Dalhuisen (2013) note 126 at 11; possibly Kevin Banks, 'NAFTA's Article 1110: Can Regulation Be Expropriation?' 5 *NAFTA: Law and Business Review of the Americas* (1999) 499–521 at 509.

[149] *Copper Mesa Mining Corporation* v. *Republic of Ecuador*, UNCITRAL, PCA 2012-2, Award of 15 March 2016, para 6.58 (emphasis added); see also Subedī (2016) note 25 at 191, 193.

[150] Ursula Kriebaum, 'Regulatory Takings: Balancing the Interests of the Investor and the State' 8 *Journal of World Investment & Trade* (2007) 717–44 at 726; see also López (2014) note 9 at 198.

[151] Zielonka (2017) note 9 at 91: 'Indem die indirekte Enteignung anhand des Vergleichsmaßstabs der direkten Enteignung beschrieben wird ... lassen sich Kontroversen über die Kriterien, welche für das Vorliegen einer indirekten

Expropriation is a single 'institute of law'. Because the three process conditions are doubled and the conditionality of *Tatbestand* and legality conditions are broken, the single institute is split in two; therefore, the police powers doctrine cannot work.[152] The second systematic limit for Type A IIA expropriation clauses is born of their micro-structure. Because direct and indirect expropriation are legally the same and are subject to the same set of legality conditions, any reading of the *Tatbestand* of indirect expropriation which establishes, explicitly or implicitly, a divergence between the two forms of expropriation goes beyond the frame of possible meanings.

7.4 All Legality Conditions Are Necessary

This issue has been the object of considerable attention in the modern debate on regulatory expropriation. However, in the current debate both those making the case for conditionality as well as those doubting or downplaying it underestimate the structural centrality of the equal conditionality of all legality conditions. In logical terms, the fulfilment of the legality conditions is a necessary condition for a legal expropriation, but only the fulfilment of *all* conditions is sufficient. Conditionality is often seen as merely one of several arguments for the sole effects doctrine which can be countered by other arguments, including policy reasoning. However, the conditionality is the paramount *structural* limit on what the *Tatbestand* of 'expropriation' can be.

It may be helpful to approach this question from the perspective of those who deny and/or de-emphasise the strict conditionality. These voices doubt the plain words of the IIA clause and give us arguments for their reading. Counter-arguments seeking to show that this doubt is not supported by the law respond to the doubters' arguments and it would be difficult to construct a narrative if the counter-arguments are presented as untethered to the doubters' legal position. In essence, doubters use two intimately interlinked and therefore difficult to separate arguments, which we will dub 'doubling' and 'selection'. Doubling in effect involves inserting some or all of the process conditions as negative criteria in the *Tatbestand*. Both tactics negate the necessity of the legality conditions, but doubling does so by making some, but not all, into

Enteignung erfüllt sein müssen, . . . auf die Frage zurückführen, inwieweit die indirekte Form der Enteignung einer direkten Enteignung entsprechen muss.'

152 Zielonka (2017) note 9 at 116, 121, 130.

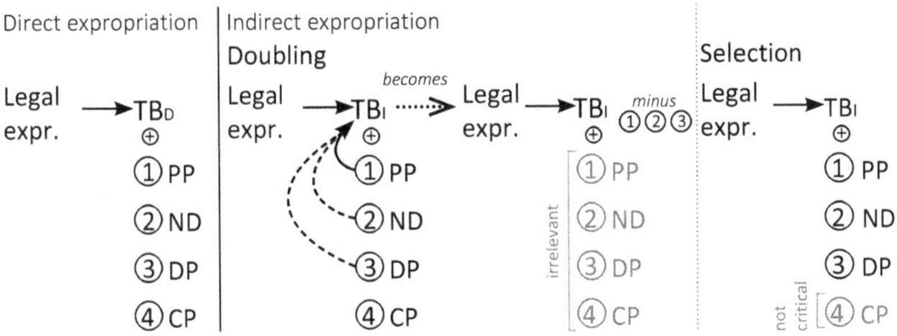

Figure 7.2 The doubling and selection tactics[153]

(negative) elements of the *Tatbestand* (Section 7.4.1). Selection does so by de-emphasising the strict necessity of one particular legality condition, namely compensation. This means creating an inequality between the process conditions, on the one hand, and the compensation condition, on the other (Section 7.4.2). Both tactics are based in essence on arguments from impracticability or ideological/policy preference. Neither tactic, it is submitted, accurately reflects the law.

7.4.1 *Doubling the Process Conditions*

In effect, proponents of the doubling argument have proceeded on the assumption that there are two stages to the indirect expropriation analysis which are strictly sequential: the definition of expropriation (*Tatbestand*) followed by the legality conditions. Sometimes this is taken further, such as when a regulatory act is not seen as 'an exception to international liability [but] … as a measure that simply does not trigger international liability'.[154] This has meant that the commonly accepted and pragmatic sequence of analysis for solving a case trumps

[153] For direct expropriation where the *Tatbestand* (TB_D) is generally not seen as an issue, it is agreed that all legality conditions, typically public purpose (PP), non-discrimination (ND), due process of law (DP) and compensation (CP) need to be cumulatively fulfilled for an act of expropriation to be legal. A. Doubling involves integrating PP (often also ND and DP), *but not CP*, into the *Tatbestand* of indirect expropriation (TB_I), which results in the legality conditions in effect being made irrelevant, as TB_I contains the integrated process conditions (PP, often also ND and DP) as negative condition. B. Selection uses other arguments to target the (immediate and co-equal) necessity of CP, such as the determination of CP only in the award of an arbitral tribunal.

[154] UNCTAD (2012) note 11 at 92; on the relationship between rule and exception see also Kammerhofer (2010d) note 77 at 49–51.

the legal structure of the norms. The dominant doubling argument could be called 'identity claim' and is expressed in the *Methanex* award: '[T]he California ban was made for a public purpose, was non-discriminatory and was accomplished with due process. Hence, Methanex's central claim under Article 1110(1) of expropriation under one of the three forms of action in that provision fails. From the standpoint of international law, the California ban was a lawful regulation and not an expropriation.'[155]

The tribunal took the exact concepts contained in the conditions in Article 1110(1)(a)–(c) NAFTA to determine the *Tatbestand* of Article 1110(1) NAFTA. Since these three were fulfilled, the measure was 'not an expropriation'. Three of the four legality conditions[156] had been reproduced *identically* in the *Tatbestand.* The opponents counter that this doubling is not possible: *inclusio unius est exclusio alterius.*[157] Doubling makes a condition redundant which the IIAs unquestionably contain; their inclusion invalidates the argument that exercises of 'police powers' are excluded from constituting expropriation. Against this predictable criticism, an alternative or supplementary argument is sometimes made, here dubbed the 'non-identity claim'. It argues that 'public interest' or '*bona fide* general regulatory measure' is not identical with 'public purpose' or the other process conditions.

1. *The identity claim.* This argument is at the root of the police powers doctrine; many have sought to counter the doctrine by taking issue with the identity claim. The identity claim is often identified as the implicit premise for the success of the police powers doctrine. Asteriti's clearly distinguishes 'regulatory expropriation … where … the expropriatory effect is a consequence of legitimate, bona fide regulation for the protection or the furtherance of the public interest' from other forms of taking. She does not shy away from making the following – 'not only descriptive…, but consciously normative…' – statement: 'I argue that the term regulatory expropriation, to the extent that it should be used at all, should only be used for legitimate exercises of regulatory authority that have an expropriatory effect, when all the other criteria for lawful expropriation are met, *except* the payment of compensation.'[158]

155 *Methanex Corporation* v. *United States of America*, NAFTA-UNCITRAL, Award of 3 August 2005, para IV-D-15.

156 Kriebaum (2008a) note 9 at 366.

157 Bray (2012) note 9 at 19.

158 Asteriti (2014) note 3 at 457.

A number of voices express the identity claim by insisting strictly on the distinction between 'the question whether there has been an expropriation ... [and] that of whether the conditions have been satisfied',[159] for example in *Fireman's Fund*: '[NAFTA Article 1110(1)] (a) through (d) do not bear on the question as whether an expropriation has occurred'.[160] Some identify one or two process conditions, mostly 'public purpose', as part of a complex criterion to exclude non-compensable regulation. In *Fireman's Fund*, the tribunal highlighted (inter alia) 'the (public) purpose and effect of the measure; whether the measure is discriminatory; the proportionality between the means employed and the aim sought to be realized; and the bona fide nature of the measure'.[161] For Coe, 'some public purposes are so compelling that a State pursuing such an end should be absolved of the duty to compensate'.[162] The 2012 UNCTAD study distinguishes between the use of the process conditions in direct and indirect expropriation cases and explicitly doubles them for the latter:

> Public purpose, non-discrimination and due process also serve as conditions for the legality of an expropriation ... However, in that context, they were designed for cases of direct expropriation where the taking itself is self-evident. For cases involving alleged regulatory expropriations, the same requirements serve to distinguish compensable expropriation from noncompensable regulation and have been recognized as such in many investment treaties and arbitral awards.[163]

2. *Countering the identity claim.* The identity claim has been criticised on the basis that this doubling runs counter to the structural limits of the traditional (Type A) IIA expropriation clause. In case-law, however, dissent tends to be voiced in an indirect manner, such as in the *Santa Elena–Unglaube* line of awards. These proceed from the fact that the expropriation clause at issue 'protects an investment from expropriation unless, inter alia, it

159 UNCTAD (2012) note 11 at 27; see also Asteriti (2014) note 3 at 469; possibly *Feldman* (2002) note 26 at 98; *EMV* (2009) note 15 at para 50.

160 *Fireman's Fund Insurance Company* v. *United Mexican States*, NAFTA-ICSID, ARB(AF)/02/1, Award of 17 July 2006, para 174.

161 *Fireman's Fund* (2006) note 160 at para 176.

162 Coe (2005) note 2 at 638; see also Sornarajah (2010) note 100 at 396; *Philip Morris* (2016) note 21 at para 305 (possibly).

163 UNCTAD (2012) note 11 at 95; see also *Methanex* (2005) note 155 at para IV-D-7 (emphasis added): 'as a matter of general international law, a *non-discriminatory* regulation for a *public purpose*, which is enacted in accordance with *due process* and, which affects, inter alios, a foreign investor or investment is not deemed expropriatory and compensable'.

is accompanied by "by prompt and adequate compensation"';[164] 'the exercise of [states'] sovereignty over natural resources or police powers' is a right to expropriate which is granted, 'provided it is done in a non-discriminatory manner and accompanied by payment of "prompt, adequate, and effective" compensation'.[165] Therefore, under Type A IIAs, 'an investor is entitled to compensation even if expropriation measures are carried out for a public purpose in accordance with the relevant legislation'.[166] As the *Santa Elena* award put it: 'International law permits ... [expropriation] for a public purpose and against the prompt payment of ... compensation ... [T]he purpose of protecting the environment ... does not alter the legal character of the taking.'[167] Strazzeri highlights the logical connectors among the four conditions in Article 1110(1) NAFTA: 'If the last element [compensation, Article 1110(1)(d)] had been joined by the disjunctive 'or,' a police power could be read into this provision, but because a, b, c, and d are joined by the conjunctive, compensation is mandatory together with the other three elements for an expropriation to be valid.'[168]

Another indirect argument against doubling the process conditions employed by some tribunals is to prioritise an enquiry into the fulfilment of the compensation condition before the *Tatbestand* and the process conditions, thereby avoiding any discussion of the police powers doctrine. The *Funnekotter* award, for example, after 'observ[ing] that the conditions enumerated in Article 6 are cumulative', announced that it 'will first examine whether or not subparagraph (c) relating to the provisions of a just compensation has been breached'. Should that be the case, 'it will not be necessary for it to consider whether ... the other conditions ... have also been breached'.[169]

[164] *Ampal-American Israel Corporation, EGI-Fund (08-10) Investors, LLC, EGI-Series Investments, LLC, and BSS-EMG Investors, LLC* v. *Arab Republic of Egypt*, ICSID, ARB/21/11, Decision on Liability and Heads of Loss of 21 February 2017, para 185 (emphasis removed); see also *Quiborax* (2015) note 26, dissenting opinion Stern at para 8.

[165] Reisman (2004) note 9 at 134.

[166] *Franz Sedelmayer* v. *Russian Federation*, SCC, Award of 7 July 1998, 73; see also *Azurix* v. *Argentina*, ICSID, ARB/01/12, Award of 14 July 2006, para 310; for a less typical expropriation clause *Les Laboratoires Servier, S.A.S., Biofarma, S.A.S., Arts et Techniques du Progrès S. A.S.* v. *Republic of Poland*, UNCITRAL, Final Award of 14 February 2012, paras 564, 569–77.

[167] *Santa Elena* (2000) note 123 at para 71; see also *Southern Pacific Properties (Middle East) Limited* v. *Arab Republic of Egypt*, ICSID, Award of 20 May 1992, paras 158–9; *Unglaube* (2012) note 123 at paras 214, 217.

[168] Strazzeri (2001–2) note 9 at 854.

[169] *Bernardus Henricus Funnekotter and others* v. *Republic of Zimbabwe*, ICSID, ARB/05/6, Award of 22 April 2009, para 98; see also *Bernhard Friedrich Arnd Rüdiger von Pezold et al.* v. *Republic of Zimbabwe*, ICSID, ARB/10/15, Award of 28 July 2015, para 498; *Georg*

But the most important argument, taking its cue from the discussion of *SD Myers* in the *Azurix* award, directly criticises the doubling of the process conditions in the *Tatbestand*. The *Azurix* tribunal held:

> The argument made by the *S.D. Myers* tribunal is somehow contradictory. According to it, the BIT would require that investments not be expropriated except for a public purpose and that there be compensation if such expropriation takes place and, at the same time, regulatory measures that may be tantamount to expropriation would not give rise to a claim for compensation if taken for a public purpose. The public purpose criterion as an additional criterion to the effect of the measures under consideration needs to be complemented.[170]

Vivendi was even more direct: 'If public purpose automatically immunises the measure from being found to be expropriatory, then there would never be a compensable taking for a public purpose.'[171] Elcombe extends this to all three process conditions:

> The three requirements set out by *Methanex* for a regulatory, non-expropriatory measure duplicate three out of the four criteria for compensable expropriations in Article 1110(1) [NAFTA]. … In fact, though, Article 1110(1) specifically applies to measures enacted '(a) for a public purpose; (b) on a non-discriminatory basis; [and] (c) in accordance with due process of law'. Following the reasoning in *Methanex* … this means that the provision cannot apply to the very measures that it expressly includes within its scope.[172]

Sustained doctrinal arguments are to be found in literature rather than in case-law, foremost in Kriebaum's 2008 book *Eigentumsschutz im Völkerrecht*. She starts by showing that then-recent cases, foremost *Methanex* and *Saluka*, advocating the so-called 'radical' police powers doctrine, have relied on the doubling tactic. 'From a doctrinal point of view, the [process conditions] are no longer used to establish whether the expropriation is lawful. Rather, they are used to determine whether an expropriation has occurred at all.'[173] She shows that the structure of the

Gavrilović and Gavrilović D.O.O. v. *Republic of Croatia*, ICSID, ARB/12/39, Award of 26 July 2018, paras 947, 949.

170 *Azurix* (2006) note 166 at para 311; see also Fortier (2004) note 130 at 309: 'an expropriation is lawful only if, *inter alia*, it is undertaken for a public purpose; if the fulfilment of a public purpose is a condition of the lawfulness of the expropriation, that purpose cannot serve, at the same time, as the justification that no compensation be due'.

171 *Compañia de Aguas Del Aconquija SA and Vivendi Universal SA* v. *Argentine Republic*, ICSID, ARB/97/3, Award of 20 August 2007, para 7.5.21.

172 Elcombe (2010) note 9 at 85.

173 Kriebaum (2007b) note 150 at 726; see also Kriebaum (2008a) note 9 at 294–5; Kriebaum (2015) note 9 at 1001–2; Zielonka (2017) note 9 at 121.

norm places limits on the possible constructions of the traditional (Type A) IIA expropriation clause:

> From the point of view of legal logic, this is not possible, because a measure being taken in a non-discriminatory manner and for a public purpose are preconditions for legal expropriation. Therefore, conforming with them cannot lead to the necessary conclusion that this was not an expropriatory measure. It is a fallacy to seek to argue that conforming with two conditions for the legality of a measure means that this measure does not exist and that therefore a third condition for legality (the compensation condition) does not have to be fulfilled.[174]

By 'confus[ing] the constitutive elements of a taking with the requirements of a lawful expropriation',[175] the proponents of the doubling tactic not only 'confuse two distinct analytical steps for a finding of expropriation'[176] but turn the structure of the Type A clause on its head. '[P]ublic interest and non-discriminatory [treatment] cannot be the answer to the question whether an expropriation has occurred',[177] because the law 'presupposes that every governmental taking will be for a public policy purpose' even while it 'guarantees compensation'.[178]

A slightly more far-ranging argument uses the reliance by IIAs on acts with a public purpose: maybe there are no non-regulatory expropriation cases, because expropriation is by definition an exercise of state powers (*acta iure imperii*).[179] Acts need to be attributable to a state in order to be able to count as an expropriation under IIAs – 'a decision of an authority of the State would be needed in order to qualify a taking of title as an

[174] 'Aus rechtslogischer Sicht ist dieser Schluss nicht zulässig, denn dass eine Maßnahme nicht diskriminierend und im öffentlichen Interesse ist, sind beides Voraussetzungen dafür, dass eine legale Enteignung vorliegt. Die Erfüllung dieser beiden Bedingungen kann daher nicht zwingend dazu führen, dass keine Enteignung vorliegt. Es ist unlogisch zu erklären, dass die Erfüllung von zwei Bedingungen für die Rechtmäßigkeit einer Maßnahme dazu führt, dass die Maßnahme gar nicht existiert und daher eine dritte Bedingung für die Rechtmäßigkeit (die Entschädigung) nicht erfüllt werden muss.' Kriebaum (2008a) note 9 at 365; see also Zielonka (2017) note 9 at 116.

[175] López (2014) note 9 at 170.

[176] Jan Paulsson, Zachary Douglas, 'Indirect Expropriation in Investment Treaty Arbitrations' in Norbert Horn (ed.), *Arbitrating Foreign Investment Disputes* (The Hague: Kluwer 2004) 145–58 at 148.

[177] Schreuer (2006) note 9 at 110.

[178] Appleton (2002–3) note 18 at 47; see also Bray (2012) note 9 at 20–1; Schreuer (2006) note 9 at 144–5.

[179] See Higgins (1983) note 9 at 331: 'Under international law standards, a regulation that amounted . . . to a taking, would need to be "for a public purpose" (in the sense of in the general, rather than for a private, interest). And just compensation would be due.'

expropriation'.[180] Also, the majority view regarding contractual expropriation is that measures need to be taken 'in the exercise of [a state's] sovereign power ("*puissance publique*")'.[181] If a sovereign act (an *actus iure imperii* as against an *actus iure gestionis*) or an exercise of *puissance publique* is required, would it not by definition fulfil the public purpose requirement? The tribunal in *Siemens* even mentioned the phrase 'police powers' and concluded that, 'in the actions listed above, Argentina acted in use of its police powers rather than as a contracting party even if it attempted at times to base its actions on the Contract'.[182]

If that is true for contractual expropriation, does it not apply a fortiori to regulatory expropriation? The *Tatbestand* of IIA expropriation clauses *requires* acts of a public purpose character, sovereign acts, acts made as exercise of the right to regulate. Rather than being *excluded* from the *Tatbestand* of (indirect) expropriation, *puissance publique* acts need to take place. Does this not strengthen the argument that IIA expropriation clauses rely on public purpose to such a degree that this element cannot serve as a negative criterion for the *Tatbestand*? However, in many cases of contractual expropriation, tribunals have avoided talking about regulatory expropriation, even though the very point of turning a contractual dispute into an expropriation is whether it is an act of *puissance publique*.[183]

3. *The* Tatbestand *cannot be immunised from the legality conditions*. The identity claim can be countered on the basis of an orthodox understanding of the rules of interpretation. In interpreting the expropriation *Tatbestand*, we must interpret it in its context, as Article 31(1) VCLT

[180] *Patrick Mitchell* v. *Democratic Republic of the Congo*, ICSID, ARB/99/7, 9 February 2004, para 70.

[181] *Impregilo SpA* v. *Islamic Republic of Pakistan*, Decision on Jurisdiction of 22 April 2005, para 281; see also *Bayindir Insaat Turizm Ticaret Ve Sanayi A.S.* v. *Islamic Republic of Pakistan*, ICSID, ARB/03/29, Award of 27 August 2009, paras 257, 444; *Siemens A.G.* v. *Argentine Republic*, ICSID, ARB/02/8, Award of 6 February 2007, para 253; *Consortium RFCC* v. *Morocco*, ICSID, ARB/00/6, Award of 22 December 2003, paras 65–9, 85–9; *Suez I* (2010) note 24 at paras 142–3; *Gold Reserve Inc.* v. *Bolivarian Republic of Venezuela*, ICSID, ARB(AF)/09/1, Award of 22 September 2014, para 664; *Crystallex International Corporation* v. *Bolivarian Republic of Venezuela*, ICSID, ARB(AF)/11/2, Award of 4 April 2016, para 692.

[182] *Siemens* (2007) note 181 at para 260; see (indirectly) also *CC/Devas (Mauritius) Ltd., Devas Employees Mauritius Private Limited, and Telcom Devas Mauritius Limited* v. *Republic of India*, UNCITRAL, PCA 2013-09, Award on Jurisdiction and Merits of 25 July 2016, para 413.

[183] The tribunal in *Gold Reserve* sought to distinguish the *acta iure imperii* question from regulatory expropriation: *Gold Reserve* (2014) note 181 at paras 663–4.

requires. The first and most important level of context is the IIA expropriation clause as a whole. In interpreting these clauses, we cannot immunise our reading of 'direct or indirect expropriation' from the legality conditions and rob them of all relevance as second-stage justification by incorporating them into the *Tatbestand*. It is ironical that some of those who demand that we interpret expropriation clauses while taking account of the widest possible context by way of systemic integration at the same time argue that we should disregard a much more intimate level of context: the provision's own legality conditions. Hoffmann, for example, points to the identity claim's argument that expropriation claims involve a two-step process:

> (i) [T]he determination whether a measure amounted to an expropriation ... and (ii) defining whether the expropriation was lawful ... If ... the criterion of "public purpose" is used to define whether an expropriation occurred, ie for step (i), it is no longer useful regarding step (ii), namely the determination of the question whether the possible expropriation was lawful – step (ii) was used to make step (i) which entails considerable difficulty for the classic concept of expropriation ...[184]

Gazzini agrees that '[s]uch an approach greatly reduces the meaning of indirect expropriation',[185] whereas Henckels sees this as a problem of the (extreme) police powers doctrine under which 'all expropriations done with a public purpose would not be compensable'.[186] This 'move' (*Verschiebung*), as Zielonka, following Kriebaum's argument, calls it, 'of the criteria for the legality of a direct expropriation from the level of exception [*Rechtfertigungsgründe*] to the threshold question [*Eingriffsebene*]' – interference with rights vis-à-vis justification – 'entails a fragmentation between the two standards for direct and indirect expropriation'[187] (Section 7.3).

[184] Hoffmann (2008) note 9 at 166.

[185] Tarcisio Gazzini, 'Drawing the Line between Non-compensable Regulatory Powers and Indirect Expropriation of Foreign Investment – An Economic Analysis of Law Perspective' 7 *Manchester Journal of International Economic Law* (2010) 36–51 at 41; see also Fortier (2004) note 130 at 309.

[186] Henckels (2012) note 4 at 225; see also Henckels (2015) note 18 at 77.

[187] 'werden also die für die Beurteilung der Rechtmäßigkeit einer direkten Enteignung maßgeblichen Kriterien von der Ebene der Rechtmäßigkeit auf die Eingriffsebene verschoben, wodurch es zu einer Fragmentierung innerhalb des Enteignungsstandards zwischen einer direkten und einer indirekten Enteignung durch regulatorische Maßnahmen kommt' Zielonka (2017) note 9 at 121; see also Ursula Kriebaum, 'Indirekte Enteignung oder zulässige Regulierung?' in Georg Nolte, Peter Hilpold (eds.), *Auslandsinvestitionen – Entwicklung großer Kodifikationen – Fragmentierung*

Rephrasing this argument in terms commensurate with this book's theoretical framework, we cannot immunise a reading of the *Tatbestand* from legality conditions. They must influence what the *Tatbestand* can be, because doing so makes a condition redundant which Type A IIA expropriation clauses unquestionably contain and which would negate the logic of the clause's structure. Justin Marlles makes the same point when he criticises *Methanex* for having 'completely abandoned Article 1110(1)(d) of NAFTA . . . There is absolutely nothing in Article 1110(1) to indicate that the "public purpose" requirement trumps the "payment of compensation" requirement.'[188] In effect, this makes not only subparagraph (d) but also (a) redundant. It is difficult to comprehend how one could argue that drafters would have wished to exclude measures of such a nature as acts of indirect expropriation when they later rely on these very criteria to determine the legality of *both* types of expropriation. Because 'public purpose' is a legality condition in most IIAs, the argument that police powers measures are a priori excluded from constituting expropriation is particularly weak.

Some writers differentiate between 'radical' and 'moderate' versions of the police powers doctrine. On the reconstruction of the moderate version by Kriebaum, '[t]ribunals . . . rely primarily on the effect of the interference. But they will also consider factors like the purpose of the measure or the existence of legitimate expectations when deciding whether an expropriation has occurred', with the 'appli[cation of] a proportionality test',[189] thus balancing between effect and purpose (Section 6.3.2), as the central element. Yet while the moderate version may at first glance seem to be different from its radical sibling, the former also rests on the same move: 'this is because "public purpose" is considered on the level of the threshold question [*Eingriffsebene*]'[190] just as with the radical police powers doctrine.

Saluka in particular based its doubling argument on a very 'optimistic' reading of the state of customary international law, which connects it to the argument from customary law as discussed in Section 7.2. The *Saluka* tribunal held a police powers exception to be 'now established in

des Völkerrechts – Status des Kosovo: Beiträge zum 31. Österreichischen Völkerrechtstag 2006 in München (2008) 18–37 at 32.

188 Marlles (2006–7) note 9 at 291, 294.

189 Kriebaum (2007b) note 150 at 727.

190 'Der Grund dafür liegt in der Berücksichtigung des Kriteriums "Zweck/öffentliches Interesse" bereits auf der Eingriffsebene.' Kriebaum (2008a) note 9 at 361; see also Zielonka (2017) at 130.

international law': 'States are not liable to pay compensation . . . when, in the normal exercise of their regulatory powers, they adopt in a non-discriminatory manner *bona fide* regulations':[191]

> In the opinion of the Tribunal, the principle that a State does not commit an expropriation and is thus not liable to pay compensation to a dispossessed alien investor when it adopts general regulations that are 'commonly accepted as within the police power of States' forms part of customary international law today. . . . The CNB's decision . . . does not fall within the ambit of any of the *exceptions* to the permissibility of regulatory action which are recognised by customary international law.[192]

Note, in particular, that *Saluka* reversed the default position: investors need to prove the applicability of exceptions to a broad right to regulate which it considered to be part of customary law. Yet the systematic argument against the doubling argument can also help to defeat the integration-of-customary-law argument:

> [T]ribunals should avoid including the customary understandings of the police power doctrine into its analysis. . . . NAFTA Article 1110(1)(a) clearly requires the tribunal to assess the 'public purpose' of the government measure. Accordingly, the *inclusio unius* maxim suggests that tribunals limit their analysis of 'public purpose' considerations in an expropriation claim to an examination of whether Article 1110(1)(a) has been satisfied.[193]

The problem is similar to arguments seeking to ensure a wide right of self-defence under Article 51 UN Charter, which – unlike Type A IIA expropriation clauses – does contain an (incorrect) reference to an 'inherent' (viz. customary) right. Any such *renvoi* is shaped and limited by the context in which it is made, as is the case for Article 51 with the phrase 'if an armed attack occurs'. Thus, even if the term 'indirect expropriation' in IIAs were to refer to one customary international law norm, the treaty would shape and restrict the incorporation clause. As I put it in a previous book:

> The 'inherent right' of self-defence . . . is only part of the Charter *because Article 51 admits it*. . . . even if the Charter itself were to refer to customary international law . . . [and] if the 'inherent right' of self-defence of some wide, pre-Charter, scope, without the need for an armed attack, had been recognised by Article 51, it would have only done so 'if an armed attack occurs'.[194]

[191] *Saluka* (2006) note 14 at para 255.
[192] *Saluka* (2006) note 14 at paras 262, 275 (emphasis added).
[193] Bray (2012) note 9 at 19; see also Elcombe (2010) note 9 at 74.
[194] Kammerhofer (2010d) note 77 at 16–17.

This is particularly so given the fact, mentioned at several points already, that the customary norm referred to is most likely even less specific than the IIA clause. In this case, whether it is an incorporation of customary law or a term of customary international law proper, 'direct or indirect expropriation' is shaped both by the public purpose condition itself as well as by the fact that the process conditions are usually connected by an 'and' to the compensation commission. If, as is variously claimed, the fulfilment of the public purpose condition for the purposes of legality is 'easy' and needs to be interpreted in a deferential manner vis-à-vis states, why should a parallel public purpose condition exist within the *Tatbestand* of expropriation which, in turn, has a narrower remit as part of an integrated police powers exception?[195] Is it therefore likely that the states parties have agreed to duplicate 'public purpose'?

Given this consideration, is it not much more likely that IIAs integrate state party claims to exercise police powers or a right to regulate *by making public purpose* (and the others) *a process condition*? Maybe Type A IIAs regulate the issue in a rather 'unbalanced' manner for today's political sensibilities precisely by *not* taking heed of *any* customary international law conceptions of police powers? Would it not be self-defeating for a treaty, on the one hand, to tacitly integrate a police powers exception (or a right to regulate) in the IIA but, on the other hand, to also include four conditions for legality, at least one of which is antithetical to such a police powers exception (or a right to regulate), that is, by making public purpose a condition in addition to compensation? Are more than two thousand Type A IIAs really testament to the fact that the legality conditions as they stand are nullified by the implicit restriction/exception to the idea of 'indirect expropriation' (only)? Hardly.

4. *The non-identity claim*. The doubling of one or more process conditions runs into the problems recounted above. The predictable countermove is that the criteria for *Tatbestand*-exclusion on the basis of a police powers exception (or a right to regulate) are similar but crucially not identical to 'public purpose', 'non-discriminatory' or 'due process'. The exception is therefore *not* doubled, because it is not based on the same exact criteria as the process conditions.

On the basis of the two-stage thesis discussed (first *Tatbestand*, then legality conditions), Clough argues that 'asking whether the regulation was conducted for a public purpose' within the legality conditions stage is

[195] Pointing to the problems of adopting such a wide approach: Kriebaum (2008a) note 9 at 294–5.

not the same as asking 'whether a regulation amounts to a taking as a matter of law'. This, in turn, 'depends on whether that type of regulation is commonly accepted to be a police power of a government'.[196] On this basis, the decisive criterion cannot be whether a regulation is made 'pursuant to a public purpose. The public purpose motivations of the host government are only relevant in determining whether a taking of property is prohibited or allowed subject to compensation.'[197] Lévesque echoes this sentiment[198] and clarifies that the criteria are not identical:

> [P]olice powers do not cover every measure adopted by the government in the public interest. If this were the case, no expropriation would ever be possible under international law as no conceptual space remains for it. . . . for an expropriation to be lawful, the state must act for a public purpose. . . . a wide discretion is left to states to determine their own interest in a measure. . . . In a nutshell, 'public interest' and 'police power' are not synonymous under international law and cannot be interchanged in this context. To hold otherwise means there could never be an expropriation, as public interest is a condition of a legal expropriation.[199]

This contains an element of circular reasoning, which becomes obvious once we turn her argument on its head: the law must acknowledge a police powers exception, because if 'public purpose' as legality condition were to be identical to the police powers exception, the law would not acknowledge a police powers exception. However, broader considerations, already discussed, militate against this alternative. There is no significant difference in whether the proposed criteria for a police powers exception are exactly identical to the process conditions. That is because Type A IIAs have already taken account of criteria in the process conditions which do not differ significantly from those proposed for the police powers exception. We cannot escape this logic by imagining that the proposed police powers-related criterion is *just sufficiently different* from 'public purpose' to succeed in undermining the legality conditions for regulatory expropriation. We cannot pretend that the process conditions are not, when read together (and public purpose in particular), identical to the criteria proposed by proponents of the police powers doctrine. The non-identity claim must face the limits established by the legality conditions: the structure of the expropriation provision presupposes that even

196 Clough (2005) note 143 at 570.
197 Clough (2005) note 143 at 570.
198 Lévesque (2004) note 5 at 300.
199 Lévesque (2004) note 5 at 306.

measures executed for a public purpose, in a non-discriminatory manner and observing due process, are compensable.

Therefore, the combination of the phrases 'indirect expropriation' in the *chapeaux*, on the one hand, and 'for a public purpose' in the legality requirements, on the other, means that regulation cannot be excepted from the scope of expropriation. This is so because 'public purpose' is already part of cumulative legality requirements, which include compensation. If 'public purpose' has been or has to be interpreted in an extremely wide and deferential manner, then all regulatory measures are included in this category. Hence, since measures need to be both for a public purpose and compensated to constitute legal expropriation, the wide meaning given to the public purpose criterion as legality condition strengthens the argument that regulatory measures were not excluded from the *Tatbestand*.

5. *Doubling the due process condition.* A minor argument against the doubling tactic takes issue with the popularity of proportionality balancing as test for non-compensable regulatory measures: proportionality analysis tracks the due process condition and thus doubles it. If IIAs require due process of law for a legal expropriation, then it cannot be doubled to serve as basis for the exclusion of certain forms of indirect expropriation.[200]

If every expropriation has to be conducted under due process,[201] and if proportionality analysis is allegedly central to international law and to the process of adjudging, then proportionality is part of the due process condition in IIAs. But if it is, not only is the tribunal empowered to thoroughly vet whether any of the four conditions are fulfilled and does not need to be 'deferential'[202] but any measures would still need to be compensated. This is so whether or not the tribunal is in fact deferential in its proportionality analysis, and even if the measures had been carried

[200] See, however, Newcombe (2005) note 17 at 39–40.

[201] Veith (1962) note 25 at 156–65.

[202] This argument is directed against statements such as the one in Henckels (2015) note 18 at 128: '[T]he broad discretion enjoyed by states in terms of the right to regulate at international law suggests that a low standard of scrutiny is appropriate in relation to this inquiry [expropriation/police powers] and that no particular area of policy should be excluded ex ante. The normative uncertainty inherent in determining whether a particular regulatory objective is legitimate means that its direct evaluation by an investment tribunal would transgress the role of national decisionmakers, particularly given arbitrators' lack of embeddedness in the state.'

out in a proportionate manner. The *Tatbestand* of indirect expropriation does not exclude measures enacted under due process.

This discussion also concerns the limits of the proportionality dogma now prevalent in international investment law writings. Kriebaum reminds us that there is a difference between how the proportionality test is used in its field of origin – (European) human rights adjudication – and in investment law adjudication: '[I]n the human rights system the proportionality test is not used to decide whether an expropriation has occurred. It is used to decide ... whether a suitable balancing of the State's interest to interfere and the property protection interest of the person hit by the interference has taken place.'[203]

Proportionality has flourished in other fields, such as human rights and constitutional law, because tribunals have had a freedom to develop or import it. In contrast, as we have seen in this chapter, international investment law places severe restrictions on how, whether, how far and where proportionality analysis may be used. There still is considerable freedom for tribunals to employ elements of this analysis. Chapters 4 and 5 discuss how the adjudicatory process provides areas of freedom; Chapter 8 provides an overview of some of these areas. However, Type A IIA expropriation clauses prescribe a 'non-proportionate'[204] regulation of expropriation. 'Non-proportionate' means a specific concept: Type A clauses are not geared towards proportionality. If an act is expropriatory, then compensation is required, whether or not the measure at issue was a proportionate measure balancing various interests. This is a counter-argument to the 'moderate' police powers doctrine – the limits posed by the IIA cannot be overcome by balancing and proportionality.

7.4.2 *Selecting from among the Legality Conditions*

Selection as a second tactic to overcome the structural limitation of traditional (Type A) IIA expropriation clauses de-emphasises the strict necessity of the compensation condition and thus puts in doubt the cumulative conditionality of all legality conditions. Essentially, it is argued that in IIAs, the payment of compensation is not as strict a requirement as the other legality conditions (see also Section 8.4). Yet mild forms of this argument with a pragmatic impetus differ from

203 Kriebaum (2007b) note 150 at 730.

204 Kriebaum styles this as an all-or-nothing (*alles-oder-nichts*) solution, eg Kriebaum (2008a) note 9 at 247, 340, 361.

designs which instrumentalise the mild form to advance the police powers doctrine; the latter in effect comes close to the doubling tactic described in Section 7.4.1. The primary argument against a different standard of compensation for unlawful as against lawful expropriations is to decrease emphasis on (the promptness of) compensation. While the promptness question is a question of filling the frame of possible meanings, the argument is used to undermine the co-equal necessity of all legality conditions.

Drawing on a long tradition stretching all the way back to *Chorzów*,[205] an important strain of case-law has held that arguments among the parties about the quantum of compensation should not be held against the respondent state. See for example *Mondev*, where the tribunal acknowledged that there is an 'obligation to compensate as a condition for a lawful expropriation' in Article 1110 NAFTA. It emphasised, however, that it need not 'occur at exactly the same time as the taking', as long as the obligation itself, rather than the precise amount, is 'recognised by the taking State at the time of the taking, or a procedure must exist at that time which the claimant may effectively and promptly invoke'.[206] It interpreted the phrase 'on payment of compensation' in Article 1110(1)(d) NAFTA to contain a requirement 'that the payment be clearly offered, or be available as compensation for taking through a readily available procedure, at the time of the taking'.[207] One reason for this pragmatic modification of the clear structure of the expropriation clause is a certain unwillingness to allow claimant investors to force respondent states into making an expropriation unlawful by drawing out any dispute on how much compensation is due. Noting the trend in case-law, Kriebaum agrees with the requirement that the state must already have acknowledged the investor's right to compensation, which will usually be absent for regulatory expropriation. 'In cases of this type, states will not assume

205 Kriebaum (2008a) note 9 at 528, citing *Factory at Chorzów (Claim for Indemnity) (Germany* v. *Poland)*, Judgment on the Merits of 13 September 1928, PCIJ Series A No 17 (1928) at 47.

206 *Mondev International Ltd.* v. *United States of America*, NAFTA-ICSID, ARB(AF)/99/2, Award of 11 October 2002, para 71; see also eg *ConocoPhillips Petrozuata B.V., ConocoPhillips Hamaca B.V., ConocoPhillips Gulf of Paria B.V. and ConocoPhillips Company* v. *Bolivarian Republic of Venezuela*, ICSID, ARB/07/30, Decision on Jurisdiction and the Merits of 3 September 2013, para 362; Matti Pellonpää, Malgosia Fitzmaurice, 'Taking of Property in the Practice of the Iran-United States Claims Tribunal' 19 *Netherlands Yearbook of International Law* 1988 (1989) 53–178 at 69–70.

207 *Mondev* (2002) note 206 at para 72.

that the measures constitute an expropriation at all . . .[I]n most cases, indirect expropriations will be unlawful.'[208]

The pragmatic sleight of hand becomes problematic when we consider what the acknowledgement that some form of compensation is due means regarding the promptness element of the Hull formula enshrined in most IIAs. Frequently, the acknowledgement will take the form of an offer. *Venezuela Holdings* drew the inevitable conclusion:

> [T]he mere fact that an investor has not received compensation does not in itself render an expropriation unlawful. An offer of compensation may have been made to the investor and, in such a case, the legality of the expropriation will depend on the terms of that offer. In order to decide whether an expropriation is lawful or not in the absence of payment of compensation, a tribunal must consider the facts of the case.[209]

The award switched the requirements twice: first, from the payment of compensation to the acknowledgement of compensation being due; second, from the fulfilment of the compensation requirement to a determination of compensation by a tribunal. On its face, we are talking about the question of compensation or reparation (Section 8.4); Brigitte Stern in her dissenting opinion to the *Quiborax* award argued that 'whether compensation or reparation is due can only be ascertained when there is a qualification of the allegedly expropriatory act, either by agreement (rare), by a national court or by an international tribunal'. Yet she accepted the far-reaching consequence that 'as long as it has not been finally determined whether there is or is not an expropriation, and whether it is or is not illegal, the obligation to compensate or repair does not arise'.[210]

This is a remarkably far-reaching statement, even if it is echoed by others. With this move, two elementary legal categories are turned into one. If the determination of the quantum of compensation by a tribunal is enough to make expropriation legal (or to make it provisionally not

[208] 'Die Staaten gehen in derartigen Fällen nicht vom Vorliegen einer Enteignung aus und sehen daher auch häufig auch keine Entschädigung vor. Somit sind indirekte Enteignungen in den meisten Fällen auch rechtswidrig.' Kriebaum (2008a) note 9 at 536; see also Thomas Rieger, *Grundsätze der Unternehmensenteignung in der Rechtsprechung des Iran–United States Claims Tribunal* (Cologne: Heymans 1997) 60–1.

[209] *Venezuela Holdings, B.V., Mobil Cerro Negro Holding, Ltd., Mobil Venezolana de Petróleos Holdings, Inc., Mobil Cerro Negro, Ltd., Mobil Venezolana de Petróleos, Inc.* v. *Bolivarian Republic of Venezuela*, ICSID, ARB/07/27, Award of 9 October 2014, para 301; see also *Koch Minerals Sàrl and Koch Nitrogen International Sàrl* v. *Bolivarian Republic of Venezuela*, ICSID, ARB/11/19, Award of 30 October 2017, para 7.27.

[210] *Quiborax* (2015) note 26, dissenting opinion Stern at para 15.

unlawful), then the tribunal would determine whether the expropriation was lawful, that is, whether it violates international law at the moment of adjudging upon the claim. If the expropriation was lawful, then the claim must be found to be without merit; if it was unlawful, then reparation is due. David Khachvani expresses the same sentiment: 'If an expropriation without compensation were lawful under international law, as suggested by some of those tribunals, they would have no jurisdiction to entertain the claim founded on the lack of compensation. Such a claim would not be capable of constituting a treaty breach and would thus fall outside their subject matter jurisdiction.'[211]

Tribunals cannot 'retroactively' convey legality by determining compensation when they adjudge the claim, for if they were to find that (at the moment of adjudging) the expropriation was lawful, their task can consist only in the rejection of the claim, never in the determination of compensation due. After all, the expropriation was lawful and international law was not breached. Investment tribunals are not claims commissions and have no mandate to determine compensation for measures irrespective of their legality. This argument is a bit like a court in a contract dispute claiming that its determination of money to be paid is the contractually obligated performance of the contract by the defendant. If so, it could not have concluded that a breach of contract had occurred and that damages are due.

While the pragmatic motives behind this move are understandable, the compensation condition is effectively negated in regulatory expropriation cases by pointing to a later tribunal decision. Accordingly, the selection tactic has been used, indirectly, by the proponents of state freedom of action. The 2015 *Tidewater* award showed sympathy for the idea that we should consider 'expropriation only wanting compensation'[212] to be legal. 'Most expropriation claims turn on the question whether a measure is expropriatory at all. ... That means that almost every decision finding expropriation would also find unlawful expropriation', which 'would make a detailed and elaborate element of the expropriation provision in modern BITs ... effectively nugatory'.[213] What the tribunal did not say is that the problem it describes will occur most acutely only in cases of regulatory

[211] Khachvani (2017) note 9 at 389.

[212] *Tidewater Investment SRL and Tidewater Caribe, C.A.* v. *Bolivarian Republic of Venezuela*, ICSID, ARB/10/5, Award of 13 March 2015, para 136, citing Jeswald W Salacuse, *The Law of International Investment Treaties* (Oxford: Oxford University Press 2010) 328.

[213] *Tidewater* (2015) note 212 at para 138.

expropriation. Again, the fulfilment of the compensation condition is moved to the determination of the arbitral tribunal:

> [S]uch a tribunal must have an opportunity to make its determination as to compensation. Where such a tribunal has done so (and assuming that the other conditions are met) the expropriation will not be illegal. . . . An expropriation only wanting fair compensation has to be considered as a provisionally lawful expropriation, precisely because the tribunal dealing with the case will determine and award such compensation.[214]

In this light, the tribunal's reliance on the expropriation-only-wanting-compensation argument means that in regulatory expropriation cases, the compensation condition is tacitly subordinated to the process conditions. George Abi-Saab's dissent in *ConocoPhillips* shows where adopting this tactic will lead: '[T]he obligation to pay compensation is not a condition of the legality of the act of nationalization, but a *secondary obligation* flowing from that act.'[215] This is a statement which does not reflect the structure of Article 6 Netherlands–Venezuela BIT 1991[216] at issue in *ConocoPhillips*. The 2012 UNCTAD study as standard-bearer for a statist reading provides a helpful summary of the more extreme tendencies inherent in the selection tactic:

> Particularly in determining the existence of an indirect expropriation and assessing a regulatory measure, the tribunal needs to first characterize the measure before looking into the existence of a duty to pay compensation. . . . [T]he duty to pay compensation is the consequence of the legal exercise of a recognized sovereign right of a State. This requirement may be met from the outset or after litigation, when the expropriatory nature of the act is established. While failure by a State to pay any compensation for a direct expropriation can be seen as rendering such an expropriation unlawful, this should not be the case when a measure at stake allegedly constitutes an indirect expropriation. Even if the measure is found by a tribunal to be expropriatory, the obligation to pay compensation should arise only as a consequence of such finding.[217]

214 *Tidewater* (2015) note 212 at paras 140, 141.

215 *ConocoPhillips* (2013) note 206, dissenting opinion Abi-Saab at para 118 (emphasis added).

216 It reads, in part: 'Neither Contracting Party shall take any measures to expropriate [etc.] . . . unless the following conditions are complied with: (a) the measures are taken in the public interest and under due process of law; (b) the measures are not discriminatory or contrary to any undertaking which the Contracting Party taking such measures may have given; (c) the measures are taken against just compensation.'

217 UNCTAD (2012) note 11 at 43–4.

According to Khachvani, Abi-Saab's 'reasoning conflates the treaty obligation to provide compensation for a taking with the obligation to pay damages for unlawful expropriation', that is, between 'the primary obligation ... from the secondary duty',[218] which may certainly play a role but is hardly the main reason, given that the distinction between compensation and reparation (Section 8.4) is at issue here.

The selection tactic is also vulnerable to an argument made earlier about non-unlawfulness making a tribunal decision moot. If, as Ratner puts it, 'nonpayment [i]s still provisionally lawful', 'it is conceptually flawed ... then to award the investor ... compensation – how can there be compensation if there is no violation of the treaty?'[219] Most 'treaty provisions on compensation do not provide for the interpretive space to say that payment includes nonpayment'[220] – unsurprisingly so. This argument cannot be successful, as it leads to substantive as well as procedural *aporia*. If expropriation is lawful, the IIA was not breached and the state owes nothing; a breach of the expropriation provision must by definition be based on an unlawful act of expropriation.

However, the main reason why the selection tactic must fail is that it breaches the structural limits of traditional (Type A) IIA expropriation clauses. The *Saint Gobain* award could, in effect, be read as a disavowal of the selection tactic on that basis. The tribunal conceded that Article 5(1)(1) France–Venezuela BIT 2001[221] 'does not ... make any reference to compensation [in its listing of legality conditions], which is rather addressed in two separate subparagraphs', prima facie making for a weaker case than in *ConocoPhillips*. This means that one could argue that the process conditions which 'preclude... from expropriating ... *per se*' differ from the compensation condition which 'relate[s] to the manner in which the expropriation has to be carried out'.[222] The tribunal was undeterred, however, and it held that the article 'has a clear

218 Khachvani (2017) note 9 at 388, 386.

219 Stephen R Ratner, 'Compensation for Expropriations in a World of Investment Treaties: Beyond the Lawful/Unlawful Distinction' 111 *American Journal of International Law* (2017) 7–56 at 44.

220 Ratner (2017) note 219 at 44–5.

221 Article 5(1) reads, in part: '[1] Les Parties contractantes ne prennent pas de mesures d'expropriation [etc.] ..., si ce n'est pour cause d'utilité publique et à condition que ces mesures ne soient ni discriminatoires, ni contraires à un engagement particulier. [2] Toutes les mesures d'expropriation qui pourraient être prises doivent donner lieu au paiement d'une indemnité prompte et adéquate ....'

222 *Saint-Gobain Performance Plastics Europe* v. *Bolivarian Republic of Venezuela*, ICSID, ARB/12/13, Award of 30 December 2016, para 599.

structure', with the compensation condition in '[s]ubparagraphs 2 and 3 provid[ing] for additional requirements and/or consequences of an expropriation'[223] to the process conditions:[224] 'In light of the unambiguous wording and structure . . ., *prima facie*, subparagraph 3 required Respondent to specify a precise figure constituting the "amount" . . . of compensation *at the time of the expropriation*'.[225] Khachvani highlights that 'the language of the relevant IIAs is clear in outlawing expropriation without compensation'.[226] In the end, the selection argument cannot overcome the structurally co-equal nature of the compensation condition. Where the treaty does not provide otherwise, compensation is on an equal footing with the other conditions. It is a primary, not a secondary duty and cannot be made optional or redundant.

This conclusion will, however, depend on the specific formulation of the IIA clause. Article III(1) US–Ecuador BIT 1993,[227] for example, which was at issue in *Burlington*,[228] specifies that the expropriation is lawful 'upon payment of compensation', rather than an 'offer' or merely 'upon compensation'. This IIA requires that the compensation must already have been paid for the expropriation to be lawful – no matter the pragmatic arguments against it. Where, on the other hand, as in Article V Spain–Argentina BIT 1991,[229] the three process conditions are mentioned as conditions of legality and then a duty of compensation is stipulated separately in the next sentence, it could be argued that compensation is a secondary duty not determinative of the legality of an expropriation – if the conditions are fulfilled, no compensation is due. Yet even on this type of wording, the better reading is still the one

223 *Saint-Gobain* (2016) note 222 at para 606.

224 The tribunal did concede, however, that there are two ways to read that paragraph and for its purposes (determining the standard of compensation) managed to avoid deciding on the issue: *Saint-Gobain* (2016) note 222 at paras 607–14.

225 *Saint-Gobain* (2016) note 222 at para 419 (emphasis added).

226 Khachvani (2017) note 9 at 388; see also Rudolf Dolzer, 'Case Comment: ConocoPhillips v Venezuela and Gold Reserve v Venezuela: Expropriation: A New Focus on Old Issues' 30 *ICSID Review* (2015) 378–83 at 381–2.

227 It reads, in part: 'Investments shall not be expropriated [etc.] . . . except: for a public purpose; in a non-discriminatory manner; upon payment of prompt, adequate and effective compensation; and in accordance with due process of law and the general principles of treatment provided for in Article II (3).'

228 *Burlington* (2012) note 27 at para 255.

229 It reads, in part: 'La . . . expropiación [etc.] . . . deberá aplicarse exclusivamente por causas de utilidad pública conforme a las disposiciones legales y en ningún caso deberá, ser discriminatoria. La Parte que adoptará alguna de estas medidas pagará al inversor o a su derecho-habiente, sin demora injustificada, una indemnización adecuada, en moneda convertible.'

proffered in the *Urbaser* award: 'When these conditions are satisfied, the host State is under an obligation to afford appropriate compensation. [If not, this] triggers the investor's right for reparation.'[230]

The reverse argument has also been made: holding the process conditions to be insignificant when compensation has been paid. Paul Comeaux and Stephan Kinsella ask: are the process conditions 'properly referred to as "requirements" of a "legal" expropriation under international law ... even if full compensation is paid?'[231] For them, the requirement of full compensation is absolute in the sense that it 'must accompany any taking, whether legal or illegal', which renders the distinction of 'limited significance'.[232] From that position, it is not too far to reach Paulsson's view that 'for practical purposes all takings become licit under international law once compensation has been paid'.[233] This view is not seriously contended and it is clear that this statement is of purely pragmatic relevance. The structure of traditional (Type A) IIA expropriation clauses privileges the compensation condition as little as it does the process conditions: they are equal and even full payment cannot make lawful an otherwise unlawful measure of expropriation, for example one that was made in a discriminatory manner.

7.5 The Influence of Treaty Clause Design

Up to this point, this chapter was concerned only with the structural limits of Type A IIA expropriation clauses, because they are by far the most used. Therefore, they are the best target for an international legal scholarship which seeks to make general statements about expropriation in international investment law, without ignoring the fact that there is no unified body of law. Before we discuss how the frame of possible meanings resulting from the structural limits has been filled in case-law (Chapter 8), we need to take account of other variants of the expropriation clause. This section will provide a brief typology of expropriation clauses and discuss whether the structural limits for Type A clauses apply to other types as well.

[230] *Urbaser S.A. and Consorcio de Aguas Bilbao Biskaia, Bilbao Biskaia Ur Partzuergoa* v. *Argentine Republic*, ICSID, ARB/07/26, Award of 8 December 2016, para 1000.

[231] Paul E Comeaux, N Stephan Kinsella, *Protecting Foreign Investment under International Law* (Dobbs Ferry: Oceana 1997) 85.

[232] Comeaux (1997) note 231 at 86.

[233] Paulsson (2006) note 62 at 10–11; see also Ratner (2017) note 219 at 8.

Beside the option of excluding expropriation as a standard of treatment in IIAs, there are four main types of expropriation provision:

- *Type A clauses*: This is the traditional IIA expropriation clause as employed for example in Article 7(1) Australia–Mexico BIT 2005 (see Section 5.5). Its structural limits were discussed at length in Sections 7.1–7.4.
- *Type B clauses*: A number of 'modern' IIAs are drafted along the lines of a model first set by the 2004 US Model BIT and the 2004 Canadian Model FIPA. These treaties follow the Type A template for the expropriation clause but insert an annex which gives further guidance. They crucially contain a default exception for general regulatory measures from the scope of indirect expropriation. Since clauses of this type constitute the majority of non-traditional regulation on expropriation in IIAs, the majority of the following discussion will focus on it.
- *Type C clauses*: In a small number of IIAs, a definition of indirect and/or regulatory expropriation is contained in the article itself, potentially also with an exception for general regulatory measures. Because it is conceivable that clauses of this type will become more popular, they will also briefly be discussed.
- *Type D treaties*: A number of IIAs include some form of general exception clauses separate from the provisions on expropriation. Sometimes, these use formulations reminiscent of Articles XX and/or XXI GATT 1947. This type of treaty is relatively widespread and has been the focus of many academic writings and a whole range of case-law, but is not the focus of this chapter. The choice not to discuss it here will briefly be explained now.

1. *Type D treaties*. A significant number of IIA clauses, such as Article XI US–Argentina BIT 1991,[234] are reminiscent of the security exceptions clause in Article XXI GATT 1947. Clauses of this type were discussed in a significant number of investment arbitrations, foremost the Argentine arbitrations following that country's 2001–2 financial crisis.[235] They have

234 'This Treaty shall not preclude the application by either Party of measures necessary for the maintenance of public order, the fulfillment of its obligations with respect to the maintenance or restoration of international peace or security, or the Protection of its own essential security interests.'

235 Eg *BG Group Plc.* v. *Republic of Argentina*, UNCITRAL, Final Award of 24 December 2007; *CMS Gas Transmission Company* v. *Argentine Republic*, ICSID, ARB/01/8, Award of 12 May 2005; *Continental Casualty Company* v. *Argentine Republic*, ICSID, ARB/03/9,

also been subject to intensive debate in scholarly writings.[236] Another example is Article 1114(1) NAFTA, whose exception has also been discussed and linked to the scope of indirect expropriation, particularly in light of the proviso that such measures be 'otherwise consistent with this Chapter'.[237] José Alvarez highlights the tension between general exception clauses and individual investor protection, arguing that it 'makes no sense ... to preclude liability for a governmental expropriation simply because ... [it is] the least restrictive measure ... to serve a public purpose' in light of the same treaty's prescription 'that governments must pay prompt, adequate, and effective compensation even for takings that serve a public purpose'.[238]

While interesting as a wider systemic argument about the global content of IIA provisions, there is a clear difference between exceptions/defences for state responsibility *after* classification as indirect expropriation and the question of the limits of the (indirect) expropriation *Tatbestand*. General exceptions do not change the *Tatbestand* of expropriation, even when they are applicable and serve to except liability where they certainly have the potential to limit or exclude the protection from uncompensated expropriation. This does not touch directly on the issues discussed here.

2. *Type B clauses.* This type of expropriation clause is the first widespread measure by states to react to the false direction (from their perspective) which arbitral case-law on regulatory expropriation has

Award of 5 September 2008; *EDF International S.A., SAUR International S.A. and León Participaciones Argentinas S.A.* v. *Argentine Republic*, ICSID, ARB/03/23, Award of 11 June 2012; *El Paso Energy International Company* v. *Argentine Republic*, ICSID, ARB/03/15, Award of 31 October 2011; *Enron Corporation Ponderosa Assets LP* v. *Argentine Republic*, ICSID, ARB/01/3, Award of 22 May 2007; *LG&E Energy Corp., LG&E Capital Corp. and LG&E International Inc.* v. *Argentine Republic*, ICSID, ARB/02/1, Decision on Liability of 3 October 2006; *Sempra Energy International* v. *Argentine Republic*, ICSID, ARB/02/16, Award of 28 September 2007.

236 Eg Titi (2014) note 9; William W Burke-White, Andreas von Staden, 'Investment Protection in Extraordinary Times: The Interpretation and Application of Non-precluded Measures Provisions in Bilateral Investment Treaties' 48 *Virginia Journal of International Law* (2008) 307–410; Andrew Newcombe, 'General Exceptions in International Investment Agreements' in Marie-Claire Cordonier Segger, Markus W Gehring, Andrew Newcombe (eds.), *Sustainable Development in World Investment Law* (Alphen aan den Rijn: Wolters Kluwer 2011) 355–70; Jürgen Kurtz, 'Adjudging the Exceptional at International Investment Law: Security, Public Order and Financial Crisis' 59 *International and Comparative Law Quarterly* (2010) 325–71.

237 Eg López (2014) note 9 at 159; Newcombe (1999) note 34 at 128; Subedī (2006) note 108 at 130–2; Zielonka (2017) note 9 at 272.

238 José E Alvarez, '"Beware: Boundary Crossings" – A Critical Appraisal of Public Law Approaches to International Investment Law' 17 *Journal of World Investment & Trade* (2016) 171–228 at 199.

taken since *Metalclad*. In an essentially conservative (using the word in its medical sense) manner, they have added information to Type A clauses, rather than completely changing them. Take for example Article 10(1) Canada–Mongolia BIT 2016, which in principle follows the Type A template. However, the article contains a footnote which reads: 'For greater certainty, paragraph 1 of Article 10 shall be interpreted in accordance with Annex B.10', which, in turn, reads, in part:

> The Parties confirm their shared understanding that:
>
> 1. indirect expropriation results from a measure or series of measures of a Party that has an effect equivalent to direct expropriation without formal transfer of title or outright seizure;
> 2. the determination of whether a measure or series of measures of a Party constitutes an indirect expropriation requires a case-by-case, fact-based inquiry that considers, among other factors:
>   1. the economic impact of the measure or series of measures, although the sole fact that a measure or series of measures of a Party has an adverse effect on the economic value of an investment does not establish that an indirect expropriation has occurred;
>   2. the extent to which the measure or series of measures interferes with distinct, reasonable investment-backed expectations; and
>   3. the character of the measure or series of measures.
> 3. Except in rare circumstances, such as when a measure or series of measures are so severe in the light of their purpose that they cannot be reasonably viewed as having been adopted and applied in good faith, non-discriminatory measures of a Party that are designed and applied to protect legitimate public welfare objectives, such as health, safety and the environment, do not constitute indirect expropriation.

Up to and including 2018, four publicly available awards on the merits had been issued on the basis of Type B clauses: *Railroad Development Corporation* (*RDC*), *Al-Tamini*, *Bear Creek* and *Aven*.[239] *RDC* and *Aven* were decided on the basis of Article 10.7 CAFTA-DR 2004, which includes Annex 10-C on expropriation (as well as Annex 10-B on customary international law). In *Aven*, the tribunal completely skirted the issue of how this type of expropriation clause had influenced its decision

[239] *Railroad Development Corporation (RDC)* v. *Republic of Guatemala*, ICSID, ARB/07/23, Award of 29 June 2012; *Adel A Hamadi Al Tamimi* v. *Sultanate of Oman*, ICSID, ARB/11/33, Award of 3 November 2015; *Bear Creek Mining Corporation* v. *Republic of Peru*, ICSID, ARB/14/21, Award of 30 November 2017; *David Aven et al.* v. *Costa Rica*, UNCITRAL, UNCT/15/3, Final Award of 18 September 2018.

not to consider Respondent's actions an expropriation, except to say that it had 'determined that Respondent has not breached its obligations under DR-CAFTA . . . under . . . Article 10.7(1) and Annex 10-C'.[240] It referred to an earlier part of its award where it had held: 'The Tribunal determines that such wetland was indeed impacted by works undertaken by Claimants, and that the reaction taken by Respondent as a consequence was merited under the laws of Costa Rica, which are not inconsistent with international law. Further, that the actions taken by the Respondent are not arbitrary nor in breach of the obligations under DR-CAFTA.'[241]

In *RDC*, the tribunal did not find a breach of Article 10.7 CAFTA-DR 2004 either, and the discussion of indirect expropriation is even less helpful, as the tribunal declined the claim on the basis of an effects argument[242] and did not even begin to take the terms of Annex 10-C (4)(b)[243] into account before it found that 'the Tribunal concludes that the effect on Claimants' investment does not rise to the level of an indirect expropriation'.[244]

In contrast to these two awards, *Bear Creek* applied Article 812 Canada–Peru FTA 2008, which includes Annex 812.1 and did discuss at length the impact of the FTA's 'more extensive and detailed definitions and rules'.[245] In analysing whether the decree at issue was an indirect expropriation, it first considered the three factors in Annex 812.1(b)(i)–(iii).[246] It quickly found the first two to be fulfilled[247] and, after exhaustive analysis, the third condition, concerning the character of the measure, was also found to be fulfilled.[248] While the party arguments on the exception clause of Annex 812.1(c) are reproduced at length, the tribunal did not consider it at all in determining whether the measure fulfilled the *Tatbestand* of indirect expropriation. It held that 'the three "factors"

240 *Aven* (2018) note 239 at para 688.
241 *Aven* (2018) note 239 at para 585.
242 Lukas Stifter, August Reinisch, 'Expropriation in the Light of the UNCTAD Investment Policy Framework for Sustainable Development' in Steffen Hindelang, Markus Krajewski (eds.), *Shifting Paradigms in International Investment Law: More Balanced, Less Isolated, Increasingly Diversified* (Oxford: Oxford University Press 2016) 81–96 at 93.
243 Equivalent to Annex B.10(3) Canada–Mongolia BIT 2016.
244 *RDC* (2012) note 239 at para 152.
245 *Bear Creek* (2017) note 239 at para 372.
246 Equivalent to Annex B.10(2)(1)–(3) Canada–Mongolia BIT 2016.
247 *Bear Creek* (2017) note 239 at paras 375–6.
248 *Bear Creek* (2017) note 239 at paras 378–414.

expressly provided in Annex 812.1(b) of the FTA for the identification of an indirect expropriation are fulfilled' and '*therefore* concludes that Supreme Decree 032 was an indirect expropriation in the sense of Article 812 and Annex 812.1 of the FTA'.[249]

Only *after* it had examined the fulfilment of the usual legality conditions and had found that the measure was unlawful[250] did it proceed to examine 'whether the measure was a valid exercise of police powers'.[251] Neither the reproduced party argument nor the tribunal mentioned the potential express incorporation of the police powers doctrine in Annex 812.1(c)[252] at this stage. Mentioning comments by the government of Canada on the police powers doctrine, the tribunal did 'not disagree with this general evaluation' but felt that the doctrine 'must be taken into account in the context of the specific provisions provided in the FTA'.[253] Peculiarly, it was more concerned with the applicability of Article 2201 Canada–Peru FTA 2008, which is roughly equivalent to the general exceptions clause in Article XX GATT 1947, than with the substantial identity of Annex 812.1(c), and it held: '[I]n substance, in view of the very detailed provisions of the FTA regarding expropriation (Article 812 and Annex 812.1) and regarding exceptions in Article 2201 expressly designated to "Chapter Eight (Investment)", the interpretation of the FTA must lead to the conclusion that no other exceptions from general international law or otherwise can be considered applicable in this case.'[254] In this manner the *Bear Creek* tribunal circumvented the difficult questions of the exact legal impact of adding, in an interpretative annex, what may amount to a severe restriction of the *Tatbestand* of indirect expropriation for general regulatory measures. The opportunity to clarify some of these questions was not taken up.

The tribunal in *Al Tamini* applied Article 10.6 Oman–US FTA 2006, which includes Annex 10-B, but quickly framed the dispute as contractual[255] and avoided discussing the Annex in depth. However, it warned the claimant

249 *Bear Creek* (2017) note 239 at paras 415, 416 (emphasis added).

250 *Bear Creek* (2017) note 239 at paras 430–49.

251 *Bear Creek* (2017) note 239 at paras 450–78.

252 Federico Ortino, 'Defining Indirect Expropriation: The Transatlantic Trade and Investment Partnership and the (Elusive) Search for "Greater Certainty"' 43 *Legal Issues of Economic Integration* (2016) 351–66 at 361–2 (referring to a similar paragraph in a 2015 EU proposal for the TTIP).

253 *Bear Creek* (2017) note 239 at para 471.

254 *Bear Creek* (2017) note 239 at para 473.

255 *Al Tamini* (2015) note 239 at paras 345–76. It concluded that '[t]he Claimant is unable to elevate a private contractual dispute with OMCO into an expropriation under international law' *Al Tamini* (2015) note 239 at para 376.

that its alternative claim 'would also have to confront the express stipulation in Annex 10-B.4(b) ... that non-discriminatory regulatory actions by a State designed and applied to protect legitimate public welfare objectives ... do not constitute indirect expropriations'.[256] While obiter, this is relatively clear language that this tribunal may have had no choice but to take the police powers exception in Annex 10-B(4)(b) seriously.

Type B expropriation clauses have three typical elements: first, they tend to claim that the content of the annex reflects customary international law; second, the annex is introduced as aid to interpretation; third, the annex is connected to a traditional Type A expropriation clause in the main text of the IIA. All three elements have given rise to controversy and are beset by theoretical problems which we have largely discussed in previous sections and chapters. We will briefly recapitulate these now before looking at what the limits of the *Tatbestand* for indirect expropriation are for Type B clauses.

Many Type B clauses contain a reference to customary law; Annex B(1) US Model BIT 2012, for example, states that 'Article 6 ... (1) is intended to reflect customary international law concerning the obligation of States with respect to expropriation', which has been read to mean that the putative 'states parties proceed from the assumption that this regulation [ie Annex B] is customary international law'.[257] In Paparinskis' words, '[t]he legal position ... is not that the newly concluded treaties contribute to new customary law ... but that they accurately and exhaustively state existing customary law to which BITs explicitly or implicitly refer'.[258] Those who believe that the police powers doctrine applies whether or not the state parties have explicitly included language to that effect in their IIA agree, but with a different emphasis:

> [S]uch clarification clauses do not constitute an exception to the treaty or to the expropriation provision. They are meant to serve merely as guidance in the assessment of whether a measure constitutes indirect expropriation. Importantly, even though the relevant clarifications are legally confined to those treaties where they are made, the exemption of good faith non-discriminatory regulatory measures exists in general customary international law on the basis on the police powers doctrine ....[259]

256 *Al Tamini* (2015) note 239 at para 368.

257 'dass die Parteien davon ausgehen, dass es sich bei dieser Regelung um Völkergewohnheitsrecht handelt' Kriebaum (2008a) note 9 at 269; see also López (2014) note 9 at 122; Paparinskis (2011b) note 1 at 324–5; Schwebel (2011) note 95 at 157; Subedī (2006) note 108 at 136; UNCTAD (2012) note 11 at 88.

258 Paparinskis (2011b) note 1 at 324–5.

259 UNCTAD (2012) note 11 at 88; see also Newcombe (2005) note 17 at 40.

Stephen Schwebel doubts that the certainty with which the reference to customary law is made in Type B treaties is warranted, 'since it is incontestable that the content of customary international law on expropriation is contentious'. The language in the various annexes stating that for general regulatory measures liability would be excluded 'except in rare instances' is particularly objectionable to him: 'Can it be plausibly maintained that the exception only for "rare circumstances" is found in customary international law?'[260] For Kriebaum, it is doubtful whether there is any agreement on the shape of customary international law on this point.[261] Even Subedī, otherwise sympathetic to the police powers doctrine, is sceptical about whether these annexes are 'an accurate reflection of the status of customary international law', pointing to the *lex specialis* character of all IIAs: '[E]xamples of *lex specialis* may in due course transform themselves into *lex generalis*, yet there is no convincing evidence to suggest at this stage [in 2006] that this has already taken place.'[262]

References in Type B clauses to customary international law are partially claims that the general law referred to is accurately described by the wording of the annexes. The arguments developed in Section 7.2 regarding the limits of the argument from customary law and in Chapter 2 regarding the limited impact of IIAs on the development of customary law are apposite here: the regulation envisaged in the annexes of Type B clauses does not reflect present customary international law. For Paparinskis, from this particular perspective 'what is important ... is not the proportion of treaties that are concluded expressly taking this position as against pre-existing treaties without such language' but rather the rising count of *opinio iuris* or state practice evidenced by states 'concluding such treaties or including such language in their Model BITs'.[263] Even if he is right in this claim, the potential impact of these new IIAs on customary international law is structurally limited. Even though states are beginning to redraft their (model) IIAs – and there is some doubt that the shift to Type B is as widespread as claimed[264] – questions of 'effectiveness' remain. Type A clauses (the foundation for Type B) are likely *inter se* abrogations. How strong an *opinio iuris*

[260] Schwebel (2011) note 95 at 157, 158.
[261] Kriebaum (2008a) note 9 at 269.
[262] Subedī (2006) note 108 at 136.
[263] Paparinskis (2011b) note 1 at 325.
[264] Alec Stone Sweet, Michael Yunsuck Chung, Adam Saltzman, 'Arbitral Lawmaking and State Power: An Empirical Analysis of Investor–State Arbitration' 8 *Journal of International Dispute Settlement* (2017) 579–609.

consuetudinalis – as against an *opinio iuris conventionalis* – can they be? What is more, is the status of Type B clauses as *opinio iuris* for future changes in customary international law not proof that the implicit police powers exception was *not* part of customary international law up to now? But this point can easily be conceded.

Across the board, Type B clauses are introduced as interpretative in nature: the Type A expropriation clause in the main text 'shall be interpreted in accordance with' the annex in question. The IIAs' self-description diverges sharply from what the expropriation clause can be in a theoretical sense. The 2012 UNCTAD study believes the self-description and cautions against reading 'such clarification clauses' as 'an exception to the treaty or to the expropriation provision. They are meant to serve merely as guidance in the assessment of whether a measure constitutes indirect expropriation.'[265] Others are far more sceptical of this claim. 'This provision ... has the appearance of an interpretive statement. However, it is, in effect, tantamount to a genuine exception to the indirect expropriation standard.'[266]

As Chapter 4 has discussed at length, rules which self-identify as 'interpretative' – whether as rules of interpretation or as interpretative declaration – are not really about interpretation as hermeneutic process, that is, part of what happens when humans try to find out what texts 'mean'. The self-description in Type B expropriation clauses is correct insofar as they are 'aimed at guiding decision-makers in future claims of indirect expropriation'.[267] Hence, if we do not believe the self-description as 'interpretative', they are treaty norms which bind arbitral tribunals to go about applying the IIA in a specific way. We are in effect confronted with an 'authentic interpretation': law which changes the law to be 'interpreted' but does so while using interpretation as rhetorical smoke-screen (Section 4.2.2). However, if we believe the self-description and take the word 'interpretation' as referring to the hermeneutic process, they are an ineffectual exhortation.

The annexes in Type B clauses are connected to a traditional Type A clause. Type A clauses, in turn, are subject to the structural limits described in Sections 7.2–7.4, which in effect contradict at least the 'general regulations' exceptions in Type B clause annexes. This 'strengthen[ing of] the continuity with past treaty practice'[268] was

[265] UNCTAD (2012) note 11 at 88.
[266] Titi (2014) note 9 at 151, see also 44.
[267] López (2014) note 9 at 199.
[268] Ortino (2016) note 252 at 354.

probably done on purpose. It has been argued that this reliance on the traditional clause will influence (our understanding of) expropriation clauses despite the restrictive language in the annexes:

> There are however, also risks . . . relying on the traditional wording may preserve the (more or less apparent) treaty's emphasis on affording a high level of protection to foreign investment to the detriment of the host State's regulatory sovereignty. In other words, mere reference to the measure's 'effect' on the investment may lead (at least some) tribunals to continue to focus on the measure's substantial adverse effect on the investment notwithstanding the legitimacy and reasonableness of the public policy being pursued by the host State.[269]

We are left with a conundrum because the states parties drafted the IIA while relying on assumptions about the content of external law which may turn out not to be true. Both the stated reliance on a (pre-existing) customary norm and the idea of interpretative guidance are highly problematic. This raises a wider question: what happens when law-makers err in theoretical matters? (Indeed, compare this with a question which is not significantly different: what happens when law-makers err in scientific matters?) Do we believe their assertion or in their prescription? Do we believe that interpretation ought to occur according to the drafters' idea of the customary law police powers exception – even if the reference is empty, because what they refer to is not part of general law? Do we ignore the truth-value and take it as a prescription of a radically different expropriation clause: modifying Type A while containing irrelevant rhetorical flourishes? *We cannot do both.*

This is decisive for the structural limits of Type B clauses. In the first case, there is no change in the structural limits of the Type A *Tatbestand*: Type B is Type A. In the second case, as López puts it, 'tribunals are generally guided towards a police-powers solution'; 'this means replacing an objective approach to the threshold question, based on the effects rule, for a subjective one, centred in the judicial analysis of the motives behind the adoption of the challenged measure'.[270] On this reading, IIAs of that type do not protect investors against the expropriatory effects of general (non-discriminatory) regulatory measures. Perhaps the problem discussed above can be analogised to a solution developed for that of erroneous final judgments.[271] On that solution, we would ask whether

[269] Ortino (2016) note 252 at 354–5.
[270] López (2014) note 9 at 161, 199.
[271] See Kammerhofer (2010d) note 77 at 191–3.

the states parties had a *voluntas eventualis* – did they want to regulate indirect expropriation in the manner they (erroneously) thought that customary international law was shaped, irrespective of whether this is true? In other words, did the parties agree that they believed that the police powers doctrine which they had laid down in the Annex accurately reflects customary international law? Did the parties agree further that, even if customary law does not bear out their belief, they want investor protection against expropriation in the IIA to be shaped in the manner which the Annex prescribes? While this is an interesting speculative enterprise, we are unlikely to ever be in a position to answer the question with any degree of certainty. It would also shift the emphasis from the words of the IIA, which is part of international law, onto our speculations of what the states parties may potentially want.

A peculiar hybrid between Type B and Type C clauses is Article 14.8 United States–Mexico–Canada Agreement (USMCA) 2018, which is accompanied by a footnote directing that it be interpreted in accordance with Annex 14-B. It is in this sense to be classified as Type B; however, Article 14.8(5) *in addition* contains a more direct link, reading: 'For greater certainty, whether an action or series of actions by a Party constitutes an expropriation shall be determined in accordance with paragraph 1 of this Article and Annex 14-B.' In this case, the annex is both guidance to interpretation *and*, it could be argued, formally made part of the prescription in Article 14.8.[272]

3. *Type C clauses.* States parties may draft widespread changes in the text of the expropriation clause itself, clarifying and modifying the (indirect) expropriation *Tatbestand*. One possible example of this type is Article 6(1)–(2) Turkey–Rwanda BIT 2016 which reads, in part:

> 1. Investments shall not be expropriated, nationalized or subject, directly or indirectly, to measures of similar effects (hereinafter referred to as expropriation) except for a public purpose, in a non-discriminatory manner, upon payment of prompt, adequate and effective compensation, and in accordance with due process of law . . .

[272] The practical relevance of this distinction is doubtful, however, as the USMCA 2018, in contrast with NAFTA 1994, no longer allows claims by investors for breach of the prohibition of indirect expropriation. See Article 14.D(1)(a)(i)(B) USMCA 2018 and Article 14.D(1)(b)(i)(B) USMCA 2018, which both read, in the relevant part: 'the claimant . . . may submit to arbitration under this Annex a claim: . . . that the respondent has breached . . . Article 14.8 (Expropriation and Compensation), except with respect to indirect expropriation'.

2. Non-discriminatory legal measures designed and applied to protect legitimate public welfare objectives, such as health, safety and environment, do not constitute indirect expropriation.

In clauses of this type, the *Tatbestand* of indirect expropriation is regulated in a restrictive manner in the article itself. Type C has not yet become particularly popular, but we can briefly discuss its structural limits. In contradistinction to Type B, where the major problem is whether the technique which the drafters have employed is adequate to ensure an outcome which is friendly to the police powers, the technique here is unquestionably legally tenable. Depending on the specific formulation employed, these IIAs do not protect against general regulatory measures. In the example given here, the IIA does not protect against measures designed and applied to protect certain 'legitimate public welfare objectives', which, in turn, is a question within the frame of possible meanings.

The only slight drawback and 'un-aesthetic' element of this way of regulating indirect expropriation is that the 'doubling' – a mere claim by scholarship and tribunals regarding Type A (Section 7.4.1) – is now contained in the text of the treaty. For Type A clauses, the doubling argument is not tenable, but when the treaty explicitly does so in Type C, some of the legality conditions – some or all process conditions – will do double duty as exclusionary elements in the *Tatbestand*. Type C clauses also treat measures of direct and of indirect expropriation in a different manner. Under Article 6(1)–(2) Turkey–Rwanda BIT 2016, the parties owe compensation for '[n]on-discriminatory legal measures designed and applied to protect legitimate public welfare objectives, such as health, safety and environment' if these are formal expropriations. Under that treaty, Turkey must pay compensation if it formally expropriates a Rwandan investor in order to protect the environment, but it does not have to do so if it protects the environment using other measures which destroy the same investment.

7.6 Conclusion

Both the micro-structure of IIA expropriation clauses and the macro-structure of international legal sources mandate limits to the possible meanings of expropriation. We are left with a significant interpretative margin, but this freedom is bounded by these limits. It is legal scholarship's primary task to identify these limits; its task is not to give one right answer for every set of facts within these limits. Those who apply the law, including arbitral tribunals, must respect the limits, but not because scholarship has said so. Scholarship has no authority in the legal sense; it is not authorised to delimit norms. Its task and its forte are to find the limits which the law itself exhibits.

In this chapter, we have identified the three most important limits to the traditional and most widespread Type A expropriation clause. Section 7.2 debunks claims that IIA expropriation clauses are necessarily identical with or contain a *renvoi* to general law, as well as that general law contains specific norms. Sections 7.3 and 7.4 demonstrate that the structure of Type A clauses mandates the equality of direct and indirect expropriation and that all legality clauses must be observed. We have also shown in Section 7.5 that differences in drafting matter but that drafters do not always produce the results they intend. The exclusion of the police powers exception (or a right to regulate) in Type A clauses[273] is not a necessary feature of *every* IIA or of international law in general. On a normativist-positivist account of international investment law, the law can and will vary. Type C clauses, for example, may distinguish between direct and indirect expropriation and double the process conditions.

We have not discussed atypical IIAs, for which the limits identified in this chapter may or may not be valid; it depends on the specific terms of the treaty, not on a priori necessities. IIAs can be drafted in a manner that incorporates the police powers doctrine, but that does not change those IIAs which do not do so. The typology employed here is a scholarly ordering of the unordered phenomenon of IIAs – the scholar seeking to typify the 'arbitrariness' of human law-making. A lepidopterologist may seek to classify species of butterflies into various *sub-genera* – yet a butterfly which does not fit into this scheme does not cease to exist because of this classification.[274] So it is here: neither does the typology presented in this chapter destroy the validity of an IIA which does not fit in nor do the types prejudge the structural limits of such a treaty. *If* a treaty fits Type A, its structure is such that it has the limits described in Sections 7.2–7.4. If it does not, some, all or none of these may apply – or the limits could be shaped in a different manner.

While this means that the law significantly limits the freedom of tribunals, particularly to follow the police powers doctrine, the sole

[273] See Kriebaum (2008a) note 9 at 422.

[274] Jörg Kammerhofer, 'Lawmaking by Scholars' in Catherine Brölmann, Yannick Radi (eds.), *Handbook on the Theory and Practice of International Lawmaking* (Cheltenham: Edward Elgar 2016) 305–25 at 315.

effects doctrine is not thereby 'mandated'. IIAs do not positively define either direct or indirect expropriation. The frame of possible meanings of what this can be and, consequently, the freedom of tribunals to decide within that frame, is significant. Expropriation is probably some form of taking of investment, but the IIA does not specify when the taking reaches the level where one can speak of expropriation. The intensity requirement developed in case-law ('substantial deprivation', Section 8.2) is one way of filling the frame of possible meaning of IIA expropriation clauses. The general and to a large extent unspecific law in these clauses is not narrowed down by the decisions of tribunals or by speculative scholarly reflection. Outside the common law, the law applied does not change by its application, even for a specific fact situation, and even if consistent jurisprudence is factually determinative of future decision-making and it is prudent to argue within that framework. Hence, all we can do at this stage with respect to the significant remaining frame of possible meanings is to document and order past decision-making; Chapter 8 will attempt to do this for three topics.

8

Expropriation Reconstructed

8.1 Introduction: Method and Topic Selection

No form of international legal scholarship can reduce the freedom of investment arbitral tribunals to zero. From time to time, this may be a subconscious goal, but such wishes do not reflect the nature of natural languages which treaties use and which scholars analyse. This goal is also belied by jurisprudence vigorously claiming its freedom, even against majorities of scholarly opinion. Tribunals, like all law-applying organs, are simultaneously bound and free. In order for their products to be part of the law, they have to accord with the limits set by both the procedural and the substantive law which they have to apply in the case before them. Yet they are also fundamentally 'free'. Their decisions are not logical deductions from higher law; they are neither the *bouche de la loi* nor the *Subsumptionsautomat* which the formalists of old would have us believe. Their decisions are constitutive because they create new norms, a new part of the legal order. Their freedom is also grounded in our use of natural languages and the inherent, irreducible and significant latitude which makes for vagueness and multivalence but also provides room for manoeuvre and creativity which is indispensable in human communication, including law-making and law-applying.

The theoretical approach which is adopted here has developed a particular understanding and method for operationalising this tension between freedom and determination: the frame of possible meanings (Section 5.1). Legal scholarship's task is to find out, for each provision of positive law which it researches, what the frame is shaped like. Law-applying organs like tribunals, in contrast, will decide, and 'any act that stays within this frame and gives it a possible sense is legal'.[1] The empowerment of law-applying organs does not stretch to giving them any 'authority' to cognise or (outside the common law) to change the frame; scholarship cannot reduce the possible meanings

[1] 'wobei jeder Akt rechtmäßig ist, der sich innerhalb dieses Rahmens hält, den Rahmen in irgendeinem möglichen Sinn ausfüllt' Hans Kelsen, *Reine Rechtslehre* (2nd edn, Vienna: Deuticke 1960) 348.

within the frame to 'one right answer'. Chapter 7 implements the Pure Theory of Law's 'frame theorem' for traditional (Type A) IIA expropriation clauses. The frame, it was argued there, of Type A clauses is shaped to a significant extent by the inter-operation of three limits to what expropriation can mean. Chapter 8, in contrast, is the attempt to show how investment arbitral tribunals have filled the frame.

A fundamental methodological question in this connection is whether the reconstruction should take the limits identified earlier into account or ignore them. On their own terms, both legal realism as well as the *Praktikerliteratur* discussed in Section 5.1 tend not to heed such limits. The first does so on the basis of the theoretical argument that 'the law in action' is more immediately relevant than abstract rules. The second does so on a subconsciously made pragmatic argument that practitioners must take account of jurisprudence, whether or not ostensible limits are transcended.

On the one hand, one could argue that fealty to the idea of providing information on the law at the level of arbitral awards must mean ignoring the limits of the 'higher' level of IIAs. On that view, the practical value of the information typically provided in legal commentaries is predictive: telling us how, in all likelihood, future decisions by the relevant tribunals will fall by looking at previous instances. If we restricted this type to results within the frame of possible meanings, we would belie this pragmatic programme. For example, it is highly likely that at least some future arbitral tribunals adjudging on Type A clauses will follow the *Methanex–Saluka* line of awards in accepting an inherent police powers exception. They will do so despite, as we have seen above, such an outcome not being supported by the substantive law they were tasked with applying: Type A clauses. This would be a valid objection if our only task were to portray the level of awards.

However, this book aims to demonstrate how legal doctrinal scholarship can operate on the basis of the Pure Theory of Law. Its fealty to the law in force, the body of positive international law which includes arbitral awards, is stronger than pragmatic considerations. Those parts of awards which go beyond the limit of the empowerment norm (in a wide sense) cannot be called part of international law.[2] On the legal theoretical approach adopted

[2] We could go further and ask whether ICSID annulment – or national domestic enforcement decisions for non-ICSID awards – establish an Error Calculus in Adolf Julius Merkl's sense or whether this is after all a case of the 'erroneous final judgment' problem, see eg Jörg Kammerhofer, 'Positivist Approaches and International Adjudication' in Hélène Ruiz Fabri (ed.), *Max Planck Encyclopedia of International Procedural Law* (Oxford: Oxford University Press 2019), available at: opil.ouplaw.com/view/10.1093/law-mpeipro/e3300.013.3300/law-mpeipro-e3300, section 3.

here, we cannot, in the end, adopt legal realism or reduce our efforts to an instance of *Praktikerliteratur*, because both ignore limits of the law and succumb to an absolutism of the individual decision.[3] The selling-points of the new doctrinal scholarship introduced in Section 5.3 are the following: it tempers universalisation by acknowledging the fragmentation of IIAs and awards; it provides generalised information about one *stratum* while showing the freedom of decision in another *stratum*; and it provides pragmatic information about the use that jurisprudence has made of this freedom, but limits it to solutions within the frame of possible meanings.

The rest of this chapter will be a selection of topics, questions or tests which have become central in investment arbitral case-law on expropriation.[4] We will elucidate expropriation clauses by presenting an overview of tribunal argument and holdings on the questions within the frame of possible meanings and by analysing and structuring jurisprudence. In contrast to Chapter 7, where arbitral awards were treated as just another source of legal arguments, this chapter will foreground them as the expression of decision-making, that is, of the creation of awards as individual norms. Accordingly, scholarly literature is relevant here only insofar as it explains, analyses and structures the case-law on a topic. For present purposes, scholarship is not a separate source of authority.

For example, whether expropriation is an interference with an investment which requires a 'substantial deprivation', while commonly accepted in jurisprudence, is a point not predetermined by traditional (Type A) IIA expropriation clauses. In Section 8.2, we will show whether and how widespread the acceptance of this test is and whether there are clusters of decisions regarding the test and fact-situations that fulfil or fail the test. In this manner, we hope to steer clear of an endless and unstructured enumeration of sets of facts and tribunal arguments. We will, on the

3 Jean d'Aspremont, 'If International Judges Say So, It Must Be True: Empiricism or Fetishism?' 4:9 *ESIL Reflections* (2015).

4 'Arbitral case-law on expropriation' is defined here as international arbitral decisions rendered until 31 December 2018 which were available publicly and to me, which have decided on the basis of an IIA and have engaged in a sustained fashion with a Type A (and, where appropriate, Type B) expropriation clause. This, in turn, is fulfilled where the tribunal developed arguments, rather than merely dismissing a claim or finding that liability established for a different head of claim liberates the tribunal from adjudicating on the expropriation claim. Inter alia, this excludes jurisprudence on the basis of customary international law, the jurisprudence of the Iran–US Claims Tribunal, human rights courts adjudicating on the protection of property, domestic arbitral tribunals and courts and certain international investment awards. This in effect also means that awards before approximately 1999 are unlikely to be considered. As a pragmatic matter, awards not available in English have also largely been excluded.

other hand, also endeavour to avoid the consciously or subconsciously normative *Rechtsdogmatik* of German-language legal scholarship which, under the guise of systematising the law, imposes its own rationality on the case-law in order to shape the application of the general law. In this light, the frequent exhortation that arbitral decisions on expropriation 'require a case-by-case, fact-based inquiry'[5] is deprived of its problematic undertones of balancing, which is seemingly able to make facts into standards without a basis in the applicable norms. A case-by-case analysis is no more than what one does in all cases of adjudging.[6]

A wide range of questions has been the subject of party arguments and tribunal reasoning in cases before investment arbitral tribunals adjudging upon IIA expropriation clauses. Many scholarly works already provide comprehensive and exhaustive overviews of tribunal jurisprudence on expropriation;[7] the following will eschew doing so. Rather, we will analyse a small number of topics within the frame of possible meanings which are of significant importance and interest for the wider issue of expropriation in

[5] United Nations Conference on Trade and Development, *Expropriation* [UNCTAD/DIAE/IA/2011/7] (2012) 57; see also August Reinisch, 'Expropriation' in Peter Muchlinski, Federico Ortino, Christoph Schreuer (eds.), *The Oxford Handbook of International Investment Law* (Oxford: Oxford University Press 2008) 407–58 at 438; Christopher S Gibson, 'Case Comment: *Yukos Universal Limited (Isle of Man) v The Russian Federation*: A Classic Case of Indirect Expropriation' 30 *ICSID Review* (2015) 303–14 at 307; Tarcisio Gazzini, 'Drawing the Line between Non-compensable Regulatory Powers and Indirect Expropriation of Foreign Investment – An Economic Analysis of Law Perspective' 7 *Manchester Journal of International Economic Law* (2010) 36–51 at 41; Meg N Kinnear, Andrea K Bjorklund, John FG Hannaford, *Investment Disputes under NAFTA: An Annotated Guide to NAFTA Chapter 11* (Alphen aan den Rijn: Kluwer 2006) 1110-17; Christina Knahr, 'Indirect Expropriation in Recent Investment Arbitration' 6:1 *Transnational Dispute Management* (2009) 3; Type B IIA clauses.

[6] L Yves Fortier, Stephen L Drymer, 'Indirect Expropriation in the Law of International Investment: I Know It When I See It, or *Caveat Investor*' 19 *ICSID Review – Foreign Investment law Journal* (2004) 293–327 at 314.

[7] Eg R Doak Bishop, James Crawford, W Michael Reisman, *Foreign Investment Disputes: Cases, Materials and Commentary* (The Hague: Kluwer 2005); Jonathan Bonnitcha, *Substantive Protection under Investment Treaties: A Legal and Economic Analysis* (Cambridge: Cambridge University Press 2014); Rudolf Dolzer, *Eigentum, Enteignung und Entschädigung im geltenden Völkerrecht* (Berlin: Springer 1985); Rudolf Dolzer, Christoph Schreuer, *Principles of International Investment Law* (2nd edn, Oxford: Oxford University Press 2012); Ursula Kriebaum, *Eigentumsschutz im Völkerrecht: Eine vergleichende Untersuchung zum internationalen Investitionsrecht sowie zum Menschenrechtsschutz* (Berlin: Duncker & Humblot 2008); Sebastián López Escarcena, *Indirect Expropriation in International Law* (Cheltenham: Edward Elgar 2014); Campbell McLachlan, Laurence Shore, Matthew Weiniger, *International Investment Arbitration: Substantive Principles* (Oxford: Oxford University Press 2007); Arnaud de Nanteuil, *L'expropriation indirecte en droit international de l'investissement* (Paris: Pedone

international investment law. Again, the structure of (Type A) IIA expropriation clauses will be our guide in selecting the topics to be discussed. Generally, expropriation clauses can be analysed in four dimensions:

- *Subject.* IIA clauses prohibit expropriation by the treaty parties, that is, by the respondent state. Hence, the subject of expropriation is the state and potential expropriatory action needs to be attributed to that state. In addition, it is argued that the quality of the state action needs to be an *actus iure imperii,* rather than *iure gestionis.*
- *Object.* IIA clauses prohibit expropriation of investments. This issue is often identified with the jurisdictional question of whether the claimant is an investor in the respondent state, but one could also view the question of the *Schutzobjekt* (the object of an expropriation) as separate, that is, that measures of expropriation are those which impact investments rather than (merely) property rights.
- *Measure.* IIAs prohibit acts of expropriation, rather than other forms of state actions impacting investments. This is a multifaceted and most problematic complex of questions, involving issues of temporality, intensity and nature of the measures.
- *Legality conditions.* IIAs prohibit expropriation, unless the legality conditions are fulfilled.

Case-law has exhibited a significant specificity in developing 'tests' and arguments on intra-frame questions. Inter alia, such tests are that 'substantial deprivation' is the relevant criterion for indirect expropriation, and which level of value-reduction or control fulfils this criterion. The four dimensions portrayed above therefore split into a host of sub-questions/topics and we will focus here on some of the more systemically relevant to showcase the combination of methods envisioned in Section 5.1. Hence, the following sections will exemplarily highlight three topics: substantial deprivation (Section 8.2), partial expropriation (Section 8.3) and the legality conditions, focusing on the difference between compensation and reparation (Section 8.4).

2014); Andrew Newcombe, Lluís Paradell, *Law and Practice of Investment Treaties: Standards of Treatment* (Alphen aan den Rijn: Kluwer 2009); Suzy H Nikièma, *L'expropriation indirecte en droit international des investissements* (Paris: Presses Universitaires de France 2012); Reinisch (2008a) note 5; Jeswald W Salacuse, *The Law of International Investment Treaties* (Oxford: Oxford University Press 2010); Muthucumaraswamy Sornarajah, *The International Law on Foreign Investment* (3rd edn, Cambridge: Cambridge University Press 2010); Sūrya Prasāda Subedī, *International Investment Law: Reconciling Policy and Principle* (3rd edn, Oxford: Hart 2016).

8.2 Substantial Deprivation

While substantial deprivation is not the only test in case-law for the intensity of measures in order to qualify as indirect expropriation, ever since the *Pope & Talbot* award in 2000 it certainly has become the most prominent one. In that award, the tribunal mentioned off-hand that the Claimant agreed with this requirement:

> While it may sometimes be uncertain whether a particular interference with business activities amounts to an expropriation, the test is whether that interference is sufficiently restrictive to support a conclusion that the property has been 'taken' from the owner. . . . Indeed, at the hearing, the Investor's Counsel conceded, correctly, that under international law, expropriation requires a 'substantial deprivation'.[8]

The phrase has been taken up by a large number of decisions since then. Case-law's privileging of that term in indirect expropriation cases raises questions on two levels. On one level, we can ask whether substantial deprivation is an issue of intensity, temporality or object of the (indirect) expropriation. On another level, we can discuss whether substantial deprivation contains sub-standards, such as control, use, benefit or value. The first set of questions will briefly be discussed in this introduction while the second will be the focus of the balance of this section.

Which part of the current mainstream judicial test is 'substantial deprivation'? While it has found widespread acceptance in case-law and academic commentary, it has only been used as a standard in a narrow set of circumstances. First, it is part of the *Tatbestand* of IIA expropriation clauses, considered alongside other factors such as permanence and the police powers doctrine.[9] Second, it is used only as a standard for indirect expropriation.[10] This is so because tribunals tend to measure direct expropriation in a much more formalistic manner[11] than indirect expropriation, which leads to a divergence in the standards for direct and indirect measures (Section 7.3) and for measures affecting only a part of the total investment (Section 8.3).

8 *Pope & Talbot Inc* v. *Government of Canada*, NAFTA-UNCITRAL, Interim Award of 26 June 2000, para 102.

9 *Burlington Resources Inc.* v. *Republic of Ecuador*, ICSID, ARB/08/5, Decision on Liability of 14 December 2012, para 506; *Quiborax S.A. and Non Metallic Minerals S.A. Claimants* v. *Plurinational State of Bolivia*, ICSID, ARB/06/2, Award of 16 September 2015, para 200.

10 See, however, *Tokios Tokelės* v. *Ukraine*, ICSID, ARB/02/18, Award of 26 July 2007, para 120: 'For *any* expropriation – *direct or indirect* – to occur, the state must deprive the investor of a "substantial" part of the value of the investment' (emphasis added).

11 Eg *Bernhard Friedrich Arnd Rüdiger von Pezold* et al. v. *Republic of Zimbabwe*, ICSID, ARB/10/15, Award of 28 July 2015, para 494.

Third, substantial deprivation is not treated as a sufficient condition but is largely seen as a necessary condition.

The substantial deprivation standard is widely identified with the sole effects doctrine. Anne Hoffmann posits that because '[t]here is a general consensus that the most significant criterion in the case law . . . is the severity or significance of the impact [of] the measure' and '[t]he effect incurred . . . is the most important criterion in current jurisprudence, in some cases the only one', we should refer to this approach as 'the sole effect doctrine'.[12] This argument turns two separate concepts into one. On the one hand, substantial deprivation is a description of a widely accepted element of the *Tatbestand* of indirect expropriation, developed in case-law, requiring further refinement and discussion and which may or may not be a necessary condition for the presence of an indirect expropriation under IIAs. The sole effects doctrine, on the other hand, much less frequently voiced in writings and jurisprudence, is the idea that a certain intensity of interference (of a non-transitory nature) is the *only sufficient condition* for the presence of an indirect expropriation. This identification may be a welcome straw-man for those wishing to strengthen the hand of the police powers doctrine, as this would degrade the intensity requirement to merely another counter-doctrine. However, as discussed in Sections 7.2–7.4, *some* form of requirement of intensity of interference – whether styled 'substantial deprivation' or otherwise – is the result of the frame of possible meanings for typical IIA expropriation clauses.[13]

Something akin to substantial deprivation is, in other words, a default element for indirect expropriation: it is what is left when we analyse what the law requires and which arguments it excludes. This holds even on a more mainstream argument, which goes as follows: (a) we cannot find an exception in the treaty at issue for certain purposes, intent or regulation; (b) many IIAs formulate indirect expropriation as 'of equivalent *effect*'; (c) by its nature, as the *EMV* tribunal put it, 'the measures must, however indirect, amount to a "taking"'.[14] Hence, effects-based reasoning comes naturally when we speak of expropriation. Talking about effects and/or the intensity

[12] Anne K Hoffmann, 'Indirect Expropriation' in August Reinisch (ed.), *Standards of Investment Protection* (Oxford: Oxford University Press 2008) 151–70 at 156; see also Knahr (2009) note 5 at 7; *Saipem S.p.A.* v. *People's Republic of Bangladesh*, ICSID, ARB/05/7, Award of 30 June 2009, para 133.

[13] See UNCTAD (2012) note 5 at 64: 'In the majority of cases to date, claims of indirect expropriation have been dismissed because the negative impact of the measure did not rise to the level of a taking.'

[14] *European Media Ventures* v. *Czech Republic*, UNCITRAL, Partial Award on Liability of 8 July 2009, para 47.

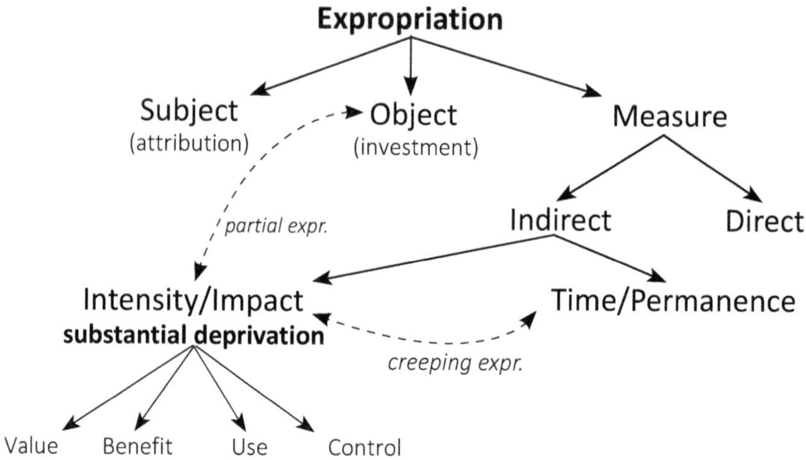

Figure 8.1 Substantial deprivation in the dimensions of expropriation

of the measure is not a 'doctrine' which can be countered by a counter-doctrine.

Generally speaking, substantial deprivation finds its place within a range of elements which constitute 'the substantive content of the indirect expropriation standard', centring on the idea of expropriation as '"dispossession," "taking," "deprivation," or "privation." Typically, an expropriation "requires a taking (which may include destruction) by a government-type authority of an investment."'[15] The overview of elements in *Fireman's Fund* is salient here as well:

> [T]he present Tribunal retains the following elements from case law. (a) Expropriation requires a taking (which may include destruction) by a government-type authority of an investment by an investor ... (c) The taking must be a substantially complete deprivation of the economic use and enjoyment of the rights to the property, or of identifiable distinct parts thereof (i.e., it approaches total impairment). (d) The taking must be permanent, and not ephemeral or temporary.... (h) The taking may be "direct" or "indirect." (i) The taking may have the form of a single measure or a series of related or unrelated measures over a period of time (the so-called "creeping" expropriation).[16]

Within the expropriation *Tatbestand* in IIAs, therefore, one state party (subject) will impact the investment (object) of the investor of another state

[15] A Devin Bray, 'Non-compensatory versus Compensatory Takings under NAFTA' 9:7 *Transnational Dispute Management* (2012) 5.

[16] *Fireman's Fund Insurance Company* v. *United Mexican States*, NAFTA-ICSID, ARB(AF)/02/1, Award of 17 July 2006, para 176.

party by measures that can be characterised as 'expropriation', either direct or indirect. Indirect expropriation measures will have two dimensions: intensity/severity and permanence; the judicial test for intensity is 'substantial deprivation'.

The various factors relevant for the question of whether the expropriation *Tatbestand* is fulfilled are closely interlinked. A certain amount of overlap is inevitable and a complete disaggregation is neither possible nor desirable. The following connections seem particularly pertinent:

- *Intensity and investment (object).* What 'ex-propriation' means depends also on what is taken – what the object of the measure is. If we are to tell when an expropriation has occurred by its effects, then the nature of the measure, particularly the intensity required, is defined by its effect *on* the object. Federico Ortino, for example, sees the various elements identified in case-law, the 'deprivation of the control, use, benefit, enjoyment, value of the investment' as part of the task of 'identifying the "object" of the deprivation',[17] rather than of the measure.
- *Intensity and partial expropriation.* A particularly important aspect and a special application of this problem is partial deprivation. Partial taking or a taking of only a part of the investment is a matter for both the intensity requirement and the object of expropriation (Section 8.3). 'The criterion of substantiality or diminution of value ... is difficult to apply without addressing the well-known "denominator" problem [– it] depends upon how the underlying property interest, or "denominator," is defined.'[18]
- *Intensity and time.* It is important to know when the crucial point has been reached where a state's actions cross the threshold. When is a taking permanent enough to be called expropriation? There is a tradition of seeing permanence as one part of substantial deprivation. The tribunal in *Philip Morris* aptly summarised that strand of jurisprudence: 'the State's measures should amount to a "substantial deprivation" ... "determinative factors" to that effect being "the

[17] Federico Ortino, 'Defining Indirect Expropriation: The Transatlantic Trade and Investment Partnership and the (Elusive) Search for "Greater Certainty"' 43 *Legal Issues of Economic Integration* (2016) 351–66 at 357.

[18] Joel C Beauvais, 'Regulatory Expropriations under NAFTA: Emerging Principles and Lingering Doubts' 10 *New York University Environmental Law Journal* (2001–2) 245–96 at 281; see also Céline Lévesque, 'Distinguishing Expropriation and Regulation under NAFTA Chapter 11: Making Explicit the Link to Property' in Kevin C Kennedy (ed.), *The First Decade of NAFTA: The Future of Free Trade in North America* (Ardsley: Transnational 2004) 293–324 at 314–15.

intensity and duration of the economic deprivation ...'".[19] Other voices[20] have separated intensity (substantial deprivation) from duration and we will follow that view here.

- *Intensity and creeping expropriation.* The total effect of several measures increasing beyond the intensity threshold vis-à-vis the special case of a creeping accretion of measures which have the effect of expropriation sits right at the border-line between the temporal and the intensity aspects.
- *Interplay of multiple factors.* Multiple factors or aspects interact when different 'parts' of the investment are impacted to different degrees at different times.

In the following, we will first look at how the general rule has been formulated in case-law (Section 8.2.1), followed by an analysis of the most important sub-standards (Section 8.2.2). This will be contrasted with an overview of what measures tribunals have actually found to constitute substantial deprivation, irrespective of their formulation of standards (Section 8.2.3).

8.2.1 The General Rule

Ever since *Pope & Talbot*, a significant part of investment tribunals adjudicating on IIA expropriation claims have used the phrase 'substantial deprivation' to describe what they consider to be the intensity standard for indirect expropriation.[21] A typical example is *Allard*: 'the first requirement for a successful claim of indirect expropriation is that ... the investor ha[s] suffered a substantial deprivation of the use or expected

[19] *Philip Morris Brands SÀRL, Philip Morris Products S.A. and Abal Hermanos S.A.* v. *Oriental Republic of Uruguay*, ICSID, ARB/10/7, Award of 8 July 2016, para 192; see also *Telenor Mobile Communications A.S.* v. *Republic of Hungary*, ICSID, ARB/04/15, Award of 13 September 2006, paras 65, 70; *Archer Daniels Midland Company and Tate & Lyle Ingredients Americas, Inc.* v. *United Mexican States*, NAFTA-ICSID, ARB(AF)/04/05, Award of 21 November 2007, para 240; Kinnear (2006) note 5 at 1110-15.

[20] *Valeri Belokon* v. *Kyrgyz Republic*, UNCITRAL, Award of 24 October 2014, para 206; *Cargill, Incorporated* v. *United Mexican States*, NAFTA-ICSID, ARB(AF)/05/2, Award of 18 September 2009, para 359; *Deutsche Bank AG* v. *Democratic Socialist Republic of Sri Lanka*, ICSID, ARB/09/2, Award of 31 October 2012, para 503; Jack Coe, Jr, Noah Rubins, 'Regulatory Expropriation and the *Tecmed* Case: Context and Contributions' in Todd Weiler (ed.), *International Investment Law and Arbitration: Leading Cases from the ICSID, NAFTA, Bilateral Treaties and Customary International Law* (London: Cameron May 2005) 597–667 at 620; Hoffmann (2008) note 12 at 158–60; López (2014) note 7 at 201.

[21] An overview of formulations used in case-law can also be found in Newcombe (2009) note 7 at 344–5.

economic benefit of the investment'.[22] Alternatively, for example 'a substantial deprivation of the Claimants' rights',[23] 'of the Claimant's investment',[24] 'of the value of an investment'[25] or 'of property forming all or a material part of the investment'[26] may be required. The exact phrasing was used by tribunals *suo voce* (that is: not reporting party positions) in at least twenty-five awards,[27] eg *AIG*, *Allard*, *Belokon*, *BG*, *Biwater Gauff*, *Bosh*, *Burlington*, *Chemtura*, *CMS*, *Copper Mesa*, *Deutsche Bank*, *El Paso*, *Foresight*, *Czescik*, *Liman*, *Merrill & Ring*, *Philip Morris*, *Pope & Talbot*, *Quiborax*, *RosInvestCo*, *Saipem*, *Sempra Energy*, *Suez I*, *Total* and *UP and CD*.[28] Linguistic variations within the

[22] *Peter A Allard* v. *Government of Barbados*, PCA 2012-06, Award of 27 June 2016, para 263.

[23] *Bosh International, Inc. and B&P, LTD Foreign Investments Enterprise* v. *Ukraine*, ICSID, ARB/08/11, 25 October 2012, para 218.

[24] *Chemtura Corporation* v. *Government of Canada*, NAFTA-UNCITRAL, Award of 2 August 2010, para 242.

[25] *Total S.A.* v. *Argentine Republic*, ICSID, ARB/04/1, Award of 27 December 2010, para 195.

[26] *Liman Caspian Oil BV and NCL Dutch Investment BV* v. *Republic of Kazakhstan*, ICSID, ARB/07/14, Award of 22 June 2010, para 293.

[27] For ease of reference, awards listed in this chapter will usually, but not necessarily, be ordered alphabetically, rather than chronologically.

[28] *AIG Capital Partners Inc. and CJSC Tema Real Estate Company* v. *Republic of Kazakhstan*, ICSID, ARB/01/6, Award of 7 October 2003 at 55; *Allard* (2016) note 22 at para 263; *Belokon* (2014) note 20 at para 206; *BG Group Plc.* v. *Republic of Argentina*, UNCITRAL, Final Award of 24 December 2007, para 271; *Biwater Gauff (Tanzania) Ltd.* v. *United Republic of Tanzania*, ICSID, ARB/05/22, Award of 24 July 2008, para 463; *Bosh* (2012) note 23 at para 218; *Burlington* (2012) note 9 at para 396; *Chemtura* (2010) note 24 at para 242; *CMS Gas Transmission Company* v. *Argentine Republic*, ICSID, ARB/01/8, Award of 12 May 2005, para 262; *Copper Mesa Mining Corporation* v. *Republic of Ecuador*, UNCITRAL, PCA 2012-2, Award of 15 March 2016, para 6.59; *Deutsche Bank* (2012) note 20 at para 503; *Tomasz Częścik and Robert Aleksandrowicz v. Republic of Cyprus*, SCC, V 2014/169, Award of 11 February 2017, para 216; *El Paso Energy International Company* v. *Argentine Republic*, ICSID, ARB/03/15, Award of 31 October 2011, para 248; *Foresight Luxembourg Solar 1 S.à.r.l., Foresight Luxembourg Solar 2 S.à.r.l., Greentech Energy System A/S, GWM Renewable Energy I S.p.A. and GWM Renewable Energy II S.p.A* v. *Kingdom of Spain*, SCC, 2015/150, Award of 14 November 2018, para 429; *Liman* (2010) note 26 at para 293; *Merrill & Ring Forestry L. P.* v. *Government of Canada*, NAFTA-UNCITRAL, Award of 31 March 2010, para 145; *Philip Morris* (2016) note 19 at para 192; *Pope & Talbot* (2000) note 8 at para 102; *Quiborax* (2015) note 9 at para 238; *RosInvestCo UK Ltd.* v. *The Russian Federation*, SCC, V 079/2005, Final Award of 12 September 2010, para 623; *Saipem* (2009) note 12 at para 133; *Sempra Energy International* v. *Argentine Republic*, ICSID, ARB/02/16, Award of 28 September 2007, para 284; *Suez, Sociedad General de Aguas de Barcelona S.A. and InterAgua Servicios Integrales del Agua S.A.* v. *Argentine Republic*, ICSID, ARB/03/17, Decision on Liability of 30 July 2010, para 123; *Total* (2010) note 25 at para 195; *UP and C.D. Holding Internationale* v. *Hungary*, ICSID ARB/13/35, Award of 9 October 2018, para 305; see also Joshua Elcombe, 'Regulatory Powers vs. Investment Protection under NAFTA's Chapter 1110: *Metalclad*, *Methanex*, and *Glamis Gold*' 68 *University of Toronto Faculty of Law Review* (2010) 71–98 at 80; Arno E Gildemeister,

substantial deprivation standard[29] were used in at least nine more awards:[30]

- *Enkev*: 'the requirement under international law for the investor to establish the substantial, radical, severe, devastating or fundamental deprivation of its rights';[31]
- *Fireman's Fund (Corn Products)*: '[t]he taking must be a substantially complete deprivation of the economic use and enjoyment of the rights to the property';[32]
- *Perenco*: '[judicial standards] tend in the direction of positing a very substantial amount of deprivation';[33]
- *Plama*: 'substantially complete deprivation of the economic use and enjoyment of the rights to the investment';[34]
- *RDC*: 'the claimant is deprived substantially of the use and benefits of the investment';[35]
- *Telenor*: 'the interference with the investor's rights must be such as substantially to deprive the investor of the economic value, use or enjoyment of its investment';[36]

'Case Comment: *Burlington Resources, Inc v Republic of Ecuador*: How Much Is Too Much: When Is Taxation Tantamount to Expropriation?' 29 *ICSID Review* (2014) 315–20 at 317; Oliver R Jones, Chido Dunn, 'Consent, Forced Renegotiation and Expropriation in International Law, 26 *Arbitration International* (2010) 391–408 at 398; Ursula Kriebaum, 'Partial Expropriation' 8 *Journal of World Investment & Trade* (2007) 69–84 at 69; Newcombe (2009) note 7 at 345; Salacuse (2010) note 7 at 308; Brigitte Stern, 'In Search of the Frontiers of Indirect Expropriation' in Arthur W Rovine (ed.), *Contemporary Issues in International Arbitration and Mediation: The Fordham Papers 2007* (Leiden: Nijhoff 2008) 29–51 at 43.

29 See also Hoffmann (2008) note 12 at 157; Kinnear (2006) note 5 at 1110-15; López (2014) note 7 at 201.

30 In this chapter, dash lists will, for ease of reference, provide quotations from case-law without following the academic custom of putting long passages in block quotes.

31 *Enkev Beheer B.V.* v. *Republic of Poland*, UNCITRAL, PCA 2013-01, First Partial Award of 29 April 2014, para 344.

32 *Fireman's Fund* (2006) note 16 at para 176; *Corn Products International, Inc.* v. *United Mexican States*, NAFTA-ICSID, ARB(AF)/04/01, Decision on Responsibility of 15 January 2008, para 91; see also *Karkey Karadeniz Elektrik Uretim A.S.* v. *Islamic Republic of Pakistan*, ICSID, ARB/13/1, Award of 22 August 2017, para 648, linking the phrase 'use and enjoyment' to contractual expropriation.

33 *Perenco Ecuador Limited* v. *Republic of Ecuador*, ICSID, ARB/08/6, Decision on Remaining Issues of Jurisdiction and on Liability of 12 September 2014, para 673.

34 *Plama Consortium Limited* v. *Republic of Bulgaria*, ICSID, ARB/03/24, Award of 27 August 2008, para 193; *Marfin Investment Group Holdings S.A., Alexandros Bakatselos and others* v. *Republic of Cyprus*, ICSID, ARB/13/27, Award of 26 July 2018, para 823.

35 *Railroad Development Corporation (RDC)* v. *Republic of Guatemala*, ICSID, ARB/07/23, Award of 29 June 2012, para 151.

36 *Telenor* (2006) note 19 at para 65.

- *Tokios Tokelės*: 'the state must deprive the investor of a "substantial" part of the value of the investment';[37]
- *Windstream*: 'the first step in the process of determining whether an effective taking has taken place is to determine whether the investor has been substantially deprived of the value of its investment'.[38]

A number of awards use phrases which could be seen as hewing reasonably close to the substantial deprivation standard, although '[t]he language chosen to express the triggering degree of deprivation is unsettled'.[39] It is an open question whether tribunals intended to propagate essentially the same standard by using these phrases. It is also unclear to which degree a neutral or favourable quotation of these phrases by later awards can be taken as endorsement – particularly if a number of different formulations is provided or if they are used obiter.

Formulations which retain the noun but drop the adjective 'substantial' are at least grammatically close:

- Taking their cue from *Tecmed*, in *Cargill II*, *Glamis Gold*, *National Grid* and *Toto*, tribunals postulated a standard of 'radical deprivation', which seems close but more restrictive than the substantial deprivation standard: 'it must be first determined if the Claimant . . . was radically deprived of the economical use and enjoyment of its investments'.[40]
- In *Venezuela Holdings*, the tribunal held that 'a measure . . . may be equivalent to an expropriation if it gives rise to an *effective deprivation* of the investment as a whole'.[41]
- In *Roussalis*, the tribunal merely spoke of 'a deprivation of the economic use and enjoyment', qualifying it further by requiring that

[37] *Tokios Tokelės* (2007) note 10 at para 120.

[38] *Windstream Energy LLC* v. *Canada*, UNCITRAL, PCA, Award of 27 September 2016, para 285.

[39] Coe (2005) note 20 at 621.

[40] *Técnicas Medioambientales Tecmed S.A.* v. *United Mexican States*, ICSID, ARB(AF)/00/2, Award of 29 May 2003, para 115; *Cargill II* (2009) note 20 at para 360; *National Grid plc* v. *The Argentine Republic*, UNCITRAL, Award of 3 November 2008, para 149; *Toto Costruzioni Generali S.p.A.* v. *Republic of Lebanon*, ICSID, ARB/07/12, Decision on Jurisdiction of 11 September 2009, para 183 (citing *National Grid*); *Glamis Gold, Ltd.* v. *United States of America*, NAFTA-UNCITRAL, Award of 8 June 2009, para 357.

[41] *Venezuela Holdings, B.V., Mobil Cerro Negro Holding, Ltd., Mobil Venezolana de Petróleos Holdings, Inc., Mobil Cerro Negro, Ltd., Mobil Venezolana de Petróleos, Inc.* v. *Bolivarian Republic of Venezuela*, ICSID, ARB/07/27, Award of 9 October 2014, para 286 (emphasis added).

a measure must have such an effect 'as if the rights related thereto, such as the income or benefits, had ceased to exist'.[42]

- A number of awards have used variations of the *Metalclad* standard: 'interference . . . which has the effect of *depriving* the owner, *in whole or in significant part*, of the use or reasonably-to-be-expected economic benefit of property',[43] such as *AES, AIG, Alpha, Anglia Auto, Azurix, A11Y, CME, CMS, E energija, Encana* and *Occidental I*.[44]

Finally, a number of awards replace the noun but retain the adjective, which may indicate a greater divergence from 'substantial deprivation': *ADM, MCI* and *Servier* use 'substantial interference';[45] *LG&E* and *Metalpar* speak of substantial impact;[46] and *Ryan* mentions 'the total loss or substantial impairment of the investment'.[47]

Some tribunals also link substantial deprivation more strongly to IIA expropriation clauses, namely by turning them into necessary or sufficient conditions for a finding of expropriation. In *Burlington*, the tribunal held that 'there can be no expropriation in the absence of substantial

[42] *Spyridon Roussalis* v. *Romania*, ICSID, ARB/06/1, Award of 7 December 2011, para 328.

[43] *Metalclad Corporation* v. *United Mexican States*, NAFTA-ICSID, ARB(AF)/97/1, Award of 30 August 2000, para 103 (emphasis added).

[44] *AES Summit Generation Limited and AES-Tisza Erömü Kft.* v. *Republic of Hungary (II)*, ICSID, ARB/07/22, Award of 23 September 2010, para 14.3.1; *AIG* (2003) note 28 at 55; *Alpha Projektholding GmbH* v. *Ukraine*, ICSID, ARB/07/16, Award of 8 November 2010, para 408; *Anglia Auto Accessories Limited* v. *Czech Republic*, SCC, V 2014/181, Final Award of 10 March 2017, para 292; *Azurix* v. *Argentina*, ICSID, ARB/01/12, Award of 14 July 2006, para 316; *A11Y Ltd.* v. *Czech Republic*, ICSID-UNCITRAL, UNCT/15/1, Award of 29 June 2018, para 196; *CME Czech Republic B.V.* v. *Czech Republic*, UNCITRAL, Partial Award of 13 September 2001, para 606; *CMS* (2005) note 28 at para 262; *UAB E energija (Lithuania)* v. *Republic of Latvia*, ICSID, ARB/12/33, Award of 22 December 2017, para 1074; *EnCana Corporation* v. *Republic of Ecuador*, UNCITRAL, LCIA UN3481, Award of 3 February 2006, para 177; *Occidental Exploration and Production Co.* v. *Ecuador*, UNCITRAL, LCIA, UN3467, Award of 1 July 2004, para 87. For an early example outside investment arbitration, see also *Elettronica Sicula SpA (ELSI) (United States of America* v. *Italy)*, Judgment of 20 July 1989, ICJ Reports (1989) 15 at 71 (para 119).

[45] *ADM* (2007) note 19 at para 240; *M.C.I. Power Group L.C. and New Turbine Inc.* v. *Republic of Ecuador*, NAFTA-ICSID, ARB/03/6, Award of 31 July 2007, para 300; *Les Laboratoires Servier, S.A.S., Biofarma, S.A.S., Arts et Techniques du Progrès S.A. S.* v. *Republic of Poland*, UNCITRAL, Final Award of 14 February 2012, para 576.

[46] *LG&E Energy Corp., LG&E Capital Corp. and LG&E International Inc.* v. *Argentine Republic*, ICSID, ARB/02/1, Decision on Liability of 3 October 2006, para 191; *Metalpar S.A. and Buen Aire S.A.* v. *Argentine Republic*, ICSID, ARB/03/5, Award on the Merits of 6 June 2008, paras 172–3.

[47] *Vincent J. Ryan, Schooner Capital LLC, and Atlantic Investment Partners LLC* v. *Republic of Poland*, ICSID, ARB(AF)/11/3, Award of 24 November 2015, para 472.

deprivation'[48] – for this tribunal, substantial deprivation is a necessary condition and must be established 'for *any* expropriation'.[49] This was criticised by the dissenting arbitrator Francisco Orrego Vicuña: ' substantial deprivation is an appropriate standard . . ., *albeit not the only one*'.[50] In contrast, in *UP and CD*, the tribunal found that 'a substantial deprivation *alone* will suffice'[51] – substantial deprivation is thus a sufficient condition. Only this can rightly be called a 'sole effects' doctrine.

Tribunals have identified substantial deprivation as concerned with economic privation, having an impact, for example on property, notwithstanding that IIA clauses explicitly define 'investment' as the object of expropriation.[52] The *Teinver* tribunal held that '[t]he essence of expropriation is a taking or deprivation of de facto or de jure rights of ownership'.[53] In *Belokon*, the tribunal held that it 'depends on whether there has been a substantial deprivation *of the benefits of property ownership*'[54] or 'of its economic rights'.[55] *Occidental I* mentioned 'that this deprivation . . . relates to the use of the property or a reasonably expected economic benefit',[56] citing *Metalclad*, which employed a similar general characterisation to those that use substantial deprivation: 'interference with the use of property which has the effect of *depriving* the owner, in whole or in *significant* part, of the use or reasonably-to-be-expected economic *benefit of property*'.[57]

The tribunal in *Biwater Gauff* (echoed by *Deutsche Bank*), in contrast, 'whilst accepting that effects of a certain severity must be shown to qualify an act as expropriatory', argued that '[a] distinction must be drawn

48 *Burlington* (2012) note 9 at para 456.

49 *Tokios Tokelės* (2007) note 10 at para 120 (emphasis added).

50 *Burlington* (2012) note 9, dissenting opinion Orrego Vicuña at para 24.

51 *UP and CD* (2018) note 28 at para 305 (emphasis added).

52 Noted eg by Kriebaum (2008a) note 7 at 309–10.

53 *Teinver S.A., Transportes de Cercanías S.A. and Autobuses Urbanos del Sur S.A.* v. *Argentine Republic*, ICSID, ARB/09/1, Award of 21 July 2017, para 937; see also *Wena Hotels Limited* v. *Arab Republic of Egypt*, ICSID, ARB/98/4, Award on the Merits of 8 December 2000, para 99; *Wena Hotels Limited* v. *Arab Republic of Egypt*, ICSID, ARB/98/4, Decision on Interpretation, 31 October 2005, paras 119–20.

54 *Belokon* (2014) note 20 at para 206 (emphasis added); see also *AIG* (2003) note 28 at 55; *BG* (2007) note 28 at paras 260–2; *Charanne B.V., Construction Investments S.A.R.L.* v. *Kingdom of Spain*, SCC, 062/2012, Award of 21 January 2016, para 460.

55 *S.D. Myers, Inc.* v. *Government of Canada*, NAFTA-UNCITRAL, Partial Award of 13 November 2000, para 283.

56 *Occidental I* (2004) note 44 at para 88.

57 *Metalclad* (2000) note 43 at para 103 (emphasis added).

between (a) interference with rights and (b) economic loss. A substantial interference with rights may well occur without actually causing any economic damage.'[58] For the tribunal, 'the absence of economic loss or damage is primarily a matter of causation and quantum – rather than a necessary ingredient in the cause of action of expropriation itself'. It felt that there could 'have been a substantial interference with an investor's rights . . . such that no economic loss actually results',[59] but which would still fulfil the indirect expropriation *Tatbestand* in the IIA.

In tribunal case-law, there are two points of convergence on what the substantial deprivation standard entails. The first could be called the 'equivalence' or 'net effect' test; the idea that substantial deprivation for indirect expropriation means that the result must in effect be the same as a direct expropriation:

- *Allard*: 'a substantial deprivation' means 'that the investor must establish that the effect of the measures . . . resembles the effect of a direct expropriation';[60]
- *ECE*: 'the interference . . . short of an outright taking of the property but equivalent in terms of its intensity, seriousness and duration of its effects, . . . may . . . give rise to a finding of an indirect expropriation';[61]
- *Electrabel*: the Claimant has 'to establish that the effect . . . was materially the same as if its investment . . . had been nationalised or directly expropriated';[62]
- *Oxus Gold* (*Foresight*, *Olin*, *Tidewater*, *Vivendi*): a measure 'must be equivalent to the effect of a direct expropriation in order to be qualified as expropriatory';[63]

[58] *Biwater Gauff* (2008) at para 464.
[59] *Biwater Gauff* (2008) at para 465; see also *Deutsche Bank* (2012) note 20 at paras 504–5.
[60] *Allard* (2016) note 22 at para 263.
[61] *ECE Projektmanagement International GmbH and Kommanditgesellschaft PANTA Achtundsechzigste Grundstücksgesellschaft mbH & Co* v. *Czech Republic*, UNCITRAL, PCA 2010-5, Award of 19 September 2013, para 4.813.
[62] *Electrabel S.A.* v. *Republic of Hungary*, ICSID, ARB/07/19, Decision on Jurisdiction, Applicable Law and Liability of 30 November 2012, para 6.53; see also *Enkev* (2014) note 31 at para 341.
[63] *Oxus Gold Plc* v. *Republic of Uzbekistan*, UNCITRAL, Award of 17 December 2015, para 745; *Foresight* (2018) note 28 at para 430; *Olin Holdings Limited* v. *Libya*, ICC, 20355/MCP, Final Award of 25 May 2018, para 165 (unclear); *Tidewater Investment SRL and Tidewater Caribe, C.A.* v. *Bolivarian Republic of Venezuela*, ICSID, ARB/10/5, Award of 13 March 2015, para 104; *Compañia de Aguas Del Aconquija SA and Vivendi Universal SA* v. *Argentine Republic*, ICSID, ARB/97/3, Award of 20 August 2007, para 7.5.24; see also Daniel Clough, 'Regulatory Expropriations and Competition under NAFTA' 6 *Journal of World Investment & Trade* (2005) 553–84 at 564; UNCTAD (2012) note 5 at 63.

- *RosInvestCo*: 'the Tribunal should evaluate whether the "net effect" of the measure ... is the same as an outright expropriation, i.e., a substantial or total deprivation of the economic value of an asset';[64]
- *Saar Papier*: '[m]easures similar to expropriation must be deemed to be measures that have an economic impact that is comparable to the economic impact of an expropriation'.[65]

The second point of convergence is the very idea behind the substantial deprivation test: deprivation must be measures of a high degree of intensity. Section 8.2.2 will show which sub-standards case-law has developed to concretise this test, but there are also a number of general observations on what this entails:

- *ADM*: 'deprives the investor of all or most of the benefits of the investment';[66]
- *CMS*: 'the enjoyment of the property has been effectively neutralized';[67]
- *Electrabel*: 'that its investment lost all significant economic value ... the substantial, radical, severe, devastating or fundamental deprivation of its rights or the virtual annihilation, effective neutralisation or factual destruction of its investment';[68]
- *Glamis Gold*: '"substantially impair[ed] the investor's economic rights, i.e. ownership, use, enjoyment or management of the business, by *rendering them useless* ..."';[69]
- *National Grid*: 'the effect that the measures concerned must have: neutralization, radical deprivation, irretrievable loss, inability to use, enjoy or dispose of the property';[70]

64 *RosInvestCo* (2010) note 28 at para 624; see also McLachlan (2007) note 7 at 298.

65 *Saar Papier Vertriebs GmbH* v. *Republic of Poland*, UNCITRAL, Final Award of 16 October 1995, para 84.

66 *ADM* (2007) note 19 at para 240.

67 *CMS* (2005) note 28 at para 262; see also *Copper Mesa* (2016) note 28 at para 6.59.

68 *Electrabel* (2012) note 62 at paras 6.53, 6.62.

69 *Glamis Gold* (2009) note 40 at para 357 (emphasis added), citing an earlier version of: Catherine Yannaca-Small, '"Indirect Expropriation" and the "Right to Regulate" in International Investment Law' in OECD (ed.), *International Investment Law: A Changing Landscape: A Companion Volume to International Investment Perspectives* (Paris: OECD 2005) 43–72 at 55; see also *Telenor* (2006) note 19 at para 65; *Suez I* (2010) note 28 at para 123; *Achmea B.V. (formerly Eureko B.V.)* v. *The Slovak Republic*, UNCITRAL, PCA 2008-13, Final Award of 7 December 2012, para 288.

70 *National Grid* (2008) note 40 at para 149.

- *Perenco*: 'deprivation need not be complete, but it must be very substantial';[71]
- *Philip Morris*: 'a major adverse impact';[72]
- *Pope & Talbot*: 'sufficiently restrictive to support a conclusion that the property has been "taken" from the owner';[73]
- *Total*: 'a total loss of value of the property'.[74]

Academic commentary has provided additional points,[75] such as that the 'interference must approach total impairment',[76] yet that substantial deprivation 'obviously does not mean ... a total taking that leaves the investor without any residual rights'[77] or that 'at least a substantial loss of control and value or severe economic impact is required'.[78] The frequent reference of tribunal definitions of the substantial deprivation test to concepts like 'use' and 'value' means that an absolute, positive, but general description of the content of the substantial deprivation test is not regarded as particularly helpful; in effect, this is why tribunal jurisprudence has developed a number of sub-standards to further refine this test.

8.2.2 Sub-standards

Sometimes, tribunals have talked in general terms about the nature of expropriation. When they did so, they tended indirectly to elucidate what elements the concept of substantial deprivation contains. For example, in *Parkerings*, the tribunal mentioned that indirect expropriation is linked to 'a deprivation of the *enjoyment of the property*'.[79] In *Mamidoil*'s 'literal translation' of expropriation, it is 'a specific effect on property itself and not a damage inflicted to property', for its indirect form consists of 'an indirect deprivation of one or several of its essential characteristics', that

[71] *Perenco* (2014) note 33 at para 673; see also *Servier* (2012) note 45 at para 576.
[72] *Philip Morris* (2016) note 19 at para 192.
[73] *Pope & Talbot* (2000) note 8 at para 102.
[74] *Total* (2010) note 25 at para 195.
[75] One helpful summary of the standard for level of interference developed in case-law can be found in Fortier (2004) note 6 at 305; see also Kriebaum (2008a) note 7 at 313–15.
[76] Coe (2005) note 20 at 621.
[77] Kriebaum (2007a) note 28 at 71; see also Kriebaum (2008a) note 7 at 315.
[78] Energy Charter Secretariat, *Expropriation Regime under the Energy Charter Treaty* (Brussels: Energy Charter Secretariat 2012) 39.
[79] *Parkerings-Compagniet AS* v. *Republic of Lithuania*, ICSID, ARB/05/8, Award of 11 September 2007, para 437 (emphasis added).

is 'its use and enjoyment, control and possession, and disposal and alienation'.[80] *Suez I* specifically linked the loss of 'the economic substance of the investment' to substantial deprivation.[81] The *Metalclad* line of cases, with its emphasis on the deprivation 'of the use or reasonably to be expected benefit of property',[82] does so as well. Because, as Rudolf Dolzer and Christoph Schreuer argue, '[t]he effect of the measure upon the economic benefit and value as well as upon the control ... is the key question ... Tribunals have accordingly based their decisions on economic considerations.'[83] Andrew Newcombe and Lluís Paradell classify the 'effects-based substantial deprivation requirement' as 'a necessary *factual* predicate for a determination of *legal liability* for expropriation',[84] which is telling. Is substantial deprivation a standard of fact or is it merely the judicial term for a range of dispositions in fact which are typically subsumed as indirect expropriation? In *Chemtura*, the tribunal held that the question of 'whether the effects of the measures challenged are to "substantially" deprive the investor ... is a matter of *degree* and not one of specific conditions'.[85]

Ortino offers useful guidance in this matter:

> The key issue here is identifying the 'object' of the deprivation. In the absence of any textual reference, investment tribunals have focused on a variety of aspects including the deprivation of the control, use, benefit, enjoyment, value of the investment. . . . Tribunals tend to list several of the factors mentioned above ... but they chose different combinations. More problematically, it is not altogether clear whether each factor is individually sufficient in order to establish an expropriation or whether they are cumulative requirements.[86]

The first quoted sentence is telling – these considerations seem to relate to the *object*, not the *modus*. But does Ortino mean the object of expropriation (the investment) or an object of deprivation as something conceptually different? The substantial deprivation standard could be structured along at least two lines: first, substantial deprivation is a significant interference (modus) with the control, use, benefit, value,

[80] *Mamidoil Jetoil Greek Petroleum Products Société S.A.* v. *Republic of Albania*, ICSID, ARB/11/24, Award of 30 March 2015, para 569.

[81] *Suez I* (2010) note 28 at para 127.

[82] *AIG* (2003) note 28 at 55; see also eg *Allard* (2016) note 22 at para 263; *Metalclad* (2000) note 43 at para 103.

[83] Dolzer (2012) note 7 at 112; see also Fortier (2004) note 6 at 300–1.

[84] Newcombe (2009) note 7 at 344.

[85] *Chemtura* (2010) note 24 at para 247.

[86] Ortino (2016) note 17 at 357.

etc. *of the investment* (object); second, to deprive an investment (object) substantially *means* affecting control, use, benefit, value, etc. to a significant degree (modus). Some support the first reading, for example Ursula Kriebaum, in an illustration in her monograph where she differentiates 'object' (investment/property) 'rights to the object' (control, use, benefit, value, etc.) and 'intensity of the measure', incorporating substantial deprivation.[87] Yet she too treats the sub-standards as in a wider sense belonging to the intensity question. Particularly in light of the fact that there is a significant conceptual overlap between 'measure' and 'object', we will proceed on the basis of the first construction.

The *Pope & Talbot* award is a leading case in this respect too; it is referred to by many awards as listing a number of indicative elements for the substantial deprivation test. However, the original award does not fully support the confident claims of later jurisprudence; its list is merely a report of a witness statement: '[t]he Investor's (and the Investment's) Operations Controller testified at the hearing that . . .'.[88] Later awards have made it quasi-canonical and we will therefore quote *Chemtura*'s restatement:

> In *Pope & Talbot*, the tribunal referred to a number of criteria to determine whether there had been an indirect expropriation, including:
>
> (i) whether the investor remained in control of its investment,
> (ii) whether it directed its day-to-day operations,
> (iii) whether its officers and employees were detained by the State,
> (iv) whether the State supervised the work of the investor's officers and employees or not,
> (v) whether the State had taken the proceeds of sales other than through taxation,
> (vi) whether the State interfered with management or shareholders' activities,
> (vii) whether the State prevented the distribution of dividends to shareholders,
> (viii) whether the State interfered with the appointment of directors or management, and
> (ix) whether the State had taken any other actions ousting the investor from full ownership and control of the investment.[89]

[87] Kriebaum (2008a) note 7 at 321.
[88] *Pope & Talbot* (2000) note 8 at para 100.
[89] *Chemtura* (2010) note 24 at para 245 (formatting changed).

For the *Enron* tribunal, this list 'is … representative of the legal standard required to make a finding of indirect expropriation. Substantial deprivation results in that light from … managing the day-to-day operations of the company, [etc.].'[90] In contrast, the *Telenor* award, like some others, preferred a list of measures which 'have been held to amount to indirect expropriation' to the list of sub-standards.[91] A wide range of factors is mentioned in case-law, but it is common to distinguish two categories: the loss of value in a wide sense and, because investments under IIAs are almost always companies, the loss of use and control;[92] legitimate expectations are sometimes added as a third group.[93] We will follow this practice below, although we will ignore legitimate expectations.

1. *Diminution of value, profits or income.* Case-law makes do with relatively abstract formulas and concepts, even at this level of specificity. This could in part be because of the strong belief in the 'fact-based' nature of the standard: most (but not all) tribunals have little patience for a prolonged discussion of the substantial deprivation standard at a relatively high level of specificity. They tend to show great alacrity in turning to the application of the law to the facts of the case, subsuming without developing a detailed judicial sub-standard, like the *Chemtura* award:

> The Tribunal is however of the view that it does not need to settle that legal controversy to decide the case before it. The determination of whether there has been a 'substantial deprivation' is a fact-sensitive exercise to be conducted in the light of the circumstances of each case. …

[90] *Enron Corporation Ponderosa Assets LP* v. *Argentine Republic*, ICSID, ARB/01/3, Award of 22 May 2007, para 245; see also *PSEG Global Inc. and Konya Ilgin Elektrik Üretim ve Ticaret Limited Sirketi* v. *Republic of Turkey*, ICSID, ARB/02/5, Award of 19 January 2007, para 278; *Sempra Energy* (2007) note 28 at para 284; *Tidewater* (2015) note 63 at para 105; *Walter Bau AG* v. *Kingdom of Thailand*, UNCITRAL, Award of 1 July 2009, para 10.16 (blind quote via *PSEG*); McLachlan (2007) note 7 at 312.

[91] *Telenor* (2006) note 19 at para 69.

[92] *ADM* (2007) note 19 at para 241; *AES* (2010) note 44 at para 14.3.1; *Plama* (2008) note 34 at paras 191–2; *Vivendi* (2007) note 63 at para 7.5.17; UNCTAD (2012) note 5 at 65; Christian Zielonka, *Der Ausgleich zwischen Investorenschutz- und Regulierungsinteressen in internationalen Investitionsschutzabkommen* (Berlin: Duncker & Humblot 2017) 98.

[93] *RosInvestCo* (2010) note 28 at para 624; see also *Hesham Talaat M. Al-Warraq* v. *Republic of Indonesia*, UNCITRAL, Final Award of 15 December 2014, para 524; Justin R Marlles, 'Public Purpose, Private Losses: Regulatory Expropriation and Environmental Regulation in International Investment Law' 16 *Journal of Transnational Law and Policy* (2006–7) 275–336 at 281.

> Given the diversity of situations that may arise in practice, it is preferable to examine each situation in the light of its own specific circumstances.[94]

Nonetheless, a few points can be made. First, while loss of use or control and loss of value or income are often named in one, sometimes the distinction is decisive.[95] Second, sometimes tribunals distinguish even on the *Tatbestand* level – rather than for the calculation of damages – between (book) value and (expected) levels of income and/or profits. For example, in *Cargill II*, the award held that 'business income of an investment is an integral part of the value ... both as an element of a larger investment involving the physical asset and as an investment in and of itself'.[96] In *ADM*, however, the question was answered in the negative: 'the test for expropriation under Article 1110 cannot be ... based exclusively on the Claimants' loss of profits, which is not necessarily a sufficient sole criterion for an expropriation'.[97] Mostly, however, tribunals have focused on the *value* of the investment *sensu largo*, for example *Burlington*: 'what appears to be decisive, in assessing whether there is a substantial deprivation, is the loss of the economic value or economic viability of the investment'.[98] In *Glamis Gold*, a lengthy comparison of value pre- and post-measures was the sole focus of the tribunal's considerations on whether the *Tatbestand* of indirect expropriation had been realised.[99]

Two negative and two positive conditions have been developed in case-law in relation to the diminution of value. The most important negative condition seems to be that the *mere* loss of (some) value of the investment is not enough. It seems to be implied in the substantial deprivation standard that a 1 per cent reduction in the value of an investment is not enough to trigger indirect expropriation. In denying that 'a mere loss of value' constituted an indirect expropriation, the *Mamidoil* tribunal felt that 'a further extension into the sphere of damages, loss of value and profitability, without regard to the substance and attributes of property, would deprive the claim of its distinct nature'.[100] What the 'mere loss' condition means exactly, however, is unclear. For

[94] *Chemtura* (2010) note 24 at para 249; see also *Tokios Tokelės* (2007) note 10 at para 120; Gibson (2015) note 5 at 306; Newcombe (2009) note 7 at 344; W Michael Reisman, Robert D Sloane, 'Indirect Expropriation and Its Valuation in the BIT Generation' 74 *British Year Book of International Law 2003* (2004) 115–50 at 122.

[95] Eg *Burlington* (2012) note 9 at para 397.

[96] *Cargill II* (2009) note 20 at paras 356, 359.

[97] *ADM* (2007) note 19 at para 248. This is echoed by UNCTAD (2012) note 5 at 66.

[98] *Burlington* (2012) note 9 at para 397; see also *Tecmed* (2003) note 40 at para 115.

[99] *Glamis Gold* (2009) note 40 at paras 361–536; see also Elcombe (2010) note 28 at 90.

[100] *Mamidoil* (2015) note 80 at para 570.

example, in *Charanne*, the tribunal held that '[a] simple decrease in the value of the ... investment cannot constitute an indirect expropriation, unless the loss of value is such that it can be considered equivalent to a deprivation of property'.[101] The *Suez I* award contains the following passage: 'The fact that the effect of such measures may have diminished the value of an investment does not in and of itself constitute an indirect expropriation.'[102]

Some tribunals go a step further. The *Philip Morris* tribunal's argument that 'as long as sufficient value remains ..., there is no expropriation'[103] is still part of the substantial deprivation standard. In contrast, the *E energija* award's holding that 'the fact that an investment has become worthless does not per se mean that there was an act of expropriation since investment always entails risk'[104] points to a stricter reading. *El Paso* looked at this issue in detail.[105] After reiterating the 'mere loss in value' doctrine, it admitted that 'some cases or general dicta ... might seem to support the idea that a substantial deprivation of the value of an investment can also be viewed as an expropriation'. It did not agree with this reading of case-law: '[F]or an expropriation to exist, the investor should be substantially deprived not only of the benefits, *but also of the use of his investment*. A mere loss of value, which is not the result of an interference with the control or use of the investment, is not an indirect expropriation.'[106]

The second and minor negative condition is that the mere loss of (additional) *profitability* does not suffice, made, for example, in *Philip Morris*: 'a partial loss of the profits that the investment would have

[101] *Charanne* (2016) note 54 at para 465: '[u]na simple disminución del valor ... de la inversión no puede por tanto caracterizar una expropiación indirecta, a menos que la pérdida de valor sea tal que se pueda considerar equivalente a una privación propiedad'; the unofficial translation is taken from *Foresight* (2018) note 28 at para 430, where the passage is quoted with approval.

[102] *Suez I* (2010) note 28 at para 126; see also Kriebaum (2008a) note 7 at 322, 324; Ursula Kriebaum, 'Expropriation' in Marc Bungenberg et al. (eds.), *International Investment Law* (Baden-Baden: Nomos 2015) 959–1030 at 984; Marlles (2006–7) note 94 at 293–4.

[103] *Philip Morris* (2016) note 19 at para 286.

[104] *E energija* (2017) note 44 at para 1077.

[105] *El Paso* (2011) note 28 at paras 249–56.

[106] *El Paso* (2011) note 28 at para 256 (emphasis added); see also *Grand River Enterprises Six Nations, Ltd., et al.* v. *United States of America*, NAFTA-UNCITRAL, Award of 12 January 2011, para 151, citing *CMS* (2005) note 28 at paras 262–4; LG&E (2006) note 46 at para 191; see also *Perenco* (2014) note 33 at para 682; *Novenergia II – Energy & Environment (SCA) (Grand Duchy of Luxembourg), SICAR* v. *Kingdom of Spain*, SCC 2015/063, Award of 15 February 2018, para 762; Kriebaum (2008a) note 7 at 324–5.

yielded absent the measure does not confer an expropriatory character on the measure'.[107] This ties in with the broader point made, inter alia, in *Waste Management*, that 'it is not the function of the international law of expropriation . . . to eliminate the normal commercial risks of a foreign investor'.[108] '[A]wards have consistently stated that not every disappointment in dealing with foreign governments will be considered an expropriation.'[109]

The first positive condition is founded on the belief that the 'question . . . whether a transfer can take place merely by a decrease in value of the original property' is 'now almost uniformly answered in the affirmative'.[110] Coe argues that if that is so, we must also 'admit. . . . . . that something short of 100% drop in value may trigger State liability'.[111] A number of awards simply apply the adjective 'substantial' (or some variant) to the drop in value required:

- *Alpha*: 'it is necessary to demonstrate that the investment has been deprived of a significant part of its value';[112]
- *Busta*: 'an expropriation takes place where an investor has been permanently deprived of the value of its investment in whole or in significant part. . . . [A] loss amounting to two-thirds of the total value . . . would represent a substantial loss of economic value';[113]
- *Cargill I*: 'the test to be applied is whether the investment, as a whole, has suffered a substantial erosion of value';[114]
- *Tokios Tokelės*: 'the state must deprive the investor of a "substantial" part of the value of the investment';[115]
- *UP and CD*: 'whether there was a substantial loss in value';[116]

[107] *Philip Morris* (2016) note 19 at para 286; see also *Burlington* (2012) note 9 at para 399; Fortier (2004) note 6 at 301; Zielonka (2017) note 92 at 100–1.

[108] *Waste Management Inc.* v. *United Mexican States*, NAFTA-ICSID, ARB(AF)/00/3, Award of 30 April 2004, para 177; see also *Marvin Roy Feldman Karpa* v. *Mexico*, NAFTA-ICSID, ARB(AF)/99/1, Award of 16 December 2002, para 112.

[109] Kinnear (2006) note 5 at 1110-17.

[110] Jones (2010) note 28 at 398.

[111] Coe (2005) note 20 at 664.

[112] *Alpha* (2010) note 44 at para 408.

[113] *I.P. Busta & J.P. Busta* v. *Czech Republic*, SCC, V 2015/014, Final Award of 10 March 2017, paras 389, 390.

[114] *Cargill, Incorporated* v. *Republic of Poland*, ICSID–UNCITRAL, ARB(AF)/04/2, Award of 29 February 2008, para 587.

[115] *Tokios Tokelės* (2007) note 10 at para 120; see also Zielonka (2017) note 92 at 99.

[116] *UP and CD* (2018) note 28 at para 333; see also Elcombe (2010) note 28 at 79–80: 'action which substantially diminishes the value of an investment'.

- *Glamis Gold*: 'whether there has been a radical diminution in value'.[117]

Other awards go further and require a total or near total destruction of value:

- *Enkev*: 'the Claimant must prove . . . that its investment . . . has lost all or almost all significant commercial value';[118]
- *Vivendi*: 'a complete or near complete deprivation of value (expropriation)';[119]
- *Oxus Gold*: 'the effective destruction of the value of the investment';[120]
- *Total*: '[a]n effective deprivation requires, however, a total loss of value of the property such as when the property affected is rendered worthless by the measure'.[121]

The second and minor positive condition is, in *Burlington*'s terms, 'the capacity to earn a commercial return', that is, 'that the investment's continuing capacity to generate a return has been virtually extinguished'.[122] An alternative formulation was employed obiter in *Metalclad*: 'negat[ing] the possibility of any meaningful return on Metalclad's investment',[123] another was employed obiter in *Tecmed*:

> [M]easures adopted by a State, whether regulatory or not, are an indirect de facto expropriation . . . if the assets or rights subject to such measure have been affected in such a way that '. . . any form of exploitation thereof . . .' has disappeared; i.e. the economic value of the use, enjoyment or disposition of the assets or rights affected by the administrative action or decision have been neutralized or destroyed.[124]

2. *Loss of use, management or control.* The second sub-standard is loss of the 'use of' and/or 'control over' the investment. As mentioned above, the idea of investments as going concern has traditionally given this aspect great importance, inter alia, in the jurisprudence of the Iran–US Claims

117 *Glamis Gold* (2009) note 40 at para 361.
118 *Enkev* (2014) note 31 at para 341.
119 *Vivendi* (2007) note 63 at para 7.5.11; see also UNCTAD (2012) note 5 at 65.
120 *Oxus Gold* (2015) note 63 at para 748.
121 *Total* (2010) note 25 at para 195; see also Stephan W Schill, 'Revisiting a Landmark: Indirect Expropriation and Fair and Equitable Treatment in the ICSID Case Tecmed' 3:2 *Transnational Dispute Management* (2006) 9–10.
122 *Burlington* (2012) note 9 at paras 397, 399.
123 *Metalclad* (2000) note 43 at para 113; see also Marlles (2006–7) note 94 at 293–4.
124 *Tecmed* (2003) note 40 at para 116.

Tribunal. There are voices which would see the loss of use and control as the *only* way to fulfil the substantial deprivation standard. The position taken by some tribunals, suggesting that loss of use and control is a necessary condition, is therefore to some extent coherent with this line of argument. They regularly posit an exclusion criterion or 'negative requirement': an investor continuing to (own and) operate the investment cannot be said to have been substantially deprived. 'In a number of cases', expropriation was held not to have occurred, 'especially so if the State did not interfere with the management and control of the investment and the investment remained operational':[125]

- *LG&E* (leading case): '[i]nterference with the investment's ability to carry on its business is not satisfied where the investment continues to operate, even if profits are diminished';[126]
- *EDF I*: '[n]o evidence has been presented to persuade us that Claimants were "substantially" deprived of their investment . . . [T]hey continued to own and operate EDEMSA';[127]
- *El Paso*: '[i]t is generally accepted that the decisive element in an indirect expropriation is the "*loss of control*" of a foreign investment, in the absence of any physical taking. ... [T]he tribunal considered that the measures adopted by the State did not deprive the investor of control over its investment and therefore concluded that there was no expropriation';[128]
- *EMV*: '[t]he Claimant retained not only legal title but full control of the investment throughout';[129]

125 Kriebaum (2015) note 102 at 986–7; see also UNCTAD (2012) note 5 at 68; Zielonka (2017) note 92 at 101–5.

126 *LG&E* (2006) note 46 at para 191, referring to *Pope & Talbot* (2000) note 8 at paras 101–2; see also *BG* (2007) note 28 at para 268; *CMS* (2005) note 28 at para 263; *Franck Charles Arif* v. *Republic of Moldova*, ICSID, ARB/11/23, Award of 8 April 2013, para 418. See for an early leading case, though not on the basis of an IIA but of a concession contract focusing on expropriatory acts preventing the exercise of effective control over the use of the property, *Revere Copper and Brass, Inc.* v. *Overseas Private Investment Corporation*, Award of 24 August 1978, 56 *International Law Reports* (1980) 258 at 291: '[T]he Jamaican Government's actions in repudiating its long term commitments to RJA have substantially the same impact on effective control over use and operation as if the properties were themselves conceded by a concession contract that was repudiated. In reaching this conclusion we are mindful that Government action impact must be on the *exercise* of control.'

127 *EDF International S.A., SAUR International S.A. and León Participaciones Argentinas S. A.* v. *Argentine Republic*, ICSID, ARB/03/23, Award of 11 June 2012, para 1113.

128 *El Paso* (2011) note 28 at paras 245, 248, referring to *Enron* (2007) note 90 at para 245; *Sempra Energy* (2007) note 28 at para 285; *Continental Casualty Company* v. *Argentine Republic*, ICSID, ARB/03/9, Award of 5 September 2008, para 276.

129 *EMV* (2009) note 14 at para 91.

- *Total* (on a different textual basis): '[t]he term "dispossession" therefore refers necessarily to the loss of the control which is characteristic of "possession" ... requiring a loss of material control over the investment'.[130]

Yet, this position is not unanimously held in awards and academic commentary; Dolzer and Schreuer's reasoning is typical for the critique:

> Control is obviously an important aspect in the analysis of a taking. However, the continued exercise of control by the investor in itself is not necessarily the sole criterion. The issue becomes obvious when a host state substantially deprives the investor of the value of the investment leaving the investor with control of an entity that amounts to not much more than a shell of the former investment. This illustrates the significance of a test which includes criteria other than control, such as economic use and benefit.[131]

Another major potential issue has been raised by Justin Marlles, who latches on to *Metalclad*'s 'emphasis on [the] use of the investment, rather than on the traditional question of control of the investment'; we should therefore 'distinguish "use" of an investment and "control" of an investment as two separate concepts': 'A foreign investor may control his or her asset but may not have a legal right, due to government regulation, to put it to its intended use':[132]

> A complete deprivation of use alone (without any diminution in control) is clearly a taking, whereas anything less than a complete use deprivation has since been found by NAFTA tribunals to be insufficient. ... On the other hand, regulations that significantly (but perhaps not completely) interfere in the internal operations of an investment or displace the claimant as the controlling shareholder doubtlessly constitute regulatory expropriation under the control standard, although the investor may retain some small ability to direct the management of the investment.[133]

On his reading of *Santa Elena* – contradicting *Feldman* – 'the loss of control must be complete before expropriation will be found ... [A] partial deprivation of control under international law would not constitute measures of sufficient extent.'[134] Equally, for Article 13 European

[130] *Total* (2010) note 25 at paras 193–4.
[131] Dolzer (2012) note 7 at 118.
[132] Marlles (2006–7) note 94 at 281–2.
[133] Marlles (2006–7) note 94 at 292–3.
[134] Marlles (2006–7) note 94 at 298.

Energy Charter Treaty 1994 (ECT), his reading of *Nykomb* (identified as the leading case) is that its 'focus on physical possession and management control, rather than on the use of the investment, remains the appropriate standard for identifying regulatory expropriation under the ECT'.[135]

While commendable as an attempt to dissect, analyse and group investment jurisprudence, it is difficult to find, in the wide range of combinations of formulations employed in case-law, this uniformity of purpose and rationality. It is submitted that this effort goes too far in attempting to promote (and impose) these notions of unity. In my analysis of the *stratum* of IIA awards, I was unable to discern, in the standards employed, a clear distinction between 'use' and 'control' or a preference for the latter over the former. An overview of case-law has to conclude that the matter is significantly less clear-cut:

- *ADM*: 'a first indication is whether the investor lost control of the investment by losing rights of ownership or management … An alternative criterion regarding intensity is whether the host State measure affects most of the investment's economic value·or renders useless the most economically optimal use of it';[136]
- *Blusun*: 'the sterilization of property …, rendering it impossible to use the property for its intended purpose, can amount to indirect expropriation';[137]
- *Burlington*: 'some tribunals have focused on the use and enjoyment of property. The loss of viability does not necessarily imply a loss of management or control. What matters is the capacity to earn a commercial return';[138]
- *Cargill II*: 'the Tribunal must find a radical deprivation of the Claimant's economic use and enjoyment of its investment';[139]
- *Copper Mesa*: 'indirect expropriation requires a substantial deprivation of the economic use and benefit of the investment';[140]
- *LG&E*: 'if due to the actions of the Respondent, the assets involved have lost their value or economic use for the Claimants';[141]
- *Nykomb*: '[t]he decisive factor for drawing the border line towards

135 Marlles (2006–7) note 94 at 324.

136 *ADM* (2007) note 19 at paras 244, 246; see also UNCTAD (2012) note 5 at 67.

137 *Blusun S.A., Jean-Pierre Lecorcier and Michael Stein* v. *Italian Republic*, ICSID, ARB/14/3, Award of 27 December 2016, para 403.

138 *Burlington* (2012) note 9 at para 397.

139 *Cargill II* (2009) note 20 at para 360; see also *Corn Products* (2008) note 32 at para 91.

140 *Copper Mesa* (2016) note 28 at para 6.122.

141 *LG&E* (2006) note 46 at para 192.

expropriation must primarily be the degree of possession taking or control over the enterprise';[142]

- *Saint Gobain*: 'the Tribunal notes that a State's de facto control of assets does not necessarily entail expropriation';[143]
- *Sempra Energy*: '[a] finding of indirect expropriation would require . . . that the investor no longer be in control of its business operation, or that the value of the business have been virtually annihilated';[144]
- *Tecmed*: 'the measures . . . are an indirect de facto expropriation if . . . the economic value of the use, enjoyment or disposition of the assets or rights affected by the administrative action or decision have been neutralized or destroyed . . . [T]he owner is also deprived of property where the use or enjoyment of benefits related thereto is exacted or interfered with to a similar extent';[145]
- *Teinver*: 'taking over management of an investment constitutes an indirect expropriation'.[146]

8.2.3 *Subsumption of Standards in Case-Law*

Have investment tribunals actually used the substantial deprivation standard and its sub-standards which they develop in their application to the cases before them? There is, after all, a conceptual difference between a standard identified by tribunals in the abstract and the one they apply. The first is an opinion of what the law requires; the second is the actual decision (law-making). Conceptual differences may result in practical differences – a tribunal may *tell* us that 'x' is the standard which an IIA requires, yet proceed to decide on a different standard. There are four logical variants:

- the tribunal finds that a standard is applicable and uses it to come to a decision;
- it finds a standard applicable, but applies a different standard to the one it has found applicable;

[142] *Nykomb Synergetics Technology Holding AB* v. *Republic of Latvia*, SCC, Award of 16 December 2003, 194.

[143] *Saint-Gobain Performance Plastics Europe* v. *Bolivarian Republic of Venezuela*, ICSID, ARB/12/13, Award of 30 December 2016, para 467.

[144] *Sempra Energy* (2007) note 28 at para 285.

[145] *Tecmed* (2003) note 40 at para 116; see also *LG&E* (2006) note 46 at para 192.

[146] *Teinver* (2017) note 53 at para 941.

- it finds a standard applicable, but does not use any standard to come to a decision;
- it does not elaborate on any standard which may be applicable, yet renders a decision nonetheless.

We will not try to classify all relevant investment awards along these lines. It is probably impossible to do so, given that many tribunals give rather terse explanations of their decision. Hence, we will give one example of each, bearing in mind, however, that the second and fourth variants will be particularly difficult to connect to that standard and that this involves a highly subjective reading which limits its usefulness.

(1) *Windstream* is one of a number of clear-cut cases of the tribunal sticking to the substantial deprivation standard. In this award, the tribunal first laid out the standard it intended to apply for indirect expropriation: 'the first step in the process of determining whether an effective taking has taken place is to determine whether the investor has been *substantially deprived* of the value of its investment'.[147] It then discussed precedents applying NAFTA which it felt had applied the standard and further elucidated its content: *ADM*, *Cargill* and *Metalclad*.[148] In turning to the application of that standard, it held:

> [N]o expropriation has taken place in this case. First, the Claimant's FIT Contract is still formally in force and has not been unilaterally terminated by the Government of Ontario; . . . while . . . the Project can no longer be completed . . ., it continues to remain open for the Parties to re-activate and, as appropriate, renegotiate the FIT Contract . . . Second, . . . the Claimant's CAD 6 million security deposit is still in place and has not been taken or rendered otherwise worthless as a result of any action taken by the Government of Ontario. . . . It therefore cannot be said that the Claimant has been substantially deprived of its investment.'[149]

(2) *WNC Factoring* is arguably an award where the tribunal supplanted another standard for the one developed in the general part of its reasoning. As explained in Section 8.1, we will ignore the tribunal's reasoning on the police powers doctrine for the present analysis. The tribunal set out the standard in a conventional form, referring to *Pope & Talbot* and

147 *Windstream* (2016) note 38 at para 285 (emphasis added).

148 *ADM* (2007) note 19 at para 240; *Cargill II* (2009) note 20 at para 360; *Metalclad* (2000) note 43 at para 103.

149 *Windstream* (2016) note 38 at para 290. *Burlington* (2012) note 9 at paras 391–540 is another example of this category, albeit a lengthy reasoning/application.

Metalclad (though not referring to substantial deprivation *eo nomine*): '"[t]he test is whether … the property has been 'taken' from the owner" … [T]he interference with the use of the property must have "the effect of depriving the owner".'[150] Yet in the passages subsuming the facts under the law, the substantial effect reasoning is curiously absent; other factors seemed to have been decisive (even subtracting the police powers doctrine). The tribunal held that 'there was no unlawful or improper conduct … [T]here was no conspiracy implicating the MoF … That being so, the events complained of were not … expropriatory acts.'[151] In summing up, the tribunal raised another issue: '[the] decision to refuse funding was not an expropriation of Škoda Export. In the absence of any obligation to provide a loan … the refusal was nothing more than a commercial decision.'[152] The question of effect/deprivation was only raised in the abstract, but did not seem to have been a factor in the tribunal's decision.

(3) In *Allard*, the substantial deprivation standard was set out in standard fashion: 'the first requirement … is that … the investor [should] have suffered a substantial deprivation of the use or expected economic benefit of the investment'.[153] When it comes to the subsumption in the following two paragraphs, however, there is no longer a discernible standard:

> Mr. Allard remains the owner … [H]e continues to operate a café, and acknowledged … that 'there is some kind of business remaining there.' It is therefore undisputed that the Claimant has not been deprived of his *entire* investment in Barbados. The argument here is that what has been expropriated is neither the land nor the café, but his ability to run an ecotourism business. This appears to imply that it is the anticipated returns of an ecotourism business that constituted the expected economic benefit of the investment.[154]

The substantial deprivation standard does not require the *entire* investment to be destroyed, as the tribunal laid down that standard. On that standard, the *Tatbestand* of indirect expropriation would arguably be fulfilled in this case. Either the tribunal supplanted another implicit

[150] *WNC Factoring Ltd (United Kingdom)* v. *Czech Republic*, UNCITRAL, PCA 2014-34, Award of 22 February 2017, para 397, referring to *Pope & Talbot* (2000) note 8 at para 102; *Metalclad* (2000) note 43 at para 103.

[151] *WNC* (2017) note 150 at para 396.

[152] *WNC* (2017) note 150 at para 400.

[153] *Allard* (2016) note 22 at para 263.

[154] *Allard* (2016) note 22 at paras 264–5.

standard or it did not decide upon the standard prescribed in the earlier paragraph.

(4) A good example for a tribunal eschewing to articulate any standard is very difficult to find, as such a lack of argument would probably fall foul of the requirement to state the reasons for an award. In the *Inmaris* award, no standard is developed in its non-redacted parts; the subsumption, however, is close to the substantial deprivation standard as analysed above. The tribunal held that the Respondent's behaviour 'deprived Claimants of access to and control over the essential asset for its investment ... Claimants' business suffered substantial harm.'[155] Therefore, the measures 'amounted to an indirect expropriation in that it destroyed the value of Claimants' contractual rights and such diminution in value ... was, for all intents and purposes, permanent'.[156] It is impossible to tell whether the tribunal might not have implicitly taken on board the parties' pleadings on the substantial deprivation standard – if that was the standard on which the parties did rely in the redacted passages – without saying in so many words.

Equally, in the *Petrobart* award, the tribunal's analysis, after stating generally that Article 13 ECT prohibits indirect expropriation as well, comes to a rather abrupt stop when it concludes, in the next paragraph:

> It is clear that there was no formal expropriation of Petrobart's investment. Nor does it appear that the measures taken by the Kyrgyz Government and state authorities, although they had negative effects for Petrobart, were directed specifically against Petrobart's investment or had the aim of transferring economic values from Petrobart to the Kyrgyz Republic. ... The Arbitral Tribunal considers that the measures taken by the Kyrgyz Republic ... did not attain the level of de facto expropriation.[157]

8.3 Partial Expropriation

Partial expropriation is the question of whether the taking of a part of an investment can ever be an (indirect) expropriation under the terms of traditional IIA clauses. Slightly polemically, one could call this international investment law's *sorites* paradox: surely, taking one paper-clip

155 *Inmaris Perestroika Sailing Maritime Services GmbH and others* v. *Ukraine*, ICSID, ARB/08/8, Award of 1 March 2012, para 300.

156 *Inmaris* (2012) note 155 at para 300.

157 *Petrobart Ltd.* v. *Kyrgyz Republic*, SCC, 126/2003, Arbitral Award of 29 March 2005, 77.

from an investor does not rise to the level of an expropriation, but if an investment consists of ten oil wells and the state directly expropriates 'only' one, how can this not be an expropriation? This is an issue which arises out of the discussion on the requisite intensity for an act of (indirect) expropriation, yet it is intimately connected to the question of the object of expropriation as well as jurisdictional questions, as the relevant yardstick for both is the 'investment'. Because it is easy to fold the *problematique* in with the substantial deprivation standard, tribunals which do not see this as a separate problem, or do not wish to discuss this separately, can easily forgo taking a position specifically on partial expropriation. It is discussed more in academic commentary than in case-law. Hence, we will begin by analysing scholarly arguments and then proceed to discuss how those ideas are reflected in case-law.

8.3.1 *The Academic Problem*

'Investment' is the key term used in IIAs; take the 2003 Cambodia–Netherlands BIT as a random example containing typical provisions and including a Type A expropriation clause: (a) It defines 'investment' in Article 1(a) in the usual expansive manner. (b) In Article 9(1), concerning the 'Settlement of Disputes between a National and a Contracting Party', the jurisdiction *ratione materiae* (and *ratione personae*) of its ISDS provisions is: 'Disputes between a national of one Contracting Party and the other Contracting Party *concerning an investment* of the former ... shall ... be submitted to international dispute settlement' (emphasis added). (c) In its expropriation provision in Article 6, the BIT defines the object of expropriation in the following manner: 'Neither Contracting Party shall take any measures depriving, directly or indirectly, nationals of the other Contracting Party *of their investments*' (emphasis added).

This is all standard fare for traditional investment treaties and would seem to strongly imply that 'investment' for the purposes of ISDS jurisdiction is exactly the same as 'investment' in terms of the required object for direct or indirect expropriation. This point was made in *EMV* with respect to the provisions of the 1989 BLEU–Czechoslowak BIT:

> Finally, it is suggested that an investment must be something which is capable of expropriation otherwise Article 3 [on expropriation] will not work. This must surely be wrong. *The whole Treaty is permeated by a single concept of investment*, which cannot in any way be controlled by Article 3, any more than it is controlled by the wider provisions of Article 2. In our

> opinion, the non-exclusive definitions [of 'investment'] in Article 1 mean what they say and they are quite broad enough to cover the different assets which the Claimant here contends constitute investments.[158]

The very possibility of the concept of partial expropriation implies a divergence in practice, rather than as a matter of the legal analysis of an IIA. On the one hand, tribunals do tend to take a 'loose', all-encompassing view of the claimant's investment for the jurisdictional phase in order not to limit themselves in the merits phase. On the other hand, tribunals construct 'investment' as the object of expropriation in a manner which requires less than the whole of the investment – as defined in the jurisdictional phase – to be taken. In other words, the object can be narrower for purposes of the expropriation *Tatbestand* than for the tribunal's jurisdiction.

The other much-discussed connection is between the object of expropriation and the intensity dimension. IIAs may prohibit the expropriation of investments, but do they require the expropriation of the *totality* of the investment – as opposed to the *total* expropriation of the investment? One of the best explanations for this conceptual slippage can be found in Ursula Kriebaum's 2007 article.[159] She starts out by explaining the generally accepted intensity standard: 'It is widely accepted that an interference ... must lead to a total or at least substantial deprivation', which '[a]t first sight ... would rule out the notion of a partial expropriation: if the investment has been affected only in part, there is no expropriation.'[160] For her, the story starts with 'the quantitative requirements'[161] (which we have called intensity requirement), because if substantial deprivation suffices – if it does not need to be total – '*almost all cases of indirect expropriation are only partial.* ... The decisive point for an expropriation is the destruction of the capability to make use of the investment in an economic sense.'[162] 'It follows that even a "total expropriation" in a traditional sense may be partial if looked at from the

[158] *EMV* (2009) note 14 at para 41 (emphasis added).

[159] Kriebaum (2007a) note 28; see also Kriebaum (2008a) note 7 at 389–404; Kriebaum (2015) note 102 at 993–5.

[160] Kriebaum (2007a) note 28 at 69.

[161] Kriebaum (2007a) note 28 at 70.

[162] Kriebaum (2007a) note 28 at 71 (emphasis added); see also Bray (2012) note 15 at 23: 'In a broad sense, almost all cases of indirect expropriation involve partial takings because the foreign investor is left with some residual rights. ... Indeed, the notions of partial and indirect expropriation go hand and hand. In this sense, an indirect expropriation will always result in a partial expropriation because only a part of the investment has been affected.'

perspective of ownership of the assets involved. What is total in this situation is merely the impossibility to make economic use of them.'[163]

Yet would she distinguish a 'genuinely' partial expropriation, where 'only parts of an overall investment are taken', such as 'the existence of several parallel investments in the same State' or 'inter-related rights in the same project',[164] from partial expropriation not properly so called – expropriation of the totality versus total expropriation? Is it coherent to distinguish in this manner? Is the question of partial expropriation not solved by applying the substantial deprivation standard for intensity in connection with a unitarian concept of the object of expropriation (investment as a whole and nothing but a whole of the investor's project in the host state)?

Another example is A Devin Bray's discussion of *Grand River*. The award concluded that '[a]n act of expropriation must involve "the investment of an investor," not part of an investment'.[165] As Bray points out, 'the tribunal also accepted that the test for an expropriation involves "the deprivation or impairment of all, or a *very significant proportion of*, an investor's interests . . ."'.[166] This can be read in two ways:

> One point of view may suggest that the *Grand River* case is representative of some confusion within NAFTA jurisprudence regarding the definition of investment, indirect expropriation and partial expropriation. It appears to stand for the paradoxical proposition that a proportion of an investment may be expropriated but a part of an investment may not. The better view, to avoid the paradox, is to recognize that *Grand River* upheld a key distinction between the second step and third step of the expropriation analysis. Specifically, by accepting that only full, stand-alone investments are protected, the reasoning of Grand River avoids situations where significant portion of a minor part of an investment may be considered as a compensable taking.[167]

The first reading echoes Dolzer and Schreuer's critique; for them, 'the Tribunal may have failed to distinguish between the questions of the definition of a taking and the extent to which an investment may have been expropriated'.[168] This, again, raises the question of the connection between partial expropriation and deprivation (ie degree of interference) of a significant part of investment, where a significant deprivation of the

[163] Kriebaum (2007a) note 28 at 72; see also Hoffmann (2008) note 12 at 159.
[164] Kriebaum (2007a) note 28 at 72.
[165] *Grand River* (2011) note 106 at para 155.
[166] Bray (2012) note 15 at 24, quoting *Grand River* (2011) note 106 at para 147.
[167] Bray (2012) note 15 at 24.
[168] Dolzer (2012) note 7 at 119.

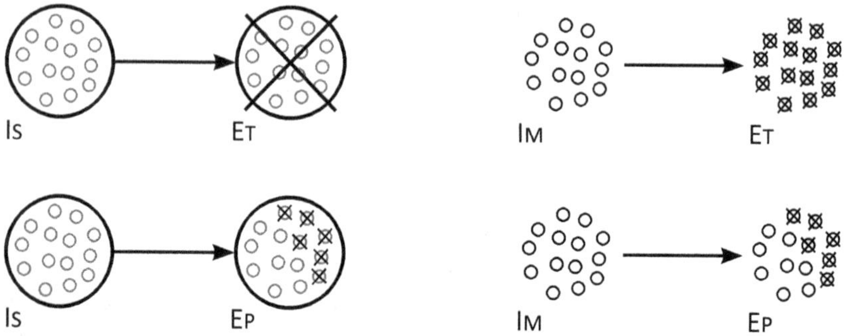

Figure 8.2 Partial expropriation[169]

total investment is an expropriation but a total deprivation of part of the investment is not an expropriation.

There seems to be a consensus in academic commentary that the solution to the partial expropriation problem is to be found in, as Newcombe and Paradell put it, 'the categorization of what has been taken and whether it is possible to divide the investment into identifiable, distinct property rights or investments'. They expand this to the entirety of the substantial deprivation debate, arguing that 'if a tribunal finds that the right affected by a government measure is an investment, then *ipso facto* there is a substantial deprivation of that investment', referring to US takings jurisprudence and warning that the 'parcel as a whole rule' applies here as well. '[T]he property owner cannot divide its bundle of property rights and argue that the strand affected by the regulation has been taken.'[170] Attempts of this nature, also called 'conceptual severance', are said to be unacceptable in international investment law, inter alia, because it 'was rejected by the Supreme Court ... [I]f every interference with the property bundle could require compensation, it would effectively force the government to "regulate by purchase".'[171] This brings us

169 I_S: investment as a singular; E_T: total expropriation; E_P: expropriation of a part; I_M: investment as a multiple.

170 Newcombe (2009) note 7 at 348; see also Andrew Newcombe, 'The Boundaries of Regulatory Expropriation in International Law' 20 *ICSID Review – Foreign Investment Law Journal* (2005) 1–57 at 44; Ortino (2016) note 17 at 356; Beauvais (2001–2) note 18 at 281: 'The finding of a complete versus partial deprivation of property rights depends upon how the underlying property interest, or "denominator," is defined.'

171 Alessandra Asteriti, 'Regulatory Expropriation Claims in International Investment Arbitrations: A Bridge too Far?' in Andrea K Bjorklund (ed.), *Yearbook on International Investment Law and Policy 2012–2013* (Oxford: Oxford University Press 2014) 451–73 at 462; see also Lévesque (2004) note 18 at 304.

back to a sub-strand of political arguments against the rejection of the police powers doctrine which were discussed in Section 7.1.

Yet what if, as Bjørn Kunoy points out, 'a foreign investor [is] simultaneously active in several different markets'? 'If one of its economic activities is subject of a dispossession, the arbitrators will not ipso facto conclude that the operator is indirectly expropriated, because the measure will only be a partial dispossession.'[172] This is 'unsatisfactory' and 'too formalistic and incontestably diminishes the scope of the notion of indirect expropriation',[173] because all measures have 'an effect on the integrality of the operator's economic activity'.[174]

It appears that a significant number of writers and tribunals have found a way out of the partial expropriation conundrum by changing the focus of the object of expropriation from the all-encompassing 'investment' to the narrower 'property' (see also Section 6.1).[175] López, for example, argues that '[t]reaties do not include an autonomous definition of property'; the answer to the question of what has been taken is therefore solved by 'a *renvoi* to municipal law'.[176] Partial expropriation then hinges on 'whether it is possible to divide the *property* into identifiable, distinct rights'.[177] Jan Paulson and Zachary Douglas recognise the potential for fragmentation (which is inherent in the switch to property): 'tribunals have resorted to subtle variations in the definition of cognizable property interests in order to justify their ultimate conclusion as to whether an expropriation has taken place'.[178]

However, the fact remains that IIAs 'tend to refer to expropriation of "investments" rather than "property"'.[179] This has not held tribunals back from arguing that, for the purposes of elucidating the *Tatbestand* of expropriation, property is the relevant concept; for example *Waste*

[172] Bjørn Kunoy, 'Developments in Indirect Expropriation Case Law in ICSID Transnational Arbitration' 6 *Journal of World Investment & Trade* (2005) 467–91 at 489.

[173] Kunoy (2005) note 172 at 490; see also Newcombe (2009) note 7 at 349.

[174] Kunoy (2005) note 172 at 489.

[175] This change is particularly relevant for those who champion the analogy to the protection of property in human rights law, see eg Thomas W Wälde, Abba Kolo, 'Environmental Regulation, Investment Protection and Regulatory Taking in International Law' 50 *International and Comparative Law Quarterly* (2001) 811–48.

[176] López (2014) note 7 at 201.

[177] López (2014) note 7 at 201 (emphasis added); see perhaps also Schill (2006) note 121 at 8.

[178] Jan Paulsson, Zachary Douglas, 'Indirect Expropriation in Investment Treaty Arbitrations' in Norbert Horn (ed.), *Arbitrating Foreign Investment Disputes* (The Hague: Kluwer 2004) 145–58 at 150; see also UNCTAD (2012) note 5 at 24.

[179] Coe (2005) note 20 at 622.

Management: 'An indirect expropriation is still a taking of property.'[180] The tribunal in *Emmis*, citing *Waste Management*, explained at length why it felt that this focus is the correct one:

> In view of the fact that the only cause of action within the Tribunal's jurisdiction is that of expropriation, Claimants must have held a property right of which they have been deprived. This follows from the ordinary meaning of the term. The *Oxford English Dictionary* defines 'expropriate' as '(of the state or an authority) take (property) from its owner for public use or benefit'/'dispossess (someone) of property'. Its origin is from the medieval Latin *expropriat-* 'taken from the owner', from the verb *expropriare*, from *ex-* 'out, from' + *proprium* 'property', neuter singular of *proprius* 'own'.[181]

But is the wording of the IIA expropriation clauses at issue in *Emmis* irrelevant? After all, Article 4(1) Netherlands–Hungary BIT 1987 provides: 'Neither Contracting Party shall take any measure depriving ... investors of the other Contracting Party *of their investments*'; Article 6(1) Swiss–Hungary BIT 1989 provides: 'Neither of the Contracting Parties shall take ... measures of expropriation ... *against investments*' (emphases added). Both speak of the deprivation/taking of 'investments', not 'property' or 'property interests', whether or not the etymology of the word 'expropriate' involves property, as the tribunal correctly pointed out. Other voices in case-law are equally unconvinced, for example *SPP*: '[n]or can the Tribunal accept the argument that the term "expropriation" applies only to *jus in rem*';[182] *SD Myers*: 'rights other than property rights may be "expropriated"';[183] *Bayindir*: '[i]t is not disputed that expropriation is not limited to *in rem* rights'.[184] Kriebaum, in analysing the case-law on this issue and finding that tribunals are split,[185] points out that IIAs at issue in these awards mention 'investment', rather than

180 *Waste Management* (2004) note 108 at para 143; see also *Emmis International Holding, B.V., Emmis Radio Operating, B.V., Mem Magyar Electronic Media Kereskedelmi és Szolgáltató Kft.* v. *Hungary*, ICSID, ARB/12/2, Award of 16 April 2014, para 160; *GAMI Investments, Inc.* v. *Government of the United Mexican States*, NAFTA-UNCITRAL, Final Award of 15 November 2004, para 126.

181 *Emmis* (2014) note 180 at para 159.

182 *Southern Pacific Properties (Middle East) Limited* v. *Arab Republic of Egypt*, ICSID, Award of 20 May 1992, para 164.

183 *SD Myers* (2000) note 55 at para 281.

184 *Bayindir Insaat Turizm Ticaret Ve Sanayi A.S.* v. *Islamic Republic of Pakistan*, ICSID, ARB/03/29, Decision on Jurisdiction, 14 November 2005, para 255.

185 Kriebaum (2008a) note 7 at 308–310, citing *pro* 'investment': *Middle East Cement Shipping and Handling Co. S.A.* v. *Arab Republic of Egypt*, ICSID, ARB/99/6, Award of 12 April 2002, para 107; *Feldman* (2002) note 108 at para 152; *Tecmed* (2003) note 40 at

'property', but comes to the conclusion that tribunals did not believe that there is a material difference between the two terms. She does so on the basis of the argument that tribunals did not care either, because they did not explain why they used 'property' rather than 'investment'.[186]

The solution first advocated by Kriebaum in her trail-blazing 2007 article – and adopted (or adapted) by others[187] – may explain why some do not accept that partial expropriation is exhausted by intensity. Starting from the position, already discussed, that if, for example, 'someone is deprived of five of ten hectares of land', one would tend to accept this as an expropriation, she argues that there is 'no good reason for a different approach in a situation where an investment can be disassembled into various specified rights'.[188] She therefore proposes that partial expropriation should be acknowledged under three cumulative conditions:

> [1] [T]he overall investment project can be disassembled into a number of discrete rights; [2] the State has deprived the investor of a right which is covered by one of the items in the definition of 'investment' in the applicable investment protection treaty; and [3] this right is capable of economic exploitation independently of the remainder of the investment.[189]

Therefore, if, in effect, plausible criteria for the partition of the object of expropriation can be given, then, in turn, partial expropriation is possible. Continuing with the analogy from scholarship on the use of force, in self-defence law a situation may constitute an armed attack only where one 'zooms out' to encompass the wider inter-state relationship, but does not where, for example, a border skirmish is seen in isolation.[190] This idea of 'zoom' may be helpful for our discussion of this solution. The more detailed one assumes an 'investment' is – say, an investment is a single oil well, rather than the sum-totality of the oil company in the

para 102; *Consortium RFCC* v. *Morocco*, ICSID, ARB/00/6, Award of 22 December 2003, para 64; *Bayindir* (2005) note 184 at para 255; *pro* 'property': *Compañia del Desarrollo de Santa Elena, S.A.* v. *Republic of Costa Rica*, ICSID, ARB/96/1, Final Award of 17 February 2000, paras 77, 78; *Pope & Talbot* (2000) note 8 at para 102; *Metalclad* (2000) note 43 at para 103; *CME* (2001) note 44 at paras 604, 606; *Ronald S. Lauder* v. *Czech Republic*, UNCITRAL, Final Award of 3 September 2001, para 200; *Waste Management* (2004) note 108 at para 159; *GAMI* (2004) note 180 at para 126; *CMS* (2005) note 28 at para 626.

186 Kriebaum (2008a) note 7 at 309–10.

187 Eg López (2014) note 7 at 202; UNCTAD (2012) note 5 at 24.

188 Kriebaum (2007a) note 28 at 83.

189 Kriebaum (2007a) note 28 at 83; see also Kriebaum (2008a) note 7 at 403.

190 Jörg Kammerhofer, *Uncertainty in International Law: A Kelsenian Perspective* (Abingdon: Routledge 2010) 31–5.

relevant country – the more likely one is to prove a significant impact on the use or enjoyment of the investment. If a measure destroys the usefulness of one of the investor's one hundred oil wells, that one well is considered as an investment, but no expropriation has occurred if the totality of the investor's activities in the host state is the relevant investment, because potentially less than 1 per cent has been taken. If we can zoom in to see concrete parts, there will be a partial expropriation, but if there are none, zooming in does not help. But how does one set the 'zoom'? Even under Kriebaum's formula, widely divergent views as to the separability are possible. The critique in *Electrabel* applies also to criteria for carving up investments:

> If it were possible so easily to parse an investment into several constituent parts each forming a separate investment . . ., it would render meaningless that tribunal's approach to indirect expropriation . . . [One] could always meet the test for indirect expropriation by slicing its investment as finely as the particular circumstances required, without that investment as a whole ever meeting that same test.[191]

The question would turn on how willing one is to see the investment as 'capable of economic exploitation independently of the remainder of the investment'.[192]

The solution will also cement the fragmentation of the concept of 'investment' in IIAs. For purposes of jurisdiction, the totality of economic activities is relevant: 'investment' *sensu largo*, as typically given in Article 1, defining terms. However, related to the object of expropriation and intensity (*Tatbestand*), a part can suffice. This divergence is connected to one of the problems of the frame of possible meanings, for whether we accept Kriebaum's position that '[n]o one will question that an expropriation has occurred if someone is deprived of five of ten hectares of land'[193] is dependent on whether it is a direct or indirect expropriation. If the five-hectare taking is done formally (a question of *direct* expropriation), no one would deny that this is an expropriation. This may occur, for example, where a state (directly) expropriates (parts of) a company in which the investor has shares, that is, when the investment is a shareholding.[194] The issue comes back to an implicit

191 *Electrabel* (2012) note 62 at para 6.57.

192 Kriebaum (2007a) note 28 at 83.

193 Kriebaum (2007a) note 28 at 83.

194 Eg *RosInvestCo* (2010) note 28 at paras 607–9; *Enkev* (2014) note 31 at paras 331–2; *Flemingo DutyFree Shop Private Limited* v. *Republic of Poland*, UNCITRAL, PCA, Award of 12 August 2016, paras 592–6.

disaggregation of direct and indirect expropriation, which is often seen as a question of interpretation, rather than a structural limit (Section 7.3). If Type A IIAs see the two forms of expropriation as equal, why should the matter be different if, say, one oil well out of one hundred were taken by formal expropriation decree or by measures having the same effect?

8.3.2 *Case-Law*

Yet in order to ascertain the *stratum* of investment arbitration decisions, we must focus on how tribunals have decided the issue of partial expropriation. In Kriebaum's helpful overview, case-law has 'dealt with the issue of partial expropriation in three disparate ways ... [It] is clearly divided'[195] into three groups, one negating the possibility of partial expropriation, a second arguing for it and a third not taking sides, but 'appl[ying] the concept implicitly and decid[ing] that expropriations had occurred in the respective cases'.[196] We will largely follow this categorisation, but limit the examples to those where the tribunal actually engaged with the concept. A negative position on partial expropriation was expressed, inter alia, in the following terms:

- *Cargill I*: 'some decisions rendered in investor-state arbitrations have accepted that specific rights relating to an investment can be expropriated separately. ... [T]he Tribunal is of the opinion that the correct approach here is to assess the investment as a whole in order to determine whether there was an expropriation';[197]
- *Electrabel*: 'the test for expropriation is applied to the relevant investment as a whole, even if different parts may separately qualify as investments for jurisdictional purposes. Here the investment held by Electrabel as a whole was its aggregate collection of interests in Dunamenti; it was thus one integral investment; and in the context of expropriation it was not a series of separate, individual investments';[198]
- *Grand River*: Article 1110 NAFTA 'speaks of "an investment," not "an investment or some portion thereof." The most natural reading of the language is that any act of expropriation will affect the totality of an investment. ... The Claimant pointed to no cases supporting the notion that state action allegedly impairing only a limited portion of

[195] Kriebaum (2007a) note 28 at 73, 82.
[196] Kriebaum (2007a) note 28 at 73.
[197] *Cargill I* (2008) note 114 at para 583, citing *Telenor* (2006) note 19 at para 67.
[198] *Electrabel* (2012) note 62 at para 6.58.

the value of an otherwise ongoing and profitable investment … can give rise to a "partial" expropriation under either NAFTA Article 1110 or general international law';[199]

- *Koch*: '[i]t is necessary to view the Respondent's measures of 11 October 2010 as the indirect expropriation of a single integrated investment. … KNI's investment cannot be sliced off and isolated, like a piece of sausage';[200]
- *Philip Morris*: 'in order to determine whether the [measure] had an expropriatory character in this case, Abal's business is to be considered as a whole';[201]
- *Telenor*: 'suggestions [of partial expropriation in case-law] have typically been made in cases where the question of partial deprivation did not arise on the facts, and were no doubt designed to avoid excluding the possibility that partial deprivation might in an appropriate case constitute expropriation. The Tribunal considers that, in the present case at least, the investment must be viewed as a whole';[202]
- *Vivendi*: '[t]he weight of authority … appears to draw a distinction between only a partial deprivation of value (not an expropriation) and a complete or near complete deprivation of value (expropriation)'.[203]

As can be seen from these statements and as discussed above, the tendency of those tribunals who deny the existence of the concept of partial expropriation is to foreground and subordinate this question under the intensity criterion. Positive statements can, inter alia, be found in the following awards:

- *GAMI* (cited by *Ampal*): '[s]hould *Pope & Talbot* be understood to mean that property is taken only if it is so affected in its entirety? … The notion must be understood as this: *the affected property* must be impaired to such an extent that it must be seen as "taken." … Other NAFTA awards have given support for the proposition that *partial* destruction of the value may be tantamount to expropriation';[204]

[199] *Grand River* (2011) note 106 at paras 147, 154.

[200] *Koch Minerals Sàrl and Koch Nitrogen International Sàrl* v. *Bolivarian Republic of Venezuela*, ICSID, ARB/11/19, Award of 30 October 2017, paras 7.47, 7.48, citing *Electrabel* (2012) note 62 at para 6.57.

[201] *Philip Morris* (2016) note 19 at para 283.

[202] *Telenor* (2006) note 19 at paras 66, 67.

[203] *Vivendi* (2007) note 63 at para 7.5.11.

[204] *GAMI* (2004) note 180 at para 126, cited by *Ampal-American Israel Corporation, EGI-Fund (08-10) Investors, LLC, EGI-Series Investments, LLC, and BSS-EMG Investors, LLC*

- *SD Myers*: 'it may be that, in some contexts and circumstances, it would be appropriate to view a deprivation as amounting to an expropriation, even if it were partial or temporary';[205]
- *Waste Management*: '[i]t is open to the Tribunal to find a breach of Article 1110 in a case where certain facts are relied on to show the wholesale expropriation of an enterprise but the facts establish the expropriation of certain assets only. Accordingly the Tribunal will consider . . . whether (even if there was no wholesale expropriation of the enterprise as such) the facts establish a partial expropriation.'[206]

A number of awards are less easy to categorise:

- *Bogdanov I*: 'the concept of indirect expropriation applies only to measures having the effect of expropriation that affect the totality or a substantial part of the investment . . . In the instant case, the value of the Transferred Assets upon which the parties agree, corresponds to . . . circa 3% of the total investment . . . This is not . . . a measure affecting the totality or a substantial part of the investment.'[207] This could be read as supporting the idea of particle expropriation, but not on the basis of such a small fraction of the investment *sensu largo*.
- *Burlington*: 'The Treaty provides that "investments shall not be expropriated." The Tribunal understands from this formulation that the focus of the expropriation analysis must be on the investment as a whole, and not on discrete parts of the investment. . . . Nevertheless, . . . the Tribunal considers that a broader view of investment must be adopted, a view that encompasses Burlington's investment "as a whole." . . . Applied to the investment as a whole, the criterion of loss of the economic use or viability of the investment implies that the investment as a whole has become unviable. The measure is expropriatory, whether it affects the entire investment or only part of it, as long as the operation of the investment cannot generate a commercial return.'[208] While sceptical of partial expropriation, the *Burlington* tribunal did seem to open the door to it if the taking affects the commercial viability of the whole.

v. *Arab Republic of Egypt*, ICSID, ARB/21/11, Decision on Liability and Heads of Loss of 21 February 2017, para 180.

205 *SD Myers* (2000) note 55 at para 283.

206 *Waste Management* (2004) note 108 at para 141.

207 *Iurii Bogdanov, Agurdino-Invest Ltd and Agurdino-Chimia JSC* v. *Republic of Moldova*, SCC, Award of 22 September 2005, 17.

208 *Burlington* (2012) note 9 at paras 257, 260, 398.

- *Merrill & Ring*: '[i]n this regard, as was also concluded in *Pope & Talbot*, the business of the investor has to be considered as a whole and not necessarily with respect to an individual or separate aspect, particularly if this aspect does not have a standalone character. It could well happen that a certain aspect is so fundamental to the business concerned that interference with it might result in a kind of compensable expropriation.'[209] Again, a negative general statement is significantly tempered.

8.4 Compensation and Reparation

Lakes of ink have been spilt on the question of the difference in kind (and degree) between the compensation condition in IIA expropriation clauses, on the one hand, and reparation for a state's breach of these IIA clauses, on the other – both in investment awards and in academic commentary. We cannot hope to achieve, within the framework of this book, the level of excellence provided by the analyses and taxonomies of case-law performed, inter alia, by Irmgard Marboe and Steven Ratner.[210] Yet there is a different point to be made within the theoretical framework developed in the previous chapters. In light of the idea, discussed throughout this book, that there are frame-relevant questions in contrast to a (wide) freedom for (judicial) organs to decide *within* that frame, we propose to look at whether this question is properly the former or the latter. We propose to analyse whether tribunals are free to set a judicial standard or are bound to take one route or another by the structure which international law provides. This is a particularly valuable target within the framework of the present book, particularly since it is intimately connected with three overarching issues identified in earlier parts: the question of the cumulative necessity of *all* legality conditions in typical IIA clauses (Section 7.4), the interrelation of treaty and customary international law (Chapter 2) and the possibility and pitfalls of analogical reasoning, in this case from private law, particularly with respect to the dichotomy between contract-mandated compensation and reparation for tortious action.

209 *Merrill & Ring* (2010) note 28 at para 144.

210 Irmgard Marboe, 'Valuation in Cases of Expropriation' in Marc Bungenberg et al. (eds.), *International Investment Law* (Baden-Baden: Nomos 2015) 1057–81 at 1063–4; Stephen R Ratner, 'Compensation for Expropriations in a World of Investment Treaties: Beyond the Lawful/Unlawful Distinction' 111 *American Journal of International Law* (2017) 7–56 at 15–17.

We will therefore eschew a discussion of the exact method of valuation, for example whether the Discounted Cash Flow method is mandated by either the IIA compensation or the state responsibility reparation, and will also not be overly concerned with the exact nature of a possible difference between the two forms, concentrating instead on the questions of identity and difference and freedom of choice on the part of tribunals. After a discussion of the problem (Section 8.4.1), we will taxonomise case-law (Section 8.4.2), then look at whether this is a matter for tribunal discretion or of the structural limits which the law provides (Section 8.4.3). As a consequence of this focus, academic commentary is more at issue than in the other sections of this chapter.

8.4.1 The Problem

The problem is engendered by the structure of Type A IIA expropriation clauses. These stipulate, for *lawful* behaviour, an alternative: either the host state does not (directly or indirectly) expropriate foreign investors or it does, but (typically) under four conditions, one of them 'compensation'. Typical compensation conditions in IIA clauses, in turn, are worded in a manner which suggests a potential for conflict with traditional conceptions of state responsibility. For one, the term used ('compensation') is identical with the one currently used in the law on state responsibility[211] as one possible consequence for *unlawful* behaviour.[212] Another issue is that the typical description of the amount of compensation for *lawful* behaviour ('fair market value'), in conjunction with modern valuation methods for going concerns and their liberal employment in investment arbitration, seems to reach – and potentially to surpass – the amount due under classical rules of state responsibility as a consequence for *unlawful* behaviour.

In addition, the leading case on state responsibility arguably suggests a distinction.[213] The Permanent Court in *Chorzów*, in an oft-cited section

[211] Article 34 Articles on the Responsibility of States for Internationally Wrongful Acts, A/RES/56/83, Annex, 12 December 2001 (ARS).

[212] Irmgard Marboe, 'Compensation and Damages in International Law – The Limits of "Fair Market Value"' 7 *Journal of World Investment & Trade* (2006) 723–59 at 755: 'the fact that the term "compensation" is used in two quite different contexts: as a prerequisite for a lawful expropriation; and for the damages due as a consequence of an internationally wrongful act or a breach of contract'.

[213] Eg Manuel A Abdala, Pablo T Spiller, '*Chorzów*'s Standard Rejuvenated: Assessing Damages in Investment Treaty Arbitrations' 25 *Journal of International Arbitration* (2008) 103–20 at 105–7; Derek William Bowett, 'State Contracts with Aliens: Contemporary Developments

of its 1928 judgment on indemnity, distinguished between two forms of taking. In the 1926 judgment on the merits, it had already found that the treaty provisions at issue, Articles 6–23 Geneva Convention concerning Upper Silesia 1922, established a regime of expropriation which 'is a derogation from the rules generally applied in regard to the treatment of foreigners' and is conditional upon 'the observance of a certain procedure',[214] which includes the payment of an 'indemnity'[215] – Article 22 speaks of 'indemnité'/'Entschädigung'. This led the Permanent Court to find that the Polish measures were 'not in conformity with Articles 6–22 of the Geneva Convention'.[216] In the 1928 judgment, it denied even the label 'expropriation' to the Polish measures: 'it is a seizure of property, rights and interests which could not be expropriated even against *compensation* [indemnité], save under the exceptional conditions fixed by Article 7 of the said Convention'.[217] Hence, the legal consequences of the Polish measures were seen as categorically different:

> [*R*]*eparation* is in this case the consequence not of the application of Articles 6 to 22 of the Geneva Convention, but of acts contrary to those articles. It follows that the compensation due to the German Government is not necessarily limited to the value of the undertaking at the moment of dispossession, plus interest to the day of payment. This limitation would only be admissible if the Polish Government had had the right to expropriate, and if its wrongful act consisted merely in not having paid to the two Companies the just price of what was expropriated; in the present case, such a limitation might result in placing Germany ... in a situation more unfavourable than that in which Germany ... would have been if

on Compensation for Termination or Breach' 59 *British Year Book of International Law* (1988) 49–74 at 59–74; Charles N Brower, Jason D Brueschke, *The Iran–United States Claims Tribunal* (The Hague: Martinus Nijhoff 1998) at 507–12; Coe (2005) note 20 at 630; Audley Sheppard, 'The Distinction between Lawful and Unlawful Expropriation' in Clarisse Ribeiro (ed.), *Investment Arbitration and the Energy Charter Treaty* (New York: JurisNet 2006) 169–99 at 181; UNCTAD (2012) note 5 at 111–12.

214 *Certain German Interests in Polish Upper Silesia (Germany* v. *Poland)*, Judgment on the Merits of 25 May 1926, PCIJ Series A No 7 (1926) at 22.

215 *Chorzów* (1926) note 214 at 33: 'Expropriation without indemnity is certainly contrary to Head III of the Convention'; see, however, August Reinisch, 'Legality of Expropriations' in August Reinisch (ed.), *Standards of Investment Protection* (Oxford: Oxford University Press 2008) 171–204 at 200–1.

216 *Chorzów* (1926) note 214 at 34, see also 81 (*dispositif*).

217 *Factory at Chorzów (Claim for Indemnity) (Germany* v. *Poland)*, Judgment on the Merits of 13 September 1928, PCIJ Series A No 17 (1928) at 46 (emphasis added); see also Martin J Valasek, 'A "Simple Scheme": Exploring the Meaning of *Chorzów Factory* for the Valuation of Opportunistic Expropriation in the BIT Generation' 4:6 *Transnational Dispute Management* (2007) 8.

> Poland had respected the said Convention. Such a consequence . . . would be *tantamount to rendering lawful liquidation and unlawful dispossession indistinguishable* in so far as their financial results are concerned.[218]

This is the origin of the idea that non-payment alone does not make a taking illegal (Section 7.4.2). Regarding the matter at hand, the Permanent Court held that there is a difference in the branches of the law between treaty-based compensation and reparation for treaty breach. All the factors discussed above combine to make the distinction problematic; Stephen Ratner summarises:

> To date, the jurisprudence has been dominated by an anachronistic and analytically unhelpful distinction between the compensation or damages to be paid for so-called 'unlawful expropriations' and those for so-called 'lawful expropriations' – concepts traceable to the venerable *Chorzów Factory* case reflexively cited by tribunals. . . . More important, tribunals disagree on whether the state expropriating 'unlawfully' or 'illegally' should have to pay more to the investor than when it expropriates 'lawfully' or 'legally' – and in particular whether the former triggers damages under customary law, whereas the latter leads only to the amount in the treaty.[219]

The exact scope of *Chorzów* and its enduring influence for the law of state responsibility are not at issue here, nor is the exact amount of compensation for lawful vis-à-vis reparation for unlawful behaviour. We are more interested in the structural problem and how it has been perceived in case-law. As a preliminary measure, we need to clarify the terminology. The ILC's 2001 Articles on the Responsibility of States (ARS) have established a system of terms for the consequences of an internationally wrongful act which is structured in the following manner: a breach has three consequences: (i) a duty of continued performance (Article 29 ARS), (ii) a duty of cessation and non-repetition (Article 30 ARS) and (iii) a duty of reparation (Articles 31, 34–9 ARS). The duty of reparation, in turn, is composed of sub-duties, most importantly: (a) restitution (Article 35 ARS), (b) compensation (Article 36 ARS) and (c) satisfaction (Article 37 ARS).[220] 'The fact that the International Law Commission . . . chose to use the term "compensation" for the consequence of an illegal act of a State perhaps has contributed to the persisting lack of clarity.'[221] Marboe proposes to use the term 'damages' in

218 *Chorzów* (1928) note 217 at 46–7 (emphasis added).

219 Ratner (2017) note 210 at 8.

220 Dolzer (2012) note 7 at 293–4.

221 Marboe (2006) note 212 at 726; see also Irmgard Marboe, 'The System of Reparation and Questions of Terminology' in Marc Bungenberg et al. (eds.), *International Investment Law* (Baden-Baden: Nomos 2015) 1031–44 at 1039.

the case where 'a State does not comply with the legal requirements of a lawful expropriation'.[222] In the interest of some coherence of the terminology traditionally employed in international investment law with the ARS system, we will use 'reparation' to denote (monetary) 'compensation' in the sense employed by Article 36 ARS. Reparation in the sense employed by Article 31 ARS, that is, including restitution and satisfaction, could then be called 'restitution *sensu largo*'. This frees up the term 'compensation' for the amount to be paid under a compensation condition in IIA expropriation clauses for 'lawful' expropriations.

8.4.2 Case-Law

A number of authors, led by Marboe and Ratner, have ably classified the case-law on the compensation–reparation dichotomy; the following will confine itself to a slight rearrangement of relevant awards and will provide relevant quotes from them. Marboe starts from non-investment jurisprudence and opines that '[t]he relevance of the distinction between lawful and unlawful expropriation for the valuation of compensation ... was not realised in the practice of international investment tribunals for some time'.[223] In line with the generally accepted opinion, she then identifies *ADC* as the leading case; she also provides seven other awards which 'confirmed the relevance of the difference between lawful and unlawful expropriation as far as the valuation of compensation is concerned'.[224] Two awards 'discussed the distinction but found that it would not be a practical issue in the case at hand'[225] and only *Rumeli* is seen as 'reject[ing] the relevance of the difference'.[226] Ratner, in contrast, warning the reader that any taxonomy is difficult, given the diversity of views and fact-situations,[227] believes that four groups can be discerned:

> *Group 1 – Compensation Based on Treaty Formula, Silence on the Lawful/ Unlawful Distinction*: Numerous IIA cases ... did not rely on any distinction between lawful and unlawful expropriations in their award of damages. The tribunals avoided addressing the distinction ...

[222] Marboe (2006) note 212 at 725.
[223] Marboe (2015b) note 210 at 1062.
[224] Marboe (2015b) note 210 at 1063–4.
[225] Marboe (2015b) note 210 at 1064.
[226] Marboe (2015b) note 210 at 1064, citing: *Rumeli Telekom A.S. and Telsim Mobil Telekomunikasyon Hizmetleri A.S.* v. *Republic of Kazakhstan*, ICSID, ARB/05/16, Award of 29 July 2008, para 793.
[227] Ratner (2017) note 210 at 15.

> *Group 2 – Lawful/Unlawful Distinction Noted, but Damages the Same as a Legal Matter:* In other cases, tribunals noted the distinction but found that it did not, as a matter of law, have an effect on damages. . . .
>
> *Group 3 – Lawful/Unlawful Distinction Noted, but Treaty Formula Used Due to Special Facts:* In a third set of cases, tribunals . . . did not rely on the distinction in the award due to the specific traits of the investment. . . .
>
> *Group 4 – Lawful/Unlawful Distinction Noted, with an Effect on Damages:* Finally, in a relatively small number of cases, the tribunal has both made a distinction between the two types of takings and used that distinction as the lodestar for determining damages.[228]

A paper by David Khachvani makes a connection between two arguments: On the one hand, 'a failure to provide compensation does not render an expropriation unlawful since the international tribunal hearing the dispute is in charge of determining the due compensation' (see Section 7.4.2). On the other hand, there is 'the failure' as he sees it 'to distinguish the primary obligation to provide compensation for a taking from the secondary duty of full reparation mandating compensation for an unlawful expropriation'.[229] In Ratner's terms, this is 'the incoherence of saying, for instance, that a violation of any of the first three (process-based) criteria of an IIA is an unlawful act while a violation of the fourth (payment) criterion alone is a lawful act'.[230] One might argue that if there is no difference between compensation and reparation, then the fourth IIA legality condition is not really conditional until after a tribunal has ruled on the compensation. This would in effect mean that the tribunal's determination is the fulfilment of the IIA compensation condition. One could even argue the reverse: if the fourth condition is somehow a lesser condition, then the difference between compensation and reparation blurs as well.

But Khachvani is mistaken to suggest that the conditionality issue *exhausts* the compensation–reparation question. His is a positive conditionality, the idea that any claim of identifying compensation vis-à-vis reparation is necessarily based on and follows *only* from the wish to see expropriation only missing compensation as 'lesser' expropriation. Because of the conditionality of *all* legality conditions, the difference in kind and value must exist. However, it is possible to argue both that the compensation condition is a strict requirement of a lawful expropriation and that compensation for lawful expropriation is the same as that for

[228] Ratner (2017) note 210 at 16–17.

[229] David Khachvani, 'Compensation for Unlawful Expropriation: Targeting the Illegality' 32 *ICSID Review* (2017) 385–403 at 386.

[230] Ratner (2017) note 210 at 20; see also Sheppard (2006) note 213 at 196.

unlawful expropriation. In other words, as discussed below, tribunals have made the determination that for expropriation, treaty-based compensation (as a primary duty) is identical in value and/or is the same thing as reparation (as a secondary duty) – and have done so independently of their position on the legality of expropriation only missing compensation.

For present purposes, awards which note the distinction but consider their case exempt due to special circumstances can be lumped together with those which explicitly deny that compensation and reparation are different (at least in terms of amount) – Group A. The *ADC*-led cluster of awards which consider the distinction to have consequences will form Group B. Ratner's Group 1 – those awards which did not mention the question – must remain outside the remit, because it is problematic to draw conclusions from a tribunal's silence.

Group A: Identity

- *BCB*: '[t]he Tribunal observes that at no point does the Treaty, being a *lex specialis*, distinguish between lawful and unlawful expropriation . . . whatever might be the merits of the distinction between lawful and unlawful expropriation under customary international law. Once the violation of the Treaty provisions regarding expropriation is established, the State has breached the Treaty. Neither is the Tribunal convinced that the generally accepted fair market value standard was intended to apply only in cases of the so-called "lawful expropriation . . ."';[231]
- *CME*: '[t]he Respondent, as a consequence of the breach of the Treaty, is under an obligation to make full reparation . . . According to Article 5 subpara. c of the Treaty, any measures depriving . . . must be accompanied "by . . . compensation. . . ." A fortiori unlawful measures of deprivation must be remedied by just compensation. . . . [T]he Respondent is obligated to compensate the Claimant by payment of a sum corresponding to the value which a restitution in kind would bear. This is the fair market value';[232]
- *Funnekotter*: '[t]he Tribunal is of the opinion that the damages suffered by the Claimants must be evaluated at the date of dispossession. This is the rule both under general international law and under Article 6(c) of the BIT . . . The identity of calculation under the BIT and general international law reinforces the Tribunal's conclusion that arguments

[231] *British Caribbean Bank Ltd.* v. *Government of Belize*, UNCITRAL, PCA 2010-18, Award of 19 December 2014, paras 260–1.

[232] *CME* (2001) note 44 at paras 615, 618 (emphasis removed).

respecting the treatment of a violation of Article 6(c) as a lawful or unlawful expropriation need not be reached';[233]

- *Gemplus*: 'the provisions on compensation in Article 5 of the two BITs . . . do not address expressly . . . unlawful expropriation in breach of Article 5(1) . . . Nonetheless, under international law, the measures of compensation in the two BITs . . . provide a useful guide to the measure of compensation for unlawful expropriation and for breach of the FET standards under these BITs';[234]
- *Guaracachi*: '[t]he BIT makes no distinction between the compensation to be provided in respect of an unlawful expropriation as opposed to a lawful one, and the Tribunal does not find any reason to believe that the illegality of the expropriation renders what the BIT deems to be "just and effective compensation" suddenly inadequate';[235]
- *Rumeli*: '[f]or expropriation, Article III of the BIT provides that "(c)ompensation shall be equivalent to the real value . . ." Article 7(2) of the FIL provides that "(t)he compensation must be equal to the fair market value . . ." . . . the expropriation of their shares in Kar-Tel, whether or not this is characterised as an expropriation calling for compensation under the BIT'[236] – 'In assessing compensation for internationally wrongful acts other than expropriation, the Tribunal considers that it should apply the principle of the *Factory at Chorzow* case';[237]
- *Rusoro*: '[t]he compensation provided for in Article VII only covers cases of expropriation. In all other breaches . . . damages must be calculated in accordance with the rules of international law [*Chorzów*] . . . The Bolivarian Republic has committed a fundamental breach of the Treaty . . . [T]he BIT mandates that Venezuela pay to the investor "adequate" compensation';[238]
- *SAUR*; *Tecmed*; *Wena*.[239]

233 *Bernardus Henricus Funnekotter and others* v. *Republic of Zimbabwe*, ICSID, ARB/05/6, Award of 22 April 2009, para 115, see also 123.

234 *Gemplus S.A., SLP S.A., Gemplus Industrial S.A. de C.V.* v. *United Mexican States*; *Talsud S.A.* v. *United Mexican States*, ICSID, ARB(AF)/04/3, ARB(AF)/04/4, Award of 16 June 2010, para 12-53.

235 *Guaracachi America, Inc. and Rurelec Plc* v. *Plurinational State of Bolivia*, UNCITRAL, PCA 2011-17, Award of 31 January 2014, para 613.

236 *Rumeli* (2008) note 226 at paras 785, 793.

237 *Rumeli* (2008) note 226 at para 792.

238 *Rusoro Mining Limited* v. *Bolivarian Republic of Venezuela*, ICSID, ARB(AF)/12/5, Award of 22 August 2016, paras 640, 646.

239 *SAUR International* v. *Argentine Republic*, ICSID, ARB/04/4, Award of 22 March 2014, paras 85–7; *Tecmed* (2004) note 40 at paras 187–8; *Wena* (2000) note 53 at para 118.

Group B: Divergence

- *ADC* (leading case): '[t]he BIT only stipulates the standard of compensation that is payable in the case of a lawful expropriation, and these cannot be used to determine the issue of damages payable in the case of an unlawful expropriation since this would be to conflate compensation for a lawful expropriation with damages for an unlawful expropriation. This would have been possible if the BIT expressly provided for such a position, but this does not exist in the present case. . . . Since the BIT does not contain any *lex specialis* rules that govern . . . the case of an unlawful expropriation, the Tribunal is required to apply the default standard contained in customary international law [*viz. Chorzów*] in the present case';[240]
- *Biwater Gauff*: '[t]he standard of compensation for unlawful expropriation (being the relevant claim here), includes full reparation . . . [which] entitles . . . to restitutionary damages which include, but are not limited to, the fair market value . . . [I]n many BIT cases, arbitral tribunals appear to have simply deployed the fair market value . . . as the measure of damages';[241]
- *ConocoPhillips*: '[t]he Tribunal . . . does not consider that the extent of the compensation payable in respect of an unlawful taking of an investment . . . is to be determined under Article 6(c): that provision establishes a condition to be met if the expropriation is in all other respects in accordance with Article 6. So, in the *Chorzów* case, the Court did not determine reparation in accordance with the provisions of the Convention before it, because it was concerned with a dispossession in breach of those provisions';[242]
- *Crystallex*: there is a 'dispute as to whether such standard [compensation under Article VII(1)] also applies to expropriations not meeting one or more of the Treaty requirements . . . [T]he Tribunal considers that in this particular case this discussion is rather theoretical and devoid of significant practical effects' – yet: 'as a general matter, the Tribunal considers that the standard of compensation contained in Article VII(1) of the Treaty is not the appropriate standard of

240 *ADC Affiliate Limited and ADC & ADMC Management Limited* v. *Republic of Hungary*, ICSID, ARB/03/16, Award of 2 October 2006, paras 481, 483.

241 *Biwater Gauff* (2008) note 28 at paras 775, 777.

242 *ConocoPhillips Petrozuata B.V., ConocoPhillips Hamaca B.V., ConocoPhillips Gulf of Paria B.V. and ConocoPhillips Company* v. *Bolivarian Republic of Venezuela*, ICSID, ARB/07/30, Decision on Jurisdiction and the Merits of 3 September 2013, para 342.

compensation in cases of breaches of that provision, i.e., when the requirements set out in Article VII(1) are not met. One particular question is whether the BIT standard is, however, applicable in cases of expropriations merely lacking compensation. This point may be left open here';[243]

- *Enkev* (obiter): 'Poland had taken the factory at *Chorzów* in violation of international law; and thus the judicial statements apply to unlawful expropriation and compensation as a form of restitution under international law. Compensation for unlawful expropriation may entail more than compensation for lawful expropriation';[244]
- *Houben*: '[l]e Tribunal considère cependant que le standard d'indemnisation prévu à l'article 4 du TBI ne s'applique qu'aux expropriations effectuées en conformité avec les autres conditions posées par cet article . . . l'article 4 ne dit rien du standard de réparation à appliquer si l'expropriation n'est pas conforme au TBI, c'est-à-dire si l'un quelconque des trois autres critères prévu par l'article 4 n'est pas rempli';[245]
- *Kardassopoulos*;[246]
- *Mondev*: '[t]here is a distinction between compensation offered or provided for a lawful taking of property and damages for the wrongful seizure of property';[247]
- *Quiborax*: 'Article VI(2) of the BIT sets out the standard of compensation for lawful expropriations . . . The treaty standard does not apply to unlawful expropriations, which are governed by the full reparation principle as articulated by the PCIJ in the *Chorzów* case and later expressed in the ILC Articles. Article VI(2) does not purport to establish a *lex specialis* for unlawful expropriations';[248]
- *Saipem*: 'Article 5(1)(3) of the BIT . . . describes the just compensation due in case of an expropriation . . . This provision is not applicable to determine the amount of compensation in the present instance because it sets out the measure of compensation for lawful expropriation which

[243] *Crystallex International Corporation* v. *Bolivarian Republic of Venezuela*, ICSID, ARB(AF)/11/2, Award of 4 April 2016, paras 842, 843, 846.

[244] *Enkev* (2014) note 31 at para 363.

[245] *Joseph Houben* v. *Republic of Burundi*, ICSID, ARB/13/7, Award of 12 January 2016, para 219.

[246] *Ioannis Kardassopoulos and Ron Fuchs* v. *Republic of Georgia*, ICSID, ARB/05/18 and ARB/07/15, Award of 3 March 2010, paras 501–17 (indirectly supporting a difference, eg when paras 517 and 514 are read together).

[247] *Mondev International Ltd.* v. *United States of America*, NAFTA-ICSID, ARB(AF)/99/2, Award of 11 October 2002, para 71.

[248] *Quiborax* (2015) note 9 at para 326.

this one is not. Hence, the Tribunal will resort to the relevant principles of customary international law and in particular to ... *Chorzów Factory*';[249]

- *Siag*: 'the Tribunal is satisfied that the compensation provisions within Article 5 of the BIT are not applicable for present purposes . . . Reading Article 5 of the BIT as a whole, it is plain that subclause (iii) is concerned with lawful expropriation ... [T]he expropriation in this case did not satisfy those conditions, and ... accordingly it was not a lawful expropriation to which Article 5 of the BIT applied' – however: 'in the present case the distinction between compensation for a lawful expropriation and compensation for an unlawful expropriation may not make a significant practical difference';[250]
- *Siemens*: '[t]he Treaty itself only provides for compensation for expropriation *in accordance with the terms* of the Treaty';[251]
- *Tidewater*: 'compensation for a lawful expropriation is fair compensation represented by the value of the undertaking at the moment of dispossession and reparation in case of unlawful expropriation is restitution in kind or its monetary equivalent'[252] – however, the tribunal was so caught up in its argument about 'provisionally lawful expropriation' (discussed in Section 7.4.2)[253] that it might in effect have blurred the distinction;
- *Tza Yap Shum*: '[e]n este caso las medidas expropiatorias no reunieron las condiciones establecidas en el artículo 4 y por lo tanto, la valoración del daño por parte del Tribunal se hará con base en el derecho internacional consuetudinario y no al artículo 4 del APPRI';[254]
- *Unglaube*: '[i]n the present case, the conduct of the State did not conform to the terms of Article 4(2). . . . [T]he Tribunal cannot accept the arguments of Respondent, for purposes of determining the amount of compensation due, that the provisions of Article 4(2) alone must govern' – however: 'this is not a matter of great consequence regarding the case before us ... [T]reaty-based compensation will often provide

[249] *Saipem* (2009) note 12 at para 201.
[250] *Waguih Elie George Siag and Clorinda Vecchi* v. *Arab Republic of Egypt*, ICSID, ARB/05/15, Award of 1 June 2009, paras 539, 541.
[251] *Siemens A.G.* v. *Argentine Republic*, ICSID, ARB/02/8, Award of 6 February 2007, para 349 (emphasis added).
[252] *Tidewater* (2015) note 63 at para 142.
[253] See also *Venezuela Holdings* (2014) note 41 at para 306.
[254] *Tza Yap Shum* v. *Republic of Peru*, ICSID, ARB/07/6, Award of 7 July 2011, para 253.

the same result as compensation based on customary international law';[255]

- *Vestey*: 'Article 5 of the BIT does not purport to establish a special regime of reparation for expropriations which are unlawful due to reasons other than the absence of compensation. … Venezuela's expropriation of Vestey's investment was not illegal only because no compensation was paid. Venezuela also failed to grant due process as required by Article 5(1) of the BIT. … Venezuela must provide full reparation under customary international law'[256] – in contradistinction to other awards espousing the legal-but-for-compensation theory, *Vestey* was clearer on the consequences flowing from an unlawful expropriation (however defined);
- *Vivendi*: '[t]he Treaty … does not purport to establish a *lex specialis* governing the standards of compensation for wrongful expropriations. [*Chorzów*] … There can be no doubt about the vitality of this statement of the damages standard under customary international law … It is also clear that such a standard permits, if the facts so require, a higher rate of recovery than that prescribed in Article 5(2) for lawful expropriations';[257]
- *Yukos*: '[t]he text of Article 13 [ECT] … provides that for "such" an expropriation, that is, for a lawful expropriation, damages shall be calculated as of the date of the taking. *A contrario*, the text of Article 13 may be read to import that damages for an unlawful taking need not be calculated as of the date of taking. … Moreover, conflating the measure of damages for a lawful taking with the measure of damages for an unlawful taking is, on its face, an unconvincing option. … The Tribunal finds that the principles on the reparation for injury as expressed in the ILC Articles on State Responsibility are relevant in this regard.'[258]

At least on this classification, a clear majority of awards since *ADC* in 2006 have drawn either a categorical or at least some sort of distinction between compensation for lawful and reparation for unlawful

[255] *Marion Unglaube and Reinhard Unglaube* v. *Republic of Costa Rica*, ICSID, ARB/08/01 and ARB/09/20, Award of 16 May 2012, paras 305, 307.

[256] *Vestey Group Limited* v. *Bolivarian Republic of Venezuela*, ICSID, ARB/06/4, Award of 15 April 2016, paras 329, 331.

[257] *Vivendi* (2007) note 63 at paras 8.2.3, 8.2.4, 8.2.5.

[258] *Yukos Universal Limited (Isle of Man)* v. *Russian Federation*, UNCITRAL, PCA AA 227, Final Award of 18 July 2014, paras 1765, 1766 (identical in all relevant aspects to *Veteran Petroleum Limited* v. *Russian Federation*, PCA AA 228, Final Award of 18 July 2014).

expropriation. Yet a number of uncertainties remain, partially connected to the legal-but-for-compensation theory, and partially owing to Group A awards tending to take less clear-cut abstract positions and to focus on the case at hand and the consequences for valuation (respectively, the lack thereof). For example, when the *CME* award found that Article 5(c) Czech Republic–Netherlands BIT required compensation which represents the genuine value, yet also held that '[a] fortiori unlawful measures of deprivation must be remedied by just compensation',[259] the identity is implied but not explicitly asserted. *Saint Gobain* is particularly opaque on this point – reporting that it 'does not have to make a finding ... as to whether the compensation standard to be applied is the standard contained in Article 5(1) ... or rather the customary international law standard'[260] while later hewing close to the ILC's ARS.[261]

8.4.3 *Judicial Standard or Structural Limit?*

Prima facie, a number of issues need to be discussed in order to decide whether the compensation–reparation duality is structurally required or a matter for tribunal discretion. For example, the various substantive differences between IIA compensation provisions vis-à-vis customary law reparation law, such as the date of valuation,[262] the subjective versus objective standards[263] or the question of *lucrum cessans* vis-à-vis *damnum emergens*,[264] seem relevant. Yet, in line with the doctrinal method of this chapter, the 'solution' is somewhat simpler, if not necessarily clearer in terms of what 'the law' requires regarding valuation and its standards. Given our analysis above of the structure of IIA expropriation clauses (at

259 *CME* (2001) note 44 at para 615.

260 *Saint-Gobain* (2016) note 143 at para 614.

261 Eg *Saint-Gobain* (2016) note 143 at para 627.

262 Eg Newcombe (2009) note 7 at 381; Marboe (2006) note 212 at 751–5; Marboe (2015b) note 210 at 1067–8, 1069–72; *ADC* (2006) note 240 at paras 496–9.

263 Dolzer (2012) note 7 at 295, 297: 'Under this principle, damages for a violation of international law have to reflect the damage actually suffered by the victim. In other words, the victim's actual situation has to be compared with the one that would have prevailed had the act not been committed. ... This subjective method includes any consequential damage but also incidental benefits arising as a consequence of the illegal act. ... Whereas damages for an illegal act look at the victim's subjective position, compensation for expropriation, as expressed in the investment's fair market value, is an objective standard that looks at the amount that a willing buyer would normally pay to a willing seller in a free transaction, at arm's length.'

264 Eg Marboe (2006) note 212 at 727–8; Reisman (2004) note 94 at 137; Sheppard (2006) note 213 at 181.

least Type A clauses), in particular of the relationship of the legality conditions in Section 7.4, it is almost trivially true that the compensation condition regulates compensation for *lawful* expropriations only, that is, expropriations meeting *all* legality conditions, including the compensation condition itself. Other articles of IIAs aside, this is *not* an issue for tribunal discretion, a choice within the frame of possible meanings in Type A clauses. The compensation condition does not itself regulate the legal consequences of a breach of the expropriation provision, that is, of an unlawful expropriation. Marboe summarises this position: 'In case of a lawful expropriation, the duty to pay compensation is the consequence of the legal exercise of a recognized sovereign right of a State. The duty to pay damages arises out of the violation of a legal obligation of that State.'[265]

This much is certain, but a new question arises: which norm(s), if any, govern the legal consequences (*Rechtsfolgen*) of an unlawful expropriation? The answer, ever since *Chorzów*, but more consistently since the completion of the ILC's State Responsibility project, has been: the customary law of reparations. Khachvani explains the *communis opinio*:

> International law . . . knows the distinction between primary and secondary norms. . . . A treaty provision requiring compensation for a taking creates a primary obligation, while the duty to provide reparation for unlawful expropriation is a secondary obligation that only applies when a breach of a primary obligation is established. Thus, the duty to pay compensation as a modality of reparation differs from the treaty obligation to provide compensation for a taking since it stems from the secondary norms of international law of state responsibility.[266]

Therefore, the customary rules of state responsibility, arguably as reflected in the ARS, are relevant to our question in two directions. Negatively, asking whether other rules are applicable instead; positively, even if no other norms are applicable, are they the law, as the mainstream assertion would have it? On the first level, the argument that the IIA compensation clause is applicable to both lawful and unlawful expropriations (identity argument) is held against its negation (divergence argument). This decision is structural. On the second level, we ask: if not the compensation clause, what law (if any) is applicable? This is no longer a structural issue. On that level, three possibilities emerge: the IIA in some form provides a *lex specialis* for unlawful expropriations, or the

[265] Marboe (2006) note 212 at 726.

[266] Khachvani (2017) note 229 at 388; see also Dolzer (2012) note 7 at 100; Valasek (2007) note 217 at 45–7.

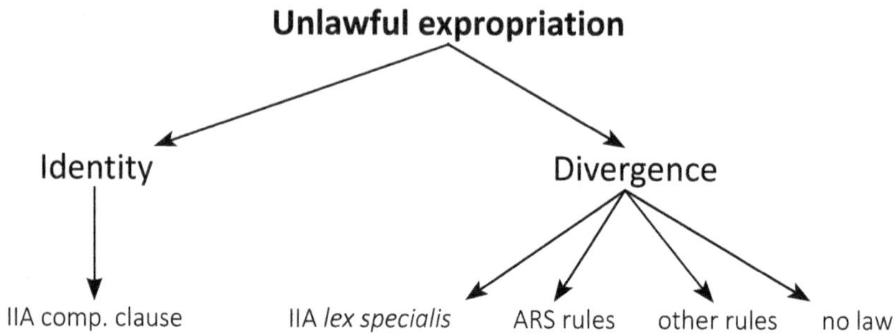

Figure 8.3 Matrix for legal consequences flowing from an unlawful expropriation

customary state responsibility rules apply as first laid down in *Chorzów* and now best embodied in the ARS, or even this is problematic.

If we take the identity argument off the table for structural reasons, the argument morphs. On that modified view, it is conceivable within the frame of meanings of IIAs that they also establish a *lex specialis* (Article 55 ARS) of IIA-state-responsibility for unlawful expropriation. The compensation condition would only serve as 'inspiration' for our reading of the IIA to *tacitly* create an IIA-specific responsibility regime. In *Crystallex*, for example, the tribunal highlighted a clause in the dispute settlement provision of the applicable BIT (Article XII(9)(a) Venezuela–Canada BIT 1996), which reads: 'A tribunal may award, separately or in combination, only: (a) monetary damages and any applicable interest'. Yet that clause 'does not . . . detail any standard of compensation . . . The only reference to a standard of compensation is the one contained in Article VII(1)',[267] the compensation condition of the BIT's expropriation clause. It found that 'the standard of compensation contained in Article VII(1) of the Treaty is not the appropriate standard of compensation . . . when [its] requirements . . . are not met'.[268] While *Crystallex* did not deal with the *lex specialis* claim, other tribunals have done so. In *Quiborax*, for example, the tribunal agreed 'with the Claimants that the BIT does not establish the standard of compensation for internationally wrongful acts. . . . Article VI(2) does not purport to establish a *lex specialis* for unlawful expropriations.'[269] The *Vivendi* award held that '[t]he Treaty . . . does not purport to establish a *lex specialis* governing the standards of compensation for wrongful expropriations'.[270] In *Vestey*, the tribunal

[267] *Crystallex* (2016) note 243 at para 841.
[268] *Crystallex* (2016) note 243 at para 846.
[269] *Quiborax* (2015) note 9 at para 326.
[270] *Vivendi* (2007) note 63 at para 8.2.3; see also *ADC* (2006) note 240 at para 483.

admitted that 'States are free to derogate from this general framework of responsibility', but felt that it could not 'follow the Respondent when it submits that the rules on compensation set in Article 5 of the BIT constitute such a derogation'.[271]

These are rather clear holdings: the likelihood that one can deduce an IIA-immanent standard faces very high evidentiary hurdles, particularly since the structure is so clear on this point and typically there are few or no other provisions which would even indirectly point to an autonomous regulation of the matter. A tacit derogation from state responsibility for the convenience of avoiding a divergence between the standards of compensation for lawful and of reparation for unlawful expropriation is highly unlikely. Better proof is required than the mere assertion; unless there is explicit language in the IIA, the establishment of a *lex specialis* regime will probably not be convincing.

The other aspect of the application of the law of state responsibility is similar to the arguments developed in Chapters 2–4 regarding the development of customary international law from IIAs and from the VCLT rules of interpretation. Even if the IIA compensation condition (or the IIA as a whole) is not applicable to unlawful expropriations, this does not automatically mean that a different set of rules applies. This is true even though the majority accepts that the customary law of state responsibility applies in the case of an unlawful expropriation,[272] for example in *Vestey*:

> Venezuela has committed an internationally wrongful act as defined by Article 2 of the ILC Articles on State Responsibility, which entails the international responsibility of the state, and gives rise to an obligation to make full reparation ... [I]t is generally accepted that the key provisions of the ILC, such as Article 31(1)[,] can be transposed in the context of the investor-State disputes.[273]

Since the rules codified in the ARS are not treaty law applicable to IIAs, a number of questions arise which are similar to those posed in previous chapters. One, as the *Vestey* tribunal mentioned in the quotation above, it could be argued that the ARS (respectively, the customary law on state responsibility) stipulates that responsibility arises only vis-à-vis other states, which would raise problems. Yet outside the etatist paradigm neither is responsibility necessarily owed towards other states nor can the idea that international law norms are normally not just owed *by*

[271] *Vestey* (2016) note 256 at para 327.
[272] Valasek (2007) note 217 at 20.
[273] *Vestey* (2016) note 256 at para 326.

a subject of international law but also *to* a subject really stand theoretical muster. This is a false analogy from the domestic private law of contracts. Quite the contrary, the idea that performance under a norm is owed *to someone* is an abnormal situation; it must be proven that a norm does so, not that it does not. Without more, the default position is that the prescriptive content of a norm is applicable to no one in particular – by default, all norms are *erga neminem*. It is entirely possible that rules of responsibility create a secondary duty of reparation *sensu largo* without legal relevance being accorded to whether the recipient of that reparation is a state, corporation or an individual. That conclusion does not change even if the duty of reparation of a bilateral IIA is properly owed *to* the other state party. The (customary *lex specialis*) rules of state responsibility could still require, as part of the secondary duty of reparation, a payment to the investor, as act of satisfaction of the primary duty owed to the other BIT party.

Two, similar problems of proof beleaguer the customary international law norms of state responsibility as other bodies of customary law, such as the law of treaties. Proof of (instances of) state practice and *opinio iuris* for a proposed norm 'x' is supplanted with proof of the ICJ and other tribunals *asserting* that 'x' is a norm of customary law. The archaic and limited nature of customary norms is underestimated and a complex modern statutory-type form of regulation is assumed for customary rules. A text – the VCLT there, the ARS here – is taken to be word-for-word identical to customary international norms. All these elements generate a significant amount of suppressed uncertainty about the validity ('whether') and exact content ('how') of the regime of legal consequences flowing from a breach of international law.

Three, another, less central set of considerations is connected to the assumption, sometimes voiced, but more often subconsciously made, that 'damages for an unlawful expropriation cannot be less than compensation for a lawful expropriation'.[274] Only an argument from necessity, couched perhaps in venerable legal maxims such as *commodum ex iniuria sua nemo habere debet*, can support such an argument. From the perspective of an analysis of positive law, however, it is possible that IIAs specify a higher level of monetary compensation for lawful acts than the customary law of responsibility does for unlawful acts. In private law, it is quite common for parties to a contract to specify, in the contract, an alternative obligation to pay compensation, sometimes called 'penalty' for breach of contract (*Vertragspönale*) which goes beyond what the law

[274] Marboe (2006) note 212 at 758.

of torts (*Schadenersatzrecht*) would require, for example where the completion of a building by a certain date is so crucial that the contractor must pay significant sums in case of delays.

The frame of possible meanings regarding the exact requirements for treaty-based compensation for lawful expropriation – and of customary law-based reparation for unlawful expropriation – is large. This creates a significant *combined* frame for valuation standards and methods. The discretion of organs (tribunals) is significant and even a tribunal pursuing the identity thesis would in all likelihood not go beyond the frame of possible meanings under the divergence thesis.

One potential and significant difference between compensation and reparation is *restitutio in integrum*. The question of restitution, more than *lucrum cessans* or any other, may be the crucial difference here: restitution is not part of the compensation condition in IIAs. It is not available for lawful behaviour under the IIA compensation regimes for a simple reason, because it would mean that the alternative offered – no expropriation or expropriation, but observance of the legality conditions – would no longer exist. States would either have to abstain from expropriating – or could do so, but only if they gave the expropriated investment back. The Iran–US Claims Tribunal in *Phillips Petroleum* confirmed this position when it held that 'the lawful/unlawful taking distinction . . . is relevant only to two possible issues: whether restitution of the property can be awarded and whether compensation can be awarded for increase of the value of the property'.[275] Under Article 35 ARS, restitution has primacy over monetary compensation:[276] 'a State responsible for an illegal expropriation is in the first place obliged to make restitution'.[277] Yet while '[i]n a number of cases, tribunals did in fact order restitution or affirmed their power to do so',[278] they have 'generally been rather reluctant to award restitution in favour of an investor'.[279] Therefore, the question of a difference does at any rate not come into play if only money is awarded, which is the vast majority of cases.

[275] *Phillips Petroleum Company, Iran* v. *Islamic Republic of Iran, National Iranian Oil Company*, Iran–USCT, Award 425-39-2 of 29 June 1989, 21 *Iran–USCT Reports* (1990) 79, para 110; see also *Funnekotter* (2009) note 233 at para 111; Valasek (2007) note 217 at 21.

[276] *Report of the International Law Commission on the Work of Its Fifty-Third Session* (23 April–1 June and 2 July–10 August 2001), A/56/10, Chapter VI: Draft Articles on State Responsibility, Commentary on Article 35 (para 3).

[277] *Yukos* (2014) note 258 at para 1766; see also Marboe (2006) note 212 at 744.

[278] Dolzer (2012) note 7 at 294.

[279] Marboe (2015a) note 221 at 1036.

Marboe brings another argument into play: '[reparation] does not only mean physical restitution of tangible assets but ... also restitution of sums of money. ... Instead of physical restitution, the replacement value ... may be appropriate.'[280] But – at least within the system as envisaged by the ILC – would this argument not conflate restitution with monetary compensation under Article 36? Would we therefore not, under the secondary law of state responsibility, have to take seriously the requirement of *restitutio ad integrum*? Would we really try to reinstate the situation-before-expropriation under Article 35 (and take the conditions therein seriously) before compensation under Article 36 is ordered? That is: if it should be possible – and it probably often is – and if they are asked to, would tribunals not be required to order the Respondent to return the investment to the Claimant, rather than immediately start calculating damages?

In addition to the large combined frame of possible meanings, the pragmatic uncertainty is also considerable on value and valuation. Ratner is surely right when he argues that 'we can never be certain whether the stated position of the tribunal is actually doing any work in arriving at the final damages number given the mystery involved in those figures'.[281] The complexity and opacity of valuation processes by tribunals, their reluctance to discuss the actual valuation, and conceivably also the lack of expertise and consequent haphazardness with which valuation decisions are made all contribute to blur the distinction.

Hence, the legal (theoretical) structural difference identified above is not as relevant as assumed, even though none of the other arguments presented in this section do, as some argue, eliminate it. Orthodox opinion shares this view, perhaps with a slightly different foundation: 'While in theory there is a distinction between compensation for lawful expropriations and reparation for unlawful ones, the typical approach is to award an investment's fair market value, regardless of the type of expropriation.'[282]

8.5 Conclusion

As expected, the freedom of tribunals within the frame, as defined in Chapter 7 and Section 8.4 is significant. As discussed, it cannot be

280 Marboe (2006) note 212 at 744.
281 Ratner (2017) note 210 at 15.
282 UNCTAD (2012) note 5 at 116.

reduced by their combined decision-making, even where the preponderance points towards a single judicial standard. Yet just as IIAs are not specific, tribunal decisions are not general law. Any analysis of expropriation law on the level of tribunal decisions/standards (the aim of this chapter) must reflect the variations and irrationalities of multiple decisions made by multiple decision-makers. This we have attempted to do for a select number of questions in connection with expropriation in international investment law.

The three examples discussed are each unique – as are other questions which we could have discussed. Virtually all tribunals and scholars agree that an investment needs to be substantially deprived (Sections 8.2) to fulfil the *Tatbestand* of indirect expropriation, but there is significant divergence in case-law as to what, exactly, this means – with respect to sub-standards and with respect to which sets of facts investment tribunals have seen as fulfilling or not fulfilling the standard. In contrast, the problem of partial expropriation and the distinction between compensation for lawful expropriation vis-à-vis reparation for unlawful expropriation, discussed in Sections 8.3 and 8.4, exhibit a different pathology. Both are particularly good examples of splits into two camps of case-law. For partial expropriation, there are those who, in the abstract, deny the possibility of partial expropriations and those who argue that this is possible. In the compensation–reparation questions, we have the identity thesis and those who see a clear divergence, though constituting a relatively clear majority. Yet at least for the compensation–reparation issue, because of the large number of other factors influencing decisions – for example the large uncertainties about valuation – the actual decision-making, rather than the abstract statements about the legal standard, is much less clearly split.

BIBLIOGRAPHY

Abdala (2008): Manuel A Abdala, Pablo T Spiller, '*Chorzów*'s Standard Rejuvenated: Assessing Damages in Investment Treaty Arbitrations' 25 *Journal of International Arbitration* (2008) 103–20.

Akehurst (1977a): Michael Akehurst, 'Custom as a Source of International Law' 47 *British Year Book of International Law 1974–75* (1977) 1–53.

Akehurst (1977b): Michael Akehurst, 'The Hierarchy of the Sources of International Law' 47 *British Year Book of International Law 1974–75* (1977) 273–85.

Al Faruque (2004): Abdullah Al Faruque, 'Creating Customary International Law through Bilateral Investment Treaties: A Critical Appraisal' 44 *Indian Journal of International Law* (2004) 292–318.

Algero (2005): Mary Garvey Algero, 'The Sources of Law and the Value of Precedent: A Comparative and Empirical Study of a Civil Law State in a Common Law Nation; 65 *Louisiana Law Review* (2005) 775–822.

Al-Mukhaizeem (2016): Bashayer Al-Mukhaizeem, 'The Dilemma of Indirect Expropriation of Host States and the Right to Regulate in the International Investment Sphere' 4:2 *Legal Issues Journal* (2016) 1–23.

Allot (1999): Philip Allott, 'The Concept of International Law' 10 *European Journal of International Law* (1999) 31–50.

Alvarez (2009): José E Alvarez, 'A BIT on Custom' 42 *New York University Journal of International Law and Politics* (2009) 17–80.

Alvarez (2016): José E Alvarez, '"Beware: Boundary Crossings" – A Critical Appraisal of Public Law Approaches to International Investment Law' 17 *Journal of World Investment & Trade* (2016) 171–228.

Appleton (2002–3): Barry Appleton, 'Regulatory Takings: The International Law Perspective' 11 *New York University Environmental Law Journal* (2002–3) 35–48.

Ascensio (2016): Hervé Ascensio, 'Article 31 of the Vienna Conventions on the Law of Treaties and International Investment Law' 31 *ICSID Review* (2016) 366–87.

Asteriti (2014): Alessandra Asteriti, 'Regulatory Expropriation Claims in International Investment Arbitrations: A Bridge Too Far?' in Andrea

K Bjorklund (ed.), *Yearbook on International Investment Law and Policy 2012–2013* (Oxford: Oxford University Press 2014) 451–73.

Auerbach (1900): Paul Auerbach, *Dispositives Recht insbesondere des BGB* (Frankfurt: Mahlau & Waldschmidt 1900).

Austin (1962): John L Austin, *How to Do Things with Words: The William James Lectures Delivered at Harvard University in 1955* (Cambridge, MA: Harvard University Press 1962).

Bankowski (1997): Zenon Bankowski, D Neil MacCormick, 'Precedent in the United Kingdom' in D Neil MacCormick, Robert S Summers (eds.), *Interpreting Precedents: A Comparative Study* (Aldershot: Ashgate 1997) 315–54.

Banks (1999): Kevin Banks, 'NAFTA's Article 1110: Can Regulation Be Expropriation?' 5 *NAFTA: Law and Business Review of the Americas* (1999) 499–521.

Bartels (2011): Lorand Bartels, 'Jurisdiction and Applicable Law Clauses: Where Does a Tribunal Find the Principal Norms Applicable to the Case before It?' in Tomer Broude, Yuval Shani (eds.), *Multi-sourced Equivalent Norms in International Law* (Oxford: Hart 2011) 115–41.

Baughen (2006): Simon Baughen, 'Expropriation and Environmental Regulation: The Lessons of NAFTA Chapter 11' 18 *Journal of Environmental Law* (2006) 207–28.

Baxter (1968): Richard R Baxter, 'Multilateral Treaties as Evidence of Customary International Law' 41 *British Year Book of International Law 1965–66* (1968) 275–300.

Baxter (1971): Richard R Baxter, 'Treaties and Custom' 129 *Recueil des Cours* (1971) 25–106.

Beauvais (2001–2): Joel C Beauvais, 'Regulatory Expropriations under NAFTA: Emerging Principles and Lingering Doubts' 10 *New York University Environmental Law Journal* (2001–2) 245–96.

Been (2003): Vicki Been, Joel C Beauvais, 'The Global Fifth Amendment? NAFTA's Investment Protections and the Misguided Quest for an International "Regulatory Takings" Doctrine' 78 *New York University Law Review* (2003) 30–143.

Behrend (1977): Jürgen Behrend, *Untersuchungen zur Stufenbaulehre Adolf Merkls und Hans Kelsens* (Berlin: Duncker & Humblot 1977).

Bernhardt (1963): Rudolf Bernhardt, *Die Auslegung völkerrechtlicher Verträge insbesondere in der neueren Rechtsprechung internationaler Gerichte* (Berlin: Duncker & Humblot 1963).

Bernhardt (1995): Rudolf Bernhardt, 'Interpretation in International Law' in Rudolf Bernhardt (ed.), *Encyclopedia of Public International Law*, vol 2 (Amsterdam: Elsevier 1995) 1416–26.

Bernhardt (2006): Rudolf Bernhardt, 'Article 59' in Andreas Zimmermann, Christian Tomuschat, Karin Oellers-Frahm (eds.), *The Statute of the International Court of Justice* (Oxford: Oxford University Press 2006) 1231–51.

Binder (1920): Julius Binder, 'Der Wissenschaftscharakter der Rechtswissenschaft' 25 *Kant-Studien* (1920) 321–65.

Bindschedler (1950): Rudolf L Bindschedler, *Verstaatlichungsmaßnahmen und Entschädigungspflicht nach Völkerrecht unter besonderer Berücksichtigung der schweizerischen Praxis über den Schutz schweizerischer Vermögenswerte im Ausland* (Zurich: Polygraphischer Verlag 1950).

Birke (1960): Wolfgang Birke, Die Konfiskation ausländischen Privatvermögens im Hoheitsbereich des konfiszierenden Staates nach Friedensvölkerrecht (PhD thesis, University of Cologne 1960).

Bishop (2005): R Doak Bishop, James Crawford, W Michael Reisman, *Foreign Investment Disputes: Cases, Materials and Commentary* (The Hague: Kluwer 2005).

Bjorklund (2008): Andrea K Bjorklund, 'Investment Treaty Arbitral Decisions as *Jurisprudence Constante*' in Colin B Picker, Isabella D Bunn, Douglas W Arner (eds.), *International Economic Law: The State and Future of the Discipline* (Oxford: Hart 2008) 265–80.

Bleckmann (1976): Albert Bleckmann, 'Völkergewohnheitsrecht trotz widersprüchlicher Praxis?' 36 *Zeitschrift für ausländisches öffentliches Recht und Völkerrecht* (1976) 374–405.

Bluntschli (1868): Johann Caspar Bluntschli, *Das moderne Völkerrecht der civilisirten Staaten als Rechtsbuch dargestellt* (Nördlingen: CH Beck 1868).

Bodansky (2015): Daniel Bodansky, 'Legal Realism and Its Discontents' 28 *Leiden Journal of International Law* (2015) 267–81.

Bonnitcha (2014): Jonathan Bonnitcha, *Substantive Protection under Investment Treaties: A Legal and Economic Analysis* (Cambridge: Cambridge University Press 2014).

Bos (1980): Maarten Bos, 'Theory and Practice of Treaty Interpretation' 27 *Netherlands International Law Review* (1980) 3–38, 135–70.

Bos (1982): Maarten Bos, 'The Identification of Custom in International Law' 25 *German Yearbook of International Law* (1982) 9–53.

Bowett (1988): Derek William Bowett, 'State Contracts with Aliens: Contemporary Developments on Compensation for Termination or Breach' 59 *British Year Book of International Law* (1988) 49–74.

Bray (2012): A Devin Bray, 'Non-compensatory versus Compensatory Takings under NAFTA' 9:7 *Transnational Dispute Management* (2012).

Brie (1899): Siegfried Brie, *Die Lehre vom Gewohnheitsrecht: Eine historisch-dogmatische Untersuchung* (Breslau: Marcus 1899).

Brierly (1955): James L Brierly, *The Law of Nations: An Introduction to the International Law of Peace* (5th edn, Oxford: Clarendon Press 1955).

Brower (1998): Charles N Brower, Jason D Brueschke, *The Iran–United States Claims Tribunal* (The Hague: Martinus Nijhoff 1998).

Brunetti (2003): Maurizio Brunetti, 'Introduction [Indirect Expropriation in International Law]' 5 *International Law Forum* (2003) 150–4.

Bullington (1927): John P Bullington, 'Problems of International Law in the Mexican Constitution of 1917' 21 *American Journal of International Law* (1927) 685–705.

Burke-White (2008): William W Burke-White, Andreas von Staden, 'Investment Protection in Extraordinary Times: The Interpretation and Application of Non-precluded Measures Provisions in Bilateral Investment Treaties' 48 *Virginia Journal of International Law* (2008) 307–410.

Busse (1993): Dietrich Busse, *Juristische Semantik: Grundfragen der juristischen Interpretationstheorie in sprachwissenschaftlicher Sicht* (Berlin: Duncker & Humblot 1993).

Byers (1999): Michael Byers, *Custom, Power and the Power of Rules: International Relations and Customary International Law* (Cambridge: Cambridge University Press 1999).

Charney (1986): Jonathan I Charney, 'International Agreements and the Development of Customary International Law' 61 *Washington Law Review* (1986) 971–95.

Cheng (1983): Bin Cheng, 'Custom: The Future of General State Practice in a Divided World' in Ronald St John Macdonald, Douglas M Johnston (eds.), *The Structure and Process of International Law: Essays in Legal Philosophy Doctrine and Theory* (The Hague: Martinus Nijhoff 1983) 513–54.

Cheng (2007): Tai-Heng Cheng, 'Precedent and Control in Investment Treaty Arbitration' 30 *Fordham International Law Journal* (2007) 1014–49.

Christie (1964): GC Christie, 'What Constitutes a Taking of Property under International Law?' 38 *British Year Book of International Law 1962* (1964) 307–38.

Clough (2005): Daniel Clough, 'Regulatory Expropriations and Competition under NAFTA' 6 *Journal of World Investment & Trade* (2005) 553–84.

Coe (2005): Jack Coe, Jr, Noah Rubins, 'Regulatory Expropriation and the *Tecmed* Case: Context and Contributions' in Todd Weiler (ed.), *International Investment Law and Arbitration: Leading Cases from the ICSID, NAFTA, Bilateral Treaties and Customary International Law* (London: Cameron May 2005) 597–667.

Collins (2014): Richard Collins, 'Classical Legal Positivism in International Law Revisited' in Jörg Kammerhofer, Jean d'Aspremont (eds.), *International Legal Positivism in a Post-Modern World* (Cambridge: Cambridge University Press 2014) 23–49.

Comeaux (1997): Paul E Comeaux, N Stephan Kinsella, *Protecting Foreign Investment under International Law* (Dobbs Ferry: Oceana 1997).

Commission (2007): Jeffery P Commission, 'Precedent in Investment Treaty Arbitration: A Citation Analysis of a Developing Jurisprudence' 24 *Journal of International Arbitration* (2007) 129–58.

Crawford (2008): James Crawford, 'Similarity of Issues in Disputes Arising under the Same or Similarly Drafted Investment Treaties' in Yas Banifatemi (ed.), *Precedent in International Arbitration: IAI Seminar Paris – December 14, 2007* (New York: Juris 2008) 97–103.

Crawford (2012): James Crawford, *Brownlie's Principles of Public International Law* (8th edn, Oxford: Oxford University Press 2012).

D'Amato (1971): Anthony A D'Amato, *The Concept of Custom in International Law* (Ithaca: Cornell University Press 1971).

d'Aspremont (2011): Jean d'Aspremont, *Formalism and the Sources of International Law: A Theory of the Ascertainment of Legal Rules* (Oxford: Oxford University Press 2011).

d'Aspremont (2012): Jean d'Aspremont, 'International Customary Investment Law: Story of a Paradox' in Tarcisio Gazzini, Eric De Brabandere (eds.), *International Investment Law: The Sources of Rights and Obligations* (Leiden: Martinus Nijhoff 2012) 5–47.

d'Aspremont (2015): Jean d'Aspremont, 'If International Judges Say So, It Must Be True: Empiricism or Fetishism?' 4:9 *ESIL Reflections* (2015).

d'Aspremont (2017): Jean d'Aspremont, 'The International Court of Justice and the Irony of System-Design' 18 *Journal of International Dispute Settlement* (2017) 366–87.

d'Aspremont (2018): Jean d'Aspremont, *International Law as a Belief System* (Cambridge: Cambridge University Press 2018).

Dalhuisen (2013): Jan H Hendrik Dalhuisen, Andrew T Guzman, 'Expropriatory and Non-expropriatory Takings under International Investment Law' 10:4 *Transnational Dispute Management* (2013).

Dahm (1958): Georg Dahm, *Völkerrecht*, vol 1 (Stuttgart: W Kohlhammer 1958).

Danilenko (1988): Gennady M Danilenko, 'The Theory of International Customary Law' 31 *German Yearbook of International Law* (1988) 9–47.

Dinstein (2002): Yoram Dinstein, 'Deprivation of Property of Foreigners under International Law' in Nisuke Ando, Edward McWhinney, Rüdiger Wolfrum (eds.), *Liber Amicorum Judge Shigeru Oda*, vol 2 (The Hague: Kluwer 2002) 849–69.

Dinstein (2007): Yoram Dinstein, 'The Interaction between Customary International Law and Treaties' 322 *Recueil des Cours 2006* (2007) 243–428.

Djeffal (2016): Christian Djeffal, *Static and Evolutive Treaty Interpretation: A Functional Reconstruction* (Cambridge: Cambridge University Press 2016).

Doehring (1976): Karl Doehring, 'Gewohnheitsrecht aus Verträgen' 36 *Zeitschrift für ausländisches öffentliches Recht und Völkerrecht* (1976) 77–95.

Dolzer (1985): Rudolf Dolzer, *Eigentum, Enteignung und Entschädigung im geltenden Völkerrecht* (Berlin: Springer 1985).

Dolzer (1986): Rudolf Dolzer, 'Indirect Expropriation of Alien Property' 1 *ICSID Review – Foreign Investment Law Journal* (1986) 41–65.

Dolzer (1995): Rudolf Dolzer, Margrete Stevens, *Bilateral Investment Treaties* (The Hague: Martinus Nijhoff 1995).

Dolzer (2002–3): Rudolf Dolzer, 'Indirect Expropriations: New Developments?' 11 *New York University Environment Law Journal* (2002–3) 64–92.

Dolzer (2012): Rudolf Dolzer, Christoph Schreuer, *Principles of International Investment Law* (2nd edn, Oxford: Oxford University Press 2012).

Dolzer (2015): Rudolf Dolzer, 'Case Comment: ConocoPhillips v Venezuela and Gold Reserve v Venezuela: Expropriation: A New Focus on Old Issues' 30 *ICSID Review* (2015) 378–83.

Douglas (2010): Zachary Douglas, 'The MFN Clause in Investment Arbitration: Treaty Interpretation Off the Rails' 2 *Journal of International Dispute Settlement* (2010) 97–113.

Dreier (2007): Horst Dreier, 'Hans Kelsens Wissenschaftsprogramm' in Helmuth Schulze-Fielitz (ed.), *Staatsrechtslehre als Wissenschaft* (Berlin: Duncker & Humblot 2007).

Dugard (2007): John Dugard, 'The Future of International Law: A Human Rights Perspective – With Some Comments on the Leiden School of International Law' 20 *Leiden Journal of International Law* (2007) 729–39.

Dumberry (2010): Patrick Dumberry, 'Are BITs Representing the "New" Customary International Law in International Investment Law?' 28 *Penn State International Law Review* (2010) 675–701.

Dumberry (2016): Patrick Dumberry, *The Formation and Identification of Rules of Customary International Law in International Investment Law* (Cambridge: Cambridge University Press 2016).

ECS (2012): Energy Charter Secretariat, *Expropriation Regime under the Energy Charter Treaty* (Brussels: Energy Charter Secretariat 2012).

Elcombe (2010): Joshua Elcombe, 'Regulatory Powers vs. Investment Protection under NAFTA's Chapter 1110: *Metalclad, Methanex,* and *Glamis Gold*' 68 *University of Toronto Faculty of Law Review* (2010) 71–98.

Ephrussi (1924): Elisabeth Ephrussi, 'Interpretation und Analogie' 4 *Zeitschrift für öffentliches Recht* (1924) 132–59.

Fitzmaurice (1952): Gerald G Fitzmaurice, 'The Law and Procedure of the International Court of Justice: Treaty Interpretation and Certain Other Treaty Points' 28 *British Year Book of International Law 1951* (1952) 1–28.

Fitzmaurice (1958): Gerald G Fitzmaurice, 'The Law and Procedure of the International Court of Justice 1951–4: Treaty Interpretation and Other Treaty Points' 33 *British Year Book of International Law 1957* (1958) 203–93.

Fitzmaurice (2010): Malgosia Fitzmaurice, Panos Merkouris, 'Canons of Treaty Interpretation: Selected Case Studies from the World Trade Organization and the North American Free Trade Agreement' in Malgosia Fitzmaurice, Olufemi Elias, Panos Merkouris (eds.), *Treaty Interpretation and the Vienna Convention on the Law of Treaties: 30 Years On* (Leiden: Martinus Nijhoff 2010) 153–237.

Fortier (2004): L Yves Fortier, Stephen L Drymer, 'Indirect Expropriation in the Law of International Investment: I Know It When I See It, or *Caveat Investor*' 19 *ICSID Review – Foreign Investment Law Journal* (2004) 293–327.

French (2006): Duncan French, 'Treaty Interpretation and the Incorporation of Extraneous Legal Rules' 55 *International and Comparative Law Quarterly* (2006) 281–314.

Friedman (1953): Samy Friedman, *Expropriation in International Law* (London: Stevens & Sons 1953).

Gaffney (2007): John Gaffney, James Loftis, 'The "Effective Ordinary Meaning" of BITs and the Jurisdiction of Treaty-Based Tribunals to Hear Contract Claims' 8 *Journal of World Investment & Trade* (2007) 5–68.

Gardiner (2008): Richard Gardiner, *Treaty Interpretation* (Oxford: Oxford University Press 2008).

Gardner (1935): John C Gardner, 'Judicial Precedent in the Making of International Public Law' 18 *Journal of Comparative Legislation and International Law* (1935) 251–9.

Gazzini (2007): Tarcisio Gazzini, 'The Role of Customary International Law in the Field of Foreign Investment' 8 *Journal of World Investment & Trade* (2007) 691–716.

Gazzini (2010): Tarcisio Gazzini, 'Drawing the Line between Non-compensable Regulatory Powers and Indirect Expropriation of Foreign Investment – An Economic Analysis of Law Perspective' 7 *Manchester Journal of International Economic Law* (2010) 36–51.

Gazzini (2016): Tarcisio Gazzini, *Interpretation of International Investment Treaties* (Oxford: Hart 2016).

Gibson (2006): Christopher S Gibson, Christopher R Drahozal, 'Iran–United States Claims Tribunal Precedent in Investor–State Arbitration' 23 *Journal of International Arbitration* (2006) 521–46.

Gibson (2015): Christopher S Gibson, 'Case Comment: *Yukos Universal Limited (Isle of Man) v The Russian Federation*: A Classic Case of Indirect Expropriation' 30 *ICSID Review* (2015) 303–14.

Gildemeister (2014): Arno E Gildemeister, 'Case Comment: *Burlington Resources, Inc v Republic of Ecuador*: How Much Is Too Much: When Is Taxation Tantamount to Expropriation?' 29 *ICSID Review* (2014) 315–20.

Godshall (2002–3): Lauren E Godshall, 'In the Cold Shadow of *Metalclad*: The Potential for Change to NAFTA's Chapter Eleven' 11 *New York University Environmental Law Journal* (2002–3) 264–316.

Griller (1990): Stefan Griller, Michael Potacs, 'Zur Unterscheidung von Pragmatik und Semantik in der juristischen Hermeneutik' in Helmuth Vetter, Michael Potacs (eds.), *Beiträge zur juristischen Hermeneutik* (Vienna: Literas 1990) 66–105.

Grisel (2014): Florian Grisel, 'The Sources of Foreign Investment Law' in Zachary Douglas, Joost Pauwelyn, Jorge E Viñuales (eds.), *The Foundations of International Investment Law: Bringing Theory into Practice* (Oxford: Oxford University Press 2014) 213–33.

Guastini (1995): Riccardo Guastini, 'Kelsen on Legal Knowledge and Scientific Interpretation' in Letizia Gianformaggio, Stanley L Paulson (eds.), *Cognition and Interpretation of Law* (Turin: Giappichelli 1995) 107–15.

Günther (1970): Herbert Günther, *Zur Entstehung von Völkergewohnheitsrecht* (Berlin: Duncker & Humblot 1970).

Gutbrod (2006): Max Gutbrod, Steffen Hindelang, 'Externalization of Effective Legal Protection against Indirect Expropriation: Can the Legal Order of Developing Countries Live Up to Standards Required by International Investment Agreements? A Disenchanting Comparative Analysis' 7 *Journal of World Investment & Trade* (2006) 59–83.

Guzman (1998): Andrew T Guzman, 'Why LDCs Sign Treaties that Hurt Them: Explaining the Popularity of Bilateral Investment Treaties' 38 *Virginia Journal of International Law* (1998) 639–88.

Guzman (2009): Andrew T Guzman, Timothy L Meyer, 'International Common Law: The Soft Law of International Tribunals' 9 *Chicago Journal of International Law* (2009) 515–35.

Haraszti (1973): György Haraszti, *Some Fundamental Problems of the Law of Treaties* (Budapest: Akadémiai Kiadó 1973).

Harten (2006): Gus Van Harten, Martin Loughlin, 'Investment Treaty Arbitration as a Species of Global Administrative Law' 17 *European Journal of International Law* (2006) 121–50.

Harvard (1935): Harvard Law School, Codification of International Law: Part III Law of Treaties, printed in 29 *American Journal of International Law Supplement* (1935) 653–1226.

Herdegen (2012): Matthias Herdegen, 'Interpretation in International Law' in Rüdiger Wolfrum (ed.), *Max Planck Encyclopedia of Public International Law*, vol 6 (Oxford: Oxford University Press 2012) 260–73.

Henckels (2012): Caroline Henckels, 'Indirect Expropriation and the Right to Regulate: Revisiting Proportionality Analysis and the Standard of Review in Investor–State Arbitration' 15 *Journal of International Economic Law* (2012) 223–55.

Henckels (2015): Caroline Henckels, *Proportionality and Deference in Investor–State Arbitration* (Cambridge: Cambridge University Press 2015).

Higgins (1983): Rosalyn Higgins, 'The Taking of Property by the State: Recent Developments in International Law' 176 *Recueil des Cours 1982* (1983) 259–391.

Hindelang (2004): Steffen Hindelang, 'Bilateral Investment Treaties, Custom and a Healthy Investment Climate: The Question of Whether BITs Influence Customary International Law Revisited' 5 *Journal of World Investment & Trade* (2004) 789–809.

Hoffmann (2008): Anne K Hoffmann, 'Indirect Expropriation' in August Reinisch (ed.), *Standards of Investment Protection* (Oxford: Oxford University Press 2008) 151–70.

Holtzendorff (1885): Franz von Holtzendorff, 'Die Quellen des Völkerrechts' in Franz von Holtzendorff (ed.), *Handbuch des Völkerrechts: Auf Grundlage Europäischer Staatspraxis*, vol 1 (Berlin: Carl Habel 1885) 67–156.

Hoof (1983): GJH van Hoof, *Rethinking the Sources of International Law* (Deventer: Kluwer 1983).

Höpfner (2008): Clemens Höpfner, *Die systemkonforme Auslegung: Zur Auflösung einfachgesetzlicher, verfassungsrechtlicher und europarechtlicher Widersprüche im Recht* (Tubingen: Mohr 2008).

ILC (1963): Yearbook of the International Law Commission 1963, vol 1: Summary Records of the Fifteenth Session 6 May–12 July 1963, UN Doc A/CN.4/SER.A/1963 (New York: United Nations 1963).

ILC (1966): International Law Commission, 'Draft Articles on the Law of Treaties with Commentaries' in International Law Commission, Report of the International Law Commission on the Second Part of Its Seventeenth Session and on Its Eighteenth Session, A/6309/Rev.1, 18 *Yearbook of the International Law Commission*, vol II (1966) 187–274.

Jabloner (2013): Clemens Jabloner, 'Richterrecht als Rechtsquelle?' in Clemens Jabloner et al. (eds.), *Gedenkschrift Robert Walter* (Vienna: Manz 2013) 185–201.

Jacob (2011): Marc Jacob, 'Precedents: Lawmaking through International Adjudication' 12 *German Law Journal* (2011) 1005–32.

Jaenicke (1960): Günther Jaenicke, 'Völkerrechtsquellen' in Hans-Jürgen Schlochauer (ed.), *Wörterbuch des Völkerrechts*, vol 3: *Rapalo-Vertrag bis Zypern* (2nd edn, Berlin: Walter de Gruyter 1960) 766–75.

Jeand'Heur (1989): Bernd Jeand'Heur, *Sprachliches Referenzverhalten bei der juristischen Entscheidungstätigkeit* (Berlin: Duncker & Humblot 1989).

Jellinek (1880): Georg Jellinek, *Die rechtliche Natur der Staatenverträge: Ein Beitrag zur juristischen Construction des Völkerrechts* (Vienna: Alfred Hölder 1880).

Jellinek (1905): Georg Jellinek, *System der subjektiven öffentlichen Rechte* (Tubingen: Mohr 1905).

Jennings (1982): Robert Y Jennings, 'What Is International Law and How Do We Tell It When We See It?' 37 *Schweizerisches Jahrbuch für internationales Recht 1981* (1982) 59–88.

Jennings (1992): Robert Y Jennings, Arthur Watts (eds.), *Oppenheim's International Law, vol 1: Peace* (9th edn, London: Longman 1992).

Jestaedt (2008): Matthias Jestaedt, 'Perspektiven einer Rechtswissenschaftstheorie' in Matthias Jestaedt, Oliver Lepsius (eds.), *Rechtswissenschaftstheorie* (Tubingen: Mohr 2008) 185–205.

Jestaedt (2011): Matthias Jestaedt, 'Wissenschaftliches Recht: Rechtsdogmatik als gemeinsames Kommunikationsformat von Rechtswissenschaft und Rechtspraxis' in Clemens Jabloner et al. (eds.), *Vom praktischen Wert der Methode: Festschrift Heinz Mayer zum 65. Geburtstag* (Vienna: Manz 2011) 169–87.

Jestaedt (2014): Matthias Jestaedt, 'Wissenschaft im Recht: Rechtsdogmatik im Wissenschaftsvergleich' 69 *JuristenZeitung* (2014) 1–12.

Jia (2010): Bing-Bing Jia, 'The Relations between Treaties and Custom' 9 *Chinese Journal of International Law* (2010) 81–109.

Jones (2010): Oliver R Jones, Chido Dunn, 'Consent, Forced Renegotiation and Expropriation in International Law' 26 *Arbitration International* (2010) 391–408.

Kadelbach (1992): Stefan Kadelbach, *Zwingendes Völkerrecht* (Berlin: Duncker & Humblot 1992).

Kammerhofer (2010a): Jörg Kammerhofer, 'Gaps, the *Nuclear Weapons* Advisory Opinion and the Structure of International Legal Argument between Theory and Practice' 80 *British Year Book of International Law 2009* (2010) 333–60.

Kammerhofer (2010b): Jörg Kammerhofer, 'Systemic Integration, Legal Theory and the ILC' 19 *Finnish Yearbook of International Law 2008* (2010) 157–82.

Kammerhofer (2010c): Jörg Kammerhofer, 'The Theory of Norm Conflict Solutions in International Investment Law' in Markus Gehring, Andrew Newcombe, Marie-Claire Cordonier Segger (eds.), *Sustainable Development in International Investment Law* (Alphen aan den Rijn: Wolters Kluwer 2010) 83–98.

Kammerhofer (2010d): Jörg Kammerhofer, *Uncertainty in International Law: A Kelsenian Perspective* (Abingdon: Routledge 2010).

Kammerhofer (2011): Jörg Kammerhofer, 'Orthodox Generalists and Political Activists in International Legal Scholarship' in Matthew Happold (ed.), *International Law in a Multipolar World* (Abingdon: Routledge 2011) 138–57.

Kammerhofer (2012): Jörg Kammerhofer, 'Law-Making by Scholarship? The Dark Side of 21st Century International Legal "Methodology"' in James Crawford, Sarah Nouwen (eds.), *Select Proceedings of the European Society of International Law: Third Volume: International Law 1989–2010: A Performance Appraisal. Cambridge, 2–4* September *2010* (Oxford: Hart 2012) 115–26.

Kammerhofer (2013): Jörg Kammerhofer, '*Robert Walter*, die Normkonflikte und der zweite Stufenbau des Rechts' in Clemens Jabloner et al. (eds.), *Gedenkschrift Robert Walter* (Vienna: Manz 2013) 237–56.

Kammerhofer (2014a): Jörg Kammerhofer, 'Die Reine Rechtslehre und die allgemeinen Rechtsprinzipien des Völkerrechts' in Nikitas Aliprantis, Thomas Olechowski (eds.), *Hans Kelsen: Die Aktualität eines großen Rechtswissenschaftlers und Soziologen des 20. Jahrhunderts* (Vienna: Manz 2014) 25–35.

Kammerhofer (2014b): Jörg Kammerhofer, 'Hans Kelsen in Today's International Legal Scholarship' in Jörg Kammerhofer, Jean d'Aspremont (eds.), *International Legal Positivism in a Post-Modern World* (Cambridge: Cambridge University Press 2014) 81–113.

Kammerhofer (2014c): Jörg Kammerhofer, Jean d'Aspremont (eds.), *International Legal Positivism in a Post-Modern World* (Cambridge: Cambridge University Press 2014).

Kammerhofer (2015): Jörg Kammerhofer, 'The Resilience of the Restrictive Rules of Self-Defence' in Marc Weller (ed.), *The Oxford Handbook of the Use of Force in International Law* (Oxford: Oxford University Press 2015) 627–48.

Kammerhofer (2016a): Jörg Kammerhofer, 'International Legal Positivism' in Florian Hoffmann, Anne Orford (eds.), *Oxford Handbook on International Legal Theory* (Oxford: Oxford University Press 2016) 407–26.

Kammerhofer (2016b): Jörg Kammerhofer, 'Lawmaking by Scholars' in Catherine Brölmann, Yannick Radi (eds.), *Handbook on the Theory and Practice of International Lawmaking* (Cheltenham: Edward Elgar 2016) 305–25.

Kammerhofer (2017a): Jörg Kammerhofer, 'Positivistische Normbegründung' in Eric Hilgendorf, Jan C Joerden (eds.), *Handbuch Rechtsphilosophie* (Stuttgart: Metzler 2017) 200–8.

Kammerhofer (2017b): Jörg Kammerhofer, 'Sources in Legal Positivist Theories: The Pure Theory's Structural Analysis of the Law' in Samantha Besson, Jean d'Aspremont (eds.), *The Oxford Handbook of the Sources of International Law* (Oxford: Oxford University Press 2017) 343–62.

Kammerhofer (2018a): Jörg Kammerhofer, 'Der Stufenbau des Völkerrechts: Strukturanalyse statt Quellenmystik' in Clemens Jabloner, Jan Kuklik, Thomas Olechowski (eds.), *Hans Kelsen in der tschechischen und internationalen Rechtslehre* (Vienna: Manz 2018) 173–90.

Kammerhofer (2018b): Jörg Kammerhofer, 'The Challenges of History in International Investment Law: A View from Legal Theory' in Stephan W Schill, Christian J Tams, Rainer Hofmann (eds.), *International Investment Law and History* (Cheltenham: Edward Elgar 2018) 164–76.

Kammerhofer (2019): Jörg Kammerhofer, 'Positivist Approaches and International Adjudication' in Hélène Ruiz Fabri (ed.), *Max Planck Encyclopedia of International Procedural Law* (Oxford: Oxford University Press 2019), available at: opil.ouplaw.com/view/10.1093/law-mpeipro/e3300.013.3300/law-mpeipro-e3300.

Kammerhofer (in press a): Jörg Kammerhofer, 'International Legal Positivist Research Methods' in Rossana Deplano, Nicholas Tsagourias (eds.), *Research Methods in International Law: A Handbook* (Cheltenham: Edward Elgar in press), available at: ssrn.com/abstract=3503295.

Kammerhofer (in press b): Jörg Kammerhofer, 'Between Pragmatism and Disenchantment: The Theory of Customary International Law after the ILC Project' in Panos Merkouris, Jörg Kammerhofer, Noora Arajärvi (eds.), *The Theory, Practice and Interpretation of Customary Law* (Cambridge: Cambridge University Press in press), available at: ssrn.com/abstract=3522535.

Kant (1781): Immanuel Kant, *Kritik der reinen Vernunft* (Riga: Hartknoch 1781/1787).

Kant (1786): Immanuel Kant, *Grundlegung zur Metaphysik der Sitten* (2nd edn, Riga: Hartknoch 1786).

Kant (1797): Immanuel Kant, *Metaphysik der Sitten* (Königsberg: Friedrich Nicolovius 1797).

Karl (1983): Wolfram Karl, *Vertrag und späte Praxis im Völkerrecht: Zum Einfluss der Praxis auf Inhalt und Bestand völkerrechtlicher Verträge* (Berlin: Springer 1983).

Kaser (1955): Max Kaser, *Das Römische Privatrecht*, vol 1: *Das altrömische, das vorklassische und klassische Recht* (Munich: CH Beck 1955).

Kaser (1986): Max Kaser, '"Ius publicum" und "ius privatum"' 103 *Zeitschrift der Savigny-Stiftung für Rechtsgeschichte Romanistische Abteilung* (1986) 1–101.

Kaufmann-Kohler (2007): Gabrielle Kaufmann-Kohler, 'Arbitral Precedent: Dream, Necessity or Excuse?' 23 *Arbitration International* (2007) 357–78.

Kaufmann-Kohler (2008): Gabrielle Kaufmann-Kohler, 'Is Consistency a Myth?' in Yas Banifatemi (ed.), *Precedent in International Arbitration: IAI Seminar Paris - December 14, 2007* (New York: Juris 2008) 137–47.

Kelsen (1920): Hans Kelsen, *Das Problem der Souveränität und die Theorie des Völkerrechts: Beitrag zu einer reinen Rechtslehre* (Tubingen: Mohr 1920) (4 *HKW* 235–572).

Kelsen (1945): Hans Kelsen, *General Theory of Law and State* (Harvard: Harvard University Press 1945).

Kelsen (1950): Hans Kelsen, *The Law of the United Nations: A Critical Analysis of Its Fundamental Problems* (New York: Praeger 1950).

Kelsen (1960): Hans Kelsen, *Reine Rechtslehre* (2nd edn, Vienna: Deuticke 1960).

Kelsen (1979): Hans Kelsen, *Allgemeine Theorie der Normen* (Vienna: Manz 1979).

Khachvani (2017): David Khachvani, 'Compensation for Unlawful Expropriation: Targeting the Illegality' 32 *ICSID Review* (2017) 385–403.

King (2014): D Brian King, Rahim Moloo, 'International Arbitrators as Lawmakers' 46 *New York University Journal of International Law and Politics* (2014) 875–910.

Kinnear (2006): Meg N Kinnear, Andrea K Bjorklund, John FG Hannaford, *Investment Disputes under NAFTA: An Annotated Guide to NAFTA Chapter 11* (Alphen aan den Rijn: Kluwer 2006).

Kishoiyian (1994): Bernard Kishoiyian, 'The Utility of Bilateral Investment Treaties in the Formulation of Customary International Law' 14 *Northwestern Journal of International Law & Business* (1994) 372–5.

Klabbers (2003): Jan Klabbers, 'International Legal Histories: The Declining Importance of *Travaux Préparatoires* in Treaty Interpretation?' 50 *Netherlands International Law Review* (2003) 267–88.

Klabbers (2005): Jan Klabbers, 'On Rationalism in Politics: Interpretation of Treaties and the World Trade Organization' 74 *Nordic Journal of International Law* (2005) 405–28.

Klabbers (2007): Jan Klabbers, 'Reluctant *Grundnormen*: Articles 31(3)(c) and 42 of the Vienna Convention on the Law of Treaties and the Fragmentation of International Law' in Matthew Craven, Malgosia Fitzmaurice, Maria Vogiatzi (eds.), *Time, History and International Law* (Leiden: Martinus Nijhoff 2007) 141–61.

Klabbers (2010): Jan Klabbers, 'Virtuous Interpretation' in Malgosia Fitzmaurice, Olufemi Elias, Panos Merkouris (eds.), *Treaty Interpretation and the Vienna Convention on the Law of Treaties: 30 Years On* (Leiden: Martinus Nijhoff 2010) 17–37.

Knahr (2009): Christina Knahr, 'Indirect Expropriation in Recent Investment Arbitration' 6:1 *Transnational Dispute Management* (2009).

Köck (1976): Heribert Franz Köck, *Vertragsinterpretation und Vertragsrechtskonvention: Zur Bedeutung der Artikel 31 und 32 der Wiener Vertragsrechtskonvention 1969* (Berlin: Duncker & Humblot 1976).

Kolb (2003): Robert Kolb, 'Selected Problems in the Theory of Customary International Law' 50 *Netherlands International Law Review* (2003) 119–50.

Koskenniemi (1989): Martti Koskenniemi, *From Apology to Utopia: The Structure of International Legal Argument* (1989, reissued: Cambridge: Cambridge University Press 2005).

Koskenniemi (2006): Martti Koskenniemi, 'Fragmentation of International Law: Difficulties Arising from the Diversification and Expansion of International Law: Report of the Study Group of the International Law Commission' in *International Law Commission, Fifty-Eighth Session, Geneva, 1 May–9 June and 3 July–11 August 2006*, A/CN.4/L.682 (2006).

Kriebaum (2007a): Ursula Kriebaum, 'Partial Expropriation' 8 *Journal of World Investment & Trade* (2007) 69–84.

Kriebaum (2007b): Ursula Kriebaum, 'Regulatory Takings: Balancing the Interests of the Investor and the State' 8 *Journal of World Investment & Trade* (2007) 717–44.

Kriebaum (2008a): Ursula Kriebaum, *Eigentumsschutz im Völkerrecht: Eine vergleichende Untersuchung zum internationalen Investitionsrecht sowie zum Menschenrechtsschutz* (Berlin: Duncker & Humblot 2008).

Kriebaum (2008b): Ursula Kriebaum, 'Indirekte Enteignung oder zulässige Regulierung?' in Georg Nolte, Peter Hilpold (eds.), *Auslandsinvestitionen – Entwicklung großer Kodifikationen – Fragmentierung des Völkerrechts – Status des Kosovo: Beiträge zum 31. Österreichischen Völkerrechtstag 2006 in München* (2008) 18–37.

Kriebaum (2015): Ursula Kriebaum, 'Expropriation' in Marc Bungenberg et al. (eds.), *International Investment Law* (Baden-Baden: Nomos 2015) 959–1030.

Kulick (2012): Andreas Kulick, *Global Public Interest in International Investment Law* (Cambridge: Cambridge University Press 2012) 77–99.

Kunoy (2005): Bjørn Kunoy, 'Developments in Indirect Expropriation Case Law in ICSID Transnational Arbitration' 6 *Journal of World Investment & Trade* (2005) 467–91.

Kunz (1953): Joseph L Kunz, 'The Nature of Customary International Law' 47 *American Journal of International Law* (1953) 662–9.

Kurtz (2010): Jürgen Kurtz, 'Adjudging the Exceptional at International Investment Law: Security, Public Order and Financial Crisis' 59 *International and Comparative Law Quarterly* (2010) 325–71.

Kurtz (2012): Jürgen Kurtz, 'Review Essay: The Shifting Landscape of International Investment Law and Its Commentary' 106 *American Journal of International Law* (2012) 686–94.

Lamond (2010): Grant Lamond, 'Persuasive Authority in the Law' 17 *Philosophy of Law* (2010) 16–35.

Lauterpacht (1927): Hersch Lauterpacht, *Private Law Sources and Analogies of International Law (With Special Reference to International Arbitration)* (London: Longmans, Green and Co. 1927).

Lauterpacht (1931): Hersch Lauterpacht, 'The So-Called Anglo-American and Continental Schools of Thought in International Law' 12 *British Year Book of International Law* (1931) 31–62.

Lauterpacht (1949): Hersch Lauterpacht, 'Restrictive Interpretation and the Principle of Effectiveness in the Interpretation of Treaties' 26 *British Year Book of International Law* (1949) 48–85.

Lauterpacht (1958): Hersch Lauterpacht, *The Development of International Law by the International Court* (London: Stevens & Sons 1958).

Lauterpacht (1970a): Hersch Lauterpacht, 'General Rules of the Law of Peace' (English ms. unpublished) in Eliuh Lauterpacht (ed.), *International Law: Being the Collected Papers of Hersch Lauterpacht*, vol 1: *The General Works* (Cambridge: Cambridge University Press 1970) 179–444.

Lauterpacht (1970b): Hersch Lauterpacht, 'International Law – the General Part' (unpublished ms.) in Eliuh Lauterpacht (ed.), *International Law: Being the Collected Papers of Hersch Lauterpacht*, vol 1: *The General Works* (Cambridge: Cambridge University Press 1970) 1–178.

Lévesque (2004): Céline Lévesque, 'Distinguishing Expropriation and Regulation under NAFTA Chapter 11: Making Explicit the Link to Property' in Kevin C Kennedy (ed.), *The First Decade of NAFTA: The Future of Free Trade in North America* (Ardsley: Transnational 2004) 293–324.

L'Hullier (1950): Jean L'Hullier, *Éléments de droit international public* (Paris: Rousseau 1950).

Linderfalk (2007): Ulf Linderfalk, *On the Interpretation of Treaties: The Modern International Law as Expressed in the 1969 Vienna Convention on the Law of Treaties* (Dordrecht: Springer 2007).

Lindquist (2005): Stefanie A Lindquist, Frank B Cross, 'Empirically Testing Dworkin's Chain Novel Theory: Studying the Path of Precedent' 80 *New York University Law Review* (2005) 1156–1206.

Lippold (2000): Rainer Lippold, *Recht und Ordnung: Statik und Dynamik der Rechtsordnung* (Vienna: Manz 2000).

López (2014): Sebastián López Escarcena, *Indirect Expropriation in International Law* (Cheltenham: Edward Elgar 2014).

Lowe (2003): Vaughan Lowe, 'Regulation or Expropriation?' 55 *Current Legal Problems 2002* (2003) 447–66.

Lowenfeld (2003): Andreas F Lowenfeld, 'Investment Agreements and International Law' 42 *Columbia Journal of Transnational Law* (2003) 123–30.

Mann (1960): FA Mann, 'State Contracts and State Responsibility' 54 *American Journal of International Law* (1960) 572–91.

Marboe (2006): Irmgard Marboe, 'Compensation and Damages in International Law – The Limits of "Fair Market Value"' 7 *Journal of World Investment & Trade* (2006) 723–59.

Marboe (2015a): Irmgard Marboe, 'The System of Reparation and Questions of Terminology' in Marc Bungenberg et al. (eds.), *International Investment Law* (Baden-Baden: Nomos 2015) 1031–44.

Marboe (2015b): Irmgard Marboe, 'Valuation in Cases of Expropriation' in Marc Bungenberg et al. (eds.), *International Investment Law* (Baden-Baden: Nomos 2015) 1057–81.

Markert (2011): Lars Markert, 'International Investment Law and Treaty Interpretation – Problems, Particularities and Possible Trends' in Rainer Hofmann, Christian Tams (eds.), *International Investment Law and*

General International Law: From Clinical Isolation to Systemic Integration? (Baden-Baden: Nomos 2011) 53–69.

Marlles (2006–7): Justin R Marlles, 'Public Purpose, Private Losses: Regulatory Expropriation and Environmental Regulation in International Investment Law' 16 *Journal of Transnational Law and Policy* (2006–7) 275–336.

Mayer (1992): Heinz Mayer, 'Die Interpretationstheorie der Reinen Rechtslehre' in Robert Walter (ed.), *Schwerpunkte der Reinen Rechtslehre* (Vienna: Manz 1992) 61–70.

Mbengue (2016): Makane Moïse Mbengue, 'Rules of Interpretation (Article 32 of the Vienna Convention on the Law of Treaties)' 31 *ICSID Review* (2016) 388–412.

McLachlan (2005): Campbell McLachlan, 'The Principle of Systemic Integration and Article 31(3)(c) of the Vienna Convention' 54 *International and Comparative Law Quarterly* (2005) 279–320.

McLachlan (2007): Campbell McLachlan, Laurence Shore, Matthew Weiniger, *International Investment Arbitration: Substantive Principles* (Oxford: Oxford University Press 2007).

McLachlan (2008): Campbell McLachlan, 'Investment Treaties and General International Law' 57 *International and Comparative Law Quarterly* (2008) 361–401.

McLachlan (2016): Campbell McLachlan, 'Is There an Evolving Customary International Law on Investment?' 31 *ICSID Review* (2016) 257–69.

McNair (1961): Arnold Duncan McNair, *The Law of Treaties* (Oxford: Clarendon Press 1961).

Mendelson (1999): Maurice H Mendelson, 'The Formation of Customary International Law' 272 *Recueil des Cours 1998* (1999) 155–410.

Merkl (1916): Adolf Julius Merkl, 'Zum Interpretationsproblem' 42 [*Grünhutsche*] *Zeitschrift für das Privat- und öffentliche Recht der Gegenwart* (1916) 535–6 (*WRS* 1059–77, I/1 *MerklGS* 63–83).

Merkl (1916–19): Adolf Julius Merkl, 'Das Recht im [Spiegel] Lichte seiner [Auslegung] Anwendung' [the title varies] 8 *Deutsche Richterzeitung* (1916) col 584–92, 9 *Deutsche Richterzeitung* (1917) col 162–76, 394–8, 443–50, 11 *Deutsche Richterzeitung* (1919) col 290–8 (*WRS* 1167–1201, I/1 *MerklGS* 85–146).

Merkl (1922): Adolf Julius Merkl, 'Gesetzesrecht und Richterrecht' 2 *Wissenschaftliche Vierteljahresschrift der Prager Juristischen Zeitschrift* (1922) 337–44 (*WRS* 1615–24, I/1 *MerklGS* 317–27).

Merkl (1923): Adolf Julius Merkl, *Die Lehre von der Rechtskraft, entwickelt aus dem Rechtsbegriff: Eine rechtstheoretische Untersuchung* (Leipzig: Deuticke 1923).

Merkl (1931): Adolf Julius Merkl, 'Prolegomena einer Theorie des rechtlichen Stufenbaues' in Alfred Verdross (ed.), *Gesellschaft, Staat und Recht: Festschrift* *für Hans Kelsen zum 50. Geburtstag* (Vienna: Springer 1931) 252–94 (*WRS* 1311–61, I/1 MerklGS 437–92).

Merkouris (2015): Panos Merkouris, *Article 31(3) VCLT and the Principle of Systemic Integration: Normative Shadows in Plato's Cave* (Leiden: Martinus Nijhoff 2015).

Mitchell (2017): Andrew D Mitchell, James Munro, 'Someone Else's Deal: Interpreting International Investment Agreements in the Light of Third-Party Agreements' 28 *European Journal of International Law* (2017) 669–95.

Mostafa (2008): Ben Mostafa, 'The Sole Effects Doctrine, Police Powers and Indirect Expropriation under International Law' 15 *Australian International Law Journal* (2008) 267–96.

Müller (1993): Friedrich Müller, *Juristische Methodik* (5th edn, Berlin: Duncker & Humblot 1993).

Müllerson (1998): Rein Müllerson, 'The Interplay of Objective and Subjective Elements in Customary Law in Karel Wellens (ed.), *International Law: Theory and Practice: Essays in Honour of Eric Suy* (The Hague: Martinus Nijhoff 1998) 161–78.

Nanteuil (2014): Arnaud de Nanteuil, *L'expropriation indirecte en droit international de l'investissement* (Paris: Pedone 2014).

Newcombe (1999): Andrew Newcombe, Regulatory Expropriation, Investment Protection and International Law: When Is Government Regulation Expropriatory and When Should Compensation Be Paid? (LL.M. thesis, University of Toronto 1999).

Newcombe (2005): Andrew Newcombe, 'The Boundaries of Regulatory Expropriation in International Law' 20 *ICSID Review – Foreign Investment Law Journal* (2005) 1–57.

Newcombe (2009): Andrew Newcombe, Lluís Paradell, *Law and Practice of Investment Treaties: Standards of Treatment* (Alphen aan den Rijn: Kluwer 2009).

Newcombe (2011): Andrew Newcombe, 'General Exceptions in International Investment Agreements' in Marie-Claire Cordonier Segger, Markus W Gehring, Andrew Newcombe (eds.), *Sustainable Development in World Investment Law* (Alphen aan den Rijn: Wolters Kluwer 2011) 355–70.

Nikièma (2012): Suzy H Nikièma, *L'expropriation indirecte en droit international des investissements* (Paris: Presses Universitaires de France 2012).

Nolte (2013): Georg Nolte, 'First Report on Subsequent Agreements and Subsequent Practice in Relation to Treaty Interpretation', *International Law Commission, Sixty-Fifth* Session, *Geneva, 6 May–7 June and 8 July–9 August 2013*, A/CN.4/660.

Nolte (2014): Georg Nolte, 'Second Report on Subsequent Agreements and Subsequent Practice in Relation to the Interpretation of Treaties', *International Law Commission, Sixty-Sixth Session, Geneva, 5 May–6 June and 7 July–8 August 2014*, A/CN.4/671 (2014).

Nolte (2015): Georg Nolte, 'Third Report on Subsequent Agreements and Subsequent Practice in Relation to the Interpretation of Treaties', *International Law Commission, Sixty-Seventh Session, Geneva, 4 May–5 June and 6 July–7 August 2015*, A/CN.4/683 (2015).

Nolte (2016): Georg Nolte, 'Fourth Report on Subsequent Agreements and Subsequent Practice in Relation to the Interpretation of Treaties', *International Law Commission, Sixty-Eighth Session, Geneva, 2 May–10 June and 4 July–12 August 2016*, A/CN.4/694 (2016).

Norton (1991): Patrick M Norton, 'A Law of the Future or a Law of the Past? Modern Tribunals and the International Law of Expropriation' 85 *American Journal of International Law* (1991) 474–505.

OECD (1968): Organisation for Economic Co-operation and Development, 'Draft Convention on the Protection of Foreign Property' reprinted in 7 *International Legal Materials* (1968) 117–43.

Öhlinger (1975): Theo Öhlinger, *Der Stufenbau der Rechtsordnung: Rechtstheoretische und ideologische Aspekte* (Vienna: Manz 1975).

Oppenheim (1905): Lassa Oppenheim, *International Law: A Treatise*, vol 1: *Peace* (London: Longmans, Green and Comp. 1905).

Orakhelashvili (2003): Alexander Orakhelashvili, 'Restrictive Interpretation of Human Rights Treaties in the Recent Jurisprudence of the European Court of Human Rights' 14 *European Journal of International Law* (2003) 529–68.

Orakhelashvili (2006): Alexander Orakhelashvili, *Peremptory Norms in International Law* (Oxford: Oxford University Press 2006).

Orakhelashvili (2008): Alexander Orakhelashvili, *The Interpretation of Acts and Rules in Public International Law* (Oxford: Oxford University Press 2008).

Orrego Vicuña (2003): Francisco Orrego Vicuña, 'Regulatory Authority and Legitimate Expectations: Balancing the Rights of the State and the Individual under International Law in a Global Society' 5 *International Law Forum* (2003) 188–97.

Ortino (2016): Federico Ortino, 'Defining Indirect Expropriation: The Transatlantic Trade and Investment Partnership and the (Elusive) Search for "Greater Certainty"' 43 *Legal Issues of Economic Integration* (2016) 351–66.

Paparinskis (2010a): Martins Paparinskis, 'Investment Protection Law and Sources of Law: A Critical Look' 103 *ASIL Proceedings* (2010) 76–9.

Paparinskis (2010b): Martins Paparinskis, 'Investment Protection Law and Systemic Integration of Treaty and Custom', *SIEL Online Proceedings Working Paper 2010/21*, available at: ssrn.com/abstract=1632559.

Paparinskis (2011a): Martins Paparinskis, 'Investment Treaty Interpretation and Customary Investment Law: Preliminary Remarks' in Chester Brown, Kate Miles (eds.), *Evolution in Investment Treaty Law and Arbitration* (Cambridge: Cambridge University Press 2011) 65–96.

Paparinskis (2011b): Martins Paparinskis, 'Regulatory Expropriation and Sustainable Development' in Marie-Claire Cordonier Segger, Markus W Gehring, Andrew Newcombe (eds.), *Sustainable Development in World Investment Law* (Alphen aan den Rijn: Wolters Kluwer 2011) 299–327.

Paparinskis (2012): Martins Paparinskis, 'Sources of Law and Arbitral Interpretations of *Pari Materia* Investment Protection Rules' in Ole Kristian Fauchald, André Nollkaemper (eds.), *The Practice of International and National Courts and the (De-)Fragmentation of International Law* (Oxford: Hart 2012) 87–116, cited from: ssrn.com/abstract=1697835.

Parlett (2016): Kate Parlett, 'Claims under Customary International Law in ICSID Arbitration' 31 *ICSID Review* (2016) 434–56.

Paulson (2018): Stanley L Paulson, 'The Purity Thesis' 31 *Ratio Juris* (2018) 276–306.

Paulsson (2004): Jan Paulsson, Zachary Douglas, 'Indirect Expropriation in Investment Treaty Arbitrations' in Norbert Horn (ed.), *Arbitrating Foreign Investment Disputes* (The Hague: Kluwer 2004) 145–58.

Paulsson (2006): Jan Paulsson, 'Indirect Expropriation: Is the Right to Regulate at Risk?' 3:2 *Transnational Dispute Management* (2006).

Paulsson (2010): Jan Paulsson, 'The Role of Precedent in Investment Arbitration' in Katia Yannaca-Small (ed.), *Arbitration under International Investment Agreements: A Guide to the Key Issues* (Oxford: Oxford University Press 2010) 699–718.

Peczenik (1997): Aleksander Peczenik, 'The Binding Force of Precedent' in D Neil MacCormick, Robert S Summers (eds.), *Interpreting Precedents: A Comparative Study* (Aldershot: Ashgate 1997) 461–79.

Pellonpää (1989): Matti Pellonpää, Malgosia Fitzmaurice, 'Taking of Property in the Practice of the Iran–United States Claims Tribunal' 19 *Netherlands Yearbook of International Law 1988* (1989) 53–178.

Petersen (2007): Niels Petersen, 'Customary Law Without Custom? Rules, Principles, and the Role of State Practice in International Norm Creation' 32 *American University International Law Review* (2007) 275–310.

Pfersmann (2009): Otto Pfersmann, 'Hans Kelsens Rolle in der gegenwärtigen Rechtswissenschaft' in Robert Walter, Werner Ogris, Thomas Olechowski (eds.), *Hans Kelsen: Leben–Werk–Wirksamkeit. Ergebnisse einer Internationalen Tagung, veranstaltet von der Kommission für Rechtsgeschichte Österreichs und dem Hans Kelsen-Institut (19.–21. April 2009)* (Vienna: Manz 2009) 367–87.

Piran (1995): Hossein Piran, 'Indirect Expropriation in the Case Law of the Iran–United States Claims Tribunal' 6 *Finnish Yearbook of International Law* (1995) 140–247.

Potacs (2015): Michael Potacs, *Rechtstheorie* (Vienna: facultas 2015).

Procès-verbaux (1920): Permanent Court of International Justice Advisory Committee of Jurists, *Procès-verbaux of the Proceedings of the Committee June 16th–July 24th 1920 with Annexes* (The Hague: van Langenhuysen 1920).

Prugger (1990): F Prugger, 'A Source Problem of International Law in the Field of Expropriation of Alien Property' 16 *Thesaurus Acroasium* (1990) 869–81.

Pulkowski (2014): Dirk Pulkowski, *The Law and Politics of International Regime Conflict* (Oxford: Oxford University Press 2014).

Radnitzky (1914): Ernst Radnitzky, 'Dispositives Völkerrecht' 1 *Österreichische Zeitschrift für öffentliches Recht* (1914) 656–74.

Ratner (2008): Stephen R Ratner, 'Regulatory Takings in Institutional Context: Beyond the Fear of Fragmented International Law' 102 *American Journal of International Law* (2008) 475–528.

Ratner (2017): Stephen R Ratner, 'Compensation for Expropriations in a World of Investment Treaties: Beyond the Lawful/Unlawful Distinction' 111 *American Journal of International Law* (2017) 7–56.

Reimann (1971): Heinrich Bernhard Reimann, *Ius cogens im Völkerrecht: Eine quellenkritische Untersuchung* (Zurich: Schulthess 1971).

Reinisch (2008a): August Reinisch, 'Expropriation' in Peter Muchlinski, Federico Ortino, Christoph Schreuer (eds.), *The Oxford Handbook of International Investment Law* (Oxford: Oxford University Press 2008) 407–58.

Reinisch (2008b): August Reinisch, 'Legality of Expropriations' in August Reinisch (ed.), *Standards of Investment Protection* (Oxford: Oxford University Press 2008) 171–204.

Reinisch (2008c): August Reinisch (ed.), *Standards of Investment Protection* (Oxford: Oxford University Press 2008).

Reinisch (2008d): August Reinisch, 'The Role of Precedent in ICSID Arbitration' *Austrian Arbitration Yearbook* (2008) 495–510.

Reinisch (2015): August Reinisch, 'The Interpretation of International Investment Agreements' in Marc Bungenberg et al. (ed.), *International Investment Law: A Handbook* (Baden-Baden: Nomos 2015) 372–410.

Reisman (2004): W Michael Reisman, Robert D Sloane, 'Indirect Expropriation and Its Valuation in the BIT Generation' 74 *British Year Book of International Law 2003* (2004) 115–50.

Restatement (1987): American Law Institute, *Restatement of the Law: The Foreign Relations Law of the United States*, vol 1 (St Paul: American Law Institute Publishers 1987).

Rieger (1997): Thomas Rieger, *Grundsätze der Unternehmensenteignung in der Rechtsprechung des Iran–United States Claims Tribunal* (Cologne: Heymans 1997).

Roberts (2001): Anthea Elizabeth Roberts, 'Traditional and Modern Approaches to Customary International Law' 95 *American Journal of International Law* (2001) 757–91.

Roberts (2013): Anthea Elizabeth Roberts, 'Clash of Paradigms: Actors and Analogies Shaping the Investment Treaty System' 107 *American Journal of International Law* (2013) 45–94.

Rosentreter (2015): Daniel Rosentreter, *Article 31(3)(c) of the Vienna Convention on the Law of Treaties and the Principle of Systemic Integration in International Investment Law and Arbitration* (Baden-Baden: Nomos 2015).

Rudden (1980): Bernhard Rudden, 'Ius cogens, ius dispositivum' 11 *Cambrian Law Review* (1980) 87–100.

Sacerdoti (1998): Giorgio Sacerdoti, 'Bilateral Treaties and Multilateral Instruments on Investment Protection' 269 *Recueil des Cours 1997* (1998) 251–460.

Salacuse (2010): Jeswald W Salacuse, *The Law of International Investment Treaties* (Oxford: Oxford University Press 2010).

Saldarriaga (2013): Andrea Saldarriaga, 'Investment Awards and the Rules of Interpretation of the Vienna Convention: Making Room for Improvement' 28 *ICSID Review* (2013) 197–217.

Sands (1999): Philippe Sands, 'Treaty, Custom and the Cross-Fertilization of International Law' 1 *Yale Human Rights & Development Law Journal* (1999) 85–105.

Sauer (1948): Ernst Sauer, *Grundlehre des Völkerrechts* (Cologne: Balduin Pick 1948).

Savigny (1840): Friedrich Carl von Savigny, *System des heutigen Römischen Rechts*, vol 1 (Berlin: Veit und Comp. 1840).

Schäffer (1973): Heinz Schäffer, 'Rechtsquellen und Rechtsanwendung' in *Verhandlungen des fünften Österreichischen Juristentages Wien 1973*, vol I.1. B (Vienna: Manz 1973).

Scheuner (1977): Ulrich Scheuner, 'Internationale Verträge als Elemente der Bildung von völkerrechtlichem Gewohnheitsrecht' in Werner Flume et al. (eds.), *Internationales Recht und Wirtschaftsordnung: Festschrift für FA Mann zum 70. Geburtstag am 11. August 1977* (Munich: CH Beck 1977) 409–38.

Schill (2006): Stephan W Schill, 'Revisiting a Landmark: Indirect Expropriation and Fair and Equitable Treatment in the ICSID Case Tecmed' 3:2 *Transnational Dispute Management* (2006).

Schill (2009): Stephan W Schill, *The Multilateralization of International Investment Law* (Cambridge: Cambridge University Press 2009).

Schill (2010): Stephan W Schill, 'International Investment Law and Comparative Public Law – An Introduction' in Stephan W Schill (ed.), *International Investment Law and Comparative Public Law* (Oxford: Oxford University Press 2010) 3–37.

Schill (2011): Stephan W Schill, 'System-Building in Investment Treaty Arbitration and Lawmaking' 12 *German Law Journal* (2011) 1083–1110.

Schiller (1938): A Arthur Schiller, 'Custom in Classical Roman Law' 24 *Virginia Law Review* (1938) 268–82.

Schlink (1989): Bernhard Schlink, 'Die Entthronung der Staatsrechtswissenschaft durch die Verfassungsgerichtsbarkeit' 28 *Der Staat* (1989) 161–72.

Schmitt (1928): Carl Schmitt, *Verfassungslehre* [1928] (9th edn, Berlin: Duncker & Humblot, 2003).

Schmitt (1932): Carl Schmitt, *Der Begriff des Politischen* [1932] (7th edn, Berlin: Duncker & Humblot 1991).

Schramm (2005): Alfred Schramm, '"Richterrecht" und Gesetzesrecht: Eine rechtsvergleichende Analyse anhand von Merkls Rechtsnormenlehre' 36 *Rechtstheorie* (2005) 185–208.

Schreuer (2006): Christoph Schreuer, 'The Concept of Expropriation under the ETC and Other Investment Protection Treaties' in Clarisse Ribeiro (ed.), *Investment Arbitration and the Energy Charter Treaty* (New York: JurisNet 2006) 108–59.

Schreuer (2008): Christoph Schreuer, Matthew Weininger, 'A Doctrine of Precedent?' in Peter Muchlinski, Federico Ortino, Christoph Schreuer (eds.), *The Oxford Handbook of International Investment Law* (Oxford: Oxford University Press 2008) 1188–1206.

Schwarzenberger (1969): Georg Schwarzenberger, 'Myths and Realities of Treaty Interpretation: Articles 27–29 of the Vienna Draft Convention on the Law of Treaties' 22 *Current Legal Problems* (1969) 205–27.

Schwebel (2004): Stephen M Schwebel, 'The Influence of Bilateral Investment Treaties on Customary International Law' 98 *American Society of International Law Proceedings* (2004) 27–30.

Schwebel (2011): Stephen M Schwebel, 'The United States 2004 Model Bilateral Investment Treaty: An Exercise in the Regressive Development of International Law' in Stephen M Schwebel, *Justice in International Law: Further Selected Writings* (Cambridge: Cambridge University Press 2011) 152–60.

Searle (1969): John R Searle, *Speech Acts: An Essay in the Philosophy of Language* (Cambridge: Cambridge University Press 1969).

Shaffer (2015): Gregory Shaffer, 'The New Legal Realist Approach to International Law' 28 *Leiden Journal of International Law* (2015) 189–210.

Shahabuddeen (1996): Mohamed Shahabuddeen, *Precedent in the World Court* (Cambridge: Cambridge University Press 1996).

Sheppard (2006): Audley Sheppard, 'The Distinction between Lawful and Unlawful Expropriation' in Clarisse Ribeiro (ed.), *Investment Arbitration and the Energy Charter Treaty* (New York: JurisNet 2006) 169–99.

Shirlow (2014): Esmé Shirlow, 'Deference and Indirect Expropriation Analysis in International Investment Law: Observations on Current Approaches and Frameworks for Future Analysis' 29 *ICSID Review* (2014) 595–626.

Sinclair (1984): Ian Sinclair, *The Vienna Convention on the Law of Treaties* (2nd edn, Manchester: Manchester University Press 1984).

Sohn (1961): Louis B Sohn, Richard R Baxter, 'Responsibility of States for Injuries to the Economic Interests of Aliens' 55 *American Journal of International Law* (1961) 545–84.

Somek (1996): Alexander Somek, *Der Gegenstand der Rechtserkenntnis: Epitaph eines juristischen Problems* (Baden-Baden: Nomos 1996).

Somek (2011): Alexander Somek, 'The Spirit of Legal Positivism', 12 *German Law Journal* (2011) 729–56.

Somek (2012): Alexander Somek, 'Legal Science as a Source of Law: A Late Reply by Puchta to Kantorowicz' (working paper 2012), available at: ssrn.com /abstract=2175235.

Somek (2018): Alexander Somek, *Wissen des Rechts* (Tubingen: Mohr 2018).

Sornarajah (2010): Muthucumaraswamy Sornarajah, *The International Law on Foreign Investment* (3rd edn, Cambridge: Cambridge University Press 2010).

Sourgens (2014): Frédéric G Sourgens, 'Law's Laboratory: Developing International Law on Investment Protection as Common Law' 34 *Northwestern Journal of International Law & Business* (2014) 181–247.

Sourgens (2015): Frédéric G Sourgens, *A Nascent Common Law: The Process of Decisionmaking in International Legal Disputes Between States and Foreign Investors* (The Hague: Nijhoff 2015).

Stern (2008): Brigitte Stern, 'In Search of the Frontiers of Indirect Expropriation' in Arthur W Rovine (ed.), *Contemporary Issues in International Arbitration and Mediation: The Fordham Papers 2007* (Leiden: Nijhoff 2008) 29–51.

Stifter (2016): Lukas Stifter, August Reinisch, 'Expropriation in the Light of the UNCTAD Investment Policy Framework for Sustainable Development' in Steffen Hindelang, Markus Krajewski (eds.), *Shifting Paradigms in International Investment Law: More Balanced, Less Isolated, Increasingly Diversified* (Oxford: Oxford University Press 2016) 81–96.

Stone (1953–5): Julius Stone, 'Fictitional Elements in Treaty Interpretation – A Study in the International Judicial Process' 1 *Sydney Law Review* (1953–5) 344–68.

Stone (1960): Julius Stone, '*Non liquet* and the Function of Law in the International Community' 35 *British Year Book of International Law 1959* (1960) 124–61.

Stone Sweet (2017): Alec Stone Sweet, Michael Yunsuck Chung, Adam Saltzman, 'Arbitral Lawmaking and State Power: An Empirical Analysis of Investor–State Arbitration' 8 *Journal of International Dispute Settlement* (2017) 579–609.

Strazzeri (2001–2): Joseph A Strazzeri, 'A *Lucas* Analysis of Regulatory Expropriations under NAFTA Chapter Eleven' 14 *Georgetown International Environmental Law Review* (2001–2) 837–59.

Suárez (1612): Francisco Suárez, *De legibus ac Deo legislatore* [1612].

Subedī (2006): Sūrya Prasāda Subedī, 'The Challenge of Reconciling the Competing Principles within the Law of Foreign Investment with Special Reference to the Recent Trend in the Interpretation of the Term "Expropriation"' 40 *International Lawyer* (2006) 121–41.

Subedī (2016): Sūrya Prasāda Subedī, *International Investment Law: Reconciling Policy and Principle* (3rd edn, Oxford: Hart 2016).

Sur (1974): Serge Sur, *L'interprétation en droit international public* (Paris: LGDJ 1974).

Talmon (2015): Stefan Talmon, 'Determining Customary International Law: The ICJ's Methodology between Induction, Deduction and Assertion' 26 *European Journal of International Law* (2015) 417–43.

Taruffo (1997): Michele Taruffo, Massimo La Torre, 'Precedent in Italy' in D Neil MacCormick, Robert S Summers (eds.), *Interpreting Precedents: A Comparative Study* (Aldershot: Ashgate 1997) 141–88.

Ten Cate (2013): Irene M Ten Cate, 'The Costs of Consistency: Precedent in Investment Treaty Arbitration' 51 *Columbia Journal of Transnational Law* (2013) 418–78.

Thaler (1982): Michel Thaler, *Mehrdeutigkeit und juristische Auslegung* (Vienna: Springer 1982).

Thirlway (1972): Hugh WA Thirlway, *International Customary Law and Codification: An Examination of the Continuing Role of Custom in the Present Period of Codification of International Law* (Leiden: AW Sijthoff 1972).

Titi (2013): Catharine Titi, 'The Arbitrator as a Lawmaker: Jurisgenerative Processes in Investment Arbitration' 4 *Journal of World Investment & Trade* (2013) 829–51.

Titi (2014): Aikaterini Titi, *The Right to Regulate in International Investment Law* (Baden-Baden: Nomos 2014).

Titi (2018): Catharine Titi, 'Refining the Expropriation Clause: What Role for Proportionality?' in Julien Chaisse (ed.), *China–European Union Investment Relationships: Towards a New Leadership in Global Investment Governance?* (Cheltenham: Edward Elgar 2018), available at and cited from: ssrn.com /abstract=2978530 (2017).

Triantafilou (2006): Epaminontas E Triantafilou, 'Taxation as Expropriation: Some Observations on *EnCana v. Ecuador*' 3:5 *Transnational Dispute Management* (2006).

Triepel (1899): Heinrich Triepel, *Völkerrecht und Landesrecht* (Leipzig: CL Hirschfeld 1899).

Trinh (2014): Hai Yen Trinh, *The Interpretation of Investment Treaties* (Leiden: Martinus Nijhoff 2014).

Troper (1997): Michel Troper, 'Precedent in France' in D Neil MacCormick, Robert S Summers (eds.), *Interpreting Precedents: A Comparative Study* (Aldershot: Ashgate 1997) 103–40.

UNCTAD (2000): United Nations Conference on Trade and Development, *Taking of Property* [UNCTAD/ITE/IIT/15] (2000).

UNCTAD (2012): United Nations Conference on Trade and Development, *Expropriation* [UNCTAD/DIAE/IA/2011/7] (2012).

UNCTAD (2014): United Nations Conference on Trade and Development, *World Investment Report 2014: Investing in the SGDs: A Plan for Action* (New York: United Nations 2014).

Valasek (2007): Martin J Valasek, 'A "Simple Scheme": Exploring the Meaning of *Chorzów Factory* for the Valuation of Opportunistic Expropriation in the BIT Generation' 4:6 *Transnational Dispute Management* (2007).

Vandevelde (1993): Kenneth J Vandevelde, 'U.S. Bilateral Investment Treaties: The Second Wave' 14 *Michigan Journal of International Law* (1993) 621–704.

Veith (1962): Werner Veith, Karl-Heinz Böckstiegel, *Der Schutz von ausländischen Vermögen im Völkerrecht* (Baden-Baden: Lutzeyer 1962).

Verdross (1926): Alfred Verdross, *Die Verfassung der Völkerrechtsgemeinschaft* (Vienna: Springer 1926).

Verdross (1937): Alfred Verdross, *Völkerrecht* (Berlin: Springer 1937).

Verwey (1984): Wil D Verwey, Nico Schrijver, 'The Taking of Foreign Property under International Law: A New Legal Perspective?' 15 *Netherlands Yearbook of International Law* (1984) 3–96.

Villiger (1997): Mark E Villiger, *Customary International Law and Treaties: A Manual on the Theory and Practice of the Interrelation of Sources* (2nd edn, The Hague: Kluwer Law International 1997).

Villiger (2011): Mark E Villiger, 'The Rules on Interpretation: Misgivings, Misunderstandings, Miscarriage? The "Crucible" Intended by the International Law Commission' in Enzo Cannizzaro (ed.), *The Law of Treaties Beyond the Vienna Convention* (Oxford: Oxford University Press 2011) 105–22.

Wagner (1999): J Martin Wagner, 'International Investment, Expropriation and Environmental Protection' 29 *Golden Gate University Law Review* (1999) 465–538.

Wälde (2001): Thomas W Wälde, Abba Kolo, 'Environmental Regulation, Investment Protection and Regulatory Taking in International Law' 50 *International and Comparative Law Quarterly* (2001) 811–48.

Wälde (2007): Thomas W Wälde, 'Specific Nature of Investment Arbitration' in Philippe Kahn, Thomas W Wälde (eds.), *New Aspects of International Investment Law* (Leiden: Brill 2007) 43–120.

Wälde (2009): Thomas W Wälde, 'Interpreting Investment Treaties: Experiences and Examples' in Christina Binder et al. (eds.), *International Investment Law for the 21st Century: Essays in Honour of Christoph Schreuer* (Oxford: Oxford University Press 2009) 724–81.

Waldock (1964): Humphrey Waldock, 'Third Report on the Law of Treaties', A.CN.4/167, A.CN.4/167/Add.1–3, 16 *Yearbook of the International Law Commission*, vol II (1964) 5–65.

Walter (1963): Robert Walter, 'Die Gewohnheit als rechtserzeugender Tatbestand' 18 *Österreichische Juristen-Zeitung* (1963) 225–32.

Walter (1964): Robert Walter, *Der Aufbau der Rechtsordnung: Eine rechtstheoretische Untersuchung auf Grundlage der Reinen Rechtslehre* (Graz: Leykam 1964).

Walter (1983): Robert Walter, 'Das Auslegungsproblem im Lichte der Reinen Rechtslehre' in Günther Kohlmann (ed.), *Festschrift für Ulrich Klug zum 70. Geburtstag* (Cologne: Peter Deubner 1983) 187–97.

Weeramantry (2012): J Romesh Weeramantry, *Treaty Interpretation in Investment Arbitration* (Oxford: Oxford University Press 2012).

Weidemaier (2010): W Mark C Weidemaier, 'Toward a Theory of Precedent in Arbitration' 51 *William and Mary Law Review* (2010) 1895–1958.

Weiler (2005): Todd Weiler, '*Methanex Corp. v. USA*: Turning the Page on NAFTA Chapter Eleven?' 6 *Journal of World Investment & Trade* (2005) 903–20.

Weiler (2013): Todd Weiler, *The Interpretation of International Investment Law: Equality, Discrimination and Minimum Standards of Treatment in Historical Context* (Leiden: Martinus Nijhoff 2013).

Weiler (2018): Todd Weiler, 'International Investment Law and International Human Rights Law: Reuniting Two Long Lost Siblings (Speaking Notes)' 15 *Transnational Dispute Management* (2018).

Weiner (2003): Allen S Weiner, 'Indirect Expropriations: The Need for a Taxonomy of "Legitimate" Regulatory Purposes' 5 *International Law Forum* (2003) 166–75.

Weisburd (1988): Arthur M Weisburd, 'Customary International Law: The Problem of Treaties' 21 *Vanderbilt Journal of Transnational Law* (1988) 1–46.

Westberg (1993): John A Westberg, 'Applicable Law, Expropriatory Takings and Compensation in Cases of Expropriation; ICSID and Iran–United States Claims Tribunal Case Law Compared' 8 *ICSID Review – Foreign Investment Law Journal* (1993) 1–28.

Weston (1975): Burns H Weston, '"Constructive Takings" under International Law: A Modest Foray into the Problem of "Creeping Expropriation"' 16 *Virginia Journal of International Law* (1975) 103–75.

Weyr (1922): Franz Weyr, 'Rechtsphilosophie und Rechtswissenschaft' 2 *Zeitschrift für öffentliches Recht* (1922) 671–82.

Wiederin (1990): Ewald Wiederin, 'Was ist und welche Konsequenzen hat ein Normkonflikt?' 21 *Rechtstheorie* (1990) 311–33.

Wiederin (1995): Ewald Wiederin, *Bundesrecht und Landesrecht: Zugleich ein Beitrag zu Strukturproblemen der bundesstaatlichen Kompetenzverteilung in Österreich und Deutschland* (Vienna: Springer 1995).

Windscheid (1862): Bernhard Windscheid, *Lehrbuch des Pandektenrechts*, vol 1 (Dusseldorf: Julius Buddeus 1862).

Winkler (1990): Günther Winkler, *Rechtstheorie und Erkenntnislehre: Kritische Anmerkungen zum Dilemma von Sein und Sollen in der Reinen Rechtslehre aus geistesgeschichtlicher und erkenntnistheoretischer Sicht* (Vienna: Springer 1990).

Wolfke (1993): Karol Wolfke, *Custom in Present International Law* (2nd edn, Dordrecht: Martinus Nijhoff 1993).

Wood (2014): Michael Wood, *Second Report on Identification of Customary International Law*, UN Doc A/CN.4/L.672, 22 May 2014.

Wood (2015): Michael Wood, *Third Report on Identification of Customary International Law*, UN Doc A/CN.4/682, 27 March 2015.

Wortley (1959): Benjamin Alexander Wortley, *Expropriation in Public International Law* (Cambridge: Cambridge University Press 1959).

Yannaca-Small (2005): Catherine Yannaca-Small, '"Indirect Expropriation" and the "Right to Regulate" in International Investment Law' in OECD (ed.), *International Investment Law: A Changing Landscape: A Companion Volume to International Investment Perspectives* (Paris: OECD 2005) 43–72.

Zemanek (1995): Karl Zemanek, 'What Is State Practice and Who Makes It?' in Ulrich Beyerlin et al. (eds.), *Recht zwischen Umbruch und Bewahrung: Völkerrecht, Europarecht, Staatsrecht: Festschrift für Rudolf Bernhardt* (Berlin: Springer 1995) 289–306.

Zielonka (2017): Christian Zielonka, *Der Ausgleich zwischen Investorenschutz- und Regulierungsinteressen in internationalen Investitionsschutzabkommen* (Berlin: Duncker & Humblot 2017).

INDEX

CAMBRIDGE STUDIES IN INTERNATIONAL AND COMPARATIVE LAW

Books in the Series

158 *International Investment Law and Legal Theory: Expropriation and the Fragmentation of Sources*
Jörg Kammerhofer

157 *Legal Barbarians: Identity, Modern Comparative Law and the Global South*
Daniel Bonilla Maldonado

156 *International Human Rights Law Beyond State Territorial Control*
Antal Berkes

155 *The Crime of Aggression under the Rome Statute of the International Criminal Court*
Carrie McDougall

154 *Minorities and the Making of Postcolonial States in International Law*
Mohammad Shahabuddin

153 *Preclassical Conflict of Laws*
Nikitas E. Hatzimihail

152 *International Law and History: Modern Interfaces* Ignacio de la Rasilla del Moral

151 *Marketing Global Justice: The Political Economy of International Criminal Law*
Christine Schwöbel-Patel

150 *International Status in the Shadow of Empire*
Cait Storr

149 *Treaties in Motion: The Evolution of Treaties from Formation to Termination*
Edited by Malgosia Fitzmaurice and Panos Merkouris

148 *Humanitarian Disarmament: An Historical Enquiry*
Treasa Dunworth

147 *Complementarity, Catalysts, Compliance: The International Criminal Court in Uganda, Kenya, and the Democratic Republic of Congo*
Christian M. De Vos

146 *Cyber Operations and International Law*
François Delerue

145 *Comparative Reasoning in International Courts and Tribunals*
Daniel Peat

144 *Maritime Delimitation as a Judicial Process*
Massimo Lando

143 *Prosecuting Sexual and Gender-Based Crimes at the International Criminal Court: Practice, Progress and Potential*
Rosemary Grey

142 *Capitalism As Civilisation: A History of International Law*
Ntina Tzouvala

141 *Sovereignty in China: A Genealogy of a Concept Since 1840*
Adele Carrai

140 *Narratives of Hunger in International Law: Feeding the World in Times of Climate Change*
Anne Saab

139 *Victim Reparation under the Ius Post Bellum: An Historical and Normative Perspective*
Shavana Musa

138 *The Analogy between States and International Organizations*
Fernando Lusa Bordin

137 *The Process of International Legal Reproduction: Inequality, Historiography, Resistance*
Rose Parfitt

136 *State Responsibility for Breaches of Investment Contracts*
Jean Ho

135 *Coalitions of the Willing and International Law: The Interplay between Formality and Informality*
Alejandro Rodiles

134 *Self-Determination in Disputed Colonial Territories*
Jamie Trinidad

133 *International Law as a Belief System* Jean d'Aspremont

132 *Legal Consequences of Peremptory Norms in International Law*
Daniel Costelloe

131 *Third-Party Countermeasures in International Law*
Martin Dawidowicz

130 *Justification and Excuse in International Law: Concept and Theory of General Defences*
Federica Paddeu

129 *Exclusion from Public Space: A Comparative Constitutional Analysis*
Daniel Moeckli

128 *Provisional Measures before International Courts and Tribunals*
Cameron A. Miles

127 *Humanity at Sea: Maritime Migration and the Foundations of International Law*
Itamar Mann

126 *Beyond Human Rights: The Legal Status of the Individual in International Law*
Anne Peters

125 *The Doctrine of Odious Debt in International Law: A Restatement*
Jeff King

124 *Static and Evolutive Treaty Interpretation: A Functional Reconstruction*
Christian Djeffal

123 *Civil Liability in Europe for Terrorism-Related Risk*
Lucas Bergkamp, Michael Faure, Monika Hinteregger and Niels Philipsen

122 *Proportionality and Deference in Investor-State Arbitration: Balancing Investment Protection and Regulatory Autonomy*
Caroline Henckels

121 *International Law and Governance of Natural Resources in Conflict and Post-Conflict Situations*
Daniëlla Dam-de Jong

120 *Proof of Causation in Tort Law*
Sandy Steel

119 *The Formation and Identification of Rules of Customary International Law in International Investment Law*
Patrick Dumberry

118 *Religious Hatred and International Law: The Prohibition of Incitement to Violence or Discrimination*
Jeroen Temperman

117 *Taking Economic, Social and Cultural Rights Seriously in International Criminal Law*
Evelyne Schmid

116 *Climate Change Litigation: Regulatory Pathways to Cleaner Energy*
Jacqueline Peel and Hari M. Osofsky

115 *Mestizo International Law: A Global Intellectual History 1842–1933*
Arnulf Becker Lorca

114 *Sugar and the Making of International Trade Law*
Michael Fakhri

113 *Strategically Created Treaty Conflicts and the Politics of International Law*
Surabhi Ranganathan

112 *Investment Treaty Arbitration As Public International Law: Procedural Aspects and Implications*
Eric De Brabandere

111 *The New Entrants Problem in International Fisheries Law*
Andrew Serdy

110 *Substantive Protection under Investment Treaties: A Legal and Economic Analysis*
Jonathan Bonnitcha

109 *Popular Governance of Post-Conflict Reconstruction: The Role of International Law*
Matthew Saul

108 *Evolution of International Environmental Regimes: The Case of Climate Change*
Simone Schiele

107 *Judges, Law and War: The Judicial Development of International Humanitarian Law*
Shane Darcy

106 *Religious Offence and Human Rights: The Implications of Defamation of Religions*
Lorenz Langer

105 *Forum Shopping in International Adjudication: The Role of Preliminary Objections*
Luiz Eduardo Salles

104 *Domestic Politics and International Human Rights Tribunals: The Problem of Compliance*
Courtney Hillebrecht

103 *International Law and the Arctic*
Michael Byers

102 *Cooperation in the Law of Transboundary Water Resources*
Christina Leb

101 *Underwater Cultural Heritage and International Law*
Sarah Dromgoole

100 *State Responsibility: The General Part*
James Crawford

99 *The Origins of International Investment Law: Empire, Environment and the Safeguarding of Capital*
Kate Miles

98 *The Crime of Aggression under the Rome Statute of the International Criminal Court*
Carrie McDougall

97 *'Crimes against Peace' and International Law*
Kirsten Sellars

96 *Non-Legality in International Law: Unruly Law*
Fleur Johns

95 *Armed Conflict and Displacement: The Protection of Refugees and Displaced Persons under International Humanitarian Law*
Mélanie Jacques

94 *Foreign Investment and the Environment in International Law*
Jorge E. Viñuales

93 *The Human Rights Treaty Obligations of Peacekeepers*
Kjetil Mujezinović Larsen

92 *Cyber Warfare and the Laws of War*
Heather Harrison Dinniss

91 *The Right to Reparation in International Law for Victims of Armed Conflict*
Christine Evans

90 *Global Public Interest in International Investment Law*
Andreas Kulick

89 *State Immunity in International Law*
Xiaodong Yang

88 *Reparations and Victim Support in the International Criminal Court*
Conor McCarthy

87 *Reducing Genocide to Law: Definition, Meaning, and the Ultimate Crime*
Payam Akhavan

86 *Decolonising International Law: Development, Economic Growth and the Politics of Universality*
Sundhya Pahuja

85 *Complicity and the Law of State Responsibility*
Helmut Philipp Aust

84 *State Control over Private Military and Security Companies in Armed Conflict*
Hannah Tonkin

83 *'Fair and Equitable Treatment' in International Investment Law*
Roland Kläger

82 *The UN and Human Rights: Who Guards the Guardians?*
Guglielmo Verdirame

81 *Sovereign Defaults before International Courts and Tribunals*
Michael Waibel

80 *Making the Law of the Sea: A Study in the Development of International Law*
James Harrison

79 *Science and the Precautionary Principle in International Courts and Tribunals: Expert Evidence, Burden of Proof and Finality*
Caroline E. Foster

78 *Transition from Illegal Regimes under International Law*
Yaël Ronen

77 *Access to Asylum: International Refugee Law and the Globalisation of Migration Control*
Thomas Gammeltoft-Hansen

76 *Trading Fish, Saving Fish: The Interaction between Regimes in International Law*
Margaret A. Young

75 *The Individual in the International Legal System: Continuity and Change in International Law*
Kate Parlett

74 *'Armed Attack' and Article 51 of the UN Charter: Evolutions in Customary Law and Practice*
Tom Ruys

73 *Theatre of the Rule of Law: Transnational Legal Intervention in Theory and Practice*
Stephen Humphreys

72 *Science and Risk Regulation in International Law*
Jacqueline Peel

71 *The Participation of States in International Organisations: The Role of Human Rights and Democracy*
Alison Duxbury

70 *Legal Personality in International Law*
Roland Portmann

69 *Vicarious Liability in Tort: A Comparative Perspective*
Paula Giliker

68 *The Public International Law Theory of Hans Kelsen: Believing in Universal Law*
Jochen von Bernstorff

67 *Legitimacy and Legality in International Law: An Interactional Account*
Jutta Brunnée and Stephen J. Toope

66 *The Concept of Non-International Armed Conflict in International Humanitarian Law*
Anthony Cullen

65 *The Principle of Legality in International and Comparative Criminal Law*
Kenneth S. Gallant

64 *The Challenge of Child Labour in International Law*
Franziska Humbert

63 *Shipping Interdiction and the Law of the Sea*
Douglas Guilfoyle

62 *International Courts and Environmental Protection*
Tim Stephens

61 *Legal Principles in WTO Disputes*
Andrew D. Mitchell

60 *War Crimes in Internal Armed Conflicts*
Eve La Haye

59 *Humanitarian Occupation*
Gregory H. Fox

58 *The International Law of Environmental Impact Assessment: Process, Substance and Integration*
Neil Craik

57 *The Law and Practice of International Territorial Administration: Versailles to Iraq and Beyond*
Carsten Stahn

56 *United Nations Sanctions and the Rule of Law*
Jeremy Matam Farrall

55 *National Law in WTO Law: Effectiveness and Good Governance in the World Trading System*
Sharif Bhuiyan

54 *Cultural Products and the World Trade Organization*
Tania Voon

53 *The Threat of Force in International Law*
Nikolas Stürchler

52 *Indigenous Rights and United Nations Standards: Self-Determination, Culture and Land*
Alexandra Xanthaki

51 *International Refugee Law and Socio-Economic Rights: Refuge from Deprivation*
Michelle Foster

50 *The Protection of Cultural Property in Armed Conflict*
Roger O'Keefe

49 *Interpretation and Revision of International Boundary Decisions*
Kaiyan Homi Kaikobad

48 *Multinationals and Corporate Social Responsibility: Limitations and Opportunities in International Law*
Jennifer A. Zerk

47 *Judiciaries within Europe: A Comparative Review*
John Bell

46 *Law in Times of Crisis: Emergency Powers in Theory and Practice*
Oren Gross and Fionnuala Ní Aoláin

45 *Vessel-Source Marine Pollution: The Law and Politics of International Regulation*
Alan Khee-Jin Tan

44 *Enforcing Obligations Erga Omnes in International Law*
Christian J. Tams

43 *Non-Governmental Organisations in International Law*
Anna-Karin Lindblom

42 *Democracy, Minorities and International Law*
Steven Wheatley

41 *Prosecuting International Crimes: Selectivity and the International Criminal Law Regime*
Robert Cryer

40 *Compensation for Personal Injury in English, German and Italian Law: A Comparative Outline*
Basil Markesinis, Michael Coester, Guido Alpa and Augustus Ullstein

39 *Dispute Settlement in the UN Convention on the Law of the Sea*
Natalie Klein

38 *The International Protection of Internally Displaced Persons*
Catherine Phuong

37 *Imperialism, Sovereignty and the Making of International Law*
Antony Anghie

36 *Principles of the Institutional Law of International Organizations*
C. F. Amerasinghe

35 *Necessity, Proportionality and the Use of Force by States*
Judith Gardam

34 *International Legal Argument in the Permanent Court of International Justice: The Rise of the International Judiciary*
Ole Spiermann

33 –

32 *Great Powers and Outlaw States: Unequal Sovereigns in the International Legal Order*
Gerry Simpson

31 *Local Remedies in International Law (second edition)*
Chittharanjan Felix Amerasinghe

30 *Reading Humanitarian Intervention: Human Rights and the Use of Force in International Law*
Anne Orford

29 *Conflict of Norms in Public International Law: How WTO Law Relates to Other Rules of International Law*
Joost Pauwelyn

28 –

27 *Transboundary Damage in International Law*
Hanqin Xue

26 –

25 *European Criminal Procedures* Edited by Mireille Delmas-Marty and J. R. Spencer

24 *Accountability of Armed Opposition Groups in International Law*
Liesbeth Zegveld

23 *Sharing Transboundary Resources: International Law and Optimal Resource Use*
Eyal Benvenisti

22 *International Human Rights and Humanitarian Law*
René Provost

21 *Remedies against International Organisations*
Karel Wellens

20 *Diversity and Self-Determination in International Law*
Karen Knop

19 *The Law of Internal Armed Conflict*
Lindsay Moir

18 *International Commercial Arbitration and African States: Practice, Participation and Institutional Development*
Amazu A. Asouzu

17 *The Enforceability of Promises in European Contract Law*
James Gordley

16 *International Law in Antiquity*
David J. Bederman

15 *Money Laundering: A New International Law Enforcement Model*
Guy Stessens

14 *Good Faith in European Contract Law*
Reinhard Zimmermann and Simon Whittaker

13 *On Civil Procedure*
J. A. Jolowicz

12 *Trusts: A Comparative Study*
Maurizio Lupoi and Simon Dix

11 *The Right to Property in Commonwealth Constitutions*
Tom Allen

10 *International Organizations before National Courts*
August Reinisch

9 *The Changing International Law of High Seas Fisheries*
Francisco Orrego Vicuña

8 *Trade and the Environment: A Comparative Study of EC and US Law*
Damien Geradin

7 *Unjust Enrichment: A Study of Private Law and Public Values*
Hanoch Dagan

6 *Religious Liberty and International Law in Europe*
Malcolm D. Evans

5 *Ethics and Authority in International Law*
Alfred P. Rubin

4 *Sovereignty over Natural Resources: Balancing Rights and Duties*
Nico Schrijver

3 *The Polar Regions and the Development of International Law*
Donald R. Rothwell

2 *Fragmentation and the International Relations of Micro-States: Self-Determination and Statehood*
Jorri C. Duursma

1 *Principles of the Institutional Law of International Organizations*
C. F. Amerasinghe